Classic
Divinatory Systems

Tarot, Cartomancy, I Ching,
Geomancy and Palmistry

Classic
Divinatory Systems

Tarot, Cartomancy, I Ching,
Geomancy and Palmistry

**Arthur Edward Waite - Cheiro
Franz Hartmann - Enos Long
P.R.S. Foli**

Classic Divinatory Systems

SOJOURNER BOOKS

© 2018 by Enos Long

All rights reserved under International and
Pan-American Copyright Conventions.
ISBN: 978-1-9994008-5-9

INTRODUCTION

According to the Oxford English Dictionary, to divine means:

The action or practice of divining; the foretelling of future events or discovery of what is hidden or obscure by supernatural or magical means; soothsaying, augury, prophecy. With a and pl., an exercise of this, a prophecy, an augury.

The word "divination" comes from the Latin *divinare* and means "to foresee, to be inspired by a god". Divination is related to *divine*, "of, relating to, or proceeding directly from God".

Many ancient cultures saw divination as a way to read subtle signs, or omens, provided by gods or spirits. In the Greco-Roman world, the gods made their wishes clear to humans by sending messages using birds (Ornithomancy is a method of divination that interprets the flight patterns of birds), dreams and many other forms. Smoke, water, flames, and other signs from nature were also used as divinatory mediums to read the divine messages.

An holistic vision of the world sees it as a place where all beings are immersed in a pattern of correspondences. A place where our thoughts can resonate with other creatures, without using causal transmission channels, simply by the fact of "being in resonance", connected through the universal web that supports all beings.

Edward Lorenz explained such phenomena as "the butterfly effect," an analogy based on a Chinese proverb that says "the slight flapping of a butterfly's wings can be felt on the other side of the world.

From a holistic viewpoint divination consists in reading the subtle signs, received through the universal network that interconnects all beings.

Ancient cultures saw the signs that anticipate what is coming as omens. Disregarding the origin of omens (whether God's messages or ripples in the universal web), divination can be see as the proper interpretation of such omens.

The divinatory systems explained in this book are called "classic", because they have existed by hundreds or even thousands or years. They offer a tried and tested way to stay in tune with the universe around us, to know where we are and where we are going. By using divination we can look behind the scenes and discover the hidden fabric that connects us with the entire world.

Divinatory Systems studied in this book

Tarot and Cartomancy

Since playing cards were introduced in Europe in the 14th century, cartomancy was used to divine by using a deck of cards. The Tarot is a special deck of cards made up of 22 figures with mystical meanings, known as Major Arcana and four suits, with 56 cards, known as the Minor Arcana.

I Ching

The *I Ching* or *Book of Changes* (also spelled *YiJing*) has been used as an oracle since the Chinese Bronze Age, three thousand years ago. The *Book of Changes* is both an oracular medium and a book of wisdom, but it doesn't try to answer why we are here or where are we going after death; instead it focuses in the business of living. It is also a human attempt to throw light in the natural laws that command change.

Astrological Geomancy

Geomancy (Greek: γεωμαντεία, "earth divination") is done by jotting down on the earth (or on paper) a number of dots at random. Astrological Geomancy extrapolates the geomantic chart to the horoscope by taking the planets associated with the geomantic figures located in the first twelve houses of the geomantic chart, and placing them in the twelve houses of the horoscope.

Palmistry

Palmistry is a different kind of divinatory system, since it is not based on artificial signs but on natural signs or patterns of the human body: the characteristics of the hand. The symbolic framework of palmistry comes from Greek mythology. The areas of the palm and fingers are related to different deities, and the appearance of each area reveals the characteristics of the corresponding aspect on the subject.

Contents

Introduction. v
Divinatory Systems studied in this book.. vi

The Pictorial Key to the Tarot

Preface 3

PART I
The Veil and its Symbols 5
§ 1. Introductory and General... 5
§ 2. The Trumps Major, otherwise Greater Arcana 7
§ 3. The Four Suits, otherwise Lesser Arcana.. 13
§ 4. The Tarot in History 13
§ 1. The Tarot and Secret Tradition.. 21

PART II
The Doctrine Behind the Veil 21
§ 2. The Trumps Major and their Inner Symbolism 25
§ 3. Conclusion as to the Greater Keys 47

PART III
The Outer Method of the Oracles 49
§ 1. Distinction between the Greater and Lesser Arcana 49
§ 2. The Lesser Arcana. Otherwise the Four Suits of Tarot Cards 50
§ 3. The Greater Arcana and their Divinatory Meanings; 70
§ 4. Some Additional Meanings of the Lesser Arcana 72
§ 5. The Recurrence of Cards in Dealing. 75
§ 6. The Art of Tarot Divination.. 76

§ 7. An Ancient Celtic Method of Divination. ... 77
§ 8. An Alternative Method of Reading the Tarot Cards ... 79
§ 9. The Method of Reading by Means of Thirty-five Cards ... 82
Bibliography. ... 83

Palmistry For All

Preface to the American Edition ... 93
Rules for Rapid Observation ... 94
The Fingers Considered Separately ... 94
Character Shown by the Thumb ... 95
Hands, Hard and Soft. ... 97
Introduction. ... 99

PART I

Palmistry or Cheiromancy ... 103
Chapter I. A Brief Résumé Of The History Of The Study Of Hands Through The Centuries To The Present Day ... 103
Chapter II. The Line Of Head Or The Indications Of The Mentality ... 106
    The Line Of Head And Its Variations. ... 107
    The Line Of Head Joined To The Line Of Life. ... 110
    Plate II. The Line of Head Joined to the Line of Life and its Terminations ... 111
    The Line Of Head Separated From The Line Of Life ... 111
    Plate III. The Line of Head Separated From the Line of Life ... 112
    The Line Of Head And Its Secondary Signs ... 113
    Plate IV. Islands on the Line of Head ... 113
    Changes In The Line Of Head. ... 114
    Plate V. More Variations of the Line of Head. ... 115
    Plate VI. The Line of Head and the Line of Heart Running Together. ... 116
    Crosses And Squares In Connection With The Line Of Head. ... 116
    Double Lines Of Head ... 117
    Plate VII. Double Lines of Head, also Crosses and Squares. ... 117
    The Line Of Head On The Seven Types Of Hands ... 118
Chapter III. The Line Of Life And Its Variations ... 119
    Plate VIII. The Line of Life and Sections of Influences from the Mounts. ... 119
    The Line Of Life ... 120
    Plate IX. The Line of Life and its Variations ... 121
    Ascending Lines ... 121
Chapter IV. The Line Of Mars Or Inner Life Line. ... 122
    Plate X. The Line of Life, the Line of Mars, and Other Signs ... 123
Chapter V. The Line Of Destiny Or Fate ... 123
    Rising From The Line Of Life ... 125

Contents

ix

- Rising From The Wrist... 125
- Rising From The Mount Of The Moon... 125
- Plate XI. The Line of Destiny and its Modifications... 125
- Plate Xii. The Line of Destiny and its Variations... 126
- Rising From The Middle Of The Palm... 127
- Plate XIII. The Line of Destiny and its Modifications... 128
- Influence Lines... 128
- Double Lines Of Fate... 128
- Plate XIV. The Line of Destiny, Islands, and Other Signs... 129

Chapter VI. The Line Of The Sun... 130
- Plate XV. The Line of Sun and its Modifications... 130

Chapter VII. The Line Of Heart As Indicating The Affectionate And Emotional Nature 132
- Plate XVI. The Line of Heart and its Variations... 133

Chapter VIII. Signs Relating To Marriage... 135
- Plate XVII. Marriage Lines. The Line Of Marriage... 135
- Influence Lines To The Fate Line On The Mount Of Venus, And Other Signs Which Also Have A Meaning In Connection With Marriage... 137
- Plate XVIII. Marriage Lines and Influence Lines which Further Help in Denoting Marriage... 137
- Influence Lines On The Mount Of Venus... 138

Chapter IX. Lines Denoting Children, Their Sex, And Other Matters Concerning Them 138

Chapter X. The Line Of Health Or The Hepatica... 139
- Plate XIX. The Line of Health... 139

Chapter XI. The Girdle Of Venus, The Ring Of Saturn, And The Bracelets... 141
- Plate XX. The Girdle of Venus, the Ring of Saturn, the Three Bracelets, the Line of Intuition and the Via Lasciva... 141
- The Ring Of Saturn... 142
- The Bracelets... 142

Chapter XII. The Line Of Intuition And The Via Lasciva... 143
- The Via Lasciva... 143

Chapter XIII. "la Croix Mystique", The Ring Of Solomon... 144
- The Ring Of Solomon... 144

Chapter XIV. Travels, Voyages And Accidents... 144
- Plate XXI. Travels, Voyages, Accidents and Descending Lines from the Mounts... 145
- Accidents... 146

Chapter XV. The Island, The Circle, The Spot, And The Grille... 146
- The Circle... 146
- Plate XXII. The Island, the Circle, the Spot, the Grille, the Star, the Square... 147
- The Spot... 147
- The Grille... 147

Chapter XVI. The Star, The Cross, The Square ... 147
    Plate XXIII. Minor Marks and Signs. ... 148
    The Cross ... 148
    The Square... 149
Chapter XVII. Different Classes Of Lines ... 149
    Plate XXIV. Minor Marks and Signs. ... 149
    Right And Left Hands ... 150
Chapter XVIII. The Great Triangle And The Quadrangle. ... 150
    The Quadrangle 150
    Plate XXV. The Great Triangle and the Quadrangle... 151
Chapter XIX. How To Tell Time And Dates Of Principal Events In The Life 151
    Plate XXVI. Time and Dates of Principal Events.. ... 151

PART II

Cheirognomy or The Science of Interpreting the Shape of Hands 153
Chapter I. The Study Of The Shape Of The Hand ... 153
    The Seven Types Of Hands 154
    The Elementary 154
        Fig. 1—The Elementary Hand.
        Fig. 2—The Square or Useful Hand. ... 154
        Fig. 3—The Spatulate Hand.
        Fig. 4—The Philosophic Hand.
    The Square Type 155
    The Spatulate Hand ... 155
    The Philosophic Hand ... 156
        Fig. 1.—The Conic or Artistic Hand ... 156
        Fig. 2.—The Psychic or Idealistic Hand... 156
        Fig. 3.—The Mixed Hand 156
    The Conic Or Artistic Hand.. ... 157
    The Psychic Or Idealistic Hand ... 157
    The Mixed Hand. ... 157
Chapter II. The Thumb.. ... 158
    Fig. 1.—The Clubbed Thumb. ... 159
    Fig. 2.—The Supple-Jointed Thumb. ... 159
    Fig. 3.—The Firm-Jointed Thumb.... 159
    Fig. 4.—The Waist-Like Thumb.... 159
    Fig. 5.—The Straight Thumb. ... 159
    Fig. 6.—The Elementary Thumb.. ... 159
Chapter III. The Fingers—length To One Another ... 160
    The Smooth And The Knotty.... 160

Contents

Chapter IV. The Nails Of The Hand ... 161
    Long Nails ... 162
    Plate V.— Part II. ... 162
    Short Nails ... 162
    Long Narrow Nails. ... 163
    Flat Nails.. ... 163
    The Moons Of The Nails.. ... 163
Chapter V. The Mounts Of The Hand And Their Meaning.. ... 163
    Plate VI.—Part II. The Mounts of the Hand.. ... 164
Chapter VI. The Mount Of Mars. ... 165
    The First Mount Of Mars. ... 165
    The Second Mount Of Mars. ... 166
Chapter VII. The Mount Of Jupiter And Its Meaning... ... 167
    Health... ... 168
    The Mount Of Jupiter (negative).. ... 168
    Health... ... 169
Chapter VIII. The Mount Of Saturn And Its Meaning.. ... 169
    Health... ... 170
    The Mount Of Saturn (negative).. ... 170
    Health... ... 170
Chapter IX. The Mount Of The Sun And Its Meaning. ... 171
    Health... ... 172
    Mount Of The Sun (negative)... ... 172
    Health... ... 172
Chapter X. The Mount Of Mercury And Its Meaning... ... 173
    The Mount Of Mercury (positive) ... 173
    Health... ... 174
    The Mount Of Mercury (negative)... ... 174
    Health... ... 175
Chapter XI. The Mount Of The Moon And Its Meaning. ... 175
    Health... ... 176
    The Mount Of The Moon (negative)... ... 176
    Health... ... 177
Chapter XII. The Mount Of Venus And Its Meaning ... 177
    Health... ... 178
    The mount of Venus (negative) ... 179
    Health... ... 179
Chapter XIII. Advice To The Student. The Best Means To Make Casts Or Take Impressions Of The Hands 179

I Ching: Oracular Interpretation

Introduction. ... 183
How to consult the Oracle. ... 187
Understanding hexagram readings ... 191
Chart of Trigrams and Hexagrams ... 196

THE 64 HEXAGRAMS

1. The Creative / Activity / Dynamic Force.. ... 197
2. The Receptive ... 200
3. Initial Difficulty. ... 203
4. Youthful Folly ... 206
5. Waiting ... 209
6. Conflict / Lawsuit. ... 211
7. The Army... ... 214
8. Union 217
9. Little Domestication. ... 220
10. Treading 223
11. Harmony / Great.. ... 226
12. Standstill / Stagnation 229
13. Fellowship.. ... 232
14. Great Possession ... 234
15. Modesty.. ... 236
16. Enthusiasm ... 238
17. Following ... 240
18. Correcting Decay / Corruption 243
19. Approach / Leadership ... 246
20. Contemplation... ... 249
21. Biting Through.. ... 252
22. Elegance / Adornment / Grace.. ... 255
23. Splitting Apart / Decay ... 257
24. Return. ... 259
25. Innocence / No expectations.. ... 262
26. Great Accumulation 265
27. Nourishment / The Jaws 268
28. Great Excess.. ... 271
29. Pit doubled / Pit within a pit... ... 274
30. The Clinging / Fire... ... 277
31. Influence / Reciprocity ... 280
32. Duration / Constancy 282
33. Retreat ... 285

34. Great Power...	287
35. Progress / Advance..	290
36. Suppressed Light...	293
37. The Family / The Clan.	296
38. Antagonism / Opposition	299
39. Hampered / Obstruction.	302
40. Liberation...	304
41. Decrease.	307
42. Increase...	310
43. Breakthrough / Resoluteness / Parting..	313
44. Close Encounter / Meeting.	316
45. Gathering together	319
46. Ascending..	322
47. Oppression / Besieged / Impasse.	325
48. The Well.	328
49. Revolution / Getting rid of.	331
50. The Cauldron / Sacrificial Vessel	334
51. Shock..	337
52. Restraint.	340
53. Gradual Development..	343
54. The Marrying Maiden...	346
55. Fullness / Abundance	349
56. Sojourner / Wanderer...	352
57. Gentle Influence / Penetration / The Wind..	355
58. Joyousness / The Lake.	358
59. Dispersion / Dissolution / The Flood...	360
60. Limitation...	363
61. Inner Truth	366
62. Excess of the Small..	369
63. Already Across ..	372
64. Before Crossing.	375

The Principles of Astrological Geomancy

Foreword..	381
Preface	383
Introduction.	385
Astrology..	387
The Seven Planets	391
Conjunctions	395

The Twelve signs of the Zodiac	397
The Symbols of Geomancy	403
Significations	404
Instructions for the Practice of Geomancy	407
Preparation	407
The Practice of Geomancy	408
Astrological Geomancy	413
Significations of the Geomantic Symbols according to their Positions	417
Astronomical Geomancy	429
Appendix. Containing 2048 Answers to Questions	433
Acquisitio	435
Amissio	441
Fortuna Major	446
Fortuna Minor	451
Populus	457
Via	462
Conjunctio	468
Carcer	474

Fortune Telling by Cards

Introduction	483
Chapter I. How we got our Pack of Cards	485
Two Systems	489
Chapter II. What the Individual Cards Signify	489
Significations of the Cards	490
Chapter III. The Selected Pack of Thirty-two Cards	493
Chapter IV. The Signification of Quartettes, Triplets, and Pairs	495
Chapter V. What the Cards can Tell of the Past, the Present, and the Future	499
Chapter VI. Your Fortune in Twenty-one Cards	503
Chapter VII. Combination of Sevens	507
Signification of Cards	508
Chapter VIII. Another Method	513
Chapter IX. A French Method	517
Chapter X. The Grand Star	521
Chapter XI. Important Questions	525
Chapter XII. How They Tell Fortunes in Italy	529
Chapter XIII. The Master Method	533
The Thirty-Six Squares and their Significance	535
Chapter XIV. Signification of Suits in the Master Method	543

Chapter XV. Combination of Nines. ... 551
Chapter XVI. Your Heart's Desire ... 555
Chapter XVII. A Rhyming Divination.. ... 559
Chapter XVIII. The Tarots ... 565
Chapter XIX. Etteilla's Method. ... 567

The Pictorial Key to the Tarot

*Being Fragments of a Secret Tradition
under the Veil of Divination*

Arthur Edward Waite

This text and the accompanying illustrations are in the public domain in the United States of America because they were published prior to 1923.

Preface

IT seems rather of necessity than predilection in the sense of apologia that I should put on record in the first place a plain statement of my personal position, as one who for many years of literary life has been, subject to his spiritual and other limitations, an exponent of the higher mystic schools. It will be thought that I am acting strangely in concerning myself at this day with what appears at first sight and simply a well-known method of fortune-telling. Now, the opinions of Mr. Smith, even in the literary reviews, are of no importance unless they happen to agree with our own, but in order to sanctify this doctrine we must take care that our opinions, and the subjects out of which they arise, are concerned only with the highest. Yet it is just this which may seem doubtful, in the present instance, not only to Mr. Smith, whom I respect within the proper measures of detachment, but to some of more real consequence, seeing that their dedications are mine. To these and to any I would say that after the most illuminated Frater Christian Rosy Cross had beheld the Chemical Marriage in the Secret Palace of Transmutation, his story breaks off abruptly, with an intimation that he expected next morning to be door-keeper. After the same manner, it happens more often than might seem likely that those who have seen the King of Heaven through the most clearest veils of the sacraments are those who assume thereafter the humblest offices of all about the House of God. By such simple devices also are the Adepts and Great Masters in the secret orders distinguished from the cohort of Neophytes as servi servorum mysterii. So also, or in a way which is not entirely unlike, we meet with the Tarot cards at the outermost gates –amidst the fritterings and débris of the so-called occult arts, about which no one in their senses has suffered the smallest deception; and yet these cards belong in themselves to another region, for they contain a very high symbolism, which is interpreted according to the Laws of Grace rather than by the pretexts and intuitions of that which passes for divination. The fact that the wisdom of God is foolishness with men does not create a presumption that the foolishness of this world makes in any sense for Divine Wisdom; so neither the scholars in the ordinary classes nor the pedagogues in the seats of the mighty will be quick to perceive the likelihood or even the possibility of this proposition. The subject has been in the hands of cartomancists as part of the stock-in-trade of their industry; I do not seek to persuade any one outside my own circles that this is of much or of no consequence; but on the historical and interpretative sides it has not fared better; it has been there in the hands of exponents who have brought it into utter contempt for those people who possess philosophical insight or faculties for the appreciation of evidence. It is time that it should be rescued, and this I propose to undertake once and for all, that I may have done with the side issues which distract from the term. As poetry is the most beautiful expression of the things that are of all most beautiful, so is symbolism the most catholic expression in concealment of things that are most profound in the Sanctuary and that have not been declared outside it with the same fulness by means of the spoken word. The justification of the rule of silence is no part of my present concern, but I have put on record elsewhere, and quite recently, what it is possible to say on this subject.

The little treatise which follows is divided into three parts, in the first of which I have dealt with the antiquities of the subject and a few things that arise from and connect therewith. It should be understood that it is not put forward as a contribution to the history of playing cards, about which I know and care nothing; it is a consideration dedicated and addressed to a certain school of occultism, more especially in France, as to the source and centre of all the phantasmagoria which has entered into expression during the last fifty years under the pretence of considering Tarot cards historically. In the second part, I have dealt with the symbolism according to some of its higher aspects, and this also serves to introduce the complete and rectified Tarot, which is available separately, in the form of coloured cards, the designs of which are added to the present text in black and white. They have been prepared under my supervision –in respect of the attributions and meanings –by a lady who has high claims as an artist. Regarding the divinatory part, by which my thesis is terminated, I consider it personally as a fact in the history of the Tarot –as such, I have drawn, from all published sources, a harmony of the meanings which have been attached to the various cards, and I have given prominence to one method of working that has not been published previously; having the merit of simplicity, while it is also of universal application, it may be held to replace the cumbrous and involved systems of the larger hand-books.

PART I
The Veil and its Symbols

§ 1. Introductory and General

THE pathology of the poet says that "the undevout astronomer is mad"; the pathology of the very plain man says that genius is mad; and between these extremes, which stand for ten thousand analogous excesses, the sovereign reason takes the part of a moderator and does what it can. I do not think that there is a pathology of the occult dedications, but about their extravagances no one can question, and it is not less difficult than thankless to act as a moderator regarding them. Moreover, the pathology, if it existed, would probably be an empiricism rather than a diagnosis, and would offer no criterion. Now, occultism is not like mystic faculty, and it very seldom works in harmony either with business aptitude in the things of ordinary life or with a knowledge of the canons of evidence in its own sphere. I know that for the high art of ribaldry there are few things more dull than the criticism which maintains that a thesis is untrue, and cannot understand that it is decorative. I know also that after long dealing with doubtful doctrine or with difficult research it is always refreshing, in the domain of this art, to meet with what is obviously of fraud or at least of complete unreason. But the aspects of history, as seen through the lens of occultism, are not as a rule decorative, and have few gifts of refreshment to heal the lacerations which they inflict on the logical understanding. It almost requires a Frater Sapiens dominabitur astris in the Fellowship of the Rosy Cross to have the patience which is not lost amidst clouds of folly when the consideration of the Tarot is undertaken in accordance with the higher law of symbolism. The true Tarot is symbolism; it speaks no other language and offers no other signs. Given the inward meaning of its emblems, they do become a kind of alphabet which is capable of indefinite combinations and makes true sense in all. On the highest plane it offers a key to the Mysteries, in a manner which is not arbitrary and has not been read in, But the wrong symbolical stories have been told concerning it, and the wrong history has been given in every published work which so far has dealt with the subject. It has been intimated by two or three writers that, at least in respect of the meanings, this is unavoidably the case, because few are acquainted with them, while these few hold by transmission under pledges and cannot betray their trust. The suggestion is fantastic on the surface for there seems a certain anti-climax in the proposition that a particular interpretation of fortune-telling –l'art de tirer les cartes– can be reserved for Sons of the Doctrine. The fact remains, notwithstanding, that a Secret Tradition exists regarding the Tarot, and as there is always the possibility that some minor arcana of the Mysteries may be made public with a flourish of trumpets, it will be as well to go before the event and to warn those who are curious in such matters that any revelation will contain only a third part of the earth and sea and a third part of the stars of heaven in respect of the symbolism. This is for the simple reason that neither in root-matter nor in development has more been put into writing, so that much will remain to be said after any pretended unveiling. The guardians of certain temples of initiation who keep watch over mysteries of this order have therefore no cause for alarm.

In my preface to The Tarot of the Bohemians, which, rather by an accident of things, has recently come to be re-issued after a long period, I have said what was then possible or seemed most necessary. The present work is designed more especially –as I have intimated– to introduce a rectified set of the cards themselves and to tell the unadorned truth concerning them, so far as this is possible in the outer circles. As regards the sequence of greater symbols, their ultimate and highest meaning lies deeper than the common language of picture or hieroglyph. This will be understood by those who have received some part of the Secret Tradition. As regards the verbal meanings allocated here to the more important Trump Cards, they are designed to set aside the follies and impostures of past attributions, to put those who have the gift of insight on the right track, and to take care, within the limits of my possibilities, that they are the truth so far as they go.

It is regrettable in several respects that I must confess to certain reservations, but there is a question of honour at issue. Furthermore, between the follies on the one side of those who know nothing of the tradition, yet are in their own opinion the exponents of something called occult science and philosophy, and on the other side between the make-believe of a few writers who have received part of the tradition and think that it constitutes a legal title to scatter dust in the eyes of the world without, I feel that the time has come to say what it is possible to say, so that the effect of current charlatanism and unintelligence may be reduced to a minimum.

We shall see in due course that the history of Tarot cards is largely of a negative kind, and that, when the issues are cleared by the dissipation of reveries and gratuitous speculations expressed in the terms of certitude, there is in fact no history prior to the fourteenth century. The deception and self-deception regarding their origin in Egypt, India or China put a lying spirit into the mouths of the first expositors, and the later occult writers have done little more than reproduce the first false testimony in the good faith of an intelligence unawakened to the issues of research. As it so happens, all expositions have worked within a very narrow range, and owe, comparatively speaking, little to the inventive faculty. One brilliant opportunity has at least been missed, for it has not so far occurred to any one that the Tarot might perhaps have done duty and even originated as a secret symbolical language of the Albigensian sects. I commend this suggestion to the lineal descendants in the spirit of Gabriele Rossetti and Eugène Aroux, to Mr. Harold Bayley as another New Light on the Renaissance, and as a taper at least in the darkness which, with great respect, might be serviceable to the zealous and all-searching mind of Mrs. Cooper-Oakley. Think only what the supposed testimony of watermarks on paper might gain from the Tarot card of the Pope or Hierophant, in connexion with the notion of a secret Albigensian patriarch, of which Mr. Bayley has found in these same watermarks so much material to his purpose. Think only for a moment about the card of the High Priestess as representing the Albigensian church itself; and think of the Tower struck by Lightning as typifying the desired destruction of Papal Rome, the city on the seven hills, with the pontiff and his temporal power cast down from the spiritual edifice when it is riven by the wrath of God. The possibilities are so numerous and persuasive that they almost deceive in their expression one of the elect who has invented them. But there is more even than this, though I scarcely dare to cite it. When the time came for the Tarot cards to be the subject of their first formal explanation, the archaeologist Court de Gebelin reproduced some of their most important emblems, and –if I may so term it– the codex which he used has served –by means of his engraved plates-as a basis of reference for many sets that have been issued subsequently. The figures are very primitive and differ as such from the cards of Etteilla, the Marseilles Tarot, and others still current in France. I am not a good judge in such matters, but the fact that every one of the Trumps Major might have answered for watermark purposes is shewn by the cases which I have quoted and by one most remarkable example of the Ace of Cups.

I should call it an eucharistic emblem after the manner of a ciborium, but this does not signify at the moment. The point is that Mr. Harold Bayley gives six analogous devices in his New Light on the Renaissance, being watermarks on paper of the seventeenth century, which he claims to be of Albigensian origin and to represent sacramental and Graal emblems. Had he only heard of the Tarot, had he known that these cards of divination, cards of fortune, cards of all vagrant arts, were perhaps current at the period in the South of France, I think that his enchanting but all too fantastic hypothesis might have dilated still more largely in the atmosphere of his dream. We should no doubt have had a vision of Christian Gnosticism, Manichæanism, and all that he understands by pure primitive Gospel, shining behind the pictures.

I do not look through such glasses, and I can only commend the subject to his attention at a later period; it is mentioned here that I may introduce with an unheard-of wonder the marvels of arbitrary speculation as to the history of the cards.

With reference to their form and number, it should scarcely be necessary to enumerate them, for they must be almost commonly familiar, but as it is precarious to assume anything, and as there are also other reasons, I will tabulate them briefly as follows:

§ 2. The Trumps Major, otherwise Greater Arcana

1. *The Magus, Magician, or juggler*, the caster of the dice and mountebank, in the world of vulgar trickery. This is the *colportage* interpretation, and it has the same correspondence with the real symbolical meaning that the use of the Tarot in fortune-telling has with its mystic construction according to the secret science of symbolism. I should add that many independent students of the subject, following their own lights, have produced individual sequences of meaning in respect of the Trumps Major, and their lights are sometimes suggestive, but they are not the true lights. For example, Éliphas Lévi says that the Magus signifies that unity which is the mother of numbers; others say that it is the Divine Unity; and one of the latest French commentators considers that in its general sense it is the will.

2. *The High Priestess, the Pope Joan*, or Female Pontiff; early expositors have sought to term this card the Mother, or Pope's Wife, which is opposed to the symbolism. It is sometimes held to represent the Divine Law and the Gnosis, in which case the Priestess corresponds to

the idea of the Shekinah. She is the Secret Tradition and the higher sense of the instituted Mysteries.

3. *The Empress*, who is sometimes represented with full face, while her correspondence, the Emperor, is in profile. As there has been some tendency to ascribe a symbolical significance to this distinction, it seems desirable to say that it carries no inner meaning. The Empress has been connected with the ideas of universal fecundity and in a general sense with activity.

4. *The Emperor*, by imputation the spouse of the former. He is occasionally represented as wearing, in addition to his personal insignia, the stars or ribbons of some order of chivalry. I mention this to shew that the cards are a medley of old and new emblems. Those who insist upon the evidence of the one may deal, if they can, with the other. No effectual argument for the antiquity of a particular design can be drawn from the fact that it incorporates old material; but there is also none which can be based on sporadic novelties, the intervention of which may signify only the unintelligent hand of an editor or of a late draughtsman.

5. *The High Priest or Hierophant*, called also Spiritual Father, and more commonly and obviously the Pope. It seems even to have been named the Abbot, and then its correspondence, the High Priestess, was the Abbess or Mother of the Convent. Both are arbitrary names. The insignia of the figures are papal, and in such case the High Priestess is and can be only the Church, to whom Pope and priests are married by the spiritual rite of ordination. I think, however, that in its primitive form this card did not represent the Roman Pontiff.

6. *The Lovers or Marriage*. This symbol has undergone many variations, as might be expected from its subject. In the eighteenth century form, by which it first became known to the world of archæological research, it is really a card of married life, shewing father and mother, with their child placed between them; and the pagan Cupid above, in the act of flying his shaft, is, of course, a misapplied emblem. The Cupid is of love beginning rather than of love in its fulness, guarding the fruit thereof. The card is said to have been entitled *Simulacyum fidei*, the symbol of conjugal faith, for which the rainbow as a sign of the covenant would have been a more appropriate concomitant. The figures are also held to have signified Truth, Honour and Love, but I suspect that this was, so to speak, the gloss of a commentator moralizing. It has these, but it has other and higher aspects.

7. *The Chariot*. This is represented in some extant codices as being drawn by two sphinxes, and the device is in consonance with the symbolism, but it must not be supposed that such was its original form; the variation was invented to support a particular historical hypothesis. In the eighteenth century white horses were yoked to the car. As regards its usual name, the lesser stands for the greater; it is really the King in his triumph, typifying, however, the victory which creates kingship as its natural consequence and not the vested royalty of the fourth card. M. Court de Gebelin said that it was Osiris Triumphing, the conquering sun in spring-time having vanquished the obstacles of winter. We know now that Osiris rising from the dead is not represented by such obvious symbolism. Other animals than horses have also been used to draw the *currus triumphalis*, as, for example, a lion and a leopard.

8. *Fortitude*. This is one of the cardinal virtues, of which I shall speak later. The female figure is usually represented as closing the mouth of a lion. In the earlier form which is printed by Court de Gebelin, she is obviously opening it. The first alternative is better symbolically, but either is an instance of strength in its conventional understanding, and conveys the idea of mastery. It has been said that the figure represents organic force, moral force and the principle of all force.

9. *The Hermit*, as he is termed in common parlance, stands next on the list; he is also the Capuchin, and in more philosophical language the Sage. He is said to be in search of that Truth which is located far off in the sequence, and of justice which has preceded him on the way. But this is a card of attainment, as we shall see later, rather than a card of quest. It is said also that his lantern contains the Light of Occult Science and that his staff is a Magic Wand. These interpretations are comparable in every respect to the divinatory and fortune-telling meanings with which I shall have to deal in their turn. The diabolism of both is that they are true after their own manner, but that they miss all the high things to which the Greater Arcana should be allocated. It is as if a man who knows in his heart that all roads lead to the heights, and that God is at the great height of all, should choose the way of perdition or the way of folly as the path of his own attainment. Éliphas Lévi has allocated this card to Prudence, but in so doing he has been actuated by the wish to fill a gap which would otherwise occur in the symbolism. The four cardinal virtues are necessary to an ideological sequence like the Trumps Major, but they must not be taken only in that first sense which exists for the use and consolation of him who in these days of halfpenny journalism is called the man in the street. In their proper understanding they are the correlatives of the counsels of perfection when these have been similarly re-expressed, and they read as follows: (a) Transcendental justice, the counter-equilibrium of the scales, when they have been overweighted so that they dip heavily on the side of God. The corresponding counsel is to use loaded dice when you play for high stakes with *Diabolus*. The axiom is *Aut Deus, aut nihil*. (b) Divine Ecstacy, as a counterpoise to something called Temperance, the sign of which is, I believe, the extinction of lights in the tavern. The corresponding counsel is to drink only of new wine in the Kingdom of the Father, because God is all in all. The axiom is that man being a reasonable being must get intoxicated with God; the imputed case in point is Spinoza. (c) The state of Royal Fortitude, which is the state of a Tower of Ivory and a House of Gold, but it is God and not the man who has become *Turris fortitudinis a facie inimici*, and out of that House the enemy has been cast. The corresponding counsel is that a man must not spare himself even in the presence of death, but he must be certain that his sacrifice shall be-of any open course-the best that will ensure his end. The axiom is that the strength which is raised to such a degree that a man dares lose himself shall shew him how God is found, and as to such refuge –dare therefore and learn. (d) Prudence is the economy which follows the line of least resistance, that the soul may get back whence it came. It is a doctrine of divine parsimony and conservation of energy, because of the stress, the terror and the manifest impertinences of this life. The corresponding counsel is that true prudence is concerned with the one thing needful, and the axiom is: Waste not, want not. The conclusion of the whole matter is a business proposition founded on the law of exchange: You cannot help getting what you seek in respect of the things that are Divine: it is the law of supply and demand. I have mentioned these few matters at this point for two simple reasons: (a) because in proportion to the impartiality of the mind it seems sometimes more difficult to determine whether it is vice or vulgarity which lays waste the present world more piteously; (b) because in order to remedy the imperfections of the old notions it is highly needful, on occasion, to empty terms and phrases of their accepted significance, that they may receive a new and more adequate meaning.

10. *The Wheel of Fortune*. There is a current *Manual of Cartomancy* which has obtained a considerable vogue in England, and amidst a great scattermeal of curious things to no purpose has intersected a few serious subjects. In its last and largest edition it treats in one section of the Tarot; which –if I interpret the author rightly– it regards from beginning to end as the Wheel of Fortune, this expression being understood in my own sense. I have no objection to

such an inclusive though conventional description; it obtains in all the worlds, and I wonder that it has not been adopted previously as the most appropriate name on the side of common fortune-telling. It is also the title of one of the Trumps Major –that indeed of our concern at the moment, as my sub-title shews. Of recent years this has suffered many fantastic presentations and one hypothetical reconstruction which is suggestive in its symbolism. The wheel has seven radii; in the eighteenth century the ascending and descending animals were really of nondescript character, one of them having a human head. At the summit was another monster with the body of an indeterminate beast, wings on shoulders and a crown on head. It carried two wands in its claws. These are replaced in the reconstruction by a Hermanubis rising with the wheel, a Sphinx couchant at the summit and a Typhon on the descending side. Here is another instance of an invention in support of a hypothesis; but if the latter be set aside the grouping is symbolically correct and can pass as such.

11. *Justice*. That the Tarot, though it is of all reasonable antiquity, is not of time immemorial, is shewn by this card, which could have been presented in a much more archaic manner. Those, however, who have gifts of discernment in matters of this kind will not need to be told that age is in no sense of the essence of the consideration; the Rite of Closing the Lodge in the Third Craft Grade of Masonry may belong to the late eighteenth century, but the fact signifies nothing; it is still the summary of all the instituted and official Mysteries. The female figure of the eleventh card is said to be Astræa, who personified the same virtue and is represented by the same symbols. This goddess notwithstanding, and notwithstanding the vulgarian Cupid, the Tarot is not of Roman mythology, or of Greek either. Its presentation of justice is supposed to be one of the four cardinal virtues included in the sequence of Greater Arcana; but, as it so happens, the fourth emblem is wanting, and it became necessary for the commentators to discover it at all costs. They did what it was possible to do, and yet the laws of research have never succeeded in extricating the missing Persephone under the form of Prudence. Court de Gebelin attempted to solve the difficulty by a tour de force, and believed that he had extracted what he wanted from the symbol of the Hanged Man –wherein he deceived himself. The Tarot has, therefore, its justice, its Temperance also and its Fortitude, but –owing to a curious omission– it does not offer us any type of Prudence, though it may be admitted that, in some respects, the isolation of the Hermit, pursuing a solitary path by the light of his own lamp, gives, to those who can receive it, a certain high counsel in respect of the *via prudentiæ*.

12. *The Hanged Man*. This is the symbol which is supposed to represent Prudence, and Éliphas Lévi says, in his most shallow and plausible manner, that it is the adept bound by his engagements. The figure of a man is suspended head-downwards from a gibbet, to which he is attached by a rope about one of his ankles. The arms are bound behind him, and one leg is crossed over the other. According to another, and indeed the prevailing interpretation, he signifies sacrifice, but all current meanings attributed to this card are cartomancists' intuitions, apart from any real value on the symbolical side. The fortune-tellers of the eighteenth century who circulated Tarots, depict a semi-feminine youth in jerkin, poised erect on one foot and loosely attached to a short stake driven into the ground.

13. *Death*. The method of presentation is almost invariable, and embodies a bourgeois form of symbolism. The scene is the field of life, and amidst ordinary rank vegetation there are living arms and heads protruding from the ground. One of the heads is crowned, and a skeleton with a great scythe is in the act of mowing it. The transparent and unescapable meaning is death, but the alternatives allocated to the symbol are change and transformation. Other heads have been swept from their place previously, but it is, in its current and patent

meaning, more especially a card of the death of Kings. In the exotic sense it has been said to signify the ascent of the spirit in the divine spheres, creation and destruction, perpetual movement, and so forth.

14. *Temperance.* The winged figure of a female –who, in opposition to all doctrine concerning the hierarchy of angels, is usually allocated to this order of ministering spirits– is pouring liquid from one pitcher to another. In his last work on the Tarot, Dr. Papus abandons the traditional form and depicts a woman wearing an Egyptian head-dress. The first thing which seems clear on the surface is that the entire symbol has no especial connexion with Temperance, and the fact that this designation has always obtained for the card offers a very obvious instance of a meaning behind meaning, which is the title in chief to consideration in respect of the Tarot as a whole.

15. *The Devil.* In the eighteenth century this card seems to have been rather a symbol of merely animal impudicity. Except for a fantastic head-dress, the chief figure is entirely naked; it has bat-like wings, and the hands and feet are represented by the claws of a bird. In the right hand there is a sceptre terminating in a sign which has been thought to represent fire. The figure as a whole is not particularly evil; it has no tail, and the commentators who have said that the claws are those of a harpy have spoken at random. There is no better ground for the alternative suggestion that they are eagle's claws. Attached, by a cord depending from their collars, to the pedestal on which the figure is mounted, are two small demons, presumably male and female. These are tailed, but not winged. Since 1856 the influence of Éliphas Lévi and his doctrine of occultism has changed the face of this card, and it now appears as a pseudo-Baphometic figure with the head of a goat and a great torch between the horns; it is seated instead of erect, and in place of the generative organs there is the Hermetic caduceus. In *Le Tarot Divinatoire* of Papus the small demons are replaced by naked human beings, male and female ' who are yoked only to each other. The author may be felicitated on this improved symbolism.

16. *The Tower struck by Lightning.* Its alternative titles are: Castle of Plutus, God's House and the Tower of Babel. In the last case, the figures falling therefrom are held to be Nimrod and his minister. It is assuredly a card of confusion, and the design corresponds, broadly speaking, to any of the designations except *Maison Dieu*, unless we are to understand that the House of God has been abandoned and the veil of the temple rent. It is a little surprising that the device has not so far been allocated to the destruction Of Solomon's Temple, when the lightning would symbolize the fire and sword with which that edifice was visited by the King of the Chaldees.

17. *The Star*, Dog-Star, or Sirius, also called fantastically the Star of the Magi. Grouped about it are seven minor luminaries, and beneath it is a naked female figure, with her left knee upon the earth and her right foot upon the water. She is in the act of pouring fluids from two vessels. A bird is perched on a tree near her; for this a butterfly on a rose has been substituted in some later cards. So also the Star has been called that of Hope. This is one of the cards which Court de Gebelin describes as wholly Egyptian-that is to say, in his own reverie.

18. *The Moon.* Some eighteenth-century cards shew the luminary on its waning side; in the debased edition of Etteilla, it is the moon at night in her plenitude, set in a heaven of stars; of recent years the moon is shewn on the side of her increase. In nearly all presentations she is shining brightly and shedding the moisture of fertilizing dew in great drops. Beneath

there are two towers, between which a path winds to the verge of the horizon. Two dogs, or alternatively a wolf and dog, are baying at the moon, and in the foreground there is water, through which a crayfish moves towards the land.

19. The Sun. The luminary is distinguished in older cards by chief rays that are waved and salient alternately and by secondary salient rays. It appears to shed its influence on earth not only by light and heat, but –like the moon– by drops of dew. Court de Gebelin termed these tears of gold and of pearl, just as he identified the lunar dew with the tears of Isis. Beneath the dog-star there is a wall suggesting an enclosure-as it might be, a walled garden-wherein are two children, either naked or lightly clothed, facing a water, and gambolling, or running hand in hand. Éliphas Lévi says that these are sometimes replaced by a spinner unwinding destinies, and otherwise by a much better symbol-a naked child mounted on a white horse and displaying a scarlet standard.

20. *The Last judgment*. I have spoken of this symbol already, the form of which is essentially invariable, even in the Etteilla set. An angel sounds his trumpet *per sepulchra regionum*, and the dead arise. It matters little that Etteilla omits the angel, or that Dr. Papus substitutes a ridiculous figure, which is, however, in consonance with the general motive of that Tarot set which accompanies his latest work. Before rejecting the transparent interpretation of the symbolism which is conveyed by the name of the card and by the picture which it presents to the eye, we should feel very sure of our ground. On the surface, at least, it is and can be only the resurrection of that triad –father, mother, child-whom we have met with already in the eighth card. M. Bourgeat hazards the suggestion that esoterically it is the symbol of evolution –of which it carries none of the signs. Others say that it signifies renewal, which is obvious enough; that it is the triad of human life; that it is the "generative force of the earth... and eternal life." Court de Gebelin makes himself impossible as usual, and points out that if the grave-stones were removed it could be accepted as a symbol of creation.

21 –which, however, in most of the arrangements is the cipher card, number nothing– *The Fool, Mate, or Unwise Man*. Court de Gebelin places it at the head of the whole series as the zero or negative which is presupposed by numeration, and as this is a simpler so also it is a better arrangement. It has been abandoned because in later times the cards have been attributed to the letters of the Hebrew alphabet, and there has been apparently some difficulty about allocating the zero symbol satisfactorily in a sequence of letters all of which signify numbers. In the present reference of the card to the letter Shin, which corresponds to 200, the difficulty or the unreason remains. The truth is that the real arrangement of the cards has never transpired. The Fool carries a wallet; he is looking over his shoulder and does not know that he is on the brink of a precipice; but a dog or other animal –some call it a tiger– is attacking him from behind, and he is hurried to his destruction unawares. Etteilla has given a justifiable variation of this card –as generally understood– in the form of a court jester, with cap, bells and motley garb. The other descriptions say that the wallet contains the bearer's follies and vices, which seems bourgeois and arbitrary.

22. *The World, the Universe, or Time*. The four living creatures of the Apocalypse and Ezekiel's vision, attributed to the evangelists in Christian symbolism, are grouped about an elliptic garland, as if it were a chain of flowers intended to symbolize all sensible things; within this garland there is the figure of a woman, whom the wind has girt about the loins with a light scarf, and this is all her vesture. She is in the act of dancing, and has a wand in either hand. It is eloquent as an image of the swirl of the sensitive life, of joy attained in the body, of the soul's intoxication in the earthly paradise, but still guarded by the Divine Watchers, as if by the powers and the graces of the Holy Name, Tetragammaton, JVHV –those four ineffable letters

which are sometimes attributed to the mystical beasts. Éliphas Lévi calls the garland a crown, and reports that the figure represents Truth. Dr. Papus connects it with the Absolute and the realization of the Great Work; for yet others it is a symbol of humanity and the eternal reward of a life that has been spent well. It should be noted that in the four quarters of the garland there are four flowers distinctively marked. According to P. Christian, the garland should be formed of roses, and this is the kind of chain which Éliphas Lévi says is less easily broken than a chain of iron. Perhaps by antithesis, but for the same reason, the iron crown of Peter may he more lightly on the heads of sovereign pontiffs than the crown of gold on kings.

§ 3. The Four Suits, otherwise Lesser Arcana

The resources of interpretation have been lavished, if not exhausted, on the twenty-two Trumps Major, the symbolism of which is unquestionable. There remain the four suits, being Wands or Sceptres —ex hypothesi, in the archæology of the subject, the antecedents of Diamonds in modern cards: Cups, corresponding to Hearts; Swords, which answer to Clubs, as the weapon of chivalry is in relation to the peasant's quarter-staff or the Alsatian bludgeon; and, finally, Pentacles —called also Deniers and Money— which are the prototypes of Spades, In the old as in the new suits, there are ten numbered cards, but in the Tarot there are four Court Cards allocated to each suit, or a Knight in addition to King, Queen and Knave. The Knave is a page, valet, or damoiseau; most correctly, he is an esquire, presumably in the service of the Knight; but there are certain rare sets in which the page becomes a maid of honour, thus pairing the sexes in the tetrad of the court cards. There are naturally distinctive features in respect of the several pictures, by which I mean that the King of Wands is not exactly the same personage as the King of Cups, even after allowance has been made for the different emblems that they bear; but the symbolism resides in their rank and in the suit to which they belong. So also the smaller cards, which —until now— have never been issued pictorially in these our modem days, depend on the particular meaning attaching to their numbers in connexion with the particular suit. I reserve, therefore, the details of the Lesser Arcana, till I come to speak in the second part of the rectified and perfected Tarot which accompanies this work. The consensus of divinatory meanings attached both to the greater and lesser symbols belongs to the third part.

§ 4. The Tarot in History

Our immediate next concern is to speak of the cards in their history, so that the speculations and reveries which have been perpetuated and multiplied in the schools of occult research may be disposed of once and for all, as intimated in the preface hereto.

Let it be understood at the beginning of this point that there are several sets or sequences of ancient cards which are only in part of our concern. The Tarot of the Bohemians, by Papus, which I have recently carried through the press, revising the imperfect rendering, has some useful information in this connexion, and, except for the omission of dates and other evidences of the archaeological sense, it will serve the purpose of the general reader. I do not propose to extend it in the present place in any manner that can be called considerable, but certain additions are desirable and so also is a distinct mode of presentation.

Among ancient cards which are mentioned in connexion with the Tarot, there are firstly those of Baldini, which are the celebrated set attributed by tradition to Andrea Mantegna, though this view is now generally rejected. Their date is supposed to be about 1470, and it is thought that there are not more than four collections extant in Europe. A copy or reproduction referred to 1485 is perhaps equally rare. A complete set contains fifty numbers, divided into five denaries or sequences of ten cards each. There seems to be no record that they were used for the purposes of a game, whether of chance or skill; they could scarcely have lent themselves to divination or any form of fortune-telling; while it would be more than idle to impute a profound symbolical meaning to their obvious emblematic designs. The first denary embodies Conditions of Life, as follows: (i) The Beggar, (2) the Knave, (3) the Artisan, (4) the Merchant, (5) the Noble, (6) the Knight, (7) the Doge, (8) the King, (9) the Emperor, (10) the Pope. The second contains the Muses and their Divine Leader: (11) Calliope, (12) Urania, (13) Terpsichore, (14) Erato, (15) Polyhymnia, (16) Thalia, (17) Melpomene, (18) Euterpe, (19) Clio, (20) Apollo. The third combines part of the Liberal Arts and Sciences with other departments of human learning, as follows: (21) Grammar, (22) Logic, (23) Rhetoric, (24) Geometry, (25) Arithmetic, (26) Music, (27) Poetry,(28) Philosophy, (29) Astrology, (30) Theology. The fourth denary completes the Liberal Arts and enumerates the Virtues: (31) Astronomy, (32) Chronology, (33) Cosmology, (34) Temperance, (35) Prudence, (36) Strength, (37) Justice; (38) Charity, (39) Hope, (40) Faith. The fifth and last denary presents the System of the Heavens (41) Moon, (42) Mercury, (43) Venus, (44) Sun, (45) Mars, (46) Jupiter, (47) Saturn, (48) A Eighth Sphere, (49) *Primum Mobile*, (50) First Cause.

We must set aside the fantastic attempts to extract complete Tarot sequences out of these denaries; we must forbear from saying, for example, that the Conditions of Life correspond to the Trumps Major, the Muses to Pentacles, the Arts and Sciences to Cups, the Virtues, etc., to Sceptres, and the conditions of life to Swords. This kind of thing can be done by a process of mental contortion, but it has no place in reality. At the same time, it is hardly possible that individual cards should not exhibit certain, and even striking, analogies. The Baldini King, Knight and Knave suggest the corresponding court cards of the Minor Arcana. The Emperor, Pope, Temperance, Strength, justice, Moon and Sun are common to the Mantegna and Trumps Major of any Tarot pack. Predisposition has also connected the Beggar and Fool, Venus and the Star, Mars and the Chariot, Saturn and the Hermit, even Jupiter, or alternatively the First Cause, with the Tarot card of the World.[1] But the most salient features of the Trumps Major are wanting in the Mantegna set, and I do not believe that the ordered sequence in the latter case gave birth, as it has been suggested, to the others. Romain Merlin maintained this view, and positively assigned the Baldini cards to the end of the fourteenth century.

If it be agreed that, except accidentally and sporadically, the Baldini emblematic or allegorical pictures have only a shadowy and occasional connexion with Tarot cards, and, whatever their most probable date, that they can have supplied no originating motive, it follows that we are still seeking not only an origin in place and time for the symbols with which we are concerned, but a specific case of their manifestation on the continent of Europe to serve as a point of departure, whether backward or forward. Now it is well known that in the year 1393 the painter Charles Gringonneur –who for no reason that I can trace has been termed an occultist and kabalist by one indifferent English writer– designed and illuminated some kind of cards for the diversion of Charles VI of France when he was in mental ill-health, and the question arises whether anything can be ascertained of their nature. The only available answer is that at Paris, in the Bibliothèque du Roi, there are seventeen cards drawn and illuminated on paper. They are very beautiful, antique and priceless; the figures have a background of gold, and are framed in a silver border; but they are accompanied by no inscription and no number.

It is certain, however, that they include Tarot Trumps Major, the list of which is as follows: Fool, Emperor, Pope, Lovers, Wheel of Fortune, Temperance, Fortitude, justice, Moon, Sun, Chariot, Hermit, Hanged Man, Death, Tower and Last judgment. There are also four Tarot Cards at the Musée Carrer, Venice, and five others elsewhere, making nine in all. They include two pages or Knaves, three Kings and two Queens, thus illustrating the Minor Arcana. These collections have all been identified with the set produced by Gringonneur, but the ascription was disputed so far back as the year 1848, and it is not apparently put forward at the present day, even by those who are anxious to make evident the antiquity of the Tarot. It is held that they are all of Italian and some at least certainly of Venetian origin. We have in this manner our requisite point of departure in respect of place at least. It has further been stated with authority that Venetian Tarots are the old and true form, which is the parent of all others; but I infer that complete sets of the Major and Minor Arcana belong to much later periods. The pack is thought to have consisted of seventy-eight cards.

Notwithstanding, however, the preference shewn towards the Venetian Tarot, it is acknowledged that some portions of a Minchiate or Florentine set must be allocated to the period between 1413 and 1418. These were once in the possession of Countess Gonzaga, at Milan. A complete Minchiate pack contained ninety-seven cards, and in spite of these vestiges it is regarded, speaking generally, as a later development. There were forty-one Trumps Major, the additional numbers being borrowed or reflected from the Baldini emblematic set. In the court cards of the Minor Arcana, the Knights were monsters of the centaur type, while the Knaves were sometimes warriors and sometimes serving-men. Another distinction dwelt upon is the prevalence of Chrstian mediæval ideas and the utter absence of any Oriental suggestion. The question, however, remains whether there are Eastern traces in any Tarot cards.

We come, in fine, to the Bolognese Tarot, sometimes referred to as that of Venice and having the Trumps Major complete, but numbers 20 and 21 are transposed. In the Minor Arcana the 2, 3, 4 and 5 of the small cards are omitted, with the result that there are sixty-two cards in all. The termination of the Trumps Major in the representation of the Last judgment is curious, and a little arresting as a point of symbolism; but this is all that it seems necessary to remark about the pack of Bologna, except that it is said to have been invented –or, as a Tarot, more correctly, modified– about the beginning of the fifteenth century by an exiled Prince of Pisa resident in the city. The purpose for which they were used is made tolerably evident by the fact that, in 1423, St. Bernardin of Sienna preached against playing cards and other forms of gambling. Forty years later the importation of cards into England was forbidden, the time being that of King Edward IV. This is the first certain record of the subject in our country.

It is difficult to consult perfect examples of the sets enumerated above, but it is not difficult to meet with detailed and illustrated descriptions –I should add, provided always that the writer is not an occultist, for accounts emanating from that source are usually imperfect, vague and preoccupied by considerations which cloud the critical issues. An instance in point is offered by certain views which have been expressed on the Mantegna codex--if I may continue to dignify card sequences with a title of this kind. It has been ruled –as we have see—in occult reverie that Apollo and the Nine Muses are in correspondence with Pentacles, but the analogy does not obtain in a working state of research; and reverie must border on nightmare before we can identify Astronomy, Chronology and Cosmology with the suit of Cups. The Baldini figures which represent these subjects are emblems of their period and not symbols, like the Tarot.

In conclusion as to this part, I observe that there has been a disposition among experts to think that the Trumps Major were not originally connected with the numbered suits. I do not wish to offer a personal view; I am not an expert in the history of games of chance, and I hate the *profanum vulgus* of divinatory devices; but I venture, under all reserves, to intimate that if later research should justify such a leaning, then –except for the good old art of fortune-telling and its tamperings with so-called destiny –it will be so much the better for the Greater Arcana.

So far as regards what is indispensable as preliminaries to the historical aspects of Tarot cards, and I will now take up the speculative side of the subject and produce its tests of value. In my preface to *The Tarot of the Bohemians* I have mentioned that the first writer who made known the fact of the cards was the archaeologist Court de Gebelin, who, just prior to the French Revolution, occupied several years in the publication of his *Monde Primitif*, which extended to nine quarto volumes. He was a learned man of his epoch, a high-grade Mason, a member of the historical Lodge of the Philalethes, and a *virtuoso* with a profound and lifelong interest in the debate on universal antiquities before a science of the subject existed. Even at this day, his memorials and dissertations, collected under the title which I have quoted, are worth possessing. By an accident of things, he became acquainted with the Tarot when it was quite unknown in Paris, and at once conceived that it was the remnants of an Egyptian book. He made inquiries concerning it and ascertained that it was in circulation over a considerable part of Europe –Spain, Italy, Germany and the South of France. It was in use as a game of chance or skill, after the ordinary manner of playing-cards; and he ascertained further how the game was played. But it was in use also for the higher purpose of divination or fortune-telling, and with the help of a learned friend he discovered the significance attributed to the cards, together with the method of arrangement adopted for this purpose. In a word, he made a distinct contribution to our knowledge, and he is still a source of reference –but it is on the question of fact only, and not on the beloved hypothesis that the Tarot contains pure Egyptian doctrine. However, he set the opinion which is prevalent to this day throughout the occult schools, that in the mystery and wonder, the strange night of the gods, the unknown tongue and the undeciphered hieroglyphics which symbolized Egypt at the end of the eighteenth century, the origin of the cards was lost. So dreamed one of the characteristic *literati* of France, and one can almost understand and sympathize, for the country about the Delta and the Nile was beginning to loom largely in the preoccupation of learned thought, and *omne ignolum pro Ægyptiaco* was the way of delusion to which many minds tended. It was excusable enough then, but that the madness has continued and, within the charmed circle of the occult sciences, still passes from mouth to mouth –there is no excuse for this. Let us see, therefore, the evidence produced by M. Court de Gebelin in support of his thesis, and, that I may deal justly, it shall be summarized as far as possible in his own words.

(i) The figures and arrangement of the game are manifestly allegorical; (2) the allegories are in conformity with the civil, philosophical and religious doctrine of ancient Egypt; (3) if the cards were modern, no High Priestess would be included among the Greater Arcana; (4) the figure in question bears the horns of Isis; (5) the card which is called the Emperor has a sceptre terminating in a triple cross; (6) the card entitled the Moon, who is Isis, shews drops of rain or dew in the act of being shed by the luminary and these-as we have seen-are the tears of Isis, which swelled the waters of the Nile and fertilized the fields of Egypt; (7) the seventeenth card, or Star, is the dog-star, Sirius, which was consecrated to Isis and symbolized the opening of the year; (8) the game played with the Tarot is founded on the sacred number seven, which was of great importance in Egypt; (9) the word Tarot is pure Egyptian, in which language Tar=way or road, and Ro=king or royal –it signifies therefore the Royal Road of Life;

(10) alternatively, it is derived from A=doctrine Rosh= Mercury =Thoth, and the article T; in sum, *Tarosh*; and therefore the Tarot is the *Book of Thoth*, or the *Table of the Doctrine of Mercury*.

Such is the testimony, it being understood that I have set aside several casual statements, for which no kind of justification is produced. These, therefore, are ten pillars which support the edifice of the thesis, and the same are pillars of sand. The Tarot is, of course, allegorical –that is to say, it is symbolism– but allegory and symbol are catholic —of all countries, nations and times they are not more Egyptian than Mexican they are of Europe and Cathay, of Tibet beyond the Himalayas and of the London gutters. As allegory and symbol, the cards correspond to many types of ideas and things; they are universal and not particular; and the fact that they do not especially and peculiarly respond to Egyptian doctrine –religious, philosophical or civil– is clear from the failure of Court de Gebelin to go further than the affirmation. The presence of a High Priestess among the Trumps Major is more easily explained as the memorial of some popular superstition –that worship of Diana, for example, the persistence of which in modern Italy has been traced with such striking results by Leland. We have also to remember the universality of horns in every cultus, not excepting that of Tibet. The triple cross is preposterous as an instance of Egyptian symbolism; it is the cross of the patriarchal see, both Greek and Latin –of Venice, of Jerusalem, for example– and it is the form of signing used to this day by the priests and laity of the Orthodox Rite. I pass over the idle allusion to the tears of Isis, because other occult writers have told us that they are Hebrew *Jods*; as regards the seventeenth card, it is the star Sirius or another, as predisposition pleases; the number seven was certainly important in Egypt and any treatise on numerical mysticism will shew that the same statement applies everywhere, even if we elect to ignore the seven Christian Sacraments and the Gifts of the Divine Spirit. Finally, as regards the etymology of the word Tarot, it is sufficient to observe that it was offered before the discovery of the Rosetta Stone and when there was no knowledge of the Egyptian language.

The thesis of Court de Gebelin was not suffered to repose undisturbed in the mind of the age, appealing to the learned exclusively by means of a quarto volume. It created the opportunity of Tarot cards in Paris, as the centre of France and all things French in the universe. The suggestion that divination by cards had behind it the unexpected warrants of ancient hidden science, and that the root of the whole subject was in the wonder and mystery of Egypt, reflected thereon almost a divine dignity; out of the purlieus of occult practices cartomancy emerged into fashion and assumed for the moment almost pontifical vestures. The first to undertake the role of *bateleur*, magician and juggler, was the illiterate but zealous adventurer, Alliette; the second, as a kind of High Priestess, full of intuitions and revelations, was Mlle. Lenormand –but she belongs to a later period; while lastly came Julia Orsini, who is referable to a Queen of Cups rather in the tatters of clairvoyance. I am not concerned with these people as tellers of fortune, when destiny itself was shuffling and cutting cards for the game of universal revolution, or for such courts and courtiers as were those of Louis XVIII, Charles IX and Louis Philippe. But under the occult designation of Etteilla, the transliteration of name, Alliette, that *perruquier* took himself with high seriousness and posed rather as a priest of the occult sciences than as an ordinary adept in *l'art de tirer les cartes*. Even at this day there are people, like Dr. Papus, who have sought to save some part of his bizarre system from oblivion.

The long and heterogeneous story of *Le Monde Primitif* had come to the end of its telling in 1782, and in 1783 the tracts of Etteilla had begun pouring from the press, testifying that already he had spent thirty, nay, almost forty years in the study of Egyptian magic, and that he had found the final keys. They were, in fact, the Keys of the Tarot, which was a book of philosophy and the *Book of Thoth*, but at the same time it was actually written by seventeen Magi in a Temple of Fire, on the borders of the Levant, some three leagues from Memphis. It contained the science of the universe, and the cartomancist proceeded to apply it to Astrology, Alchemy, and fortune-telling, without the slightest diffidence or reserve as to the fact that he was driving a trade. I have really little doubt that he considered it genuine as a *métier*, and that he himself was the first person whom he convinced concerning his system. But the point which we have to notice is that in this manner was the antiquity of the Tarot generally trumpeted forth. The little books of Etteilla are proof positive that he did not know even his own language; when in the course of time he produced a reformed Tarot, even those who think of him tenderly admit that he spoiled its symbolism; and in respect of antiquities he had only Court de Gebelin as his universal authority.

The cartomancists succeeded one another in the manner which I have mentioned, and of course there were rival adepts of these less than least mysteries; but the scholarship of the subject, if it can be said to have come into existence, reposed after all in the quarto of Court de Gebelin for something more than sixty years. On his authority, there is very little doubt that everyone who became acquainted, by theory or practice, by casual or special concern, with the question of Tarot cards, accepted their Egyptian character. It is said that people are taken commonly at their own valuation, and –following as it does the line of least resistance– the unsolicitous general mind assuredly accepts archæological pretensions in the sense of their own daring and of those who put them forward. The first who appeared to reconsider the subject with some presumptive titles to a hearing was the French writer Duchesne, but I am compelled to pass him over with a mere reference, and so also some interesting researches on the general subject of playing-cards by Singer in England. The latter believed that the old Venetian game called Trappola was the earliest European form of card-playing, that it was of Arabian origin, and that the fifty-two cards used for the purpose derived from that region. I do not gather that any importance was ever attached to this view.

Duchesne and Singer were followed by another English writer, W. A. Chatto, who reviewed the available facts and the cloud of speculations which had already arisen on the subject. This was in 1848, and his work has still a kind of standard authority, but –after every allowance for a certain righteousness attributable to the independent mind– it remains an indifferent and even a poor performance. It was, however, characteristic in its way of the approaching middle night of the nineteenth century. Chatto rejected the Egyptian hypothesis, but as he was at very little pains concerning it, he would scarcely be held to displace Court de Gebelin if the latter had any firm ground beneath his hypothesis. In 1854 another French writer, Boiteau, took up the general question, maintaining the oriental origin of Tarot cards, though without attempting to prove it. I am not certain, but I think that he is the first writer who definitely identified them with the Gipsies; for him, however, the original Gipsy home was in India, and Egypt did not therefore enter into his calculation.

In 1860 there arose Éliphas Lévi, a brilliant and profound *illuminé* whom it is impossible to accept, and with whom it is even more impossible to dispense. There was never a mouth declaring such great things, of all the western voices which have proclaimed or interpreted the science called occult and the doctrine called magical. I suppose that, fundamentally speaking, he cared as much and as little as I do for the phenomenal part, but he explained the phenomena with the assurance of one who openly regarded charlatanry as a great means to an end, if used in a right cause. He came unto his own and his own received him, also at his proper valuation, as a man of great learning –which he never was– and as a revealer of all mysteries without having been received into any. I do not think that there was ever an instance of a writer with greater gifts, after their particular kind, who put them to such indifferent uses. After all, he was only Etteilla a second time in the flesh, endowed in his transmutation with a mouth of gold and a wider casual knowledge. This notwithstanding, he has written the most comprehensive, brilliant, enchanting *History of Magic* which has ever been drawn into writing in any language. The Tarot and the de Gebelin hypothesis he took into his heart of hearts, and all occult France and all esoteric Britain, Martinists, half-instructed Kabalists, schools of *soi disant* theosophy –there, here and everywhere– have accepted his judgment about it with the same confidence as his interpretations of those great classics of Kabalism which he had skimmed rather than read. The Tarot for him was not only the most perfect instrument of divination and the keystone of occult science, but it was the primitive book, the sole book of the ancient Magi, the miraculous volume which inspired all the sacred writings of antiquity. In his first work Lévi was content, however, with accepting the construction of Court de Gebelin and reproducing the seventh Trump Major with a few Egyptian characteristics. The question of Tarot transmission through the Gipsies did not occupy him, till J. A. Vaillant, a bizarre writer with great knowledge of the Romany people, suggested it in his work on those wandering tribes. The two authors were almost coincident and reflected one another thereafter. It remained for Romain Merlin, in 1869, to point out what should have been obvious, namely, that cards of some kind were known in Europe prior to the arrival of the Gipsies in or about 1417. But as this was their arrival at Lüneburg, and as their presence can be traced antecedently, the correction loses a considerable part of its force; it is safer, therefore, to say that the evidence for the use of the Tarot by Romany tribes was not suggested till after the year 1840; the fact that some Gipsies before this period were found using cards is quite explicable on the hypothesis not that they brought them into Europe but found them there already and added them to their stock-in-trade.

    We have now seen that there is no particle of evidence for the Egyptian origin of Tarot cards. Looking in other directions, it was once advanced on native authority that cards of some kind were invented in China about the year A.D. 1120. Court de Gebelin believed in his zeal that he had traced them to a Chinese inscription of great imputed antiquity which was said to refer to the subsidence of the waters of the Deluge. The characters of this inscription were contained in seventy-seven compartments, and this constitutes the analogy. India had also its tablets, whether cards or otherwise, and these have suggested similar slender similitudes. But the existence, for example, of ten suits or styles, of twelve numbers each, and representing the avatars of Vishnu as a fish, tortoise, boar, lion, monkey, hatchet, umbrella or bow, as a goat, a boodh and as a horse, in fine, are not going to help us towards the origin of our own Trumps Major, nor do crowns and harps –nor even the presence of possible coins as a synonym of deniers and perhaps as an equivalent of pentacles– do much to elucidate the Lesser Arcana. If every tongue and people and clime and period possessed their cards –if with these also they philosophized, divined and gambled– the fact would be interesting enough, but unless they were Tarot cards, they would illustrate only the universal tendency of man to be pursuing the same things in more or less the same way.

    I end, therefore, the history of this subject by repeating that it has no history prior to the fourteenth century, when the first rumours, were heard concerning cards. They may have existed for centuries, but this period would be early enough, if they were only intended for people to try their luck at gambling or their luck at seeing the future; on the other hand, if they contain the deep intimations of Secret Doctrine, then the fourteenth century is again early enough, or at least in this respect we are getting as much as we can.

PART II
The Doctrine Behind the Veil

§ 1. The Tarot and Secret Tradition

THE Tarot embodies symbolical presentations of universal ideas, behind which lie all the implicits of the human mind, and it is in this sense that they contain secret doctrine, which is the realization by the few of truths imbedded in the consciousness of all, though they have not passed into express recognition by ordinary men. The theory is that this doctrine has always existed –that is to say, has been excogitated in the consciousness of an elect minority; that it has been perpetuated in secrecy from one to another and has been recorded in secret literatures, like those of Alchemy and Kabalism; that it is contained also in those Instituted Mysteries of which Rosicrucianism offers an example near to our hand in the past, and Craft Masonry a living summary, or general memorial, for those who can interpret its real meaning. Behind the Secret Doctrine it is held that there is an experience or practice by which the Doctrine is justified. It is obvious that in a handbook like the present I can do little more than state the claims, which, however, have been discussed at length in several of my other writings, while it is designed to treat two of its more important phases in books devoted to the Secret Tradition in Freemasonry and in Hermetic literature. As regards Tarot claims, it should be remembered that some considerable part of the imputed Secret Doctrine has been presented in the pictorial emblems of Alchemy, so that the imputed *Book of Thoth* is in no sense a solitary device of this emblematic kind. Now, Alchemy had two branches, as I have explained fully elsewhere, and the pictorial emblems which I have mentioned are common to both divisions. Its material side is represented in the strange symbolism of the *Mutus Liber*, printed in the great folios of Mangetus. There the process for the performance of the great work of transmutation is depicted in fourteen copper-plate engravings, which exhibit the different stages of the matter in the various chemical vessels. Above these vessels there are mythological, planetary, solar and lunar symbols, as if the powers and virtues which -according to Hermetic teaching –preside over the development and perfection of the metallic kingdom were intervening actively to assist the two operators who are toiling below. The operators –curiously enough– are male and female. The spiritual side of Alchemy is set forth in the much stranger emblems of the *Book of Lambspring*, and of this I have already given a preliminary interpretation, to which the reader may be referred (See the Occult Review, vol. viii, 1908). The tract contains the mystery of what is called the mystical or arch-natural elixir, being the marriage of the soul and the spirit in the body of the adept philosopher and the transmutation of the body as the physical result of this marriage. I have never met with more curious intimations than in this one little work. It may be mentioned as a point of fact that both tracts are very much later in time than the latest date that could be assigned to the general distribution of Tarot cards in Europe by the most drastic form of criticism.

They belong respectively to the end of the seventeenth and sixteenth centuries. As I am not drawing here on the font of imagination to refresh that of fact and experience, I do not suggest that the Tarot set the example of expressing Secret Doctrine in pictures and that it was followed by Hermetic writers; but it is noticeable that it is perhaps the earliest example of this art. It is also the most catholic, because it is not, by attribution or otherwise, a derivative of any one school or literature of occultism; it is not of Alchemy or Kabalism or Astrology or Ceremonial Magic; but, as I have said, it is the presentation of universal ideas by means of universal types, and it is in the combination of these types –if anywhere– that it presents Secret Doctrine.

That combination may, *ex hypothesi*, reside in the numbered sequence of its series or in their fortuitous assemblage by shuffling, cutting and dealing, as in ordinary games of chance played with cards. Two writers have adopted the first view without prejudice to the second, and I shall do well, perhaps, to dispose at once of what they have said. Mr. MacGregor Mathers, who once published a pamphlet on the Tarot, which was in the main devoted to fortune-telling, suggested that the twenty-two Trumps Major could be constructed, following their numerical order, into what he called a "connected sentence." It was, in fact, the heads of a moral thesis on the human will, its enlightenment by science, represented by the Magician, its manifestation by action –a significance attributed to the High Priestess-its realization (the Empress) in deeds of mercy and beneficence, which qualities were allocated to the Emperor. He spoke also in the familiar conventional manner of prudence, fortitude, sacrifice, hope and ultimate happiness. But if this were the message of the cards, it is certain that there would be no excuse for publishing them at this day or taking the pains to elucidate them at some length. In his *Tarot of the Bohemians*, a work written with zeal and enthusiasm, sparing no pains of thought or research within its particular lines-but unfortunately without real insight –Dr. Papus has given a singularly elaborate scheme of the Trumps Major. It depends, like that of Mr. Mathers, from their numerical sequence, but exhibits their interrelation in the Divine World, the Macrocosm and Microcosm. In this manner we get, as it were, a spiritual history of man, or of the soul coming out from the Eternal, passing into the darkness of the material body, and returning to the height. I think that the author is here within a measurable distance of the right track, and his views are to this extent informing, but his method –in some respects- confuses the issues and the modes and planes of being.

The Trumps Major have also been treated in the alternative method which I have mentioned, and Grand Orient, in his *Manual of Cartomancy*, under the guise of a mode of transcendental divination, has really offered the result of certain illustrative readings of the cards when arranged as the result of a fortuitous combination by means of shuffling and dealing. The use of divinatory methods, with whatsoever intention and for whatever purpose, carries with it two suggestions. It may be thought that the deeper meanings are imputed rather than real, but this is disposed of by the fact of certain cards, like the Magician, the High Priestess, the Wheel of Fortune, the Hanged Man, the Tower or *Maison Dieu*, and several others, which do not correspond to Conditions of Life, Arts, Sciences, Virtues, or the other subjects contained in the denaries of the Baldini emblematic figures. They are also proof positive that obvious and natural moralities cannot explain the sequence. Such cards testify concerning themselves after another manner; and although the state in which I have left the Tarot in respect of its historical side is so much the more difficult as it is so much the more open, they indicate the real subject matter with which we are concerned. The methods shew also that the Trumps Major at least have been adapted to fortune-telling rather than belong thereto. The common divinatory meanings which will be given in the third part are largely arbitrary attributions, or the product of secondary and uninstructed intuition; or, at the very most, they belong to the subject on a lower plane, apart from the original intention. If the Tarot were of fortune-telling in the root-matter thereof, we should have to look in very strange places for the motive which devised it –to Witchcraft and the Black Sabbath, rather than any Secret Doctrine.

The two classes of significance which are attached to the Tarot in the superior and inferior worlds, and the fact that no occult or other writer has attempted to assign anything but a divinatory meaning to the Minor Arcana, justify in yet another manner the hypothesis that the two series do not belong to one another. It is possible that their marriage was effected first in the Tarot of Bologna by that Prince of Pisa whom I have mentioned in the first part. It is said that his device obtained for him public recognition and reward from the city of his adoption, which would scarcely have been possible, even in those fantastic days, for the production of a Tarot which only omitted a few of the small cards; but as we are dealing with a question of fact which has to be accounted for somehow, it is conceivable that a sensation might have been created by a combination of the minor and gambling cards with the philosophical set, and by the adaptation of both to a game of chance. Afterwards it would have been further adapted to that other game of chance which is called fortune-telling. It should be understood here that I am not denying the possibility of divination, but I take exception as a mystic to the dedications which bring people into these paths, as if they had any relation to the Mystic Quest.

The Tarot cards which are issued with the small edition of the present work, that is to say, with the *Key to the Tarot*, have been drawn and coloured by Miss Pamela Colman Smith, and will, I think, be regarded as very striking and beautiful, in their design alike and execution. They are reproduced in the present enlarged edition of the Key as a means of reference to the text. They differ in many important respects from the conventional archaisms of the past and from the wretched products of colportage which now reach us from Italy, and it remains for me to justify their variations so far as the symbolism is concerned. That for once in modern times I present a pack which is the work of an artist does not, I presume, call for apology, even to the people –if any remain among us– who used to be described and to call themselves "very occult." If any one will look at the gorgeous Tarot valet or knave who is emblazoned on one of the page plates of *Chatto's Facts and Speculations concerning the History of Playing Cards*, he will know that Italy in the old days produced some splendid packs. I could only wish that it had been possible to issue the restored and rectified cards in the same style and size; such a course would have done fuller justice to the designs, but the result would have proved unmanageable for those practical purposes which are connected with cards, and for which allowance must be made, whatever my views thereon. For the variations in the symbolism by which the designs have been affected, I alone am responsible. In respect of the Major Arcana, they are sure to occasion criticism among students, actual and imputed. I wish therefore to say, within the reserves of courtesy and *la haute convenance* belonging to the fellowship of research, that I care nothing utterly for any view that may find expression. There is a Secret Tradition concerning the Tarot, as well as a Secret Doctrine contained therein; I have followed some part of it without exceeding the limits which are drawn about matters of this kind and belong to the laws of honour. This tradition has two parts, and as one of them has passed into writing it seems to follow that it may be betrayed at any moment, which will not signify, because the second, as I have intimated, has not so passed at present and is held by very few indeed. The purveyors of spurious copy and the traffickers in stolen goods may take note of this point, if they please. I ask, moreover, to be distinguished from two or three writers in recent times who have thought fit to hint that they could say a good deal more if they liked, for we do not speak the same language; but also from any one who, now or hereafter, may say that she or he will tell all, because they have only the accidents and not the essentials necessary for such disclosure. If I have followed on my part the counsel of Robert Burns, by keeping something to myself which I "scarcely tell to any," I have still said as much as I can; it is the truth after its own manner, and as much as may be expected or required in those outer circles where the qualifications of special research cannot be expected.

In regard to the Minor Arcana, they are the first in modern but not in all times to be accompanied by pictures, in addition to what is called the "pips" –that is to say, the devices belonging to the numbers of the various suits. These pictures respond to the divinatory meanings, which have been drawn from many sources. To sum up, therefore, the present division of this key is devoted to the Trumps Major; it elucidates their symbols in respect of the higher intention and with reference to the designs in the pack. The third division will give the divinatory significance in respect of the seventy-eight Tarot cards, and with particular reference to the designs of the Minor Arcana. It will give, in fine, some modes of use for those who require them, and in the sense of the reason which I have already explained in the preface. That which hereinafter follows should be taken, for purposes of comparison, in connexion with the general description of the old Tarot Trumps in the first part. There it will be seen that the zero card of the Fool is allocated, as it always is, to the place which makes it equivalent to the number twenty-one. The arrangement is ridiculous on the surface, which does not much signify, but it is also wrong on the symbolism, nor does this fare better when it is made to replace the twenty-second point of the sequence. Etteilla recognized the difficulties of both attributions, but he only made bad worse by allocating the Fool to the place which is usually occupied by the Ace of Pentacles as the last of the whole Tarot series. This rearrangement has been followed by Papus recently in *Le Tarot Divinatoire*, where the confusion is of no consequence, as the findings of fortune telling depend upon fortuitous positions and not upon essential place in the general sequence of cards. I have seen yet another allocation of the zero symbol, which no doubt obtains in certain cases, but it fails on the highest planes and for our present requirements it would be idle to carry the examination further.

§ 2. The Trumps Major and their Inner Symbolism

I - The Magician

A youthful figure in the robe of a magician, having the countenance of divine Apollo, with smile of confidence and shining eyes. Above his head is the mysterious sign of the Holy Spirit, the sign of life, like an endless cord, forming the figure 8 in a horizontal position. About his waist is a serpent-cincture, the serpent appearing to devour its own tail. This is familiar to most as a conventional symbol of eternity, but here it indicates more especially the eternity of attainment in the spirit. In the Magician's right hand is a wand raised towards heaven, while the left hand is pointing to the earth. This dual sign is known in very high grades of the Instituted Mysteries; it shews the descent of grace, virtue and light, drawn from things above and derived to things below. The suggestion throughout is therefore the possession and communication of the Powers and Gifts of the Spirit. On the table in front of the Magician are the symbols of the four Tarot suits, signifying the elements of natural life, which lie like counters before the adept, and he adapts them as he wills. Beneath are roses and lilies, the *flos campi* and *lilium convallium*, changed into garden flowers, to shew the culture of aspiration. This card signifies the divine motive in man, reflecting God, the will in the liberation of its union with that which is above. It is also the unity of individual being on all planes, and in a very high sense it is thought, in the fixation thereof. With further reference to what I have called the sign of life and its connexion with the number 8, it may be remembered that Christian Gnosticism speaks of rebirth in Christ as a change "unto the Ogdoad." The mystic number is termed Jerusalem above, the Land flowing with Milk and Honey, the Holy Spirit and the Land of the Lord. According to Martinism, 8 is the number of Christ.

Divinatory Meanings

Skill, diplomacy, address, subtlety; sickness, pain, loss, disaster, snares of enemies; self-confidence, will; the Querent, if male.

Reversed: Physician, Magus, mental disease, disgrace, disquiet.

II - The High Priestess

She has the lunar crescent at her feet, a horned diadem on her head, with a globe in the middle place, and a large solar cross on her breast. The scroll in her hands is inscribed with the word *Tora*, signifying the Greater Law, the Secret Law and the second sense of the Word. It is partly covered by her mantle, to shew that some things are implied and some spoken. She is seated between the white and black pillars –J. and B.– of the mystic Temple, and the veil of the Temple is behind her: it is embroidered with palms and pomegranates. The vestments are flowing and gauzy, and the mantle suggests light –a shimmering radiance. She has been called occult Science on the threshold of the Sanctuary of Isis, but she is really the Secret Church, the House which is of God and man. She represents also the Second Marriage of the Prince who is no longer of this world; she is the spiritual Bride and Mother, the daughter of the stars and the Higher Garden of Eden. She is, in fine, the Queen of the borrowed light, but this is the light of all. She is the Moon nourished by the milk of the Supernal Mother.

In a manner, she is also the Supernal Mother herself –that is to say, she is the bright reflection. It is in this sense of reflection that her truest and highest name in bolism is *Shekinah* –the co-habiting glory. According to Kabalism, there is a *Shekinah* both above and below. In the superior world it is called *Binah*, the Supernal Understanding which reflects to the emanations that are beneath. In the lower world it is *Malkuth* –that world being, for this purpose, understood as a blessed Kingdom that with which it is made blessed being the Indwelling Glory. Mystically speaking, the *Shekinah* is the Spiritual Bride of the just man, and when he reads the Law she gives the Divine meaning. There are some respects in which this card is the highest and holiest of the Greater Arcana.

Divinatory Meanings

Secrets, mystery, the future as yet unrevealed; the woman who interests the Querent, if male; the Querent herself, if female; silence, tenacity; mystery, wisdom, science.

Reversed: Passion, moral or physical ardour, conceit, surface knowledge.

III - The Empress

A stately figure, seated, having rich vestments and royal aspect, as of a daughter of heaven and earth. Her diadem is of twelve stars, gathered in a cluster. The symbol of Venus is on the shield which rests near her. A field of corn is ripening in front of her, and beyond there is a fall of water. The sceptre which she bears is surmounted by the globe of this world. She is the inferior Garden of Eden, the Earthly Paradise, all that is symbolized by the visible house of man. She is not *Regina coeli*, but she is still *refugium peccatorum*, the fruitful mother of thousands. There are also certain aspects in which she has been correctly described as desire and the wings thereof, as the woman clothed with the sun, as *Gloria Mundi* and the veil of the *Sanctum Sanctorum*; but she is not, I may add, the soul that has attained wings, unless all the symbolism is counted up another and unusual way. She is above all things universal fecundity and the outer sense of the Word. This is obvious, because there is no direct message which has been given to man like that which is borne by woman; but she does not herself carry its interpretation.

In another order of ideas, the card of the Empress signifies the door or gate by which an entrance is obtained into this life, as into the Garden of Venus; and then the way which leads out therefrom, into that which is beyond, is the secret known to the High Priestess: it is communicated by her to the elect. Most old attributions of this card are completely wrong on the symbolism –as, for example, its identification with the Word, Divine Nature, the Triad, and so forth.

Divinatory Meanings

Fruitfulness, action, initiative, length of days; the unknown, clandestine; also difficulty, doubt, ignorance.

Reversed: Light, truth, the unraveling of involved matters, public rejoicings; according to another reading, vacillation.

IV - The Emperor

He has a form of the *Crux ansata* for his sceptre and a globe in his left hand. He is a crowned monarch —commanding, stately, seated on a throne, the arms of which axe fronted by rams' heads. He is executive and realization, the power of this world, here clothed with the highest of its natural attributes. He is occasionally represented as seated on a cubic stone, which, however, confuses some of the issues. He is the virile power, to which the Empress responds, and in this sense is he who seeks to remove the Veil of Isis; yet she remains *virgo intacta*.

It should be understood that this card and that of the Empress do not precisely represent the condition of married life, though this state is implied. On the surface, as I have indicated, they stand for mundane royalty, uplifted on the seats of the mighty; but above this there is the suggestion of another presence. They signify also —and the male figure especially— the higher kingship, occupying the intellectual throne. Hereof is the lordship of thought rather than of the animal world. Both personalities, after their own manner, are "full of strange experience," but theirs is not consciously the wisdom which draws from a higher world. The Emperor has been described as (a) will in its embodied form, but this is only one of its applications, and (b) as an expression of virtualities contained in the Absolute Being —but this is fantasy.

Divinatory Meanings

Stability, power, protection, realization; a great person; aid, reason, conviction; also authority and will.

Reversed: Benevolence, compassion, credit; also confusion to enemies, obstruction, immaturity.

V - The Hierophant

He wears the triple crown and is seated between two pillars, but they are not those of the Temple which is guarded by the High Priestess. In his left hand he holds a sceptre terminating in the triple cross, and with his right hand he gives the well-known ecclesiastical sign which is called that of esotericism, distinguishing between the manifest and concealed part of doctrine. It is noticeable in this connexion that the High Priestess makes no sign. At his feet are the crossed keys, and two priestly ministers in albs kneel before him. He has been usually called the Pope, which is a particular application of the more general office that he symbolizes. He is the ruling power of external religion, as the High Priestess is the prevailing genius of the esoteric, withdrawn power. The proper meanings of this card have suffered woeful admixture from nearly all hands. Grand Orient says truly that the Hierophant is the power of the keys, exoteric orthodox doctrine, and the outer side of the life which leads to the doctrine; but he is certainly not the prince of occult doctrine, as another commentator has suggested.

He is rather the *summa totius theologiæ*, when it has passed into the utmost rigidity of expression; but he symbolizes also all things that are righteous and sacred on the manifest side. As such, he is the channel of grace belonging to the world of institution as distinct from that of Nature, and he is the leader of salvation for the human race at large. He is the order and the head of the recognized hierarchy, which is the reflection of another and greater hierarchic order; but it may so happen that the pontiff forgets the significance of this his symbolic state and acts as if he contained within his proper measures all that his sign signifies or his symbol seeks to shew forth. He is not, as it has been thought, philosophy-except on the theological side; he is not inspiration; and he is not religion, although he is a mode of its expression.

Divinatory Meanings

Marriage, alliance, captivity, servitude; by another account, mercy and goodness; inspiration; the man to whom the Querent has recourse.

Reversed: Society, good understanding, concord, overkindness, weakness.

VI - The Lovers

The sun shines in the zenith, and beneath is a great winged figure with arms extended, pouring down influences. In the foreground are two human figures, male and female, unveiled before each other, as if Adam and Eve when they first occupied the paradise of the earthly body. Behind the man is the Tree of Life, bearing twelve fruits, and the Tree of the Knowledge of Good and Evil is behind the woman; the serpent is twining round it. The figures suggest youth, virginity, innocence and love before it is contaminated by gross material desire. This is in all simplicity the card of human love, here exhibited as part of the way, the truth and the life. It replaces, by recourse to first principles, the old card of marriage, which I have described previously, and the later follies which depicted man between vice and virtue. In a very high sense, the card is a mystery of the Covenant and Sabbath.

The suggestion in respect of the woman is that she signifies that attraction towards the sensitive life which carries within it the idea of the Fall of Man, but she is rather the working of a Secret Law of Providence than a willing and conscious temptress. It is through her imputed lapse that man shall arise ultimately, and only by her can he complete himself. The card is therefore in its way another intimation concerning the great mystery of womanhood. The old meanings fall to pieces of necessity with the old pictures, but even as interpretations of the latter, some of them were of the order of commonplace and others were false in symbolism.

Divinatory Meanings

Attraction, love, beauty, trials overcome.
Reversed: Failure, foolish designs. Another account speaks of marriage frustrated and contrarieties of all kinds.

VII - The Chariot

An erect and princely figure carrying a drawn sword and corresponding, broadly speaking, to the traditional description which I have given in the first part. On the shoulders of the victorious hero are supposed to be the *Urim* and *Thummim*. He has led captivity captive; he is conquest on all planes –in the mind, in science, in progress, in certain trials of initiation. He has thus replied to the sphinx, and it is on this account that I have accepted the variation of Éliphas Lévi; two sphinxes thus draw his chariot. He is above all things triumph in the mind.

It is to be understood for this reason (a) that the question of the sphinx is concerned with a Mystery of Nature and not of the world of Grace, to which the charioteer could offer no answer; (b) that the planes of his conquest are manifest or external and not within himself; (c) that the liberation which he effects may leave himself in the bondage of the logical understanding; (d) that the tests of initiation through which he has passed in triumph are to be understood physically or rationally; and (e) that if he came to the pillars of that Temple between which the High Priestess is seated, he could not open the scroll called *Tora*, nor if she questioned him could he answer. He is not hereditary royalty and he is not priesthood.

Divinatory Meanings

Succour, providence also war, triumph, presumption, vengeance, trouble.
Reversed: Riot, quarrel, dispute, litigation, defeat.

VIII - Strength, or Fortitude

A woman, over whose head there broods the same symbol of life which we have seen in the card of the Magician, is closing the jaws of a lion. The only point in which this design differs from the conventional presentations is that her beneficent fortitude has already subdued the lion, which is being led by a chain of flowers. For reasons which satisfy myself, this card has been interchanged with that of justice, which is usually numbered eight. As the variation carries nothing with it which will signify to the reader, there is no cause for explanation. Fortitude, in one of its most exalted aspects, is connected with the Divine Mystery of Union; the virtue, of course, operates in all planes, and hence draws on all in its symbolism. It connects also with *innocentia inviolata*, and with the strength which resides in contemplation.

These higher meanings are, however, matters of inference, and I do not suggest that they are transparent on the surface of the card. They are intimated in a concealed manner by the chain of flowers, which signifies, among many other things, the sweet yoke and the light burden of Divine Law, when it has been taken into the heart of hearts. The card has nothing to do with self-confidence in the ordinary sense, though this has been suggested –but it concerns the confidence of those whose strength is God, who have found their refuge in Him. There is one aspect in which the lion signifies the passions, and she who is called Strength is the higher nature in its liberation. It has walked upon the asp and the basilisk and has trodden down the lion and the dragon.

Divinatory Meanings

Power, energy, action, courage, magnanimity; also complete success and honours.
Reversed: Despotism, abuse if power, weakness, discord, sometimes even disgrace.

IX - The Hermit

The variation from the conventional models in this card is only that the lamp is not enveloped partially in the mantle of its bearer, who blends the idea of the Ancient of Days with the Light of the World It is a star which shines in the lantern. I have said that this is a card of attainment, and to extend this conception the figure is seen holding up his beacon on an eminence. Therefore the Hermit is not, as Court de Gebelin explained, a wise man in search of truth and justice; nor is he, as a later explanation proposes, an especial example of experience. His beacon intimates that "where I am, you also may be."

It is further a card which is understood quite incorrectly when it is connected with the idea of occult isolation, as the protection of personal magnetism against admixture. This is one of the frivolous renderings which we owe to Éliphas Lévi. It has been adopted by the French Order of Martinism and some of us have heard a great deal of the Silent and Unknown Philosophy enveloped by his mantle from the knowledge of the profane. In true Martinism, the significance of the term *Philosophe inconnu* was of another order. It did not refer to the intended concealment of the Instituted Mysteries, much less of their substitutes, but –like the card itself– to the truth that the Divine Mysteries secure their own protection from those who are unprepared.

Divinatory Meanings

Prudence, circumspection; also and especially treason, dissimulation, roguery, corruption.

Reversed: Concealment, disguise, policy, fear, unreasoned caution.

X - Wheel of Fortune

In this symbol I have again followed the reconstruction of Éliphas Lévi, who has furnished several variants. It is legitimate –as I have intimated– to use Egyptian symbolism when this serves our purpose, provided that no theory of origin is implied therein. I have, however, presented Typhon in his serpent form. The symbolism is, of course, not exclusively Egyptian, as the four Living Creatures of Ezekiel occupy the angles of the card, and the wheel itself follows other indications of Lévi in respect of Ezekiel's vision, as illustrative of the particular Tarot Key. With the French occultist, and in the design itself, the symbolic picture stands for the perpetual motion of a fluidic universe and for the flux of human life. The Sphinx is the equilibrium therein. The transliteration of *Taro* as *Rota* is inscribed on the wheel, counterchanged with the letters of the Divine Name –to show that Providence is implied through all. But this is the Divine intention within, and the similar intention without is exemplified by the four Living Creatures. Sometimes the sphinx is represented couchant on a pedestal above, which defrauds the symbolism by stultifying the essential idea of stability amidst movement.

Behind the general notion expressed in the symbol there lies the denial of chance and the fatality which is implied therein. It may be added that, from the days of Lévi onward, the occult explanations of this card are –even for occultism itself– of a singularly fatuous kind. It has been said to mean principle, fecundity, virile honour, ruling authority, etc. The findings of common fortune-telling are better than this on their own plane.

Divinatory Meanings

Destiny, fortune, success, elevation, luck, felicity.
Reversed: Increase, abundance, superfluity.

XI - Justice

As this card follows the traditional symbolism and carries above all its obvious meanings, there is little to say regarding it outside the few considerations collected in the first part, to which the reader is referred.

It will be seen, however, that the figure is seated between pillars, like the High Priestess, and on this account it seems desirable to indicate that the moral principle which deals unto every man according to his works– while, of course, it is in strict analogy with higher things; –differs in its essence from the spiritual justice which is involved in the idea of election. The latter belongs to a mysterious order of Providence, in virtue of which it is possible for certain men to conceive the idea of dedication to the highest things. The operation of this is like the breathing of the Spirit where it wills, and we have no canon of criticism or ground of explanation concerning it. It is analogous to the possession of the fairy gifts and the high gifts and the gracious gifts of the poet: we have them or have not, and their presence is as much a mystery as their absence. The law of Justice is not however involved by either alternative. In conclusion, the pillars of Justice open into one world and the pillars of the High Priestess into another.

Divinatory Meanings

Equity, rightness, probity, executive; triumph of the deserving side in law.
Reversed: Law in all its departments, legal complications, bigotry, bias, excessive severity.

XII - The Hanged Man

The gallows from which he is suspended forms a *Tau* cross, while the figure –from the position of the legs– forms a fylfot cross. There is a nimbus about the head of the seeming martyr. It should be noted (1) that the tree of sacrifice is living wood, with leaves thereon; (2) that the face expresses deep entrancement, not suffering; (3) that the figure, as a whole, suggests life in suspension, but life and not death. It is a card of profound significance, but all the significance is veiled. One of his editors suggests that Éliphas Lévi did not know the meaning, which is unquestionable nor did the editor himself. It has been called falsely a card of martyrdom, a card a of prudence, a card of the Great Work, a card of duty; but we may exhaust all published interpretations and find only vanity. I will say very simply on my own part that it expresses the relation, in one of its aspects, between the Divine and the Universe.

He who can understand that the story of his higher nature is imbedded in this symbolism will receive intimations concerning a great awakening that is possible, and will know that after the sacred Mystery of Death there is a glorious Mystery of Resurrection.

Divinatory Meanings

Wisdom, circumspection, discernment, trials, sacrifice, intuition, divination, prophecy.

Reversed: Selfishness, the crowd, body politic.

XIII - Death

The veil or mask of life is perpetuated in change, transformation and passage from lower to higher, and this is more fitly represented in the rectified Tarot by one of the apocalyptic visions than by the crude notion of the reaping skeleton. Behind it lies the whole world of ascent in the spirit. The mysterious horseman moves slowly, bearing a black banner emblazoned with the Mystic Rose, which signifies life. Between two pillars on the verge of the horizon there shines the sun of immortality. The horseman carries no visible weapon, but king and child and maiden fall before him, while a prelate with clasped hands awaits his end.

There should be no need to point out that the suggestion of death which I have made in connection with the previous card is, of course, to be understood mystically, but this is not the case in the present instance. The natural transit of man to the next stage of his being either is or may be one form of his progress, but the exotic and almost unknown entrance, while still in this life, into the state of mystical death is a change in the form of consciousness and the passage into a state to which ordinary death is neither the path nor gate. The existing occult explanations of the 13th card are, on the whole, better than usual, rebirth, creation, destination, renewal, and the rest.

Divinatory Meanings

End, mortality, destruction, corruption also, for a man, the loss of a benefactor for a woman, many contrarieties; for a maid, failure of marriage projects.

Reversed: Inertia, sleep, lethargy, petrifaction, somnambulism; hope destroyed.

XIV - Temperance

A winged angel, with the sign of the sun upon his forehead and on his breast the square and triangle of the septenary. I speak of him in the masculine sense, but the figure is neither male nor female. It is held to be pouring the essences of life from chalice to chalice. It has one foot upon the earth and one upon waters, thus illustrating the nature of the essences. A direct path goes up to certain heights on the verge of the horizon, and above there is a great light, through which a crown is seen vaguely. Hereof is some part of the Secret of Eternal Life, as it is possible to man in his incarnation. All the conventional emblems are renounced herein.

So also are the conventional meanings, which refer to changes in the seasons, perpetual movement of life and even the combination of ideas. It is, moreover, untrue to say that the figure symbolizes the genius of the sun, though it is the analogy of solar light, realized in the third part of our human triplicity. It is called Temperance fantastically, because, when the rule of it obtains in our consciousness, it tempers, combines and harmonises the psychic and material natures. Under that rule we know in our rational part something of whence we came and whither we are going.

Divinatory Meanings

Economy, moderation, frugality, management, accommodation.
Reversed: Things connected with churches, religions, sects, the priesthood, sometimes even the priest who will marry the Querent; also disunion, unfortunate combinations, competing interests.

XV - The Devil

The design is an accommodation, mean or harmony, between several motives mentioned in the first part. The Horned Goat of Mendes, with wings like those of a bat, is standing on an altar. At the pit of the stomach there is the sign of Mercury. The right hand is upraised and extended, being the reverse of that benediction which is given by the Hierophant in the fifth card. In the left hand there is a great flaming torch, inverted towards the earth. A reversed pentagram is on the forehead. There is a ring in front of the altar, from which two chains are carried to the necks of two figures, male and female. These are analogous with those of the fifth card, as if Adam and Eve after the Fall. Hereof is the chain and fatality of the material life.

The figures are tailed, to signify the animal nature, but there is human intelligence in the faces, and he who is exalted above them is not to be their master for ever. Even now, he is also a bondsman, sustained by the evil that is in him and blind to the liberty of service. With more than his usual derision for the arts which he pretended to respect and interpret as a master therein, Éliphas Lévi affirms that the Baphometic figure is occult science and magic. Another commentator says that in the Divine world it signifies predestination, but there is no correspondence in that world with the things which below are of the brute. What it does signify is the Dweller on the Threshold without the Mystical Garden when those are driven forth therefrom who have eaten the forbidden fruit.

Divinatory Meanings

Ravage, violence, vehemence, extraordinary efforts, force, fatality; that which is predestined but is not for this reason evil

Reversed: Evil fatality, weakness, pettiness, blindness.

XVI - The Tower

Occult explanations attached to this card are meagre and mostly disconcerting. It is idle to indicate that it depicts min in all its aspects, because it bears this evidence on the surface. It is said further that it contains the first allusion to a material building, but I do not conceive that the Tower is more or less material than the pillars which we have met with in three previous cases. I see nothing to warrant Papus in supposing that it is literally the fall of Adam, but there is more in favour of his alternative –that it signifies the materialization of the spiritual word. The bibliographer Christian imagines that it is the downfall of the mind, seeking to penetrate the mystery of God. I agree rather with Grand Orient that it is the ruin of the House of We, when evil has prevailed therein, and above all that it is the rending of a House of Doctrine. I understand that the reference is, however, to a House of Falsehood. It illustrates also in the most comprehensive way the old truth that "except the Lord build the house, they labour in vain that build it."

There is a sense in which the catastrophe is a reflection from the previous card, but not on the side of the symbolism which I have tried to indicate therein. It is more correctly a question of analogy; one is concerned with the fall into the material and animal state, while the other signifies destruction on the intellectual side. The Tower has been spoken of as the chastisement of pride and the intellect overwhelmed in the attempt to penetrate the Mystery of God; but in neither case do these explanations account for the two persons who are the living sufferers. The one is the literal word made void and the other its false interpretation. In yet a deeper sense, it may signify also the end of a dispensation, but there is no possibility here for the consideration of this involved question.

Divinatory Meanings

Misery, distress, indigence, adversity, calamity, disgrace, deception, ruin. It is a card in particular of unforeseen catastrophe

Reversed: According to one account, the same in a lesser degree also oppression, imprisonment, tyranny.

XVII - The Star

A great, radiant star of eight rays, surrounded by seven lesser stars – also of eight rays. The female figure in the foreground is entirely naked. Her left knee is on the land and her right foot upon the water. She pours Water of Life from two great ewers, irrigating sea and land. Behind her is rising ground and on the right a shrub or tree, whereon a bird alights. The figure expresses eternal youth and beauty. The star is *l'étoile flamboyante*, which appears in Masonic symbolism, but has been confused therein. That which the figure communicates to the living scene is the substance of the heavens and the elements. It has been said truly that the mottoes of this card are "Waters of Life freely" and "Gifts of the Spirit."

The summary of several tawdry explanations says that it is a card of hope. On other planes it has been certified as immortality and interior light. For the majority of prepared minds, the figure will appear as the type of Truth unveiled, glorious in undying beauty, pouring on the waters of the soul some part and measure of her priceless possession. But she is in reality the Great Mother in the Kabalistic *Sephira Binah*, which is supernal Understanding, who communicates to the *Sephiroth* that are below in the measure that they can receive her influx.

Divinatory Meanings

Loss, theft, privation, abandonment; another reading says-hope and bright prospects,

Reversed: Arrogance, haughtiness, impotence.

XVIII - The Moon

The distinction between this card and some of the conventional types is that the moon is increasing on what is called the side of mercy, to the right of the observer. It has sixteen chief and sixteen secondary rays. The card represents life of the imagination apart from life of the spirit. The path between the towers is the issue into the unknown. The dog and wolf are the fears of the natural mind in the presence of that place of exit, when there is only reflected light to guide it.

The last reference is a key to another form of symbolism. The intellectual light is a reflection and beyond it is the unknown mystery which it cannot shew forth. It illuminates our animal nature, types of which are represented below –the dog, the wolf and that which comes up out of the deeps, the nameless and hideous tendency which is lower than the savage beast. It strives to attain manifestation, symbolized by crawling from the abyss of water to the land, but as a rule it sinks back whence it came. The face of the mind directs a calm gaze upon the unrest below; the dew of thought falls; the message is: Peace, be still; and it may be that there shall come a calm upon the animal nature, while the abyss beneath shall cease from giving up a form.

Divinatory Meanings

Hidden enemies, danger, calumny, darkness, terror, deception, occult forces, error. *Reversed*: Instability, inconstancy, silence, lesser degrees of deception and error.

XIX - The Sun

The naked child mounted on a white horse and displaying a red standard has been mentioned already as the better symbolism connected with this card. It is the destiny of the Supernatural East and the great and holy light which goes before the endless procession of humanity, coming out from the walled garden of the sensitive life and passing on the journey home. The card signifies, therefore, the transit from the manifest light of this world, represented by the glorious sun of earth, to the light of the world to come, which goes before aspiration and is typified by the heart of a child.

But the last allusion is again the key to a different form or aspect of the symbolism. The sun is that of consciousness in the spirit - the direct as the antithesis of the reflected light. The characteristic type of humanity has become a little child therein –a child in the sense of simplicity and innocence in the sense of wisdom. In that simplicity, he bears the seal of Nature and of Art; in that innocence, he signifies the restored world. When the self-knowing spirit has dawned in the consciousness above the natural mind, that mind in its renewal leads forth the animal nature in a state of perfect conformity.

Divinatory Meanings

Material happiness, fortunate marriage, contentment.
Reversed: The same in a lesser sense.

XX - The Last Judgment

I have said that this symbol is essentially invariable in all Tarot sets, or at least the variations do not alter its character. The great angel is here encompassed by clouds, but he blows his bannered trumpet, and the cross as usual is displayed on the banner. The dead are rising from their tombs —a woman on the right, a man on the left hand, and between them their child, whose back is turned. But in this card there are more than three who are restored, and it has been thought worth while to make this variation as illustrating the insufficiency of current explanations. It should be noted that all the figures are as one in the wonder, adoration and ecstacy expressed by their attitudes. It is the card which registers the accomplishment of the great work of transformation in answer to the summons of the Supernal —which summons is heard and answered from within.

Herein is the intimation of a significance which cannot well be carried further in the present place. What is that within us which does sound a trumpet and all that is lower in our nature rises in response —almost in a moment, almost in the twinkling of an eye? Let the card continue to depict, for those who can see no further, the Last Judgment and the resurrection in the natural body; but let those who have inward eyes look and discover therewith. They will understand that it has been called truly in the past a card of eternal life, and for this reason it may be compared with that which passes under the name of Temperance.

Divinatory Meanings

Change of position, renewal, outcome. Another account specifies total loss though lawsuit.

Reversed: Weakness, pusillanimity, simplicity; also deliberation, decision, sentence.

0 (zero) - The Fool

With light step, as if earth and its trammels had little power to restrain him, a young man in gorgeous vestments pauses at the brink of a precipice among the great heights of the world; he surveys the blue distance before him-its expanse of sky rather than the prospect below. His act of eager walking is still indicated, though he is stationary at the given moment; his dog is still bounding. The edge which opens on the depth has no terror; it is as if angels were waiting to uphold him, if it came about that he leaped from the height. His countenance is full of intelligence and expectant dream. He has a rose in one hand and in the other a costly wand, from which depends over his right shoulder a wallet curiously embroidered. He is a prince of the other world on his travels through this one-all amidst the morning glory, in the keen air. The sun, which shines behind him, knows whence he came, whither he is going, and how he will return by another path after many days. He is the spirit in search of experience. Many symbols of the Instituted Mysteries are summarized in this card, which reverses, under high warrants, all the confusions that have preceded it.

In his *Manual of Cartomancy*, Grand Orient has a curious suggestion of the office of Mystic Fool, as apart of his process in higher divination; but it might call for more than ordinary gifts to put it into operation. We shall see how the card fares according to the common arts of fortune-telling, and it will be an example, to those who can discern, of the fact, otherwise so evident, that the Trumps Major had no place originally in the arts of psychic gambling, when cards are used as the counters and pretexts. Of the circumstances under which this art arose we know, however, very little. The conventional explanations say that the Fool signifies the flesh, the sensitive life, and by a peculiar satire its subsidiary name was at one time the alchemist, as depicting folly at the most insensate stage.

Divinatory Meanings

Folly, mania, extravagance, intoxication, delirium, frenzy, bewrayment.
Reversed: Negligence, absence, distribution, carelessness, apathy, nullity, vanity.

XXI - The World

As this final message of the Major Trumps is unchanged –and indeed unchangeable– in respect of its design, it has been partly described already regarding its deeper sense. It represents also the perfection and end of the Cosmos, the secret which is within it, the rapture of the universe when it understands itself in God. It is further the state of the soul in the consciousness of Divine Vision, reflected from the self-knowing spirit. But these meanings are without prejudice to that which I have said concerning it on the material side.

It has more than one message on the macrocosmic side and is, for example, the state of the restored world when the law of manifestation shall have been carried to the highest degree of natural perfection. But it is perhaps more especially a story of the past, referring to that day when all was declared to be good, when the morning stars sang together and all the Sons of God shouted for joy. One of the worst explanations concerning it is that the figure symbolizes the Magus when he has reached the highest degree of initiation; another account says that it represents the absolute, which is ridiculous. The figure has been said to stand for Truth, which is, however, more properly allocated to the seventeenth card. Lastly, it has been called the Crown of the Magi.

Divinatory Meanings

Assured success, recompense, voyage, route, emigration, flight, change of place.

Reversed: Inertia, fixity, stagnation, permanence.

§ 3. Conclusion as to the Greater Keys

There has been no attempt in the previous tabulation to present the symbolism in what is called the three worlds –that of Divinity, of the Macrocosm and the Microcosm. A large volume would be required for developments of this kind. I have taken the cards on the high plane of their more direct significance to man, who –in material life– is on the quest of eternal things. The compiler of the *Manual of Cartomancy* has treated them under three headings: the World of Human Prudence, which does not differ from divination on its more serious side; the World of Conformity, being the life of religious devotion; and the World of Attainment, which is that of "the soul's progress towards the term of its research." He gives also a triple process of consultation, according to these divisions, to which the reader is referred. I have no such process to offer, as I think that more may be gained by individual reflection on each of the Trumps Major. I have also not adopted the prevailing attribution of the cards to the Hebrew alphabet –firstly, because it would serve no purpose in an elementary handbook; secondly, because nearly every attribution is wrong. Finally, I have not attempted to rectify the position of the cards in their relation to one another; the Zero therefore appears after No. 20, but I have taken care not to number the World or Universe otherwise than as 21. Wherever it ought to be put, the Zero is an unnumbered card.

In conclusion as to this part, I will give these further indications regarding the Fool, which is the most speaking of all the symbols. He signifies the journey outward, the state of the first emanation, the graces and passivity of the spirit. His wallet is inscribed with dim signs, to shew that many sub-conscious memories are stored up in the soul.

PART III
The Outer Method of the Oracles

§ 1. Distinction between the Greater and Lesser Arcana

IN respect of their usual presentation, the bridge between the Greater and Lesser Arcana is supplied by the court cards –King, Queen, Knight and Squire or Page; but their utter distinction from the Trumps Major is shewn by their conventional character. Let the reader compare them with symbols like the Fool, the High Priestess, the Hierophant, or –almost without exception– with any in the previous sequence, and he will discern my meaning. There is no especial idea connected on the surface with the ordinary court cards; they are a bridge of conventions, which form a transition to the simple pretexts of the counters and denaries of the numbers following. We seem to have passed away utterly from the region of higher meanings illustrated by living pictures. There in was a period, however, when the numbered cards were also pictures, but such devices were sporadic inventions of particular artists and were either conventional designs of the typical or allegorical kind, distinct from what is understood by symbolism, or they were illustrations –shall we say?– of manners, customs and periods. They were, in a word, adornments, and as such they did nothing to raise the significance of the Lesser Arcana to the plane of the Trumps Major; moreover, such variations are exceedingly few. This notwithstanding, there are vague rumours concerning a higher meaning in the minor cards, but nothing has so far transpired, even within the sphere of prudence which belongs to the most occult circles; these, it is true, have certain variants in respect of divinatory values, but I have not heard that in practice they offer better results. Efforts like those of Papus in *The Tarot ol the Bohemians* are strenuous and deserving after their own kind; be, in particular, recognizes the elements of the Divine Immanence in the Trumps Major, and he seeks to follow them through the long series of the lesser cards, as if these represented filtrations of the World of Grace through the World of Fortune; but he only produces -an arbitrary scheme of division which he can carry no further, and he has recourse, of necessity, in the end to a common scheme of divination as the substitute for a title to existence on the part of the Lesser Arcana. Now, I am practically in the same position; but I shall make no attempt here to save the situation by drawing on the mystical properties of numbers, as he and others have attempted, I shall recognize at once that the Trumps Major belong to the divine dealings of philosophy, but all that follows to fortune-telling, since it has never yet been translated into another language; the course thus adopted will render to divination, and at need even to gambling, the things that belong to this particular world of skill, and it will set apart for their proper business those matters that are of another order. In this free introduction to the subject in hand, it is only necessary to add that the difference between the fifty-six Lesser Arcana and ordinary playing-cards is not only essentially slight, because the substitution of Cups for Hearts, and so forth, constitutes an accidental variation, but because the presence of a Knight in each of the four suits was characteristic at one time of many ordinary packs, when this personage usually replaced the Queen. In the rectified Tarot which illustrates the present handbook, all numbered cards of the Lesser Arcana –the Aces only excepted– are furnished with figures or pictures to illustrate-but without exhausting –the divinatory meanings attached thereto.

Some who are gifted with reflective and discerning faculties in more than the ordinary sense –I am not speaking of clairvoyance may observe that in many of the Lesser Arcana there are vague intimations conveyed by the designs which seem to exceed the stated divinatory values. It is desirable to avoid misconception by specifying definitely that, except in rare instances –and then only by accident– the variations are not to be regarded as suggestions of higher and extradivinatory symbolism. I have said that these Lesser Arcana have not been translated into a language which transcends that of fortune telling. I should not indeed be disposed to regard them as belonging in their existing forms to another realm than this; but the field of divinatory possibilities is inexhaustible, by the hypothesis of the art, and the combined systems of cartomancy have indicated only the bare heads of significance attaching to the emblems in use. When the pictures in the present case go beyond the conventional meanings they should be taken as hints of possible developments along the same lines; and this is one of the reasons why the pictorial devices here attached to the four denaries will prove a great help to intuition. The mere numerical powers and bare words of the meanings are insufficient by themselves; but the pictures are like doors which open into unexpected chambers, or like a turn in the open road with a wide prospect beyond.

§ 2. The Lesser Arcana.
Otherwise the Four Suits of Tarot Cards

The Lesser Arcana will now be described according to their respective classes by the pictures to each belonging, and a harmony of their meanings will be provided from all sources.

Such are the intimations of the Lesser Arcana in respect of divinatory art, the veridic nature of which seems to depend on an alternative that it may be serviceable to express briefly. The records of the art are ex hypothesi the records of findings in the past based upon experience; as such, they are a guide to memory, and those who can master the elements may— still *ex hypothesi*—give interpretations on their basis. It is an official and automatic working. On the other hand, those who have gifts of intuition, of second sight, of clairvoyance—call it as we choose and may—will supplement the experience of the past by the findings of their own faculty, and will speak of that which they have seen in the pretexts of the oracles. It remains to give, also briefly, the divinatory significance allocated by the same art to the Trumps Major.

THE SUIT OF WANDS

King

The physical and emotional nature to which this card is attributed is dark, ardent, lithe, animated, impassioned, noble. The King uplifts a flowering wand, and wears, like his three correspondences in the remaining suits, what is called a cap of maintenance beneath his crown. He connects with the symbol of the lion, which is emblazoned on the back of his throne.

Divinatory Meanings: Dark man, friendly, countryman, generally married, honest and conscientious. The card always signifies honesty, and may mean news concerning an unexpected heritage to fall in before very long.
Reversed: Good, but severe; austere, yet tolerant.

Queen

The Wands throughout this suit are always in leaf, as it is a suit of life and animation. Emotionally and otherwise, the Queen's personality corresponds to that of the King, but is more magnetic.

Divinatory Meanings: A dark woman, countrywoman, friendly, chaste, loving, honourable. If the card beside her signifies a man, she is well disposed towards him; if a woman, she is interested in the Querent. Also, love of money, or a certain success in business.
Reversed: Good, economical, obliging, serviceable. Signifies also –but in certain positions and in the neighbourhood of other cards tending in such directions– opposition, jealousy, even deceit and infidelity.

Knight

He is shewn as if upon a journey, armed with a short wand, and although mailed is not on a warlike errand. He is passing mounds or pyramids. The motion of the horse is a key to the character of its rider, and suggests the precipitate mood, or things connected therewith.

Divinatory Meanings: Departure, absence, flight, emigration. A dark young man, friendly. Change of residence.
Reversed: Rupture, division, interruption, discord.

Page

In a scene similar to the former, a young man stands in the act of proclamation. He is unknown but faithful, and his tidings are strange.

Divinatory Meanings: Dark young man, faithful, a lover, an envoy, a postman. Beside a man, he will bear favourable testimony concerning him. A dangerous rival, if followed by the Page of Cups. Has the chief qualities of his suit. He may signify family intelligence.

Reversed: Anecdotes, announcements, evil news. Also indecision and the instability which accompanies it.

Ten

A man oppressed by the weight of the ten staves which he is carrying.

Divinatory Meanings: A card of many significances, and some of the readings cannot be harmonized. I set aside that which connects it with honour and good faith. The chief meaning is oppression simply, but it is also fortune, gain, any kind of success, and then it is the oppression of these things. It is also a card of false-seeming, disguise, perfidy. The place which the figure is approaching may suffer from the rods that he carries. Success is stultified if the Nine of Swords follows, and if it is a question of a lawsuit, there will be certain loss.

Reversed: Contrarieties, difficulties, intrigues, and their analogies.

Nine

The figure leans upon his staff and has an expectant look, as if awaiting an enemy. Behind are eight other staves – erect, in orderly disposition, like a palisade.

Divinatory Meanings: The card signifies strength in opposition. If attacked, the person will meet an onslaught boldly; and his build shews, that he may prove a formidable antagonist. With this main significance there are all its possible adjuncts –delay, suspension, adjournment.

Reversed: Obstacles, adversity, calamity.

Eight

The card represents motion through the immovable-a flight of wands through an open country; but they draw to the term of their course. That which they signify is at hand; it may be even on the threshold.

Divinatory Meanings: Activity in undertakings, the path of such activity, swiftness, as that of an express messenger; great haste, great hope, speed towards an end which promises assured felicity; generally, that which is on the move; also the arrows of love.

Reversed: Arrows of jealousy, internal dispute, stingings of conscience, quarrels; and domestic disputes for persons who are married.

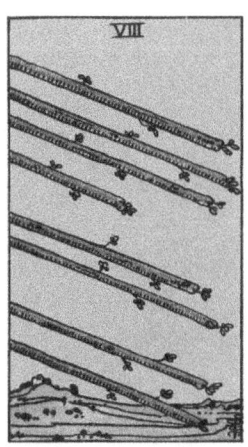

Seven

A young man on a craggy eminence brandishing a staff; six other staves are raised towards him from below.

Divinatory Meanings: It is a card of valour, for, on the surface, six are attacking one, who has, however, the vantage position. On the intellectual plane, it signifies discussion, wordy strife; in business —negotiations, war of trade, barter, competition. It is further a card of success, for the combatant is on the top and his enemies may be unable to reach him.

Reversed: Perplexity, embarrassments, anxiety. It is also a caution against indecision.

Six

A laurelled horseman bears one staff adorned with a laurel crown; footmen with staves are at his side.

Divinatory Meanings: The card has been so designed that it can cover several significations; on the surface, it is a victor triumphing, but it is also great news, such as might be carried in state by the King's courier; it is expectation crowned with its own desire, the crown of hope, and so forth.

Reversed: Apprehension, fear, as of a victorious enemy at the gate; treachery, disloyalty, as of gates being opened to the enemy; also indefinite delay.

Five

A posse of youths, who are brandishing staves, as if in sport or strife. It is mimic warfare, and hereto correspond the
Divinatory Meanings: Imitation, as, for example, sham fight, but also the strenuous competition and struggle of the search after riches and fortune. In this sense it connects with the battle of life. Hence some attributions say that it is a card of gold, gain, opulence.

Reversed: Litigation, disputes, trickery, contradiction.

Four

From the four great staves planted in the foreground there is a great garland suspended; two female figures uplift nosegays; at their side is a bridge over a moat, leading to an old manorial house.

Divinatory Meanings: They are for once almost on the surface —country life, haven of refuge, a species of domestic harvest-home, repose, concord, harmony, prosperity, peace, and the perfected work of these.

Reversed: The meaning remains unaltered; it is prosperity, increase, felicity, beauty, embellishment.

Three

A calm, stately personage, with his back turned, looking from a cliff's edge at ships passing over the sea. Three staves are planted in the ground, and he leans slightly on one of them.

Divinatory Meanings: He symbolizes established strength, enterprise, effort, trade, commerce, discovery; those are his ships, bearing his merchandise, which are sailing over the sea. The card also signifies able co-operation in business, as if the successful merchant prince were looking from his side towards yours with a view to help you.

Reversed: The end of troubles, suspension or cessation of adversity, toil and disappointment.

Two

A tall man looks from a battlemented roof over sea and shore; he holds a globe in his right hand, while a staff in his left rests on the battlement; another is fixed in a ring. The Rose and Cross and Lily should be noticed on the left side.

Divinatory Meanings: Between the alternative readings there is no marriage possible; on the one hand, riches, fortune, magnificence; on the other, physical suffering, disease, chagrin, sadness, mortification. The design gives one suggestion; here is a lord overlooking his dominion and alternately contemplating a globe; it looks like the malady, the mortification, the sadness of Alexander amidst the grandeur of this world's wealth.

Reversed: Surprise, wonder, enchantment, emotion, trouble, fear.

Ace

A hand issuing from a cloud grasps a stout wand or club.

Divinatory Meanings: Creation, invention, enterprise, the powers which result in these; principle, beginning, source; birth, family, origin, and in a sense the virility which is behind them; the starting point of enterprises; according to another account, money, fortune, inheritance.

Reversed: Fall, decadence, ruin, perdition, to perish also a certain clouded joy.

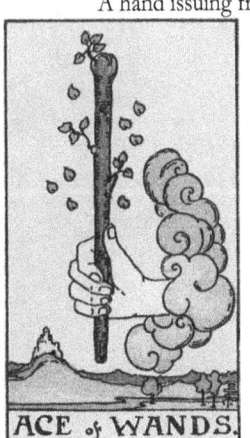

THE SUIT OF CUPS

King

He holds a short sceptre in his left hand and a great cup in his right; his throne is set upon the sea; on one side a ship is riding and on the other a dolphin is leaping. The implicit is that the Sign of the Cup naturally refers to water, which appears in all the court cards.

Divinatory Meanings: Fair man, man of business, law, or divinity; responsible, disposed to oblige the Querent; also equity, art and science, including those who profess science, law and art; creative intelligence.

Reversed: Dishonest, double-dealing man; roguery, exaction, injustice, vice, scandal, pillage, considerable loss.

Queen

Beautiful, fair, dreamy —as one who sees visions in a cup. This is, however, only one of her aspects; she sees, but she also acts, and her activity feeds her dream.

Divinatory Meanings: Good, fair woman; honest, devoted woman, who will do service to the Querent; loving intelligence, and hence the gift of vision; success, happiness, pleasure; also wisdom, virtue; a perfect spouse and a good mother.

Reversed: The accounts vary; good woman; otherwise, distinguished woman but one not to be trusted; perverse woman; vice, dishonour, depravity.

Knight

Graceful, but not warlike; riding quietly, wearing a winged helmet, referring to those higher graces of the imagination which sometimes characterize this card. He too is a dreamer, but the images of the side of sense haunt him in his vision.

Divinatory Meanings: Arrival, approach —sometimes that of a messenger; advances, proposition, demeanour, invitation, incitement.

Reversed: Trickery, artifice, subtlety, swindling, duplicity, fraud.

Page

A fair, pleasing, somewhat effeminate page, of studious and intent aspect, contemplates a fish rising from a cup to look at him. It is the pictures of the mind taking form.

Divinatory Meanings: Fair young man, one impelled to render service and with whom the Querent will be connected; a studious youth; news, message; application, reflection, meditation; also these things directed to business.

Reversed: Taste, inclination, attachment, seduction, deception, artifice.

Ten

Appearance of Cups in a rainbow; it is contemplated in wonder and ecstacy by a man and woman below, evidently husband and wife. His right arm is about her; his left is raised upward; she raises her right arm. The two children dancing near them have not observed the prodigy but are happy after their own manner. There is a home-scene beyond.

Divinatory Meanings: Contentment, repose of the entire heart; the perfection of that state; also perfection of human love and friendship; if with several picture-cards, a person who is taking charge of the Querent's interests; also the town, village or country inhabited by the Querent.

Reversed: Repose of the false heart, indignation, violence.

Nine

A goodly personage has feasted to his heart's content, and abundant refreshment of wine is on the arched counter behind him, seeming to indicate that the future is also assured. The picture offers the material side only, but there are other aspects.

Divinatory Meanings: Concord, contentment, physical bien-être; also victory, success, advantage; satisfaction for the Querent or person for whom the consultation is made.

Reversed: Truth, loyalty, liberty; but the readings vary and include mistakes, imperfections, etc.

Eight

A man of dejected aspect is deserting the cups of his felicity, enterprise, undertaking or previous concern.

Divinatory Meanings: The card speaks for itself on the surface, but other readings are entirely antithetical –giving joy, mildness, timidity, honour, modesty. In practice, it is usually found that the card shews the decline of a matter, or that a matter which has been thought to be important is really of slight consequence –either for good or evil.

Reversed: Great joy, happiness, feasting.

Seven

Strange chalices of vision, but the images are more especially those of the fantastic spirit.

Divinatory Meanings: Fairy favours, images of reflection, sentiment, imagination, things seen in the glass of contemplation; some attainment in these degrees, but nothing permanent or substantial is suggested.

Reversed: Desire, will, determination, project.

Six

Children in an old garden, their cups filled with flowers.

Divinatory Meanings: A card of the past and of memories, looking back, as –for example– on childhood; happiness, enjoyment, but coming rather from the past; things that have vanished. Another reading reverses this, giving new relations, new knowledge, new environment, and then the children are disporting in an unfamiliar precinct.

Reversed: The future, renewal, that which will come to pass presently.

Five

A dark, cloaked figure, looking sideways at three prone cups two others stand upright behind him; a bridge is in the background, leading to a small keep or holding.

Divinatory Meanings: It is a card of loss, but something remains over; three have been taken, but two are left; it is a card of inheritance, patrimony, transmission, but not corresponding to expectations; with some interpreters it is a card of marriage, but not without bitterness or frustration.

Reversed: News, alliances, affinity, consanguinity, ancestry, return, false projects.

Four

A young man is seated under a tree and contemplates three cups set on the grass before him; an arm issuing from a cloud offers him another cup. His expression notwithstanding is one of discontent with his environment.

Divinatory Meanings: Weariness, disgust, aversion, imaginary vexations, as if the wine of this world had caused satiety only; another wine, as if a fairy gift, is now offered the wastrel, but he sees no consolation therein. This is also a card of blended pleasure.

Reversed: Novelty, presage, new instruction, new relations.

Three

Maidens in a garden-ground with cups uplifted, as if pledging one another.

Divinatory Meanings: The conclusion of any matter in plenty, perfection and merriment; happy issue, victory, fulfilment, solace, healing,

Reversed: Expedition, dispatch, achievement, end. It signifies also the side of excess in physical enjoyment, and the pleasures of the senses.

Two

A youth and maiden are pledging one another, and above their cups rises the Caduceus of Hermes, between the great wings of which there appears a lion's head. It is a variant of a sign which is found in a few old examples of this card. Some curious emblematical meanings are attached to it, but they do not concern us in this place.

Divinatory Meanings: Love, passion, friendship, affinity, union, concord, sympathy, the interrelation of the sexes, and – as a suggestion apart from all offices of divination– that desire which is not in Nature, but by which Nature is sanctified.

Ace

The waters are beneath, and thereon are water-lilies; the hand issues from the cloud, holding in its palm the cup, from which four streams are pouring; a dove, bearing in its bill a cross-marked Host, descends to place the Wafer in the Cup; the dew of water is falling on all sides. It is an intimation of that which may lie behind the Lesser Arcana.

Divinatory Meanings: House of the true heart, joy, content, abode, nourishment, abundance, fertility; Holy Table, felicity hereof.

Reversed: House of the false heart, mutation, instability, revolution.

THE SUIT OF SWORDS

King

He sits in judgment, holding the unsheathed sign of his suit. He recalls, of course, the conventional Symbol of justice in the Trumps Major, and he may represent this virtue, but he is rather the power of life and death, in virtue of his office.

Divinatory Meanings: Whatsoever arises out of the idea of judgment and all its connexions-power, command, authority, militant intelligence, law, offices of the crown, and so forth.

Reversed: Cruelty, perversity, barbarity, perfidy, evil intention.

Queen

Her right hand raises the weapon vertically and the hilt rests on an arm of her royal chair the left hand is extended, the arm raised her countenance is severe but chastened; it suggests familiarity with sorrow. It does not represent mercy, and, her sword notwithstanding, she is scarcely a symbol of power.

Divinatory Meanings: Widowhood, female sadness and embarrassment, absence, sterility, mourning, privation, separation.

Reversed: Malice, bigotry, artifice, prudery, bale, deceit.

Knight

He is riding in full course, as if scattering his enemies. In the design he is really a prototypical hero of romantic chivalry. He might almost be Galahad, whose sword is swift and sure because he is clean of heart.

Divinatory Meanings: Skill, bravery, capacity, defence, address, enmity, wrath, war, destruction, opposition, resistance, ruin. There is therefore a sense in which the card signifies death, but it carries this meaning only in its proximity to other cards of fatality.

Reversed: Imprudence, incapacity, extravagance.

Page

A lithe, active figure holds a sword upright in both hands, while in the act of swift walking. He is passing over rugged land, and about his way the clouds are collocated wildly. He is alert and lithe, looking this way and that, as if an expected enemy might appear at any moment.

Divinatory Meanings: Authority, overseeing, secret service, vigilance, spying, examination, and the qualities thereto belonging.

Reversed: More evil side of these qualities; what is unforeseen, unprepared state; sickness is also intimated.

Ten

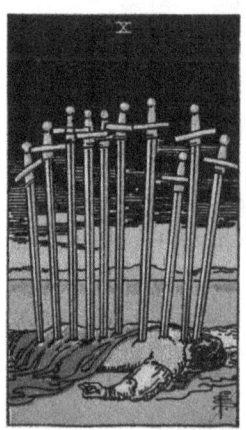

A prostrate figure, pierced by all the swords belonging to the card.

Divinatory Meanings: Whatsoever is intimated by the design; also pain, affliction, tears, sadness, desolation. It is not especially a card of violent death.

Reversed: Advantage, profit, success, favour, but none of these are permanent; also power and authority.

Nine

One seated on her couch in lamentation, with the swords over her. She is as one who knows no sorrow which is like unto hers. It is a card of utter desolation.

Divinatory Meanings: Death, failure, miscarriage, delay, deception, disappointment, despair.

Reversed: Imprisonment, suspicion, doubt, reasonable fear, shame.

Eight

A woman, bound and hoodwinked, with the swords of the card about her. Yet it is rather a card of temporary durance than of irretrievable bondage.

Divinatory Meanings: Bad news, violent chagrin, crisis, censure, power in trammels, conflict, calumny; also sickness.

Reversed: Disquiet, difficulty, opposition, accident, treachery; what is unforeseen; fatality.

Seven

A man in the act of carrying away five swords rapidly; the two others of the card remain stuck in the ground. A camp is close at hand.

Divinatory Meanings: Design, attempt, wish, hope, confidence; also quarrelling, a plan that may fail, annoyance. The design is uncertain in its import, because the significations are widely at variance with each other.

Reversed: Good advice, counsel, instruction, slander, babbling.

Six

A ferryman carrying passengers in his punt to the further shore. The course is smooth, and seeing that the freight is light, it may be noted that the work is not beyond his strength.

Divinatory Meanings: journey by water, route, way, envoy, commissionary, expedient.

Reversed: Declaration, confession, publicity; one account says that it is a proposal of love.

Five

A disdainful man looks after two retreating and dejected figures. Their swords lie upon the ground. He carries two others on his left shoulder, and a third sword is in his right hand, point to earth. He is the master in possession of the field.

Divinatory Meanings: Degradation, destruction, revocation, infamy, dishonour, loss, with the variants and analogues of these.

Reversed: The same; burial and obsequies.

Four

The effigy of a knight in the attitude of prayer, at full length upon his tomb.

Divinatory Meanings: Vigilance, retreat, solitude, hermit's repose, exile, tomb and coffin. It is these last that have suggested the design.

Reversed: Wise administration, circumspection, economy, avarice, precaution, testament.

Three

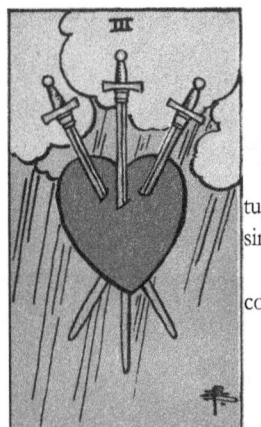

Three swords piercing a heart; cloud and rain behind.

Divinatory Meanings: Removal, absence, delay, division, rupture, dispersion, and all that the design signifies naturally, being too simple and obvious to call for specific enumeration.

Reversed: Mental alienation, error, loss, distraction, disorder, confusion.

The Pictorial Key to the Tarot

Two

A hoodwinked female figure balances two swords upon her shoulders.

Divinatory Meanings: Conformity and the equipoise which it suggests, courage, friendship, concord in a state of arms; another reading gives tenderness, affection, intimacy. The suggestion of harmony and other favourable readings must be considered in a qualified manner, as Swords generally are not symbolical of beneficent forces in human affairs.

Reversed: Imposture, falsehood, duplicity, disloyalty.

Ace

A hand issues from a cloud, grasping as word, the point of which is encircled by a crown.

Divinatory Meanings: Triumph, the excessive degree in everything, conquest, triumph of force. It is a card of great force, in love as well as in hatred. The crown may carry a much higher significance than comes usually within the sphere of fortune-telling.

Reversed: The same, but the results are disastrous; another account says –conception, childbirth, augmentation, multiplicity.

THE SUIT OF PENTACLES

King

The figure calls for no special description the face is rather dark, suggesting also courage, but somewhat lethargic in tendency. The bull's head should be noted as a recurrent symbol on the throne. The sign of this suit is represented throughout as engraved or blazoned with the pentagram, typifying the correspondence of the four elements in human nature and that by which they may be governed. In many old Tarot packs this suit stood for current coin, money, deniers. I have not invented the substitution of pentacles and I have no special cause to sustain in respect of the alternative. But the consensus of divinatory meanings is on the side of some change, because the cards do not happen to deal especially with questions of money.

Divinatory Meanings: Valour, realizing intelligence, business and normal intellectual aptitude, sometimes mathematical gifts and attainments of this kind; success in these paths.

Reversed: Vice, weakness, ugliness, perversity, corruption, peril.

Queen

The face suggests that of a dark woman, whose qualities might be summed up in the idea of greatness of soul; she has also the serious cast of intelligence; she contemplates her symbol and may see worlds therein.

Divinatory Meanings: Opulence, generosity, magnificence, security, liberty.

Reversed: Evil, suspicion, suspense, fear, mistrust.

Knight

He rides a slow, enduring, heavy horse, to which his own aspect corresponds. He exhibits his symbol, but does not look therein.

Divinatory Meanings: Utility, serviceableness, interest, responsibility, rectitude-all on the normal and external plane.

Reversed: inertia, idleness, repose of that kind, stagnation; also placidity, discouragement, carelessness.

Page

A youthful figure, looking intently at the pentacle which hovers over his raised hands. He moves slowly, insensible of that which is about him.

Divinatory Meanings: Application, study, scholarship, reflection another reading says news, messages and the bringer thereof; also rule, management.

Reversed: Prodigality, dissipation, liberality, luxury; unfavourable news.

Ten

A man and woman beneath an archway which gives entrance to a house and domain. They are accompanied by a child, who looks curiously at two dogs accosting an ancient personage seated in the foreground. The child's hand is on one of them.

Divinatory Meanings: Gain, riches; family matters, archives, extraction, the abode of a family.

Reversed: Chance, fatality, loss, robbery, games of hazard; sometimes gift, dowry, pension.

Nine

A woman, with a bird upon her wrist, stands amidst a great abundance of grapevines in the garden of a manorial house. It is a wide domain, suggesting plenty in all things. Possibly it is her own possession and testifies to material well-being.

Divinatory Meanings: Prudence, safety, success, accomplishment, certitude, discernment.

Reversed: Roguery, deception, voided project, bad faith.

Eight

An artist in stone at his work, which he exhibits in the form of trophies.

Divinatory Meanings: Work, employment, commission, craftsmanship, skill in craft and business, perhaps in the preparatory stage.

Reversed: Voided ambition, vanity, cupidity, exaction, usury. It may also signify the possession of skill, in the sense of the ingenious mind turned to cunning and intrigue.

Seven

A young man, leaning on his staff, looks intently at seven pentacles attached to a clump of greenery on his right; one would say that these were his treasures and that his heart was there.

Divinatory Meanings: These are exceedingly contradictory; in the main, it is a card of money, business, barter; but one reading gives altercation, quarrels –and another innocence, ingenuity, purgation.

Reversed: Cause for anxiety regarding money which it may be proposed to lend.

Six

A person in the guise of a merchant weighs money in a pair of scales and distributes it to the needy and distressed. It is a testimony to his own success in life, as well as to his goodness of heart.

Divinatory Meanings: Presents, gifts, gratification another account says attention, vigilance now is the accepted time, present prosperity, etc.

Reversed: Desire, cupidity, envy, jealousy, illusion.

Five

Two mendicants in a snow-storm pass a lighted casement.

Divinatory Meanings: The card foretells material trouble above all, whether in the form illustrated –that is, destitution –or otherwise. For some cartomancists, it is a card of love and lovers-wife, husband, friend, mistress; also concordance, affinities. These alternatives cannot be harmonized.

Reversed: Disorder, chaos, ruin, discord, profligacy.

Four

A crowned figure, having a pentacle over his crown, clasps another with hands and arms; two pentacles are under his feet. He holds to that which he has.

Divinatory Meanings: The surety of possessions, cleaving to that which one has, gift, legacy, inheritance.

Reversed: Suspense, delay, opposition.

Three

A sculptor at his work in a monastery. Compare the design which illustrates the Eight of Pentacles. The apprentice or amateur therein has received his reward and is now at work in earnest.

Divinatory Meanings: Métier, trade, skilled labour; usually, however, regarded as a card of nobility, aristocracy, renown, glory.

Reversed: Mediocrity, in work and otherwise, puerility, pettiness, weakness.

Two

A young man, in the act of dancing, has a pentacle in either hand, and they are joined by that endless cord which is like the number 8 reversed.

Divinatory Meanings: On the one hand it is represented as a card of gaiety, recreation and its connexions, which is the subject of the design; but it is read also as news and messages in writing, as obstacles, agitation, trouble, embroilment.

Reversed: Enforced gaiety, simulated enjoyment, literal sense, handwriting, composition, letters of exchange.

Ace

A hand –issuing, as usual, from a cloud– holds up a pentacle.

Divinatory Meanings: Perfect contentment, felicity, ecstasy; also speedy intelligence; gold.

Reversed: The evil side of wealth, bad intelligence; also great riches. In any case it shews prosperity, comfortable material conditions, but whether these are of advantage to the possessor will depend on whether the card is reversed or not.

§ 3. The Greater Arcana and their Divinatory Meanings;

Such are the intimations of the Lesser Arcana in respect of divinatory art, the veridic nature of which seems to depend on an alternative that it may be serviceable to express briefly. The records of the art are *ex hypothesi* the records of findings in the past based upon experience; as such, they are a guide to memory, and those who can master the elements may –still *ex hypothesi*– give interpretations on their basis. It is an official and automatic working. On the other hand, those who have gifts of intuition, of second sight, of clairvoyance –call it as we choose and may– will supplement the experience of the past by the findings of their own faculty, and will speak of that which they have seen in the pretexts of the oracles. It remains to give, also briefly, the divinatory significance allocated by the same art to the Trumps Major.

1. **THE MAGICIAN.** Skill, diplomacy, address, subtlety; sickness, pain, loss, disaster, snares of enemies; self-confidence, will; the Querent, if male.
   Reversed: Physician, Magus, mental disease, disgrace, disquiet.
2. **THE HIGH PRIESTESS.** Secrets, mystery, the future as yet unrevealed; the woman who interests the Querent, if male; the Querent herself, if female; silence, tenacity; mystery, wisdom, science.
   Reversed: Passion, moral or physical ardour, conceit, surface knowledge.
3. **THE EMPRESS.** Fruitfulness, action, initiative, length of days; the unknown, clandestine; also difficulty, doubt, ignorance.
   Reversed: Light, truth, the unraveling of involved matters, public rejoicings; according to another reading, vacillation.
4. **THE EMPEROR.** Stability, power, protection, realization; a great person; aid, reason, conviction; also authority and will.
   Reversed: Benevolence, compassion, credit; also confusion to enemies, obstruction, immaturity.
5. **THE HIEROPHANT.** Marriage, alliance, captivity, servitude; by another account, mercy and goodness; inspiration; the man to whom the Querent has recourse.
   Reversed: Society, good understanding, concord, overkindness, weakness.
6. **THE LOVERS.** Attraction, love, beauty, trials overcome.
   Reversed: Failure, foolish designs. Another account speaks of marriage frustrated and contrarieties of all kinds.
7. **THE CHARIOT.** Succour, providence also war, triumph, presumption, vengeance, trouble.
   Reversed: Riot, quarrel, dispute, litigation, defeat.
8. **FORTITUDE.** Power, energy, action, courage, magnanimity; also complete success and honours.
   Reversed: Despotism, abuse if power, weakness, discord, sometimes even disgrace.
9. **THE HERMIT.** Prudence, circumspection; also and especially treason, dissimulation, roguery, corruption.
   Reversed: Concealment, disguise, policy, fear, unreasoned caution.
10. **WHEEL OF FORTUNE.** Destiny, fortune, success, elevation, luck, felicity.
    Reversed: Increase, abundance, superfluity.
11. **JUSTICE.** Equity, rightness, probity, executive; triumph of the deserving side in law.
    Reversed: Law in all its departments, legal complications, bigotry, bias, excessive severity.
12. **THE HANGED MAN.** Wisdom, circumspection, discernment, trials, sacrifice, intuition, divination, prophecy.
    Reversed: Selfishness, the crowd, body politic.
13. **DEATH.** End, mortality, destruction, corruption also, for a man, the loss of a benefactor for a woman, many contrarieties; for a maid, failure of marriage projects.
    Reversed: Inertia, sleep, lethargy, petrifaction, somnambulism; hope destroyed.
14. **TEMPERANCE.** Economy, moderation, frugality, management, accommodation.
    Reversed: Things connected with churches, religions, sects, the priesthood, sometimes even the priest who will marry the Querent; also disunion, unfortunate combinations, competing interests.

15. **THE DEVIL.** Ravage, violence, vehemence, extraordinary efforts, force, fatality; that which is predestined but is not for this reason evil
    Reversed: Evil fatality, weakness, pettiness, blindness.
16. **THE TOWER.** Misery, distress, indigence, adversity, calamity, disgrace, deception, ruin. It is a card in particular of unforeseen catastrophe
    Reversed: According to one account, the same in a lesser degree also oppression, imprisonment, tyranny.
17. **THE STAR.** Loss, theft, privation, abandonment; another reading says-hope and bright prospects,
    Reversed: Arrogance, haughtiness, impotence.
18. **THE MOON.** Hidden enemies, danger, calumny, darkness, terror, deception, occult forces, error.
    Reversed: Instability, inconstancy, silence, lesser degrees of deception and error.
19. **THE SUN.** Material happiness, fortunate marriage, contentment.
    Reversed: The same in a lesser sense.
20. **THE LAST JUDGMENT.** Change of position, renewal, outcome. Another account specifies total loss though lawsuit.
    Reversed: Weakness, pusillanimity, simplicity; also deliberation, decision, sentence.
0. **THE FOOL.** Folly, mania, extravagance, intoxication, delirium, frenzy, bewrayment.
    Reversed: Negligence, absence, distribution, carelessness, apathy, nullity, vanity.
21. **THE WORLD.** Assured success, recompense, voyage, route, emigration, flight, change of place.
    Reversed: Inertia, fixity, stagnation, permanence.

It will be seen that, except where there is an irresistible suggestion conveyed by the surface meaning, that which is extracted from the Trumps Major by the divinatory art is at once artificial and arbitrary, as it seems to me, in the highest degree. But of one order are the mysteries of light and of another are those of fantasy. The allocation of a fortune-telling aspect to these cards is the story of a prolonged impertinence.

§ 4. Some Additional Meanings of the Lesser Arcana

WANDS

King. Generally favourable may signify a good marriage.
   Reversed: Advice that should be followed.
Queen. A good harvest, which may be taken in several senses.
   Reversed: Goodwill towards the Querent, but without the opportunity to exercise it.
Knight. A bad card; according to some readings, alienation.
   Reversed: For a woman, marriage, but probably frustrated.
Page. Young man of family in search of young lady.
   Reversed: Bad news.
Ten. Difficulties and contradictions, if near a good card.
Nine. Generally speaking, a bad card.

Eight. Domestic disputes for a married person.
Seven. A dark child.
Six. Servants may lose the confidence of their masters; a young lady may be betrayed by a friend.
Reversed: Fulfilment of deferred hope.
Five. Success in financial speculation.
Reversed: Quarrels may be turned to advantage.
Four. Unexpected good fortune.
Reversed: A married woman will have beautiful children.
Three. A very good card; collaboration will favour enterprise.
Two. A young lady may expect trivial disappointments.
Ace. Calamities of all kinds.
Reversed: A sign of birth.

CUPS

King. Beware of ill-will on the part of a man of position, and of hypocrisy pretending to help.
Reversed: Loss.
Queen. Sometimes denotes a woman of equivocal character.
Reversed: A rich marriage for a man and a distinguished one for a woman.
Knight. A visit from a friend, who will bring unexpected money to the Querent.
Reversed: Irregularity.
Page. Good augury; also a young man who is unfortunate in love.
Reversed: Obstacles of all kinds.
Ten. For a male Querent, a good marriage and one beyond his expectations.
Reversed: Sorrow; also a serious quarrel.
Nine. Of good augury for military men.
Reversed: Good business.
Eight. Marriage with a fair woman.
Reversed: Perfect satisfaction.
Seven. Fair child; idea, design, resolve, movement.
Reversed: Success, if accompanied by the Three of Cups.
Six. Pleasant memories.
Reversed: Inheritance to fall in quickly.
Five. Generally favourable; a happy marriage; also patrimony, legacies, gifts, success in enterprise.
Reversed: Return of some relative who has not been seen for long.
Four. Contrarieties.
Reversed: Presentiment.
Three. Unexpected advancement for a military man.
Reversed: Consolation, cure, end of the business.
Two. Favourable in things of pleasure and business, as well as love; also wealth and honour.
Reversed: Passion.

Ace. Inflexible will, unalterable law.

Reversed: Unexpected change of position.

SWORDS

King. A lawyer, senator, doctor.

Reversed: A bad man; also a caution to put an end to a ruinous lawsuit.

Queen. A widow.

Reversed: A bad woman, with ill-will towards the Querent.

Knight. A soldier, man of arms, satellite, stipendiary; heroic action predicted for soldier.

Reversed: Dispute with an imbecile person; for a woman, struggle with a rival, who will be conquered.

Page. An indiscreet person will pry into the Querent's secrets.

Reversed: Astonishing news.

Ten. Followed by Ace and King, imprisonment; for girl or wife, treason on the part of friends.

Reversed: Victory and consequent fortune for a soldier in war.

Nine. An ecclesiastic, a priest; generally, a card of bad omen.

Reversed: Good ground for suspicion against a doubtful person.

Eight. For a woman, scandal spread in her respect.

Reversed: Departure of a relative.

Seven. Dark girl; a good card; it promises a country life after a competence has been secured.

Reversed: Good advice, probably neglected.

Six. The voyage will be pleasant.

Reversed: Unfavourable issue of lawsuit.

Five. An attack on the fortune of the Querent.

Reversed: A sign of sorrow and mourning.

Four. A bad card, but if reversed a qualified success may be expected by wise administration of affairs.

Reversed: A certain success following wise administration.

Three. For a woman, the flight of her lover.

Reversed: A meeting with one whom the Querent has compromised; also a nun.

Two. Gifts for a lady, influential protection for a man in search of help.

Reversed: Dealings with rogues.

Ace. Great prosperity or great misery.

Reversed: Marriage broken off, for a woman, through her own imprudence.

PENTACLES

King. A rather dark man, a merchant, master, professor.

Reversed: An old and vicious man.

Queen. Dark woman; presents from a rich relative; rich and happy marriage for a young man.

Reversed: An illness.

Knight. An useful man; useful discoveries.

Reversed: A brave man out of employment.

Page. A dark youth; a young officer or soldier; a child.
Reversed: Sometimes degradation and sometimes pillage.

Ten. Represents house or dwelling, and derives its value from other cards.
Reversed: An occasion which may be fortunate or otherwise.

Nine. Prompt fulfilment of what is presaged by neighbouring cards.
Reversed: Vain hopes.

Eight. A young man in business who has relations with the Querent; a dark girl.
Reversed: The Querent will be compromised in a matter of money-lending.

Seven. Improved position for a lady's future husband.
Reversed: Impatience, apprehension, suspicion.

Six. The present must not be relied on.
Reversed: A check on the Querent's ambition.

Five. Conquest of fortune by reason.
Reversed: Troubles in love.

Four. For a bachelor, pleasant news from a lady.
Reversed: Observation, hindrances.

Three. If for a man, celebrity for his eldest son.
Reversed: Depends on neighbouring cards.

Two. Troubles are more imaginary than real.
Reversed: Bad omen, ignorance, injustice.

Ace. The most favourable of all cards.
Reversed: A share in the finding of treasure.

It will be observed (1) that these *additamenta* have little connexion with the pictorial designs of the cards to which they refer, as these correspond with the more important speculative values; (2) and further that the additional meanings are very often in disagreement with those previously given. All meanings are largely independent of one another and all are reduced, accentuated or subject to modification and sometimes almost reversal by their place in a sequence. There is scarcely any canon of criticism in matters of this kind. I suppose that in proportion as any system descends from generalities to details it becomes naturally the more precarious; and in the records of professional fortune-telling, it offers more of the dregs and lees of the subject. At the same time, divinations based on intuition and second sight are of little practical value unless they come down from the region of universals to that of particulars; but in proportion as this gift is present in a particular case, the specific meanings recorded by past cartomancists will be disregarded in favour of the personal appreciation of card values.

This has been intimated already. It seems necessary to add the following speculative readings.

§ 5. The Recurrence of Cards in Dealing

In the Natural Position

4 Kings = great honour; 3 Kings = consultation; 2 Kings = minor counsel.
4 Queens = great debate; 3 Queens = deception by women; 2 Queens = sincere friends.
4 Knights = serious matters; 3 Knights = lively debate; 2 Knights = intimacy.

4 Pages = dangerous illness; 3 Pages = dispute; 2 Pages = disquiet.
4 Tens = condemnation; 3 Tens = new condition; 2 Tens = change.
4 Nines = a good friend; 3 Nines = success; 2 Nines = receipt.
4 Eights = reverse; 3 Eights = marriage 2 Eights = new knowledge.
4 Sevens = intrigue; 3 Sevens = infirmity; 2 Sevens = news.
4 Sixes = abundance; 3 Sixes = success; 2 Sixes = irritability.
4 Fives = regularity; 3 Fives = determination; 2 Fives = vigils.
4 Fours = journey near at hand; 3 Fours = a subject of reflection; 2 Fours = insomnia.
4 Threes = progress; 3 Threes = unity 2 Threes = calm.
4 Twos = contention; 3 Twos = security; 2 Twos = accord.
4 Aces = favourable chance; 3 Aces = small success; 2 Aces = trickery.

Reversed

4 Kings = celerity; 3 Kings = commerce 2 Kings = projects.
4 Queens = bad company; 3 Queens = gluttony; 2 Queens = work.
4 Knights = alliance 3 Knights = a duel, or personal encounter; 2 Knights = susceptibility.
4 Pages = privation 3 Pages = idleness 2 Pages = society.
4 Tens = event, happening; 3 Tens disappointment; 2 Tens = expectation justified.
4 Nines = usury; 3 Nines imprudence; 2 Nines = a small profit.
4 Eights = error; 3 Eights a spectacle; 2 Eights = misfortune.
4 Sevens = quarrellers; 3 Sevens = joy; 2 Sevens = women of no repute.
4 Sixes = care; 3 Sixes = satisfaction 2 Sixes = downfall.
4 Fives = order; 3 Fives = hesitation; 2 Fives = reverse.
4 Fours = walks abroad; 3 Fours = disquiet; 2 Fours = dispute.
4 Threes = great success; 3 Threes = serenity; 2 Threes = safety.
4 Twos = reconciliation; 3 Twos apprehension; 2 Twos = mistrust.
4 Aces = dishonour; 3 Aces debauchery; 2 Aces = enemies.

§ 6. The Art of Tarot Divination

We come now to the final and practical part of this division of our subject, being the way to consult and obtain oracles by means of Tarot cards. The modes of operation are rather numerous, and some of them are exceedingly involved. I set aside those last mentioned, because persons who are versed in such questions believe that the way of simplicity is the way of truth. I set aside also the operations which have been republished recently in that section of The Tarot of the Bohemians which is entitled "The Divining Tarot"; it may be recommended at its proper value to readers who wish to go further than the limits of this handbook. I offer in the first place a short process which has been used privately for many years past in England, Scotland and Ireland. I do not think that it has been published –certainly not in connexion with Tarot cards; I believe that it will serve all purposes, but I will add by way of variation-in the second place what used to be known in France as the Oracles of Julia Orsini.

§ 7. An Ancient Celtic Method of Divination

This mode of divination is the most suitable for obtaining an answer to a definite question. The Diviner first selects a card to represent the person or, matter about which inquiry is made. This card is called the Significator. Should he wish to ascertain something in connexion with himself he takes the one which corresponds to his personal description. A Knight should be chosen as the Significator if the subject of inquiry is a man of forty years old and upward; a King should be chosen for any male who is under that age a Queen for a woman who is over forty years and a Page for any female of less age.

The four Court Cards in Wands represent very fair people, with yellow or auburn hair, fair complexion and blue eyes. The Court Cards in Cups signify people with light brown or dull fair hair and grey or blue eyes. Those in Swords stand for people having hazel or grey eyes, dark brown hair and dull complexion. Lastly, the Court Cards in Pentacles are referred to persons with very dark brown or black hair, dark eyes and sallow or swarthy complexions. These allocations are subject, however, to the following reserve, which will prevent them being taken too conventionally. You can be guided on occasion by the known temperament of a person; one who is exceedingly dark may be very energetic, and would be better represented by a Sword card than a Pentacle. On the other hand, a very fair subject who is indolent and lethargic should be referred to Cups rather than to Wands.

If it is more convenient for the purpose of a divination to take as the Significator the matter about which inquiry is to be made, that Trump or small card should be selected which has a meaning corresponding to the matter. Let it be supposed that the question is: Will a lawsuit be necessary? In this case, take the Trump No. 11, or justice, as the Significator. This has reference to legal affairs. But if the question is: Shall I be successful in my lawsuit? one of the Court Cards must be chosen as the Significator. Subsequently, consecutive divinations may be performed to ascertain the course of the process itself and its result to each of the parties concerned.

Having selected the Significator, place it on the table, face upwards. Then shuffle and cut the rest of the pack three times, keeping the faces of the cards downwards.

Turn up the top or FIRST CARD of the pack; cover the Significator with it, and say: This covers him. This card gives the influence which is affecting the person or matter of inquiry generally, the atmosphere of it in which the other currents work.

Turn up the SECOND CARD and lay it across the FIRST, saying: This crosses him. It shews the nature of the obstacles in the matter. If it is a favourable card, the opposing forces will not be serious, or it may indicate that something good in itself will not be productive of good in the particular connexion.

Turn up the THIRD CARD; place it above the Significator, and say: This crowns him. It represents (a) the Querent's aim or ideal in the matter; (b) the best that can be achieved under the circumstances, but that which has not yet been made actual.

Turn up the FOURTH CARD; place it below the Significator, and say: This is beneath him. It shews the foundation or basis of the matter, that which has already passed into actuality and which the Significator has made his own.

Turn up the FIFTH CARD; place it on the side of the Significator from which he is looking, and say: This is behind him. It gives the influence that is just passed, or is now passing away.

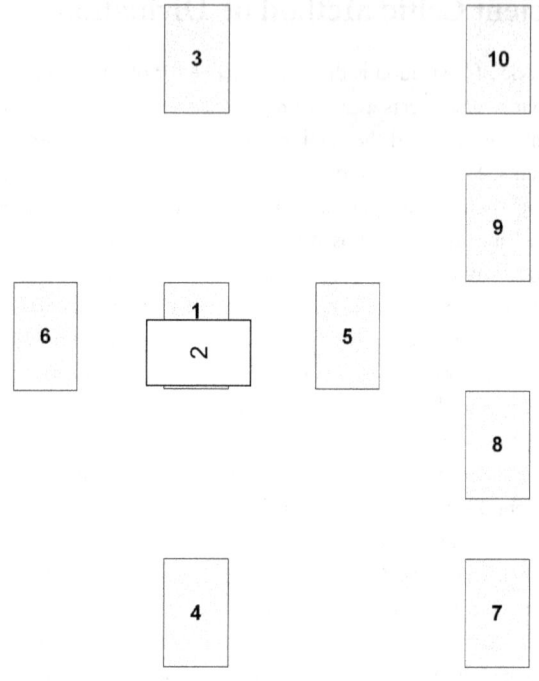

The Significator

1. That covers him.
2. What crosses him.
3. What crowns him.
4. What is beneath him.
5. What is behind him.
6. What is before him.
7. Himself.
8. His house.
9. His hopes or fears.
10. What will come.

N.B. If the Significator is a Trump or any small card that cannot be said to face either way, the Diviner must decide before beginning the operation which side he will take it as facing.

Turn up the SIXTH CARD; place it on the side that the Significator is facing, and say: This is before him. It shews the influence that is coming into action and will operate in the near future.

The cards are now disposed in the form of a cross, the Significator –covered by the First Card– being in the centre.

The next four cards are turned up in succession and placed one above the other in a line, on the right hand side of the cross.

The first of these, or the SEVENTH CARD of the operation, signifies himself –that is, the Significator– whether person or thing-and shews its position or attitude in the circumstances.

The EIGHTH CARD signifies his house, that is, his environment and the tendencies at work therein which have an effect on the matter –for instance, his position in life, the influence of immediate friends, and so forth.

The NINTH CARD gives his hopes or fears in the matter.

The TENTH is what will come, the final result, the culmination which is brought about by the influences shewn by the other cards that have been turned up in the divination.

It is on this card that the Diviner should especially concentrate his intuitive faculties and his memory in respect of the official divinatory meanings attached thereto. It should embody whatsoever you may have divined from the other cards on the table, including the Significator itself and concerning him or it, not excepting such lights upon higher significance as might fall like sparks from heaven if the card which serves for the oracle, the card for reading, should happen to be a Trump Major.

The operation is now completed; but should it happen that the last card is of a dubious nature, from which no final decision can be drawn, or which does not appear to indicate the ultimate conclusion of the affair, it may be well to repeat the operation, taking in this case the Tenth Card as the Significator, instead of the one previously used. The pack must be again shuffled and cut three times and the first ten cards laid out as before. By this a more detailed account of "What will come" may be obtained.

If in any divination the Tenth Card should be a Court Card, it shews that the subject of the divination falls ultimately into the hands of a person represented by that card, and its end depends mainly on him. In this event also it is useful to take the Court Card in question as the Significator in a fresh operation, and discover what is the nature of his influence in the matter and to what issue he will bring it.

Great facility may be obtained by this method in a comparatively short time, allowance being always made for the gifts of the operator-that is to say, his faculty of insight, latent or developed-and it has the special advantage of being free from all complications.

On the left page you can see a diagram of the cards as laid out in this mode of divination. The Significator is here facing to the left (the second card is crossed over the first one).

§ 8. An Alternative Method of Reading the Tarot Cards

Shuffle the entire pack and turn some of the cards round, so as to invert their tops. Let them be cut by the Querent with his left hand.

Deal out the first forty-two cards in six packets of seven cards each, face upwards, so that the first seven cards form the first packet, the following seven the second, and so on-as in the following diagram:

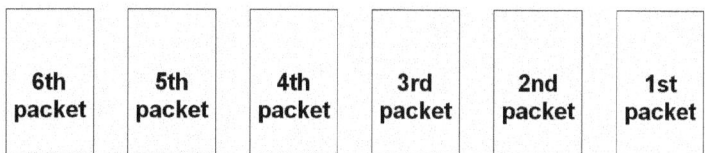

Take up the first packet; lay out the cards on the table in a row, from right to left; place the cards of the second packet upon them and then the packets which remain. You will thus have seven new packets of six cards each, arranged as follows:

Take the top card of each packet, shuffle them and lay out from right to left, making a line of seven cards.

Then take up the two next cards from each packet, shuffle and lay them out in two lines under the first line.

Take up the remaining twenty-one cards of the packets, shuffle and lay them out in three lines below the others.

You will thus have six horizontal lines of seven cards each, arranged after the following manner.

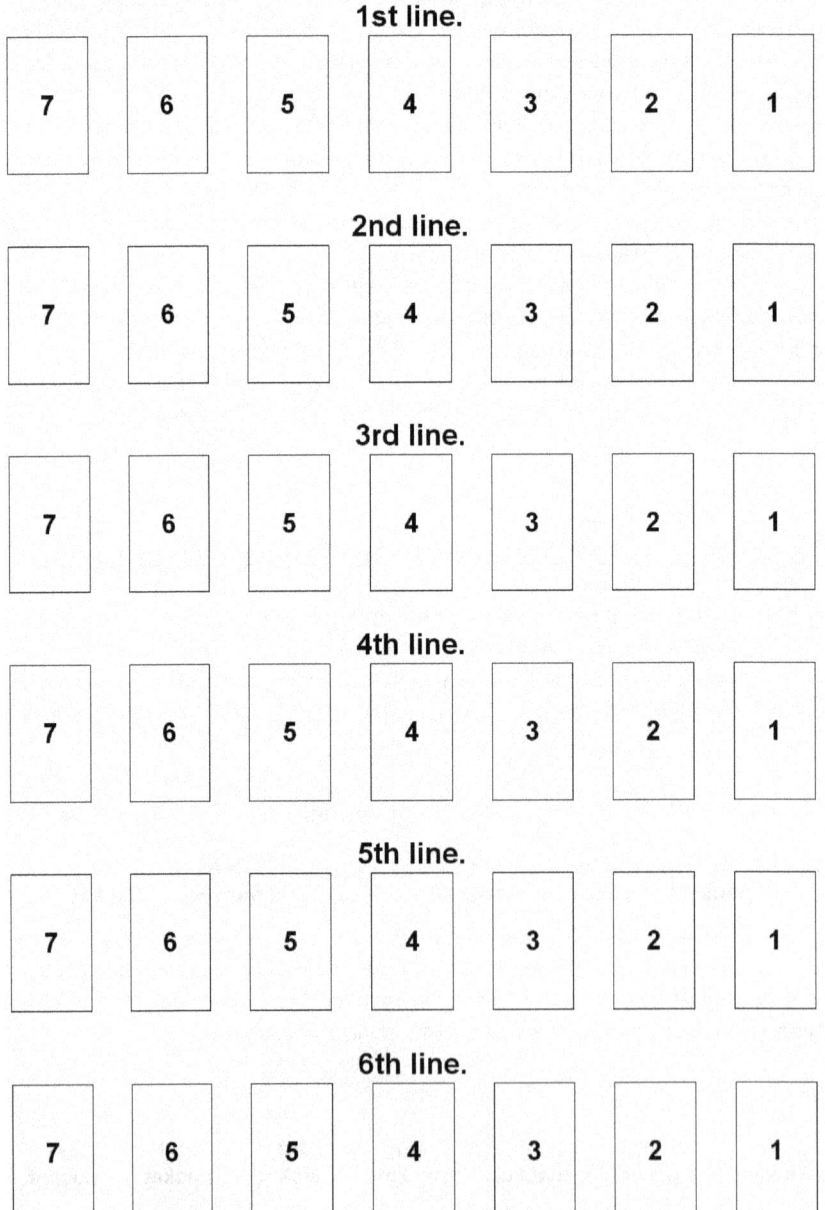

In this method, the Querent –if of the male sex– is represented by the Magician, and if female by the High Priestess; but the card, in either case, is not taken from the pack until the forty-two cards have been laid out, as above directed. If the required card is not found among those placed upon the table, it must be sought among the remaining thirty-six cards, which have not been dealt, and should be placed a little distance to the right of the first horizontal line. On the other hand, if it is among them, it is also taken out, placed as stated, and a card is drawn haphazard from the thirty-six cards undealt to fill the vacant position, so that there are still forty-two cards laid out on the table.

The cards are then read in succession, from right to left throughout, beginning at card No. 1 of the top line, the last to be read being that on the extreme left, or No. 7, of the bottom line.

This method is recommended when no definite question is asked-that is, when the Querent wishes to learn generally concerning the course of his life and destiny. If he wishes to know what may befall within a certain time, this time should be clearly specified before the cards are shuffled.

With further reference to the reading, it should be remembered that the cards must be interpreted relatively to the subject, which means that all official and conventional meanings of the cards may and should be adapted to harmonize with the conditions of this particular case in question –the position, time of life and sex of the Querent, or person for whom the consultation is made.

Thus, the Fool may indicate the whole range of mental phases between mere excitement and madness, but the particular phase in each divination must be judged by considering the general trend of the cards, and in this naturally the intuitive faculty plays an important part.

It is well, at the beginning of a reading, to run through the cards quickly, so that the mind may receive a general impression of the subject-the trend of the destiny –and afterwards to start again– reading them one by one and interpreting in detail.

It should be remembered that the Trumps represent more powerful and compelling forces –by the Tarot hypothesis– than are referable to the small cards.

The value of intuitive and clairvoyant faculties is of course assumed in divination. Where these are naturally present or have been developed by the Diviner, the fortuitous arrangement of cards forms a link between his mind and the atmosphere of the subject of divination, and then the rest is simple. Where intuition fails, or is absent, concentration, intellectual observation and deduction must be used to the fullest extent to obtain a satisfactory result. But intuition, even if apparently dormant, may be cultivated by practice in these divinatory processes. If in doubt as to the exact meaning of a card in a particular connexion, the Diviner is recommended, by those who are versed in the matter, to place his hand on it, try to refrain from thinking of what it ought to be, and note the impressions that arise in his mind. At the beginning this will probably resolve itself into mere guessing and may prove incorrect, but it becomes possible with practice to distinguish between a guess of the conscious mind and an impression arising from the mind which is sub-conscious.

It is not within my province to offer either theoretical or practical suggestions on this subject, in which I have no part, but the following additamenta have been contributed by one who has more titles to speak than all the cartomancists of Europe, if they could shuffle with a single pair of hands and divine with one tongue.

NOTES ON THE PRACTICE OF DIVINATION

1. Before beginning the operation, formulate your question definitely, and repeat it aloud.
2. Make your mind as blank as possible while shuffling the cards.
3. Put out of the mind personal bias and preconceived ideas as far as possible, or your judgment will be tinctured thereby.
4. On this account it is more easy to divine correctly for a stranger than for yourself or a friend.

§ 9. The Method of Reading by Means of Thirty-five Cards

When the reading is over, according to the scheme set forth in the last method, it may happen-as in the previous case-that something remains doubtful, or it may be desired to carry the question further, which is done as follows:

Take up the undealt cards which remain over, not having been used in the first operation with 42 cards. The latter are set aside in a heap, with the Querent, face upwards, on the top. The thirty-five cards, being shuffled and cut as before, are divided by dealing into six packets thus:

Packet I consists of the first SEVEN CARDS.

Packet II consists of the SIX CARDS next following in order; *Packet III* consists of the FIVE CARDS following; *Packet IV* contains the next FOUR CARDS; *Packet V* contains Two CARDS; and *Packet VI* contains the last ELEVEN CARDS. The arrangement will then be as follows:

Packet VI.	Packet V.	Packet IV.	Packet III.	Packet II.	Packet I.
11 cards	2 cards	4 cards	5 cards	6 cards	7 cards

Take up these packets successively; deal out the cards which they contain in six lines, which will be necessarily of unequal length.

THE FIRST LINE stands for the house, the environment and so forth.

THE SECOND LINE stands for the person or subject of the divination.

THE THIRD LINE stands for what is passing outside, events, persons, etc.

THE FOURTH LINE stands for a surprise, the unexpected, etc.

THE FIFTH LINE stands for consolation, and may moderate all that is unfavourable in the preceding lines.

THE SIXTH LINE is that which must be consulted to elucidate the enigmatic oracles of the others; apart from them it has no importance.

These cards should all be read from left to right, beginning with the uppermost line.

It should be stated in conclusion as to this divinatory part that there is no method of interpreting Tarot cards which is not applicable to ordinary playing-cards, but the additional court cards, and above all the Trumps Major, are held to increase the elements and values of the oracles.

And now in conclusion as to the whole matter, I have left for these last words –as if by way of epilogue– one further and final point. It is the sense in which I regard the Trumps Major as containing Secret Doctrine. I do not here mean that I am acquainted with orders and fraternities in which such doctrine reposes and is there found to be part of higher Tarot knowledge. I do not mean that such doctrine, being so preserved and transmitted, can be constructed as imbedded independently in the Trumps Major. I do not mean that it is something apart from the Tarot. Associations exist which have special knowledge of both kinds; some of it is deduced from the Tarot and some of it is apart therefrom; in either case, it is the same in the root-matter. But there are also things in reserve which are not in orders or societies, but are transmitted after another manner. Apart from all inheritance of this kind, let any one who is a mystic consider separately and in combination the Magician, the Fool, the High Priestess, the Hierophant, the Empress, the Emperor, the Hanged Man and the Tower. Let him then consider the card called the Last Judgment. They contain the legend of the soul. The other Trumps Major are the details and –as one might say– the accidents. Perhaps such a person will begin to understand what lies far behind these symbols, by whomsoever first invented and however preserved. If he does, he will see also why I have concerned myself with the subject, even at the risk of writing about divination by cards.

Bibliography

A CONCISE BIBLIOGRAPHY OF THE CHIEF WORKS DEALING WITH THE TAROT AND ITS CONNEXIONS

As in spite of its modest pretensions, this monograph is, so far as I am aware, the first attempt to provide in English a complete synoptic account of the Tarot, with its archæological position defined, its available symbolism developed, and –as a matter of curiosity in occultism– with its divinatory meanings and modes of operation sufficiently exhibited, it is my wish, from the literate standpoint, to enumerate those text-books of the subject, and the most important incidental references thereto, which have come under my notice. The bibliographical particulars that follow lay no claim to completeness, as I have cited nothing that I have not seen with my own eyes; but I can understand that most of my readers will be surprised at the extent of the literature –if I may so term it conventionally– which has grown up in the course of the last 120 years. Those who desire to pursue their inquiries further will find ample materials herein, though it is not a course which I am seeking to commend especially, as I deem that enough has been said upon the Tarot in this place to stand for all that has preceded it. The bibliography itself is representative after a similar manner. I should add that there is a considerable catalogue of cards and works on card-playing in the British Museum, but I have not had occasion to consult it to any extent for the purposes of the present list.

I. *Monde Primitf, analysé et comparé avec le Monde Moderne.* Par M. Court de Gebelin. Vol. 8, 40, Paris, 1781.

The articles on the *Jeu des Tarots* will be found at pp. 365 to 410. The plates at the end shew the Trumps Major and the Aces of each suit. These are valuable, as indications of the cards at the close of the eighteenth century. They were presumably then in circulation in the South of France, as it is said that at the period in question they were practically unknown at Paris. I have dealt with the claims of the papers in the body of the present work. Their speculations were tolerable enough for their mazy period; but that they are suffered still, and accepted indeed without question, by French occult writers is the most convincing testimony that one can need to the qualifications of the latter for dealing with any question of historical research.

II. The Works of Etteilla. *Les Septs Nuances de l'œuvre philosophique Hermitique; Manière de se récréer avec le Jeu de Cartes, nommeés Tarots; Fragments sur les Hautes Sciences; Philosophie des Hautes Sciences; Jeu des Tarots, ou le Livre de Thoth; Leçons Théoriques et Pratiques du Livre de Thoth* –all published between 1783 and 1787.

These are exceedingly rare and were frankly among the works of *colportage* of their particular period. They contain the most curious fragments on matters within and without the main issue, lucubrations on genii, magic, astrology, talismans, dreams, etc. I have spoken sufficiently in the text of the author's views on the Tarot and his place in its modern history. He regarded it as a work of speaking hieroglyphics, but to translate it was not easy. He, however, accomplished the task that is to say, in his own opinion.

III. *An Inquiry into the Antient Greek Game, supposed to have been invented by Palamedes.* [By James Christie.] London: 40, 1801.

I mention this collection of curious dissertations because it has been cited by writers on the Tarot. It seeks to establish a close connexion between early games of antiquity and modern chess. It is suggested that the invention attributed to Palamedes, prior to the Siege of Troy, was known in China from a more remote period of antiquity. The work has no reference to cards of any kind whatsoever.

IV. *Researches into the History of Playing Cards.* By Samuel Weller Singer. 40, London, 1816.

The Tarot is probably of Eastern origin and high antiquity, but the rest of Court de Gebelin's theory is vague and unfounded. Cards were known in Europe prior to the appearance of the Egyptians. The work has a good deal of curious information and the appendices are valuable, but the Tarot occupies comparatively little of the text and the period is too early for a tangible criticism of its claims. There are excellent reproductions of early specimen designs. Those of Court de Gebelin are also given *in extenso.*

V. *Facts and Speculations on Playing Cards.* By W. A. Chatto. 8vo, London, 1848.

The author suggested that the Trumps Major and the numeral cards were once separate, but were afterwards combined. The oldest specimens of Tarot cards are not later than 1440. But the claims and value of the volume have been sufficiently described in the text.

VI. *Les Cartes à Jouer el la Cartomancie.* Par D. R. P. Boiteau d'Ambly. 40, Paris, 1854.

There are some interesting illustrations of early Tarot cards, Which are said to be of Oriental origin; but they are not referred to Egypt. The early gipsy connexion is affirmed, but there is no evidence produced. The cards came with the gipsies from India, where they were designed to shew forth the intentions of "the unknown divinity" rather than to be the servants of profane amusement.

VII. *Dogme el Rituel de la Haute Magie.* Par Éliphas Lévi, 2 vols., demy 8vo, Paris, 1854.

This is the first publication of Alphonse Louis Constant on occult philosophy, and it is also his *magnum opus*. It is constructed in both volumes on the major Keys of the Tarot and has been therefore understood as a kind of development of their implicits, in the way that these were presented to the mind of the author. To supplement what has been said of this work in the text of the present monograph, I need only add that the section on transmutations in the second volume contains what is termed the *Key of Thoth*. The inner circle depicts a triple *Tau*, with a hexagram where the bases join, and beneath is the Ace of Cups. Within the external circle are the letters TARO, and about this figure as a whole are grouped the symbols of the Four Living Creatures, the Ace of Wands, Ace of Swords, the letter *Shin*, and a magician's candle, which is identical, according to Lévi, with the lights used in the Goetic Circle of Black Evocations and Pacts. The triple *Tau* may be taken to represent the Ace of Pentacles. The only Tarot card given in the volumes is the Chariot, which is drawn by two sphinxes; the fashion thus set has been followed in later days. Those who interpret the work as a kind of commentary on the Trumps Major are the conventional occult students and those who follow them will have only the pains of fools.

VIII. *Les Rômes*. Par J. A. Vaillant. Demy 8vo, Paris, 1857.

The author tells us how he met with the cards, but the account is in a chapter of anecdotes. The Tarot is the sidereal book of Enoch, modelled on the astral wheel of Athor. There is a description of the Trumps Major, which are evidently regarded as an heirloom, brought by the gipsies from Indo-Tartary. The publication of Lévi's *Dogme et Rituel* must, I think, have impressed Vaillant very much, and although in this, which was the writer's most important work, the anecdote that I have mentioned is practically his only Tarot reference, he seems to have gone much further in a later publication –*Clef Magique de la Fiction et du Fait*, but I have not been able to see it, nor do I think, from the reports concerning it, that I have sustained a loss.

IX. *Histoire de la Magie*. Par Éliphas Lévi. 8vo, Paris, 1860.

The references to the Tarot are few in this brilliant work, which will be available shortly in English. It gives the 21st Trump Major, commonly called the Universe, or World, under the title of *Yinx Pantomorph* –a seated figure wearing the crown of Isis. This has been reproduced by Papus in *Le Tarot Divinataire*. The author explains that the extant Tarot has come down to us through the Jews, but it passed somehow into the hands of the gipsies, who brought it with them when they first entered France in the early part of the fifteenth century. The authority here is Vaillant.

X. *La Clef des Grands Mystères*. Par Eliphas Lévi. 8vo, Paris, 1861.

The frontispiece to this work represents the absolute Key of the occult sciences, given by William Postel and completed by the writer. It is reproduced in The Tarot of the Bohemians, and in the preface which I have prefixed thereto, as indeed elsewhere, I have explained that Postel never constructed a hieroglyphical key. Eliphas Lévi identifies the Tarot as that sacred alphabet which has been variously referred to Enoch, Thoth, Cadmus and Palamedes. It consists of absolute ideas attached to signs and numbers. In respect of the latter, there is an extended commentary on these as far as the number ig, the series being interpreted as the Keys of Occult Theology. The remaining three numerals which complete the Hebrew alphabet are called the Keys of Nature. The Tarot is said to be the original of chess, as it is also of the Royal Game of Goose. This volume contains the author's hypothetical reconstruction of the tenth Trump Major, shewing Egyptian figures on the Wheel of Fortune.

XI. *L'Homme Rouge des Tuileyies.* Par P. Christian. Fcap. 8vo, Paris, 1863.

The work is exceedingly rare, is much sought and was once highly prized in France; but Dr. Papus has awakened to the fact that it is really of slender value, and the statement might be extended. It is interesting, however, as containing the writer's first reveries on the Tarot. He was a follower and imitator of Lévi. In the present work, he provides a commentary on the Trumps Major and thereafter the designs and meanings of all the Minor Arcana. There are many and curious astrological attributions. The work does not seem to mention the Tarot by name. A later Histoire de la Magie does little more than reproduce and extend the account of the Trumps Major given herein.

The History of Playing Cards. By E. S. Taylor. Cr. 8vo, London, 1865.

XII. This was published posthumously and is practically a translation of Boiteau. It therefore calls for little remark on my part. The opinion is that cards were imported by the gipsies from India. There are also references to the so-called Chinese Tarot, which was mentioned by Court de Gebelin.

XIII. *Origine des Caries à Jouer.* Par Romain Merlin. 40, Paris, 1869.

There is no basis for the Egyptian origin of the Tarot, except in the imagination of Court de Gebelin. I have mentioned otherwise that the writer disposes, to his personal satisfaction, of the gipsy hypothesis, and he does the same in respect of the imputed connexion with India; he says that cards were known in Europe before communication was opened generally with that world about 1494. But if the gipsies were a Pariah tribe already dwelling in the West, and if the cards were a part of their baggage, there is nothing in this contention. The whole question is essentially one of speculation.

XIV. *The Platonist.* Vol. II, pp. 126-8. Published at St. Louis, Mo., U.S.A., 1884-5. Royal 4to. This periodical, the suspension of which must have been regretted by many admirers of an unselfish and laborious effort, contained one anonymous article on the Tarot by a writer with theosophical tendencies, and considerable pretensions to knowledge. It has, however, by its own evidence, strong titles to negligence, and is indeed a ridiculous performance. The word Tarot is the Latin *Rota* = wheel, transposed. The system was invented at a remote period in India, presumably –for the writer is vague– about B.C. 300. The Fool represents primordial chaos. The Tarot is now used by Rosicrucian adepts, but in spite of the inference that it may have come down to them from their German progenitors in the early seventeenth century, and notwithstanding the source in India, the twenty-two keys were pictured on the walls of Egyptian temples dedicated to the mysteries of initiation. Some of this rubbish is derived from P. Christian, but the following statement is peculiar, I think, to the writer: "It is known to adepts that there should be twenty-two esoteric keys, which would make the total number up to 100." Persons who reach a certain stage of lucidity have only to provide blank pasteboards of the required number and the missing designs will be furnished by superior intelligences. Meanwhile, America is still awaiting the fulfilment of the concluding forecast, that some few will ere long have so far developed in that country "as to be able to read perfectly... in that perfect and divine sibylline work, the Taro." Perhaps the cards which accompany the present volume will give the opportunity and the impulse!

XV. *Lo Joch de Naips.* Per Joseph Brunet y Bellet. Cr. 8vo, Barcelona, 1886.

With reference to the dream of Egyptian origin, the author quotes E. Garth Wilkinson's *Manners and Customs of the Egyptians* as negative evidence at least that cards were unknown in the old cities of the Delta. The history of the subject is sketched, following the chief authorities, but without reference to exponents of the occult schools. The mainstay throughout is Chatto. There are some interesting particulars about the prohibition of cards in Spain, and the appendices include a few valuable documents, by one of which it appears, as already mentioned, that St. Bernardin of Sienna preached against games in general, and cards in particular, so far back as 1423. There are illustrations of rude Tarots, including a curious example of an Ace of Cups, with a phoenix rising therefrom, and a Queen of Cups, from whose vessel issues a flower.

XVI. *The Tarot: Its Occult Signification, Use in FortuneTelling, and Method of Play.* By S. L. MacGregor Mathers. Sq. 16mo, London, 1888.

This booklet was designed to accompany a set of Tarot cards, and the current packs of the period were imported from abroad for the purpose. There is no pretence of original research, and the only personal opinion expressed by the writer or calling for notice here states that the Trumps Major are hieroglyphic symbols corresponding to the occult meanings of the Hebrew alphabet. Here the authority is Lévi, from whom is also derived the brief symbolism allocated to the twenty-two Keys. The divinatory meanings follow, and then the modes of operation. It is a mere sketch written in a pretentious manner and is negligible in all respects.

XVII. *Traité Méthodique de Science Occulte.* Par Papus. 8vo, Paris, 1891.

The rectified Tarot published by Oswald Wirth after the indications of Éliphas Lévi is reproduced in this work, which –it may be mentioned– extends to nearly 1,100 pages. There is a section on the gipsies, considered as the importers of esoteric tradition into Europe by means of the cards. The Tarot is a combination of numbers and ideas, whence its correspondence with the Hebrew alphabet. Unfortunately, the Hebrew citations are rendered almost unintelligible by innumerable typographical errors.

XVIII. *Éliphas Lévi: Le Livre des Splendeurs.* Demy 8vo, Paris, 1894.

A section on the Elements of the Kabalah affirms (a) That the Tarot contains in the several cards of the four suits a fourfold explanation of the numbers 1 to 10; (b) that the symbols which we now have only in the form of cards were at first medals and then afterwards became talismans; (c) that the Tarot is the hieroglyphical book of the Thirty-two Paths of Kabalistic theosophy, and that its summary explanation is in the *Sepher Yelzirah*; (d) that it is the inspiration of all religious theories and symbols; (e) that its emblems are found on the ancient monuments of Egypt. With the historical value of these pretensions I have dealt in the text.

XIX. *Clefs Magiques et Clavicules de Salomon Par Éliphas Lévi.* Sq. 12mo, Paris, 1895.

The Keys in question are said to have been restored in 1860, in their primitive purity, by means of hieroglyphical signs and numbers, without any admixture of Samaritan or Egyptian images. There are rude designs of the Hebrew letters attributed to the Trumps Major, with meanings –most of which are to be found in other works by the same writer. There are also combinations of the letters which enter into the Divine Name; these combinations are attributed to the court cards of the Lesser Arcana. Certain talismans of spirits are in fine furnished with Tarot attributions; the Ace of Clubs corresponds to the *Deus Absconditus*, the First Principle. The little book was issued at a high price and as something that should be reserved to adepts, or those on the path of adeptship, but it is really without value –symbolical or otherwise.

XX. *Les xxii Lames Hermétiques du Tarot Divinatoire*. Par R. Falconnier. Demy 8vo, Paris, 1896.

The word Tarot comes from the Sanskrit and means "fixed star," which in its turn signifies immutable tradition, theosophical synthesis, symbolism of primitive dogma, etc. Graven on golden plates, the designs were used by Hermes Trismegistus and their mysteries were only revealed to the highest grades of the priesthood of Isis. It is unnecessary therefore to say that the Tarot is of Egyptian origin and the work of M. Falconnier has been to reconstruct its primitive form, which he does by reference to the monuments –that is to say, after the fashion of Éliphas Lévi, he draws the designs of the Trumps Major in imitation of Egyptian art. This production has been hailed by French occultists as presenting the Tarot in its perfection, but the same has been said of the designs of Oswald Wirth, which are quite unlike and not Egyptian at all. To be frank, these kinds of foolery may be as much as can be expected from the Sanctuary of the Comédie-Française, to which the author belongs, and it should be reserved thereto.

XXI. *The Magical Ritual of the Sanctum Regnum, interpreted by the Tarot Trumps*. Translated from the MSS. of Éliphas Lévi and edited by W. Wynn Westcott, M.B. Fcap. 8vo, London, 1896.

It is necessary to say that the interest of this memorial rests rather in the fact of its existence than in its intrinsic importance. There is a kind of informal commentary on the Trumps Major, or rather there are considerations which presumably had arisen therefrom in the mind of the French author. For example, the card called Fortitude is an opportunity for expatiation on will as the secret of strength. The Hanged Man is said to represent the completion of the Great Work. Death suggests a diatribe against Necromancy and Goëtia; but such phantoms have no existence in "the *Sanctum Regnum*" of life. Temperance produces only a few vapid commonplaces, and the Devil, which is blind force, is the occasion for repetition of much that has been said already in the earlier works of Lévi. The Tower represents the betrayal of the Great Arcanum, and this it was which caused the sword of Samael to be stretched over the Garden of Delight. Amongst the plates there is a monogram of the Gnosis, which is also that of the Tarot. The editor has thoughtfully appended some information on the Trump Cards taken from the early works of Lévi and from the commentaries of P. Christian.

XXII. *Comment on devient Alchimiste*. Par F. Jolivet de Castellot. Sq. 8vo, Paris, 1897.

Herein is a summary of the Alchemical Tarot, which-with all my respect for innovations and inventions-seems to be high fantasy; but Etteilla had reveries of this kind, and if it should ever be warrantable to produce a Key Major in place of the present Key Minor, it might be worth while to tabulate the analogies of these strange dreams. At the moment it will be sufficient to say that there is given a schedule of the alchemical correspondences to the Trumps Major, by which it appears that the juggler or Magician symbolizes attractive force; the High Priestess is inert matter, than which nothing is more false; the Pope is the Quintessence, which –if he were only acquainted with Shakespeare– might tempt the present successor of St. Peter to repeat that "there are more things in heaven and earth, Horatio." The Devil, on the other hand, is the matter of philosophy at the black stage; the Last judgment is the red stage of the Stone; the Fool is its fermentation; and, in fine, the last card, or the World, is the Alchemical Absolute-the Stone itself. If this should encourage my readers, they may note further that the particulars of various chemical combinations can be developed by means of the Lesser Arcana, if these are laid out for the purpose. Specifically, the King of Wands = Gold the Pages or Knaves represent animal substances the King of Cups = Silver; and so forth.

XXIII. *Le Grand Arcane, ou l'occultisme dévoilé.* Par Éliphas Lévi. Demy 8vo, Paris, 1898.

After many years and the long experience of all his concerns in occultism, the author at length reduces his message to one formula in this work. I speak, of course, only in respect of the Tarot: he says that the cards of Etteilla produce a kind of hypnotism in the seer or seeress who divines thereby. The folly of the psychic reads in the folly of the querent. Did he counsel honesty, it is suggested that he would lose his clients. I have written severe criticisms on occult arts and sciences, but this is astonishing from one of their past professors and, moreover, I think that the psychic occasionally is a psychic and sees in a manner as such.

XXIV. *Le Serpent de la Genêse –Livre II; La Clef de la Magie Noire.* Par Stanislas de Guaita. 8vo, Paris, 1902.

It is a vast commentary on the second septenary of the Trumps Major. Justice signifies equilibrium and its agent; the Hermit typifies the mysteries of solitude; the Wheel of Fortune is the *circulus* of becoming or attaining; Fortitude signifies the power resident in will; the Hanged Man is magical bondage, which speaks volumes for the clouded and inverted insight of this fantasiast in occultism: Death is, of course, that which its name signifies, but with reversion to the second death; Temperance means the magic of transformations, and therefore suggests excess rather than abstinence. There is more of the same kind of thing –I believe– in the first book, but this will serve as a specimen. The demise of Stanislas de Guaita put an end to his scheme of interpreting the Tarot Trumps, but it should be understood that the connexion is shadowy and that actual references could be reduced to a very few pages.

XXV. *Le Tarot: Aperçu historique.* Par. J. J. Bourgeat. Sq. 12MO, Paris, 1906.

The author has illustrated his work by purely fantastic designs of certain Trumps Major, as, for example, the Wheel of Fortune, Death and the Devil. They have no connexion with symbolism. The Tarot is said to have originated in India, whence it passed to Egypt. Éliphas Lévi, P. Christian, and J. A. Vaillant are cited in support of statements and points of view. The mode of divination adopted is fully and carefully set out.

XXVI. *L'Art de tirer les Caries.* Par Antonio Magus. Cr. 8vo, Paris, n.d. (about 1908).

This is not a work of any especial pretension, nor has it any title to consideration on account of its modesty. Frankly, it is little –if any– better than a bookseller's experiment. There is a summary account of the chief methods of divination, derived from familiar sources; there is a history of cartomancy in France; and there are indifferent reproductions of Etteilla Tarot cards, with his meanings and the well-known mode of operation. Finally, there is a section on common fortune-telling by a piquet set of ordinary cards: this seems to lack the only merit that it might have Possessed, namely, perspicuity; but I speak with reserve, as I am not perhaps a judge possessing ideal qualifications in matters of this kind. In any case, the question signifies nothing. It is just to add that the concealed author maintains what he terms the Egyptian tradition of the Tarot, which is the Great Book of Thoth. But there is a light accent throughout his thesis, and it does not follow that he took the claim seriously.

XXVII. *Le Tarot Divinatoire: Clef du tirage des Caries et des sorts*. Par le Dr. Papus. Demy 8vo, Paris, 1909.

The text is accompanied by what is termed a complete reconstitution of all the symbols, which means that in this manner we have yet another Tarot. The Trumps Major follow the traditional lines, with various explanations and attributions on the margins, and this Plan obtains throughout the series. From the draughtsman's point of view, it must be said that the designs are indifferently done, and the reproductions seem worse than the designs. This is probably of no especial importance to the class of readers addressed. Dr. Papus also presents, by way of curious memorials, the evidential value of which he seems to accept implicitly, certain unpublished designs of Éliphas Lévi; they are certainly interesting as examples of the manner in which the great occultist manufactured the archæology of the Tarot to bear out his personal views. We have (a) Trump Major, No. 5, being Horus as the Grand Hierophant, drawn after the monuments; (b) Trump Major, No. 2, being the High Priestess as Isis, also after the monuments; and (c) five imaginary specimens of an Indian Tarot. This is how *la haute science* in France contributes to the illustration of that work which Dr. Papus terms *livre de la science éternelle*; it would be called by rougher names in English criticism. The editor himself takes his usual pains and believes that he has discovered the time attributed to each card by ancient Egypt. He applies it to the purpose of divination, so that the skilful fortune-teller can now predict the hour and the day when the dark young man will meet with the fair widow, and so forth.

XXVIII. *Le Tarot des Bohémiens*. Par Papus. 8vo, Paris, 1889. English Translation, second edition, 1910.

An exceedingly complex work, which claims to present an absolute key to occult science. It was translated into English by Mr. A. P. Morton in 1896, and this version has been re-issued recently under my own supervision. The preface which I have prefixed thereto contains all that it is necessary to say regarding its claims, and it should be certainly consulted by readers of the present Pictorial Key to the Tarot. The fact that Papus regards the great sheaf of hieroglyphics as "the most ancient book in the world," as "the Bible of Bibles," and therefore as "the primitive revelation," does not detract from the claim of his general study, which –it should be added– is accompanied by numerous valuable plates, exhibiting Tarot codices, old and new, and diagrams summarizing the personal theses of the writer and of some others who preceded him. *The Tarot of the Bohemians* is published at 6s. by William Rider & Son, Ltd.

XXIX. *Manuel Synthétique et Pratique du Tarot*. Par Eudes Picard. 8vo, Paris, 1909.

Here is yet one more handbook of the subject, presenting in a series of rough plates a complete sequence of the cards. The Trumps Major are those of Court de Gebelin and for the Lesser Arcana the writer has had recourse to his imagination; it can be said that some of them are curious, a very few thinly suggestive and the rest bad. The explanations embody neither research nor thought at first hand; they are bald summaries of the occult authorities in France, followed by a brief general sense drawn out as a harmony of the whole. The method of use is confined to four pages and recommends that divination should be performed in a fasting state. On the history of the Tarot, M. Picard says (a) that it is confused; (b) that we do not know precisely whence it comes; (c) that, this notwithstanding, its introduction is due to the Gipsies. He says finally that its interpretation is an art.

Palmistry For All

Cheiro
(William John Warner)

This text and the accompanying illustrations are in the public domain in the United States of America because they were published prior to 1923.

Preface to the American Edition

There is no country in the world where the "study of character" is more indulged in than in the United States of America. During my many visits there I could not help remarking how even the "hardest headed" business men used any form of this study that they could get hold of to help them in their business dealings with other men and also in endeavouring to ascertain the character of their clerks and employees.

In looking over the records of my career I find that in the course of my visits to America I gave private lessons to the heads of two hundred and seventy business establishments in New York, one hundred and thirty-five in Boston, and three hundred and forty-two in Chicago.

All these men were large employers of labour and what they principally wanted was, to have some help beyond that of their own judgment in dealing with those with whom they came in contact in the regular course of their business careers. In no other country did I find the same interest taken in the study of character from a practical standpoint.

It is for this reason that I write a special Preface for this Edition, believing as I do that my American readers will appreciate the added information I may be able to give regarding the obtaining by a mere glance at a hand a quick grasp of the leading characteristics of the persons with whom they are thrown into contact, or for whatever reason they choose to make use of this study.

Everyone knows that "the face can wear a mask," that a person may be a good actor and put on a certain expression that may deceive even the best judgment.

But hands cannot change as the result of a mere effort to please; *the character they express is the real nature of the individual*—the true character that has been formed by heredity or that has grown up with the person by long years of habit.

The characteristics alluded to below are those which may be easily observed and which are aids to a rapid judgment of character and which I have never before been able to give to the public in such a concise way.

The more elaborate details concerning the ultimate success of the person one is talking to, their more intimate character and their future development will be found in their proper place, in the subsequent chapters.

Rules for Rapid Observation

The Fingers

Observe the fingers. If they look short and stumpy in proportion to the rest of the palm—one may be sure that the individual to whom they belong is of an animal nature, possessing coarse instincts, devoid of real intellectuality, and belonging to the lower order of humanity.

If the fingers and the palm appear equal in length, the owner belongs to a more cultured race. He has inherited from a more intellectual line of ancestors and for all work requiring intelligence and a higher mentality he or she could be depended on, whereas the first-mentioned type could not—no matter how well he might talk or advocate his own superiority.

If the fingers look unusually long and thin, and in this way out of proportion to the palm, the man or woman will err on the side of too much ideality and refinement and is not suited to business or work requiring "level headedness" and practicality. It would be useless, for example, to put such a person in charge of work-people or over work-rooms. His ideality and refinement would be thrown away in such positions, and even with the best will in the world he would be completely out of harmony with his surroundings.

Such a man, however, could be depended upon in all positions requiring personal mental work, research, science, literature, philosophy, educational work or, in fact, anything relating to the higher qualities of the mind.

If his fingers, in addition to their length, were also knotty or jointed (joints much pronounced), he could be depended on to a still greater extent for all work requiring great thoughtfulness, detail, and concentration of mind.

If, on the other hand, these long fingers were smooth jointed, he would, while having the same desire for ideality and for everything intellectual, be impulsive and inspirational, would lack a sense of detail and a love for detail in his own work, would be visionary, artistic, emotional. Such a person would be suited to artistic work, such as painting, making designs, models, etc., but could not be trusted to perform anything requiring detail, research or science, and would be utterly useless in any position where discipline or control of others were required.

The Fingers Considered Separately

Let us now observe the fingers separately from the rest of the hand.

The first finger is considered as the Dictator, the Lawgiver, the finger of Ambition, the Indicator, the Pointer, etc.

If this finger is unusually long and nearly equals the second, all these tendencies are extremely pronounced.

Therefore, if your employee has this finger long, you can safely entrust him with control over, and charge of others. You will be amazed how well he or she will make rules and regulations and see that they are obeyed; but beware, Mr. Employer, lest your first finger is short in proportion as that of your employee is long, for, if such be the case, you too will have "to toe the line" and you may find yourself in a very disagreeable position.

But let me give you a further warning: Should this man or woman have a first finger that is long and crooked, you will assuredly find out to your cost that the personal ambitions of such individual are "crooked." Such an employee would be perfectly unscrupulous in finding out your secrets and getting you into his power.

If the second finger is straight and well shaped, its owner will be very serious, a little inclined to melancholy, but will pay due regard to whatever responsibilities with which he may be entrusted, but again beware if this finger is crooked. In this case the owner would be, however, more subject to what may be called "a crooked fate" than willfully "wrong." Such people are, as a rule, the children of strange circumstances over which they seem to have no control. They are continually getting themselves into trouble and into false positions, but, I must admit, more by a strange fatality of things than by their own willful actions. Nevertheless, such infelicities might be very unpleasant for their employer, especially if he has more heart than brains.

The third finger, if extremely long and straight, indicates an extraordinary desire for glory, celebrity, publicity and the like; and although this might be an extremely good quality in the case of an actor, preacher, politician or public man, it may be most undesirable if such a person is to occupy the position of a private secretary, or the confidential clerk to some family lawyer.

If this finger is crooked as well as very long, all the above qualities will be intensified and exaggerated. The love of spending money and fondness for show will also be more marked, the gambling tendencies very pronounced. No position involving the handling of money, should be entrusted to the possessor of such a finger.

The fourth, or little finger, if long (passing the nail joint of the third) is indicative of power of speech and subtlety in choice of language—the saying "to twist a person round one's little finger" originated from this very sign. Such people have a marvellous gift of speech, eloquence and flow of language, valuable gifts, of course, for orators and public persons, but not desirable qualities in a wife if a man is fond of sleep.

A short "little finger" denotes the reverse of the above. Such persons find the greatest difficulty in expressing what they want to say, but they can write better than speak and should be encouraged to do so.

These individuals have, however, not much power over others and the shorter the "little finger" is, the more timid and sensitive they are in the presence of strangers. If this finger is crooked, then these weaknesses are all the more emphasised, but if formed *crooked and long* the power of eloquence is also crooked. Such people will tell any "fairy tale" to suit their purpose—they are natural born liars and the position of President of the Ananias Club is their rightful inheritance.

The first and third fingers absolutely of equal length is the best sign of *an equally balanced mind*, but such a sign is rather rare to find.

When the fingers are very supple in the joints and turn backwards or outwards from the palm, it is an indication of a quick wit and clever brain; but such persons lack continuity of purpose. They have no "hold," as it were, on any one thing.

Fingers slightly curved inwards towards the palm, denote persons slow to grasp an idea, or a subject, but such people have retentive memories and "hold" or grip, as it were, any one thing they may take up.

Character Shown by the Thumb

The thumb is in itself more expressive of character than any other member of the hand. It was D'Arpentigny who wrote "the thumb individualises the man."

Medical science has proved that there is such a thing as a "thumb centre" in the brain and any pressure or disease in that part of the brain *shows its effect in the thumb*.

A large well-made thumb is the outward and visible sign of a strong-willed, determined person, be he man or woman.

The longer the thumb, the more the power of will rules the actions; the shorter the thumb, the more brute force and obstinacy sways the nature.

The shorter and more thick-set the nail phalange is, giving the appearance of a club, the more ungovernable is the person in his or her temper. Such people have no control over themselves and under the least opposition will fly into a blind rage of fury. This curious formation has been called the "Murderer's Thumb" because so many who have committed murder in a mad fit of passion have been found with this curious formation.

An employee with this class of thumb should never be given any position of authority over others, for he could not curb his ungovernable temper. He would also be absolutely unbalanced in his jealousy, and no woman who has the ambition to live to the usual "threescore-years-and-ten" should risk marriage to a man with one of these thumbs. But as "love is blind" it is useless, I know, to give advice in such a case.

The first joint or nail phalange of the thumb, when long and thin, denotes the opposite of the above characteristics. In such cases the person has the most absolute control over his temper, his will power is also strong but quick and unobtrusive, and in a firm, determined way people with such a thumb manage others and bend those around them to their purpose.

The second joint, if delicately shaped, almost "waist like," indicates tact, diplomacy, and gentleness, also subtlety in argument; but if this part of the thumb be full looking or equal in size to that of the nail phalange, it denotes the person who cares nothing for tact but who, on all occasions, will speak his mind plainly, and with brutal frankness.

When the thumb looks as if it were "tied in" close to the hand, the person is timid, easily frightened by both people and circumstances, narrow-minded in his views, and miserly in his habits. It is a well-established fact that the thumbs of all misers are "tied in" and cramped-looking. It is perhaps this very fear of things and people that in the end makes them misers with their gold.

One need never waste one's time asking a person with one of these cramped-looking thumbs to do a favour, and may God help the business man or woman who ever gets into such a person's clutches!

A thumb with the nail joint supple (bending backwards or as it is also called "double jointed") indicates a character the exact opposite of that associated with the "tied in" thumb. Possessors of such a thumb are generous, adaptable to others, extravagant, and impetuous in their actions and decisions. They promise things quickly and are more often heard to say "Yes" than "No"; but if they have time for reflection, they very often go back on their promises.

Individuals having a "stiff-jointed" thumb, on the contrary, cannot easily adapt themselves to others. They are distant and more reserved with strangers. When asked to do a thing, they generally first say "No," but on reflection or when reasoned with, they often give in to the other and generally regret having done so. It is useless to oppose such people—if one cannot lead them, it is no use attempting to force them against their will.

This type has more self-control than the type of people with the "supple jointed" formation, and is not so generous or extravagant. Individuals of this group, however, make more reliable friends, so their friendship, though difficult to obtain, is generally worth having.

A thumb standing very far out from the hand (almost at right angles to the palm) is not a good sign for ordinary success. Such people go to extremes in everything they do and are generally fanatics in religion, social reform, or whatever line of thought occupies their attention.

Hands, Hard and Soft

Even in the simple act of shaking hands, one can form conclusions about character.

Beware of any man or woman whose hand seems to slip from yours when you grasp theirs in greeting. Such persons are deceptive and treacherous. They may smile at you with their lips, but instinctively they regard you as their prey and will only use you for their own object.

A soft, fat hand is the indication of an indolent and more or less lazy person.

A firm hand is the sign of an energetic, reliable nature.

A very thin hand denotes a restless energetic disposition, but one that is given to worry, and fretting and is generally discontented.

A thin hand that feels listless in one's grasp denotes a weak constitution that has only sufficient energy to live.

A cold, clammy hand is also a sign of poor health, but generally that of a very sensitive and nervous person.

A person who keeps his hands closed while talking, is distrustful in his nature, has little self-reliance and can seldom be relied on by others.

A man or woman who gives a good firm grasp of the hand, is self-confident, energetic, and generally reliable.

When all the fingers (especially if the fingers be long) are seen always clinging, sticking, as it were, or folding over one another it denotes very doubtful qualities in the nature of their possessor and a decided tendency towards thieving and general lack of moral principal.

Remember that the hands *are the immediate servants or instruments of the brain*. There are more motive and sensory nerves from the brain to the hand than to any other portion of the body and, whether sleeping or waking, they continually and unconsciously reflect the thought and character of the mind or soul of the individual.

It will, then, be seen from these observations that without looking at the lines of the hand, one may be able to obtain certain details of character that are more trustworthy than those given by the face, and that these rules, if followed, should be of the greatest assistance and value to people in all walks of life.

Many of these observations are further amplified in subsequent chapters of this work. There is not a single one of these rules that has not been proved by me in my long professional career, and knowing that they will bear the strictest inquiry and observation, it gives me pleasure now to offer them to the readers of the American Edition of *Palmistry for All*.

CHEIRO.

LONDON.

Introduction

It was on July 21, 1894, that I had the honour of meeting Lord Kitchener and getting the autographed impression of his right hand, which I now publish for the first time as frontispiece to this volume. The day I had this interview, Lord Kitchener, or, as he was then, Major-General Kitchener, was at the War Office, and to take this impression had to use the paper on his table, and, strangely enough, the imprint of the War Office may be seen at the top of the second finger—in itself perhaps a premonition that he would one day be the controlling force of that great department.

Lord Kitchener was at that moment Sirdar of the Egyptian Army. He had returned to England to tender his resignation on account of some hostile criticism about "the Abbas affair," and so I took the opportunity of his being in England to ask him to allow me to add his hand to my collection, which even then included some of the most famous men and women of the day.

As Mr. T.P. O'Connor, in writing recently of Lord Kitchener, said: "One of his greatest qualities, at once useful and charming, is his accessibility. Anybody who has anything to say to him can approach him; anybody who has anything to teach him will find a ready and grateful learner."

My experience can indeed bear out the truth of this clear judgment of one of the leading traits in Lord Kitchener's character. That very year, 1894, was a notable one in his life; his strong-willed action over the Abbas affair was completely vindicated; he was made a K.C.M.G., and returned to Egypt with more power than ever.

Once in his presence he put me completely at my ease, and in a few moments he appeared to be deeply interested in observing the difference between the lines in his own clearly-marked palm and those in dozens of other impressions that I put before him.

He was then almost forty-four years of age, and I remember well how I explained the still higher positions and responsibilities that his path of Destiny mapped out before him. The heaviest and greatest of all would, I told him, be undertaken in his sixty-fourth year (1914), but how little either of us thought then that in that year the most terrible war of the century would have broken out.

Believing, as I do, in the Law of Periodicity playing as great a rôle in the lives of individuals as it does in nations, it is strange to notice that the same radix numbers that governed Lord Kitchener's career when he was planning out the Egyptian campaign, which resulted in his great victories of Atbara and Omdurman in 1896 and 1897, are exactly the same for him in 1914-1915, and 1916 gives again the same radix number that in 1898 saw him receive a vote of thanks from both Houses of Parliament, and a gift of £30,000 from the State.

From the standpoint of those interested in this strange study of hands, the accompanying impression of Lord Kitchener's cannot help but be regarded as of great importance. In it, the rules of Palmistry that I have given in the following pages are borne out in all their details.

Returning to the impression of this remarkable hand; even in shape alone one may read by the rules of this science the following clearly-marked characteristics:

Length of fingers—intellectuality (page 134), strong determination and will-power (chapter on the Thumb, page 127), mentality and firm determination of purpose (*see* Line of Head, page 17).

The remarkable Line of Fate running up the centre of the hand and turning towards the first finger, denotes ambition and domination over others (page 52).

The Line of Success and Fame, starting on the hand from the Line of Life and ascending to the base of the third finger, exactly coincides with the period in Lord Kitchener's career when he began to find recognition and success (page 63).

As in my larger work on this subject I published Gladstone's hand as a remarkable illustration of the truth that may be found in this study, so in this present work with the same confidence I give this illustration of Lord Kitchener's as another proof of character indicated in the shape and lines of the hand, and as it has been said so often that "Character is Destiny," so it is surely not illogical to point out that in following the rules laid down by this study one may obtain a clear idea of the destiny that the Character, Will, and Individuality trace out in advance—tracks, as it were, stretching far out into the distant future for the engine of purpose and achievement to find already laid and ready to be used at the "appointed time."

In conclusion, as I have now completely retired from all professional work, I may be allowed to point out that I am not publishing this book with the idea of seeking clients. I have no desire but to see this strange study taken up as a useful and practical means of obtaining an exact judgment of the character, qualities, and hidden tendencies that might otherwise be ignored.

I think that if all parents knew at least something of Palmistry, the vast majority of children would be more usefully trained and their proper tendencies developed.

It is often too late when a child discovers—and most probably by accident—some tendency or talent that had never been suspected by its parents.

It is no wonder that so few persons find their true vocations in the world, when it is remembered the random, haphazard way in which children are brought up—educated for the most part in some scholastic mill that grinds down all to the same dead level of mediocrity, and then turns them into the Army, the Church, or into trade.

If, on the contrary, all these studies that teach the understanding of character were more encouraged, parents would have less excuse for the supreme ignorance they now show as to the real nature of those children who hold them responsible for their entry into the battlefield of existence.

These same parents would lift up their voices in righteous indignation if soldiers were sent into battle untrained, without their proper equipment, and yet these same parents have never, in the whole course of their lives, made the simplest study of any one of those many subjects by which they could in knowing the nature of their child, have strengthened weak points in the fortress of character, or by developing some talent or gift, doubly armed him for his entry into the battle of life.

It is from this standpoint that I earnestly hope this study of hands may some day be taken up. It was from this standpoint that I interested such men as Gladstone, Professor Max Muller, of Oxford, Lord Russell, when he was Lord Chief Justice, King Edward VII., and many others too numerous to mention; and lastly, it is from the same standpoint that I have now written this book, which under the title of *Palmistry for All*, will, I hope, appeal to all classes, and cause such an interest in the Study of Character that, instead of such an art being left in the hands of a few, it will, on the contrary, become universally used for the benefit of all.

CHEIRO

NOTE.—Cheiro retired from all professional work some time ago, and the public is therefore warned against persons pretending that they are the real "Cheiro," and endeavouring to pass themselves off as the author of his well-known works.

PART I
Palmistry or Cheiromancy

Chapter I
A Brief Résumé Of The History Of The Study Of Hands Through The Centuries To The Present Day

The success I had during the twenty-five years in which I was connected with this study was, I believe, chiefly owing to the fact that although my principal study was the lines and formation of hands, yet I did not confine myself alone to that particular page in the book of Nature. I endeavoured to study every phase of thought that can throw light on human life; consequently the very ridges of the skin, the hair found on the hands, all were used as a detective would use a clue to accumulate evidence. I found people were sceptical of such a study only because they had not the subject presented to them in a logical manner.

There are hundreds of facts connected with the hand that people have rarely, if ever, heard of, and I think it will not be out of place if I touch on them here. For instance, in regard to what are known as the corpuscles, Meissner, in 1853, proved that these little molecular substances were distributed in a peculiar manner in the hand itself. He found that in the tips of the fingers they were 108 to the square line, with 400 papillæ; that they gave forth certain distinct crepitations, or vibrations, and that in the red lines of the hand they were most numerous and, strange to say, were found in straight individual rows in the lines of the palm. Experiments were made as to these vibrations, and it was proved that, after a little study, one could distinctly detect and recognise the crepitations *in relation to each individual*. They increased or decreased in every phase of health, thought, or excitement, and were extinct the moment death had mastered its victim. About twenty years later, experiments were made with a man in Paris, who had an abnormally acute sense of sound (Nature's compensation for want of sight, as he had been born blind). In a very short time this man could detect the slightest change or irregularity in these crepitations, and through the changes was able to tell with wonderful accuracy about how old a person was, and how near they were to illness, and even death.

The study of these corpuscles was also taken up by Sir Charles Bell, who, in 1874, demonstrated that each corpuscle contained the end of a nerve fibre, and was in immediate connection with the brain. This great specialist also demonstrated that every portion of the brain was in touch with the nerves of the hand and more particularly with the corpuscles found in the tips of the fingers and the lines of the hand.

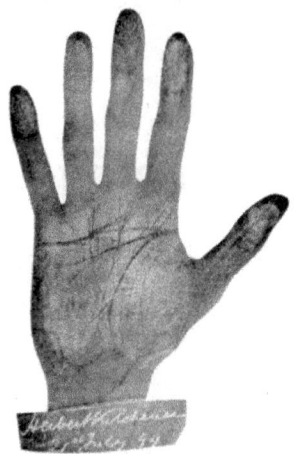

LORD KITCHENER'S HAND.

The detection of criminals by taking impressions of the tips of the fingers and by thumb marks is now used by the police of almost every country, and thousands of criminals have been tracked down and identified by this means.

To-day, at Scotland Yard, is to be seen almost an entire library now devoted to books on this side of the subject and to the collections that the police have made, and yet, in my short time, I remember how the idea was scoffed at when Monsieur Bertillon and the French police first commenced the detection of criminals by this method. If the ignorant prejudice against a complete study of the hand were overcome, the police would be greatly assisted by studying the lines of the palm, and acquiring a knowledge of what these lines mean, especially as regards mentality and the inclination of the brain in one direction or another.

It is a well-known fact that, even if the skin be burned off the hands or removed by an acid, in a short time the lines will reappear exactly as they were before, and the same happens to the ridges or "spirals" in the skin of the inside tips of the fingers and thumb.

The scientific use of such a study could also be made invaluable in foreseeing tendencies towards insanity, etc.

Sir Thomas Browne, in his *Religio Medici*, after referring to Physiognomy, says:

"Now there are besides these characters in our faces certain mystical figures in our hands, which I dare not call mere dashes, strokes *à la volée* or at random, because delineated by a pencil that never works in vain, and hereof I take more particular notice because I carry that in mine own hand which I could never read nor discover in another."

But prejudice is a hard thing to combat, and, in consequence, a study which could render untold aid to humanity has been neglected in modern times. Yet it cannot be denied that this strange study was practised and followed by some of the greatest teachers and students of other civilizations.

Whether or no these ancient philosophers were more enlightened than we are has long been a question of dispute, but the one point and the most important one which has been admitted is, that in those days the greatest study of mankind was man. It is, therefore, reasonable to suppose that their conclusions are more likely to be correct than those of an age like our own—famous chiefly for its implements of destruction, its warships, its dynamite, and its cannon.

This study of hands can be traced back to the very earliest, most enlightened forms of civilization. It has been practised by the greatest minds in all those civilizations, minds that have left their mental philosophies and their monuments for us to marvel at. India, China, Persia, Egypt, Rome—all in their study of mankind have placed the greatest store in their study of the hand.

During my stay in India, I was permitted by some Brahmans (descendants of the Joshi Caste, famous from time immemorial for their knowledge in occult subjects) with whom it was my good fortune to become intimately acquainted, to examine and make extracts from an extraordinary book on this subject which they regarded as almost sacred, and which belonged to the great past of the now despised Hindustan.

As the wisdom of the Hindus spread far and wide across the earth, so the theories and ideas about this study spread and were practised in other countries. Similar to the way in which religion suits itself to the conditions of the country in which it is propagated, so has it divided itself into various systems. It is, however, to the days of the Greek civilization that we owe the present clear and lucid form of the study. The Greek civilization has, in many ways, been considered the highest and most intellectual in the world, and here it is that Palmistry or Cheiromancy (from the Greek χείϱ, the hand) grew and found favour in the eyes of those who have given us laws and philosophies that we employ to-day and whose works are taught in all our leading colleges and schools.

It is a well-known and undisputed fact that the philosopher Anaxagoras not only taught but practised this study. We also find that Hispanus discovered on an altar dedicated to Hermes a book on Cheiromancy, written in gold letters, which he sent as a present to Alexander the Great, as "a study worthy of the attention of an elevated and enquiring mind." Instead of it being followed by the "weak-minded," we find, on the contrary, that it numbered amongst its disciples such men of learning as Aristotle, Pliny, Paracelsus, Cardamis, Albertus Magnus, the Emperor Augustus, and many others of note.

This brings us down to the period when the power of the Church was beginning to be felt outside the domain and jurisdiction of religion. It is said that the early Fathers were jealous of the influence of this old-world science. Whether this be true or not, we find that it was bitterly denounced and persecuted by the early Church. It has always been, that the history of any dominant creed or sect is the history of opposition to knowledge, unless that knowledge come through it. This study, therefore, the offspring of "pagans and heathens," was not even given a trial. It was denounced as sorcery and witchcraft; the devil was conjured up as the father of all such students, and the result was that through this bitter persecution, the study was outlawed, and fell into the hands of vagrants, tramps, and gipsies. In spite of this persecution it is interesting and significant to notice that almost the first book ever printed was a work on Palmistry, *Die Kunst Ciromantia*, printed in Augsburg, in the year 1475.

In examining this subject it will be found that in the study of mankind it came to be recognised that, as there was a natural position on the face for the nose, eyes, lips, etc., so also on the hand was there a natural position for what is known as the Line of Head, Line of Life, and so on. If these were found in some unnatural position they would equally be the indications of unnatural tendencies. It doubtless took years of study to name these lines and marks, but it must be remembered that this curious study is more ancient than any other in the world.

In the original Hebrew of the Book of Job (chap. xxxvii., ver. 7), we find these significant words: "God caused signs or seals on the hands of all the sons of men, that the sons of men might know their works."

As the student of anatomy can build up the entire system from the examination of a single bone, so may a person by a careful study of an important member of the body such as the hand, apart from anything superstitious or even mystical, build up the entire action of the system and trace every effect back to its cause.

To-day the science of the present is coming to the rescue of the so-called superstition of the past. All over the world scientists are little by little sweeping aside prejudice and beginning to study occult questions. Perhaps the "whys and wherefores" of such things may one of these days be as easily explained as are those wireless waves of electricity that carry messages from land to land.

Chapter II
The Line Of Head Or The Indications Of The Mentality

The object of the following chapters is to give clear and unmistakable instruction on the lines and markings of the hands, both from the student's standpoint and from that of the general reader. This is not usually the course adopted in books printed on this subject which have to appeal to a general public.

During my twenty-five years' professional experience in England, America, and other countries, I have carefully noted down the questions that are not answered in books published on this subject. I have also recorded what are the difficulties that arise in the minds of those students who meet this, that, or the other mark or line and search in vain for some explanation as to its meanings. I may add that there is not a single point on which I give information that has not been proved by me from probably thousands of cases that have come before me during my own professional experience.

As regards illustrations, I have endeavoured to make these of the simplest and clearest kind possible. I have every confidence that if they are carefully studied, no student can fail to grasp this subject in a masterful manner, and that whoever acts upon the advice I give in these pages, cannot fail to become successful as an interpreter of this study.

In all my work I regard the Line of Head (page 106) or the Line of Mentality as the most important sign that can be found in the hand.

A Line of Head is like the needle in the compass, without a true knowledge of which it is impossible to grasp the "direction of the subject." I have seen more mistakes caused by a lack of grasp of this point than by anything else.

I have seen, for example, many students make the mistake of paying great attention to what looked like a good Line of Sun or Success, and, at the same time, not noticing a weak, badly formed Line of Head, which contradicted the promise of success given by the various lines. If, on the other hand, the student had first noticed the Line of Head, he would have been able to tell the subject that the promise of success was not backed up by the intelligence or the mentality.

As regards the future being foreshadowed, it has been demonstrated that the brain is always growing, changing, increasing, or diminishing. These changes commence years before the effect is shown by the thoughts or actions of the individual. A boy ten years old may at that point commence a development which will not be felt until he is thirty, and then it may change his whole life and career. As this development commences at ten, even at that age it has affected certain nerves, and they in their turn have already affected the Line of Head—a full twenty years before the point of change or action has been reached. It therefore follows that the future may be seen and told by a careful examination of the hand which, as Aristotle has said, is the "organ of all organs, the active agent of the passive powers of the entire system."

The Line Of Head And Its Variations

The Line of Head (page 106), or indication of the Mentality of the subject, must in all cases be considered as the most important line on the hand. The greatest attention should be paid to it, so as to obtain a clear grasp of the Mentality under consideration.

The two hands must be carefully compared—the left showing the inherited tendencies, the right the developed or cultivated qualities. The slightest change or deviation in the markings from the left to the right should be carefully noted down or remembered.

The direction or the termination or end of the line should, above all, be distinctly noted, for the all-important reason that this shows the direction that the Mentality is inclined to develop towards. For example, if found with the end of the line sloping downwards in the left hand, and having become straight or lying across the palm in the right—the student is safe in concluding that the subject has not been able to follow his natural bent, but by the force of circumstances has been obliged to make himself more practical, to study business methods, and to have undertaken a training towards practicality and level-headedness in order to rise equal to the circumstances that he found himself forced to meet.

In this way the student obtains an insight into the earlier conditions of the life under examination that is invaluable, especially when there is, as will be found in many cases, no Line of Destiny visible in the early years.

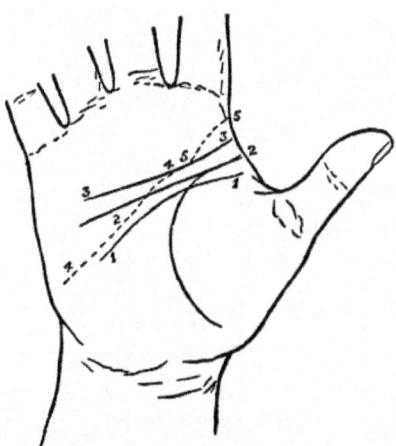

PLATE I. THE THREE PRINCIPAL POSITIONS FOR THE COMMENCEMENT OF THE LINE OF HEAD.

If, on the contrary, the Line of Head is found exactly in the same position on the right hand as on the left, or even very nearly so, the student can be sure that there was little or no strain in the early years, but that the subject had easy conditions which were favourable, and which allowed him to develop his natural bent of Mentality.

If, however, it is found that the left hand shows a forked ending to the Line of Head, namely, one end sloping downwards and the other end straight, or nearly so, and that the right hand shows only the straight line, then the student may decide that the subject inherited from the parents two natures, the imaginative and the practical, and that he chose to develop the latter, either in the direction of business or science.

In such a case, the student may state with confidence that the parents of the subject were decidedly opposite in their characteristics. If the line has become straight in the right hand the subject takes more after the side that was practical.

In the case of boys or men it must be remembered that they will take more after their mother's mental peculiarities, and in the case of girls or women that they more generally take after the mental qualities of the father.

On a man's left hand that has the forked ending with the upper end straight, or nearly so, the student can state that the mother was the more practical of the parents. If on the right hand the same mark has become clearest the man developed, followed, or cultivated the mental qualities of the mother more than those of the father. When reading a woman's hand the reverse will apply.

If, on the contrary, the lower line was the more developed on the right hand, then the subject, if a man, had developed the imaginative or artistic qualities of the mother, and *vice versa* if the subject be a girl or a woman.

When the Line of Head looks light or faint on the left, and strong and clear on the right, the student can safely state that the subject did not inherit any strong mental bent from either parent, but has cultivated and developed his own mentality.

In such a case the subject has been a hard mental student, and has become mentally superior to his or her parents. This is often found in the case of "self-made" men or women, who have had little or no education in their early life or in their home, but who from an innate love of education developed themselves mentally. Such a sign would speak volumes for the will power and ambition of the subject under examination.

If the Line of Head is lighter and poorer on the right hand than on the left, the student can state that the subject has not made the most of his opportunities mentally, and that he has not, and never will, equal the brain power and education of his or her parents.

In such a case one may also be sure that the subject has not a very strong will power —at least mentally— although he might be very obstinate by nature, which will be seen from the quality exhibited by the nail phalange of the thumb (page 96).

A poor or non-developed Line of Head in the right hand of any man or woman is also the indication of a lack of purpose or ambition —there being no ambition where a want of mental desire and development is so distinctly shown.

A clean cut deep Line of Head is a more powerful sign of mentality than when the line is very broad, or lying, as it were, merely on the surface of the palm.

A wide broad line shows less concentration and a more vacillating changeable nature. This rule applies with equal truth to all the lines on the palm.

Broad, coarse-looking lines are more a constitutional sign than a mental indication. They are often found in cases where the subject leads a robust outdoor life, and those who have developed the physical side of their nature more than the mental.

Great brain workers usually have thin, fine, clean-looking lines, and especially that of the Line of Head.

It will thus be seen that by observation the student will be enabled to class the sort of life led by the person under examination. No matter how intellectual a man or woman may look, the lines on the hand will indicate whether or not they have developed their intellectuality. In this way it will be seen that a study of the hand becomes a far more accurate guide than the study of the face. Many men and women may have handsome, intellectual faces and yet prefer sport or outdoor life to any mental pursuit or exercise.

Turning from an examination of the direction of ending of the Line of Head, the student must next examine the indications of the beginnings of this important Line. For example, the Line of Head may commence in three distinct different ways.

(1) From inside the Line of Life (1-1, Plate I.).

(2) Joined to the Line of Life (2-2, Plate I.).

(3) And outside the Line of Life (3-3, Plate I.).

The first is the most uncertain of all. It denotes an over-sensitive, over-cautious, timid person. It also indicates a highly nervous, easily excited individual, one who has little control over himself or his temper, who is easily put out over trifles, and liable to do the most erratic things, or fly off at a tangent when irritated. Such people are always in trouble, generally fighting or quarrelling with those about them and over things that are of no consequence. They are likewise so easily wounded in their feelings, that even a look or an imagined slight will put them out of humour or upset them for days.

If this Line of Head farther out in the palm become straight, it denotes that the subject will, later, by the development of his intelligence largely overcome this failing of over-sensitiveness. If the line slope much or bend down towards the wrist or on to the Mount of Luna (the Mount of Imagination), then the subject will become still worse with his advancing years. If the Line of Head is also poorly marked, or with "hairlines" from it, it is often the indication of some form of insanity which is likely to cause the subject to be placed under restraint in later life.

If, with this latter indication, the student also finds all the upward main lines, such as the Line of Destiny, etc., fading out past the middle of the palm, the indication of insanity and restraint becomes all the more certain.

This class of Head Line is largely found in cases where the subject is naturally inclined towards drink and intemperance of every description.

Even in cases where there are good lines running up the palm, it will usually be found that the subject gives way to occasional fits of intemperance or the desire for drugs. The qualities of the fiery Mount of Mars, from which such a Line of Head starts inside the Life Line, is largely the cause of the peculiarities above indicated. The opposite Mount of Mars (page 163) on the side of the hand, on the contrary, gives mental control, so that even when the Line of Head runs out straight on the palm it partakes of this "Mental Mars" quality, and so denotes that later on in years the subject with such a Line of Head will be able to develop mental control. The sloping Line of Head, however, would denote that the subject allows himself to turn, as it were, away from mental control, and so lets the earlier tendencies become his master.

This point alone is worthy of the consideration of all parents, and if observed by them would do much to help such children to develop mental control over themselves. The accompanying plates show this formation of the Line of Head in all its variations.

The Line Of Head Joined To The Line Of Life

The position of this line indicates in all cases a highly sensitive disposition, which inclines towards the side of caution and also lacks self-confidence (2-2, Plate I.). Even the cleverest people with this sign seem to rein themselves in too tightly, and are always inclined to undervalue their capabilities and talents.

When, with the same indication, the line is also sloping slightly downwards, the sensitiveness is still more increased. This form is largely found on the hands of artists, painters, and those who even in other walks of life have the sensitive artistic temperament, even though it may not have been developed to a larger extent. If, on the contrary, the Line of Head joined to the Line of Life runs straight out across the hand towards the mental Mount of Mars (2-2, Plate I.), the subject, though still extremely sensitive, has got greater courage of his opinions. Such people do not get credit for being as highly sensitive as do the other people with the line sloping downwards towards the Mount of Imagination. The straighter the Head Line is found, the subject can be more relied on to carry out his determination, and often these highly sensitive and even nervous people are found doing very determined work in connection with some battle for principle or for right which they believe it their moral duty to carry out. If this class of Line of Head, however, go very far across the hand and straight on to the Mental Mount of Mars, it indicates an extremely strong-willed determined person who has the power to hide his sensitiveness and nervousness and stake everything for what he believes his duty to carry out.

The difference in the observation of these two distinct classes of individuals, namely, those with the Line of Head joined but sloping, and the Line of Head joined and straight across the hand, has caused many exponents of this study to make great mistakes in the judgment of their subject. When, as is very often the case, the Line of Head is forked (3-3, Plate II.), also when joined and when these forked lines are equal to one another, especially in cases where the Line of Head is joined to the Line of Life showing the sensitive temperament, this forked mark often indicates a certain want of decision. The subject is inclined to balance too much between the two qualities of brain, the practical and the imaginative. As to what they should do for the best, in such cases it is always wise to advise the subject to act according to first impulse either in dealing with practical or imaginative things. By so doing they employ, as it were, the intuition of the brain, and by using it do not waver and vacillate by too much reasoning over the question or endeavouring to see both sides of it at once. When the sloping Line of Head has a gentle curve downwards towards the Mount of the Moon (1-1, Plate II.), distinct control over the imagination is indicated. The student will then know that the subject simply uses his imagination when he wishes to do so instead of being controlled by it. But the contrary is the case when the line bends too far down this Mount (4-4, Plate II.). In this case the subject is the slave of his imagination and generally does erratic and peculiar things or can only work in moods of the moment. People of this latter class seldom, if ever, produce the great results in the world of art or imagination as do those who have the line simply curving downwards into this Mount.

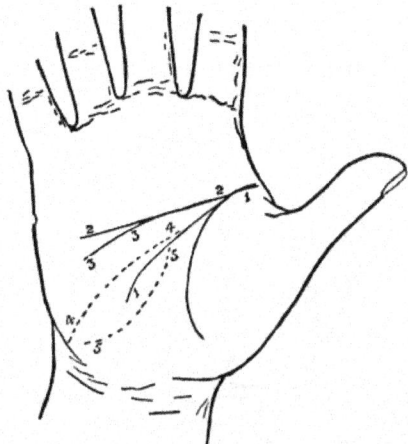

PLATE II. THE LINE OF HEAD JOINED TO THE LINE OF LIFE AND ITS TERMINATIONS.

When the Line of the Head bends completely down and turns with a curve, as it were, under the base of the Mount of Luna (5-5, Plate II.), the tendency is to extreme morbid imaginings and such extreme sensitiveness, that people on whose hands it is found generally separate themselves from the rest of their fellows, and either retire from the world altogether and live a solitary life or else make their exit by the gate of suicide. The latter is, in fact, generally the ending of such lives. Their extreme sensitiveness evidently renders life for them almost unbearable. But this formation must not be confounded with the Line of Head curving downwards through the upper part of the Mount (4-4, Plate II.). In this latter case, it can even descend as far down as the wrist itself, and, unless it has an island or star at the end of the line, there is not the danger of suicide. In all such cases, however, there is extreme imagination, extreme sensibility, and a tendency to melancholy and morbidness, but there is no indication of the brain breaking down under strain as there is in the other case of what is known as the distinct tendency for self-murder.

The Line Of Head Separated From The Line Of Life

The Line of Head is more frequently found connected with than separated from the Line of Life. When the space is not very wide (3-3, Plate I.), it is an excellent mark to have, giving independence of thought, quickness of judgment, and a certain mental daring that is invaluable in fighting the battle of life. When the Line of Head is at the same time lying fairly straight across the palm, such individuals have an immense power over others, but their capabilities are always more distinctly shown if they should in any form go in for some kind of public life. People possessing this mark are rather less "hard students" than those with the Line of Head and Line of Life joined together, but they have such brilliancy and quickness of thought that they seem to see in a flash that which takes the other class hard work to attain. But these people with the "open Line of Head" must, above all things, have purpose in their life. Without purpose they are rather like a ship drifting on an idle sea. They may spend their life in an aimless way unless "the call" comes to them or the tide of ambition turns their way and carries them onward.

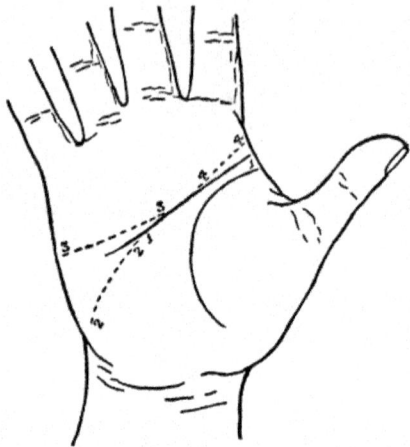

PLATE III. THE LINE OF HEAD SEPARATED FROM THE LINE OF LIFE.

The same class of line but sloping is the more uncertain of the two characters, because the person is still more inclined to work only by moods. If the mood or the desire does not come, such people, although always brilliant and clever, may often waste their lives doing nothing.

Those people with the Line of Head "open" and ascending slightly upwards towards or on to the Mental Mount of Mars (3-3, Plate III.), are self-appointed leaders, organizers of any public movement. They will sacrifice everything, home, affection, and all ties for what they believe is their public duty in connection with the work that they have undertaken.

The Line of Head very open and separate from the Line of Life denotes a character with too little caution or sensitiveness (4-4, Plate III.). The subject will go to the opposite extreme of him with the Line of Head and Line of Life joined. When the space is very wide it denotes excessive impetuosity and lack of continuity of purpose, a person who pushes himself forward on all occasions, a great desire for notoriety and one continually changing his plans as far as the world is concerned. When this line is excessively open or separate from the Line of Life, the brain seems to be an extremely excitable one. The subject suffers greatly from excessive blood to the head, mental hysteria, sleeplessness, and all things that affect the brain. If the Line of Head is badly formed with islands, or a broad line with breaks and hair lines (1-1, Plate IV.), it is just as much a mark of another form of insanity as the Line of Head curving downwards at the wrist, but with the line mentioned the type is inclined to be morbid with a tendency to suicide.

This other Line of Head with islands indicates the character that will be more likely to be excitable and fly into a temper and kill other people. A Line of Head not too widely separated and either one end of it commencing on the Mount of Jupiter, or with its main branch from the Mount of Jupiter (4-4, Plate III.), is one of the most brilliant marks of all. The student must, however, carefully establish this difference of the Line of Head in his own mind, as well as the termination or the ending of this line. Once he has these two points firmly established, he has gained the great keynote to this subject. When once this part is mastered, he has a sure foundation to work on.

My next remarks will relate to the minor marks and their meaning, and to islands or breaks on or in the Line of Head.

The Line Of Head And Its Secondary Signs

What are known as "islands" in the Line of Head are very important, especially if they are considered both in relation to the age at which they occur, and also in relation to the mentality itself.

In the first place the principal rule the student must bear in mind is, that islands must be considered as showing a weakness in any line wherever they may be found, and are to be considered unfortunate signs.

On the Line of Head when found in the form of a continuous chain (1-1, Plate IV.), all through the line, they denote mental weakness, but generally produced by ill-health which more immediately affects the brain.

Such mental weakness or "brain illness," if found with nails showing very small "moons" or none at all, denotes an anæmic condition of the blood that affects the brain, a low condition of vitality and bad circulation, which seems to starve the brain of blood and prevents such people from making any continuous effort in regard to study or will power, and causes them to act in an erratic fashion.

If at the same time the Line of Head is seen placed very high on the hand, this sign is worse still in its meaning, and such subjects are inclined to be "half mad" in periods.

When the Line of Head is widely separated from the Line of Life, then this chain formation of islands is still more accentuated and more difficult to cure. Such subjects have periods of mental excitability which it seems impossible for them to control, and in such moments they are liable to fly off at a tangent and commit mad or rash acts, but acts generally dangerous to other people.

When, however, the Line of Head is very sloping (2-2, Plate IV.), with this formation of islands the subject is inclined to have fits of depression and melancholy, during which he is likely to shrink away from people or make an attempt against his own life. "Suicide while temporarily insane" is the verdict of the jury in such cases.

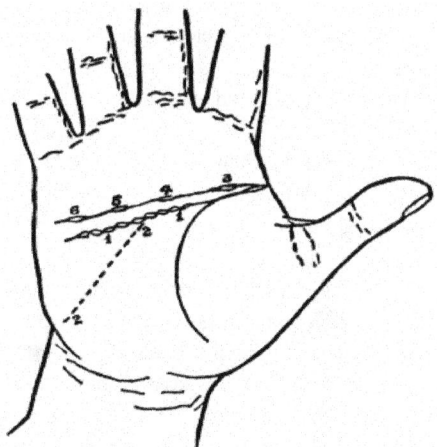

PLATE IV. ISLANDS ON THE LINE OF HEAD.

Another important point of consideration in relation to the islands in the Line of Head, is to note their position on the line itself, or under what finger they make their appearance. When these islands are found at the commencement of the line under the first finger or Mount of Jupiter (3, Plate IV.), it will be found that the subject in early life was delicate mentally, and displayed no energy of will; no desire to study, was listless and without ambition.

Under the second finger on the Mount of Saturn (4, Plate IV.), the subject, on the contrary, is inclined to suffer from severe headaches, morbidness, melancholy, and a tendency for inflammation, especially at the base of the head.

If the line looks weak or frays into little hair lines from this point out, it shows that the subject will never recover thoroughly from this malady.

Under the third finger, the Mount of Sun (5, Plate IV.), an island shows a very curious fact, namely that the person is inclined to suffer from weakness of the eyes and short-sight. If many of these islands are marked it generally foreshadows a still greater tendency to blindness and weakness of the sight.

Islands under the fourth finger, the Mount of Mercury (6, Plate IV.), and the extremity of the Head Line denote weakness of the brain in old age, and a highly nervous worrying disposition. If very badly marked they denote that in the latter part of life the subject may be disposed to insanity proceeding from a worrying disposition, and often from the over-straining of the mental faculties. It will thus be seen that every portion of this remarkable line may be divided into sections to obtain marvellous detail in making predictions for the future.

This line can further be divided, showing with considerable clearness the ages at which troubles or changes in the mentality may be expected.

Under the first finger the period of the life indicated is the first 21 years, the second period contains another section of the three 7's, and lasts until 42 years of age; the third period of 7's which will be found under the third finger indicates the section from 49 to 63, and the fourth section which takes in the remainder of the hand, under the fourth finger, stands for the period from 70 up to the end.

Changes In The Line Of Head

Another extremely interesting point in studying the Line of Head is to take notice of certain changes in its position, or lines either dropping or rising from it, which will also be found to give very remarkable information. For example: if a sloping Line of Head at any point in its track seems to curve or slightly bend upwards (1-1, Plate V.), it indicates that about that period of the person's life some unusual strain will be forced upon him. If this curved line is clearly marked and not interfered with by things that look like blotches in it, the person, although of a completely opposite turn of mind to the practical, will yet rise superior to the occasion, and for the time being will develop a practical or business-like way of looking at things which may even be the very reverse of the nature.

If, however, instead of the curve or bend a fine line is seen leaving the Head Line in an upward direction (2-2, Plate V.), that period will leave a definite mark on the subject's entire character for the remainder of his life. In some cases these fine lines will, after a few years, appear to develop more strongly, and may even become a kind of second Head Line. This would denote that the person continues to cultivate the practical side of his nature that was at that period called into existence.

If one were examining a straight Line of Head and noticed a curve downward or a fine line growing downwards from it (3-3, Plate V.), the natural interpretation of such a mark would be that at that date in the person's career he had become less practical, or for the time being developed the more imaginative qualities of the mentality. In this latter case, curiously enough, it often denotes that the person had at that period of his life become more wealthy or prosperous, and so he was able to develop the artistic side of his nature. It is logical to assume that he could only have done this if the strain in the practical battle had been lessened about that time, but this must only be presumed if, at about the same date, the Sun Line (Plate XV.) were seen clearly marked or suddenly appearing on the hand, then the student can be positive in assuming that at that date greater ease and comfort came into the subject's life and he consequently turned to the more imaginative side of existence.

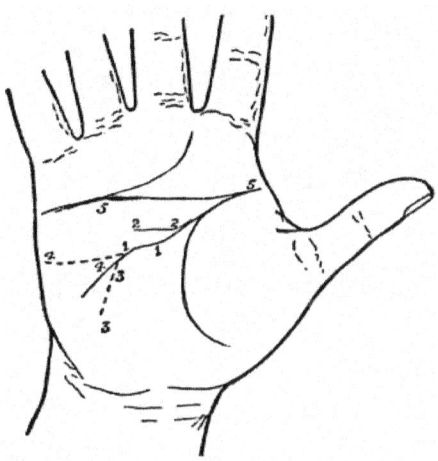

Plate V. MORE VARIATIONS OF THE LINE OF HEAD.

If the Line of Head itself should curve upward, especially at the end towards the fourth finger or Mount of Mercury (4-4, Plate V.), it denotes almost without exception that the longer the person lives the more his desire for money and his determination to possess it will become stronger every year.

If the Line of Head apparently partly leaves its natural place, which will be seen by an examination of the left hand, and completely rises as it were to the Line of Heart (5-5, Plate V.), the person will develop an enormous fixity of purpose for some one desire. He will apparently and deliberately control the affectionate side of his nature by his will power, and will stick at nothing to obtain the realisation of whatever his desire may be. If this mark is found on a square thick-set material looking hand, it is a foregone conclusion that the subject has set his determination on some material object, such as wealth, and he will stop at nothing, even crime, in carrying out his aim. If this mark is found on a long hand the object of the ambition is certain to be connected with intellectual power over people and absolute determination to accomplish whatever the purpose of the career may be.

This mark must not be confounded with one clear line running across the hand from side to side (Plate VI.), because in this case the Line of Head has not risen out of its position, but simply denotes tremendous intensity of character, for good or evil as the case may be; such a person would exhibit great power of concentration, and if he concentrated his mentality on any purpose he would unite with it his heart nature. But if he had set his heart or affections on any person, he would unite with that desire the whole force of his mental nature. In this case it is as if these two sides of the mentality, the sentimental and the mental, were linked or in some way united together. Such persons I have always found possess greater intensity of purpose than any other, but I have never found it a very happy mark to possess.

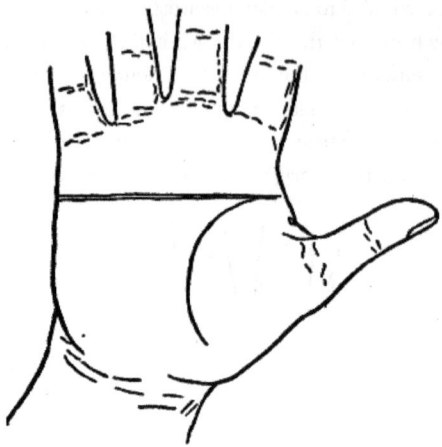

PLATE VI. THE LINE OF HEAD AND THE LINE OF HEART RUNNING TOGETHER.

In the first place, this peculiar type of person appears to be so rare in life that he seems to have no companions and for that reason has always the feeling of being intensely lonely and isolated from others. He is usually also in every way super-sensitive and easily wounded in his feelings. I have seldom found these people successful, unless when acting alone, but if linked with others by partnership in business, etc., they seem to feel their personality cramped, and the partnership as a rule seldom results happily. In considering this, the student must carefully observe whether this one line across the hand lies across the centre where the Head Line would naturally be, or whether it lies higher up towards the base of the fingers where the Heart Line is generally found. If the former case, one may be sure that it is a question of head and mentality and very little heart; but if the latter, it is a question of more intensity of feeling emotion and affection than of mental intensity.

Crosses And Squares In Connection With The Line Of Head

Small, sharply-defined crosses in any position just over or touching the Line of Head are generally signs of accidents to the Head itself.

Under Jupiter (1, Plate VII.), they usually are brought about by blows caused generally by the subject's desire to rule and to be too dogmatic or tyrannical.

Under Saturn (2, Plate VII.), crosses indicate injuries to the head from accidents by animals, blows by treachery, mine explosions, etc., and generally relate to accidents of a treacherous nature.

Under the Mount of the Sun (3, Plate VII.), these crosses have been found to relate to accidents to the head from sudden falls, such as the subject striking his head by falling, concussion of the brain, etc.

Under the Mount of Mercury (4, Plate VII.), these sharply defined crosses relate to injuries to the head due to accidents generally produced by scientific experiments or some hazardous business venture.

Small defined squares touching the Line of Head (5, Plate VII.), are in all cases signs of preservation, and they relate to the particular qualities of the Mount of the hand under which they are found. (*See* chapter on Mounts, page 163)

Double Lines Of Head

Double Lines of Head (6-6, Plate VII.), are as rarely found as are cases of the single line right across the hand. In all cases where the Double Line of Head stands out distinct and clear as two separate lines, the object will be found to have a dual mentality. He is usually capable of an enormous amount of mental work and is of that class of people who carry out two separate mental lives with success. It is often found with one line joined to the Line of Life and the other rising from the Mount of Jupiter; if such is the case, the interpretation would be that one side of the nature is extremely sensitive and cautious, while the other is self-confident with a great desire to rule or enforce its mental ideas on the world.

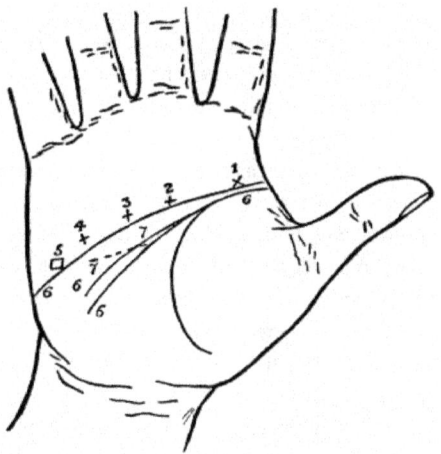

Plate VII. DOUBLE LINES OF HEAD, ALSO CROSSES AND SQUARES.

Although such a sign as the Double Line of Head gives a remarkable degree of mentality, yet I have always found it a more successful sign to find one clear Line of Head well marked on the hand than the two Lines of Head in any of their positions.

Another form of the Double Line of Head (7-7, Plate VII.), is one where the main line seems to separate about the middle of the hand, and where one branch goes across the hand and the other descends towards the Mount of the Moon. In such a case we get the double mental personality, but one which is more under the control of the will of the subject, whereas the two double distinct lines denote that the two mental personalities seem to act independently one from the other.

It has been considered by many ancient authorities that the Double Line of Head, when found with two distinct lines, is a sign of the inheritance of great riches or power. I have generally found, however, that what it means is, that although the financial results of such a person's life may be either great wealth or power, yet he may inherit it from his mental right and not from his birth right.

The Line Of Head On The Seven Types Of Hands

There are seven distinct types of hands, bearing in their own way more or less relationship to the Seven Races of Humanity.

These seven types of hands are as follows:

I.—The Elementary or Lowest type.

II.—The Square, also called the Useful or Practical.

III.—The Spatulate or Active.

IV.—The Philosophic.

V.—The Conic or Artistic.

VI.—The Psychic or Idealistic.

VII.—The Mixed Hand.

As a rule the Line of Head is generally found in accordance with the type of hand on which it is seen, namely, lying straight or what is called "level-headed" on the Square-looking or Practical hand; or sloping, and thus indicating the more imaginative qualities on the Philosophic, Conic, or Psychic types.

Consequently, if it be found on a hand in what may be called opposition to its class, such a Line of Head immediately possesses a greater significance.

For example, if a sloping Line of Mentality were seen on the Square or Practical hand, it would indicate that though the bases of that man or woman's thoughts and plans were of the practical kind, yet they possessed a far greater power of imagination than any casual observer would at first sight give them credit for.

On the contrary, if the Line of Head were found straight or level on the Spatulate, Philosophic, Conic, or Psychic types, it would denote that the person in question was usually level-headed and practical, even in their highest dreams of philosophy or idealistic creations.

On the Elementary hand the Line of Head is usually found short, straight, and coarse-looking, often nothing more than a short deep-set furrow. Consequently, if found long and clear, it would indicate a superior mental development in a coarse brutal or animal nature.

If in a Square-looking hand the Line of Head were found sloping instead of long and straight, it would denote an unusual development of the artistic and imaginative qualities, but always with the practical and logical basis for its support.

On the Spatulate hand the natural indication of the Line of Head is long, clear and sloping, but if found straight or level it would indicate a practical development of the brain endeavouring to set off the active energy and originality indicated by the Spatulate formation.

On the Philosophic type, the hand of the thinker and philosopher, the usual position of the Line of Mentality is long and sloping, but if found straight or level it indicates a mental development of the logical and practical qualities which might not be expected in such a class or type.

The same rules hold good with the Conic and Psychic, but with what is called the Mixed type, the best Line of Head to find would be one, long straight and level-looking, because this class, being a mixture as it were of all the others, would require a practical or level-headed mentality to hold its own amid the mixture of tendencies which the last type personifies.

Chapter III
The Line Of Life And Its Variations

The Line of Life is that line which runs round the base of the thumb and lies directly over a large blood-vessel called the great Palmer Arch (1-1, Plate VIII.). This blood-vessel is more directly connected with the heart, stomach, and vital organs which may have given use to its term "The Vital," as used by the ancients.

It is reasonable to assume that it is this intimate connection with the vital organs of the body which enables it to foretell the length of life from *natural causes*.

If the student will bear this in mind it will make clear and plain to him many difficulties in connection with predictions as to health and disease, and he will follow more easily the following explanations.

The first rules to master are, that to be normal the Line of Life should be long, clearly marked, and without any irregularities or breaks of any kind. Such a formation would indicate length of life, vitality, freedom from illness, and strength of constitution (1-1, Plate VIII.).

Bearing the first observation in mind it will be noticed that as the Line of Life represents the stomach and the vital organs, when well marked the stomach and digestion must necessarily be in a good condition.

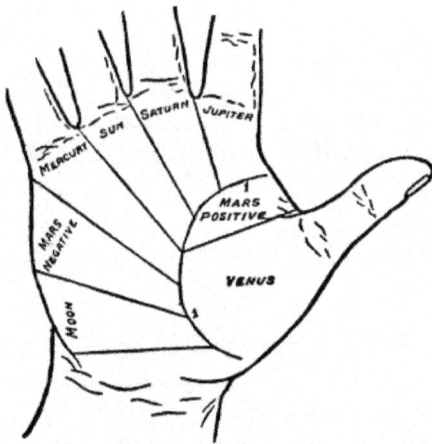

PLATE VIII. **THE LINE OF LIFE AND SECTIONS OF INFLUENCES FROM THE MOUNTS.**

When made up of little pieces or linked like a chain, it is a certain sign of poor health, weak stomach and lack of vitality.

At this point I must ask the most careful attention to the following rules—which no other book on the subject contains, and which I have not published in any of my other writings, viz.: as the Line of Life seems in every sense to be the representative on the hand of the body or trunk of the man—so the position of these breaks, marks, links, or islands denotes the portion of the body most affected.

Before we go further I must also impress on the student to grasp the fact that every line or sign on the hand plays a dual rôle. By one of their rôles these lines indicate the disease the person is most liable to for the entire run of the life, and in another rôle these lines indicate the date when the illness will reach its greatest gravity.

To explain carefully this strange phenomenon of nature, I have divided this line into sections (*see* Plate VIII.), and although I am not writing on astrology in these pages, yet all believers in that science may be interested to find how wonderfully these twin sciences agree when the comparison is pointed out by an impartial observer such as I claim to be.

In Plate VIII. are shown the Sections of the Line of Life with their various tendencies divided by the mounts at the base of the fingers. This will materially assist the student to comprehend their significance and, together with the influence of the month of birth as set out in the chapters on the Mounts of the Hand (page 163), will enable him to obtain an accuracy on all matters relating to health, diseases, and dangers to the life that up till now has never been attained.

We will now proceed to consider the details as regards the Line of Life itself.

The Line Of Life

It is very important at the outset to consider the qualities of this very important line. In some hands it is broad and shallow on the surface of the hand, in others it is deep and fine; the appearance of this line is very often deceptive, and leads students astray when they have not had their attention called to its appearance.

The broad, shallow Line of Life often leads people to suppose that it is a sign of a very healthy, robust constitution; but, on the contrary, such an indication is not nearly as good a sign as a clear, thin, deep line. The broad Life Line seems to belong to people who have more robust animal strength, whereas the finer line relates to people who have more nerve or will-force. Under any strain of ill-health, it is the finer line that will hold out, whereas the broad-looking line has not the same resisting force.

Very broad lines on the hand denote more muscular strength than will power, and I cannot impress this difference too strongly on the minds of my readers. If the line is made of chain formation (1-1, Plate IX.), it is a sure sign of a tendency to bad health, and especially so if the hand be soft. The same marks on a hard, firm hand would not indicate as much delicacy, because hard, firm hands denote in themselves a robust constitution.

Another important point to consider is, whether the Line of Life goes straight up to the side of the Mount of Venus and narrows that Mount (2-2, Plate IX.), or whether it forms a well-defined curve or semicircle out into the palm (3-3, Plate IX.). In the first case it indicates a naturally more delicate constitution, and less force of animal magnetism. This explanation will be readily understood by readers when I again call their attention to the fact that one of the most important blood-vessels going from the body to the hand is called the Great Palmer Arch, which carries the blood up to the hand towards the root of the thumb, and carries the circulation back on the other side of the Arch almost underneath the Line of Life. It will, therefore, be seen that people who have a weaker constitution are more likely to have this Great Palmer Arch narrower in construction than those who have a robust constitution and strong circulation of the blood. This is the reason why, when the Mount of Venus is large and wide on the hand, it gives rise to the idea that it indicates a more passionate animal nature than when this mount is thin and narrow.

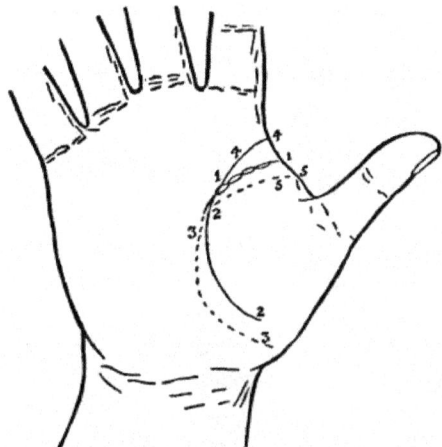

PLATE IX. THE LINE OF LIFE AND ITS VARIATIONS.

While speaking on this particular point, I must also call attention to the fact that when the Line of Head is curved downwards instead of running straight across the palm, that it seems to be more attracted to the qualities indicated by the Mount of Venus and gives more to the imaginative, romantic nature, showing a greater tendency to fall in love, than with people who possess the Line of Head running straight across the hand, as if it were not attracted to the qualities indicated by the Mount of Venus. It will thus be seen that every point of this study bearing on character can be reasoned out from a logical standpoint. This places the study upon a higher foundation than when it is considered purely from the superstitious standpoint with which it has so long been associated.

If the Line of Life is seen to rise high on the hand towards the Mount of Jupiter (4-4, Plate IX.), the subject has more control over himself, and his life is more governed by the ambitious side of his nature. When, however, the Line of Life rises lower down on the palm, more from the Mount of Mars (5-5, Plate IX.), it gives less control over the temper. When this sign is noticed, especially in the case of young persons, it will be found that they are more quarrelsome, more disobedient, and have less ambition in connection with their studies.

Ascending Lines

When the Line of Life is found with a number of ascending lines, even if they are small, it denotes a life of greater energy; and the dates at which these lines ascend from the Line of Life may always be considered points at which the subject has made a particular effort towards whatever may have been the special purpose of his destiny at that moment. When these lines are seen ascending towards or on the Mount of Jupiter (1-1, Plate X.), it indicates the desire and ambition to rise in life, especially in some way that would give the subject control or authority over others. If one of the lines be found partly arrested or stopped at the Line of Head (2-2, Plate X.), it indicates that the subject has by some mental error of judgment or stupidity, broken or prevented the effort, which started well, from reaching a successful termination. If one of these lines reaches and stops at the Line of Heart, it indicates that the affections have, or will, interfere with the subject's special effort in whatever direction this line indicates. If one of these lines crosses and joins the line of Fate (3-3, Plate X.), it indicates and gives two distinct dates which are very curious in their meaning. The first date it gives is when this line leaves the Line of Life on its way towards the Line of Fate. The date of this start towards the Line of Fate will be given on the Line of Fate itself, right opposite where this line begins to grow from the Line of Life. This mark will denote that the subject has made a determined effort at that moment in his career to make his own destiny, and to break free from the circumstances or people that surround him or tie him down.

It is always a successful sign when this line is found to join the Line of Fate, especially if the Line of Fate looks stronger at or about this point of the junction.

The second date is given at the period in the Line of Life when one is reading down the Line of Life itself. The singular point about this is that a repetition of circumstances will be found to occur in the destiny. Suppose, for example, one saw this line going towards the Fate Line at twenty-six years of age—a circumstance or repetition of the occurrence will be found to occur at almost double that age, namely, fifty-two years of age, which would give a more or less exact date of this occurrence when reading the Line of Life. As an illustration to help the reader I may say that I have generally found that this mark will indicate that the subject has, in the first instance, broken free from some tie at an early date, and that a similar occurrence will take place at the second date, viz., late in life, when again the subject seems to break free from some tie, and goes out more into the world for himself.

This curious sign very often helps in deciding matters as regards marriage. The man, or woman, will apparently assert his independence more, and leave the ties of home life, and again go out in the world and fight the battle for himself, as he did in the earlier part of his existence, when he probably left his parents' influence and forged ahead for himself.

When the ascending line is seen crossing over towards the Mount of Saturn, and running as an independent line not joined to the Line of Fate (6, Plate X.), it will be found that the subject has carried out a kind of second fate. The date when this line left the Line of Life will give the first date of its commencement, *i.e.*, opposite it on the Fate Line. If the line be a good one it would give its second date when reading down the Line of Life, where, if the line were good, it carried out this second fate to a successful culmination.

Chapter IV
The Line Of Mars Or Inner Life Line

What is called the Line of Mars is that line that is found only on some hands encircling the Mount of Venus and inside the Line of Life.

This Line, which rises on the Mount of Mars, from which it derives its name, when found clear and strong appears to back up and reinforce the Line of Life (4-4, Plate X.). It indicates great vitality, power of resistance to illness and disease, and is not found on all hands.

It is an excellent sign on the hands of soldiers, or in connection with all persons who follow a dangerous calling.

All breaks or bad marks indicated on the Line of Life are minimized on the hands that have this Inner Life Line, or Line of Mars.

As its name implies, in character it denotes a robust and rather fighting disposition, a person naturally inclined to rush into dangers and quarrels, and if deeply marked and reddish in colour it increases all indications of accidents and dangers shown on other parts of the hand.

When a branch seems to shoot off from this line and runs on to the Mount of Luna (5-5, Plate X.), it foreshadows restlessness and an intense craving for excitement. With a weak-looking Line of Mentality it is a sure sign of a craving for drink and intemperance of all kinds, and at the point where it breaks through the Line of Life, it generally indicates death brought on by the intemperance this mark foreshadows.

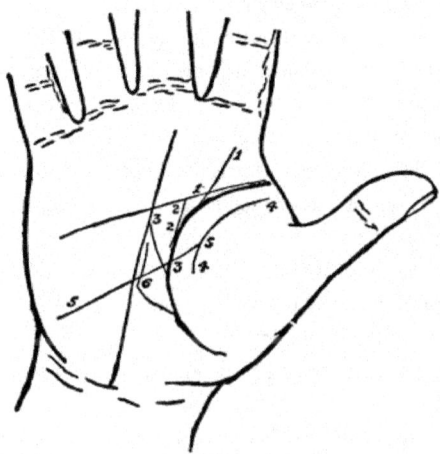

PLATE X. THE LINE OF LIFE, THE LINE OF MARS, AND OTHER SIGNS.

It is generally found on short, thick-set square hands or short hands, but when found on a long, thin, and narrow palm, it indicates great vitality and resistance to disease, a nervous, highly-strung, and rather irritable disposition.

Any broken Life Line with this Line of Mars behind it may indicate great danger of death where the break appears, but a danger that will be overcome through the vitality indicated by this Inner Life Line or Line of Mars.

Chapter V
The Line Of Destiny Or Fate

The Line of Destiny, otherwise called the Line of Fate (1-1, Plate XI.) is naturally one of the most important of the principal lines of the hand.

Although one may never be able to explain why it is, this line undoubtedly appears to indicate at least the main events of one's career.

It may be found on the hand even at the moment of birth, clearly indicating the class of Fate or Destiny that lies in the far distant future before the individual.

In some cases it may look faint or shadowy, as if the path of Destiny were not yet clearly defined, while in other instances almost every step of the road is chiselled out with its milestones of failure or success, sorrow or joy, as the case may be.

That some human beings seem to be more children of Fate than others has been admitted by almost all thinkers, but why they should be so has been the great question that baffles all students of such subjects.

There are some who appear to have no Fate, and others who seem to carve their Destiny from day to day.

I have seen hundreds of cases where every step of the journey was indicated from childhood to the grave; others where only the principal changes in the career were marked in advance. There are, again, others where nothing seemed decided, and where the events indicated by the Line of Fate appeared to change from year to year.

The why and wherefore of such things may be impossible to fathom, but there are so many mysteries in Life itself that one more or less does not seem to matter.

Some of the greatest teachers and philosophers have come to the conclusion that Fate exists for all. In the 17th Article of Religion in the Episcopal Church it is stated, and in no uncertain manner, that "Predestination to life is the everlasting purpose of God." All through the Bible the Destiny of nations and of men is clearly laid down, and from the first chapter of Genesis to the last page of Revelation the trials, tribulations, and pathway of the Jews was prophesied and predicted ages in advance.

Thousands of years before the birth of Christ, it was foretold in Holy Writ in what manner He should be born, and in what manner He should die. It was predicted that a Virgin should conceive and that a Judas should betray, and that both were necessary "that the Scriptures might be fulfilled."

In more recent ages thousands and thousands of predictions have been fulfilled, and all point to some mysterious agency that underlies the purpose of humanity, and that nothing from the smallest to the greatest is left to blind chance.

It may be that the Soul—in being part of the Universal Soul of all things—*knows all things*, and so through the instrumentality of the brain writes its knowledge of the Future in advance.

To the mysteries of the mind there are no limits. Medical science has, in late years, gone so far as to prove that there must be an advance growth or change in the brain cells years before action or change in character become the result of such development. For all we know, every deed in our careers is the result of some such mental change, and as there are more super-sensitive nerves from the brain to the hand, it may then follow that such changes and subsequent actions in our lives may be written in our hands even long years in advance.

It may be, then, that to all living beings there is a Destiny "that shapes our ends, rough hew them as we will."

I would, however, humbly suggest that each of us endeavour by knowledge to find what our Fate may be, and like loyal workmen accept whatever the task should prove, and so carry it out to the utmost of our ability, willing to leave the final result to the Master that thought fit to employ us in the working out of His design.

All such questions as these the student of this subject must settle in his own mind, for when he or she once broaches this study of Fate, he will be assailed on all sides, and the student must be prepared to give "an answer for the faith that is in him."

In studying the hand it will be found that the Line of Fate may rise from the following distinct positions:

It may rise from and out of the Line of Life (2-2, Plate XI.), straight up from the wrist (1-1, Plate XI.), from the Mount of the Moon (3-3, Plate XI.), or from the middle of the palm.

The following is the meaning of these principal positions:

Rising From The Line Of Life

Rising from the Line of Life (2-2, Plate XI.), the subject's success will be made by personal effort and merit; the early years of such a Fate will be cramped and difficult; circumstances and the early surroundings will not be favourable, and such people will be greatly hampered or sacrificed to the wishes and plans of their parents or relatives. If the Line of Fate, however, should run on clear and strong from where it leaves the Line of Life, then the subject will overcome all such difficulties and win success by his own personal effort and merit, and not depend on what is termed luck at any time in the career.

Another striking and important point is that the date or years marked on the Line of Fate of such a breaking out into the palm, will be found to coincide with the year in the subject's life in which he asserted his independence or launched out into what he more particularly wanted to do. (*See* also end of chapter on Time, page 151.)

In any case this date as indicated will be found to be one of the most important in his career (for how to obtain dates and years *see* Chapter XIX).

Rising From The Wrist

When the Line of Fate rises from the Wrist (1-1, Plate XI.) and goes straight up the centre of the palm to the Mount of Saturn, provided at the same time the Line of Sun (4-4, Plate XI.) is found well marked, luck, brilliance, and success will attend the Destiny, and extreme good fortune may be anticipated.

Rising From The Mount Of The Moon

Rising from the Mount of the Moon (3-3, Plate XI.) the Fate will be more eventful, changeable, and largely depending on the fancy and caprice of other people.

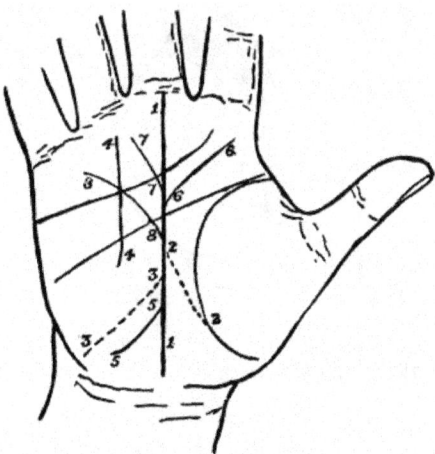

PLATE XI. THE LINE OF DESTINY AND ITS MODIFICATIONS.

If such a line be found joining the Line of Heart (1-1, Plate XII.), it foretells a happy and prosperous marriage, but one in which idealism, romance, and some fortunate circumstances play their rôle, and one which results more from the caprice or fancy of the person of the other sex.

If the Line of Fate be itself straight but with a line running in and joining it from the Mount of the Moon (5-5, Plate XI.), it indicates that the influence of some outside person has helped the subject's Fate, and it is generally an indication of the influence of another sex to the one on whose hand it appears.

When this line of influence from the Mount of the Moon does not, however, blend with the Fate Line (2-2, Plate XII.), it denotes that the other person's life will always remain distinct, and the influence will last only for the length of time that it runs by the side of the subject's Fate.

When this influence line cuts the Line of Fate and, leaving it, travels on for some distance towards the Mount of Jupiter (3-3, Plate XII.) it tells that the person whose influence it denotes will only be attracted to the subject by personal ambition—that this person will use the subject for the furthering of his own aims and ambitions, and will desert the subject when she is of no further use. This is more commonly seen on the hand of a woman than on that of a man.

If the Line of Fate ascending the hand sends an offshoot from it on or towards any of the Mounts, such as to Jupiter, the Sun, or Mercury, then the Destiny will be more largely associated with the quality that the Mount it approaches symbolises.

For example: If such a line be seen approaching or going towards Jupiter (6-6, Plate XI.) it denotes responsibility, power of command over others, or some high position which will commence to be realised from the date when the offshoot leaves the Line of Fate. If such a mark continues its course and finishes on the Mount of Jupiter, it is one of the most magnificent signs of success that can be found for that particular aim or purpose.

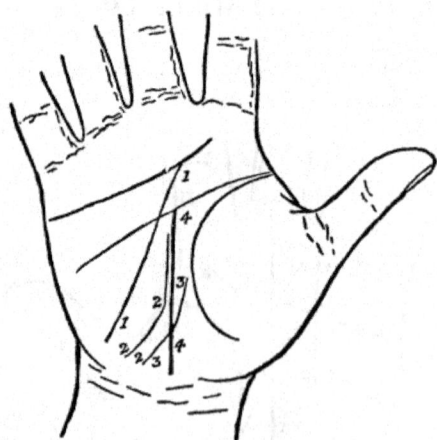

PLATE XII. THE LINE OF DESTINY AND ITS VARIATIONS.

If this offshoot ascends towards the Mount of the Sun (7-7, Plate XI.) the success will be in the direction of riches and public life, which will give great publicity or renown; this is also a magnificent sign of success.

If the offshoot goes towards the Mount of Mercury (8-8, Plate XI.), the success it indicates will be more in the direction of some special achievement either in science or commerce.

If the Line of Fate itself should not ascend towards its habitual position on the Mount of Saturn, but, instead, run up towards or on to any other Mount, then the whole effort of the life will be tinged with whatever quality that particular Mount signifies. Such an indication must not, however, be considered as the certain or sure sign of success as when the Line of Fate keeps to its own place and sends branches to some particular Mount.

When the Line of Fate ascends the hand without branches and runs like a lonely path up and on to the Mount of Saturn, such a person will be like a child of Fate chained to an iron road of circumstances. It will be impossible for him to avert the trials of his Destiny or mitigate them in any way. He will receive no help from others, and little will ever happen except to bring him sorrow or tragedy. Such a mark of Fate through the hand must never be considered as "a good line of Destiny."

To have a really good Line of Fate it should not be too heavily marked, but just clear and distinct, and, above all, be accompanied by a Line of Sun in some form or other.

If a Line of Fate run over the Mount of Saturn and up into the base of the finger, it is an unfortunate sign, as everything the subject undertakes will get out of his control, and he will not apparently know how or when to stop in whatever he takes up.

When the Line of Fate appears to be stopped by the Line of Heart, the career will always be ruined through or by the affections being badly placed.

When, however, it joins the Line of Heart and they together ascend the Mount of Jupiter (1-1, Plate XII.), the subject will have happiness through his affections and will be helped by love and affection to attain his highest ambitions. He will also be extremely lucky through the friendship and love of those he meets, and will be greatly benefited and helped by others.

When the Line of Fate appears to be stopped by the Line of Head (4-4, Plate XII.), it foretells that his career will be spoiled by the subject's own stupidity or mental foolishness.

Rising From The Middle Of The Palm

When the Line of Fate only makes its appearance far up in the centre of the palm, in what is called the Plain of Mars, it indicates a hard early life and that the subject must always have a hard fight to gain his ends; but should the Line ascend clearly and strongly from the Plain of Mars and have a branch to or on towards the Mount of the Sun, such a person will be the architect of his own fortunes, and without help or assistance will win success and fortune by his own personal hard work and merit.

When the Line of Fate rises from the Line of Head and when it is well marked, everything will come to the subject late in life and only then by his own brains.

When the Line of Fate is seen with one branch on the Mount of Venus and the other on the Mount of the Moon (1-2, Plate XIII.) it indicates a career of romance and passion, by which the whole of the Destiny will be swayed.

When the Line of Fate itself rises inside the Life Line on the Mount of Venus (2-2, Plate XIII.), passionate love will affect the whole career, and such persons, it will be found, usually place their affections on impossible people or on those who are in some way tied up by marriage or who otherwise are unable to gratify the love that the other person demands. This is a most unlucky sign for affection to find in the hands of a woman.

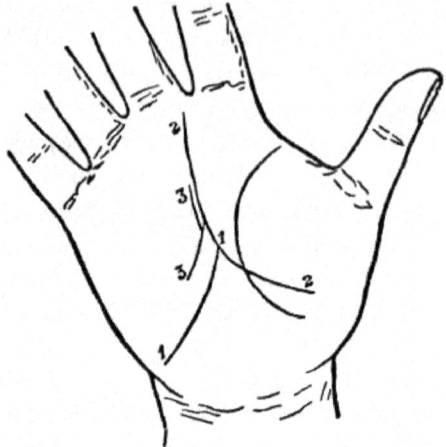

PLATE XIII. THE LINE OF DESTINY AND ITS MODIFICATIONS.

When the Line of Fate is broken or made up in little bits, the career will be found full of troubles, breaks, and nothing that one gets will last long enough to bring any settled or continuous success.

A break in the Fate Line is not always a bad sign to have, provided that one side begins before the other ends; in such a case it foretells a complete change in surroundings and position, and if the new line looks good and straight it will be found to mean that the change will bring about an advancement in position commencing at the date when the second line first makes its appearance (for dates on the Line of Fate *see* Chapter XIX).

Influence Lines

When any small line joins the Fate Line or goes on with it as an attendant line, such a mark usually indicates marriage at the date when these lines join (3-3, Plate XIII.). If, on the contrary, these lines do not join, marriage with the person is not likely to occur although the affection and influence will be present in the career.

When one of these influence lines appears by the side of the Fate Line and crosses through it towards or on to the Mount of Mars, it indicates that the influence thus shown will turn to hate and will injure the career of the person on whose hand it is found (1-1, Plate XIV.).

Double Lines Of Fate

When the Line of Fate is itself double (2-2, Plate XIV.), it is a sign of what is called "a double life," but if, after running side by side for some length these two lines join or become one, it foretells that "the double life" has been caused by some great affection, that circumstances prevented a union, but that the preventing cause will be removed at the point where these two lines join.

When, however, a double Line of Fate is clearly marked, especially if they incline towards different mounts of the hand, such a mark indicates that two careers would be carried out simultaneously—one perhaps as a hobby and the other as the principal career.

When the Line of Fate is extremely faint or just barely traced through the palm, it will be found to indicate a general disbelief in the idea of Fate and Destiny. It is often found on the hands of very materialistic persons, those who rebel against the idea that they are governed in any way by Fate or by any power save themselves.

When this is found, and at the same time a good clear Line of Head, such people will be sure to win success by their mentality alone, but the details of their destiny will not be able to be told, and one must content oneself with chiefly describing their characteristics, peculiarities, etc.

When no Line of Fate whatever is found and only a very ordinary Line of Head, then there will be nothing very particular to say about the Destiny; such people, as a rule, lead very colourless lives, nothing seems to affect them much one way or the other, and they will be found to have very little purpose to illumine the drab monotony of their existence.

An island (3, Plate XIV.) is an extremely bad sign to find in the Line of Fate.

When found at the very beginning of the line (4, Plate XIV.) it indicates some mystery regarding the commencement of such careers, such as illegitimate birth.

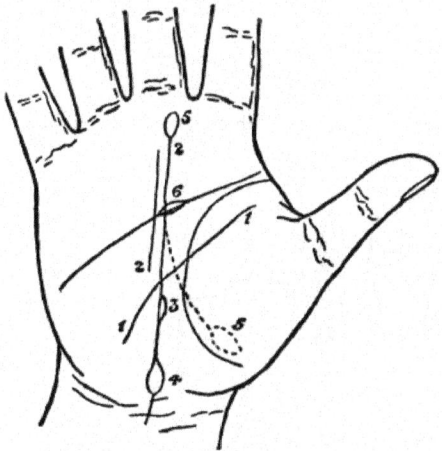

PLATE XIV. THE LINE OF DESTINY, ISLANDS, AND OTHER SIGNS.

An island, when found on a woman's hand connecting the Fate Line with the Mount of Venus, is an almost certain indication of her seduction (5, Plate XIV.).

An island in any part of the Plain of Mars indicates a period of great difficulty, loss in one's career, and in consequence, generally loss of money (3, Plate XIV.).

An Island on the Fate and Head Lines together means loss also, but more brought on by the person's own stupidity or lack of intelligence (6, Plate XIV.).

An island over the Fate and Heart Lines indicates loss and trouble connected with affairs of the heart or brought about by the affections.

An island on the Mount of Saturn or towards the end of the Line of Fate (5, Plate XIV.) foreshadows that the career will finish in poverty and despair (for more details concerning the meaning of "islands" in general, *see* Chapter XV).

When the Line of Fate finishes suddenly with a cross, some great fatality may be expected, but when the cross is found on the Fate Line and on the Mount of Saturn, the ending of such a Destiny will be some terrible tragedy, generally one of public disgrace and public death.

Chapter VI
The Line Of The Sun

The Line of the Sun, which is otherwise called the Line of Success or the Line of Brilliancy (1-1, Plate XV.), is one of the most important marks on the hand to consider.

It has in its symbolism almost the same significance as the Sun itself has to the Earth.

Without this line the life has no happiness, no sunshine, as it were, and even the greatest talents lie in darkness and do not produce their fruit.

Amateurs, in looking at hands, often make the greatest mistakes in seeing what appears to be "a good Line of Fate," and in consequence rush off and predict great success and fortune, whereas, as I explained in the preceding chapter, a Fate Line unaccompanied by the Line of Sun may simply mean a fatalistic life full of sorrow and darkness.

The quality that the Line of Sun denotes is, what is generally called "luck"; with a well-marked Sun Line even a poor Line of Head promises more success, and it is the same with the Line of Fate.

People with the Sun Line appear to have more magnetism, more influence over others. They more easily secure recognition, reward, riches, and honours.

They also have a happier and brighter disposition, and this has naturally a great deal to do with what is called success.

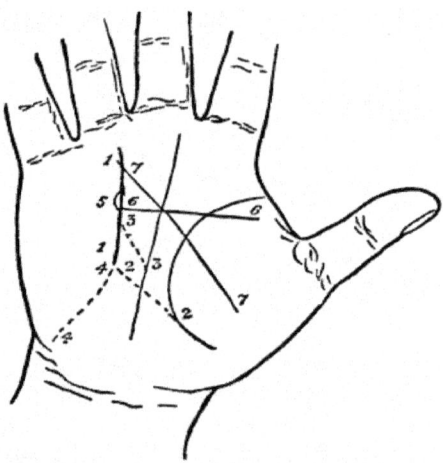

PLATE XV. THE LINE OF SUN AND ITS MODIFICATIONS.

From whatever date in the hand the Line of Sun appears, things become brighter, more prosperous and important. The Line of the Sun may rise from the following positions:

From the Line of Life, the Line of Fate, the Plain of Mars, the Mount of the Moon, the Line of Head, and from the Line of Heart, or it may only appear as a small line on its own Mount.

Rising from the Line of Life (2-2, Plate XV.), it promises success from whatever the life is that is led, but not from "luck."

From the Line of Fate (3-3, Plate XV.), it is a sure sign of recognition for the career adopted, but brought about by the personal effort of the subject.

From the Plain of Mars, and not connected with the other lines, it foretells success after difficulties.

From the Mount of the Moon (4-4, Plate XV.), success is more a matter due to the caprice of others. It is more changeable and uncertain and is by no means such a sure sign of riches or solid position. It is more the sign of success as a public favourite, and is often found in the hands of those who depend on the public for their livelihood, such as actors and actresses, singers, and certain classes of artists, speakers, clergymen, etc. For all such professions it is, however, fortunate, and an extremely lucky sign to have, as it promises in all cases luck, brilliancy, and recognition in the world.

Rising from the Line of Head, the Sun Line gives success from the mental efforts and qualities, but not until after the middle of life is past. It is found on the hands of brain workers, students of some particular branch of study, writers, scientists, etc.

From the Line of Heart, success will come late in life in some way depending on, or through, the affections. In such cases it generally promises a very happy marriage late in life, but it is always a certain sign of eventual ease, happiness, and worldly comfort.

Marked only on its own Mount, the Line of Sun promises happiness and success, but so late in life as to make it hardly worth having.

When the third finger—called the finger of the Sun—is much longer than the first with the Line of Sun well marked, the gambling instincts will be much in evidence. Nearly all successful gamblers for money have these two indications.

When, however, the third finger is equal to the second, the love of amassing wealth will be the dominant passion of the life.

When the third finger is extremely long and twisted or crooked, the person will endeavour to obtain money at any cost. This malformation is much seen in the hands of thieves or criminals who are likely to commit any crime for the sake of money. Note—if the Line of Head is very high on the palm, and more especially if it rises upwards at the end (3-3, Plate III.), these evil qualities will be still more accentuated.

When a hand is found to be artistic in its shape, with pointed fingers or long and narrow, the Line of Sun on such a formation promises rather success and brilliancy in Art, on the Stage, or in Public Singing, than in anything else.

The real musician's hand, such as the composer's or player's, is however rarely a long, thin-shaped hand, because such persons must have a more scientific nature. This quality is not found with those who possess the long, slender, very artistic-shaped hand, who depend more on their emotional temperament than on scientific study for their foundation.

On extremely long, thin hands, those that belong to what is called the Psychic Type,[4] the Line of Sun has very little meaning except that of temperament, such persons being too idealistic to care for either wealth, position, or worldly success. They have as a rule, simply bright, happy, sunny dispositions if this line is marked on their hands, and they go through life as in a dream, and their dreams are to them the only things that matter (*see* Types of Hands, Part II., page 153).

A curious characteristic, however, and one that has not been noticed by other writers on this subject, is, that on all hands where the Sun Line is seen, the nature of such people is much more sensitive to environment than that of those persons who do not possess this Line. For this reason the Line has been considered a sign of the artistic nature. But what is known as the "artistic nature" may show itself only in the love of beautiful things, harmony of surroundings, and such like; whereas the people who do not possess any mark of the Sun Line, seldom even notice their surroundings and would live equally happy in the most squalid homes. They would not trouble whether their curtains were black, green, yellow, or some fearful conglomeration of all three.

When many lines are found on the Mount of the Sun, they show also the artistic nature, but one where the multiplicity of aims and ideas will prevent any real success.

Two or three Sun Lines, when running parallel and evenly together, are good and indicate success in two or three different lines of work; but one good, straight, clear line is the best sign to have.

An "island" on any part of the Line of the Sun destroys the position and success promised, but only during the period where the island appears (5, Plate XV.). In nearly all cases it denotes public scandal, and when very clearly marked a *cause célèbre* or something of that sort.

All opposition lines, viz., those that cross over from the thumb side of the hand, and especially those from the Mount of Mars or from its direction, are bad (6-6 Plate XV.). If these opposition lines pass through, cut, or interfere with the Line of Sun in any way, they denote the jealousy or interference of people against one.

Curiously enough, these opposition lines from the Mount of Mars relate to the interference of members of the same sex as the subject; while, if they come from the Mount of Venus, they relate to the opposite sex of the individual on whose hand they appear (7-7, Plate XV.).

A "star" found on the Line of Sun is one of the luckiest and most fortunate signs to have.

A "square" is a sign of preservation against the attacks of enemies or efforts to assail one's position.

A "cross" is an unfortunate sign, and denotes difficulties and annoyance, but only relating to one's name or position.

On a "hollow hand," the Line of Sun loses all power, and its good promises are never fulfilled.

The complete absence of the Line of Sun on an otherwise well-marked hand, indicates that no matter how clever or talented these people may be, the recognition of the world will be difficult or even impossible to gain. In other words, their life will remain in darkness; people will not see their work and the "Sun of Success" will never dawn on their pathway of labour.

Chapter VII
The Line Of Heart As Indicating The Affectionate And Emotional Nature

The Line of Heart is that Line which runs across the hand under the fingers and generally rises under the base of the first, and runs off the side of the hand under the base of the fourth or little finger (1-1, Plate XVI.).

The Line of Heart relates purely to the affectionate disposition, in fact, to the mental side of the love nature of the subject. It should be borne in mind that, by lying as it does on that part of the hand above the Line of Head, it is consequently on the portion of the hand that relates to mental characteristics and not to the physical.

The Line of Heart should be deep, clear, and well coloured. It may arise from the extreme outside of the Mount of Jupiter (2, Plate XVI.), from the centre of this Mount, from the space between the first and second fingers (3, Plate XVI.), from the face of the Mount of Saturn (4, Plate XVI.), or from directly under this Mount (5, Plate XVI.).

From the outside of the Mount of Jupiter, it denotes the blind enthusiast in affection, a man or woman who places his or her ideal of love so high that neither fault nor failing is seen in the being worshipped. With these people their pride in the object of their affection is beyond all reason, and all such extremists as a rule suffer terribly through their affections.

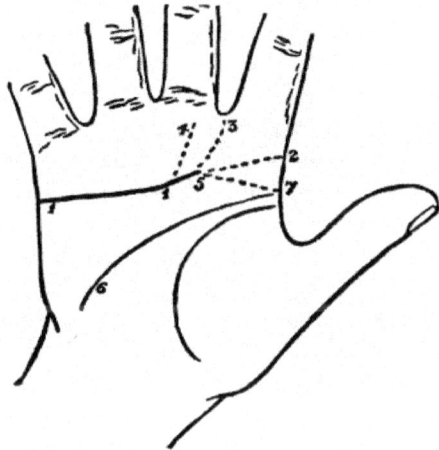

PLATE XVI. THE LINE OF HEART AND ITS VARIATIONS.

From the centre of the Mount of Jupiter, the Heart Line gives more moderation, but also great ideality, and is one of the best of the variations of this Line that we are about to consider.

People with such a Heart Line are firm and reliable in their affections, they have an unusually high code of honour and morality. They are ambitious that the person they live with be great, noble, and successful. They seldom marry beneath their station in life, and they have fewer love affairs than any other class.

If they once really love, they love for ever. They do not believe in second marriages, and the divorce courts are seldom troubled with their presence.

The Heart Line rising from between the first and second fingers, gives a calmer but a very deep nature in all matters of the affections (3, Plate XVI.).

These people seem to strike the happy medium between the ideality and pride given by Jupiter, and the more selfish love nature given when the line rises from Saturn.

They are not very demonstrative when in love, but they are capable of the very greatest sacrifices for those they care for. They do not expect the person on whom they bestow their affection to be a god or a goddess.

When the Line of Heart rises on the Mount of Saturn the subject will be rather selfish in all questions of affection (4, Plate XVI.). These people are not self-sacrificing, like the previous type. They are inclined to be cynical, reserved, undemonstrative but very insistent in trying to gain the person they want. They will let nothing stand in their way, but once they have obtained their object they show little tenderness or devotion.

They are very unforgiving if they discover any lapses on the part of their partner, but as they are "a law unto themselves," they close their eyes to their own shortcomings.

The Line of Heart that rises from under the base of the Mount of Saturn (5, Plate XVI.), exhibits all the foregoing characteristics, but in a much more intensified form. Such persons live for themselves, and care little whether those around them are happy or not.

The shorter the Line of Heart is on the Hand, the less the higher sentiments of the affection make themselves manifest.

When the Line of Heart is found in excess, namely, extremely long—it denotes a terrible tendency toward jealousy (2, Plate XVI.), and this is alarmingly increased if the Line of Head on the same hand is very sloping towards the Mount of the Moon (6, Plate XVI.). In such a case the imagination will run away with itself where jealousy is concerned.

When the Line of Heart is found curving downward at the base of the Mount of Jupiter (7, Plate XVI.), it tells of a strange fatality in that person, of meeting with great disappointment in love, and even with those they trust in friendship. He seems to lack perception, in knowing whom to love. His affections are nearly always misplaced or never returned.

These people have, however, as a rule, wonderfully kind, affectionate dispositions. They have little pride about whom they love and they generally marry beneath their station in life.

A Line of Heart made up like a chain, or by a crowd of little lines running into it, denotes flirtations and inconstancy in the love nature, and seldom has any lasting affection.

A Line of Heart from Saturn in holes or links like a chain, especially when it is broad, denotes an absolute contempt for the subject's opposite sex. It is one of the signs of mental degeneration as far as love is concerned.

When this Line is pale and broad, without any depth, it denotes a nature *blasé* and indifferent with no depth of affection.

When very low down on the hand, almost touching the Line of Head, the heart will always interfere with the affairs of the head.

When it lies very high on the hand and the space is narrowed only by the Head Line being abnormally high and out of its place, it indicates the reverse of the above, and that the affairs of the heart are ruled by the head. Such persons are extremely calculating in all matters of love.

When only one deep, straight line is found across the hand from side to side, the two lines both Head and Heart appear to blend together. This denotes an intensely self-concentrated nature. If such a subject loves, he unites with it all the forces of his mind, and if he put his mind on any subject, he throws his whole heart and soul into whatever it may be (Plate VI.).

These people are also terribly head-strong and self-willed in all they do. They do not seem to know what fear means in any sense—they are dangerous lovers and husbands to trifle with, for they will stop at nothing if their blood is once roused.

They are also dangerous to themselves. They rush blindly into danger, and they usually meet with terrible accidents and injuries, and very often suffer a violent death.

When the Line of Heart commences with a fork, one branch on Jupiter and the other between the first and second fingers, it is an excellent sign of a well-balanced, happy, affectionate disposition, and a good promise of great happiness in all matters of affection.

When the Line of Heart is very thin and with no branches, it denotes coldness and want of heart.

When there is no Line of Heart whatever, it is a sign of a cold-blooded, unemotional nature. Such people can, however, be brutally sensual and especially so if the Mount of Venus is high (*see* Mounts, page 177).

A broken Heart Line is a certain sign that some terrible tragedy in the affections will at some time or other overwhelm the subject.

It may not often be found nowadays, but I have seen it in some few cases, and these persons never recovered the loss of the loved one or ever had love in their lives again.

Chapter VIII
Signs Relating To Marriage

What is called the Line of Marriage is that mark or marks, as the case may be, found on the side of the Mount under the fourth finger (1, Plate XVII.).

I will first proceed to give all the details possible about these lines, and then call my reader's attention to the other marks on the hand that qualify these Lines of Marriage, and further add a wealth of information regarding them.

The Line, or Lines, of Marriage may be found as very short marks almost on the very side of the hand, or they may appear as quite long lines rising from the side of the hand into the face of the Mount of Mercury, or, in some cases, going farther still into the hand itself.

Only the clearly formed lines relate to marriage, the short ones to deep affection, or marriage contemplated, but never entered into (2, Plate XVII.).

When the deep line is found lying close to the line of Heart, the marriage will take place early in life, but the other marks I am going to explain later will give more accurate dates as to when the event will occur.

For a happy marriage the lines on the Mount of Mercury should be straight and clear, without breaks or irregularities of any kind (1, Plate XVII.).

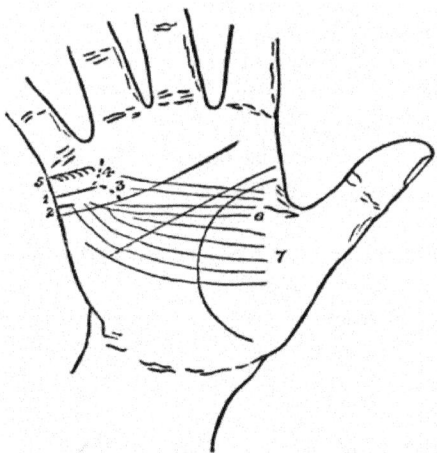

PLATE XVII. MARRIAGE LINES. THE LINE OF MARRIAGE.

When the Line of Marriage curves or droops downwards (3, Plate XVII.), the person on whose hand this appears will outlive the other.

When the line turns upward in the reverse direction, the possessor is not likely ever to marry (4, Plate XVII.).

When the line is clear and distinct, but has a lot of little lines dropping from it, it foreshadows trouble and anxiety in the marriage, but brought on by the delicacy and ill-health of the partner (5, Plate XVII.).

When the line has a curve at the end, and if a cross or line be found cutting into this curve (2, Plate XVIII.), the partner will die by accident or a sudden illness of some kind. But when the Marriage Line ends in a long, gradual curve into the Heart Line, the death of the partner will come about by gradual ill-health or illness of a very long duration.

When the line has an "island" at the beginning, then the marriage will be for a long time delayed, and the two persons will be much separated at the commencement of their married life.

When the "island" is found about the middle of the Marriage Line, some great trouble and separation will take place about the middle of the married life (3, Plate XVIII.).

When the "island" is found towards the end of the line, the marriage will most probably end in trouble and separation one from the other.

When the Line of Marriage divides into the form of a fork (4, Plate XVIII.), the two people will live apart from one another, but when the fork turns downwards towards the Line of Heart a legal separation may be anticipated (5, Plate XVIII.).

When this fork is more accentuated, and turns down more into the hand, divorce may be expected, and especially so if one end of this fork stretches across the hand in the direction of the Plain of Mars, or the Mount of Mars (5, Plate XVIII.).

In many cases a fine line may be found crossing the entire palm, from the Marriage Line, and in such a case the greatest animosity and bitterness will enter into the fight for freedom and divorce. In such an example there is never any hope of reconciliation.

When the Line of Marriage is full of little islands, or linked like the loops of a chain, the subject should be warned not to marry at any time, as such a union would be full of the greatest unhappiness and continual separations.

When the line, which is otherwise well marked, appears about the centre to break in two, it foreshadows a fatality or break-up in an otherwise happy married life.

When the Line of Marriage itself, or an offshoot from it, goes into the hand, and joins or ascends upward with the Line of Sun, it promises that its possessor will marry some one of great wealth or distinction (6, Plate XVIII.).

When this above-mentioned line bends downward and cuts the Line of Sun, it denotes that the person on whose hand it is found will lose his position by the marriage he will make.

When any line from the top of the Mount of Mercury falls down into the Marriage Line, it shows that there will be great obstacles to overcome in whatever marriage the subject enters, but if the Line of Marriage is a good one, then such obstacles will be overcome.

When there is another line much slighter in appearance lying close to the upper side of the Marriage Line, it foretells some influence that will come into the subject's life after marriage.

All lines that cross the hand from the Mount of Mars (6, Plate XVII.), and rise up towards the Line of Marriage denote the interference of people with the marriage. These lines give the date of the interference when they cross the Line of Destiny; they cause quarrels when they come from Mars; from Venus they also denote annoyances, but not of such a vindictive nature (7, Plate XVII.).

Influence Lines To The Fate Line On The Mount Of Venus, And Other Signs Which Also Have A Meaning In Connection With Marriage

The student may also get very great help in ascertaining details about the likely marriage of the person whose hands he is examining by the following:

Fine Influence Lines seen joining the Line of Fate (7, Plate XVIII.), relate to persons who come into and affect the Destiny.

If the Line of Influence is very strong where it joins the Fate Line, and if at about the same date a clear Marriage Line is seen on the Mount of Mercury, the date of marriage may be more accurately predicted by the place on the Fate Line where the Influence Line joins it.

A great wealth of detail may also be made out from observing these Influence Lines to the Destiny:

Coming over from the Mount of the Moon, there is always something romantic about the union. The person on whose hand this Line appears will as a rule meet his affinity when traveling or away from his home.

If the Influence Line has an "island" marked on it, the influence will then be a bad one, or, at least, the person will have had some scandal connected with his or her past life (8, Plate XVIII.). If the Line of Fate looks weaker or more uncertain after the union is marked, then such a marriage has not brought good or success to the subject. If, on the contrary, the Line of Fate looks better or stronger after the Influence Line has joined it, then this union will prove of advantage to the person whose hand is being examined.

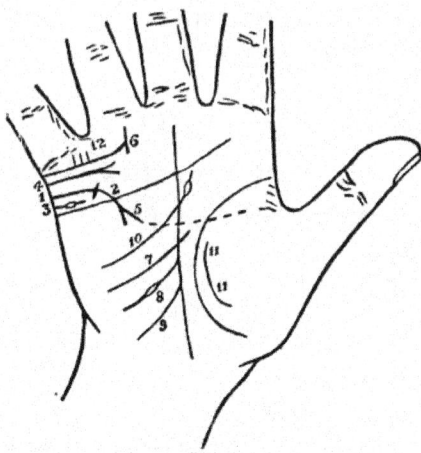

PLATE XVIII. MARRIAGE LINES AND INFLUENCE LINES WHICH FURTHER HELP IN DENOTING MARRIAGE.

This increase of wealth or power is still more accentuated if at the same time it is observed that a Sun Line has made its appearance.

If the Influence Line should cut through the Fate Line, and appear on the thumb side of it, the affection will seldom last as long, or be so happy (7, Plate XVIII.). If a still wider separation of the Influence Line and the Fate Line appear as these two lines ascend the hand together, the separation of interests and destiny of the two persons will be still more marked as the years proceed.

If an Influence Line approaches close to the Line of Fate, and runs parallel with it for some time but does not join it, some great obstacle will prevent a marriage ever taking place (*see* also page 128).

If an Influence Line terminates in an "island," the influence itself will itself get into trouble, generally disgrace of some character (10, Plate XVIII.). For further particulars refer back to chapter on the Line of Destiny, where these Influence Lines are also referred to (page 128).

Influence Lines On The Mount Of Venus

These are fine lines that run parallel with the Line of Life (11-11, Plate XVIII.), but they must not be confounded with the Line of Mars, or "Sister Life Line," which commences higher up nearer the Mount of Mars.

These Venus Influence Lines are more often found with those persons who have what is called the "Venus temperament," or who are intensely emotional and passionate.

When many of such lines are seen, the subject cannot live without love, and will have many "affairs" at the same time.

As such an Influence Line runs parallel with the Life Line, or turns away from it, so it can be judged how long such an influence will last, and with fair accuracy the date when it will occur (for dates *see* page 151).

These Influence Lines, however, never have the same importance or meaning as those previously ascribed to the Line of Fate.

In my large work on this subject, Cheiro's *Language of the Hand*, I have been able to go into still greater detail with regard to all these Influence Lines.

Chapter IX
Lines Denoting Children, Their Sex, And Other Matters Concerning Them

The Lines relating to children are those finely marked upright lines found immediately above the Line of Marriage (12, Plate XVIII.). A very good plan, in trying to see these Lines, is to press this portion of the hand with the tips of the fingers, and then note which of these small lines stand out the most clearly.

Sometimes they are extremely deeply marked, and as a rule much more so on a woman's hand than on a man's. In many cases it is necessary to employ a magnifying glass in order to see them.

Broad and deep lines denote male children, fine and narrow lines, females.

When they appear as straight lines they denote strong healthy children, but when very faint or crooked, the children indicated are always delicate.

When the first part of the little line (taking it upward from the Line of Marriage) is marked with a small "island," such a child will be very delicate in its early life, but if the line appears well marked when the "island" is passed, the probability is that it will grow up strong and healthy. When ending or broken at the "island" the child will never grow up.

When one line stands out very clear and distinct among the others, the child the mark indicates will be more to the parent, and will be more successful than any of the others.

To know the number of children anyone will have, it is necessary to count these lines from the outside of the hand in towards the palm.

A person with the Mount of Venus very flat on the hand, and very poorly developed, is not likely to have any children at all, and this is all the more certain if the first Bracelet is found rising up like an arch into or towards the palm (*see* page 142).

Chapter X
The Line Of Health Or The Hepatica

There has been very considerable discussion among students of this subject as to the part of the hand on which the Line of Health (1-1, Plate XIX.) commences.

My own theory, and one that I have proved by over twenty-five years' experience and also watching its growth on the hands of children, is, that it rises at the base of or on the face of the Mount of Mercury, and as it grows across the hand and attacks the Line of Life, it foreshadows the development of illness or germ of disease, which, at the date of its coming in contact with the Line of Life, will reach the climax of its attack.

The Line of Life, it must be remembered, merely relates to the promised length of life from heredity and natural causes, but the Line of Health denotes the effect of the class of life the subject has led. Where these two lines come together, if one is of equal strength to the other, will be the date of death, even though the Line of Life should pass this point and appear to be a much greater length (2, Plate XIX.).

The Line of Mercury, or of Health, relating as it does to the nervous system, and also to the mind (Mercury), lends itself to the supposition that the all-knowing subconscious brain is cognisant, even at an early age, of the force of resistance in the nervous system. It may know how long this force will last, when it will be exhausted, and consequently may mark the hand long years in advance.

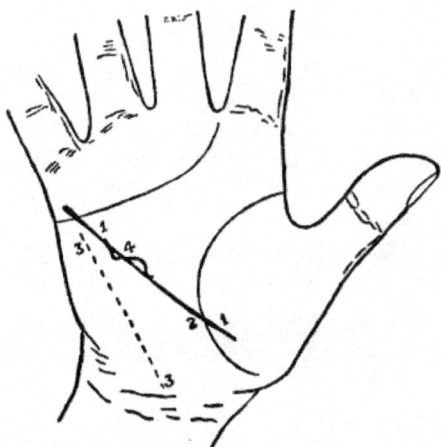

PLATE XIX. THE LINE OF HEALTH.

The Line of Health is one of the lines of the hand most subject to changes. It is the thermometer of the life showing its "rise and fall" as the case may be. I have seen this mysterious line look deep and threatening during the early years of a life, and completely fade away as greater health and strength took possession of the body.

Again, I have often seen it look deeper and more ominous as the wear and tear, especially of the nervous system, began to make itself manifest, or when the subject over-taxed his mental strength.

Further, it is an excellent sign to be without this line altogether. Its absence denotes an extremely robust, strong constitution, and a healthy state of the nervous system.

If a hand has the Line of Health, the best position for it is to lie straight down the hand, and not approach or touch the Line of Life (3-3, Plate XIX.). When found crossing the hand, and touching or throwing branches across to the Line of Life, it foretells that there is some illness at work which is undermining the health.

If it rises and seems like a branch from the Heart Line, especially if both these lines are broad in appearance and with the Health Line running down the palm coming in contact with the Line of Life, it is a certain indication of weakness or disease of the heart.

The student should always observe the kind of nails there are on the hand when thinking out the diseases indicated by the Line of Health.[6]

[6] *See* Chapter on Nails, page 161.

When the finger nails are short, without moons, and round, and the Line of Health is strongly marked, he may be sure that nervous weak action of the heart is decidedly threatened.

When the nails are long and almond-shaped, there is danger of weakness and delicacy of the lungs. With the same shape of nails, and with islands in the upper part of the Health Line (4, Plate XIX.), consumption of the lungs and tuberculosis will make itself manifest.

When the nails are very flat, and especially shell-shaped (*see* Plate V., Part II.), and the Line of Health is deeply marked, paralysis and the worst forms of nerve diseases are threatening the subject.

When this line is very red in small spots, especially when pressed, rheumatic fever is indicated.

When twisted, irregular, and yellowish in colour, the subject will suffer from biliousness and liver complaints.

When found heavily marked, and only joining the Heart and Head Lines together, it foreshadows brain-fever, especially when any islands are marked on the Line of Head.

The Line of Health, running straight down the hand but not touching the Line of Life, indicates that though the constitution may not be robust, it is wiry, and there is great reserve resistance to disease.

In connection with the examination of the Line of Health, the student must always look for other indications to the rest of the lines of the hand, more especially to the Line of Life and Line of Head. For instance, when the Line of Life looks very chained and weak, the Health Line on a hand will naturally increase the danger of delicate health; and when found with a Line of Head full of little islands, or like a chain, such a Health Line more clearly foreshadows brain disease, severe headaches, etc.

By a study of this line the most valuable warnings may be given of approaching ill-health. Whether persons will follow the warnings or not is a question. My experience is that they do not and will not, and therefore, whatever is indicated will most probably come to pass.

Providence places many signposts and warnings in our paths, but human nature is either too blind or too self-confident to notice them until it is too late.

Chapter XI
The Girdle Of Venus, The Ring Of Saturn, And The Bracelets

These marks are classed among the minor lines of the hands, but they often have a significance that is of the greatest importance.

The Girdle of Venus is that broken or sometimes unbroken kind of semi-circular line that is found rising from the base of the first finger to the base of the fourth (1-1, Plate XX.).

I have not in my experience found this mark to indicate the gross sensuality that is so often ascribed to it by other writers. It should be remembered that the hand is divided by the Line of Head, as it were, *into two hemispheres, the lower and the upper.*

The lower relates to the physical or more animal side of the nature, and the upper to the intellectual. Following this arrangement, it is only reasonable to assume that this mark under consideration, viz., the Girdle of Venus, relates more to the mental side of the symbolism of the Venus nature.

I have found that persons with this sign are more mentally sensual than physically so. They love to read or write books on the subject of the "sex problem," but they are not inclined to put their theories and ideas into practice, at least with their own lives.

The qualities, however, that this mark represents are much more active and dangerous when this Girdle forms itself from the Mount of Saturn to that of Mercury. The imaginings of such people are then morbid and unhealthy.

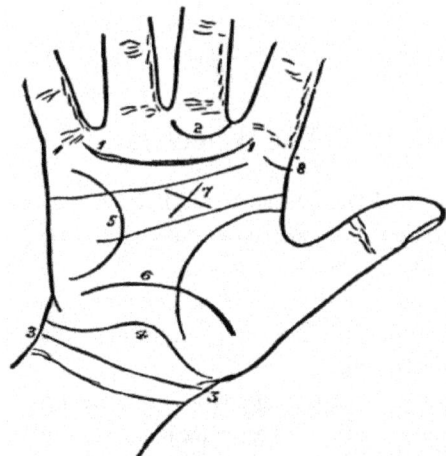

PLATE XX. THE GIRDLE OF VENUS, THE RING OF SATURN, THE THREE BRACELETS, THE LINE OF INTUITION AND THE VIA LASCIVA.

To those who study Astrology, the inference that I draw from the connection of these two parts of the hand will become clear and reasonable.

When broken or made up of little pieces, the Girdle of Venus has little meaning except to show a hysterical temperament, with a leaning towards the tendencies I have mentioned above.

These persons in all cases suffer enormously from moods, they are very difficult to live with, and when the Girdle of Venus runs off the side of the hand and passes out through the Marriage Lines, their moody, changeable natures generally make marriage for them an unusually unhappy experience.

The Ring Of Saturn

What is called the Ring of Saturn (2, Plate XX.) is very seldom found, and it is by no means a good sign to have. It is also a semi-circular line, but found lying across the Mount of Saturn.

In all my experience I have never been able to come across any person with this mark who succeeded in life or was able to carry any one of his plans to a successful termination.

These people seem cut off from their fellow beings in some peculiar and extraordinary way. They are isolated and alone, and they appear to realise their lonely position keenly. They are gloomy, morbid, and Saturnine in character. They seldom marry, and when they do it is always a ghastly failure.

They are terribly obstinate and headstrong in all their actions, they resent the least advice or interference in their plans. Their lives generally close in suffering, poverty, or by some sinister tragedy or fatality.

It is the most unfortunate mark ever to find.

The Bracelets

The Bracelets (3-3, Plate XX.) are of very little importance except to throw light on certain points of health. There are supposed to be three of these lines or bracelets at the wrist, which were called by the Greeks the Bracelets of Health, Wealth, and Happiness.

It is certainly very seldom that they can be found together, for experience in life does not give much hope that these three much-sought-after possessions can ever be found together on this side of the grave.

Delving back into the ancient legends of Greece, we find one very significant point in reference to the first bracelet, the one nearest the palm, which represents Health.

It appears that at one period of the ancient Greek civilization all women had to come to the priest at their Temple to have their hands examined before they were allowed to marry. If the priest found this first Bracelet out of its place and rising up into the hand in the shape of an arch (4, Plate XX.), he would not allow the woman possessing this sign to be married under any circumstance, the idea being that it represented some internal malformation that would prevent her bringing children into the world. In such cases these women were made Vestal Virgins in the temples. Perhaps the old Greek Priest was right in his idea, for if this first Bracelet is found rising into the hand in the form of an arch, both men and women possessing it are delicate internally, and especially so in matters relating to sex.

Chapter XII
The Line Of Intuition And The Via Lasciva

The Line of Intuition (5, Plate XX.) is seldom found on other types of hand than those of the Philosophic, the Conic, and the Psychic, but it is sometimes found on the Spatulate.

It takes more or less the formation of a semi-circle from the face of the Mount of Mercury to that of the Mount of the Moon, or may be found on the Mount of the Moon alone. It must not be confounded with the Hepatica, or Line of Health, but is found as a distinct mark in itself.

It denotes an extra highly-strung sensitive temperament, also presentiments, inspiration, clairvoyance of the highest kind, clear vivid dreams which often come to pass, intuition as to how things should be done, and very often manifests itself in inspired speaking and writing of the loftiest character.

It is much more often found on women's hands than on men's, although many cases have come under my notice of its being unusually clearly marked on some men's hands. In each case the possessor of it had most remarkable powers and unusual faculties, as well as the gift of intuition, even concerning purely mundane subjects that in an ordinary state they knew nothing whatever about.

I use the words "ordinary state" advisably here, because such people are not always in the condition of mind when these strange faculties may be employed. Several of these men were absolutely uneducated, and yet at times, when thrown into an inspired state, they were able to explain the most intricate problems with the greatest accuracy. If asked, however, from where they obtained their knowledge, they were only able to reply that "it came to them" when in certain moods.

One man I knew well had such remarkable dreams of coming events that he was able to warn many people weeks and months in advance of dangers that lay before them, and his warnings in many cases saved life.

With all people who were gifted in this way I have noticed that they completely lost their strange powers the moment they indulged in alcohol of any kind.

The Via Lasciva

This is a strange mark (6, Plate XX.) which takes the form also somewhat of a semi-circle, but in this case it connects the Mount of the Moon with that of Venus, or it may simply run off the hand from the lower part of the Mount of Luna into the wrist.

The first-mentioned formation indicates unbridled sensuality and passion, and where it cuts through the Line of Life it indicates death, but one usually brought about in connection with the licentiousness that it denotes.

This Line running from the Mount of the Moon into the wrist denotes the most sensual dreams, desires, and imaginings, but, unlike the other class, it is usually only dangerous to the person on whose hand it is found.

In both cases there is generally a tendency towards the taking of drugs such as opium, morphine, especially when the hand is noted to be soft, full, and flabby. With a firm hard palm the subject usually indulges in excessive drinking fits, and when under drink seems to have no control whatever.

If the Line of Head is found weak-looking, full of islands and descending downwards on the Mount of the Moon, insanity or the worst form of degeneracy will sooner or later destroy the whole character and career.

Chapter XIII
"la Croix Mystique", The Ring Of Solomon

What is called "La Croix Mystique" is found in the quadrangle of the hand between the Lines of Heart and Head (7, Plate XX.).

It is more usually found in the centre of this part of the hand, but it may be also found nearer the one side of the quadrangle or the other.

This mark denotes a natural gift or talent for mysticism and occultism of all kinds.

When placed nearer Jupiter, it denotes the employment of these studies more to gratify the subject's own pride or ambition than the following out of such things for their own sake.

When it is in the centre of the quadrangle, across the Line of Fate, or immediately under the Mount of Saturn, such studies become more of a religion or are followed for their own worth and the influence and truth of occultism will play a leading rôle in the whole career. Most likely the possessor of this mark will follow it as a profession, or will crystallise his researches into the form of books.

When this mark lies lower down in the quadrangle, nearer to the Mount of the Moon, the subject will study some form of occultism more from a superstitious standpoint than any other. None the less, he will be likely to succeed in doing so, and influence other people through his studies, and with this latter form he will be more likely to write beautiful mystic poetry with the prophetic note running through it very strongly.

The Ring Of Solomon

The Ring of Solomon is also one of these strange marks of mysticism and occultism, but in this latter case, owing probably to the qualities signified by the Mount of Jupiter, its possessor will aim at having the power of a master or an adept in such subjects (8, Plate XX.).

Chapter XIV
Travels, Voyages And Accidents

Travels and voyages may be seen on the hand by the little lines that leave the Line of Life and bend over towards the Mount of the Moon and also by the lines found on this Mount (2, Plate XXPlate XXI.).

When these fine lines of travel are seen on the Line of Life, by referring to the map showing dates (Plate XXVI.), it may be possible to obtain a very clear idea of when these travels take place.

When, however, the Line of Life itself divides, and one branch of it leans over towards or on to the Mount of the Moon (I, Plate XXI.), it denotes that the entire life will be full of change and travel. In such a case it will not be possible, except by the use of some gift such as clairvoyance, to tell accurately in advance the dates of voyages that will be undertaken.

Palmistry for All 145

If the Line of Life apparently leaves its ordinary course and sweeps over to the Mount of the Moon, the life will be one continual round of travel. The person will settle nowhere, and the end of the life in such a case will take place in some land far distant from the place of birth.

If the Line of Life has no line or branch leaving it and going in an opposite direction, but keeps to the form of a semi-circle round the Mount of Venus, then such a life will be remarkably free from change and travel, and the person will remain all his life in the land of his birth (3-3, Plate XXI.).

When a travel Line from the Line of Life ends in a small cross the journey undertaken will end in disappointment (4, Plate XXI).

When the Line ends in a square, there will be great danger to the subject on such a journey, but he will escape, as the square is a sign of preservation from danger.

When the Line ends in an island, the journey will end in loss (5, Plate XXI.).

When the Travel Line crosses over near or on to the Mount of the Moon and ends in a fork or a circle, there will be great danger of the subject losing his life in undertaking such a journey.

There is always more danger in traveling on water when the subject is found to be born in the following dates:

(1) Between the 21st of June and the 21st of July.

(2) The 21st of October and the 21st of November.

(3) Between the 21st of February and the 21st of March.

There is more likelihood of danger from collision of trains and accidents on land when the subject is born between:

(1) The 21st of April and 21st of May.

(2) The 21st of August and the 21st of September.

(3) The 21st of December and the 21st of January.

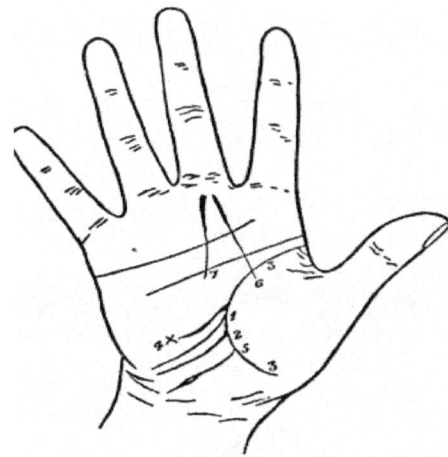

PLATE XXI. TRAVELS, VOYAGES, ACCIDENTS AND DESCENDING LINES PROM THE MOUNTS.

Danger from storms, tornadoes, thunder and lightning, is more likely to occur when people are traveling whose birthdays fall between:

(1) The 21st of May and the 21st of June.

(2) The 21st of September and the 21st of October.

(3) The 21st of January and the 21st of February.

Accidents

Accidents are generally marked by lines descending from the Mount of Saturn and touching the Line of Life (6, Plate XXI.).

When falling on the Line of Head, they increase the danger to the head itself (7, Plate XXI.).

Descending lines are those that look thicker on the Mount and taper as they come downwards.

Chapter XV
The Island, The Circle, The Spot, And The Grille

The Island is never a fortunate sign. Where ever it makes its appearance, it reduces the promise of the Line or Mount on which it may be found.

On the Line of Life it shows delicacy or illness at that particular date where it appears (1, Plate XXII.).

On the Line of Head, weakness of the brain, danger of brain illness (2, Plate XXII.).

On the Line of Heart, weakness of the heart (3, Plate XXII.), and especially so when under the Mount of the Sun.

On the Line of Fate, heavy loss in worldly matters, worry, and anxiety about the subject's destiny (4, Plate XXII.).

On the Line of Sun, loss of position and generally by some scandal (5, Plate XXII.).

On the Line of Health, serious illness (6, Plate XXII.); if on the upper part of the Line and with small round finger-nails, throat and bronchial troubles. With long nails, delicacy of the lungs and chest. With short nails without moons, bad circulation and weak action of the heart; and with very flat nails, nerve diseases and paralysis (*see* Nails, page 161).

Lower down on the Line of Health on the Mount of the Moon, it indicates a grave tendency towards kidney and bladder troubles (7, Plate XXII.).

Any Line that forms itself into an island or that runs into one, is a bad sign for that Line or particular part of the hand on which it is found. An island on any of the Mounts weakens the qualities of what the Mount expresses.

The Circle

On the Mount of the Sun the Circle is favourable (8, Plate XXII.) in all other positions it is unfavourable. On the Mount of the Moon it threatens death from drowning.

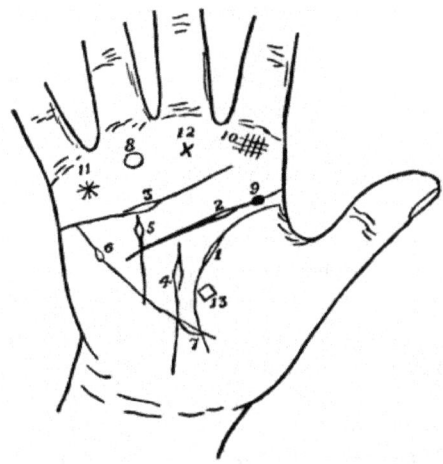

PLATE XXII. THE ISLAND, THE CIRCLE, THE SPOT, THE GRILLE, THE STAR, THE SQUARE.

The Spot

The Spot is a sign of temporary arrest of the qualities of any Line on which it may be found.

On the Line of Head, shock or injury. (9, Plate XXII.)
On the Line of Life, sudden illness.
On the Line of Health, fever.
On all the other Lines it appears to have less significance.

The Grille

The Grille (10, Plate XXII.) is very often seen on the Mounts of the Hand. It denotes difficulties and obstacles in connection with whatever the Mount represents, and a lack of success in whatever quality or talent the Mount symbolises.

Chapter XVI
The Star, The Cross, The Square

The Star (11, Plate XXII.) is with only one exception a most fortunate mark to possess. On the Mount of Jupiter, the Star promises added honour, power, and position.

On the Mount of Sun, it gives riches and glory, but generally associated with a public life.

On the Mount of Mercury, unusual success in commerce, business, science, or great eloquence, according to other indications of the hand. (11, Plate XXII.)

On the Mount of Mars under Jupiter, great distinction and celebrity in martial life or in some one decisive battle, which gives renown to the rest of the career, like a Wellington at Waterloo.

On the Mount of Mars under Mercury, it gives honour won by the mentality fighting the battle of life (*see* Mounts, page 163).

On the Mount of the Moon it is a sign of great celebrity arising from the qualities of this Mount, viz., through the imagination or inventive faculties.

On the Mount of Venus the Star on the centre of this Mount is also a sign of success, but in relation to animal magnetism and sensuality it gives extraordinary success with the opposite sex.

On the Mount of Saturn it is the one unfavourable sign of this particular mark, and on this Mount it gives distinction, but one to be dreaded. Such a person will be the plaything of destiny, a man cast for some terrible part in the tragedy of life. Such a man's life will end in some terrible disaster, but one which will cause his name to be on everyone's lips. A king perhaps, but one crowned by doom.

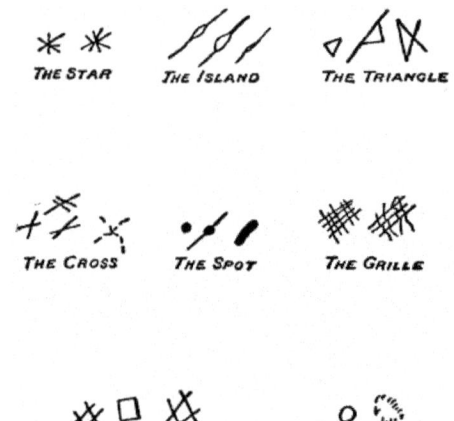

PLATE XXIII. MINOR MARKS AND SIGNS.

The Cross

This sign is the direct opposite to the preceding sign, and has only one favourable position, viz., on the Mount of Jupiter where it indicates some extraordinary fortunate affection which will come into the life. On all the other Mounts it is evil.

On the Mount of Saturn, violent death. (12, Plate XXII.)

On the Mount of Sun, disappointment in riches.

On the Mount of Mercury, dishonesty.

On the Mount of Mars (under Mercury) great opposition.

On the Mount of Mars (under Jupiter) violence and even death from quarrels.

On the Mount of the Moon it denotes a fatal influence to the imagination. Such a man will deceive himself. When low down on this Mount it foreshadows death by drowning.

On the Mount of Venus it indicates some fatal influence of the affections.

Above the Line of Head it foretells an accident or injury to the head.

Above the Line of Heart, the sudden death of some loved one.

The Square

The Square (13, Plate XXII.) is usually called the Mark of Preservation. It shows escape from dangers at that particular moment where it appears.

When on the Line of Life it means preservation from death. (13, Plate XXII.)

On the Line of Fate, preservation from loss, and so on with each quality represented by the different lines.

Chapter XVII
Different Classes Of Lines

The lines on the palm should be clearly marked, a good pink or reddish colour, and they should be free from breaks, crosses, holes or irregularities of all kinds.

When very pale in colour they show lack of force and loss of energy, and often poor health.

When extremely red they indicate excessive energy and a rather violent disposition.

When yellow in colour they denote a tendency to biliousness and liver complaints, and tell in consequence of a melancholy morose nature.

Forked lines are generally good and increase the quality of the special indication. When at the end of the Line of Head, the fork gives more of what is called a dual mentality and less power of concentration on any one subject. (Plate XXIV.)

Spots on a Line weaken it and arrest its growth.

Tasselled Lines (Plate XXIV.) are not good signs. They weaken any indication the line itself denotes, and at the end of a Life Line they foreshadow loss of all nervous energy.

Wavy Lines (Plate XXIV.) show uncertainty, lack of decision and want of force.

Broken Lines (Plate XXIV.) destroy the meaning of the line at the particular place where the break appears, but if one line ends above the other, the break is not so bad and the quality of the line will be continued.

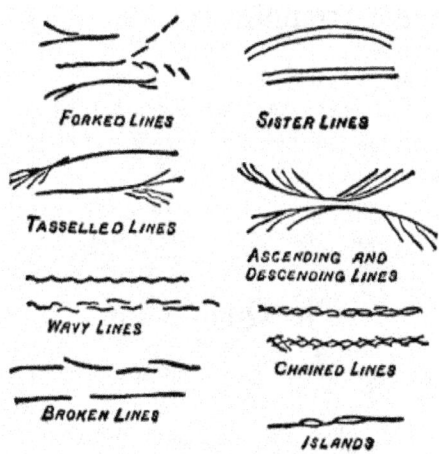

PLATE XXIV. MINOR MARKS AND SIGNS.

Sister Lines (Plate XXIV.) increase or double the power of any line, and when lying close together at the Line of Head, they give it great power and promise.

Islands (Plate XXIV.) are always evil and denote weakness or failure of the Line or Mount on which they may be found.

Ascending Lines (Plate XXIV.) are good from any line from which they spring. From the Line of Life they denote increased energy wherever they make their appearance. If they run up to any particular Mount or part of the hand, they show that the increased effort or energy will be in that particular direction.

Descending Lines (Plate XXIV.) are the reverse and mean loss of power.

Chained Lines show lack of force or fixity of purpose. (Plate XXIV.).

When the entire hand is covered with a network of small lines, it denotes a highly nervous disposition and usually great mental worry and lack of decision.

Right And Left Hands

Both the hands should be examined together to see if they accord. When they do, the indication of whatever the mark is, is more decided.

When something is marked on the left hand and not on the right, the tendency will be in the nature, but unless it is also marked on the right hand it will never bear fruit or come to any result. When the two hands are exactly alike, it denotes that the subject has not developed in any way from what heredity or Nature gave to him.

It must be remembered that we use the left side of the brain more than we do the right, and the nerves cross and go to the right hand. Consequently, it is this hand which denotes the developed or active brain, the left only giving the natural tendencies or inclinations.

To be scientific and accurate the student of this subject must always keep this rule before his mind and not be led away in his judgment by some "marvellously good line" that the subject may proudly call his attention to in the left hand, for such a mark will have no actual result unless it is also found on the right hand.

Chapter XVIII
The Great Triangle And The Quadrangle

The Great Triangle is formed by the lines of Head, Life, and Health (Plate XXV.). The larger this triangle is, the better will be the health, for the reason that the Line of Health will be further removed from the Life Line. The views of life will also be broader and the field of action as it were less limited.

When the upper angle (made by the Head and Life Lines) is acute, the subject will be more nervous, timid, and sensitive.

The Quadrangle

The Quadrangle, as its name implies, is that space lying between the Lines of Head and Heart. (Plate XXV.)

To be well marked, it should be even in shape and not narrow at either end.

When marked in this way it denotes balance of judgment, level-headedness in all things, and is a most excellent sign to have.

It represents man's disposition or mental attitude towards his fellow men. When extremely narrow it indicates narrowness of views and bigotry in regard to religion.

When excessively wide, it denotes a lack of judgment in all things and too much looseness of views for one's good.

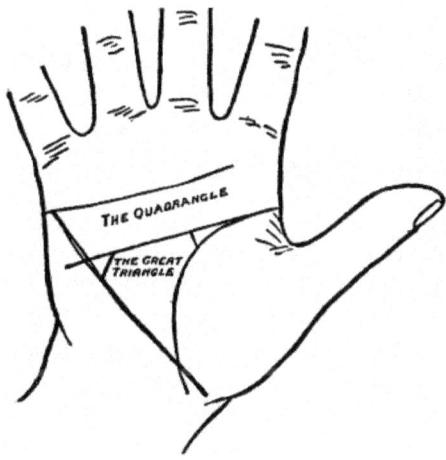

PLATE XXV. THE GREAT TRIANGLE AND THE QUADRANGLE.

Chapter XIX
How To Tell Time And Dates Of Principal Events In The Life

The most correct way in which to tell time by the hand is to divide the Line of Life into periods of seven years, and also the Line of Fate, following the accompanying design (Plate XXVI.).

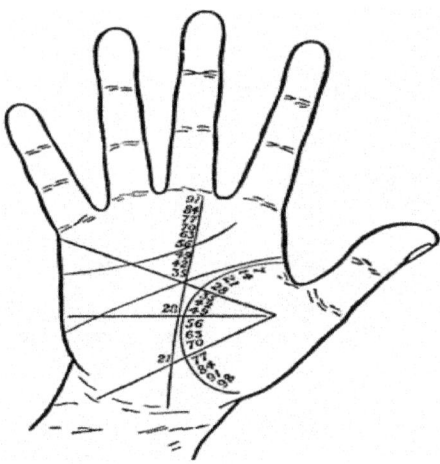

PLATE XXVI. TIME AND DATES OF PRINCIPAL EVENTS.

The Line of Head may also be divided into sections of seven years (*see* page 151).

This division into periods of seven is the most natural one of all, as the entire nature changes every seven years. Long experience has proved that, by dividing the hand in the manner shown in the accompanying illustration, the best possible results as regards dates are obtained.

I have also made the following curious observation concerning the most important years in people's careers, which I now publish in this work for the first time.

People born on the 1st, 10th, 19th, and 28th of any month, and especially in the months of July, August, and January, will find the following years of their lives the most eventful:

1st, 7th, 10th, 16th, 19th, 28th, 34th, 37th, 43d, 46th, 52d, 55th, 61st, and 70th.

Those born on the 2d, 11th, 20th, and 29th of any month, but more especially in July, August, and January, will find the following years of their lives the most eventful:

2d, 7th, 11th, 16th, 20th, 25th, 29th, 34th, 38th, 43d, 47th, 52d, 56th, and 70th.

Those born on the 3d, 12th, 21st, and 30th of any month, but more especially in the months of December and February, will find the following years of their lives the most eventful:

3d, 12th, 21st, 30th, 39th, 48th, 57th, 66th, and 75th.

Those born on the 4th, 13th, 22d, and 31st, especially in the months of July, August, and January, will find the followings years of their lives the most eventful:

1st, 4th, 10th, 13th, 19th, 22d, 28th, 31st, 37th, 40th, 46th, 49th, 55th, 58th, 64th, 67th, 73d, and 76th.

Those born on the 5th, 14th, and 23d of any month, but especially in the months of June and September, will find the following years of their lives the most eventful:

5th, 14th, 23d, 32d, 41st, 50th, 59th, 68th, and 77th.

Those born on the 6th, 15th, and 24th of any month, but especially in the months of May and October, will find the following years of their lives the most eventful:

6th, 15th, 24th, 33d, 42d, 51st, 60th, 69th, 78th, and 87th.

Those born on the 7th, 16th, and 25th of any month, especially in the months of July, August, and January, will find the following years of their lives the most eventful:

2d, 7th, 11th, 16th, 20th, 25th, 29th, 34th, 38th, 43d, 47th, 56th, 61st, 65th, 70th, 74th, and 79th.

Those born on the 8th, 17th, and 26th of any month, but more especially in the months of January, February, July, and August, will find the following years of their lives the most eventful:

8th, 17th, 26th, 35th, 44th, 53d, 62d, 71st, and 80th.

Those born on the 9th, 18th, and 27th of any month, but more especially in the months of April, October, and November, will find the following years of their lives the most eventful:

9th, 18th, 27th, 36th, 45th, 54th, 63d, 72d, and 81st.

This curious system it will be seen has embraced every day of every month that people can be born on. It is based on a strange law of periodicity that after years of study I have found extremely accurate and wonderful in its meaning.

PART II
Cheirognomy or The Science of Interpreting the Shape of Hands

Chapter I
The Study Of The Shape Of The Hand

We now leave the domain of what must be considered Palmistry, the study of the Lines of the Palm—or Cheiromancy, as it was called by the Greeks from the word χείρ, the hand, and proceed to consider the meanings that can be derived from the shapes of the hands, fingers, etc., which is called Cheirognomy.

These two studies may be taken up separately, but by a knowledge of both the student will be doubly armed, especially in the reading of character.

To a judge of horseflesh the limbs of the horse give him such a fund of information as to the animals' breed, training, etc., that it enables him to draw conclusions that he could not otherwise obtain.

In the same way the shape of the hand gives an enormous wealth of information as to breed and peculiarities of human beings.

In a book of this nature I shall be able to give only the leading traits denoted by each type, but if readers wish to carry out this study further, I must refer them to my larger works on the subject, in which the shapes of the hands are described in the fullest detail.

The most casual observation of character as shown by the formation of hands will soon convince any person of the value of this study. Even in itself it possesses the most far-reaching possibilities in helping to a clear understanding of the difference that exists in races, their various blends of types, that have now spread themselves by intermarriage and travel over the surface of the earth.

For example, the difference in the shape of the hands of the French and German or the French and English races would convince any thinking person that temperament and disposition are indeed largely indicated by the shape of the hand itself.

It is even a remarkable thing that though work and exercise may enlarge and broaden the hand, yet the type to which it belongs is never destroyed, but can be easily detected by anyone who has made a study of such matters.

The Seven Types or Shapes of Hands are as follows:

(1) The Elementary—or lowest type.

(2) The Square—or the useful hand.

(3) The Spatulate—or nervous active type.

(4) The Philosophic—or jointed hand.

(5) The Conic—or the artistic type.

(6) The Psychic—or the idealistic hand.

(7) The Mixed Hand.

THE SEVEN TYPES OF HANDS

The Elementary

As its name implies, the Elementary is the lowest type of all. It is just a little above the brute creation. This type is extremely short (Plate I., Part II.), thick set and brutal-looking. In passing I must draw the reader's attention to the fact that the shorter and thicker the hand is, the nearer the person is to the animal.

In examining this type one can therefore only expect to find it the expression of all that is coarse, brutal, and animal.

People having such hands naturally have very little mental development or ability. They are found engaged in occupations requiring only unskilled labour and the very lowest even of that.

They are violent in temper, and have little or no control over their passions or their anger. They are coarse in their ideas, possess little or no sentiment, no imagination or feeling, and it has been found that even the nerve system of such types is more or less in a state of non-development. They do not feel pain as the higher types of humanity feel it, and have little ambition except to eat, drink, and sleep.

Note.—The thumb is extremely short and low-set with the Elementary type.

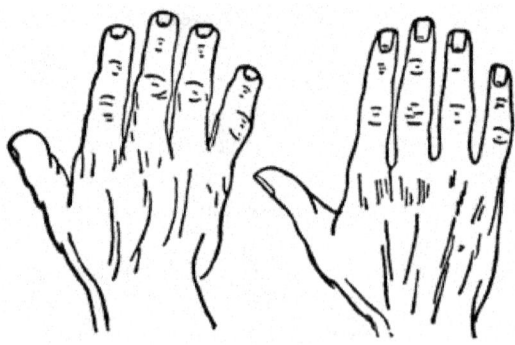

Fig. 1—THE ELEMENTARY HAND.
Fig. 2—THE SQUARE OR USEFUL HAND.

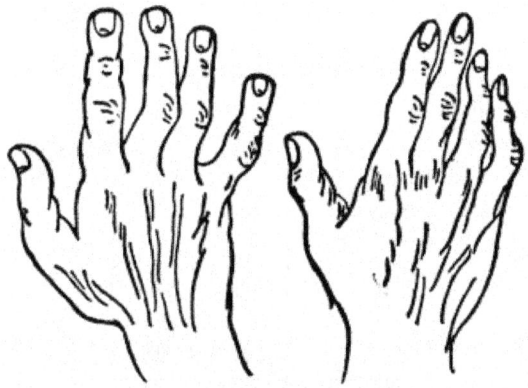

Fig. 3—THE SPATULATE HAND.
Fig. 4—THE PHILOSOPHIC HAND.
Plate I.—Part II.

The Square Type

The Square type (Plate I., Part II.,) is so designated on account of the palm being like a square in shape, or at least nearly so. Such a hand in fact "looks square." It is rather straight or even at the wrist, at the base of the fingers, and also at the sides. The fingers themselves also have a "square-cut" appearance. The thumb is, however, nearly always long, well-shaped, and set high on the palm, and stands well out from the palm.

The Square Hand is also called the practical or useful hand. People who possess this type are essentially practical, logical, and rather materialistic. They belong to the earth and the things of the earth. They have little imagination or idealism, they are solid, serious workers, methodical and painstaking in all they do. They believe in things only by proof and by their reason. They are often religious and even superstitious, but more from habit than from anything else.

They are determined and obstinate, especially if their thumbs are long and the first joint stiff (*see* Chapter on Thumbs, page 158).

They succeed in all lines of work that do not require imagination or the creative faculties, and as business men, lawyers, doctors, scientists, they do extremely well, and are generally to be found in such callings.

The Spatulate Hand

The Spatulate or active nervous type (Plate I., Part II.) is usually crooked or irregular looking, with large tips or pads at the ends of the fingers, rather like the spatula chemists use and from which peculiarity this type gets its name. The people who possess this type are in fact always "pounding" at something. They are full of untiring energy, enormous workers in everything they take up, and generally remarkable for their originality.

They are not built on the hard set square lines of the former type. These persons have enormous imagination, their creative faculties largely developed. They are inventive, unconventional, emotional, demonstrative, and in fact the complete opposite in character to the class who possesses the square type of hand.

The Spatulate type has also the palm irregular in shape. It may be wider at the base of the fingers than at the wrist, or it may be found *vice versa*.

In the first case they are then more practical in their work and views and less impulsive. With the larger development at the wrist, they are more carried away with their impulses, hasty and impetuous in temper, speech, and action.

The Philosophic Hand

The Philosophic Hand (Plate I., Part II.) received this name from the Greek φιλοσ—love, and σοφιχ—wisdom. When the Greeks made a study of hands they noticed that all those persons who possessed this type had a bent for philosophy in their blood that nothing could eradicate.

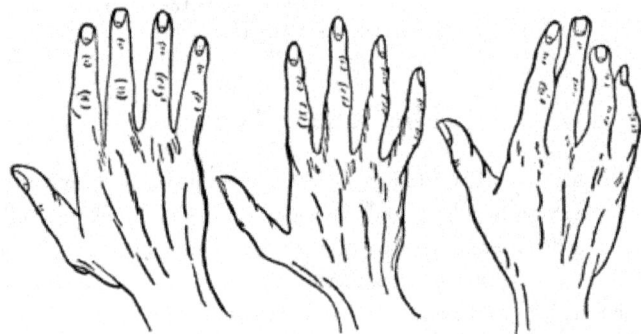

FIG. 1.—THE CONIC OR ARTISTIC HAND.
FIG. 2.—THE PSYCHIC OR IDEALISTIC HAND.
FIG. 3.—THE MIXED HAND.
PLATE II.— PART II.

The Philosophic Hand is long, bony, and angular with knotty joints, and is as a general rule fairly thin. People with this type of hand are always studious. They are great readers and usually have a strong tendency towards literature. They love sedentary work, and have a somewhat lonely, ascetic disposition. Perhaps on account of this quality they are very often found in church-life, or largely associated with religious movements. The monks of old, I mean those who compiled those wonderful manuscripts on doctrine, science, art, alchemy, and occult matters, all had this class of hand. In our modern times this type may be easily recognised, and the qualities it expresses remain the same even in the age of money-getting and machinery.

It is, however, more usual nowadays to find a slight modification of the true philosophic hand in that of the hand with the palm square and with the fingers only belonging to the philosophic type. In such cases the practical nature is a basis or foundation on which the studious mind builds its theories, its religion, its literary achievements, or its scientific researches.

As a rule the Line of Head on such hands is rather sloping, but it may also be found almost straight, and when it is, a more "level-headed" disposition will make more practical use of the studious nature. But speaking generally, people with this type of hand rarely accumulate as much wealth as those possessing the Square Hand.

The knotted or jointed fingers give carefulness and detail in work or study. They arrest the impulse of the brain, and so acquire time for thought and reflection.

The Philosophic Hand is one of the highest developments of the mental side of the human family.

The Conic Or Artistic Hand

The Conic, also called the Artistic, Hand (Plate II., Part II.), is always graceful looking, with the fingers tapering and pointed. It has, not only on account of its appearance but also because of the qualities it represents, been called the Artistic Hand.

Its possessor may not always paint pictures or design beautiful things, but he will have the emotional, artistic temperament, which loves beautiful surroundings, and is most sensitive to colour, music, and all the fine arts. It largely depends on the kind of Head Line and the will power shown by it, to determine whether its owner will develop the natural artistic temperament that he or she possesses.

Such hands being generally full, fleshy, or soft, there is always a decidedly pronounced indolence in the nature which, if not overcome, combats the hard work necessary to achieve any real result. All very emotional people have more or less the characteristics of this type, but great numbers simply squander their time in the appreciation of art, rather than in making the effort in themselves to create it.

The harder and firmer this type of hand is, the more likely it is to find that its possessor will really make something out of his artistic temperament.

The Psychic Or Idealistic Hand

This type (Plate II., Part II.), may in many ways be considered as the highest development of the hand on the purely mental plane, but from a worldly standpoint it is the least successful of all. Its possessors live in a world of dreams and ideals. They know little or nothing about the practical or purely material side of existence, and when they have to earn their own bread they gain so little that they usually starve.

These beautiful hands do not appear made for work in any sense. They are also too spiritual and frail to deal blows and hold their own in the battle of life. If they are supported by others, or have money of their own to live on, all may be well, and in such cases they will be likely to develop strange psychic gifts dealing with visions and ideals that some few may hear and understand. But if not, their fate as a rule is a sad one, they will easily be pushed aside by the rougher types of humanity or, in sheer helplessness, take their own lives, and so end the unequal struggle.

In constitution they are seldom strong physically, and consequently they are doubly unfitted for the struggle for existence.

The Mixed Hand

What is called the "Mixed Hand" (Plate II., Part II.), is an aggregation of all the types, or at least, some of them.

It is very often found having all the fingers different from one another, as for example one pointed, one square, or spatulate, and so on. Or sometimes the palm may be of one type, say spatulate, with all the fingers mixed.

Such persons are always versatility itself, but so changeable in purpose that they rarely succeed in making much out of any talents they may possess. They can generally do a little of everything but nothing well. They can talk on any subject that may crop up, but never impress their listeners with depth of thought on any subject.

It is only when the Line of Head is found on such hands clear and straight that there is a likelihood of these persons developing some one talent out of the versatility that this type gives.

Chapter II
The Thumb

In the judgment of character by the formation of the Hand, the Thumb is of about the same importance as the nose is to the face. It must be understood to represent the natural Will Power, whereas the Line of Head represents the Mental Will.

In my larger works on this subject I have gone into very deeply the medical reasons why character should be expressed by the Thumb and the extraordinary rôle it has played in civilization, and also in the various religions of the world.

The Thumb proper represents the three great worlds of ideas, viz., Love, Logic, and Will (Plate VI., Part II.).

Love is represented by the base of the Thumb which is covered on the hand by the Mount of Venus.

Logic is the middle phalange, and Will is the top or nail portion.

When these divisions are found large, the qualities are increased; when small, they play a smaller rôle in the life of the individual.

There are two distinct classes of Thumbs, the supple-jointed and the firm-jointed.

The former of these divisions is the Thumb bending outwards and supple at the joint underneath the nail (Fig. 2, Plate III.).

This denotes a nature pliable and adaptable to others, very broad-minded, rather unconventional, and not obstinate in its views of life. These characteristics will be increased if the Head Line be found sloping and bending downwards. If, however, the Line of Head be found lying straight across the palm, they are more conventional. The "supple-jointed" thumb also denotes generosity of mind both as regards thought and money. In all ways these people are more extravagant than people who have the straight firm-jointed thumb. In other words they "give more" even in what they think as well as in what they do.

The nearer the Thumb approaches the side of the hand, or the more it looks tied down or cramped to the palm, the more the subject is inclined to grasp or hold. The true miser has always a thumb cramped towards the hand, and the nail phalange as a rule slightly turned in, as if the mind wanted to grab hold or retain.

The supple-jointed Thumb is more impulsive in its desire to give than is the stiff-jointed class, whereas the latter type demands reflection before he even gives an opinion.

If a favour should be asked of the man with the supple-jointed Thumb, one should remember that he is more inclined to give in on the impulse of the moment, and if one does not press one's point home at once, he is likely first to promise, and later, on reflection, change his mind.

The man with the stiff-jointed Thumb (Fig. 3, Plate III.) on the contrary, is more likely to refuse at first and on reflection to agree to the proposition; but if he does make up his mind, he will stick to his judgment or opinion, and the more he is opposed the more determined he will be to hold to his view.

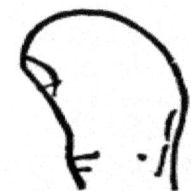

Fig. 1.—THE CLUBBED THUMB.

Fig. 2.—THE SUPPLE-JOINTED THUMB.
Fig. 3.—THE FIRM-JOINTED THUMB.

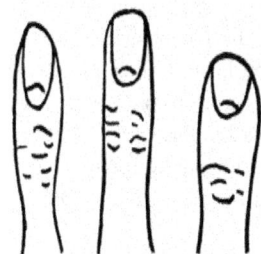

Fig. 4.—THE WAIST-LIKE THUMB.
Fig. 5.—THE STRAIGHT THUMB.
Fig. 6.—THE ELEMENTARY THUMB.
Plate III.— Part II.

The firm-jointed thumb is then the outward sign of a more resisting nature, and the longer the first or nail phalange is, the stronger and more powerful the Will force.

These people seldom make friends so easily or rapidly as those belonging to the other type. On a railway journey they rarely begin a conversation with a fellow traveler, and if they have to do so it will generally be in the form of an argument that "the window must be left open or shut," as the case may be. Heaven help the other poor traveler if he should also happen to have a stiff thumb, and oppose his ideas to those of the first.

The supple-jointed class, on the contrary, enter readily into conversation with strangers, and they often make their greatest friends while traveling. They are affable, charming companions, and give in readily to the wishes of others. In fact, this quality inclines to a weakness that should be guarded against. Among all those men and women who take the "easiest way" a large majority will be found to have very supple-jointed thumbs. This, however, will be greatly qualified by the position and appearance of the Line of Head, the indicator of the developed mental Will.

To have a supple lower or middle joint does not relate to the Will but to the phalange of Logic of the possessor. When this second joint is found supple the subject adapts himself to circumstances rather than to persons. He reasons out that he must bend or adapt himself to the conditions or circumstances of the life in which he is placed.

The Clubbed Thumb (Fig. 1, Plate III.), is so called from its being thick like a club. People possessing this class of Thumb belong to the Elementary type as far as Will is concerned. They are brutal and like animals in their unreasonable obstinacy. If they are opposed they fly into ungovernable passions and blind rages. They have no control over themselves, and are liable to go to any extreme of violence or crime during one of their tempers. In fact the clubbed-shaped Thumb has also been designated "the murderer's thumb" on account of so many murderers having been found with this formation.

The possessor of a Clubbed Thumb could not, however, plan out or premeditate a crime, for he would not have the determined Will or power of reason to think it out.

The shorter the Thumb, the nearer the possessor is to the brute in passion and lack of self-control.

The "waist-like" Thumb (Fig. 4, Plate III.), and the "straight" formation (Fig. 5), must also be considered as the opposite of one another in their characteristics, but in this case the difference is in the quality of Logic or Reason. The former will not use or depend much on such things, he will rely, on the contrary, on tact and diplomacy to gain his point or win his way. The second class have little or no tact, but in all matters depend on argument and reason.

The third phalange of the Thumb, which is placed under the designation of Love (Plate VI., Part II.), when found long, denotes more control over the quality of Love or Sensuality; when short and thick-set, the passion or sensual nature is more brutal and animal.

The space at my disposal in this work will not allow me to go deeper into all the shades of character that can be made out by a study of the Thumb alone, but I think I have said enough to show my readers the great truth in D'Arpentigny's words that "the Thumb individualises the man."

Chapter III
The Fingers—length To One Another

The Smooth And The Knotty

The First Finger is called the Finger of Jupiter.

The Second is called the Finger of Saturn.

The Third is called the Finger of The Sun.

The Fourth is called the Finger of Mercury.

The Finger of Jupiter, when long, gives love of power and command over others. When short it denotes dislike of responsibility and lack of ambition.

The Finger of Saturn when long gives prudence, love of solitude and a reserved, studious disposition. When short it denotes frivolity and general lack of seriousness in all things.

The Finger of the Sun when long gives love of the beautiful, desire for celebrity and fame, but when excessively long, the tendency inclines more toward notoriety, risk in speculation, the love of money and gambling. When short it denotes a dislike of all these things.

The Finger of Mercury when long gives mental power, grasp of languages, and power of expression, especially in speech. When short it denotes difficulty in speaking, and in the expression of thoughts. When crooked, with an irregular Head Line, it is an evil sign of the Mentality.

The fingers should be long in proportion to the palm; they then denote greater intellectuality and mental power. When short and stubby looking, the subject is inclined to animalism and gross materialism.

When the fingers lean towards one another, they take after the qualities expressed by the finger towards which they lean.

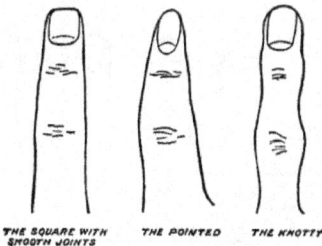

PLATE IV.—PART II. DIFFERENT SHAPES OF FINGERS.

A wide space between the thumb and first finger denotes independence of will and fearlessness.

When wide between the first and second fingers, independence of thought; between the second and third fingers, independence of circumstances; and wide between the third and fourth fingers, independence of action.

When the fingers are found loose and inclined to curve backwards, the subject is "open-minded" and quick to grasp ideas or suggestions. They will not, however, have the more methodical stick-at-it quality of those whose fingers are found firm and stiff.

When the fingers are curved inwards, the subject is slower to grasp new ideas, very cautious, and inclined to hold on to what he knows or what he has.

Smooth-jointed fingers are more impulsive than those with "knotty joints". The "knotty joints" arrest the impetuousness of the disposition and give reflection, love of detail in all their work and are more frequently found in the hands of all great organisers and those who require thought and reflection in carrying out their plans.

Chapter IV
The Nails Of The Hand

A study of the Nails of the Hand is a remarkably accurate guide to many diseases. This part of Palmistry is now recognised by the majority of medical men, who seldom fail quietly to observe the appearance of the nails on a patient's hand.

They are peculiarly indicative of hereditary diseases, especially lungs, heart, nerves, and spine.

They are divided into four very distinct classes. Long, Short, Broad, and Narrow.

Long Nails

When the Nails are found very long, the general constitution never appears to be so strong as when they are medium in size.

Persons with long Nails are more liable to all diseases of the Lungs and Chest (Plate V., Part II.), and still more so when these long Nails are seen ribbed or fluted, with the ribs running upward from the base to the edge of the nail.

The same type of Nail, but shorter in appearance, indicates that the delicacy lies higher up towards the throat, and denotes tendencies for laryngitis, inflammation of the throat, and all bronchial troubles.

When especially long Nails are bluish in colour, they denote a still more delicate constitution, coupled with poor circulation of the blood.

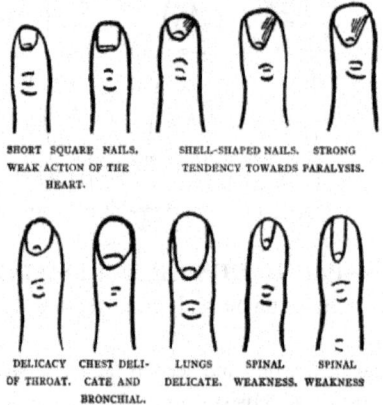

SHORT SQUARE NAILS. WEAK ACTION OF THE HEART. SHELL-SHAPED NAILS. STRONG TENDENCY TOWARDS PARALYSIS.

DELICACY OF THROAT. CHEST DELICATE AND BRONCHIAL. LUNGS DELICATE. SPINAL WEAKNESS. SPINAL WEAKNESS

PLATE V.— PART II.

Short Nails

Nails short in appearance denote a tendency towards weak action of the heart, more especially so when the "moons" are very small or barely noticeable. When the Nails appear very flat and sunk into the flesh at the base they denote nerve diseases. When they are "ribbed" across the Nail from side to side, the danger is still more apparent.

When a deep furrow is found across the Nail, it is a sign in any hand that an unusual call has recently been made on the nervous system by illness. If the following rule be studied, the date of this illness or strain can be very clearly indicated.

As it takes about nine months for a nail to grow out from the base to the outer edge, the nail can easily be divided into sections. When the furrow or very deep "rib" is seen close to the edge, the illness took place about nine months ago; when the furrow is seen about the centre, the date was about from four to five months, and when at the base, about one month previously.

White spots on the Nails are a sign of general delicacy, and when the Nail is seen covered with small white flecks, the whole nervous system is in a low state of health.

Long Narrow Nails

Very narrow Nails (Plate V., Part II.), show spinal weakness, and when extremely curved and very thin they indicate curvature of the spine and great delicacy of the constitution.

Flat Nails

When the Nails appear very flat and inclined to lift themselves up from the flesh towards their outer edge, the threatened danger is towards paralysis, and still more so when they look like a shell and are pointed towards the base (Plate V., Part II.). When these Nails are without any signs of moons, and whitish or bluish in colour, the disease is in a very advanced stage.

The Moons Of The Nails

Large "Moons" always denote strong action of the heart and rapid circulation of the blood, but when unusually large they indicate too much pressure on the heart, rapidity in its beat, the valves over-strained and danger of bursting some blood vessel in the heart or in the brain.

Small "Moons" indicate the reverse of this; they always denote poor circulation, weak action of the heart and anæmia of the brain.

When close to death the "Moons" are the first to take on a bluish look, and later on the entire Nail becomes blue or almost black in colour.

Chapter V
The Mounts Of The Hand And Their Meaning

The Mounts of the Hand (Plate VI., Part II.) vary in the most remarkable manner in accordance with the character and dispositions of races and their different temperaments.

In almost all the Southern and more emotional races, these Mounts are more noticeable than those belonging to Northern countries. It has been observed that all people with the Mounts apparent or prominent are more swayed by their feelings and emotions than those people who have flat palms and undeveloped Mounts.

The names given to the Mounts of the Hand are those also given to the seven principal planets that sway the destiny of our earth, viz., the Sun, Moon, Venus, Mercury, Mars, Jupiter, and Saturn.

These names were given to the Mounts by the Greek students of this subject, and were associated by them with the qualities attributed to these seven planets, such as:

Venus	=	Love, sensuality and passion.
Mars	=	Vitality, courage, fighting, etc.
Mercury	=	Mentality, commerce, science.
Moon	=	Imagination, romance, changeability.
Sun	=	Brilliancy, fruitfulness, success.
Jupiter	=	Ambition, power, domination.
Saturn	=	Reserve, melancholy, seriousness.

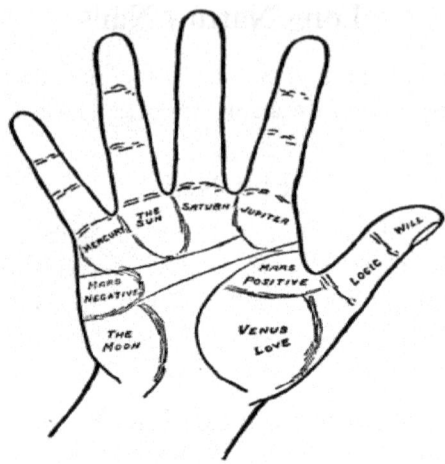

PLATE VI.—PART II. THE MOUNTS OF THE HAND

In my own long experience I could not help but remark the intimate relation between the effect of these great planets of our Universe and humanity in general. Although it would not be within the scope of this work to teach also Astrology in these pages, I must, however, in order to help all earnest students and readers of this book, put before them the following curious evidence of the influence of the planets on our lives. This is also demonstrated by the position and shape of the Mounts on the Hand, and, as far as I know, has never been published in any book dealing with Palmistry before.

In the accompanying pages it will be noticed that I have for the first time dealt with these Mounts as Positive and Negative. The following explanation of my reason for doing this should be of the greatest assistance to my readers, and will also be useful in showing the close relationship between the two sciences Astrology and Palmistry.

There are, it is well-known, in the Zodiac which surrounds our earth, what are called "the twelve Houses" of the seven principal planets of our Solar System.

The Zodiac itself is described both by Astronomers and Astrologers as a pathway in the Universe, about sixteen degrees broad, in which the planets travel. It is divided into twelve Signs or Houses of thirty degrees each, and our Sun enters a new sign on an average of every thirty days. At the end of twelve months it has completed the zodiacal circle of 360 degrees, or one Solar year.

The Sun, the creator of life, and itself the greatest mystery of our Universe, is in bulk 330,000 times larger than our earth. It therefore follows that in entering a new sign of the Zodiac, it changes the magnetic vibrations of the effect of each sign towards our earth. Consequently it is reasonable to presume that a person born, say in April, and another in May, would have very different characteristics and naturally a distinct destiny, because character is Fate or Destiny.

My readers will now easily follow me when I state that, especially as regards health and disease, the following tables concerning the Mounts of the Hand, taken in conjunction with the date of birth, will enable them, when reading the hand, to tell many things with an accuracy that will be most convincing both to themselves and to their hearers.

Chapter VI
The Mount Of Mars

This Mount has two positions on the palm (Plate VI., Part II.); the first is to be found immediately under the upper part of the Line of Life, and the other opposite to it in the space lying between the Line of Heart and the Line of Head. The first relates to the physical characteristics and the second to the mental.

The first if large is Positive, and it has more importance when the person is born between the dates of March 21st and April 21st, and in a minor way until April 28th, which portion of the year in the Zodiac is called the House of Mars (Positive).

The second is considered Negative, and it has more importance when the person is born between October 21st and November 21st, and in a minor way until November 28th, because in the Zodiac this portion of the year is denoted as the House of Mars (Negative).

We will now consider the difference of these two positions, how distinctly they affect the mind and temperament, and also their relation as to health and tendency towards disease.

The First Mount Of Mars

In the first Mount of Mars, at the commencement of the Line of Life, and especially when the subject is born in the House of Mars (March 21st to April 21st, and in a minor way until the 28th), he possesses a strong martial nature which will make its tendencies manifest in all actions of the life, whether the man be a business man, a soldier, or a leader of men in any line whatever.

These subjects are born fighters in every sense of the word. They brook little or no control in all their affairs; they aspire to be leaders in whatever career they undertake, and with even average intelligence they generally become heads of business houses or organisations and take on large responsibilities.

They have great obstinacy of purpose and determination, they resent all criticism, they are decided and dogmatic in all their views, and seldom ask the advice of others, until it is too late to alter their purpose for good or evil.

They must do everything their own way, and as they always believe their way is the only right one they resent the slightest interference from others, and will even turn on their best friend who may attempt to dissuade them from their plans or purpose.

They can only be handled or managed by kindness, patience, tact, or by their affections.

The slightest attempt to fight or coerce them will bring them up "in arms" in a moment. The temper is hasty and explosive, but at the same time quickly over, and when the storm subsides they bitterly regret the outburst of passion and the cruel things they may have said in the heat of the moment.

As a rule these people are good-natured and generous, but spasmodic and impulsive in all their actions. Their greatest fault lies in their impulsiveness and lack of self-control, and unless a good Line of Head be shown on the hands, they rush madly into all kinds of difficulties and dangers and often make a complete muddle of their opportunities and the magnificent powers of leadership that they nearly all possess.

These people as a rule are unhappy in their love affairs or domestic life. They rarely meet women who understand them, and if they are lucky enough to escape opposition from their wives, they usually meet with it in their children.

In health they are prone to fevers and blood diseases, especially in their early life. In youth they are also very liable to fits, epilepsy, severe headaches, often water on the brain, and suffer greatly with their teeth.

In old age they have a grave liability towards apoplexy, vertigo, pains in the head and softening of the brain, and especially so if on their hands the Line of Head looks frayed, or made up of little pieces like a chain.

Such people should be advised to cultivate repose self-control, and above all to avoid wines, spirits, and stimulants of all kinds, to which as a rule these natures are very much inclined.

They should endeavour to sleep more than any other class, to take more recreation and exercise in the open air, and above all things to curb their pride and control their temper.

The higher types of these subjects and those among them who practise self-restraint, can rise to almost any height in life and do great things for the benefit of their fellow men.

The Second Mount Of Mars

The second Mount of Mars, lying between the Heart and Head Line (Plate VI., Part II.), is more important when the subject is born between the dates of 21st October and the 21st November and until November 28th. In the Zodiac this period of the year is called the House of Mars Negative or Mental.

In character they are the complete opposite of the former type, all the Mars qualities being in the mind and in the mental attitude towards people and things.

The latter type are mentally very courageous, and possess *moral courage* more than physical. They hate to have scenes, or to be mixed up with physical violence or bloodshed.

They love to fight mentally, however, and in debates or arguments they also fight to the finish. They are more quietly determined than the former class of Mars subjects. They are even more obstinate in their views, but conceal their opinions, and often pass for assenting parties when in reality they are but waiting for the right opportunity to strike their "mental blow" and confuse their opponent.

These people make better organisers than leaders, and their mental martial spirit often finds a splendid field for their talents as the brain behind an army. In plans, tactics and strategy, in carefully thought-out stores of ammunitions, provisions, or in financial schemes that may bring ruin or discomfiture on a more warlike enemy.

When not highly cultivated or developed, they employ cunning and craft of every description to carry out their plans. They will stop at nothing to carry out their purpose. They can be the most treacherous and deadly enemies of all, and poison in opposition to the sword is one of the chief weapons they most readily employ.

All these Mars Negative people have a mysterious power of magnetism, which they seem almost unconsciously to use in their dealings with others. They make natural hypnotists and thought-readers, and have strong leanings towards occultism and secret societies of all kinds. When on a highly developed plane, they use these wonderful qualities for the good of others, especially if they take up the study of medicine or science, for which work they seem usually well suited.

Mars Negative people are generally so versatile and many-sided that they are the most difficult of all to place in some special career. If a good Line of Head be found on the hand, then there is nothing in the world of mental endeavour in which they will not make a success. It is a curious fact that these people seldom carry out what they were first trained for, and in fact in the course of their lives they are likely to change their profession or vocation as many times as the proverbial cat has lives.

The worst fault of this type is that they are rather too adaptable to their surroundings and to the people with whom they come in contact. If they are thrown with evil-minded persons they are inclined to adapt themselves to their companions and even attempt to "go one better," but if in contact with good influences they just as rapidly develop the best that is in them.

Their period of the Zodiac has from time immemorial been symbolised in their lower development as the figure of a scorpion wounding its own tail, and in their higher development that of an eagle with its head pointing upwards to the sky.

Such symbols perfectly illustrate the dual nature of the type under consideration. In their lower aspect no type can be more vicious or harmful, even to wounding themselves and bringing about their own destruction. In their higher form, however, there is probably no class whose spiritual nature can, like the eagle, soar to such heights or be so free from earthly ties.

Mars Negative people, especially when young, should above all things be carefully brought up with good companions. They should be especially warned to control their sex nature and be kept aloof from all perverse persons and evil books.

As regards health, this type is usually inclined to be both slight and delicate in their early years, but generally incline towards corpulency after passing middle life. Both the men and women have a likelihood of weakness or illness in the sex organs, especially in youth, also in the kidneys and the bladder, while in advanced years the stomach and digestive organs become disordered. All through their lives they should be most careful and abstemious in their diet.

Chapter VII
The Mount Of Jupiter And Its Meaning

The Mount of Jupiter is found at the base of the first finger (Plate VI., Part II.). When large, it shows desire to dominate, to rule and command others, to lead and organise, and to carry out some distinct object. But these good qualities will only be employed if the Line of Head is clear and long. When this line is poor and badly formed, then a large Mount of Jupiter gives pride, excess of vanity, a self-confident and a self-opinionated person. But on what is known as a good well-marked hand, there is no Mount more excellent and no surer indication of success from sheer strength of character and purpose.

This Mount may be considered Positive when a person is found born between November 21st and December 20th, and in a minor way until the 28th. These persons are naturally ambitious, fearless and determined in all they undertake, but in acting on their impulses, they generally "hit too straight from the shoulder," or show their ambition too plainly, and so arouse antagonism, opposition, and enmity.

They concentrate all their attention on whatever they may be doing at the moment and see no way but their own, especially if they feel the least opposition to their plans. They are, however, honourable and high principled in almost all they undertake and respond to any trust or confidence placed in them.

They are usually extremely truthful and bitterly resent any attempt at deception, and do not hesitate to unmask any effort to deceive others, even when such an action on their part may ruin their own plans.

They have great enterprise in business and all matters requiring organisation, and easily become the heads of businesses, or hold responsible positions in government offices or under the government. They rarely become politicians, for the simple reason that they cannot bear to bend to any party plans or schemes.

They are perhaps the most independent of all types in choosing their own careers. Because their father may have happened to be a clergyman will be no reason for them to follow his example or even hold the same views on religion.

It is for this reason that in early life such subjects are a cause of worry and anxiety to their parents; but they should always be allowed to choose their own career and even change it a dozen times if they wish, until at last they find their true vocation.

The great fault of this class is that they are inclined to go to extremes in all things, and in doing so exhaust their efforts, and then change and fly off in another direction. But in all cases where the Line of Head is well-marked, especially when lying straight across the palm, there is no height in position or responsibility that they may not reach.

Health

These subjects are more inclined to suffer with rheumatism and acid complaints than from any other form of disease, also inflammation of the tongue and throat, boils, carbuncles, eczema, and all skin troubles.

The Mount Of Jupiter (negative)

The Mount of Jupiter may be considered negative or mental when the subject is born between the dates of February 19th and March 20th, and in a slighter degree until the 28th.

In this case the ambition takes rather the mental form than what might be termed material. Brain work and brain development is more their speciality than other forms of effort.

They seem to possess a kind of natural understanding of things and easily acquire all sorts of knowledge about a large variety of things, especially the history of countries, races, peoples, geographical, botanical, and geological researches.

In spite of this mental ambition, these people are usually so very sensitive and so lacking in self-confidence that they find the greatest difficulty in carrying out their plans and making people believe in their projects. For this reason they appear to shrink from coming before the public, and have to stand aside and see others getting the credit for what really was their plan.

A great number of literary people, composers and artists are born in this period and exhibit all the qualities that it represents. It is again a strong clear Line of Head which, if found on the hand, will determine whether the mental will power is sufficient to make this type overcome its natural sensitiveness and use the great qualities they have to carry out their aims and ambitions.

Health

People born in this period suffer largely from despondency, insomnia, and a feeling of martyrdom. Like the Positive type of the same Mount, they are also much inclined towards rheumatism and disorders brought on through the blood.

They also suffer from internal chills, liver, and very often jaundice. Climate has the greatest possible effect upon their health, so they should endeavour to live in a bright, dry atmosphere and have plenty of air and exercise, and variety of change and travel.

Chapter VIII
The Mount Of Saturn And Its Meaning

The Mount of Saturn is found at the base of the second finger (*see* Plate VI., Part II.). Its chief characteristics are love of solitude, prudence, quiet determination, the study of serious sombre things, the belief in fatalism and in the ultimate destiny of all things.

A complete absence of this Mount indicates a more or less frivolous way of looking at life, while an exaggeration of it denotes an exaggeration of all the qualities it represents.

The Mount of Saturn may be considered Positive when the subject is found to be born between the following dates, December 21st and January 20th, and during the subsequent seven days while this period is fading out and being overlapped by the period following.

People born in these dates have strong will force and mentality, but they usually feel exceptionally lonely and isolated in going through life.

They are very much children of fate and circumstances, over which they appear to have no control, and seem to make or mar their careers independently of their strong will.

In character they are usually remarkable for their independence of thought and action, they also detest being under the restraint of others.

For kindness and sympathy they will do almost anything, but they usually feel so isolated that they scarcely believe in the affections that may be offered.

They have strange ideas of love and duty, and for this reason they are usually called somewhat peculiar by those few who attempt to penetrate their isolation.

They have a deeply devotional nature, even when appearing not to be religious, and they make every effort to do good, especially to the masses, even when there may be no likelihood of their getting recognition or reward for their efforts.

Such people as a rule feel the responsibilities of life too heavily and in consequence often become despondent and gloomy or retire into their own shell.

If at all inclined to be very religious, they generally go to extremes and become fanatical in any Church they may adopt.

Mysticism and occultism of all kinds appeal very strongly to their inner nature, but here again they are also inclined to go to extremes.

They almost worship clever, intellectual people, and are deep thinkers in all matters that interest them, but they cannot brook interference in their views from others.

They are often found holding positions of great responsibility, but in all matters fatalism seems to play a strange rôle in their life. They seem chosen to be the instrument or mouthpiece of Destiny, often hurling thousands to destruction in what they believe is their duty. If called upon to make a sacrifice of their own flesh and kin they will be the first to plunge the knife into the heart of their dearest.

Nearly all people born in this period are strange, strong characters, equally feared, loved, and hated.

Health

The chief tendencies towards illness with persons born in this period are towards rheumatism, gout, pains and swellings in the feet and legs, also accidents to the feet, knees, and limbs, trouble with the liver and kidneys, ruptures, and disease of the teeth and ears.

The Mount Of Saturn (negative)

The Mount of Saturn may be considered negative or mental when the person is found born between the dates of January 21st and February 18th, and also for the seven days following.

These people are like the preceding type in almost all things, except that the same things appear to affect them more mentally than physically.

They also feel lonely in life, but more mentally than the former type—they seem to feel less companionship in their ideas and thoughts, whereas the former feel it more in their lives and careers.

These latter types are more sensitive and very easily wounded in their feelings.

They read character instinctively and seem to "see through" people too easily to be really happy. They bitterly resent being taken in or deceived, and when they think they have been, they astonish people by the bitterness of their resentment.

They make loyal, true friends, if their feelings are once aroused, and they will undergo any sacrifice for the sake of a friend, but they will stop at nothing to avenge an injury if they think they have been deceived.

They are usually very active for the public good, and they give a good deal of their time and money to doing good, but in their own way. Like the positive type of Saturn they have very decided views of their own about religion and especially the regular observances and ceremonials of Church life.

They are very different from the previous type in that they usually take a keen interest in public meetings and large gatherings of people. They love theatres, concerts, and places of amusement, and yet always if they told the truth, they feel alone in life.

They have a quiet controlling power with their eyes, and although highly nervous people themselves, yet they have the greatest control over excitable and nervous patients and also over the insane. It is a strange fact that in the run of their careers they seem fated to be brought into contact with such cases.

Health

These people suffer most from the nerves of the stomach and the digestive organs, and ordinary remedies seem to fail entirely to relieve them.

They have as a rule poor circulation of the blood, cold feet and hands, very delicate teeth, and suffer much from accidents and hurts to the feet, ankles and limbs.

They seldom feel strong in health and yet they have enormous power of resistance, and when a call is made on their will power, they usually astonish every one by what they can stand, especially if they in any way think that their duty or principles are involved or at stake.

Chapter IX
The Mount Of The Sun And Its Meaning

The Mount of the Sun is found under the base of the third finger. To this Mount the Greeks also gave the name of Mount of Apollo (Plate VI., Part II.).

When large or well developed it indicates glory, publicity, a desire to shine before one's fellows. It is always considered a good Mount to have large.

It also indicates enthusiasm for the beautiful in all things, whether one follows an artistic calling or not. People with this Mount large, even if they have success in practical life, build beautiful houses or have artistic surroundings of some sort. They also have an expansive temperament, are generous and luxurious in all their tastes. They are bright and sunny by nature and have a forceful, happy, lucky personality.

This Mount may be considered Positive when the subject is found to be born between the dates of July 21st and August 20th, and generally until the 28th of this month, which portion of the Zodiac is called the "House of the Sun."

These people represent what may be called the heart force of the human race, and as a rule are generous and sympathetic even to an extreme.

They have great force of character and personality, and even when constrained by circumstances to exist in the lower walks of life, they play, even there, a rôle distinct from their fellows, and their clean-cut, well-marked personality is sure to make itself manifest.

At heart they are really most sympathetic, though they often seem to hide this quality on account of their strong sense of trying to force people to do what is right towards others.

They have no mercy for "weaklings" or evaders of the truth, and in brutal frankness they will even denounce their own children should they find them falling into evil ways.

They display the greatest loyalty if any friend of theirs is attacked, especially if in an underhand way. They love intensely and they hate intensely. Theirs is no middle path, for they must be either at one extreme or the other.

Although truthful and naturally honest they often get terribly deceived, and the danger is with such people that towards the sunset of their lives, the glorious Sun that has shone, as it were, through them gets darkened by the deceit and treachery of others and sets in clouds, or gets hidden before the ending of life's pathway comes to view.

Many of these people who have cheered others, who have brought their grand sunshine of good into the hearts of others, cannot cheer themselves when the twilight comes, and so they often fall victims to gloom and melancholy, and many commit suicide.

Among other marked characteristics these people are extremely proud and would sooner die than ask favours from others. They are extremely easily wounded through their pride and are unusually sensitive.

Impetuous and hot-tempered, they make many enemies, and when engaged in public life, which they are usually well fitted for, they often find themselves bitterly attacked in the most unscrupulous manner.

Health

Those born in the dates I have given, or who have the Mount of the Sun large, are most inclined to suffer with pains, palpitations, and trouble of the heart, head, and ears; with inflammation of the eyes, kidneys, and swellings and injuries to the feet.

Mount Of The Sun (negative)

This Mount may be considered Negative when the subject is found born between January 21st and February 18th, and for the seven days following.

In this case they are far more successful when managing for others than for themselves.

They are usually found most active in their plans towards the relief of all distress and for what they believe to be the public good.

They are also often as a class found in governmental positions, or as leaders of some party or section of public opinion. Usually they take the part of the "under dog," and cause themselves to be greatly abused and disliked by the richer and more powerful classes.

They seldom attract wealth as do those of the Positive type, who are usually lucky in money, and when they do they are inclined to impoverish themselves in their efforts to help those around them, or in the execution of their philanthropic plans for the good of the poorer classes.

In strange apparent contradiction to this, these people are usually excellent in business and in their financial plans, but again it is more for others than for themselves. Many of them make fortunes for others and keep the merest pittance for their own homes.

As a rule, they find great pleasure in public ceremonies, and meetings of all kinds. They love theatres and all places where large numbers of people congregate, and when wound up to the occasion they can display great eloquence, power of argument, and influence in debates. They rarely hold the positions they win for the run of their careers, they seem to play the rôle of the moment, and when that is passed they just as quickly retire into obscurity or into a quiet private life, and often end their days in the most unusual or unheard-of places.

Quite the reverse of the Positive type, these people seldom if ever commit suicide; on the contrary, they can endure any kind of martyrdom or suffering. They are buoyed up with the feeling they have done their duty to their fellow beings, and this feeling seems to sustain them against all disappointments, or losses or attacks on their name.

Health

These children of the Negative period of the Sun suffer mostly with the stomach and internal organs, also with poor circulation of blood, loss of natural heat, and with liver and kidney complaints.

They are also prone to have accidents to their bones, especially to limbs, knees, and ankles.

Very dry climates and plenty of sunlight is their greatest safeguard against all their maladies.

Chapter X
The Mount Of Mercury And Its Meaning

The Mount of Mercury is found under the base of the fourth finger (Plate VI., Part II.). On a good hand it is a favourable Mount to have, but on a hand shewing evil tendencies, especially mental, it increases the bad indications.

It seems to relate more to the mind than anything else. It gives quickness of brain, wit, thought, eloquence. It also relates to adaptability in science and commerce, but if evilly afflicted, it denotes mental excitability, nervousness, lack of concentration, trickiness in business, and everything that is unreliable in character.

This Mount should always be considered with the kind of Line of Head found on the hand.

With a Line of Head long and well marked, it increases all the promise of mental aptitude and success, but with a weak, badly marked, or irregular Head Line, it augments all its weak or bad indications.

The Mount Of Mercury (positive)

This Mount can be considered positive when the subject is found to be born between the dates of May 21st and June 20th, and until the 27th of that month, but during the last seven days its influence is considered dying out and not so strong.

People born in this period are represented in the Zodiac by the symbolism of the twins. It is a curious fact that all persons born in this part of the year are singularly dual in character and temperament. One side of their nature may, in fact, be described as perpetually pulling against the other, and although nearly always possessed with unusual intelligence, they often spoil their lives by lack of continuity in their plans and in their purpose.

They seldom seem to have a fixed idea of what they really want. They change their plans or their occupations at a moment's notice, and unless they chance to be very happily married, they are just as uncertain in marriage.

They are the most difficult of all classes to understand. In temperament they are hot and cold in the same moment, they may love passionately with one side of their nature and just as quickly dislike with the other.

They are very critical, and especially notice small faults or mannerisms in others, and they can express their views with a sarcasm that is as cutting as it is clever.

In all business dealings or affairs where a subtle, keen mentality is useful, they can out-distance all rivals, provided they are sufficiently interested to enter into the competition.

They are excellent in diplomacy and are gifted talkers, but they usually leave their listeners at the end of their conversation no wiser than they were at the beginning.

If taken as they are and with their moods, they are the most delightful people imaginable, but one must never expect them to be the same to-day that they were yesterday.

They believe that they are the most truthful persons in the world, and so they may be at the moment they are telling the story, but to them moments seem entire lives, and so in a day or a week the same story may have a totally different colouring.

None of these people will probably admit this to be true of his character, but a little study will convince anyone that it is a fairly accurate description of this subject's chief characteristics.

Mental work, especially the class of mental work that requires quickness of wit and change, appeals to them more than any other. They make clever actors, barristers, and a certain class of public speakers, also diplomatists, stock brokers, company promoters, or inventors of new methods in business. In all careers that require keenness of brain, they can attain success, provided they have developed a sufficient amount of will power and continuity of purpose to stick long enough to any one thing.

Health

Everything that can affect the nerves and the nervous system especially, afflicts these people.

Indigestion caused by nervous worry or anxiety, catalepsy, paralysis, afflictions of the tongue, stammering, insomnia, vivid dreams; to all such things they are specially liable. They are also inclined towards delicacy of the throat and bronchial tubes, and particularly to trouble with the nose and eyes.

The Mount Of Mercury (negative)

This Mount may be considered negative when the persons are born between August 21st and September 20th, and until the 27th, but these last seven days of this period are not so marked, but take more from the characteristics of the incoming sign.

People belonging to this negative type of the Mount of Mercury have all the good points of the positive class, and even some added in their favour. For example, they stick longer and with more continuity to whatever study or career they adopt. They have hardly the quickness or the brilliancy of the first type, but they have a more solid, plodding course of action, and as a general rule they make more out of their lives.

They are also more materialistic and practical in their views of life, but they analyse and reason everything from their own way of thinking outwards towards others. If they see a thing is right, it is right to them, and for this reason they are often found doing exactly the opposite from what one would expect.

Women born in this period are especially curious puzzles. They are either extremely virtuous or the direct opposite, either extremely truthful and conventional or the reverse; but whether good or bad, they are all a law unto themselves, and in all things they usually think of themselves first.

People born in this period often abandon their husbands or their children just because they think they ought to do so. They also are liable to change their religious views half way through life, or from the most conventional suddenly become the reverse. In the same way women who have commenced their career by leading unconventional lives, may just as suddenly become religious and enter some extremely severe order or community.

Again, as in the positive type, it is the Line of Head that must be carefully considered if one should endeavour to form an estimate of what they will eventually become.

If it be clear and straight, their best qualities will, as a rule, come to their rescue; but if weak or poorly marked, it is more than likely, especially with this class, that the evil side of the nature will in the end predominate.

Health

These people are more open to mental suggestion as far as health is concerned than any other class.

If they think they are ill it is quite sufficient that they are so, and they can become cured in exactly the same manner.

In reality they have excellent constitutions, except when they are ruined by taking drugs and medicines.

As they always imagine that they have something the matter, they are invariably the willing prey of quack doctors and every new cure that is advertised.

They can hardly pass a chemist's shop without buying something, and if they sit next to a doctor at a dinner table, they are certain to walk off with some prescription.

Their greatest fault is that they will persist in talking to everyone of their supposed ailments or afflictions, for the slightest ache, pain, or anything that concerns them, has the most exaggerated importance in their mind.

On the contrary, Nature can do more for these people than for any other class of humanity. Peace of mind, a country life, and plenty of fresh air will banish all their ills and ailments into oblivion.

But, if badly mated, or living in unhappy surroundings, their health quickly breaks up, and if they cannot make a change into happier conditions, then no medicine in all the world can help them.

Chapter XI
The Mount Of The Moon And Its Meaning

The Mount of the Moon, or as it is also called the Mount of Luna, is found on the base of the hand under the end of the Line of Head (Plate VI., Part II.).

This Mount relates to everything that has to do with the imaginative faculties, the emotional artistic temperament, romance, ideality, poetry, change of scenery, travel, and such like.

This Mount may be considered positive when it looks high or well-developed, and also when the subject is found to be born between the dates of June 21st and July 20th, and until July 27th.

People who belong to this positive class are gifted with strong imagination which tinges everything they do or say. They are intensely romantic, but idealistic in their desires, and have not that passionate or sensual nature that is given by the Mount of Venus on the opposite side of the palm.

As a rule they have the inventive faculties well developed, and succeed in inventions and in all new ideas in whatever careers they may have entered.

Even business people born in this period are remarkable for their originality, and the inventive manner in which they will tackle the most practical affair.

They are, however, inclined to speculate or gamble even with their chances, also in stocks, business or, in fact, anything in which they are engaged.

Although their imagination is large, they often achieve great success and make money in business. Some great financiers and heads of large organisations have been born in this period and have also had the Mount of Luna very highly developed on their hands.

It has been said "that what one sees in one's dreams one shall gain in reality," but the fact remains that imaginative people have been found among the most successful of all classes. Imagination may be another name for Inspiration.

People born in this period are seldom hide-bound by any rule of thumb or set convention. They love what is new in everything, and perhaps for this reason they love travel and change, and generally see the greater part of this planet before they voyage over the last river of all.

Change in every way affects their careers as it also does their lives. Even the successful members of this period have more ups and downs than almost any other class.

They rarely, however, give in to the blows of Fate. Their imagination probably helps them through, and they seldom remain down or down-hearted for long.

Inventors, a large number of artists, musicians, and composers are found among people of this type, but almost without exception they have a love of mystic and occult things, and their dreams and visions are tangible and clear.

These Children of the Moon owe much to the influence of their planet that they are even more magnetic and successful when the Moon appears in the heavens. Even their health appears to change and become better under her benign influence, and they should always be advised to commence their plans or operations when their planet is to be seen illuminating the skies.

That the Moon plays an important rôle in the affairs of this earth cannot for a moment be doubted. Recent discoveries are every day revealing more and more that her strange magnetic influence has a power almost beyond belief in its effect upon the growth of vegetables, and even inanimate things.

There are other thinkers besides those interested in occult subjects who have noticed the effect of this planet on mundane things. If the Moon can affect vegetables, eggs, and the growth of chickens, as it is proved to do, how much more easily and wonderfully it must affect the grey matter of the human brain, which is the most subtle and mysterious essence of all.

People born in the period I have mentioned should be most careful of those with whom they associate, because they are extraordinarily sensitive to the magnetism of others.

They should, if possible, avoid marrying early in life unless they are absolutely sure they have met their affinity. These natures both change and develop rapidly, and they have a strong tendency to "grow away" from those with whom they associate in early life. It is the same with partners in business; they should be as much as possible "on their own" or, if partnerships are made, they should not be of a binding or restricting order, and provision should always be made for the partnership to be dissolved when it has become irksome.

Health

These Children of the Moon are chiefly inclined towards all watery ailments and inflammatory diseases. In early life they are prone towards having water on the brain, gastric and dysentery attacks, and later in life, inflammation of the lungs and chest, pleurisy, and dropsy.

The Mount Of The Moon (negative)

This Mount is considered negative when it appears very flat on the hand, and it may also be taken as negative when people are found to be born between the dates of January 21st and February 20th, and in a minor degree, until about February 27th.

People born between these dates have good mental powers, but their imaginative faculties are seldom as much in evidence as is so strongly the case with the positive period.

These persons, on the contrary, are good and quiet reasoners-out of problems and matters relating to the organisation of business, and are also excellent in all forms of government work. They make splendid heads of departments and rise to any responsibility very quickly and easily.

They are high-minded and have very decided views on love, duty, and social life. They make great efforts to do good to others, but as a rule their best work is done towards helping the masses more than individuals.

They are extremely kind-hearted and love to give a helping hand when they can, but at the same time they have an unfortunate knack of making many bitter enemies, and when holding government positions they are most bitterly attacked by the opposition press. Their work seldom receives its proper recognition and reward until they have passed from their sphere of influence, or have left this world of mistrust and ingratitude.

They generally make excellent speakers, but more from "plain speaking," in a particular way of their own.

As a rule they espouse the unpopular cause and take the part of the under dog in the fight.

They make devoted and loyal friends once their friendship is aroused, but at the same time they are extremely sensitive and easily wounded by those they care for.

They are strongly inclined to be religious and generally bring their religious views into all they do. They are in danger of becoming too fanatical, and when opposed, they become extremely obstinate, dogmatic, and hard to manage.

Heavy responsibility for others suits them best of all, especially if such responsibility lies in the form of government work, or in some position of management.

Health

These people usually worry themselves into bad health. They overwork themselves and bring on nervous breakdowns, palpitation and weakness of the heart, and often paralysis. They suffer with the nerves of the stomach, acidity of the blood, rheumatism, liver complaints, and gout. They are particularly liable to meet with accidents to the feet, ankles, and limbs.

They should be very guarded when traveling by water, for they seldom get through life without sooner or later experiencing grave danger of drowning.

Chapter XII
The Mount Of Venus And Its Meaning

The portion of the palm under the base of the Thumb and inside the Line of Life is called the Mount of Venus (Plate VI., Part II.).

When well-formed and not too large, it denotes a desire for love and companionship, the desire to please, worship of beauty in every form, the artistic and emotional temperament, and it is usually very prominent in the hands of all artists, singers, and musicians.

This Mount, the science of Physiology teaches, covers one of the most important blood vessels in the palm, viz., the "Great Palmer Arch." If this loop or arch is large, it indicates a plentiful supply of blood and strong active circulation; consequently, the health is more robust. It is found that persons possessing this Mount well developed, being in active strong health, are naturally more full of passion than those individuals in poor health, and who, in consequence, have this portion of the hand either flat or poorly developed. Hence, when this Mount is large it has been considered to show passion and larger sensuality than when flat, flabby, or non-developed.

This Mount is therefore called Positive when high or large, and Negative when small or flat.

With the rest of the hand normal, this Mount well shaped is an excellent sign to have, as it denotes magnetism and attraction of one sex to the other, but if found together with vicious or abnormal signs in the hand, it increases those tendencies.

When considered with the birth date, as alluded to in the former chapters, it helps to throw considerable light on characteristics that might otherwise be overlooked.

The student may consider it Positive when the subject is born between April 20th and May 20th, and in a minor way until May 27th, the chief characteristics of this period being as follows:

These persons have a curious dominating power over others, and are found rather inclined to be too dogmatic in their opinions, and also often too unyielding and tyrannical. They are considered stiff-necked and obstinate, but the strange thing is that when they love they become the most abject slaves of all to the object of their devotion, and they will consider no sacrifice too great for that one being who holds or attracts their affection.

They are hospitable and generous, and especially love to entertain their friends. They make wonderfully good hosts, have great taste about food, and love to give excellent dinners.

They dress with great taste, and are generally considered richer than they really are, and they can make a good show on very little.

They are impulsive in their likes and dislikes, rather too frank and outspoken, quick in temper, and when their blood is up they have no restraint on what they say.

Their passion or temper is, however, quickly over, and when the storm is passed they are most regretful for the wounds their temper may have caused.

These types are most easily influenced by their surroundings, and become morbid and depressed when they are forced to live in gloomy and uncongenial conditions.

Neither the man nor woman born in this period should marry early, for their first attempt is usually a mistake. They are so independent in character that, especially if they marry early and find their mistake, they lead unconventional lives and get severely criticised in consequence.

They are inclined to be very jealous when their affections are roused, especially if the peace of the home is in any way disturbed.

Health

People born in this period have usually short or round-shaped nails which indicate a tendency to suffer with complaints of the throat and nose.[8] They also suffer, as a rule, with pains in the head and ears, swellings in the neck, and have a tendency towards tumours, appendicitis, and other internal troubles, chiefly relating to the intestines (*see* Chapter on Nails, page 161).

The mount of Venus (negative)

This Mount may be considered Negative when the subject is born between the dates of September 21st and October 20th, and in a minor way until October 27th, and with people born in this period it is seldom found so prominent. The fact is, that the affections these subjects possess may be just as intense, but more mental than physical.

Their love is spiritual rather than sensual, and they crave more for soul companionship than for that of the physical senses.

Of course there are exceptions to all rules, but these exceptions can be easily seen by watching if the Mount of Venus is large with people born in this period.

All mental characteristics rule, however, very strongly. Those born in this latter period have keen intuition and a mental balance of all things not given to the other class. They have presentiments and psychic experiences, dreams, clairvoyance, and such like, which they often spoil by their reasoning faculties, and they endeavour to answer all problems through the medium of their mind or mental faculties.

In love they are nearly always unhappy. They cannot "let themselves go," like the Positive Venus type. They hesitate and miss their opportunities whilst they think or reason, and so love goes by and often leaves them nothing but regret. They should be advised to act more on their first impressions and intuition, and take the opportunities that Fate throws in their way.

They occupy themselves very much with all mental questions concerning their fellow beings. They are often found studying Law, but more with the desire of improving it for others than for their own personal advantage.

They have a great desire for knowledge, and often spend their lives in studying abstruse subjects, but always weighing and balancing each point in the most conscientious manner. They make excellent doctors, judges, lawyers, but more as masters of some particular branch than that of gaining worldly advantage.

Health

The people born in this period are inclined to suffer from lack of physical strength, exhaustion of the nerves, depression of spirits, melancholia, intense feeling of loneliness, and such like. Also severe headaches, pains in the back, loins, and kidneys; just as in the case of those of the other period of this Venus sign they have a great tendency, especially the women, to suffer from internal ailments, and often undergo severe operations.

Chapter XIII
Advice To The Student. The Best Means To Make Casts Or Take Impressions Of The Hands

I would strongly advise students of this subject to make casts of hands in plaster of Paris, wax, or any other suitable material, in order to make a library or collection, both for their own private study, and also as a valuable record of their work.

Before I read any hands professionally, I had some thousands of casts, impressions on paper, and photographs of hands in my possession, and I found that I derived the most valuable aid from being able to analyse and study their shapes and markings at my leisure.

In making casts I would advise the very finest plaster of Paris to be used. When the plaster is worked up to the proper consistency, it is necessary to rub a fine oil into the hand before bringing it into contact with the plaster, as otherwise the hair may stick and so cause trouble and annoyance.

Dental wax heated in hot water and made very soft is also an excellent material to make moulds from, especially as it does not make a mess, and is very little trouble to employ.

The great disadvantage of making a collection of casts arises from the large space that such a collection will eventually occupy. To avoid this the student can also make a library of impressions of hands on paper, and keep them marked and numbered in a series of albums or scrap-books that may easily be obtained at any stationer's.

The best means of taking these impressions is to obtain a small gelatine roller used by printers for fine work, such as die stamping, a tube of printer's ink, and a small sheet of glass to roll the ink out until it covers the surface of the roller in an even way.

The roller may then be passed over the surface of the palm, the hand pressed firmly down on a smooth sheet of white paper, and with a little practice, most excellent impressions can easily be obtained.

When the impression is dry it can be dated, numbered, and placed in an album for reference.

In order to remove the black ink from the hand, powdered washing soap, well brushed into the hand with a nail brush, and a little hot water is all that will be found necessary.

These impressions taken with printer's ink are far better than those taken by smoking a sheet of paper by camphor, or by a candle, or any other means.

The best time for examining hands is during the day, first because the light is better and, above all, because the circulation of the blood does not redden the entire palm as it does at night, and the finer lines can consequently easily be detected.

As I described earlier in these pages, the right and left hands should be examined together to note what difference there may be in the shape and position of the lines, but the markings on the right hand are the only ones to be relied on.

Lastly, do not be for ever on the lookout for faults and failings in the subject whose hands you may be examining, remember no one is perfect, and that faults and failings may in the end be as stepping stones "by which we rise from our dead selves to higher things."

I Ching
Oracular Interpretation

Enos Long

Introduction

The *Yijing* or *Book of Changes* (previously spelled as *I Ching*) was intended as a strategic oracle for feudal lords in the Chinese Bronze Age, three thousand years ago, but with the pass of the centuries the book was evolving and become more philosophical, under the influence of Confucianism.

The *Book of Changes* is both an oracular medium and a book of wisdom, but it doesn't try to answer why we are here or where are we going after death; instead it focuses in the business of living. It is also a human attempt to throw light in the natural laws that command change.

Change is the natural state of this world. All things live in continuous flow. All beings are born, grow, evolve and finally decay and die. By observing the natural cycles, the sages of ancient times achieved an intuitive understanding of the laws that regulate change. Change is not chaotic, but it follows a pattern of development. Change is inevitable; situations never are completely static and unchanging

The 64 hexagrams (or sections) of the *Yijing* are a description of the different ways in which situations can evolve, they describe the steps of change and tell us how to act effectively at every moment.

Since change happens through time, each hexagram describes different times. There are times for advancing, times for retreating, times for peace, times for war, and so on. Each hexagram depicts a different time, a different pattern of change. This idea has echoes in the Bible (Ecclesiastes 3:1-8):

> *For everything there is a season, and a time for every purpose under heaven: a time to be born, and a time to die; a time to plant, and a time to pluck up that which is planted; a time to kill, and a time to heal; a time to break down, and a time to build up; a time to weep, and a time to laugh; a time to mourn, and a time to dance; a time to cast away stones, and a time to gather stones together; a time to embrace, and a time to refrain from embracing; a time to seek, and a time to lose; a time to keep, and a time to cast away; a time to tear, and a time to sew; a time to keep silence, and a time to speak; a time to love, and a time to hate; a time for war, and a time for peace.*

Knowing which kind of time we are experiencing allows us to take both preventive measures and to plan the best course of action in advance. In that way we can take the best course between the rough waves of life. Sometimes we may have a smooth sailing, and ride along with the tides with little effort, but in other cases we will have to work hard to manage well the situation.

Content and Structure

The *Yijing* describes change as a permanent cycle between two principles, one active and energetic and the other passive and yielding. Those two principles are the building blocks of the 64 hexagrams of the Book of Changes, they are called *yang* and *yin*. The next table shows how *yang* and *yin* look when drawn as hexagram's lines.

Figure	Description	Attributes
▬ ▬	Yin line	Feminine, passive, dark, cold, soft.
▬▬▬	Yang line	Masculine, active, light, hot, hard.

Yin and *yang* are relative and changing attributes that interact constantly. Firm and dominant behaviors are *yang*, weak and subordinate are *yin*. *Yang* and *yin* flow constantly, *yang* mutates into *yin* and vice-versa. The flow of *yang* and *yin* is evident in the adaptation to the needs of each moment; some situations require *yang* boldness, and other *yin* tolerance.

All hexagrams are drawings composed by six *yang* and *yin* lines (except the hexagrams 1 and 2, which are pure *yang* and pure *yin*).

The *yang* and *yin* lines form a binary system; by combining both types of lines in six different positions, 64 different hexagrams are created, forming the structure of the *Yijing*. All hexagrams are interconnected between them; when the oracle answers a question it is usual to receive a pair of hexagrams, which describes the flow of the situation.

Each line in an hexagram describes a step in a situation. The lines are counted from bottom to top, being the bottom line the first one. The *Yijing* hexagrams describe how a situation develops in time, starting with the first line and how it evolves until reaching its sixth line.

Each one of the 64 hexagrams has some texts attached to its drawing:

- The hexagram title, known as "hexagram tag", which is composed of the first one or two Chinese characters that form the Judgment.
- The *Judgment* (*guaci*), that describes the characteristics of the situation and its prognosis, either good or bad.
- The *Image* (*daxiang*), which analyzes the relation of the trigrams that comprise the hexagram and suggests the best course of action based on the symbolic value of them –you will learn more about the trigrams later–.
- Also there are six other texts (*yaoci*), one for each line, which describe the opportunities and dangers of each step.

Notice that this book always shows the original *Yijing* text as indented lines, our own commentaries to the *Yijing* are show below the indented lines for each text (Judgment, Image and Lines).

Example (from the hexagram 45):

Fourth Nine

Great good fortune.
No defect.

All the text following the two lines above (without indentation) is our commentary. "Great good fortune. No defect" is the original text.

Reality and discourse

The authors of the *Yijing* had different values from our contemporary society. They lived in a highly hierarchical, patriarchal and feudal society.

Because of this, some ideas or terminology used in this translation may be offensive or strange to a contemporary sensibility. In my comments on the *Yijing* original text, I try to show the original ideas from a modern point of view. I have used gender-neutral words as much as the English language allows me, without damaging the style of the text. Nevertheless, I have been as faithful to the original book text as I can, because my intention is to offer a reliable translation; otherwise my book would be a different book, and could not be called *I Ching* or *Yijing*.

The fundamental principles of life have not changed since the *Book of Changes* was written, we are no better or worse than our remote predecessors. The profound perceptions about human relations that the *Yijing* offers us are still valid and can be applied to our lives in the same way they were in ancient China.

Today as yesterday, fate is determined by both factors outside our reach and by our own capacity. The *Yijing* can help us to understand better the relation between external reality and our will, and because that it is an invaluable tool that will enhance the quality of our lives if we hear its message.

The Name of the Book

I used *I Ching* as title, because it's the title most people know. Here, inside this book I prefer to call it *Yijing*, because that is the accepted way of writing the pronunciation of the original Chinese name today, using the *pinyin* system. Note that *I Ching* and *Yijing* are simply two different ways of writing the pronunciation of the Chinese name in Western letters.

The name of the *Book of Changes*, written in traditional Chinese characters is:

Abridged Version

I CHING: Oracular Interpretation is an abridged version of **I Ching: Natal Chart and Oracular Interpretation**, by Enos Long.

How to consult the Oracle

It has been said that the answer is always hidden inside the question, meaning that you can only get the right answer if you know how to express your question clearly or if you know the right question.

The *Yijing* will not answer your questions unequivocally but instead it will tell you a moral history, sometimes including several protagonists and possible outcomes. It is your task to put yourself inside the history, to understand which part is yours and which is the relation between answer and question.

The oracle will chart for you the possibilities and dangers lurking ahead; if you open your intuition you will understand the message. Perhaps the answer will not be clear at first, but if you keep meditating over it, at some point you will grasp it.

The questions should be clear cut, avoiding asking about several possibilities at once. If you want to know which option is best, you should ask about one option first and then ask again about the other choice in a second consult; never include several alternatives in the same question. Think carefully what you want to ask, take your time; do not ask the oracle in a hurry or in a disturbed emotional state.

Examples:

Should I buy the car that John sells? This question is concise and will simplify understanding of the answer.

Should I go to Paris or Londres for my next holiday? This sort of question will prevent you from getting a clear answer.

Also you could simply ask the oracle to describe the situation, optionally giving a time frame.

Example:

What are my chances for getting a new job in the next six months?

Always write down your question before beginning your consult, afterwards you may write the answer in the same paper sheet.

Notice that the oracle may mirror your fears and expectancies in its answer, casting light over your hopes and fears.

In all cases the answer is mainly about you and your interaction with the world around you. The oracle cannot change an objective situation, but can help you to make the most within your circumstances, indicating both your shortcomings and strong points.

Sometimes you will apprehend intuitively the meaning of the answer at once, other times you may have to ponder about it for several days until at least you find what the answer means for you.

Getting your Yijing reading

The consultation process will generate six numbers, and you will draw a hexagram according to them.

Some people like to follow a predefined ritual before divination; if you are inclined to do so, the ritual may help you to put your mind at ease.

Indeed focusing your mind is what matters most, if you concentration wanders during the consultation it may affect the final outcome. In an ideal world you should not consult the *Yijing* if you are not relaxed and without distractions, an altered state of mind doesn't improve the practice of divination.

Using the coins to get an oracular reading

It is said that this method has been in use since the fourth century BC, the yarrow-stalks method is older, but because the coin-tossing method is faster and easier it is more widely used at the present time.

Traditionally three Chinese coins are used, but you can use any kind of coins, provided that all them are equal.

The coins should be tossed six times on a flat surface to get the six lines of a hexagram. You will draw the hexagram from bottom to top, according to how the coins fall, as the following table shows:

Coins	Numbers	Results
Three tails	2+2+2=6	A changing *yin* line —✗—
Three heads	3+3+3=9	A changing *yang* line —⊖—
2 tails and 1 head	2+2+3=7	A static *yang* line ▬▬▬
2 heads and 1 tail	3+3+2=8	A static *yin* line ▬ ▬

As you can see tails are worth 2 and heads 3; when you add the numbers for the three coins you will get 6, 7, 8 or 9 for each coin toss.

Broken lines are *yin* and whole lines are *yang*. If there are one or more changing lines, they will generate a second hexagram, with all changing lines inverted: *yin* will become *yang* and vice versa.

I Ching: Oracular Interpretation

After you toss the coins six times you will have a six lines drawing which depicts the oracle answer.

Example (the first column shows the line number and coin toss value for that line):

	Hex. 55	Hex. 21
L6: 6	━╳━	━━━━━
L5: 8	━━ ━━	━━ ━━
L4: 7	━━━━━	━━━━━
L3: 9	━━◯━━	━━ ━━
L2: 8	━━ ━━	━━ ━━
L1: 7	━━━━━	━━━━━

As you can see, the changing lines are drawn differently from the non-changing lines, adding an X or a circle in the middle.

In the previous example, the hexagram on the left (55) is the first one that you will draw. In this example, it has two changing lines: a *yang* line in the third position and a *yin* line in the sixth position.

The second hexagram (21) is similar to the first, but the two changing lines are replaced with their opposite ones. If the changing line is *yang*, replace it with a *yin* line and vice versa.

If there are no changing lines, you will get a single hexagram.

After drawing the hexagram/s see the Chart of the Trigrams and Hexagrams, to get the number/s of the hexagram/s.

Returning to the previous example, where we got the hexagram 55 that mutates to the 21; we must read the Judgment, the Image and the third and sixth lines of the hexagram 55, but only the Judgment and the Image of the hexagram 21.

The hexagram 55 is the starting point of a situation that will lead to hexagram 21, which describes the final situation. Note that both hexagrams can be linked in other ways, see **Understanding hexagram readings** to learn how to interpret hexagram readings better.

What are changing lines

We get a changing line when a coin toss has three tails or three heads –6 or 9 value–. The changing lines generate a second hexagram; if there are no changing lines, we get a single hexagram, which depicts a slowly evolving situation.

Changing lines are the steps of change that are activated in the hexagram reading; because that we will experience only the situations described by the changing lines we got.

Changing lines are also the lines more charged with energy. *Yang* and *yin* always change, *yang* mutates into *yin* and vice-versa. When the *yang* or *yin* lines are strongly charged with energy, they flip, mutating into its opposite, that is the reason changing lines generate a second hexagram.

Understanding hexagram readings

The interpretation of oracular responses is more of an art than a science, use the guidelines outlined below as useful tools to structure and analyze the answer got from the oracle, rather than absolute rules.

General guidelines

Although basically you would only need to read the changing lines, Judgment and Image, if you are not familiar with the Book of Changes, it would be good to read the entire hexagram, because that way you will get a clearer idea of the time you will have to live through.

After reading the full text of the hexagrams (it can be one or two, if there are changing lines), concentrate on the specific parts referring to the reading you got; first read the Judgment and the Image of the first hexagram, if there are changing lines, read them –only in the first hexagram– and then read the Judgment and the Image of the second hexagram.

If you got only one hexagram, the situation will not change very quickly and you should only read the Judgment and the Image to know how the circumstances will develop and what kind of behaviour is most appropriate.

If you got two hexagrams, the first hexagram describes the immediate situation and the second its future development, although both may be linked in other ways, see *How to interpret the second hexagram*, further down in this same section.

Sometimes the oracle will be easily understood as you read it, you will be able to see clearly how the answer you get applies to your life.

Other times, the answer may seem like a coded message, which has little to do with the reality that surrounds you; in that case, keep the oracular response in your mind, as a pending matter; meditate on it, don't dismiss it. Let some time go by, maybe you could reread the answer the next day. If you persist, at the some moment, you will be able to see clearly how the hexagram reading applies to your life.

How to interpret the changing lines

It is useful to apply some rules to avoid contradictions in the interpretations of answers with several changing lines and thus better understand the readings.

Always remember that the lines are numbered from bottom to top.

If the number of changing lines is between one and five, you must read all the changing lines in the first hexagram.

Note that if only the first or sixth line changes or if more than 4 lines are change, the emphasis will be on the second hexagram.

When several lines change, the top line is the most important, because it defines the conclusion of the situation. If there is a contradiction between the top line and other changing lines or the Judgment or Image, take the text from the top line as the most valid oracle.

Note that, within each hexagram the lines are identified with titles such as: First Six, Third Nine, Top Six, etc. This is because only changing lines are read, which are those with a value of 6 (*yin* lines) or 9 (*yang* lines). So "First Six" means the changing *yin* line in the first place, "Third Nine" means the changing *yang* line in the third place and "Top Six", means the changing *yin* line in the sixth place.

Alternative procedures for interpreting changing lines

Each changing line links the first hexagram with a second hexagram. If several lines change, a second hexagram would be produced, but each of these changing lines can also be changed individually –without modifying the other lines– generating a different hexagram for each line, read only the text of the changed line in that hexagram, it will serve as an additional explanation for the text of the original changing line.

Use this method with caution and only when several lines mutate and the meaning of a line needs to be clarified.

No line changes

There's only one hexagram. Read the Judgment and the Image. The situation is stable or may evolve slowly.

Only one line changes

Read the text of the changing line in the first hexagram, as well as the Judgment and Image of both hexagrams. The line takes precedence over the Judgment. In case of contradiction between the line and the Judgment, take the line as the valid oracle.

If the changing line is the top line, in the sixth position, the time of the first hexagram is passing; in that case read only the text of the changing line and the Judgment and Image of the second hexagram.

Two, three or four lines change

Read the changing lines in the first hexagram, in addition to reading the Judgment and the Image in both hexagrams.

Five lines change

Read the changing lines in the first hexagram, in addition to reading the Judgment and the Image in both hexagrams.

The situation described by the first hexagram will soon be over.

All lines change

The situation described by the first hexagram will conclude soon, so the second hexagram is the most important. Do not read the changing lines, only read the Judgment and Image of each hexagram.

Note: The hexagrams 1 and 2 have an special text to read when all lines mutate.

Only the first line changes

The first line has not yet entered fully into the situation, so you may pass to the second hexagram, without fully experiencing the time described by the first one.

Only the last line changes

The last line is saying goodbye to the situation, which is why you may pass to the second hexagram, without fully experiencing the time described by the first one.

Relationships between changing lines

The lines describe the evolution of the situation, from the bottom to the top, each line illustrates a different moment of the situation —which may be good or bad— but they also describe relationships between different people.

The lines have a natural hierarchy, which is why they often describe relationships between people of different social positions.

The first line represents someone in a low social position, with little experience, a beginner or someone who has no power. It can also indicate an influence or a person that is just entering the situation now.

The second line symbolizes a wife, an assistant, an employee with some responsibility, an official who is located far from the center of power, someone who has an internal task within an organization or a family.

The third line is placed in a transition point and can represent an intermediary.

The fourth line represents a minister, an executive officer who works in a position close to an authority figure, such as a leader, a manager or a ruler.

The fifth line represents a manager, a governor, a king, a leader or the head of a group or family.

The sixth line represents a sage, a spiritual leader, a counselor, or someone who has distanced himself from the situation. Sometimes it can represent someone who went too far and who becomes a transgressor.

Adjacent lines can be linked through a bond of solidarity, especially between *yang* and *yin* lines.

The lines in the positions 1st, 2nd, and 3rd are related to the lines in the 4th, 5th and 6th positions by a correspondence relationship. *Yang* lines correspond to *yin* lines and vice versa.

For all these reasons, the changing lines can describe the dynamics of a situation, showing its protagonists in action and how they relate to each other.

How to interpret the second hexagram

If there are one or more changing lines, you will have to interpret two hexagrams.

If you get two hexagrams, the first hexagram describes the immediate situation and the second its future development, although both can be linked in other ways.

In some situations the first hexagram describes the situation in the outside world (objective reality), and the second indicates the feelings and tendencies in the mind of the consultant (subjective reality).

Note that, as we indicated earlier, in the event that more than 4 lines mutate, the emphasis will be on the second hexagram.

The Trigrams

Each hexagram is composed of two trigrams, one corresponds to the three lower lines and the other to the three upper lines.

The interaction of both trigrams determines the character of the hexagram. In the Image, this interaction is used as an example to follow appropriate behavior for each hexagram.

The trigrams are associated with many symbolic meanings, which can greatly enrich the interpretation of the hexagrams.

The lower trigram is related to the inner world: feelings, judgments and hopes and the superior to the external world: the objective situation.

A practical example

The following oracular answer is an answer to the question: *Job Possibilities*. We got the hexagram 55, **Fullness**; which has two changing lines and thus originates a second hexagram, the 21, **Biting Through**. The first column shows the line number and value obtained for each line.

	Hex. 55	Hex. 21
L6: 6	―✕―	―――
L5: 8	― ―	― ―
L4: 7	―――	―――
L3: 9	―o―	― ―
L2: 8	― ―	― ―
L1: 7	―――	―――

Fullness describes a time with many opportunities, but it is also full of inconveniences, and it will not last long, so it is important to take advantage of it well before it ends.

Biting Through indicates that firm measures must be used to remove an obstacle.

The two lines that change in *Fullness* are:

- *Third line:* Unfavorable conditions will block any attempt on your part to overcome them. The broken arm means that your influence and power will be diminished if you try to make a failed attempt to move forward.

- *Sixth line:* This line describes someone who, instead of facing the problems of daily life, takes refuge in the memories of the past, withdrawing from the outside world.

This is a possible synthesis of the meanings of all the parts of this response:

You will have good opportunities to progress in your work (Judgment and Image of hex. 55), but you will have to overcome some obstacles to achieve it (indicated by the hexagram 21 and the image of 55). Do not delay, but do not act without preparation; If you are not careful, the impediments will stop you and may even harm you (3rd line).

Keep a positive attitude, focused on the means at your disposal to advance, do not escape reality by taking refuge in false illusions of superiority (6th line).

The third and sixth lines are linked by a correspondence relationship; the third line symbolizes an employee in a transition position (the consultant), who does not have much power; the sixth line is a weak and inoperative boss who does not fulfill his duty and who can block the employee advance by refusing to accept reality.

If you waste the moment for advancement, you will lose the opportunity. If you can take advantage of the opportunities, you will obtain important, although transitory, advantages. You can benefit in the long term, because you will get a significant improvement in your reputation and, over time, this will open your way to a wider circle of action.

Chart of Trigrams and Hexagrams

Upper ▶ Lower ▼	Quian	Zhen	Kan	Gen	Kun	Xun	Li	Dui
Quian	1	34	5	26	11	9	14	43
Zhen	25	51	3	27	24	42	21	17
Kan	6	40	29	4	7	59	64	47
Gen	33	62	39	52	15	53	56	31
Kun	12	16	8	23	2	20	35	45
Xun	44	32	48	18	46	57	50	28
Li	13	55	63	22	36	37	30	49
Dui	10	54	60	41	19	61	38	58

Each hexagram is composed by two trigrams, one comprises the lower three lines of the hexagram and the other corresponds to the three upper lines.

The above table shows all possible combinations of the eight trigrams, in that way you can find easily the number for any hexagram drawing.

1

qián
The Creative / Activity / Dynamic Force

This is one of the eight hexagrams that are comprised by the same trigram repeated twice, in this case *qián*, The Creative.

Associated meanings

Spirit power, creative, force, dynamic, strong action, vigor, constant, heaven, heavenly generative principle (male), father, sovereign, power above the human, yang power, active, vigorous appearance.

Judgment

> The Creative.
> Outstanding success.
> The determination is favorable.

This hexagram is comprised of six solid, *yang* lines, representing light, action and strength. It describes a great accumulation of energy and consequently the need for steadfast action to channel such power in the proper direction.

The figure of the dragon appears as protagonist in five of the seven line statements (only the first and second hexagrams have seven line statements).

The Chinese dragon, different from the western dragon, is not evil, but beneficial. It is a legendary animal, a powerful force that surges from the waters, and is associated with rain, floods, heaven and the hexagram 1. It also has supernatural godly power. It is at home either under the waters or flying in heaven and has supernatural energy. Also it is related with the supreme authority (the emperor).

In this hexagram the dragon symbolizes somebody with its same qualities, and the lines show its ascension from a low position (under the water) up to the sky.

This is one of the few hexagrams that mention the "four cardinal virtues": *yuan*: outstanding (fundamentality, primal, originating, spring season, head, sublime, great, grand); *heng*: success (prevalence, growing, penetrating, treat, offering, sacrifice); *li*: determination (perseverance, constancy, correct and firm) and *heng*: favorable (advantageous, suitable, beneficial, lucky). One or more of the cardinal virtues appear in 50 different hexagrams, but only the hexagrams 1, 2 (with some modification), 3, 17, 19, 25 and 49 have the four virtues in its Judgment. Since the *Han* Dynasty onwards they have become keywords of Confucian thought, four qualities or virtues applicable both to Heaven and to the noble-minded person.

In the Confucian tradition the dragon is associated with the four cardinal virtues. Any oracle encompassing the four cardinal virtues indicates that success is granted, but only if you don't stray from the good; for this reason determination in the right way is the key to success.

The Image

> Heaven action is strong and dynamic.
> Thus the noble never ceases to strengthen himself.

In the same way that heaven revolves daily, the creative person should be ready for incessant action, a movement that keeps going along through time, renovating itself each day.

Strong action should be matched to the needs of each moment. The creative person should keep touch with reality and with other people as well.

First Nine

> Submerged dragon.
> Do not act.

The dragon is at home either under the waters or flying in heaven.

It was believed that dragons caused rain when they ascended into the sky, hence they were beneficial since the rain watered the crops.

In this line the dragon is hibernating; still not ready to make its mark in the world. It means that the time is not yet ripe for action and that you should wait and keep a low profile until you are ready.

Second Nine

> Dragon in the field.
> It is favorable to see the great man.

You are entering your field of action in life, where you will find your peers.

The word translated as "field" also means "hunt". The hunt symbolizes the search for your destiny and your vocation.

To see the great man means that having a mentor would be very useful at this stage; but it also indicates that you should rise spiritually and in understanding.

Third Nine

> The noble is active throughout the day.
> At night he is cautious, as if in danger.
> No defect.

You will be creatively active all day long. Enduring strength and alertness will keep you out of trouble.

A wide scope of opportunities will spread before you along with your reputation.

Do not procrastinate nor allow others to influence you improperly. You will have to marshal wisely your resources to keep pace with your responsibilities.

Fourth Nine

> Hesitates before jumping over the chasm.
> No defect.

You will test your capability for success, deciding your future.
The choice is yours; you can ascend and play an important role in the world, gaining fame and power or stay low and dedicate yourself to personal matters.

Fifth Nine

> Dragon flying in the sky.
> It is favorable to see the great man.

To fly in the sky means to have reached a high position in the place where you belong, because the sky is the natural world of the dragon.
The sky is the highest sphere where only dragons, that is to say, the most capable and creative persons can abide.
The flying dragon symbolizes an outstanding person at work, having great influence and being an example for other people. The flying dragon also indicates that you can advance freely and achieve lofty goals with ease.
To see the great man means that still after having reached such a high place, having a guide would be very useful.

Top Nine

> Arrogant dragon.
> There will be occasion for repentance.

If you go too far in your ambition you will lose contact with the real world and will get lost.
Arrogance will sever your links with other people and when you most need them you will not get any help.
If you recognize your limits and do not forget your fellow men you may still prevent trouble.

All lines are Nine

> A group of dragons without heads.
> Auspicious.

Only the first two hexagrams, The Creative and The Receptive have an additional line statement, to be read when all lines change.
Each dragon is strong; a group of dragons is a powerful force that hardly can be stopped.
To be without heads means that the dragons act by common accord, without having a chief among them.
When all lines mutate *The Creative* changes into the hexagram 2: *The Receptive*. By combining the strength of *The Creative* with the devotion of the *The Receptive* you will achieve a perfect balance and will be able to handle any situation easily, hence the prospects will be entirely good.

kūn
The Receptive

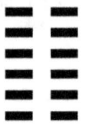

This is one of the eight hexagrams that are comprised by the same trigram repeated twice, in this case *kūn*, The Receptive.

Associated meanings

Earth, nature; receptiveness, responsiveness, compliance, acquiescence, docility, devotion, subordinate; matter, field, spatial extension; feminine, nurturing, mother, yin force.

Judgment

> The Receptive.
> Outstanding success favorable for the determination of a mare.
> If the noble takes the lead he goes astray,
> but if he follows, he finds a master.
> It is favorable to find friends in the west and south;
> avoid friends in the east and north.
> A quiet determination is auspicious.

A mare is strong but docile. Hence, do not try to impose your will but follow someone's example or guide.
You are part of a group or team and you should work for the good of the whole, not just for your own personal gain or benefit.
If you have employment, it would be best for you to progress inside the place where you are working instead of trying to go ahead on your own. If you are part of a family, be loyal with them and do you share of the work for the sake of your family.
South-west means going towards other people and to work with them, north-east indicates advancing in solitude.
Going with friends signifies to surrender to a community-sense work, where solidarity and cooperation are involved.
Quiet determination means that you should do what is required from you and persevere with steadfast and calm resolve.

This is one of the few hexagrams that mention the "four cardinal virtues": *yuan*: outstanding (fundamentality, primal, originating, spring season, head, sublime, great, grand); *heng*: success (prevalence, growing, penetrating, treat, offering, sacrifice); *li*: determination (perseverance, constancy, correct and firm) and *heng*: favorable (advantageous, suitable, beneficial, lucky). One or more of the cardinal virtues appear in 50 different hexagrams, but only the hexagrams 1, 2 (with some modification), 3, 17, 19, 25 and 49 have the four virtues in its Judgment. Since the *Han* Dynasty onwards they have become keywords of Confucian thought, four qualities or virtues applicable both to Heaven and to the noble-minded person.

Any oracle encompassing the four cardinal virtues indicates that success is granted, but only if you don't stray from the good; for this reason determination in the right way is the key to success.

The Image

> The earth condition is receptive obedience.
> Thus the noble, who has a munificent character, sustains all living creatures.

Like the earth nurtures all beings, the virtuous person will be generous and tolerating, helping and guiding all living beings.
Be open-minded and compassionate to the needs of other persons.
Do you duty for the sake of others more than for your own advancement.

First Six

> Walking on hoarfrost one reaches hard ice.

Walking on hoarfrost (*lu shuāng*) has several connotations:
- The coming winter; signs of decay.
- An approaching marriage. Two *ShiJing* (The Classic of Poetry) odes use the same characters with that meaning.
- Ceremonial walking on hoarfrost for the autumnal sacrifices.

The first meaning is the more common interpretation, here walking on hoarfrost indicates that danger is coming and good conditions are coming to an end, because the hard and cold winter is approaching. Be alert for signs of trouble and do not let matters slip out of hand.
Also the reference to hard ice may indicate that your advance will be stopped cold soon.

Second Six

> Right, square and large, inexperienced.
> But nothing will be not favorable.

The square is a symbol of earth. An alternative translation would be: "honorable, straightforward and extensive, without practice". In any case the line means that by being correct and strong you can make all things flourish easily.
Be sincere and follow your instincts, you will do the right thing.

Third Six

> Hidden brilliance.
> The determination is suitable.
> If you are in the service of a king you will not have achievements,
> but will carry to conclusion.

Concentrate your efforts in your duty and do not seek distinctions for yourself.
Your talents will be rewarded when the time is ripe, for now it would be best for you to focus in servicing others.
If you are not independent but work for somebody, you will do a good job, but you will not get any credit for it at the present time.

Fourth Six

> A tied up bag.
> No defect, no praise.

Keep your opinions and plans private. Do not draw attention to yourself.
Caution is advised, do not commit, keep your neutrality and distance until the situation clears.

Fifth Six

> Yellow lower garment.
> There will be outstanding happiness.

Yellow is the color of the earth and indicates moderation and following the middle path between the extremes.
Also, the yellow lower garment symbolizes humility and virtue in somebody that occupies a place of honor (the fifth line is the ruler's place).
If you are sincere but polite, people will respond well to you sensible approach.

Top Six

> Dragons fight in the open country.
> Their blood is black and yellow.

The *yin* principle is the complement of the *yang* force, but it should be subservient and do not take the lead.
Here a mad fight between the two forces, the true *yang* dragon and the rebel *yin* false dragon will cause calamity. Black is the color of heaven and yellow is the color of the earth, they identify the true and false dragons.
An unpleasant and violent competition for power will only cause misery for both sides. Be cooperative, not competitive.

All lines are Six

> Long term determination is favorable.

Only the first two hexagrams, The Creative and The Receptive have an additional line statement, to be read when all lines change.
Final success will be achieved through the practice of constant determination.
You are doing things just fine, keep in the same line and you will have lasting success.

zhūn
Initial Difficulty

Associated meanings

Difficult; to sprout, begin to grow; leadership; assemble, accumulate, hoard; to garrison soldiers, massed, bunched.

Judgment

> The Initial Difficulty.
> Outstanding success.
> The determination is favorable.
> It should not be pursued any goal.
> It is favorable to appoint officials.

In the first stages of growth, immature beings and new ventures need nurturing, care and firm determination.

This is the right moment to set the basis of future developments, to affirm the innate potential, as the root must be steady into the soil before sprouting. The situation is unstable and the task couldn't be done without the help of collaborators. Goals cannot be attained until some order and development is achieved. That means that long term planning is required.

This is one of the few hexagrams that mention the "four cardinal virtues": *yuan*: outstanding (fundamentality, primal, originating, spring season, head, sublime, great, grand); *heng*: success (prevalence, growing, penetrating, treat, offering, sacrifice); *li*: determination (perseverance, constancy, correct and firm) and *heng*: favorable (advantageous, suitable, beneficial, lucky). One or more of the cardinal virtues appear in 50 different hexagrams, but only the hexagrams 1, 2 (with some modification), 3, 17, 19, 25 and 49 have the four virtues in its Judgment. Since the *Han* Dynasty onwards they have become keywords of Confucian thought, four qualities or virtues applicable both to Heaven and to the noble-minded person.

Any oracle encompassing the four cardinal virtues indicates that success is granted, but only if you don't stray from the good; for this reason determination in the right way is the key to success.

The Image

>   Clouds and thunder: The image of the Initial Difficulty.
>   Thus the noble sorts the threads of warp and woof.

The competent person should order and classify things in order to convert potential capabilities into a real force.

Clouds and thunder is a reference to the two constituent's trigrams which depict a situation with plenty of possibilities but also in a chaotic state. To sort the threads of warp and woof is a metaphor for the act of government.

Resolute leadership is a required to order the situation and achieve final success.

First Nine

>   Looking to overcome an obstacle.
>   It is favorable to maintain the determination.
>   It is favorable to appoint assistants.

It may be necessary to try different approaches before being able to surpass an obstacle; hence some hesitation will be unavoidable, but the final goals should not be forgotten.

By recognizing the merits of your subordinates and making them feel useful, you can get help from them and establish a good foundation for further expansion.

Second Six

>   Difficulties impeding progress.
>   Horse and cart separate.
>   It's not a villain, but a pretender.
>   The girl has determination and does not plight her troth.
>   After ten years she will pledge herself.

The horse separated from the cart symbolizes the difficulty in making cooperative efforts work.

An obstacle still impedes the advance and some misunderstandings are complicating the teamwork.

Somebody will provide help from an unexpected quarter. The newcomer will not be appreciated at a first glance, you may hesitate, waiting for the right moment before taking on any obligations or to compromise your will.

The Chinese character translated as "plight" also means "conceive", "breed", indicating that you will achieve a fruitful alliance at the end.

Ten years indicates a long period, like in the hexagrams 24.5 and 27.3.

Third Six

>   Chasing the deer without forester, entering in the depths of the forest.
>   The noble sees the signs and desists.
>   If he went forward, he would regret it.

Blinded by your desire, you may advance in dangerous and unknown ground without taking the proper precautions or lacking a good guide. The deer represents the desire; the forest symbolizes the unknown and the dangers ahead where you may be taken by your ambition. The signs are subtle indications that –if disregarded– will lead you amiss.

Fourth Six

> Horse and cart separate.
> Look for the union.
> Advance brings happiness.
> Everything will be auspicious and without blemish.

The forces at your disposal are scattered and discordant. The cart symbolizes a project that cannot advance forward for lack of union.

You are not qualified to solve the problems by yourself, getting an ally is the only way to resume your advance and carry out things to a successful end.

Fifth Nine

> Difficulties dispensing favors.
> Determination in small matters is auspicious.
> Determination in major ways brings misfortune.

Preserve your energy, wait for a more propitious time. For now only small things can be done successfully. Big achievements will fail.

You will not be able to help others in any significant way.

Top Nine

> Horse and cart separate.
> Tears of blood are spilled.

Blood tears represent an exaggerated attitude; more stressful in the lament than what really corresponds. You have gone too far and now you are mired in difficulties.

There are no helpers and you will find no suitable place for moving, but neither remaining in your current position will do you any good.

If you yield to reality and give up your obstinacy you will be able to start anew.

4

méng
Youthful Folly

Associated Meanings

Ignorance, immaturity, inexperience; cover, hidden, in darkness; go with covered eyes against; deception, conceal, cheat.

Judgment

> The Youthful Folly is successful.
> It is not I who seek the young fool, the young fool seeks me.
> At the first oracle I inform, but a second or third time is troublesome;
> and I do not instruct the annoying.
> The determination is favorable.

Immaturity is a learning stage. A young fool can be successful; because the close contact with experience will help him to acquire some wisdom. Also, the learning process should be taken care showing respect to the master; otherwise the teacher's effort will be wasted Unruly students will bring humiliation over themselves.

The Oracle speaks here, telling the people who seek its advice to take seriously its instruction and to avoid asking the same question again and again. In such case they would just waste their time.

The Image

> Under the mountain flows a spring: The image of the Youthful Folly.
> Thus the noble makes his actions resolute and cultivates his virtue.

The mountain is strong, consolidated, but the spring flowing out of it runs in search of the formation of its own course. The spring runs the risk of stagnation, as when the youthful inexperience takes the wrong road, delaying the maturation process.

To cultivate one's virtue means to develop the own strong points or natural gifts. That is the way to success.

First Six

To develop the foolish man it will be favorable to discipline him.

> The fetters must be removed,
> otherwise there will be regret.

Discipline is good for strengthening the will, but it shouldn't be carried too far. If the restrains (symbolized by the fetters) are excessive they will sap the student creativity and good will. After all, discipline is an excellent tool but not a goal in itself.

Second Nine

> Supporting the Youthful Folly is auspicious.
> To take a wife is auspicious.
> A son can take care of the family.

The student weakness should be tolerated. Expecting too much and too soon from people that are starting to learn is not a realistic expectancy.

The wife is here a symbol of weakness, to be able to take one indicates a kindly and considerate attitude, how a stronger being can manage a relation with a weaker person.

The pupil that is educated with kindness, in turn will be able to take care of his own family in the same way.

Third Six

> Do not marry a girl who, on seeing a man of metal,
> loses her self-possession.
> No place is favorable.

This line describes how a weaker person can lose his will and blindly imitate or follow a stronger person as a role model. It is not right to allow other person to follow you in such a slavish way. That kind of situation doesn't lead to success or to a sustainable relation.

Also, sometimes a weaker person can relate to a stronger or richer one only with the idea of getting selfish advantages. In such case nothing good will come of that relationship.

Fourth Six

> Trapped by his folly he will suffer shame.

A fool who is not ready to give up his foolish ways and is too proud to change, will arrive to a dead end, losing touch with reality and becoming trapped in his own fantasies. No other outcome than shame is possible.

Fifth Six

> Children's folly is auspicious.

Being flexible, willing to learn and accepting guidance will be favorable.

An open-minded person knows his limitations and where to look for help. This describes the exact inverse situation of the previous line.

Top Nine

> Punishing Youthful Folly.
> It is not favorable to commit harassment,
> but it is favorable to defend yourself against transgressors.

When a fool is stubborn he may require punishment, but only to the point that is required to curb his bad behavior. The amount of punishment depends on the person; in some cases a light punishment may be enough in other cases stronger punishments may be more appropriate. Punishment is the last resort and should not be applied as revenge or in anger.

The same Chinese word is translated as "harassment" and "transgressors", literally means "bandit, invader, enemy, robber, violent people, outcasts, plunderers". The basic meaning would be: do not become a bandit, defend against bandits.

5

xū
Waiting

Associated Meanings

Wait, tarry, stop; get wet; serve.

Judgment

Waiting.
With brilliance and sincerity you will succeed.
The determination is favorable.
It is favorable to cross the great river.

Waiting is not the same than giving up. Having clarity of purpose one can wait patiently, looking carefully at the situation to see when the right moment for advance comes.
In ancient China, crossing rivers, either at a ford or when the river was frozen, was not an easy task. It implicated dangers and hardships; hence crossing the great river means to carry out a difficult undertaking.

The Image

Clouds ascend to heaven: The image of Waiting.
Thus the noble drinks, eats and parties.

Clouds gathering in the sky symbolize a process or situation that is evolving slowly. The conclusion of that process will be rain, which also indicates the liberation of the stress.
To drink eat and party means to be at ease and to have a good and optimist state of mind. The waiting time can be enjoyed, and normal live must go on without being put on hold until your goals are attained.
Nourish yourself and keep in touch with other people while you wait.

First Nine

Waiting in the suburbs.
It is favorable to have perseverance.
No defect.

Your life is still undisturbed and nothing unusual happens yet.
If you stay away from danger and remain committed to your daily chores you will have no trouble.

Second Nine

> Waiting in the sand.
> They say little things.
> Finally there will be good fortune.

Waiting in the sandbank, near the river means that you are about to cross the river. Crossing a river symbolizes undertaking a dangerous enterprise. Some people may not understand your goals or distrust your capability to perform them, but their gossip will have no importance. In time you will carry out successfully your objective.

Third Nine

> Waiting in the mud attracts bandits.

You advanced too far and too soon and now you are in a vulnerable position. You are in danger of being attacked or slandered.
The way out of the bad actual situations is not clear; you are obstructed for the time being. Utter prudence and circumspection are advised.

Fourth Six

> Waiting in blood.
> Outside the pit!

To be in a bloody pit means that you have fallen in a trap or are in a critical situation. Rushing things only will worsen your problems. Keep your head cool, let things take its course and wait until you can see a clear way out.

Fifth Nine

> Waiting with wine and food.
> The determination is favorable.

Waiting in the middle of abundance, you can replenish your strength and enjoy the current moment. You are at the proper place, enjoy it while you can.

Top Six

> One falls into the pit.
> Three uninvited guests arrive.
> Treat them with respect and in the end there will be good fortune.

The character translated as "pit" here (and also in the fourth line) in addition means "cave, hole, underground dwellings". It indicates that you are trapped in darkness, you cannot see the way out and there is no hope left.
The three uninvited guest indicate new persons, ideas or influences that will change entirely and unexpectedly the situation for good.
If you treat the unexpected guests in the proper way, you will gain insight and will be able to come out of the pit.

6

sòng
Conflict / Lawsuit

Conflict, litigation, dispute, quarrel, to demand justice, accusation, arguing, grievance.

Judgment

> Conflict.
> You are sincere but you are hold back.
> Cautiously stopped halfway brings good fortune.
> Going to the end is ominous.
> It is advantageous to see the great man.
> It is not favorable to cross the great river.

Righteousness it not enough to win the conflict and no matter if you win, the costs may be higher than the advantages.
The Judgment suggests stopping halfway; that means to find a middle ground where both litigants can agree.
The great man is a mediator that can help both sides to find a peaceful solution.
The fact that it is not favorable to cross the great river indicates that to take the conflict ahead is not convenient. Going to the end –not reaching a compromise– would be disastrous; there is danger of a never ending conflict that will drag you down for a long time.
This hexagram is related with civil lawsuits, the other hexagram with a similar meaning is the number 21: **Biting through**, which indicates a criminal lawsuit.

The Image

> Sky and water move in opposite directions: The image of the Conflict.
> Thus the noble, in all his tasks, plans well before starting.

The sky is located far above the waters, and water always goes down; this symbolizes two parties –litigants– with opposite goals and perspectives.
In order to prevent conflicts it is necessary to plan ahead and to delimitate clearly the responsibilities and duties of every involved person. Stating your position clearly at the beginning, also will minimize the danger of any future confrontations.

First Six

> If one does not perpetuate the affair, there will be some gossip,
> but eventually it will be auspicious.

This is the initial stage of the conflict where it is still feasible to stop it without negative effects. At this point it would be easy to find mutual understanding with minimal discussions and without losing face.

Second Nine

> One cannot succeed in the suit and escapes back to his home.
> The inhabitants of his city, three hundred families,
> will not suffer misfortune.

Confronted with a superior power the only reasonable action is to go back to a safe position. A conflict can expand towards the surroundings and it may harm people that are not directly related to it, hence a prompt retreat will secure the safety of your friends and associates. Returning home also indicates to take a low profile approach.
In ancient China, the man who lost the litigation should have to pay a fine or commute a harsh penalty by payment. His vassals –the inhabitants of his city– would be forced to pay the fine for his feudal lord, hence if the lord retreats before losing his case they would suffer no harm.

Third Six

> Subsisting on old virtue.
> Determination in front of danger.
> There will be good fortune in the end.
> If you are in the service of a king
> you will not be able to complete your work.

The traditional ways are the safest option, especially when confronting powerful contenders. This is not the right time to improve or change anything; the situation cannot be improved yet but it can be sustained. Steady but traditional work will achieve the best results in the end. Behave with restraint and modesty to avoid attracting unwanted attention.

Fourth Nine

> One cannot win the fight.
> Turns back and accepts fate.
> Changes his attitude and finds peace.
> The determination is auspicious.

When the right is not on your side, the correct thing to do is to resign and go back.
Accepting fate and resigning your ambitions will bring peace to you. It is auspicious to act that way.

Fifth Nine

> Litigating.
> Outstanding fortune.

The fifth line is the ruler of the hexagram and it symbolizes a just arbiter situated in an elevated position.

To resolve the conflict in a fair way you should recourse to a just person in position of authority. It is important not only to search for a proper mediator but to take the right course towards the desired goal.

Justice will be done. If you are in the right you will be highly successful.

Top Nine

> If you get rewarded with a leather belt,
> by late morning it will have been snatched away three times.

The leather belt is a symbol of rank and authority.

To lose it several times means that the victory will not be sustainable, that the conflict will never end.

shī
The Army

Associated meanings

Army, troops, legion, militias, a disciplined group, multitude; master, leader; take as a master, imitate, follow a role model or norm; military virtues.

Judgment

> The Army.
> The determination brings good fortune for a strong man.
> No defect.

An army requires strong leadership and clarity of purpose, expressed with firm determination. Good organization and strict discipline are needed to avoid the army becoming a mob. Caution is required to avoid falling in danger.

The Image

> The earth contains water inside it: The image of The Army.
> Thus the noble takes care of and increases the crowd.

The trigram *Kan* appears in the lower part of this hexagram. *Kan* the symbol of moving water, but also indicates danger; the trigram *Kun* is the upper trigram and it symbolizes the Earth. The Army is like water put in movement, powerful and dangerous, but in this case, it remains hidden in the depths of the Earth until it is mobilized. A strong leader can drive the masses and gives them direction, like water channeled in a precise direction.
The noble indicates a person of high ideals and capacity that supports and contains the people like the Earth contains the water. He knows how to attract followers to his cause and how to motivate and direct them.

First Six

> The Army should set forward in orderly rows.
> If discipline is bad there will be misfortune.

The Army requires organization and discipline, in other way it will never work properly. From the start, clear rules and goals must be established; rushing ahead without planning or lacking discipline should be disastrous.

Second Nine

> In the midst of The Army.
> Good fortune.
> No defect.
> The king gives rewards and promotions thrice.

This is the position of the leader, the only *yang* line in this hexagram. The king giving rewards and promotions symbolizes a ruler who supports and promotes an able person as leader of the army (the second line); it also means to receive blessings from heaven.

Third Six

> Perhaps The Army carries a corpse in the carriage.
> Ominous.

Note that in ancient China sometimes a child impersonated the dead during sacrifices. From this viewpoint carrying a corpse may mean that the army leader is no present but is substituted for another one during battle, who is not up to the task. Hence, this line may indicate deficient leadership, lack of capacity and misunderstandings in the handling of the resources at your disposal.
Such lack of leadership will be disastrous.

Fourth Six

> The Army camps on the left.
> No defect.

To camp on the left means to withdraw to the barracks. By avoiding battle you can keep clear from trouble.

Fifth Six

> There is game in the field.
> It is favorable to capture them for questioning.
> No defect.
> The eldest son should lead The Army,
> if the younger brother leads, the carriages will be used to carry corpses.
> The determination is ominous.

The "game in the field" means that there is no way to postpone facing an important problem and that your adversary is in the open.
To "capture for questioning" means that you should analyze the situation carefully before taking action.
It is important to wait until the new facts are understood clearly before taking action, to solve the present crisis and start the fight.
The eldest son is a symbol of good leadership; without it defeat will be the final result.

"The determination is ominous" means that you must exercise restraint in battle and stop advancing as soon as your goals are accomplished. It also indicates the need for self-discipline and moderation to avoid dangerous excesses.

Top Six

> The great king has the mandate to found a state and inherit the house.
> Small men should not be used.

After achieving your goals you should consolidate your situation. Distribute your resources wisely to avoid further problems.

Both inferior people and low desires should be kept in check.

bǐ
Union

Associated meanings

Union, go together with, joining with others, put together, holding together, assemble, associate with, alliance, combine, ally with, pair, match.

Judgment

> Union brings happiness.
> Look deep and divine to see if you have great long-term determination;
> if so there will be no defect.
> They will come from the lands without peace.
> Those who arrive late will have misfortune.

In order to achieve union you should feel confident that it is good for you; because only with no doubts you will be able to have enough determination to accomplish a worthy union.

The phrase "lands without peace" refers either to people with doubts or to unruly people; if they muster enough confidence, they will join the group, but if they hesitate for too long or refuse to comply with the ruler, they will miss the opportunity.

The text describes the summons from a ruler to his tribal chieftains. Those who arrive late will not be well received and may be even punished. There is a proper time for joining a group, those who enter too late will not be able to become full members.

The Image

> On earth there is water: The image of Union.
> So the kings of old established ten thousand different states
> and kept close relations with all the feudal lords.

The earth supports the water, which in turn humidifies earth, fertilizes it; this shows how a proper union can benefit all participants.

Then thousand indicates a large number. There are masses of water on the earth just as there are many countries on the world. In the same way than flowing water, friendly cultural and commercial relationships between different nations fertilize the world.

In the same way a leader maintains mutually beneficial relations with his associates, keeping the communication channels well opened like flowing waterways. It is important to cooperate between people and assign each one the proper task.

First Six

> If there is sincerity, the Union will be without defect.
> Full of sincerity as an overflowing earthenware vessel.
> Finally, through others, happiness will come.

Sincerity is essential to keep good relations with friends and associates. The earthenware vessel symbolizes a sincere and true approach, full of substance and not a mere appearance. It shows that something of real value is offered and that there is no disguise. Having such a good attitude and offering a real value you will gain the trust from everybody and the reunion will bring happiness to all parties.

The overflowing earthenware vessel also indicates that your capacity for sincerity will attract people. The mention to "others" means that valuable people outside of your usual sphere of acquaintances will be attracted..

Second Six

> Union from the inside.
> The determination is fortunate.

Affinity with a certain person (the fifth *yang* line, the one with a superior position) will be firstly manifested inwardly as a shared feeling. Such sincere relationship will bring good fortune.

"Union from the inside" also indicates that you should remain loyal to your comrades and close friends.

Third Six

> Union with worthless people.

The two Chinese characters translated as "worthless people" also mean: "bandit, disreputable or despicable people". It may indicate that you give trust to the wrong people and that you are being deceived.

No prognostication is appended, but mixing with bad company will prevent you from establishing relations with better people and surely will not lead you to a positive outcome.

Fourth Six

> Solidarity with people outside.
> Determination brings good fortune.

Manifesting openly your affinity with other persons will bring good fortune. Also it may mean that you are establishing a positive connection with somebody who is outside of your normal sphere of acquaintances.

This line also depicts the moment when the decision of joining somebody or to pursue some goal is openly taken.

Fifth Nine

> Manifest Union.
> The king uses beaters for hunting prey on three sides,

> but lets the animals in front of him go.
> The villagers are not wary.
> Good fortune.

"The ancient rule for hunting expeditions was that after the beating was completed and the king was ready to commence taking game, one side of the enclosure into which it had been driven was left open and unguarded. This was proof of the royal benevolence which didn't want to make an end of all the creatures inside". (*Legge*)

As the leader, he motivates people and puts them in motion, but without forcing the final decision on anybody.

The people related to him ("the villagers": people in the same organization or family) know and trust him.

This union between high (the leader, the fifth line) and low (the people) brings good fortune. Here the union is completely voluntary; people decide by themselves if they want to join the leader, and they do so because they believe in him.

Top Six

> Union without a leader.
> Misfortune.

The union was not achieved because lack of a focusing point and bad leadership. The consequences are isolation and regret.

The lack of a leader may be caused for disagreement among members or groups within an organization, such conflicts will conduce to a complete breakdown.

9

xiǎo chù
Little Domestication

Associated meanings

Accumulate, nurture, support, cultivate, farming, domesticate take care of little things. All done in small scale.

Judgment

> Little Domestication is successful.
> Dense clouds, no rain from our western borders.

The clouds in the sky indicate partial results, a work in progress that still cannot bring out the desired outcome. Rain symbolizes the positive consequence of your efforts.
Only small steps can be taken at this time, this is not the proper time for great expenditures or a full scale advance.
Exercise restraint and moderation. Long term planning is required. For now you can only set the groundwork to consolidate the requirements for a future expansion.
It is important to give attention to details and to keep the final goal in mind. Gather information, polish your plans and be sure that nothing will be left to chance when you can at last make a bold advance.

The Image

> The wind crosses the sky: The image of Little Domestication.
> Thus the noble refines the outward manifestation of his virtue.

Although you don't have yet the means to produce big effects, you can use your knowledge to improve your image and promote your goals.
The outward manifestation of virtue implies things like kindness, politeness, good social graces and tolerance.

First Nine

> Returns to the own road.
> How could it be wrong?
> Good fortune.

It is preferable to go back instead of being exposed to danger. This means you should exercise self-restraint.

The term translated as "own" also means "source, origin", meaning that you should go back to your own vocation or to the original point from where you have strayed.

It also indicates returning to normal life after being stranded.

Second Nine

> Led to return.
> Good fortune.

After looking at how other people in similar position than you behave, you will decide to go back.

Also your own experience may teach you that the conditions are not right at this time and that by going back you will avoid trouble and be successful.

This moment marks the end of a cycle. The next time you may have better results, but for now it is time to reshuffle and deal again.

Third Nine

> Rays are removed from the carriage wheels.
> Man and wife avert their eyes from each other.

The carriage with the spokes of its wheels removed points to a project that has been stopped completely. No matter how much power is applied to move forward a carriage, if the wheels are broken it will not advance at all.

The man and his wife that do not look at each other symbolize lack of cooperation, indifference, people with different objectives or having severe dissensions. Also the man-wife conflict may symbolize lack of understanding and good will between a boss and an employee.

Fourth Six

> If you are sincere, the blood disappears and concerns are cast aside.
> No defect.

Sincerity can act as a soothing factor. After trust is restored the risk of spilling blood will be avoided and all involved people will feel at ease.

Only by being truthful and inspiring confidence in others, you will be able to defuse this conflict and avoid further mistakes.

Fifth Nine

> If you are sincere with your neighbors
> the alliance will bring prosperity for all.

You sincerity will draw other people to collaborate with you.

By sharing your prosperity you will increase it.

Top Nine

> The rain fell and he could rest.
> His spiritual power brings him recognition.
> The determination is dangerous for a wife.

The moon is almost full.
Enterprises are unfortunate.

By the sum of small steps a project or plan has been driven to completion. The rain symbolizes relaxation after a storm and shows that it is time to stop and rest.

The Chinese character translated as "spiritual power", also means "moral integrity, ability, character, virtue". It indicates that your value is recognized and people trust you.

The mention to a wife indicates that all achievements were produced not for the use of force, but on the contrary, by careful, measured steps, not with *yang* bravado but with *yin* cunning and perseverance. The *yin* power is at its strongest when the moon is almost full, so now it is the proper time to cease advancing; continuing ahead would be counter-productive and would put in danger all your present achievements.

The moon almost full indicates that a cycle is ending and changes are coming.

lǔ
Treading

Associated meanings

Step on, track, walk or follow a trail or way, stepping on the tiger's tail; footwear, shoes; conduct, behavior, ceremonies.

Judgment

> Treading the tiger's tail.
> The man is not bitten.
> Success.

Stepping on the tiger's tail means that you will cope with a perilous endeavor or circumstance. It also indicates to conduct yourself correctly, to behave properly in the face of danger.
This is not a good time to be adversarial, but to remain constant in your beliefs or convictions and to advance with politeness and care.
The tiger symbolizes a powerful and wild force; when facing individuals that are equally dangerous, you should proceed in a way that doesn't antagonize them, advancing softly and with utmost care, but with firmness. In that way, although the tiger will notice that somebody is treading over its tail, it will tolerate it.

The Image

> Above the sky, down the lake: The image of Treading.
> Thus the noble distinguishes between high and low
> and makes certain the will of the people.

The distance between heaven and the lake symbolizes the range of different behaviors in human society. The noble takes in account such differences and understands that each person acts according to his will. Indeed the Chinese word translated as "will", also means "purpose, goal, determination". Hence the noble tries to understand the different purposes and goals that motivate people and to take in account the feelings and the expectations of them, acting tactfully and with care, especially when facing dangerous persons.

First Nine

> Simple Treading.
> Advance without defect.

You are taking the first steps and since you still don't have any heavy responsibilities on your shoulders, you are free to follow your own feelings and to take life easily. Such easy going attitude is correct at this point.

Second Nine

> Treading a smooth and easy way.
> The determination of a lonely man brings good fortune.

The word translated as "lonely" also means "dark, solitary, secluded". The "lonely man" indicates a wise man that follows his own path without asking for fame, fortune or worldly recognition. Because he is unassuming and doesn't ask too much, his way is easy. His way is also smooth because he follows what he really feels and has no doubts.

Third Six

> A one-eyed man can see, a lame can tread.
> The tiger bites such a one who treads on his tail.
> Misfortune. A warrior acts as if he were a great lord.

Trying to live beyond your capabilities or forces will lead to disaster. Ignoring your limitations, like a man blind in an eye who thinks that his sight is excellent or a lame that believes he can run, will be unfortunate. To act as a lord means to act boldly.
The tiger biting such overconfident fellow indicates an important setback or loss.
This line can be translated in different ways: "a warrior acting like a great lord" would indicate overconfidence and recklessness, but it also may be translated as: "a warrior that acts in behalf of his prince"; this second translation supplies an alternative interpretations; it indicates a man who sacrifices himself doing something that he is not able to handle, but not motivated by foolishness but because he is following his duty.

Fourth Nine

> Steps on the tiger's tail with great caution.
> At the end there will be good fortune.

The situation is difficult and you are under pressure, but with extreme caution and circumspection you still can succeed.

Fifth Nine

> Resolute Treading.
> The determination is dangerous.

You are firmly resolved to carry on with the task at hand, but such strict determination may be dangerous because it will not allow you enough flexibility to make adjustments along the way. A breakthrough point is close. Be ready to notice any changes in the circumstances; reevaluate your situation on a daily basis and be flexible in dealing with it.

Top Nine

>Watch the trodden path and examine the omens.
>The cycle starts back.
>Great good fortune.

When you are at the end of the road it is time to stop and review the path taken. If the consequences of your actions are good that would be a good omen. New paths will open up with plenty of possibilities ahead.

tài
Harmony / Great

Associated meanings

Great, extensive, exalted, superior, prosperous, successful; harmony, peace, quiet; liberal; extreme, influential, spread out and reach everywhere, permeate, pervade.

Judgment

> Harmony.
> The petty depart and the great are coming.
> Good fortune and success.

People from all walks of life can cooperate with solidarity. There is no place for meanness or petty selfish interests.
The great that are coming means that the result of such harmony will be very good and will bring prosperity for everybody.
This is a period of material and spiritual balance where everything is in its proper position.
It is an excellent time for teamwork and reaching accords. A culture of sharing and cooperation will drive your business ahead.
Harmony and tolerance makes social interaction easy. Grievances go away and people trust each other.

The Image

> Heaven and earth are closely related: The image of Harmony.
> Thus the sovereign regulates and completes the course of Heaven and Earth, and assists Heaven and Earth in the right way;
> thereby helping the people.

Heaven and earth represent the forces of *yang* and *yin,* male and female, activity and passivity. They are complementary forces and when they relate to each other harmoniously all people prosper.

For the ancient Chinese, the interaction of heaven and earth produced the seasons. The sovereign regulated the activity in his domains to match the course of the seasons and the pass of the time.

Applied to actual circumstances this teaches us to follow the course of nature, to not strive against it but to flow along with nature and make good use of the favorable circumstances.

First Nine

> When reeds are pulled,
> they pull up others of the same kind together with them.
> Enterprises bring good fortune.

The roots of reeds are intertwined, so when one strand is pulled out it will take other grasses alongside. When somebody starts some endeavor in flourishing times, such action has a summoning effect and others will follow the good example and cooperate freely.

Second Nine

> Bear with the uneducated, wade the river, do not neglect the distant.
> Thus factions disappear.
> One get honors if stays in the middle path.

To wade the river means to go beyond your area of expertise, to enter a new field of action, to learn something new.

To "wade the river" can be also translated as "put to use those who wade the river". In such case that would be another reference to the uneducated, since people who wade the river, do so because they don't have boats or a carriage; they are uncultured people.

This is a good moment to make long-term plans and to take precautions against contingencies. You will need to include people of different backgrounds in your plans to make them work; do not use only your friends or the people that you already know. Sometimes valuable helpers and friends can be found behind a rough façade. Do not be prejudiced when you meet new people. Be ready to accept people from all walks of life. Think outside the box.

Third Nine

> There are no plains without slopes.
> There is no going forth without a return.
> Fortitude under trying conditions.
> No defect.
> Do not regret this truth.
> Enjoy the happiness you still possess.

All things in life are subjected to change and finally pass away. By fully accepting the transient nature of life you will be able to fully enjoy the good moments and to be strong when bad times come.

Fourth Six

> Flapping, fluttering.
> Not using his own rich resources to deal with his neighbors.
> Without having to ask gets confidence.

Flapping and fluttering indicates fluctuations and hesitation.

Seek a way to establish a good relation with others without pushing your weight around. In that way you will get the trust of others who will see that you are sincere and humble.

Fifth Six

> The sovereign *Yi* gives his daughter in marriage.
> This brings happiness and great fortune.

An alliance between low and high will bring prosperity to all people involved.

Top Six

> The wall falls back into the pit.
> Do not use the army now.
> Proclaim your commands only in your own town.
> The determination brings humiliation.

The "walls" refers to the city walls, battlements or ramparts. The typical fortification for a city was a high wall surrounded by a pit.

A natural cycle is at its end. The falling city walls symbolize some plan or structure that is crumbling down and cannot be sustained by force anymore. It indicates as well that you are now in a vulnerable position.

You should concern yourself with your immediate surroundings and put order there. If you are overextended you will be shamed.

Do not try to fix your troubles by the use of force.

pǐ
Standstill / Stagnation

Associated meanings

Standstill, stagnation, obstruction, hindrance, stoppage, blocked, dead end; bad, wrong.

Judgment

> Standstill.
> Worthless people are unfavorable to the determination of the noble.
> The great is going away, the petty is coming.

This is a period of stoppage, when able persons are hindered by evil and small-minded people. There is lack of cooperation and the tide of events favors petty people. Those with a self-serving agenda will obstruct the efforts of the best minded persons.
Growth is not possible anymore; the prevalence of selfish people makes this a time of decay, because their intolerance and greed will block any intent of progress.
Personal difficulties will hinder your plans. From a psychological viewpoint, you may be lured by other people or by your own low desires to take the wrong path. Do not try to force the advance, be patient and wait until the situation improves.

Image

> Heaven and earth are not related: The image of Standstill.
> Thus the noble, restrains his virtue, and avoids calamities.
> He does not accept receiving rank or salary.

Heaven and earth represent high and low. When high and low do not cooperate, when people from different walks of life plot against and mistrust each other, things don't prosper and nothing good can be achieved.
Weakness (the three lower *yin* lines) is within and strength (the three upper *yang* lines) is outside, indicating morally weak people in a situation of power.
The Chinese character translated as "virtue" in: "the noble restrains his virtue", also may be translated as "capabilities, qualities". It means that when advancing is not possible without compromising your moral standing, you should withdraw and do not lend you own capabilities

to evil associates or worthless friends. It is better to take a low profile approach and avoid displaying your talents.

You may be sorely tempted, but by keeping apart from the bad people that are in power, you will avoid falling in trouble.

The temporal progression of the situation described by the *Yijing* hexagrams is always from bottom to top, lines enter the hexagram at the base and leave it at the top; because that the three first lines are considered to be "inside" and the three upper lines are "outside".

First Six

> When reeds are pulled,
> they pull up others of the same kind together with them.
> The determination brings good fortune and success.

This is the beginning of a stagnation period. The pulled reeds dragging other herbs indicate a capable person withdrawing from the bad company, avoiding getting involved in weakness, dragging out of the public life other good people with him. Success, under these circumstances, means to be free of wrongdoings and avoiding shame.

Second Six

> They support and tolerate.
> Good fortune for the petty.
> By accepting the Standstill the great man will have success.

Small people will adapt to and follow any leader, without thinking twice in the final consequences. But the *Yijing* is written for high minded people, who in this time should avoid getting involved in the generalized misconduct.

Accepting the Standstill means to fully realize that this is not the proper time for action, that you should stand aside until the Standstill ends. Keep your hands clean and do not involve yourself in any wrongdoings.

Third Six

> They bear the shame.

Those who are in posts above his capabilities will be humiliated. People who raised using flattery and obsequiousness will not be able to handle well their responsibilities and will disgrace themselves.

Fourth Nine

> Who follows the commands of Heaven will have no defect.
> His comrades will share the blessings.

The phrase "commands of Heaven", may be translated as well as "fate" or "orders from above". It means that if you follow truthfully your real vocation or your duty you will be blameless and you will benefit your companions as well.

Fifth Nine

> The Standstill is stopping.
> Good fortune for the great man.

> It can fail! It can fail!
> Tie it to a luxuriant mulberry tree.

Finally there is a way to put an end to the Standstill. But it is up to the great person (the fifth line usually symbolizes a person in a commanding position, like a king or a ruler) to put things to right. The phrase "tie it to a luxuriant mulberry tree" means that all possible precautions should be taken to prevent failure, since stopping the standstill is not an easy task.

Also to tie something to a tree indicates that you should focus and concentrate all your resources in a single objective in order to succeed, avoiding dispersing them.

Tying a talisman to a tree is some kind of protective magic that still is used in some places, and the fifth line may reflect that ancient belief.

Top Nine

> The Standstill is overthrown.
> First standstill, afterwards joy.

This is the end of the stagnation period, when the roads are unlocked and it is possible to move ahead again.

tóng rén
Fellowship

Associated meanings

Gather people, assemble, join, partake in; identical, together, fellowship; in agreement, identified.

Judgment

> Fellowship in the fields.
> Success.
> It is advantageous to cross the great river.
> The determination brings good fortune for the noble.

People assemble naturally when a common purpose joins them, when they share a common vision and commitment. The fact that the union is in the fields indicates that it is a union of people of similar standing.

A group of like-minded people can achieve big success if all them work for the sake of the group and avoid in-fighting and hidden agendas.

In ancient China, crossing rivers, either at a ford or when the river was frozen, was not an easy task. It implicated dangers and hardships; hence crossing the great river means to carry out a difficult undertaking.

Determination is required to keep things going smoothly and to stay in the right path.

The Image

> Heaven and fire: The image of the Fellowship.
> Thus the noble organizes the clans and discriminates among things.

The fire under heaven symbolizes a gathering point, a point of interest that attracts and unites people.

A gathering of people should be organized and every person should be given the task more appropriate for their abilities.

By following specific goals and rules of behavior the group gathered together will become a fellowship instead of a mob.

First Nine

> Fellowship in the front door.
> No defect.

The union is forming in the open, not behind closed doors. There are no hidden agendas. To pass over the door indicates entering in the fellowship, to cross a threshold, taking on a new relationship and making a commitment.

Second Six

> Fellowship in the clan.
> Shame.

Selfish purposes will weak the community and will make way to factions that in the end may break the group. Those with egoist and mean ends will be sorry.

Third Nine

> He hides weapons in the bush and climbs the high hill,
> but for three years he will not rise.

This line describes somebody that retreats from social life and seeks a secure position, afraid of others.
Mistrust and conflicts are inspiring paranoid attitudes in some persons. Instead cooperating, people are wary and try to get the upper hand on others. There is no communication, everybody is isolated.
The three years indicate a full period that will pass before the impasse is left behind.

Fourth Nine

> He climbs to his wall he but cannot attack.
> Good fortune.

You feel alienated from others and distrust them. But before attacking them you will realize that such thing is not possible, and finally you will reach an agreement. Good fortune is the result of stopping the conflict and resuming cooperation.

Fifth Nine

> The men in Fellowship first weep and mourn, but then laugh.
> Great armies come across.

You are separated from the group where you belong. Conflicts keep divided the people and cause unnecessary suffering. If you take the first step, making clear your commitment, that will bring joy to all the people involved; laugh symbolizes the relaxation and happiness after the fellowship is restored, when an agreement is achieved; like powerful armies that stop being belligerent and join in peace.

Top Nine

> Fellowship in the field.
> No repentance.

The fellowship in the field means reaching a proper and convenient union, but without intimacy. The time for a close fellowship has passed, but in spite of that you can cooperate with others in a good way.

dà yǒu
Great Possession

Associated meanings
Great possession, great wealth, abundance; sovereignty,

Judgment
> Great Possession.
> Outstanding success.

Clarity and creative strength combined will give you plenty of possibilities to achieve your objectives.
You have many resources and the know-how to use them well, that will bring about outstanding success.

The Image
> Fire at the top of heaven: The image of Great Possession.
> Thus the noble punishes evil and promotes good,
> following the good will of Heaven.

Fire at the top of heaven indicates that you have clarity of mind, which makes you able to have an acute perception of what happens around you. It also means that you are in the spotlight, in the sight of every one.
Such keen awareness and visibility also increases your responsibility to make good use of your wealth and insight, curbing evil and promoting what is good.

First Nine
> No relationship with harmful things.
> No defect.
> There will be hardship but no defect.

You are a beginner, endowed with great resources. Until now you have not faced great trouble and your record is clean

If you are alert and don't misuse your resources you will make no mistakes in spite of the hard times coming.

Second Nine

> A great carriage for carrying things.
> One has a goal.
> No defect.

The words "a great carriage", suggest that you have not only plenty of resources but that you are able to put them to good use effectively; because they can mobilized swiftly and applied where you need them.

Having a goal, without any defects, means that you can apply you energies positively in one single direction, with clear purpose, and without making mistakes.

Third Nine

> A prince presents his offerings to the Son of Heaven.
> A petty man is not able to do so.

Wealthy people should put his wealth to the service of higher purposes, like a prince presenting offerings to the emperor.

Offering to the Son of Heaven indicates to use your wealth not only for yourself but to benefit others as well, to act with greatness.

Monopolizing all resources for egoist purposes is the mark of a small-minded person.

Fourth Nine

> He is not arrogant.
> No defect.

The Chinese character translated as "arrogant" also means "fullness, plenitude". Besides the basic meaning of not being boastful, proud or overbearing, it also indicates that you know how to control yourself, and will not exceed the proper measure.

Fifth Six

> His sincerity will earn the trust and respect of others.
> Good fortune.

Your sincerity will make people trust you. Dignified, but accessible and humble, you will gain the admiration of the people around you.

Top Nine

> He has the protection of Heaven.
> Good fortune.
> Nothing that is not favorable.

To have the protection of Heaven means that you will receive recognition and support from high spheres. It also indicates divine help or blessings.

Because you have plenty and resources and a keen mind, everything will be favorable.

qiān Modesty

Associated meanings

Modest, humble, yielding, moderate, temperate, unassuming, reverent.

Judgment

> Modesty.
> Success.
> The noble carries things to completion.

Modesty allows carrying things through without putting the ego in the way. By concentrating in the work at hand and avoiding conflicts with others, modest people can enjoy a very balanced lifestyle.

Modesty doesn't meant that you are insecure of weak, only that you know how to relate with other people and how to project a non-threatening image that draws the better in other people and has a soothing effect around.

The Image

> A Mountain in the middle of the earth: The image of Modesty.
> Thus the noble reduces what is excessive and increases what is insufficient.
> Weighs and distributes things evenly.

A mountain hidden under the earth is the image of a self-effacing attitude, it means no ostentation, also it symbolizes hidden treasures, resources at your disposal that you held in reserve. You don't boast about your virtues –what is excessive– but instead work on your weak points, increasing what is insufficient. In this way you will keep improving yourself and will avoid arousing jealousy.

First Six

> An extremely modest noble can cross the great river.
> Good fortune.

In ancient China, crossing rivers, either at a ford or when the river was frozen, was not an easy task. It implicated dangers and hardships; hence crossing the great river means to carry out a difficult undertaking.

Modesty opens the way to achieve great enterprises.

Second Six

> Modesty expresses itself.
> The determination is fortunate.

The Chinese character translated as "expresses" literally means the "cry of a bird", indicating that modesty is calling out publicly. It indicates that your achievements will speak for themselves and make evident to everybody your worth. If you keep up your commitment and your work you will be fortunate.

Third Nine

> A noble meritorious for his modesty carries things to completion.
> Good fortune.

You occupy a place of honor. Persevere in your efforts until you achieve your goals.

An alternative translation would be "working modesty", instead "meritorious modesty". In both cases the meaning is diligent work.

You will be supported by the people because they respect your accomplishments and devotion to your work.

After you accomplish your objectives do not forget your loyalty and commitments.

Fourth Six

> Nothing that is not favorable for manifested modesty.

Your sincere commitment and dedication will make you very successful. The Chinese character translated as "manifested" also means "display, fly a banner", that means that you should make yourself known publicly and display your work.

Fifth Six

> Without wealth can employ his neighbors.
> It is advantageous to take the offensive.
> Nothing that is not favorable.

Do not be reactive but proactive. Do not limit yourself to fix the troubles as they appear, but act with strength and determination to avoid things getting out of hand.

Modesty doesn't mean weakness or submission. Use whatever means you need to restore justice but without using excessive or uncontrolled force.

Top Six

> Manifest Modesty.
> It is favorable to launch armies to punish the capital city.

To punish the capital city indicates self-discipline, since the capital is at the heart of the country. It means that when something is wrong you shouldn't blame others but look inside yourself or inside your own intimate circle for the cause of the trouble.

yù
Enthusiasm

Associated meanings

Joy, happy, amusement, recreation, enthusiasm, contentment, at ease; think beforehand, take precautions, anticipate, planning ahead.

Judgment

> Enthusiasm.
> It is favorable to appoint officers and to set the army in motion.

A strong leader stirs with happiness and passion the people who follow him. To appoint officers means to choose capable persons who share the same ideal as helpers.
Setting the army indicates not only to enlist troops, and to organize them in a capable force but to go ahead with some project.
Proper timing is very important, acting before the right moment comes or being late will make you fail.

The Image

> Thunder comes out from the earth: The image of Enthusiasm.
> So the kings of old made music to honor merit, and lavishly offered it
> to the Supreme Lord to be worthy of their dead ancestors.

Music, like thunder, indicates something that attracts the attention of people. Music awakes feelings within and influences and puts people in a receptive mood. Music symbolizes an attractive and harmonic message that makes all listeners vibrate in the same tune. In that way people can collaborate more effectively, and share a higher purpose than selfish interest.

First Six

> Manifest Enthusiasm is ominous.

Showing off your achievements or bragging about your connections will put you at odds with the people around you. Such conduct would be a source of trouble.

Second Six

> Solid as a rock.
> His chance will come before the end of the day.
> The determination brings good fortune.

"Solid as a rock" means that you should trust your own judgment and do not deviate from your chosen path. Do not let other people or passing fads deviate you from your objectives. You should be ready to advance or retreat as the situation evolves, without hesitation and without heeding what other persons say, acting always with determination.

Third Six

> Enthusiasm that looks upward brings repentance.
> Hesitation brings remorse.

Lack of autonomy and indecision will make you to lose a good opportunity.
Procrastinators will not be rewarded.

Fourth Nine

> Enthusiasm causes great things.
> Do not hesitate.
> Friends are quick to join your side.

The right time for action has come, take your chance before the opportunity fades.
A true leader will be sure of his way and will attract like-minded people around him with excellent final results.

Fifth Six

> Determination.
> Persistently ill but not dying.

To be ill without dying indicates a period of stoppage, your will experience pressure and trouble but your determination will keep you going.

Top Six

> Confused Enthusiasm.
> But if one changes course after it is over, there will be no defect.

The time of the Enthusiasm is ending. If you don't adapt to the new circumstances but instead press ahead blindly it would be a mistake. You will have a final chance to make amendments, do not waste it.

17

suí
Following

Associated meanings

Follow, pursue, conform to, accord with, respond, follow a way or religion, accepting guidance, acquiring followers.

Judgment

> Following has outstanding success.
> The determination is favorable.
> No defect.

Continuity, persistence and flexible adaptation to the demands of the changing times are the keys to success in this time.

Following has a dual aspect, to be followed and to follow; hence knowing when to follow and when to lead others is very important. Following also is related with helping and serving other people.

Before getting your own followers you should know how to follow the right track, being open-minded and flexible enough as to hear what other persons have to say and to change course when it is needed.

This is one of the few hexagrams that mention the "four cardinal virtues": *yuan*: outstanding (fundamentality, primal, originating, spring season, head, sublime, great, grand); *heng*: success (prevalence, growing, penetrating, treat, offering, sacrifice); *li*: determination (perseverance, constancy, correct and firm) and *heng*: favorable (advantageous, suitable, beneficial, lucky). One or more of the cardinal virtues appear in 50 different hexagrams, but only the hexagrams 1, 2 (with some modification), 3, 17, 19, 25 and 49 have the four virtues in its Judgment. Since the *Han* Dynasty onwards they have become keywords of Confucian thought, four qualities or virtues applicable both to Heaven and to the noble-minded person.

Any oracle encompassing the four cardinal virtues indicates that success is granted, but only if you don't stray from the good; for this reason determination in the right way is the key to success.

The Image

In the middle of the lake is the thunder: The image of Following.
Thus the noble, at dusk, enters and rests in peace.

Chinese people believed that in winter the thunder (*yang*, creative energy), rested in the depths of the lake.

Notice that the characters translated as "at dusk" also may be translated as "when it is time to be reticent" or "when you are in darkness". Therefore, the meaning of the image is that you should rest and restore energies when it is not propitious to go ahead.

There is a time for action and a time for resting, the wise person should grasp intuitively the right moment, since the meaning of Following is to be in touch with the time. The important thing is to be adaptable enough as to pursue the right course of action at every moment.

First Nine

The situation is changing.
The determination is favorable.
Going outside to find associates is worthwhile.

This is a good moment to broaden your horizons, meet new people and accept new influences. To be ready for the coming opportunities you should be open to new alternatives, reconsider your priorities and goals, do not stick blindly to outmoded ideas.

Use your self-determination to select what is good for you and choose your goals wisely.

Second Six

He clings to the boy and lets go the strong man.

The boy symbolizes a trivial, immature, superficial choice and the strong man a sound and wise alternative or decision.

Relating with nice and care-free people only for the sake of having a good moment is not bad, at least if done occasionally; but if you choose such persons as your day-to-day relationships you will miss far more valuable people.

The essential point is that to get better things you have to discontinue your relations with low quality elements.

Third Six

He is involved with the strong man and lets go the boy.
By following one gets what one seeks for.
The determination is favorable.

This situation is the inverse of the previous line. It indicates a good and wise choice, a mature decision.

This is a good time to outgrow relationships and habits that are no longer suitable for a mature person.

By following a good model with perseverance you will achieve your goals advantageously.

Fourth Nine

By following there will be a catch.
The determination is ominous.

> He is truthful and bright on the way.
> How could there be defect in this?

The Chinese word translated as "catch" also means "hit the mark, find, succeed". You may find or achieve some tangible thing, succeed in your pursuit or catch a perception or an idea. Things will go well for a while, but if you are complacent, in the end you will have trouble.
Keep up your standards and do not trust blindly the people around you, some of your supporters may have hidden agendas.

Fifth Nine

> Sincerity leads to excellence.
> Good fortune.

Pursuing a higher goal with sincerity will help you to get the trust of others and achieve good fortune.
Notice that this line may be translated alternatively as "Faithfulness is rewarded". Hence, commitment and dedication to your duty will bring you success.

Top Six

> Strong ties between those who follow the same path.
> The king makes an offering in the Western Mountain.

The top line frequently describes a sage of somebody who is outside the situation, since the time of the hexagram is ending at this point.
You may be called from your retirement to help others.
The figure of the king making an offering in the Western Mountain indicates that your work or your ideas will be recognized by the authorities and set as an example to be imitated for others.

18

gŭ
Correcting Decay / Corruption

Associated meanings

Decay, corruption, poisonous worms in the food or the stomach, poison, evil influence, seduction, madness, insanity, curse, spell. The central meaning of the hexagram is to correct the corruption inherited from the past.

Judgment

> Correcting Decay has outstanding success.
> It is favorable to cross the great river.
> Before the first day three days.
> After the first day three days.

Decay may have been caused by carelessness, mistakes or lack of flexibility when facing changing situations.

Before correcting a spoiled situation it is important to understand the causes of it, which is the reason the Judgment says: "before the first day three days". Also, when correcting decay, people will need some time to adjust to the new rules, things cannot be fixed in no time; hence the text says "after the first day three days".

Correcting a spoiled situation implies to keep the foundation, but to eliminate all rotten parts; to keep the essence of the thing, but to get rid of the corruption that crept inside along the time. Renovating a situation that was neglected for too long takes time and requires a great effort, but the results will be good if you are willing to do a thorough job, such kind of job is indicated by the phrase "It is favorable to cross the great river".

In ancient China, crossing rivers, either at a ford or when the river was frozen, was not an easy task. It implicated dangers and hardships; hence crossing the great river means to carry out a difficult undertaking.

The Image

> The wind blows under the mountain: The image of Corruption.
> Thus the noble puts in motion the people and cultivates their moral values.

The wind blowing in the base of mountain gives the idea of stagnation, of air trapped in a valley. In the same way people may get trapped in outmoded ideas and bad habits, unable to change and improve. They should be awakened and learn new and better ways of doing things; that is the meaning of the text in the Image. New values and positive action should replace the lassitude and negative attitudes of the past.

First Six

> Correcting the decay left by his father.
> Since there is a son the father will have no defect.
> Danger.
> Good fortune in the end.

The mention to the father indicates mistakes caused for ways that are no longer valid; trouble that comes from the past. What is needed is a renovation and since the time of decay if just beginning, fixing the wrong things shouldn't be too difficult; in that way the father will have no defect.

On the other hand, if things are left to themselves, without any correction, there will be danger of stagnation. The more time passes the more difficult will be fixing the problems inherited from the past.

Second Nine

> Correcting the decay left by his mother.
> One shouldn't be too hard.

The mention to the mother and the warning about avoiding being too hard, indicates that the mistakes to be corrected should be handled with softness and gentleness, without making the people involved to lose face.

A tempered approach, taking in consideration the limitations of the people who caused the trouble, is the best option.

Third Nine

> Correcting the decay left by his father.
> There will be some regrets, but no great defect.

You may need to step in some toes to fix problems that have been neglected for a long time. You will have no help from others and some people may even complain, saying that you are too harsh, but the important thing is to fix the issues, so in the end all will go well because you have enough will and strength to straighten up the situation.

Fourth Six

> Tolerating the decay left by his father.
> He will regret going this way.

Inactivity will get you to nowhere. Weakness and rigid adhesion to the past only will cause your current troubles to grow worse.

Fifth Six

> Correcting the decay left by his father.
> You get praises.

Long standing problems should be corrected with the help of others. To get praises means that you efforts will be recognized and supported by others.

Top Nine

> Does not serve kings or lords.
> He seeks much higher goals.

The last line many times indicates somebody who is outside the situation. Here it symbolizes a wise person detached from worldly affairs, focused in spiritual goals and self-improvement.

lín
Approach / Leadership

Associated meanings

Approach, becoming great, oversee, supervise, inspect, leadership.

Judgment

> Approach.
> Outstanding Success.
> The determination is favorable.
> On the eighth month there will be misfortune.

You should be ready to make the most of the new opportunities that area approaching, because they will not last a long time. Eight months represents an ephemeral period, after it ends, the growth and prosperity will stop.

The three lower lines symbolize people that are prospering. The three upper lines indicate persons of higher rank who work with the three lower lines, helping and overseeing them.

This is one of the few hexagrams that mention the "four cardinal virtues": yuan: outstanding (fundamentality, primal, originating, spring season, head, sublime, great, grand); heng: success (prevalence, growing, penetrating, treat, offering, sacrifice); li: determination (perseverance, constancy, correct and firm) and heng: favorable (advantageous, suitable, beneficial, lucky). One or more of the cardinal virtues appear in 50 different hexagrams, but only the hexagrams 1, 2 (with some modification), 3, 17, 19, 25 and 49 have the four virtues in its Judgment. Since the Han Dynasty onwards they have become keywords of Confucian thought, four qualities or virtues applicable both to Heaven and to the noble-minded person.

Any oracle encompassing the four cardinal virtues indicates that success is granted, but only if you don't stray from the good; for this reason determination in the right path is the key to success.

The Image

> Above the lake is the earth: The image of Approach.
> Thus the noble is tireless in his efforts to educate the people
> and doesn't know boundaries in protecting and supporting them.

The image of this hexagram shows a hidden body or water, located under the earth. It symbolizes a type of leadership based on nurturing and educating the people, as a gardener waters the garden to make plants grow.

Like a garden, this time will flourish only for a while, until fall comes, hence no time should be wasted.

This is a good moment for supporting and teaching people, delegating authority in them. In that way they will grow as fully responsible persons.

First Nine

> Joint approach.
> The determination is favorable.

Your influence will attract like-minded people; joining forces with them will benefit everybody. Be ready to cooperate with others, but keep your own goals in mind.

Second Nine

> Joint approach.
> Good fortune.
> Everything is favorable.

You will get recognition from your superiors. Since you have the strength and knowledge to push forward your projects, nothing will stop your advance.

Third Six

> Sweet approach.
> No goal is favorable.
> If he becomes anxious about it, there will be no defect.

Becoming too cozy and over-confident would be an error, but if you are really sorry for your carelessness you can still avoid making big mistakes.

Be wary of flattery and do not be lazy or rash.

Fourth Six

> Approach reaches its climax.
> No defect.

The fact that the approach is at its climax and that there is no defect indicates that you can handle the situation with ease, being able to lead your subordinates well. All is running smoothly, if you keep focused in your duty you will have no trouble.

Fifth Six

> Wise approach.
> It is fitting for a lord.
> Good fortune.

A wise leader can employ others in order to serve him, trusting and promoting the capable persons (the second *yang* line) and because that he will be successful.

Top Six

> Sincere and generous approach.
> Good fortune.
> No defect.

A generous and humble sage is a blessing for the people whom he teaches (the first and second lines). He is ready to share his experience with others in order to help worthy people with his wisdom.

guān
Contemplation

Associated meanings

Contemplate, look at, observe, watch, regard, examine, evaluate; scenery, sight, aspect.

Judgment

> Contemplation.
> The ablution was done but not yet the offering.
> His dignified appearance inspires confidence.

The sacrificial rituals in ancient China started with a purification ceremony. Here is described the moment between such ceremony and the offering, the sacrifice preparations were started but it still has not been performed.
Besides knowledge, the act of quiet contemplation can provide spiritual balance and insight. After acquiring such spiritual insight, one becomes a living example for other people, like the worshiper in the Judgment, who symbolizes a highly developed person performing an important task. Such person will be publicly looked on and will inspire trust in the spectators. Contemplation means to acquire knowledge about something by carefully observing it, but it is not possible to look at something without changing it, because the observer will also be seen by others.

The Image

> The wind moves upon the earth: The image of Contemplation.
> Thus the ancient kings inspected all regions looking at the people
> and giving instruction.

The wind moving upon the earth means to look far away, trying to understand the customs of other people with an open mind. The ancient kings symbolize wise persons that know how to adapt ancient wisdom to the reality of the people, to instruct and guide them.
From a personal viewpoint, the image is telling us to widen our horizons, to take a fresh look at the situation, and also to adapt and apply old beliefs to the current situation.

First Six

> Childish contemplations.
> No defect for the small man.
> For the noble is humiliating.

Lack of understanding is not a fault for an ignorant or young person. Some persons may have limited understanding of the situation, lacking analytical capacity. Indeed ignorance would be excusable in young people, but in a mature individual it would be shaming, since such person should know better.

In any case, the one described here doesn't understand the situation, and because that he will not be able to act correctly.

Second Six

> Furtive contemplation.
> The determination is favorable for a woman.

The Chinese word translated as "furtive", also indicates to "peep through a door crack". In ancient China women neither could leave her homes nor have a superior education, hence it would not be expected from them to have wide knowledge of the world; for that reason furtive contemplation is related to a woman.

Indeed somebody looking through a door crack cannot have a good knowledge of what is looked upon, since such person cannot see the whole scene. Hence, this line indicates somebody –either a man or a woman– who has a narrow field of view and cannot understand the whole situation.

You may lack knowledge or be limited by dogmatism, looking on reality from a distorted viewpoint. This kind of limited contemplation would be excusable in somebody with limited possibilities, like a woman in ancient China, but not in a capable person.

Also this line may point to some kind of spying in favor of a weak faction.

Third Six

> Looking at the progress and setbacks in my life.

Some maturity has been reached at this point. It is time to try to make sense of your past life, to understand and eventually change the way you behave.

Making a realistic balance of your possibilities will make clear to you what you can do from now on.

Fourth Six

> Contemplation of the glory of the kingdom.
> It is favorable to act as a guest of a king.

Contemplation of the glory of the kingdom means to broaden your horizons and discover new possibilities. You can use your talents to support a worthy cause or business.

The phrase rendered as "favorable to act as a guest of a king", also may be translated as "favorable for having audience with the king"; it means that you can progress by contacting the right person who is in a position of authority.

Fifth Nine

> Contemplation of my life.
> The noble has no defect.

You occupy an elevated position. Your decisions affect not only your own life but also other people.

The text says "no defect" because you will keep clean or errors by watching with attention the result of your actions. Only by contemplating the effect of your actions you will know if you did the right thing.

Top Nine

> Contemplation of his life.
> The noble has no faults.

The sixth line many times depicts a wise person who is not concerned by worldly matters.
You can see with detachment and a good perspective not only what happens around you but also your own actions, because you no longer care for success and money. As a result you can see things as they really are. Your clarity will prevent you from making any mistakes.

"Knowing others is intelligence; knowing yourself is true wisdom. Mastering others is strength; mastering yourself is true power." (*Laozi*)

shì hé
Biting Through

Associated meanings

To bite through, crush between the teeth, consuming, union by gnawing, remove the obstacles so the jaws come together.

Judgment

> Biting Through is successful.
> It is favorable to administer justice.

This hexagram is related with criminal lawsuits, the other hexagram with a similar meaning is the number 6: **The Conflict**, which indicates a civil lawsuit.

Biting Through indicates that energetic measures must be applied to correct a wrong. There is some obstruction, some dysfunctional element that should be punished or removed. The bite indicates a fast and energetic action, applying justice with strength to fix some issue. It also indicates that this is the time to take a stand and fight for what you believe in.

The first and last lines are those who receive punishment, the other lines are the ones administering justice.

The Image

> Thunder and lightning: The image of the Biting Through.
> Thus the ancient kings applied punishments with intelligence
> and enacted laws.

Thunder is shocking and represents the force of the law in action, lighting indicates clarity: laws should be clearly defined to make it clear what is lawful and what is not and should have real force behind them.

The ancient kings symbolize a pattern or model of good governance, which we should strive to follow.

To apply punishment with intelligence means to not act arbitrarily and to measure carefully the kind and degree of the punishment to be applied, on a case by case basis.

To enact the laws means to put the laws in action without delay and to be ready to do what is needed to restore justice.

First Nine

> His feet are trapped by fetters
> and his toes are mangled.
> No defect.

Being the first line the movement is only starting here, hence the punishment is applied as a preventive action, trapping the feet means to prevent a transgression. The fetters indicate a punitive action that stops a first-time transgressor from continuing with his bad behavior. The first line, being in a low position, is associated with the feet in several hexagrams.

The transgressor becomes free of blame because he is stopped in his tracks and prevented from committing further transgressions.

Second Six

> Biting Through tender flesh, the nose is destroyed.
> No defect.

Tender flesh indicates that there are no complications, the facts are clear. To destroy the nose may indicate that you you're too enthusiastic and lacking in sensibility, being too hard; or it may mean that cutting out the nose was the punishment applied in this case. In any case, the punishment is right. The line says "no defect" because there are more than enough arguments to condemn the transgressor.

Third Six

> Biting Through dried meat finds poison.
> A little humiliation.
> No defect.

You face a long time neglected problem and some things that come to the light may cause trouble. The person to be punished will not submit meekly and instead will try to get back to you. Since you lack enough power to fully correct the issues that you are facing, you will lose some face but in the end you will not make any mistakes.

Fourth Nine

> Biting Through bone-dry meat he gets metal arrows.
> Fortitude under trying conditions is favorable.
> Good fortune.

To get metal arrows indicates that to overcome strong resistance and to manage an old problem, which is tough as dried meat, you need to have the proper elements (the **hexagram 40.2** also mentions getting arrows, but golden instead metallic). The arrows symbolize speed, guidance, hardness and penetration; they indicate as well that you should be very determined and tough to be able to apply the proper punishment effectively.

"Of old, in a civil case, both parties, before they were heard, brought to the court an arrow (or a bundle of arrows), in testimony of their rectitude, after which they were heard; in a criminal case, they in the same way deposited each thirty pounds of gold, or some other metal." (*Legge*)

Fifth Six

> Biting Through dry meat he gets yellow metal.
> The determination is dangerous.
> No defect.

This line represents the regent, but as a weak, *yin* line, he will be disposed to leniency. To get yellow metal indicates that you should take precautions. Be ready to be impartial and just, and have ready the proper means before facing dangerous situations.

"The determination is dangerous" means that it would be perilous to force the situation or to go to extremes. Keep your balance and you will make no mistakes.

Top Nine

> He carries a yoke that make his ears disappear.
> Ominous.

An obstinate wrongdoer who doesn't heed any warnings only will have misfortune. The fact that the yoke cover his hears indicates that he is not able to hear or learn, that he will not correct his ways because he is deafened by his stubbornness.

bì
Elegance / Adornment / Grace

Associated meanings

Ornate, elegant, brilliant; embellish, adorn; good manners, finesse, diplomatic maneuvering.

Judgment

> Elegance.
> Success
> It is favorable to have a goal in minor matters.

Social etiquette norms are useful to regulate the behavior of people for the benefit of the common good. Thus grace helps to keep the social order.

Applied to the current situation, it means that you should handle it with finesse and charm; this is not the proper time for assertive or bold behavior but for tactful and elegant conduct. Your relations with other people will be better if you are polite and have educated manners. Avoid taking important decisions or handling difficult affairs.

The Image

> Fire at the foot of the mountain: The image of Elegance.
> Thus the noble regulates the crowds with enlightenment.
> But doesn't dare to decide criminal cases.

The fire illuminates and highlights the mountain, in the same way, by emphasizing the desired behavior, with charm and persuasion, a sage guides the people. This means using soft, persuasive methods, to teach and convince the people.
Nevertheless, such soft methods cannot be used to handle hardened criminals.

First Nine

> He gives Elegance to his feet, leaves the carriage and walks.

To leave the carriage means to get down to essentials, to discard some things and simplify your life. To give elegance to his feet suggests to use your own means for advancing, to use your own resources instead relying on others for getting an easy ride.

Second Six

> He gives Elegance to his beard.

To gave elegance to his beard means to follow some rules or traditions required in some places. Your position is weak and dependent so you need to conform to the customs established by your superiors or by society.

Third Nine

> Adorned with moisture.
> Long-term determination is fortunate.

You have a very elegant and comfortable way of life. However you ought to keep your constancy to avoid being weakened by your opulent lifestyle. If you keep up your strength and determination you will be fortunate.

Fourth Six

> Adorned in white.
> A white horse soaring.
> He is not a robber, but a suitor.

The sudden appearance of a newcomer –adorned with simple white elegance, but with soaring thoughts and objectives–, may cause some doubts, but his sincere wish is to cooperate. In time, he will be accepted and the obstructions will disappear.
You may hesitate before taking an important decision. May be somebody offered you something or asked for your friendship or love.
Getting the trust of another person will take some time.

Fifth Six

> Elegance in hills and gardens.
> The silk bundle is meager.
> Humiliation, but good fortune at the end.

Hills and gardens also can be translated as "native forest" or "wild park". In any case it indicates a quiet place, outside the active city life. It symbolizes a secluded circle where you want to enter, a natural and spiritual place. But you don't have much to offer, your material resources are meager, and you may feel humiliated because that. In the end such things will not matter because you will be accepted.
To look for the hills and gardens also may indicate a search of peace, to move away from the mundane noise.

Top Nine

> Simple elegance.
> No defect.

Many times the sixth line is beyond the situation. In this case it is beyond adorning.
Simplicity is the only thing that you need. By being completely sincere you will make no mistakes.

23

bō
Splitting Apart / Decay

Associated meanings
Flay, strip, peel; pluck, lay bare, strip (as clothes or badges of office); split, slice, crack; disintegration.

Judgment
> Splitting Apart.
> It is not favorable to go anywhere.

This is a time of decay, when evil men prosper and destroy the support that good people have. Interpersonal relations are hampered, each person is for himself; trust is scarce and people don't cooperate between them any longer. This declination process cannot be stopped, so instead wasting time and energy in fighting it, the best course of action is to remain calm and stay out of trouble until it ends.

The Image
> The mountain lies on earth: The image of Splitting Apart.
> Thus by means of being munificent with those below them,
> the superiors secure the peace and stability of their own position.

To keep your position safe you have to secure your foundations. Make sure that you keep the support of the people from whom you depend for your needs. Be ready to make concessions to others instead fighting and keep a low profile.

First Six
> Splitting Apart the legs of the bed.
> Determination leads to destruction.
> Ominous.

A bed that is disintegrated bit by bit symbolizes how the situation is undermined gradually by evil men, from the periphery (the legs) up to the center (the skin, in the fourth line).
Splitting apart the bed's legs indicates a systematic plan of action for depriving you of your support. Also, since the bed is a place for resting, your tranquility and peace are threatened as well.

There is nothing you can do except to be alert and wait. Any offensive action will only make worse your plight.

Second Six

> Splitting Apart the bed's frame.
> Determination leads to destruction.
> Ominous.

The situation worsens and the attack is affecting the very frame that supports your position. You will be left without supporters and defenseless.
Be flexible; try to see a way to retreat to a safe place. If you try to fight to maintain your position you will be crushed.

Third Six

> Splitting Apart them.
> No defect.

Do not let others sway you from your principles. You are surrounded by bad people, but if you break your bond with them you will make no mistakes.

Fourth Six

> The bed is peeled down to the skin.
> Ominous.

In ancient times the bed mattress was an animal skin stretched across the frame. If that skin was destroyed the bed became useless.
The bad times are at its worst. Decay affects you directly; you have no support and nowhere to rest. There is no way to escape from the trouble now.

Fifth Six

> A string of fishes.
> Favors by means of the ladies of palace.
> Nothing that is not favorable.

Decay is ending. The string of fishes symbolizes people that are starting to cooperate following a good lead. The ladies of palace are symbolized by the five *yin* lines that are now stopping their hostility and instead cooperating for the good of all. Receiving favors by the ladies of palace means to be endorsed, to be introduced to the center of power. New opportunities for moving things forward will appear.

Top Nine

> A large fruit still uneaten.
> The noble gets a carriage; the petty man shelter is split apart.

The large fruit symbolizes great achievements and indicates a great person among many others who are inferior.
Also, the large fruit is the symbol of the new opportunities for advancement that will open up. The noble getting a carriage indicates that capable persons are now in power, with plenty of support and moving ahead. On the other side, the petty people that thrived in the bad times will lose all their ill-gotten gains.

fù
Return

Associated meanings

Return, turn back; repeat; restore, revert, renewal.

Judgment

> Return.
> Success.
> Exit and entry without harm.
> Friends come.
> No defect.
> Back and forth along the way.
> In seven days will return.
> It is favorable to have where to go.

This hexagram is related with the month of the Winter Solstice, the time in the year when days start to grow longer and the *yang* power, symbolized by the thunder and the first line, returns. The "seven days" reference may refer to a short time or to the start of a new cycle, like the seventh day when the moon reaches a major phase after the new moon. Besides this hexagram, the Chinese character for seven only appears in the hexagrams 51 and 63, in the second line in both cases. Here it indicates the beginning of a new cycle and a return. It is related with the return of money in the hexagram 51 and with the return of a curtain in the hexagram 63. The return is a natural occurrence, the days will be getting longer at the winter solstice, but spring still is several months off. For this reason it would be useless to try to force matters, since the situation will develop at its own pace.

Exit and entry without harm means that after a period of stagnation, there will appear opportunities and things will start to move ahead. People will join in groups to collaborate spontaneously.

Since the *yang* energy still is not firmly established, there will be adjustments to be done and you may have to try different ways until finding the proper one, but in the end you will find a worthy goal, which is the reason the text says "it is favorable to have where to go".

The Image

> The thunder in the middle of the earth: The image of Return.
> So on the day of the solstice, the ancient kings closed the border crossings.
> Merchants and travelers did not travel
> and the ruler did not visit his dominions.

The ancient kings closed the entry points of the realm at the winter solstice to allow people rest.

The return is a period of renewal, a recovery after a time of weakness or estrangement. At the beginning of such moments it is important to rest for a while, to halt all activity to nourish the returning energy (*yang* principle) in order to allow it to grow, to be ready for intense activity at the proper time, later.

First Nine

> Returning before going too far.
> There will be no need for repentance.
> Outstanding good fortune.

Mistakes should be corrected before they complicate the situation further. When an error is corrected without hesitation, reacting on time, there will be no cause for shame and you will secure a good result.

Second Six

> Quiet return.
> Good fortune.

The Chinese character translated as "quiet" also means "resign, release, let go". This means that you will be able to relax, reconsider and finally go back. It also indicates avoiding trouble and to be happy with the outcome of the situation.

Third Six

> Repeated return.
> Danger.
> No repentance.

Insecurity and vacillation will make you to waste your time, but at least, if you see and correct your mistakes you will avoid having further trouble, hence there will be no reason for repentance.

The Chinese character translated here as "repeated" also means "on the brink of, river bank, shore", so the line may alternatively read "returning from the brink of water". The meaning in such case is to return from a dangerous position, to step back from the brink of a dangerous body of water, since moving water is a symbol of danger in the *Yijing*.

Fourth Six

> Returns alone by the middle of the road.

You are subjected to different influences, but you will choose to follow your own course, and as result you will return alone. The line doesn't say if your new course is good or bad, but walking by the middle of the road (avoiding the extremes) indicates good balance and composure, which can never be a bad thing.

Fifth Six

> Earnest return.
> No defect.

The Chinese character for "earnest" also means "honest, solid, and sincere". It indicates that the return is a true one and that it is done without doubts, with full commitment.

Top Six

> The return goes astray.
> Ominous.
> Calamities and errors.
> If he puts armies on the march, in the end will suffer a great defeat,
> whose misfortune will extend to the ruler of the state.
> For ten years he will not be able to attack.

Being the last line in the hexagram, the return here is done from the most distant point. Because you are confused and have advanced too far in the wrong direction, you will miss the proper moment and the right path for returning.

Putting armies in the march means to put considerable resources in the wrong place. If you insist obstinately in such aggressive and wrong behavior you will suffer big losses.

Ten years indicates a long period, like in hexagrams 3.2 and 27.3, but in this case it also means that you will be powerless for a long time after suffering a resounding defeat.

25

wú wàng
Innocence /
No expectations

Associated meanings

Innocent behavior, no expectancy, acting spontaneously, wholehearted sincerity; unexpected happenings.

Judgment

> Innocence.
> Outstanding success.
> The determination is favorable.
> If he is not honest he has misfortune.
> It is favorable to have a goal.

Innocence means genuine, without fakery, without guile or pretensions. Innocent action signifies following your natural instincts when facing the unexpected. Doing what you really want to do, without expectations, just for the sake of it.

Being in touch with the time is the key point here. The time of innocence requires intuition, sincerity and adaptability to the changing circumstances, not following a script.

This is one of the few hexagrams that mention the "four cardinal virtues": *yuan*: outstanding (fundamentality, primal, originating, spring season, head, sublime, great, grand); *heng*: success (prevalence, growing, penetrating, treat, offering, sacrifice); *li*: determination (perseverance, constancy, correct and firm) and *heng*: favorable (advantageous, suitable, beneficial, lucky). One or more of the cardinal virtues appear in 50 different hexagrams, but only the hexagrams 1, 2 (with some modification), 3, 17, 19, 25 and 49 have the four virtues in its Judgment. Since the *Han* Dynasty onwards they have become keywords of Confucian thought, four qualities or virtues applicable both to Heaven and to the noble-minded person.

Any oracle encompassing the four cardinal virtues indicates that success is granted, but only if you don't stray from the good; for this reason determination in the right way is the key to success.

The Image

> The thunder moves under heaven and all things partake of innocence.
> Thus the ancient kings, in excellent harmony with the seasons,
> nurtured all beings.

The thunder under the heavens means power and creativity.
The ancient kings symbolize a pattern or model of good governance, in tune with the rhythms of nature.
In the same way, you should be in harmony with the tides of change, accepting people and the ever changing world on its own terms.
Do not try to adapt people and reality to your own conditions; you should be flexible enough as to perceive intuitively the best way to relate with the changing circumstances around you.

First Nine

Going forward with innocence brings good fortune.
Acting with spontaneity, following your natural impulses will be lucky. Do not repress yourself, be flexible and open to change.
You will accomplish your wishes.

Second Six

> Harvest without plowing.
> The fields are ready for use without having been prepared.
> It is favorable to have a goal.

To harvest without plowing and having the fields ready without preparing them beforehand indicates that you work on behalf of another and you don't initiate the action yourself. But you will do what you are asked for because you want to do it, not because of greed or blind obedience.
Another alternative translation would be "not doing the plowing for the sake of the harvest, nor doing the clearing for the sake of having a mature field", meaning that you will do what you have to do, without caring for the possible benefits, without expectations, simply taking pride in doing a good job.
The line also means to get good rewards after little effort or simply getting lucky, but it is important to focus properly in your goals.

Third Six

> Unexpected disaster.
> The cow tied by someone, is the traveler's gain and the villager's misfortune.

The loss of somebody is the gain of other person. Good time for the wanderer and losses for the sedentary person.
Some may benefit from your bad luck, but your troubles are not your fault. Alternatively you may have gains at the expense of other people.

Fourth Nine

> If you can keep your determination there will be no defect

An alternative translation would be "can be determined", or "an augury can be made". The meaning is that you choose what to do you should stick to your own decision and do not let it waver. Stick to your own vocation and advice, be true to yourself.

Fifth Nine

> Unexpected illness.
> Do not take medicine and you will rejoice.

Unexpected trouble unfolds. Let the situation take its own course, do not interfere and the problems will improve by themselves.

Top Nine

> Innocent action brings misfortune.
> No place is favorable.

Stop right now. Following your natural impulses only will get you into trouble. The time for innocent behavior is gone. Wait until new opportunities arise, until then do nothing.

I Ching: Oracular Interpretation

dà chù
Great Accumulation

Associated meanings

The taming power of the great, controlled power, great domestication, great restraint (what is restrained accumulates its strength), big accumulation, great nurturing, gathering up and developing resources for future use.

Judgment

> Great Accumulation.
> The determination is favorable.
> Not eating at home brings good fortune.
> It is favorable to cross the great river.

Before accomplishing great achievements, you should muster your resources. Do not act before making appropriate preparations.

To leave your own home in order to look for sustenance means to expand, to overcome your current limits.

In ancient China, crossing rivers, either at a ford or when the river was frozen, was not an easy task. It implicated dangers and hardships; hence crossing the great river means to carry out a difficult undertaking.

The Image

> Heaven in the middle of the mountain: The image of Great Accumulation.
> Thus, the noble is acquainted with many words and deeds of the past
> and cultivates his character.

Heaven in the middle of the mountain symbolizes hidden treasures. Knowledge from the past is a valuable treasure that not only has intellectual value but also can be applied to the present. Before embarking in a new venture gather as much information as possible about it and also look at how similar projects have fared in the past.

The Chinese character translated as "character" also means "ability, aptitude, quality"; increasing your knowledge will surely make you more able and confident. Also, the deeds of other people in the past will provide you with good role models to follow.

First Nine

> Danger.
> It is best to halt.

It should be better to wait for a change in the current conditions, because there are dangerous obstacles ahead blocking your path.

Second Nine

> The axle brackets are removed from the carriage.

The axle brackets are two pieces of wood underneath a cart, which hold the axle firmly on both sides. If they are removed the carriage will not move, no matter how much power is applied to push or drag it.

You will not receive any warnings before your are stopped, and your advance will be completely checked since the repressing power is incontestable. It is time to submit and wait, storing up resources for future usage.

Third Nine

> Good horses that run one after another.
> Fortitude under trying conditions.
> Exercise every day with chariots and defensive measures.
> It is favorable to have a goal.

The blockage is removed and you can advance along with other people of the same mind, like horses running together.

Danger and further difficulties lurk ahead, do not be reckless. Your determination will be tested.

To make your plans work, mobility, speed and good defensive measures will be required.

It is imperative that you take precautions and every conceivable defensive measure. Training with chariots indicates that you should check and recheck your plans, make sure that they will work as intended, and also to be ready to make adjustments on the go.

Fourth Six

> The protective covering of the horns of the calf.
> Outstanding good fortune.

Preventing a young bull from goring anyone with his horns before they have grown indicates that precautionary measures should be applied long before real danger is present, to prevent trouble in advance. Also it means than you should control the people under your responsibility to avoid potential trouble.

In the same way, applying this to you inner self, you should exercise self-control and avoid taking any action before you are ready for it.

The main theme of this hexagram is to accumulate power by restraining and channeling properly your strength without wasting it prematurely, and in that way avoiding falling into danger.

Fifth Six

> The tusks of a castrated boar.
> Good fortune.

The raw power has been tamed; the energy is sublimated and now it can be used without danger.

Danger can be external, coming from other people; or internal, if you lose control of your passions.

Here the danger is neutralized in his source and at last you can apply the power successfully. Good fortune is the result of regulating effectively your energy and using it for the good.

Top Nine

> Attains the way of heaven.
> Success.

An alternative translation would be "receives the blessings from heaven". At this point all obstacles have been overcome and you will find the appropriate way of expression to fulfill your potentialities. The way of heaven means to have a very broad scope of action.

The "way of heaven" also may indicate that you will fulfill your destiny and that you are following commands from above. The Chinese character translated as "heaven", *tiān*, only appears three times as a religious concept (instead the physical sky) in the Judgment and lines, once in this hexagram and two more times in the hexagram 14. In this context it means "divine, power above the human".

27

yí
Nourishment / The Jaws

Associated meanings

Nourish, feed, to care for in the early years of life; the jaws, the chin, the cheeks, jawbones.

Judgment

> Nourishment.
> Determination brings good fortune.
> Watch what you nourish
> and what you are looking to fill your mouth with.

This hexagram is related to nourishment, which includes not only material food but emotional and spiritual nourishment as well.

The three lower lines nourish themselves (material nourishment) and the three upper lines nourish other people (spiritual nourishment).

Choosing the right source of nourishment for your spirit is important, since it will determine the kind of people that you will become.

To watch the nourishment means not only to select the right values for your spiritual nourishment, but also the right food for your table. Also you shouldn't take your nourishment at the expense of other people.

The Image

> Under the mountain is the thunder: The image of Nourishment.
> Thus the noble is careful with what he says,
> and restrained in his drinking and eating.

Your words affect the people around you, they can nourish others emotional and spiritually or damage them. The kind of food you incorporate into your body may damage you if you are not temperate. In both cases the jaws are used either for taking food or for saying words. Also, the things you watch and hear are part of the nourishment of your spirit.

First Nine

> You let your magic turtle go and look at me with your jaws hanging.
> Misfortune.

Losing the magic turtle indicates that you are not taking care of your responsibilities as you should. The magic turtle symbolizes your intelligence and initiative. You should be able to take care of yourself easily; you have the means to do that. But instead you look at other people with envy. Such dependent attitude will be bad for you.

Take control of your own life and accept responsibility for your own decisions.

Turtle shells were used as an oracular medium long before the *Yijing* was in use. During the *Shang* and *Zhou* dynasties, ox shoulder blades and turtle's shells were used to divine. With time, the *Zhou* dynasty replaced that method by yarrow stalks to query the *Yijing*. Hence, the magic turtle indicates oracular powers and spiritual insight. Also the turtles were a symbol of longevity.

Second Six

> Forages in the summit.
> Turns away from the path and goes to the summit for Nourishment.
> Going forward brings misfortune.

You are seeking nourishment in the wrong place instead doing the job of providing for yourself as you should do. If you continue on the wrong path you will face misfortune.

The Chinese word translated as "summit", in this context also indicates danger of falling down or being overthrow. If you do not know any limit and measure and take excessive risks, you will fall down.

Third Six

> Rejects Nourishment.
> The determination brings misfortune.
> Do not act for ten years.
> Nothing at all is favorable.

Seeking the wrong nourishment with persistence will trap you in a vicious cycle that will damage your health.

Ten years indicates a long period, like in the hexagrams **3.2** or **24.5**.

Fourth Six

> Forages in the summit.
> Staring like a tiger, with greed and insatiable desire to chase.
> No defect.

The summit is a high place which allows a clear view all around, it indicates clarity of mind and intent. The tiger is a symbol of extreme *yang*, powerful and energetic, but in this case such strong desire is oriented toward nourishing others in the right way, for that reason there you will make no mistakes.

The fourth line symbolizes a minister who is working for his king, looking out for reliable helpers.

Fifth Six

> Moving away from the path.
> The determination brings good fortune.
> He cannot cross the great river.

To move away from the path indicates that you cannot find a way to help and nourish others under the current circumstances and you will have to look for unconventional ways to comply with your responsibilities. You will need the help of a wise person (the sixth line) who will guide you with his experience and knowledge.

Not crossing the river means to recognize your own limitations and to avoid doing dangerous things that are beyond your means, but instead to seek guidance.

Top Nine

> The source of Nourishment.
> Danger, but good fortune.
> It is favorable to cross the great river.

You have the power to educate, guide and nourish other people. Do not take your responsibilities lightly, if you are careful you will have success.

In ancient China, crossing rivers, either at a ford or when the river was frozen, was not an easy task. It implicated dangers and hardships; hence crossing the great river means to carry out a difficult undertaking.

28

dà kuo
Great Excess

Associated meanings

Overload, critical mass, excess of the great, major superiority, preponderance of the great, inner preponderance.

Judgment

> Great Excess.
> The main beam sags.
> It is favorable to have a goal.
> Success.

The four internal *yang* lines in this hexagram symbolize a supporting beam that is overloaded. The *yin* lines on the bottom and the top are the weak support of the inner *yang* lines. The text says "the main beam sags", it means that the load is too heavy for the supporting beam, which is straining beyond its endurance.

The *yang* lines symbolize power, energy that is reaching the breaking point. This is an extraordinary time because the abundance or *yang* energy, but it also requires extraordinary measures to avoid trouble and balance the situation because the foundation is not stable.

You are overburdened and stressed; to be successful you should decide what to do and then advance towards your goal without wasting any time. It is time to take prompt action, but with utmost care and without violence.

The Image

> The lake covers the trees: The image of Great Excess.
> Thus the noble remains alone without fear
> and retreats from the world without regret.

The lake covering the trees symbolizes a situation that has reached a critical point, that is no longer under control.

The threes under water also indicate that you are isolated and cannot act effectively. Actually you should stop and take distance from your daily troubles for a while; you cannot deal with all the obligations that are wearing you down.

You should decide what you can do and discard what you cannot handle anymore; no matter if that means that you have to leave things or some people behind or if you defy conventional wisdom or political correctness.

First Six

> Use a white reeds offering mat.
> No defect.

The first line is where the movement starts but it also indicates a humble position. Poor people used to place their offerings on mats of grasses, while wealthy people used bronze ritual vessels for that.

The mat or reeds symbolizes taking careful precautions before doing anything. If you advance with caution and sincerity you will make no mistake.

"To place the things on the ground might be considered sufficient; but when he places beneath them mats of the white grass, what occasion for blame can there be? Such a course shows the height of carefulness. The white grass is a trivial thing, but, through the use made of it, it may become important. He who goes forward using such careful art will not fall into any error." (*Ten Wings, Xiaoxiang I*).

Second Nine

> New shoots grow from a withered willow.
> An old man gets a young wife.
> Nothing that is not favorable.

This line indicates that something that looked withered is being renewed; an unusual alliance is putting new energy into your life.

Also it may indicate that you will look at your life with new eyes and new interests after forming a partnership with a younger or inexpert person.

Third Nine

> The main beam sags.
> Misfortune.

If you go too far and are stubborn and inflexible; the price for your arrogance will be failure. Know your limits and ask for help when needed, otherwise you will struggle with more than you can manage.

Fourth Nine

> The main beam bulges upward.
> Good fortune.
> If there is something else, it will be regretful.

The main beam bulges upward because it is supported from below. It forms an arch and in that way it can support more weight than before.

If you make good use of your current position of strength you will have good fortune, but if you misuse your resources trying to get advantages only for yourself, forgetting your supporters, you will be sorry. Know your limits or you will have trouble.

Fifth Nine

> A withered willow produces flowers.
> An old woman gets a young husband.
> Neither failure nor praise.

An old man can have children with a young wife (like the second line suggests), but an old woman cannot do the same with a young husband.

The union described in this line cannot generate good and lasting results, only something evanescent as flowers, which symbolize temporary pleasure. If you try to fix your problems only on the surface, for show, in the long run you will get nowhere.

This line occupies the place of the ruler; a decadent ruler cannot fix his problems by getting help from a strong subject.

Top Six

> Excess when fording the river.
> The water covers the top of the head.
> Misfortune.
> No defect.

If you cope with a dangerous endeavor at any cost (like wading a river that is too deep) it will cost your dearly. You may have to sacrifice too much, because you are not up to the task and you will not be able to finish it successfully.

It is only you who can decide if the sacrifices that you are facing are worthwhile.

29

xí kǎn
Pit doubled / Pit within a pit

This is one of the eight hexagrams that are comprised by the same trigram repeated twice, in this case *kan*, The Abysmal.

Associated meanings

Entrapment, perilous passage, danger, critical time, sinking, pit, trap, snare, pitfall, mastering pitfalls. The meanings are intensified because the first character in the hexagram tag means "repeated", hence it gives the idea a of a long stretch of danger. Pits were dug in the ground to keep prisoners jailed in ancient China.

Judgment

> The Pit doubled.
> If you follow what you feel in your heart you will succeed.
> Moving forward brings rewards.

The situation is dangerous and difficult. To be successful in these critical times you should emulate water, which is the symbol of danger but also tells us how to overcome perilous times. Water flows unceasingly and always is true to itself, it fills every crevice following its course, without ever turning back.
To ride successfully this time you should not retreat, but to advance unceasingly like flowing water, facing every turn of the way with resolution. Follow what your heart tells you and be true to yourself.
You may make mistakes and will be exposed to danger, but if you keep your determination and continue pushing ahead with determination, you will prevail against the odds.

The Image

> The water flows to reach the goal: The image of the Pit doubled.
> Thus the noble maintains constantly his virtuous conduct,
> and practices the job of teaching.

Like the water flowing non-stop, filling all holes in its way, you should take care or every detail. This is not a good time for cutting corners, but to act earnestly and with devotion to the task or duty that you are committed for.

Water flowing unremittingly also symbolizes teaching by example, by repetition.

First Six

> The Pit doubled.
> One falls into a pit at the bottom of the cave.
> Misfortune.

After losing your way you have fallen into a pattern of repetitive mistakes that have trapped you like if you were in the bottom of a double pit. The situation is very serious, if you do not realize how bad it is and do something about it, you will have serious trouble.

Second Nine

> The Pit is dangerous.
> You can only get small gains.

When confronting dangerous obstacles you can only do small things. Do not try to solve all your problems in a hurry. For now you only can manage to improve a few things, making your situation safer by small steps.

The Chinese word translated as "dangerous" also means "steep, a precipice". Hence the danger of falling down the abyss.

Third Six

> Coming to the Pit.
> Deep and dangerous Pit.
> Enters a pit in the cave.
> Do nothing.

You are trapped in a dangerous situation which you do not understand completely. Anything that you try to do to extricate yourself only will worsen your position. You cannot leave from where you are without external help, so until you get it just relax and wait.

Fourth Six

> A jug of wine over a bowl of rice.
> Using clay pots, delivered jointly by the window.
> At the end there will be no defect.

Proceed with utter simplicity, directness and honesty. You may feel that what you have to offer is not much, but the important thing is to be truthful, that will be enough to avoid making any mistakes.

In another interpretation level, pits were often used as prison cells and this line shows somebody giving help to a person that is imprisoned or trapped in a bad situation, nourishing the prisoner with material or spiritual food.

Fifth Nine

> The Pit does not overflow.
> Only is filled to the brim.
> No defect.

You will get out of your current difficulties. The situation will worsen only up to some point, an then it will stabilize and improve by itself.

Be careful to avoid any excesses, do not overextend yourself.

Top Six

> Tied with a braided rope and a black cord.
> Abandoned in a thorny bush.
> For three years you get nothing.
> Misfortune.

If you insist in going the wrong way you will be punished and trapped by your own folly. You will be stopped and immobilized for a full period because you have broken the law.

The thorny bush suggests that you will be kept captive or trapped in some bad situation (the two Chinese characters translated as "thorny bush" also mean "to keep a prisoner captive in a place").

Three years indicate a full period of stoppage.

30

lí
The Clinging / Fire

This is one of the eight hexagrams that are comprised by the same trigram repeated twice, in this case *lí*, The Clinging.

Associated meanings

Brightness, radiance, clarity; attach, cling, a net, allegiance; name of a bird (oriole or some kind of owl), bird of omen. The modern meaning is to leave.

Judgment

> The Clinging.
> The determination is favorable.
> Taming a cow brings good fortune.

Enlightenment and allegiance are the main themes of this hexagram.
A tamed cow indicates docility and compliance; also it means to know when you should be ready to make concessions.
To have determination but to be compliant as well means that you should do what duty demands, to adhere closely to what is the correct thing to do.
The Clinging also depicts the ability to catch insights and perceptions, like a net, using them to follow the proper path of enlightenment.

The Image

> Brightness duplicated: The image of The Clinging.
> Thus the great man maintains its clarity,
> illuminating the four cardinal points.

The lower trigram symbolizes clarity within, and the upper external clarity. The meaning of this, applied to human life is that, only having internal insight, knowing yourself well (as indicated by the lower trigram), you will be able to shed light over the world around you (symbolized by the upper trigram) and to understand it in depth.

Fire is consuming, and consequently this hexagram speaks about the transience of life. Only if the fire of enlightenment clings to your life, you will make sense and a good use of it.

First Nine

> Walking with hesitant and cautious steps.
> If you take care there will be no defect.

This line symbolizes sunrise time and the start of a day or a journey through life.
You are beginning your journey still ignoring your destiny and your path. For that reason it is only natural to be cautious and to hesitate for a while. The important thing is to have proper care, if you take reverent attention to the task at hand you will not fail.

Second Six

> Yellow glow.
> Outstanding good fortune.

This line symbolizes the middle of the day when the Sun shines.
You have reached a good understanding. The yellow color symbolizes taking the proper way, the middle path between the extremes, indicating good balance.

Third Nine

> In the light of the setting sun, if he does not drum the pot and sing,
> he will regret the approach of old age.
> Misfortune.

This line symbolizes the setting Sun and the end of a cycle.
A moment of splendor is fading; you can either enjoy the present or be sorry because the good times are going to end soon.
It doesn't matter what you do, you will lose something, but if you accept your fate with docility you will suffer less.

Fourth Nine

> Comes abruptly, as with fire and death and thus is discarded.

This line describes a rapid ascension, propelled with violence and extreme brightness. Such an accelerated process will not have enough time to consolidate, it will burn quickly, like a straw fire, and extinguish itself with the same velocity.
The person described here will be discarded because he didn't take the proper measures to get support. At the end he will be isolated and forgotten.

Fifth Six

> Torrents of tears with sorrow and lamentations.
> Good fortune.

Looking over your past mistakes you will regret bitterly them when you see the things that you have done with a new clarity.
After the darkest hour a new dawning is coming.

Top Nine

> The king sends him to attack.
> It is worthwhile to execute the leaders and capture
> those that are not of the same evil sort.
> No defect.

Some problems should be taken care off. To be sent by the kind means that you have real authority and no doubts. Executing only the leaders means to get to the root of the problem, and avoids wasting time with small details.

Killing the leaders may be also translated as "sever the heads"; this phrase emphasizes the need to deal with the cause of the problem, not its manifestations.

31

xián

Influence / Reciprocity

Four hexagrams are related with marriage and the preliminary steps leading to it: 31-Influence, depicts the initial attraction and courtship in a couple; **32-Duration**, indicates the institution of marriage; **53-Gradual Development**, shows the steps and ceremonies leading to marriage and **54-The Marrying Maiden**, describes a young maiden entering an older man's house as a secondary wife.

Associated meanings

Influence, wooing, joined, together, reciprocity, mutual attraction, to unite, feelings, sensitivity.

Judgment

> Influence. Success.
> The determination is favorable.

Taking a wife brings good fortune.
Influence is reciprocal; it involves not only influencing others, but also being open to influences from other people.
In this context determination means to be ready to follow the natural course of development of the relationship, without having any secret designs about it.
"Taking a wife" not only means marriage but also may refer to many other kinds of long lasting relationships based on mutual openness, like friendships, family relations, business relations, etc.

The Image

> A lake on the mountain: The image of Influence.
> Thus the noble is open-minded and welcoming for people.

In the same way that water collects in a mountain lake because it is concave, leaving space for storing water, being open-minded will attract people to you. The word translated as "open-minded" also means "humble, modest, pure, unprejudiced".
Such forgiving and receptive attitude will allow you to connect deeply and sincerely with other persons.

First Six

>Influence in the big toe of the foot.

The big toe alone cannot move the rest of the body.
At this point your influence is hardly noticeable. You may want to establish a relation with other person who seems to be agreeable, but nobody has made yet any concrete move.

Second Six

>Influence in the calves.
>Misfortune.
>Keeping still brings good fortune.

Advancing before the proper time would cause trouble.
Keep your independence and stay in your own place. Do not let others involve you in a course of action that will compromise you.

Third Nine

>Influence on the thighs.
>He holds close to what he follows.
>Going ahead causes humiliation.

Do not act rashly. Take enough time to evaluate the situation before doing anything.
Being open to influences is good, but losing your self-control and becoming a puppet of other people or being enslaved by your own desires would be humiliating.

Fourth Nine

>The determination brings good fortune.
>Regret vanishes.
>Restless and indecisive comes and goes.
>Only is friends can follow his plans.

Your doubts and lack of resolve are stopping you. This is the proper time to act with determination, choose the path to follow and keep to it.
Since you do not have a wide sphere of influence, only those closely associated with you will support your actions.
The word translated as "follow" also means "adhere, obey, pursue".

Fifth Nine

>Influence in the back of the neck.
>There is no repentance.

The back of the neck can also be translated as "the flesh along the spine above the heart". In either case it means that the influence comes from the heart, from a true source. You have reached a firm decision and have clarity of mind. Such firmness of purpose will allow you to expand your influence steadily.

Top Six

>Influence in the jaws, cheeks and tongue.

If you try to influence others only using words with no substance behind them, you will not make any lasting effects.

32

héng
Duration / Constancy

Four hexagrams are related with marriage and the preliminary steps leading to it: **31-Influence**, depicts the initial attraction and courtship in a couple; 32-Duration, indicates the institution of marriage; **53-Gradual Development**, shows the steps and ceremonies leading to marriage and **54-The Marrying Maiden**, describes a young maiden entering an older man's house as a secondary wife.

Associated meanings

Duration, persistence, endurance, steadiness, constancy, continuity, for a long time, perpetuation.

Judgment

> Duration. Success.
> No defect.
> The determination is favorable.
> It is favorable to have a place to go.

You should not try to change your status, continue doing the same thing; keep to the right path, focused on your objectives.
To achieve duration you should be ready to adapt to the changing times, but always being true to your goals and commitments.
Traditionally this hexagram is related to marriage, as a long lasting relation that requires constant care and adaptation to endure through the years. Long term relationships require shared goals and constant commitment to be workable.

The Image

> Thunder and wind: The image of the Duration.
> Thus the noble stands up and does not change its course.

Duration is a dynamic process; keeping still would mean stagnation, but being steady following your goals is the way to achieve duration.

I Ching: Oracular Interpretation

Being flexible and yet persistent you can maintain constancy for a long time. You should keep focused on your objectives but be ready to make any necessary adjustments along the way.

First Six

> He goes too far.
> The determination brings misfortune.
> No target is favorable.

The Chinese word translated as "too far" also means "ask too much, overstep, go beyond". It describes an individual that is too hasty and overzealous.

You are in a low position and you want easy and fast results, but if you don't wait for the right moment and know no boundaries you will commit mistakes that will land you in plenty of trouble.

Second Nine

> Regret disappears.

If you learn how to be steadfast and keep committed to your goals without making mistakes, you will have no regrets.

You have a strong character but your position still is low, hence prudence and self-improvement are required. You know that you will have a chance to succeed, but it will take some time.

Third Nine

> His character is not constant.
> He may have to bear the shame.
> The determination is humiliating.

To be unhappy with the present situation, dreaming with unrealizable goals and to be dependent of external approval, weakens the character and humiliation is the logical consequence.

If you do not have constancy and fail to meet your commitments you will not achieve anything of value and will be shamed.

Fourth Nine

> No animals in the hunt.

Not finding game in the hunt means that your efforts are misplaced or your expectations are out of touch with reality. As a result you will fail.

Perseverance is not enough, you should be flexible enough as to change your approach when you see that what you do is not working properly.

Fifth Six

> Perseverance in constancy is auspicious for a wife but wrong for a master.

The wife symbolizes a person in a subordinate position, as wives were in ancient China. This means lack of character or initiative. Also indicates incapacity to adapt to new circumstances.

If you are following the lead of others, not having much character or initiative wouldn't be a fault, but if you are expected to take decisions or you have responsibilities over other people, such deficiency would be wrong.

Top Six

> Constantly agitated.
> Misfortune.

If you do not calm down and stop your agitation for a bit, your anxiety will bring you misfortune.

To be agitated constantly indicates lack self-control and being reckless.

dùn
Retreat

Associated meanings

Retreat, escape, evade, strategic withdrawal; hide away, skulk.

Judgment

> The Retreat.
> Success.
> Determination in small matters is favorable.

The two *yin* lines on the bottom of this hexagram represent petty persons that are advancing and forcing better people to retire.
In this time, the only way to avoid losses –for good people– is to withdraw, to stop advancing and retiring to a secure position. By retreating you will avoid failure and also will save face. Retreat also means to keep a low profile, to stay in the background.
Retreating is not the same thing than giving up. Retreating is a strategic move that preserves your strength and lets you plan your future comeback at the proper time.
Determination in small matters means that ambitious goals cannot succeed now, only small things can be done.

The Image

> Mountain under heaven: The image of Retreat.
> Thus the noble keeps the petty afar,
> not with hatred but with reserve.

Stern reserve will prevent undesirable people from coming near you. Avoid open confrontations but keep them away by staying out of reach. Do not let them involve you in their petty schemes.

First Six

> At the tail of the Retreat.
> Danger.
> Do not try to undertake anything.

It is too late to retreat safely. By being at the tail of the retreat you are in direct contact with your pursuers and in danger.
You waited for too long, now you must stay quiet until you can see clearly what has to be done. Retreating hastily only would worsen your problems.
The trouble following you may be some unsolved conflict from the past.

Second Six

> Clutching a yellow ox leather no one can remove.

Yellow symbolizes balance, it is the color of the middle and in this case it indicates that you are following the right path and you will stay firmly in it.
This line also indicates that a person in an inferior position (the second line) holds strongly to someone in an elevated position (the fifth line).
Following this idea you should get help from a person more experienced and powerful than you and hold loyal to him.

Third Nine

> An entangled retreat is stressing and dangerous.
> It is favorable to take charge of servants and maids.

An entangled retreat means that your choices are limited. Your freedom is severely restricted by the sentimental attachments or obligations that you have with inferior people.
Until you recover your freedom only small things can be done.

Fourth Nine

> Retreats from what he is fond of.
> Good fortune for the noble, decline for the vulgar.

To retire from what one likes is not easy. A vulgar man, attached to his pleasures would not be able to do so, since it requires a strong will and commitment to duty to detach yourself from something enticing.
This kind of retreat should be performed with courtesy, without bitterness but with resolve.
You will be able to live well without the person that you are leaving behind, but it is the vulgar who depends on you who will not be able to prosper after you leave.

Fifth Nine

> Excellent retreat.
> The determination is favorable.

The word translated as "excellent" also means "joyful, happy", meaning that this a friendly retreat, performed in the right moment, without causing any conflicts and with firm determination. In that way you will leave behind no enemies, but people with good will.
Notwithstanding such friendly retreat it is favorable to keep firm your determination.

Top Nine

> Fruitful retreat.
> Nothing that is not favorable.

You will be able to retire happily and successfully. Your future prospects are excellent.

34

dà zhuàng
Great Power

Associated meanings

Power, strength, strong, robust, big, full grown male, in the prime of life.

Judgment

> Great Power.
> The determination is favorable.

Having plenty of strength any action that you take will have strong effects. But having power and knowing how to use it are two different things.
Determination here means to persevere in the right path, to apply your power in a wise manner, only in that way you will be successful.

The Image

> The thunder at the top of the sky: The image of Great Power.
> Thus the noble does not tread any path that deviates
> from the established order.

Great Power can be really useful only when you are able control it, without causing damage to others or to yourself. Without wisdom and self-control Great Power only causes trouble. Only by avoiding straying from the correct path and abusing your strength, you will perfect your power; otherwise you will complicate your life and create unending conflicts with other people.

First Nine

> Power in the toes.
> To push ahead brings misfortune.
> Have confidence.

The toes indicate the first stage of development. You are in no condition to apply your strength effectively, because you have no connections and you still lack self-control.

Use your power to improve yourself, resist the urge or use your power before you are ready for handling it, or it will be wasted. Be aware of your limitations and wait for more propitious circumstances.

Second Nine

>The determination is favorable.

The obstacles to your advance are vanishing. At this point it is important to avoid being overconfident but instead exercising moderation.
By avoiding excesses you will have long-standing success.

Third Nine

>A common man uses the power.
>The noble does not act like that.
>The determination is dangerous.
>A ram butts the fence and his horns get stuck.

Power should be used with moderation to avoid trouble.
To persist in blatant use of power would be dangerous, because when you try to fix a problem with brute force you will cause unnecessary resentment among people.
This hexagram uses the image of a ram as a symbol of abuse of power and lack of self-control, since the shape of the six lines, with two broken lines at the top suggest a ram with its horns at the top.
Getting stuck in the fence means that you will create unforeseen complications if you wield power with arrogance and show disregard for others

Fourth Nine

>The determination is favorable.
>Regret vanishes.
>The fence is broken and will not entangle you anymore.
>The power lies in the axle-brace of a great carriage.

The mention to "determination" and the fact that "regret vanishes" indicates that you will make no mistakes and will progress with ease in the correct path.
In the same way that a carriage rolling smoothly, supported by its axle, you can move forward with your plans without anything hindering you, because there are no obstacles stopping you any more.

Fifth Six

>Loses the goat at *Yi*.
>There is no repentance.

Yi was the name of a place. Losing the goat at *Yi* means to overcome bad character traits as stubbornness and arrogance although there is also the idea of losing strength or power.
Now you can handle the situation with proper balance and harmony, making no mistakes, because you are strong but flexible.

Top Six

> The ram butts the fence.
> Cannot retreat and cannot push through.
> Nothing is favorable.
> Fortitude under trying conditions.
> Good fortune.

You have reached a standstill. You went too far and got stopped, now you cannot advance more but neither can retreat.

Stop trying to fix your troubles using force, reconsider the situation and accept your limitations. Try to see the different sides of the issue and look for a new approach.

jìn
Progress / Advance

Associated meanings

Progress, advance, promotion, flourishing, increasing.

Judgment

> Progress.
> The Marquis of *Kang* is honored with numerous horses.
> On the same day he is received three times.

The Marquis of *Kang* symbolizes a person whose importance is recognized by the authorities, who support him. Being received three times indicates that he works closely with his superiors and that his progress is continuous.

You should wait for the sanction of the authority before advancing, because albeit you have a high position, it is a dependent one.

The horses symbolize power and means for advancing. The most valuable means that you can have are the people at your service. Hence you should cooperate with other people, for the good of the organization to which you belong.

Kang Hou, the Marquis of *Kang*, was the title of *Feng*, the ninth son of King *Wen*. His name only appears in the Judgment of this hexagram. Most possibly, by the time the text of the this hexagram was written, *Feng* still was the Marquis of *Kang*. Afterwards he was bestowed the fief of *Wei*, since then he was known as the Marquis of *Wei*, and his previous title was forgotten from history. Many *Yijing* versions, following Wilhelm, translate *Kang* as "vigorous", because in Wilhelm time it wasn't know that *kang hou* was the title of *Feng*.

The Image

> The brightness of the sun rises over the earth: The image of Progress.
> Thus the noble himself makes clear his talents.

After you perfect yourself and establish a reputation you will be in condition to get support from the authorities in your field of activity.

Once you have gained some recognition from your superiors, your talents will serve to illuminate not only your way but also to help other people.

On other interpretation level, to "make clear his talents" indicates that before having any repercussion in the world you need to have a clear view of your strengths and weaknesses, know what you want and what are your chances of getting it.

First Six

> Progressing but repressed.
> The determination is favorable.
> Be tolerant of lack of confidence.
> No defect.

At the beginning of the progress you will not have yet earned the confidence of others. Possibly you lack enough experience and because that you cannot get enough support.

Be faithful to your own expectations. Continue working with determination to turn your vision into reality.

Second Six

> Progressing with grief.
> The determination is favorable.
> Receives a great blessing from her ancestor.

Progressing with grief means that you have to make some sacrifices to continue advancing forward.

Your progress is difficult because you are still alone, not receiving any help or cooperation from others.

At some time you will receive help, may be from a woman or a motherly figure. Also the "great blessing from her ancestor" may indicate that you will get an inheritance or will receive recognition from your predecessor.

Third Six

> All agree and trust.
> Regret disappears.

You gained the trust and cooperation of your peers. By working with other people you will be able to carry out your goals successfully.

"Regret disappears" means that all involved people share the same objectives and that they have no doubts about them.

Fourth Nine

> Progressing as a squirrel.
> The determination is dangerous.

The word translated as squirrel indicates a rodent of some sort. Such animals were seen as a plague since they destroyed the crops. The squirrel symbolizes a dishonest and aggressively greedy behavior.

The sense of this time is to progress along with other people, not to monopolize all goods for yourself. If you continue behaving rapaciously you will be punished.

Fifth Six

> Regret disappears.
> Do not worry about loss or gain.
> Going forward brings happiness.
> Nothing that is not favorable.

"Regret disappears" indicate that you have no doubts; you are fully focused in your duty, without being obsessed with the chances of gain or loss, victory or failure.

Your commitment and fine balance will make you happy and successful. You will make no mistakes.

Top Nine

> Progressing with the horns.
> Use them only to punish your own city.
> Danger, but there will be good fortune.
> No defect.
> The determination is humiliating.

Punishing your own city means to discipline yourself and the people under your leadership.

The time for progress is ending. Since you cannot advance more, use your energy to put in order your own sphere of influence.

This is the last line of the hexagram, so there is danger of matters getting out of hand, but that would not justify you to use extreme measures to punish others. If you do that you will be humiliated.

36

míng yí
Suppressed Light

Associated meanings

Darkening of the light, hiding the light, brightness dimmed, light suppressed, hiding one's brilliance; censorship.

Judgment

> Suppressed Light.
> Fortitude under trying conditions brings good fortune.

You are coping with adverse circumstances. Neither your words nor your deeds will be appreciated by others.
Lowly people will harass and keep grievances against you. Avoid attracting attention to yourself; do not exhibit your knowledge or your talents, since that would draw hostility upon you.
Do not tell other people about your opinions or plans; keep true to your objectives and continue ahead following your own way, firmly, but quietly.
Suppressed Light also may indicate that the situation is not clear or your perception is clouded.

The Image

> Light has come into the earth: The image of the Suppressed Light.
> Thus the noble deals with the masses, concealing his talents,
> but still illuminating.

Keep a low profile. Light hidden under the earth means that in times of intellectual decadence it is dangerous to show your brilliance.
Bear with patience the ignorance of others and do not try to correct or criticize them. It is preferable that they take you for a fool rather than antagonizing them. The important thing is to keep your clarity of mind for yourself.

First Nine

> Suppressed Light during the flight.
> He lowers his wings.

> The noble goes along the road for three days without food,
> but has somewhere to go.
> The host gossips about him.

Some danger or an unexpected contingency will compel you to scale down your plans. Lowering the wings indicates that you cannot advance for the moment and you have to descend, avoid attracting attention and resigning some ambitions.

You will not abandon your objectives. The three days on the road without food indicate that you will persevere in spite of the lack of resources, being faithful to your goals.

People will not understand and will criticize you, that is other reason for keeping a low profile.

Second Six

> Suppressed Light.
> Wounded in the left thigh.
> Rescued by a powerful horse.
> Good fortune.

To be wounded in a leg means that resistance against you is mounting; it will decrease your means and hurt your capacity for advancing, but it will not disable you entirely.

The left is the direction of retreat, hence to be wounded in the left thigh may indicate that you are wounded from your back, that you didn't see the blow coming.

The horse is a symbol of courage, spirit and moral strength to resist opposition; it means that if you keep up your resolution you will surmount the difficulties and will even help those under your responsibility. The horse also indicates that you will improve your mobility and capacity for advancing.

Third Nine

> Suppressed Light during the hunt in the south.
> The great leader is caught.
> Cannot be hurriedly determined.

The hunt means to search for a way to solve the present difficulties. In ancient China the south was placed at the top of the maps, thus this indicates that you are hunting for a person in an elevated position, who is the source of all the troubles.

Only when the "Lord of Darkness" (the sixth, top line), is finally uncovered you will find a way to fully understand and control the situation.

To solve the current bad situation you should not be too hasty, the problems that you are trying to fix have existed for a long time and they should be corrected gradually.

Fourth Six

> Enters the left side of the belly.
> Grasps the heart of the Suppressed Light.
> Leaves the gate and courtyard.

You will get to the bottom of the matter; the heart of darkness is the central point, from where you will know everything. The mention to the "heart" and "the left side of the belly" indicate that you have access to the inner machinations of the one that is the source of all darkness. You are close to a dangerous and evil person and even may have his confidence.

At that point you will know that there is nothing more to do there, it is time for a new stage. Leave your position (the gate and courtyard) and escape from there.

Fifth Six

> Suppressed Light (as) Prince *Ji*.
> The determination is favorable.

Prince *Ji* was the minister the last *Shang* king, a tyrant who allowed no opposition. Because of his family connections he couldn't withdraw from the court and instead feigned madness to avoid being involved with the evil king, but remain safe.

Your situation is very complicated; you cannot withdraw from a dangerous situation and making public what you really think should put you in danger. Following Prince *Ji* example, the best way out of danger is to conceal your brightness under a dull or crazy exterior.

Be cautious and do not enter in conflict with other people, let them think that you are inoffensive and clueless. Stay clear from involving yourself with any evil doings.

Top Six

> No light, but darkness.
> First ascended to heaven.
> Later sank into the earth.

After darkness reaches its climax it will begin to fall. This describes a person who achieved a high position but used his power wrongly to suppress the truth.

The situation was totally wasted because lack of vision and wrong handling, and for that reason it now starts to disintegrate.

The fall of the dark forces, in turn, will open the road for progress.

37

jiā rén
The Family / The Clan

Associated meanings

Family, house people, household, home, to keep a home; clan, close-knit group.

Judgment

> The Family.
> The determination is favorable for a woman.

In ancient China all members of a household subordinated themselves to the head of the family, hence this hexagram describes a hierarchical structure, where all members cooperate between them and obey the leader of the group. It can describe any close-knit group or hierarchical human association.

The determination of a woman refers to the proper conduct of a subordinate, as women were in ancient China; it means to take care of supporting, preserving and nurturing the members of the group or family. The duties of a subordinate are oriented towards the inside of the group, since it is the household's head the one who will take care of the group's interaction with the outside.

The Image

> The wind comes from the fire: The image of The Family.
> So the noble's speech is anchored in reality and his actions have duration.

Following traditional Confucian thinking, the relationships within a family mirror the human connections in larger groups, like a business or a country. Also they are analog to the internal workings of the psyche, where the conscience is the master and our passions are the household people.

Making your words true and your behavior consistent is very important inside the family because you cannot influence in a good way your family if you are not steady and trustworthy. People who lead another people, either in a family, or in any other kind of human group need to keep good discipline in the group. If you are not consistent or are too permissive you will not be able to lead any human group effectively.

First Nine

> With firm boundaries in The Family regret vanishes.

The first line of a hexagram always describes the first developments of a situation.
In this case clear responsibilities and limits should be established for everyone in the group from the start. This will avoid conflicts and discussions in the future. Also it is best to prevent problems than correcting them after they have got entrenched.

Second Six

> Unpretentious.
> Stays inside preparing food.
> The determination is favorable.

To stay inside preparing food indicates that you have to support others and you are not independent.
Do not try to bend the rules to follow your whims. Learn to follow the rules and fulfill your duty first.
Stay in the background; do not try to call attention over yourself.

Third Nine

> A family run with stern severity will cause regrets,
> but there will be good fortune.
> Women and children chuckling and giggling will end in shame.

Women and children symbolize lack of discipline, overindulgence and disordered behavior.
Sometimes it is difficult to get the proper balance between discipline and laxity. If you are too hard with others they will complain, but if the family or group gets disorganized and chaotic this will cause sorrow in the long run.
Try to avoid the extremes, do not be too harsh or too indulgent, but when in doubt stick to the rules. The basic idea here that it is better to err on the side of discipline instead being too lax.

Fourth Six

> A thriving family.
> Great good fortune.

The fourth line is the place of the minister, a person with important responsibilities, who runs effectively the internal side of an organization.
In a traditional family this is the place of the wife, who makes the household thriving by keeping things in order and supporting everybody.
Your service is vital; it will be much appreciated and will contribute greatly to the success of your family or group. At this point there are no conflicts, the people for whom you work for are trusting and cooperative.

Fifth Nine

> The king approaches his family.
> Do not worry.
> Good fortune.

The king symbolizes a respected and wise person who benefits the family or group with good leadership.
In turn, the people in the family trust and welcome their leader.
Good fortune is the result of good leadership and people willing to cooperate with each other.

Top Nine

> He inspires confidence and respect.
> At the end there will be good fortune.

Your qualities and the excellence of your work are recognized. People will follow your example without questions because they trust you.

kuí
Antagonism / Opposition

Associated meanings

Diverging, extraordinary, opposition, polarization, estrangement, alienation, disharmony; to look askance, as in disapproval.

Judgment

> Antagonism.
> Good fortune in small matters.

Antagonism means that people have misunderstandings and diverging objectives; as a result they are estranged, opinions are polarized and it is difficult to find common ground.

When people cannot work together only small things can be done, therefore instead trying to fix the whole problem, you should concentrate in solving small matters and finding common ground in the least contended issues.

Antagonism only can be overcame by leaving behind the misunderstandings and finding a way to cooperate. Be tolerant, avoid confrontation and make an effort to understand the point of view of your antagonists.

This hexagram mentions chance meetings, gains and strange loses in several lines. Be adaptable and open to new opportunities.

From a psychological viewpoint antagonism characterizes somebody who cannot decide what to do and has a split personality.

The Image

> Fire is above, lake below: The image of Antagonism.
> Thus the noble is companionable, but maintains its uniqueness.
> It is important to see the common factors for all sides of a situation.

You have your unique viewpoint, but with empathy and tolerance you will be able to understand and accept the position of other people and to share some things with them, disregarding the fact that your own opinion may be different.

First Nine

> Repentance fades.
> Do not chase the horse that got away.
> It will return on its own.
> You will find bad people, but you will not make mistakes.

Do not try to force back estranged subjects. Sometimes misunderstandings will make some people break away, but in time they will return to your side.
Hostile people should be handled with diplomacy. The important thing is to avoid mistakes that would magnify the alienation of other persons.
A lost horse also is an image of distress and loss of strength.

Second Nine

> He meets his master in an alley.
> No defect.

A fortuitous encounter will allow you to encounter a kindred spirit at an unlikely place.
You may find a valuable person in the least expected place, and receive guidance and support from him.
Good prospects.

Third Six

> He sees his cart pulled back.
> His oxen and his men arrested, marked and mutilated.
> There is no (a good) start but (a good) end.

In ancient China criminals were tattooed in the forehead or mutilated depending on the crime committed by them.
This line indicates loss of position. You will be punished and humiliated. Your projects will be stopped.
Your advance will be blocked until you get help from a superior force.
The Chinese character translated as "mutilated" literally means "to cut off the nose". The character translated as "marked" means to be branded on the forehead or to cut off the head's hair or the top knot. This knot was a symbol of status, so it means that the subject status is diminished or its pride is injured.

Fourth Nine

> Isolated by antagonism.
> One meets an outstanding man (that can become a) truthful partner.
> Danger.
> No defect.

Mistrust and alienation keep people apart, isolated.
By establishing an alliance with a very good person you will overcome the antagonism.
Breaking the distrust will not be easy, as any alliance implies risks, but the goal is worthwhile and joining will be no mistake.

Fifth Six

> Repentance fades.
> In the temple of the clan they eat meat.
> How could it be a mistake to go there?

To meet in the temple of the clan means to become part of a close-knit group. To eat meat indicates abundance.

Troubles disappear when you find a good human group to belong to.

Top Nine

> Isolated by antagonism.
> He sees (the other as) a pig covered with mud, a carriage full of demons.
> First tenses his bow, but then puts it aside.
> It is not a robber but a marriage suitor.
> Going forward rain falls.
> Good fortune.

A dangerous conflict will be avoided when you overcome disagreements and irrational hatreds. Do not act rashly, think again and you will find that your apparent enemy can become a good partner.

The rain falling down symbolizes relaxation and the clearing of all misunderstandings and hatreds, but you have to take the first step forward to solve the troubles.

39

jiăn
Hampered / Obstruction

Associated meanings

Lame, hobble, stumble, limp, proceed haltingly, impasse, obstruction, impediment, obstacle; troubles, difficulties.

Judgment

> Hampered.
> The south-west is favorable; the north-east is not advantageous.
> It is favorable to see the great man.
> Determination brings good fortune.

In the *Yijing* south-west indicates retreat and north-east advance, thus the message is clear, the path forward is blocked.

The north indicates isolation and the south the community. You cannot continue alone, you will need help from somebody who has authority and is more knowledgeable than you; also you should be in touch with other persons, do not become isolated, seek cooperation with another people.

To retire means to reconsider your position and look for alternative ways to carry on your objectives. It also means to detach yourself from your current troubles. Stop struggling, relax and look for new options.

To see the great mean also indicates that you have to grow and mature before being ready for advancing.

The Image

> Above the mountain there is water: The image of Hampered.
> Thus the noble goes back to himself to cultivate his nature.

When you face an insurmountable obstacle you have to change your approach. To do so you should adjust your view of the situation, to modify your perception and expectations.

The phrase "to cultivate his nature" actually means to adapt and evolve, to grow internally and learn new ways to face the world.

Indeed external obstacles will provide the stimuli for personal growth, which in turn will help you to overcome such obstacles.

First Six

> Going forward is Hampered, going back brings praise.

Advancing will put you in trouble, stay where you are or retreat. Have patience and do not be rash.

Second Six

> The king's servant (is struggling with) difficulties.
> Not because of himself.

You are duty bound to take action, no matter the obstacles facing you. You will have to face plenty of difficulties because holding back is not a choice.

Third Nine

> Going forward is Hampered.
> He comes back.

Going back means to reconsider your previous decision and accept that you made a mistake. Retreat; you do not have the resources to go forward. By going back you will escape danger and return to normality.

Fourth Six

> Going forward is Hampered.
> Coming back meets companions.

You cannot continue forward on your own because your path is hampered and you will be isolated if you continue advancing.
Return and cooperate with other people in order to muster enough resources and strength to overcome the obstacles ahead.

Fifth Nine

> When the Obstruction is greater, friends will come over.

The fifth line is the ruler of the hexagram; hence you are the one who is trying to correct the current troubles.
You need collaborators and friends to overcome adversity with their help.

Top Six

> Going forward is Hampered, coming back brings great good fortune.
> It is favorable to see the great man.

You are not directly affected by the current troubles, but you feel that it is your duty to help others in this time of hardship.
To see the great man indicates that you have to look for a capable helper to fix the issues.

40

jiě
Liberation

Associated meanings

Deliverance, getting free, release from adversity, untie, loosen, divide, sever, disjoin, untangle, untie a knot, unravel a complication.

Judgment

> Liberation.
> The south-west is favorable.
> If there is nowhere to go return brings good fortune.
> If there is somewhere to go, to be early brings good fortune.

Liberation is the aftermath of the previous hexagram: 39 - *Hampered*. It means release from bondage and hardship.
In the *Yijing* south-west indicates retreat and the community, thus it means that to get free from troubles you should retreat, move away from a situation that is bad for you and avoid being isolated.
A stressful and complicated situation can be unraveled by taking a step back and looking for a new approach.
Take care of not leaving behind loose ends after the situation starts to untangle and you can leave. If there is anything that requires your attention before turning back, you should attend to it promptly.

The Image

> Thunder and rain in action: The image of Liberation.
> Thus the noble forgives excesses and excuses offenses.

Thunder and rain clean the atmosphere, they represent liberation from stress and anxiety, since a storm clears the air.
To get proper release from a time of conflict and troubles, you should leave behind hatreds, misgivings and ill feelings, cultivating instead tolerance and being broad-minded.

A new cycle is starting, and you should face it without carrying worries and resentments from the past.

First Six

> No defect.

Relax and restore your energies.
Everything is going well, you will make no mistakes.

Second Nine

> One catches three foxes in the hunt and gets a golden arrow.
> Determination brings good fortune.

The hunt is the will to purge the situation from undesirable elements, either internal or external: the three foxes.
The foxes symbolize greed, ignorance and fear. They are elements of corruption, which create difficulties and harm the progress.
The golden arrow was bestowed to people who did great things (the **hexagram 21.4** also mentions getting arrows, but they are metallic instead of golden), this means that after removing the bad factors (the foxes) you will get rewards. To persevere in the hunt and catch the foxes will bring good fortune.

Third Six

> One who bears a burden on his back but rides on a carriage attracts bandits.
> The determination is humiliating.

In ancient China, carriages were only used by high-ranking people, hence a baggage bearer had no place into them.
This line describes a low rank person, who sneaked into an elevated position, but he is not ready for his new responsibilities and it shows.
Since his appearance doesn't match reality he will receive no help but instead draw bandits and transgressors around him. If he persists in his charade he will be exposed for what he is and will be shamed.
The line also indicates a debasement of correct behavior, such as impersonating righteousness.

Fourth Nine

> Deliver yourself from your big toe.
> Then a trusty companion will come.

The big toe helps to walk, but here the big toe indicates dependence on an inferior and unreliable element.
It may be a habit, some people, or anything that you use as a prop for advancing, but it is surely damaging your prospects.
It is time to look elsewhere for support and discard such unworthy element. After you get rid of it, new possibilities will be opened to you and you will get help from good people.

Fifth Six

> Only the noble can have liberation.
> Good fortune.
> Inferior people trust him.

Only you can disengage yourself from links with inferior people and degrading habits.
If you are strong enough to liberate yourself you will be successful. Those inferior people whose links you severed will understand that you are in earnest and will not stop your parting.

Top Six

> The prince shoots at a hawk on a high wall and hits the target.
> Nothing that is not favorable.

The hawk symbolizes an evil element in a high position and the last obstacle in your deliverance. Shooting and hitting the hawk indicates that you should use the appropriate means to take down what is hampering your progress.
There will be no further problems.

41

sŭn
Decrease

Associated meanings
Decrease, diminish, lessen, damage, loss, reduction, sacrifice, sublimation.

Judgment
Decrease with sincerity brings outstanding good fortune.
No defect.
Can be determined.
It is favorable to have somewhere to go.
What should be done?
Two bowls can be used for the offering.

All things increase and decrease periodically with the pass of time, but if you adjust your behavior to the needs of the current time you will be successful in the long run.
In times of shortage what matters most is your attitude. You cannot ignore reality and must be ready to accept some losses and give up some comfort. To be sincere means to accept your position; do not live in the past and make good use of the little things you still have.
Decrease also indicates that you should balance your resources. What exceeds should be restrained, and what is deficient increased.
The bowls were ritual vessels used to offer cooked grain to the spirits. They show the need to give up something and to do more with less, since the bowls were used for modest offerings.

The Image
Down the mountain is the lake: The image of the Decrease.
Thus the noble controls his anger and restrains his passions.

The lake waters evaporate and fertilize the mountain. In the same way you should apply self-control and keep in check your passions and anger. In return, the restricted energy can be used to improve your spiritual growth.
What is inferior is decreased to increase a superior cause. This is not the time for sensual gratifications and indulgence, but for restrain and servicing the needs of other people.

First Nine

> There is no defect if after finishing your work you go quickly,
> but think about how much you can sacrifice.

Helping other people after doing your tasks is fine and good. In this case the first line (a person who is in a low position), is helping the fourth line (somebody in a more elevated, directive position).
When you help your superiors you must draw the line at some point. Do not let others abuse you and neither be servile towards them.

Second Nine

> The determination is favorable.
> Going forward with violence brings misfortune.
> Without loss one may increase.

It is favorable to keep to your normal tasks, but to take on new risky or aggressive endeavors would be unfortunate.
Do not innovate, instead carry on with your current duties; with your work you can help others.

Third Six

> Three men walking along the road together are decreased,
> but one man walking gains a companion.

Increase conduces to decrease and decrease leads to increase, following the normal cycles.
If you are alone you will find company, but if you are part of group, it will be decreased.
This line speaks about keeping a proper balance in social relations. You should be perceptive enough to know where it is time to enter a group and when you should leave.

Fourth Six

> As a result of reducing his anxiety, he will have joy quickly.
> No defect.

The word translated as "anxiety" also means "defect, stress, affliction, haste, illness". It means that if you relax a bit and are more accessible, your troubles will decrease and you will be less stressed.

Fifth Six

> Someone increases him by ten pairs of tortoise shells.
> Nobody can resist.
> Outstanding happiness.

Tortoise shells were both used as currency and for divination. Ten pairs of tortoise shells mean a great number of good omens and to receive an important amount of resources or money. They also indicate that fate is on your side, you will receive blessings from above. Nothing can stand in the way of your success and happiness.

Top Nine

> There is no Decrease but increase.
> No defect.
> The determination brings good fortune.
> It is favorable to have where to go.
> One gets servants but not a household.

The time for decrease is ending. What you do will benefit everybody without decreasing yourself. You will make no mistakes and having a worthy goal to follow will allow you to do still more.

To get servants but not a household means that you are working for the public good, unselfishly.

yì
Increase

Associated meanings

Increase, augment, expansion, progress, benefit, profit, advantage, more and more.

Judgment

> Increase.
> It is favorable to have where to go.
> It is favorable to cross the great river.

In this time people in high position are dedicated to strengthen the people under them, cooperating freely and helping out more humble people.
There is a spirit of collaboration for the greater good because people see that the leadership objectives are beneficial for everyone, not only a few.
But this good time will not last for long, increase means a favorable opportunity that should be used before it vanishes.
To have where to go means that you should have a definite goal where to concentrate your efforts to reap the benefits of this time.
Since the meaning of Increase is cooperation, it is also related with providing services to others and working for the greater good.
In ancient China, crossing rivers, either at a ford or when the river was frozen, was not an easy task. It implicated dangers and hardships; hence crossing the great river means to carry out a difficult undertaking.

The Image

> Wind and thunder: The image of Increase.
> Thus the noble moves toward the good when he sees it;
> and corrects any excesses.

Wind and thunder symbolize complementary forces that cooperate between them to undertake something.

The noble always looks for positive things and improvements to be done, but also is ready to correct mistakes and transgressions.

To be ready to make continuous adjustments and improvements, avoiding excesses and overindulgence, is the way to success.

First Nine

> It is favorable to begin great endeavors.
> Outstanding good fortune.
> No defect.

You will receive great support and already have plenty of resources to enable you to carry out great endeavors with very good results.

Increase is a time for concentrating in your duty and servicing others, there is no margin for selfish attitudes.

Second Six

> Someone increases him by ten pairs of tortoise shells.
> Nobody can resist.
> Long-term determination brings good fortune.
> Used by the king in an offering to the Divine Ruler.
> Good fortune.

Tortoise shells were used both as currency and for divination. Ten pairs of tortoise shells mean a great number of good omens and to receive an important amount of resources or money. They also indicate that fate is on your side, you will receive blessings from above.

Nothing can stand in the way of your success and great happiness.

Long-term determination means that long-term planning and endurance is required.

To be used in an offering to God means that your reputation will be greatly increased and your deeds recognized by the higher authorities.

Third Six

> Increased by unfortunate events.
> If your service is sincere there is no defect.
> Walk in the middle and report to the prince with a jade baton.

Although the situation is not good, you will make the most of it. Others may have losses but you will benefit from the adverse circumstances.

The important thing is to avoid using the misfortune of others for selfish aggrandizement, but instead having a service mindset.

If you behave with moderation your will receive recognition and support from your superiors.

Fourth Six

> If you walk in the middle and report to the prince, he will follow.
> It is favorable to be assigned to relocate the capital.

This line is the place of an officer who works as a consultant or mediator, providing guidance to the direction of his organization.

To walk in the middle means to have a balanced approach. As a mediator you have to understand how different people see the situation and avoid taking sides, but you your principal duty is

to serve loyalty the prince —your superiors— giving him a non-partisan report of the current circumstances.
Your proposal will be well accepted and you will be trusted for carrying on important projects.

Fifth Nine

> If you have a sincere and kind heart you do not need to ask.
> Outstanding good fortune.
> One has sincerity and is favored with spiritual power.

If you act moved by a sincere desire to help others you will have no doubts and will not need to ask the oracle about your plans.
People will trust you because they will sense your goodwill. Your influence will grow, that will be your spiritual power.
Your wishes will become true for the benefit of all people around you, since your will is oriented towards the common good.

Top Nine

> He increases no one.
> Perhaps somebody will attack him.
> Doesn't keep his heart constant.
> Misfortune.

Acting with greed will isolate you and make you hated.
By failing to help others and acting with injustice you may attract just retribution from the people that you are harming.
If you do not learn to share with others you will have many troubles.

43

guài
Breakthrough / Resoluteness / Parting

Associated meanings

Breakthrough, make a breach, split, cut off, pull off, flight, run away; resolute, decisive.
The ancient form of the character for this hexagram tag seems to show an archer's thumb ring or thimble, which was called *jué*. The meaning breakthrough may come from the bursting loose of the bow string.

Judgment

> Breakthrough.
> Proclaim the matter truthfully in the king's court.
> Danger.
> Report to your own city.
> It is not favorable to resort to weapons.
> It is favorable to have where to go.

Breakthrough means that the situation is more than ripe for change.
Tension has accumulated for a long time and the last remaining bad influences (symbolized by the sixth line) should be resolutely eradicated. It is not possible to reach compromises of any sort with evil forces; they should be eliminated by using soft power, and diplomacy, but not violence.
This is a decisive moment; you can't stand aside any longer. You have to make a stand and voice publicly your views.
To proclaim the issue in the king's court means that the crisis should be handled by common accord and publicly. In the same way, to report to your own city stresses out the importance of gathering support from your own sphere of influence before taking a public stand. Also it is important to have definite objectives.
From a psychological viewpoint, breakthrough indicates that vices and weaknesses should be not tolerated inside your own self.

The Image

> The lake rises above the heaven: The image of the Breakthrough.
> Thus the noble distributes benefits downward,
> while avoiding presumption of virtue.

The lake waters evaporate and generate clouds in heaven. Those clouds symbolize the tension that has accumulated, which can generate a dangerous outburst of rain.

To prevent such violent outbursts the noble doesn't hoard things for himself, but shares them with others.

Not presuming of virtue means to avoid boasting and not having selfish attitudes.

First Nine

> Powerful in the toes.
> He goes forward but cannot triumph, and makes a mistake.

To be powerful in the toes means that you are overeager to advance, but the conditions for a successful advance are not yet in place. You need more planning, also your position is not consolidated enough to allow you advancing successfully.

Acting now would be a mistake, if you are not able to stop yourself you will fail.

Make an effort to control your emotions and behaving more calmly.

Second Nine

> Cries of alarm at evening and night.
> If you are armed there is nothing to fear.

The situation is neither safe nor stable. Do not lower your guard and look out for signs of trouble.

To be armed means to be ready to face emergencies, contingency planning is critical for long-term success.

Third Nine

> To be powerful in the cheeks brings misfortune.
> The noble is perfectly resolved.
> Walks alone in the rain, wet and grieved.
> No defect.

To be powerful in the cheeks indicates a pushy or overbearing temperament; such character traits will cause you trouble.

You will have to endure some level of conflict with other people and sacrifice some comforts to keep up your resolution, but you will make no mistake.

To minimize the unavoidable troubles, try to be tolerant of the limitations of the other people. They neither will understand nor support you but that is not reason for being harsh with them.

Fourth Nine

> There is no flesh on his buttocks.
> Walks haltingly and leading a sheep.
> Regret disappears.
> Hearing complaints, not to be believed.

You were stubborn and insisted in doing things your own way for a long time. You never listened to good advice.
Now you don't have strength enough to continue forward on your own and you will have to accept unquestioningly the terms of others.
In ancient China to lead a sheep being half dressed was a ceremony that indicated surrender, to ask mercy from a conqueror.
To resign independence and your own goals is a hard thing to do, but you have no other choices left to you.

Fifth Nine

> A goat mountain breaks through and goes along the middle of the road.
> No defect.

Finally a breakthrough is achieved; the weak line at the top of the hexagram symbolizes an open way ahead.
To go along the middle of the road indicates balance and commitment to solid principles. For that reason there will be no fault.

Top Six

> There is no cry.
> At the end there will be misfortune.
> All seems good but there is unexpected trouble ahead.

The word "cry" means to cry for help or to make some signal. You will not have any warning of a coming danger and you will not receive any help, as a result you will suffer misfortune.
Being the only *yin* line in the hexagram, the sixth line symbolizes an inferior person who will be rejected by the other five *yang* lines and will suffer for it.

44

gòu
Close Encounter / Meeting

Associated meanings
Couple, mate, meet, meeting of opposites, interlock, locking, coming to meet, brief encounter, temptation.

Judgment
> Close encounter.
> The woman is powerful.
> Do not take her as wife.

The structure of this hexagram is the inverse of the previous one, where the only *yin* line is at the top. Here the *yin* force is entering from the bottom, in 43 it is leaving.

Close encounter describes a time when opposite forces meet: the first *yin* line is entering the situation and meeting the other *yang* lines.

The first line symbolizes an inferior element, and because it is a *yin* line in low position, it is symbolized by a loose woman. The present danger is to become infatuated with this seemingly weak and attractive element, because she is more powerful and dangerous that she looks.

Not taking her as wife means that the inferior element may have a proper place in your life but only for a brief time and under some restrictions. But there is no chance of having a good and lasting relationship, since she would bring shame on your life and may even subjugate you. Although the inferior element is symbolized by a woman, in real life it may refer to persons of any sex or to any type of situation where some kind of temptation or foul play is happening. From a psychological point of view, the first line symbolizes a primal force of the unconscious that, if not checked properly can take command of the whole self with destructive results.

The Image
> Under the sky is the wind: The image of Close Encounter.
> Thus the sovereign dispenses his orders to the four corners of the world.

The sovereign position is at the highest point of the social order, his subjects are below him. Like the wind, which connects the sky with the things below, stirring what it touches, the sovereign influences people by using his laws; he goes to the encounter of his subjects by mean of his laws.

In the same way that an encounter between opposites can be bad or good, laws affect the life of the people in different ways, depending on the goodness of the current government.

First Six

> Tie it to a metal brake.
> The determination brings good fortune.
> If it moves in any direction evil will appear.
> When one relies on a skinny pig it will falter.

It is better to apply restrain than to fall into danger.

Here the inferior element is compared to a skinny pig. If it is not controlled properly, in the end it will break havoc.

It cannot be trusted, it seems inoffensive and lean but it will grow more powerful and cause trouble if is not stopped now.

Second Nine

> There is a fish in the wrapping
> No defect.
> Not fitting for guests.

The second *yang* line is keeping the first yin *line* isolated. It means that you should prevent inferior influences from increasing, keeping them in place, to protect other people (the guests).

Third Nine

> There is no flesh on his buttocks and he walks unsteadily.
> Danger.
> There will be no great defect.

You are sorely tempted but you will not be able do what you want because you lack enough strength.

In the end, the circumstances will prevent you from doing anything dangerous.

Fourth Nine

> There are no fish in the wrapping.
> This causes misfortune.

If you are too self-righteous and lack tolerance with the common folk you will lose their support when you more need it.

Lack of cooperation and understanding between people from different walks of life will cause trouble.

Fifth Nine

> A melon wrapped in willow leaves.
> Hidden brilliance.
> It falls from Heaven.

The melon symbolizes something that needs a period of maturation, without being seen.

A melon, like a fish, is something that can be spoiled or can decompose easily. To wrap the melon indicates that it is not only preserved but also hidden.

The wrapped melon also symbolizes keeping good relations with your subordinates, protecting them.

Be prudent, cultivate your talents and your plans without ostentation, avoid pushing others.

If you are careful and discreet, when all things are in place you will achieve your objectives with ease, as if they fell from the sky into your hands.

Top Nine

> Close encounter with his horns.
> Some regrets.
> No defect.

A close encounter with the horns means the interlocking of horns by two animals fighting one another. The top line is often associated with horns or the top of the head and also with extreme attitudes.

You do not suffer fools gladly and will stop inferior people who make advances on you with severity.

Although you are not doing anything bad, your attitude will generate friction with some people and in the long run you behavior will generate some troubles in your life.

cuì
Gathering together

Associated meanings

Collect, assemble, gather together, massing, bunched, thick, dense, crowd, collection, group.

Judgment

> Gathering together.
> Success.
> The king approaches his temple.
> It is favorable to see the great man.
> Success.
> The determination is favorable.
> Offering great sacrifices brings good fortune.
> It is favorable to have where to go.

People gather together in families, organizations and states. The king is a leader that gathers people around him.

To join a mass of people, a sense of shared purpose and identity is required. The temple symbolizes such central point, which focuses the attention of the people in a single point and motivates them.

Seeing the great man may mean that you should ask for support from a wise person, but it also indicates that you should rise spiritually and intellectually to be able to gather other people around you. If you can do that you will have success.

Sacrifices are required from people in communities; all members should curb their own selfish desires up to a point, to contribute to the shared purpose that unifies the community.

To have determination and a definite goal is required to keep people working together for the greater good.

The Image

> The lake rises above earth: The image of Gathering together.
> Thus the noble gets his weapons in order,
> to be on guard against the unexpected.

The lake is a mass of water gathered together in one place.
Water can cause dangerous floods; in a group of people the danger comes from the conflicts that may arise between them.
To prevent unexpected dangers you should be alert and ready to make adjustments to avoid personal conflicts from escalating into nasty fights.

First Six

> One has confidence but not to the end, hence there will be confusion.
> Gathering together.
> One calls out, after one handclasp he will laugh.
> Do not worry.
> Going has no defect.

To be sincere, but not to the end, means that you are confused and insecure, fearing rejection. You still don't know to which group you belong or who you should follow.
To call out means to request admission to a group clearly. This will bring happiness.

Second Six

> Drawn out.
> Good fortune.
> No defect.
> If he is sincere it is favorable to make a small offering.

A friend or some acquaintance may ask you to join some group, or some authority in an organization may summon you to take part with others in some activity.
May be you cannot offer much, but your sincerity and good will be more than enough to be admitted into the gathering and your participation will be propitious.

Third Six

> Gathering together between moans.
> Nothing is favorable.
> Going is without defect.
> Small humiliation.

Entering the group where you want to belong is difficult and you will have some trouble being accepted.
You should find some kind of sponsor to help you entering there. You will make no mistake if you go that way, although you will lose some face.

Fourth Nine

> Great good fortune.
> No defect.

You have an important mission in the group, supporting and working closely with the group leader, helping him to gather followers.
Your generous efforts will conduce you to great success.

Fifth Nine

> Gathering together has a good position.
> No defect.
> There is no trust.
> Having outstanding long term determination regret disappears.

This line symbolizes the leader who gathers people around a shared goal, but some of them may have joined the group only to get some rewards and do not really share the group's goals. In time, by keeping committed to the group objectives, the leader will gain the trust of all people in the gathering. Until that moment the group will not work as a unified force.

Top Six

> Sighing and moaning, copious tears.
> No defect.

You are sorry and frustrated because your contributions to the group are not recognized and you are left alone.

May be there is some conflict between you and the other people; try to understand what is preventing your from participating as a full member of the group.

If you are sincere, let them know that you want to join the group and that you are hurt. In the end, you will have a good chance of being admitted inside.

shēng
Ascending

Associated meanings

Climb, push upwards, ascend, rise, go up, arise.
The lower trigram for this hexagram is *xùn,* The Gentle, whose natural symbol is wood; the upper trigram is *kūn,* The Earth. This hexagram shows wood growing in the earth.

Judgment

> Ascending has outstanding success.
> It is useful to see the great man.
> Do not worry.
> Marching forth toward the south brings good fortune.

Ascending is a steady and continuous form of progress, not swift, but unstoppable.
To see the great man means not only to seek advice and help from those who can support and guide you but also to rise to the occasion, to meet the challenge of this propitious time.
This is a good moment to ascend in your organization or to make your business grow. Your progress will be steady and you will get support along the way.
You should not worry because you already have the necessary potentiality for success; it is only matter of developing yourself with determination. Departing toward the south means to undertake the necessary actions to reach your goals, the south is related with the community and the north with solitude.

The Image

> In the middle of the earth grows wood: The image of Ascending.
> Thus the noble, with yielding character,
> accumulates the small to achieve the great.

A tree seed growing below the earth is not seen, and its growth is unceasing but slow. It pushes upward until breaks ground and it adapts its way to the terrain. If it finds an obstacle, searches for a way around, but always pushing upward, towards the sun, which was traditionally placed in the south in ancient Chinese maps.

Ascending shows how by the sum of many imperceptible steps you can achieve great elevation, in the same way than a growing tree.

First Six

> Trusted and ascending.
> Great good fortune.

The first line symbolizes the root. It is the beginning of the ascension and it is very successful because people in high places will support it.

Second Nine

> If one is sincere it is favorable to present a small offering.
> No defect.

The second and third lines symbolize the tree trunk.
Even a small contribution will be favorable because it will show your sincerity and that you have the potential to still give more.
You will not make mistakes because what you do is the true expression of your potentialities.

Third Nine

> One ascends into an empty city.

To ascend into an empty city means to advance easily, without resistance and to take possession of a vacated territory.
This line doesn't tell if there will be fortune or misfortune, thus you may suspect that the situation is too good to be true, nevertheless such opportunity should not be discarded, but you should be careful.
In another interpretation level to ascend into an empty city may indicate to rise under a ruler who is going to fall or to follow a pipe dream.

Fourth Six

> The King presents an offering on Mount *Qi*.
> Good fortune.
> No defect.

The fourth line is the place of the minister, who is privileged to take part in the ceremony when the king sacrifices to his ancestors.
The king represents a powerful person; to be along him in an important occasion means that you have been favored and honored by him.
In a practical level this means that you will fulfill your wishes and will ascend to a high position.

Fifth Six

> The determination brings good fortune.
> One ascends on stairs.

To ascend with determination and on stairs indicates that you know clearly what you have to do. It also means to complete all stages carefully without skipping a single step. Do not look for shortcuts, take care of every detail.
You ascension will be achieved by entrusting responsibilities on others and by acting with softness and constancy.

Top Six

Ascending in the dark.
It is favorable an untiring determination.

The good times are coming to an end. You do not know what lies ahead. Do not stop ascending now, but be alert.
In this case, an untiring determination means to take all possible precautions to avoid danger.

kùn
Oppression / Besieged / Impasse

Associated meanings

Oppression, obstruction; besieged, surrounded, beset; entangled, burdened, harassed; distress, exhaustion, anxiety, hardship, adversity.
The Chinese character constituents for this hexagram tag are: *mù*, "tree", and *wéi*, "enclosure, surround": a tree enclosed in a restricted space, where it cannot spread its branches nor grow.

Judgment

> Oppression.
> Success.
> The determination brings good fortune to the great man.
> No defect.
> Talk is not to be trusted.

You are caught by oppressive forces that are beyond your control and hinder you; neither advance nor withdraw is possible.
Good fortune means here to keep your willpower intact and never give up.
Words will make no effect, since you will not be trusted, instead they may make your situation worse.
Since you cannot neither change the current situation nor escape, the only way out is to endure the hard times until them improve.
If you keep up the faith in yourself you will prevail in the end.

The Image

> The lake has no water: The image of Oppression.
> Thus the noble will sacrifice his own life to achieve his objective.

The water sipping from the lake will make it dry and lifeless; this symbolizes lack of nourishment and support that may exhaust you.

The oppression is a test of your character. The external things that you may lose are not important in the long run, the critical thing is to not surrender to the pressure mounting around you; stand up and do not give up your goals.

First Six

> Buttocks oppressed by a tree stump.
> Enters a dark valley and is not seen for three years.

Oppression has sapped your willpower; to sit down uncomfortably on a tree stump means that your will is exhausted.
Entering a dark valley symbolizes a period of depression and defeatist attitudes. To overcome it, try to look ahead to a brighter future and do not isolate yourself. Three years indicate a long time.
In another interpretation level this may indicate a stint in jail or to be under some kind of restriction. The dark valley may depict a hole a in the ground; pits were used to hold prisoners in ancient China. The wooden stick indicates that punishment is used to overcome your will, as when the guards beat up a prisoner with a stick.

Second Nine

> Oppressed between wine and food.
> Scarlet knee bands arrive from all sides.
> Offering a sacrifice is favorable.
> Marching forth will bring misfortune.
> No defect.

The wine and food indicate that you have a comfortable position, but your oppression is an internal state. You feel entangled with the boring circumstances of your life. Those who wore scarlet knee bands were men of rank and authority, to be approached by them means that you will be offered an opportunity to carry on some important endeavor.
To offer a sacrifice means to work for the sake of others, giving generously from your time and resources, but you have to wait for a clear sign before committing. Do not act rashly, only for your own benefit.
An alternative translation would be "oppressed by wine and food", meaning that you have been too self-indulgent and as a result you are entangled in sensual pleasures.

Third Six

> Oppressed by stones.
> Leans on thorny bushes and thistles.
> Enters his house but does not see his wife.
> Misfortune.

Being restless and irresolute, you will receive no support because you are looking for it in the wrong places. To be oppressed by stones and prickled by thorns indicates that you are expecting support from those that will not help you.
Calm down and reevaluate your priorities before it is too late.
In another interpretation level, to lean on thorns may indicate a period in prison, since prisons were surrounded by thorny bushes. You may not find any support or solace after you recover your freedom and return to your previous home.

Fourth Nine

> He comes very slowly, oppressed in a golden carriage.
> Humiliation, but it will be carried to conclusion.

To be in a golden carriage indicates a high social position and riches. You have good intentions and want to help a friend in need (symbolized by the first line) but you are afraid of criticism from powerful people and you delay doing the right thing.
At the end you will do what you should have done in the first place, but your lack of fortitude will shame you.

Fifth Nine

> His nose and feet are severed.
> Oppressed by scarlet knee bands.
> The joy comes slowly.
> It is favorable to present offerings and libations.

You are oppressed from above and below. The cut nose indicates that your perception of detail is obliterated. The cut feet mean that your movement is restrained. Those who wore scarlet knee bands were men of high position; they may be bureaucrats or people with power over you.
Because you cannot overcome the superior powers that oppress you, the only way out is to accept your situation in life and learn to live in reduced circumstances.
Focus in your spiritual development and keep up your composure. With the pass of time things will slowly improve.
In another interpretation level, to be oppressed by scarlet knee bands may mean to be burdened by the responsibilities of your job.

Top Six

> Oppressed by climbing plants.
> He is anxious and insecure.
> He says to himself that movement will bring regret.
> With repentance, marching forth brings good fortune.

Climbing plants symbolize restrictions that can be easily torn.
The oppression has ended, but you continue to fear it and don't dare to move.
The situation has changed for the better, be ready to cope with new challenges and to learn something new. You need to reevaluate your perspective and overcome your fears; that is the meaning of the word "repentance" in this context.
By moving forward you will leave all your troubles in the past.

jĭng
The Well

In ancient times wells were placed in the center of a grid of nine fields. The center field, which had the well, was property of the feudal lord and the eight families living around it cultivated that field in common, in benefit of his lord and had shared use of the well.

Associated meanings

Water well, wellspring, life water, nourishment, foundation or source of life, inner source of truth, nucleus.

Judgment

> The Well.
> Changing the town, not changing the well.
> No loss, no gain.
> Going to take water from the well nearly dry.
> If the rope does not reach the water or the jar breaks, misfortune.

The well is the foundation of life, a non-changing nucleus that remains the same through life, your roots in life.
The well also represents the government of a city or the head of a family, if it fails to provide nourishment for the people, it should be corrected or replaced.
Changing the town but not changing the well indicates that although you may make big changes in your external life, your essence will remain the same through your whole life.
Reaching the water means to reach the truth, and to receive real nourishment from the sources of life, to get in contact with your inner sources.
When the rope is not long enough or the jar breaks the truth is not reached, because you don't know how or you are not are able to do it.

The Image

> Wood above the water: The image of the Well.
> Thus the noble encourages people at their work
> to cooperate among themselves.

A well is to the people around it, and to society in general, what a ruler is to the people. The value of the well depends on the water being actually raised, not empty promises.

In the same way, the principles of government must be actually carried out. If they are not working as intended, the people will not get nourishment and will stop cooperating between themselves.

To keep the social order healthy, cooperation between people and good communication between rulers and citizens is required.

The same principles apply to both countries, organizations, families and any other human groups.

First Six

> One does not drink from a muddy well
> There are no animals (birds) in an old well.

A muddy well symbolizes a misuse of resources. If you do not take care of your own development your life will be useless, both for yourself and for other people.

It also symbolizes a source that is not providing nourishment anymore or –in the external level– a man with authority who is corrupt and useless and because that has been left alone.

Second Nine

> Shooting fishes in the well.
> The jar is broken and leaks.

A well is not the proper place to shoot fishes (they were shoot using arrows with attached strings). You are squandering away your talents in trivial pursuits.

The broken and leaking jar indicates that you are not using the correct method to get to the source of nourishment.

If you continue neglecting your potentialities you will not accomplish anything worthwhile and will stay in darkness.

You should set yourself higher goals.

Third Nine

> The well is cleaned but its water is not drunk.
> Our hearts grieve, because the water might be drawn out and used.
> If the king were clear-minded all would receive the blessings.

A well that is cleaned means plenty of potentialities and assets that have been restored, but sadly your person and abilities are still ignored by the authorities.

Do not disregard the opportunities for progress that you may find along the way. Use productively your resources, apply them to useful pursuits and do not isolate yourself.

Fourth Six

> The well is lined.
> No defect.

The well is under restoration, that is a good thing and hence, doing so will mean no mistake.
It is time to put your life in order, reform what is wrong and develop your capacities.
You will not be able to do anything useful until your get your life organized.

Fifth Nine

The well has clear, cold spring water for drinking.

This line is the place of the ruler. You have the potential capacity to be a leader and to nurture the people. Both your work and words can benefit others, like pure drinkable water.

Still, there is not mention here about good fortune, since your capabilities have yet to be applied to the real world.

Top Six

> Taking water from the well.
> Not covering.
> It inspires confidence.
> Outstanding good fortune.

Notice that this is the only line where the well water is actually reached and used productively. The well is accessible to everyone without hindrance.

In the same way, a leader of people inspires trust and is generous and tolerant with everyone. Because there is a pure and nourishing source available for everyone and a spirit of cooperation prevails, outstanding good fortune is the outcome.

gé
Revolution /
Getting rid of

Associated meanings

Change, change of seasons; revolution, metamorphosis, overthrow; skin or hide, rawhide, leather, hide without the hair; flay, peel off, skinning, molting.

Judgment

>The Revolution is trusted after it has been accomplished.
>Outstanding good fortune.
>The determination is favorable.
>Repentance fades.

Revolution indicates a great personal change, a change in some external social structure or adjustment to new circumstances.

People will support the new order only after it is established and it will take time to win their trust. Hence, although radical change is needed, it should be done on a timely basis, or you will not have enough support and so the revolution will fail.

After the change is accomplished successfully, repentance will fade, since only then the revolution will be justified.

This is one of the few hexagrams that mention the "four cardinal virtues": *yuan*: outstanding (fundamentality, primal, originating, spring season, head, sublime, great, grand); *heng*: success (prevalence, growing, penetrating, treat, offering, sacrifice); *li*: determination (perseverance, constancy, correct and firm) and *heng*: favorable (advantageous, suitable, beneficial, lucky). One or more of the cardinal virtues appear in 50 different hexagrams, but only the hexagrams 1, 2 (with some modification), 3, 17, 19, 25 and 49 have the four virtues in its Judgment. Since the *Han* Dynasty onwards they have become keywords of Confucian thought, four qualities or virtues applicable both to Heaven and to the noble-minded person.

Any oracle encompassing the four cardinal virtues indicates that success is granted, but only if you don't stray from the good; for this reason determination in the right way is the key to success.

The Image

> Within the lake is fire: The image of the Revolution.
> Thus the noble regulates the calendar and makes clear the seasons.

The lower trigram is fire and above it is located the trigram of the lake. Fire and water are antagonistic, putting fire below water either makes the water boil or extinguishes the fire. Fire within the lake indicates conflict and change.

In the natural world the seasons bring ordered change to Earth. Each season starts a new renovation cycle, involving life and death. Notice that the character translated as "seasons" also means "time, epoch, opportune moment".

In the same way that proper timing is important to synchronize the crops with the seasons; when implementing important changes, finding the correct moment is of the utmost importance.

Most persons will resist change until it is firmly established, providing people with an ordered and timely transition will soothe them.

First Nine

> The Revolution is tied with a yellow cow hide.

The time for change has not arrived yet. Yellow indicates balance and moderation. To be tied in a yellow hide indicates that you should not advance, but wait for a propitious moment.

Second Six

> Revolution after the end of the day.
> It is favorable to attack.
> No defect.

Depending on the translation, the first line may read either the "end of the day" or "your own day".

In any case it means that the time will be ripe for change soon.

A full renovation is required and it will be auspicious. To attack means to advance boldly, you will make no mistakes moving forward now.

Third Nine

> Attacking brings misfortune.
> The determination is dangerous.
> Only after you have spoken about three times the revolution will be trusted.

If you act before you are ready, lacking the necessary support, you will fail.

To speak about three times means to check your plans and evaluate the perspectives carefully and to reach firm agreement with all involved people before acting. You have to be sure that you have enough support before making any bold movement forward. Make sure that you are trusted and that you can trust your followers as well.

Fourth Nine

> Repentance fades.
> There is confidence.
> Reforming the form of government brings good fortune.

A substantial transformation is possible now.
The Chinese character translated as "form of government" also means "heaven's will, fate, highest law". It means either to implement a radical change to modify the orientation of your life, or a profound change in the structure of an organization or human group.

Fifth Nine

> The great man changes like a tiger.
> Even before asking the oracle he has confidence.

The great man indicates a highly principled person.
To change like a tiger means to innovate, adapt to new circumstances, to be ready to meet new challenges. The tiger symbolizes raw power; it is an emblem of bravery, ferocity and strength. Having confidence before asking the oracle means that you are not only free of any doubts but also you are in tune with the times and you know perfectly what you should do to have success. Your firm convictions and high ideals will help you to get the support of the people.

Top Six

> The noble changes as a leopard.
> The petty man changes its face.
> Attacking brings misfortune.
> The determination brings good fortune.

The revolution is already done. Now people should adapt to the new order.
The leopard symbolizes versatility, beauty and independence. To change like a leopard means to innovate, adapt to new circumstances with elegance. Also, to change like a leopard traditionally means to go from rags to riches.
Since attacking brings misfortune, change should be carried on without violence, with diplomacy. Also, since the main transformation has been already performed; to push ahead with more radical changes would be dangerous, only minor adjustments should be done now. The change will bring good fortune only if performed deeply and with sincerity, like a leopard; passive acceptance or faking a change, like a petty man, will not do. Inferior people will only change their appearance, but not their hearts; they are not trustworthy.

50

dǐng
The Cauldron / Sacrificial Vessel

Associated meanings

Cauldron; three-legged bronze cauldron with two ears; establish, renew, transform. Sacred bronze vessels were used during by the *Shang* and *Zhou* dynasties to offer sacrificial meals to the spirits in rituals.

Judgment

> The Cauldron.
> Outstanding good fortune.
> Success.

In ancient China, when a dynasty began, the first thing done was to cast a new cauldron with the fundamental laws inscribed on it, to symbolize the new epoch begun under the new king. Thus, when starting new life cycle (after Revolution, the previous hexagram) you should transform yourself to be able to face the new conditions and establish them firmly.

The Cauldron symbolizes purification, like it happened during sacrifice offerings; it also means initiation and transformation. The Cauldron also indicates something that tempers, transforms and harmonizes its contents.

In another interpretation level you are the sacrificial vessel, hence the Cauldron means the full realization of your potential, to develop your talents and gifts.

The Image

> Fire over wood: The image of the Cauldron.
> Thus the noble corrects his position to consolidate his fate.

Fire over wood suggests the idea of cooking. The head of the family cooked his sacrifices to the spirits and served the food from the Cauldron into the bowls of the guests

Nourishing people with consecrated food indicates spiritual development, maturing and learning how to realize the innate potential: the fate.

The hexagram 48: **The Well** indicates the nourishment of the people in general, but the Cauldron means the spiritual nourishment of noble persons.

Wood keeps the fire running, in the same way the noble cultivates his fate with his acts, making sure he is on the correct path.

Fire over wood also indicates the importance of the correct placement of things. Thus, the noble rectifies the position of the people, to fully realize their potential.

First Six

> The Cauldron is lying upside down.
> It is favorable to remove debris.
> One takes a concubine to bear a child.
> No defect.

A Cauldron lying upside down means to produce a radical change of attitude when starting a new cycle in life. This transposition of values means that much of what previously was seen as good (the old content of the cauldron), it is no longer useful, and that what was previously disdained (the concubine) now has good development possibilities (the son).

In times of renovation, unorthodox methods should be used, what was low (the concubine, or handmaiden in other translations) will generate new opportunities and what was of high value is now worthless.

Second Nine

> The Cauldron is full.
> My counterpart is anxious, but cannot get at me.
> Good fortune.

Your achievements may cause resentment in some people. The anxious counterpart (comrade or enemy in other translations) means somebody who wants to take from you the content of the Cauldron, without having any rights to it.

But they cannot get what belongs to you. Continue ahead with dedication and you will be fortunate.

Third Nine

> The handles of the Cauldron are removed.
> Progress is impeded.
> The fat pheasant meat is not eaten.
> Rain falls all around, and regrets disappear.
> Finally there will be good fortune.

The missing handles mean that your talents are not appreciated and because that they are misused or are unproductive.

The meat not eaten indicates lost opportunities and wasted resources.

The rain symbolizes clearing up misunderstandings and overcoming conflicts.

At the end your true value will be recognized and you will be able to make good use of your talents and abilities.

Fourth Nine

> The Cauldron legs are broken.
> The stew is spilled and stains the Prince's figure.
> Misfortune.

The broken legs mean lack of support that make your plans fail, lack of judgment, wrong start, overambitious plans that you are not qualified to handle.

The stained figure (or punishment by branding in other translations) means that as a result of your failure your reputation will be in tatters and you may be even punished.

Fifth Six

> The Cauldron has yellow handles and metal carrying-bars.
> The determination is favorable.

The carrying-bars pass through the handles (ears) of the Cauldron and allow its proper use. This line is the place of the ruler, who is represented by the carrying-bars; his helpers are the cauldron handles. Yellow symbolizes balance and modesty.

An open-minded and wise ruler will attract good people to cooperate with him.

Top Nine

> The Cauldron has carrying-bars of jade.
> Great good fortune.
> Nothing that is not favorable.

The jade carrying-bars are impervious to corrosion, they are hard, smooth, and have a soft luster; they symbolize an advisor who can handle with great strength and compliance the more delicate tasks. He is free of partiality and can do his work with the summit of perfection.

The sixth line of a hexagram frequently symbolizes a sage who is outside the situation and helps the ruler with his wisdom, as happens in this case.

zhèn
Shock

This is one of the eight hexagrams that are comprised by the same trigram repeated twice, in this case *zhèn*, The Arousing.

Associated meanings

Shock; clap of thunder; fear, awe inspiring, to terrify; stimulation, movement, quake, excitation, upheaval; to quicken; endow, succor.

Judgment

> Shock. Success.
> The arrival of Shock causes great fear.
> But afterwards there are laughing words.
> Shock terrifies for a hundred *li*.
> But he doesn't drop the libation in the sacrificial ladle.

An unexpected violent disruption in your life will shock you.
Uncertainty and awe inspiring changes will shake the structure of your life. Laughing words indicate the excitement mixed with fear that such times arouse.
Notice that shock may came in waves, in such case you will experience several periods of fear followed by distension moments when you will laugh.
To avoid dropping the sacrificial ladle means to keep your balance and to be ready to face the new times.
These are interesting times, if you are able to adapt to the new circumstances you will grow as a person.

The Image

> The thunder repeated: the image of Shock.
> Thus the noble with apprehension and fear, puts his life in order
> and evaluates himself.

The duplicated trigram that forms this hexagram is exciting, arousing and shaking.

Thunder repeated means that your daily routine will be unsettled by unexpected events; they may be the result of completely unpredictable factor or they may happen because you chose to ignore some facts and hence you are no ready to handle its consequences.

These events may be unexpected situations, seemly fortuitous events, or a person that enters your life disrupting it.

At this moment you cannot ignore any longer what is happening. You have to grow and learn how to cope with the challenge.

To put your life in order means to be ready to adjust your attitude and your beliefs and to leave behind what is not useful anymore.

First Nine

> The arrival of Shock causes great fear.
> But afterwards there are laughing words.
> Good fortune.

The words in this line are similar to the text of the Judgment.
At first, shock will terrify you but after the first effect passes you will adapt and relax.
The new fearful things that have irrupted in your life will be indeed a blessing in disguise.

Second Six

> Shock comes with risk.
> You lose one hundred thousand cowries and climb the nine hills
> Do not go in pursuit.
> In seven days you will get them.

You will be greatly disturbed and suffer some emotional or material losses, represented by the lost cowries (they were a form of coin).
If you accept your losses and instead striving to recover them, retreat until the danger is gone, all will end well.
In another level, to climb the hills indicates the need to grow and mature to be able to handle the new situation.
The seven days represent a necessary cycle, which cannot be skipped. After it ends you will get back what you lost before.
Besides this hexagram, the Chinese character for seven only appears in the **hexagram 24**, in the Judgment and in the second line of the **hexagram 63**. Here it indicates the return of money, in the hexagram 24 is related with a return and in the hexagram 63 with the return of the curtain of a carriage.

Third Six

> Shock stimulates and terrifies one.
> If shock excites one to action, there will be no defect.

Shock is dangerous, but if it awakens you to the need to change and adapt to the new times, you will make no mistake.
You may get confused at first, but after you recover your balance you will find a way to handle the disturbing events.
If you take no action, ignoring the need for change, you will be ashamed.
On other level, to take action also may mean to leave the place of danger, to run away.

Fourth Nine

> After Shock mud.

You are mired in doubt and confusion, because you lost your chance for escaping the turmoil. Try to recover your balance and composure and to find new solutions for your troubles or your life will stagnate.

Fifth Six

> Shock comes and goes.
> Danger.
> But nothing is lost.
> There are things to do.

You are in the middle of great turmoil and danger, but if you stay focused in your objectives and keep balanced and rolling with the waves you will do well.

Top Six

> Shock causes fear and agitation.
> One looks around in terror.
> Marching forth brings misfortune.
> The shock does not reach you but your neighbor.
> No defect.
> There is talk of marriage.

Shock has reached its highest point and unrest and confusion are extensive. Because people are afraid and unsettled they will be prone to act without thinking, making still worse their situation.

You have a chance to stay out of that collective psychosis. Do not follow the masses, but keep yourself calm and withdrawn.

The talk of marriage indicates plans or a chance to establish an alliance to overcome the current commotion.

gèn
Restraint

This is one of the eight hexagrams that are comprised by the same trigram repeated twice, in this case *gèn*, Keeping Still.

Associated meanings

Keeping still, limit, check, hold steady, restrain, being quiet, non-action, stop; mind at peace, meditation.

Judgment

> Restraining his back. Doesn't feel his body.
> Goes to his courtyard and doesn't see his people. No defect.

Besides its literal sense, restraining the back means to keep both action and stillness in the proper place.
Not feeling his body and not seeing his people indicates to avoid following blindly impulsive instincts or the call of the group; to let things happen without reacting to them.
Restrain can be applied in two levels: inner restraint means to keep the mind in peace and outer restraint means to stay focused in what you are doing.
By mastering restrain you will be free of anxiety in two ways:
Your mind will not wander and worry about all the possible outcomes on your current situation.
You will not care about what other people think about you, because you will be focused in what you are doing not in how you look or what others may say about you.

The Image

> Joined mountains: The image of Restraint.
> Thus the noble doesn't let his thoughts wander beyond his position.

A range of mountains stays in place as an insurmountable barrier. It teaches us how to put a stop to our wandering thoughts.

Not allowing the thoughts to wander means to put a stop to vain speculations, to restrain the mind from idly rambling, to stay focused in the matters at hand, and to stay in the here and now.

It also means being realistic, to avoid chasing illusions.

First Six

> Restraining his toes.
> No defect.
> Long term steadiness is favorable.

You will be tempted to take action, but still this is not the right time to proceed forward.
If you keep your position steadily you will not make any mistakes.

Second Six

> Restraining his calves doesn't help the one he follows.
> His heart is not happy.

The second line symbolizes a follower of the person indicated by the third line, the second line would like to help the third one, but it is unable to do so.

You are carried in the wake of a powerful will. The calves cannot move independently from the legs, they are dependent. In the same way you cannot stop the movement that has already started because a force more powerful than you is pushing ahead.

Third Nine

> Restraining his hips.
> Tears his lumbar area.
> Danger.
> The heart is suffocated.

Here restraint is applied to the wrong point and with excess.

In the external world, this indicates an unyielding attitude and lack of adaptation to reality. If you do not know how to bend you will break.

Internally, it means an excessive repression of your feelings. This unwholesome attitude will generate too much stress and will suffocate your spirit.

Fourth Six

> Restrains his body.
> No defect.

To maintain still the body means to control the whole individuality in a balanced manner, without being influenced by external factors.

It also indicates that you know how to relax and rest properly.

Fifth Six

> Restrains his jaws.
> What he says is orderly.
> Repentance fades.

To restrain the jaws means to not indulge in idle chatter and to think before speaking.

Speaking orderly signifies to say the proper words and also to avoid saying things that will cause unrest between the people.

Top Nine

> Earnest restrain.
> Good fortune.

Your deep inner composure allows you to contemplate with equanimity and an impartial perspective all things that happen to yourself and in the world in general.
Such attitude will bring good fortune to you and the people around you.

53

jiàn
Gradual Development

Four hexagrams are related with marriage and the preliminary steps leading to it: **31-Influence**, depicts the initial attraction and courtship in a couple; **32-Duration**, indicates the institution of marriage; 53-Gradual Development, shows the steps and ceremonies leading to marriage and **54-The Marrying Maiden**, describes a young maiden entering an older man's house as a secondary wife.

Associated meanings

Gradual development, gradually, increasingly, advance by degrees, slow growth; moisten, dip down into, imbue; influence. Advance like the water, infiltrating gradually.

Judgment

> Gradual Development.
> The maiden's marriage brings good fortune.
> The determination is favorable.

In traditional Chinese society after a maiden was engaged, a number of ceremonies had to be performed before her marriage.
In the same way, Gradual Development requires proceeding on a step-by-step basis. Preliminary steps cannot be skipped if you want to lay solid bases for any project. In time your determination will allow reaching the concretion point, symbolized by the marriage of the maiden.

The Image

> On the mountain is a tree: The image of Gradual Development.
> Thus the noble dwells in virtue and so improves the manners of the people.

Gradual Development indicates a slow but impressive ascent, from the low riverbanks up to the highlands. In the same way that a growing tree, you should progress slowly and properly, establishing firm bases for your development.

The slow growing of a tree also indicates how a sage, gradually along his own development, influences other people improving their life and teaching them. In time, your ascent will put you as a prominent role model for the people around you, such as a grown tree on a high place, which can be seen from afar.

First Six

> The goose gradually moves toward the riverbank.
> The small child is in danger and will be spoken against.
> No defect.

The goose appears in all the lines of this hexagram, symbolizing the steps in Gradual Development, from the water to the sky.

The goose is an animal that can swim in water, walk on land of fly on the sky. The goose is safer on water or when flying than in land, where it is in danger from its predators. Here it approaches a dangerous limit, symbolized by the riverbank.

This is the beginning of Gradual Development, you are alone and entering a new territory, attractive, but full of unknown perils.

You will be criticized, because you are crossing a line and daring to try something new. You are inexperienced and people will not trust you, hence you will face some trouble.

If you follow your goals with determination you will learn new things and will do well, without making any mistakes.

Second Six

> The goose gradually moves towards a big rock.
> Eats and drinks joyfully.
> Good fortune.

You have reached some security here and you can look to the future with hope. The big rock represents a stable and secure base, a place where your basic necessities are satisfied.

The Chinese character translated as "joyfully" also means feasting, which gives the idea of a social reunion.

Also the same character, which is repeated twice, is an onomatopoeia for the honking sound of geese. It has been said that geese call other of their same kind when they find food, to share it, hence this line suggest sharing happily the good things of life with other people.

Third Nine

> The goose gradually moves to the highlands.
> The man goes on an expedition but does not return;
> the woman is pregnant but does not give birth.
> Misfortune.
> It is favorable to fend off bandits.

The highlands are not a proper place for a goose, because there is no food or shelter for it there. To go to the highlands or on an expedition (notice that the word "expedition" may be also translated as "go to war") means to start some bold and risky advance without proper preparation.

If you start a conflict or try to something dangerous beyond your real possibilities, you will fail. The not returning man indicates loses and lack of support; the woman not giving birth symbolizes a plan that doesn't fructify.

By trying to force advance where it is not possible to do so you will lose your way.
To fend off bandits means that instead following ahead with impossible goals you should protect what you have already got.

Fourth Six

> The goose gradually moves towards a tree.
> It may find a flat branch.
> No defect.

A flat branch in a tree is not the best place for a goose, but in times of hardship and danger you should be flexible, and accept what you can get.
The important thing is to find shelter, it may not be the perfect place for you but if it puts your out of danger is a good option.
The flat branch also indicates temporary solutions.

Fifth Nine

> The goose gradually moves towards the top of the hill.
> The woman cannot conceive for three years.
> Finally, nothing can stop it.
> Good fortune.

Conceiving a child symbolizes accomplishing the desires of your heart, but there are some obstacles that will stop that from happening for a time.
The *yin* line in the second place symbolizes a woman, who is separated from the fifth *yang* line –which is on the hilltop– by the intermediate lines. Applied to human relations it means that deceitful people or misunderstandings will create barriers that will prevent you for a time from achieving what you wish.
Also, the top of the hill indicates a person in a high position, who may become isolated and suffer abuse and slander from invidious people.
In the end all obstacles will be overcame and you will have good fortune.

Top Nine

> The goose gradually moves towards the highlands.
> Its feathers can be used to practice the rites.
> Good fortune.

The highlands are the culmination of Gradual Advance.
To use the feathers of the goose for the rites means that your advancement makes you an example and also an inspiration for others; in a more mundane level it may indicate a consummated marriage.

54

guī mèi
The Marrying Maiden

Four hexagrams are related with marriage and the preliminary steps leading to it: **31-Influence**, depicts the initial attraction and courtship in a couple; **32-Duration**, indicates the institution of marriage; **53-Gradual Development**, shows the steps and ceremonies leading to marriage and 54-The Marrying Maiden, describes a young maiden entering an older man's house as a secondary wife.

The two Chinese characters for this hexagram tag are: *guī*: "send in marriage" and *mèi*: "maiden, daughter, younger sister".

In ancient China a noble could have several wives and a ruler should have not less than three, all from the same family. The secondary wives were called younger sisters, since they usually were normally junior sisters, step-sisters or cousins of the primary bride.

The secondary wives were subservient to the principal wife, whose children had precedence over the other children.

Associated meanings

The marriage of the younger sister, the second wife, playing a subordinate role, concubine.

Judgment

> The Marrying Maiden.
> Marching forth brings misfortune.
> Nothing that is favorable.

A girl entering a household as a secondary wife symbolizes becoming part of a human group in a subservient, informal or temporary position.

Taking an unassuming attitude and doing what is expected from you is the best choice when you are a subordinate.

Do not assume inappropriate prerogatives and do not undermine the people above you by influencing your common boss bypassing them.

The Image

On the lake is the thunder: The image of the Marrying Maiden.
Thus the noble persists to the end and knows the cause of the damage.

Thunder symbolizes the eldest son, who is leading the lake, the younger sister. This shows a young girl entering the house of an elder man in a low position, like a secondary wife or concubine.

Applied to current times, when entering in non-symmetric relationships, on the weaker side, you should be very careful to avoid damage, and behave with endurance.

Notice that neither good fortune nor blame is mentioned here. This kind of position is fraught with disadvantages, but as in most situations, with the proper attitude –patient and tactful in this case–, you can get the most of it.

This sentence also gives the idea of a transitory union that can't last forever because its initial flaws are the seeds of its final destruction.

First Nine

She marries as a concubine.
A lame man can walk.
Marching forth brings good fortune.

The first line indicates a person with low social standing, as a concubine who has a humble position in a household. You are becoming part of some group, but you have little influence and you are very low in the pecking order.

Nevertheless, in spite of the disadvantages you can advance successfully, like a lame man who cannot walk fast but still advances on.

This is a good moment to start something new, if you are humble you will advance unimpeded, for that reason, marching forth brings good fortune.

Yi was the name of the penultimate *Shang* Emperor who gave a bride to the lord of *Zhou*. The **hexagram 11.5** has a similar oracle.

Second Nine

A one-eyed man can see.
The determination of a solitary man is favorable.

The one-eyed man that can see means to lose a partner and becoming solitary, to be in disadvantage or to suffer some loss or disappointment. Also it indicates having only a partial view of the situation.

To be determined as a solitary man indicates to go ahead on your own, without asking for help, in isolation.

In another interpretation level this line may indicate that if you do not have good prospects it is better to remain alone.

Third Six

The Marrying Maiden in servitude.
She returns and marries as a secondary wife.

To marry in servitude indicates a failing union or project; hence you will return back and accept a secondary role.

The sense of this line is that after your main ambition is thwarted you may go back and accept a compromise, taking the best possible alternative.

Fourth Nine

> The Marrying Maiden delays marriage, waiting for the right time.
> There will be a late marriage.

It is better to wait until you have a good opportunity instead compromising yourself with something that is below you.
In the end you will achieve your wishes.

Fifth Six

> The emperor *Yi* gives his daughter in marriage.
> The sleeves of her dress were less gorgeous than her bridesmaid's.
> The moon is almost full.
> Good fortune.

The bridesmaids were secondary wives. In this case the more important thing –the daughter of the emperor– looked less attractive or was more humble than a less important factor –the bridesmaid–.
Appearance is not the main theme here, but modesty and a having a service vocation; that is what will allow you to complete a cycle –as the reference to the full moon indicates– and to be successful.

Top Six

> The woman has a basket, but it contains no fruit.
> The man stabs a sheep but it does not bleed.
> Nothing is favorable.

The empty basket indicates falsity and meanness, the sheep that doesn't bleed is an insincere sacrifice, since the animal was already dead.
Also, the empty basket symbolizes an infertile womb and the non-bleeding sheep a man with no seed.
Lack of real commitment and hypocritical attitudes will poison any good chances in a marriage or union of any type.

55

fēng
Fullness / Abundance

Associated meanings

Abundance, fullness; luxurious, bountiful, fruitful, prolific, ripe, full; prosperity, affluence; reaching the zenith. Some scholars think it describes a solar eclipse, which serves as an analogy for the eclipse of the influence or capable men.

Judgment

> Fullness has success.
> The king is coming.
> Do not be sad.
> Suitable at midday.

Both the king and the reference to the sun at midday denote personal growth and elevation. You will reach a high point in your life, but since the sun starts descending as soon it reaches its zenith, it will be a transient moment of glory as well. That is the reason for the warning: do not be sad.

Also the sun gives warmth and light to all things; it shares its energy with all human beings. Do not try to hoard the fullness of this moment, it is not possible and such behavior goes against the requirements of this time. On the contrary, be ready to help and sustain others, share your blessings with an open heart.

The Image

> Thunder and lightning culminate altogether: The image of Fullness.
> Thus the noble decides legal cases and applies punishments.

Thunder and lightning symbolize power exercised from a superior and enlightened position. In several lines of Fullness, lack of clarity and suspicions make difficult the interaction between people.

Legal cases and punishments are the main tools to restore the public trust and to avoid lowly persons from interfering and darkening the light of justice.

First Nine

> Meets the master that is his match.
> Even if they are together for a ten-day week there will be no mistake.
> Going forward attains rewards.

You will meet somebody that shares your values and views –the fourth line– but is placed in a position higher than yours; this person will help you to realize your goals.
The ten-day week describes a period without harm that is granted between both parties. It will be a temporary meeting but you will complete a full cycle in that time.
The ten days together will allow you to accomplish a shared project with help from your master.
If you try to prolong the allowed time together, to reach still more benefits, you will attract calamity over yourself.
In ancient China the ten days weeks in use was based only on numeric considerations, without any astronomic relation.

Second Six

> The curtain has such fullness that the Big Dipper could be seen at noon.
> Going forwards attains distrust and hatred.
> Manifest sincerity will have good fortune.

The text of this line has several possible translations, but the general meaning is that your advance will be checked because you are distrusted. The curtains are prejudices and envy that will keep your merits unnoticed by your superiors.
Direct action will not work well, but if you demonstrate your sincerity by doing worthy deeds, finally you will be successful and will gain the trust of your superiors.
The Big Dipper is a cluster of seven stars in the constellation *Ursa Major*, four forming the bowl and three the handle of a dipper-shaped configuration, also called Plow or Plough.

Third Nine

> The covering has such fullness that the dimmest starts could be seen at noon.
> Breaks his right arm.
> No defect.

Unfavorable conditions will block any intent on your part to overcome them. The broken arm means that your influence and power will be diminished after an unsuccessful intent for advancing.
The dimmest starts symbolize petty people who will prosper meanwhile you are obstructed. Nevertheless, you will make no mistake.

Fourth Nine

> The curtain has such fullness that the Big Dipper could be seen at noon.
> He meets his master in secret.
> Good fortune.

The darkness can be overcame with the help of a powerful ally, the fifth line, who is the ruler. You will complement well the qualities of your master and by joining your efforts in a concerted way you will advance successfully.
To meet in secret stresses out the need for extreme care and caution.

Fifth Six

>Brilliance is coming.
>You will have blessings and fame.
>Good fortune.

You will get over the pressing darkness with the help of capable helpers and the application of your inner abilities.

Your merits will be recognized and honored and with the cooperation of your supporters you will achieve great accomplishments.

Top Six

>A large canopy hides his house.
>He peeks from his door, silent and with no one at his side.
>For three years he sees nothing.
>Misfortune.

Instead of facing the troubles of daily life you prefer to abode in the past, being afraid of the external world.

You are becoming isolated because you are not ready to share your blessings but look at others with arrogance and contempt.

Your rigid attitude will keep you apart from other people for a full period of seclusion.

56

lǚ

Sojourner / Wanderer

Associated meanings

Sojourner, guest, to lodge, wanderer, traveler, stranger, outsider, exile, expatriate, stay away from home, transition, temporary situation, wandering troops.

Judgment

> The Sojourner.
> Success in small things.
> The determination of the Sojourner brings good fortune.

You are residing in a strange land. Because you don't have support from your family or a wide network of friends, your perspectives are restricted, thus only small things can be done.
The determination of the Sojourner indicates adaptation to the limits of your current situation and to act accordingly to your possibilities.
As a Sojourner you are looking for a place to call home and perhaps employment as well. Until you secure a good place for settling, you should be satisfied with small comforts and avoid asking too much from people. You are a stranger and you will be respected only if you behave with dignity and modesty.
In another interpretation level this hexagram indicates a transitional phase, a temporary situation that will pass in time.

The Image

> Above the mountain is fire: The image of the Sojourner.
> Thus the noble applies punishments with clarity
> and doesn't prolong litigations.

Conflicts may have unpredictable and dangerous results, like a fire on a mountain summit that is swayed by the winds, they can easily grow beyond your control.
Fire will only last while it has something to burn, in the same way punishments should only be applied for a short while and when there is no other chance.

You may have to defend yourself, but you do not have the resources to sustain protracted conflicts.

First Six

> The Sojourner is too fussy.
> He will bring calamity upon himself.

The character translated as "fussy" also means "trivial, petty, annoying, touchy, contemptible". The general idea is that the Sojourner has an exaggerated opinion of his own importance and he is an annoyance to other people, a troublemaker.

Notice that being this the first line, it depicts a person of scarce resources and low social position. Such a petty person will fall in disgrace because his inappropriate behavior.

Second Six

> The Sojourner comes to a resting place.
> Keeps his belongings safely and gets a young and loyal servant.

You will find a good place to stop for a while.

The character translated here as "belongings" also means "money, means of livelihood and property"; besides its literal meaning, it symbolizes your resources, knowledge, and ability. To keep your belongings safe also means that you are coping well with your journey, that you behave with self-possession and modesty.

To get a young servant indicates that you will receive support, which will be good within its limits, since a young servant wouldn't be highly qualified.

Third Nine

> The Sojourner burns his resting place.
> He loses his young servant.
> The determination is dangerous.

To burn the resting place indicates a violent and overbearing behavior that will undermine your own security.

If you treat other people with arrogance and insensitivity you will lose their cooperation.

If you follow such wrong path, you will be alienated from other people, and will find only trouble in your future.

Fourth Nine

> The Sojourner stays at one place and obtains property and an ax.
> My heart is not happy.

You have found a temporary resting place and some security.

Still uneasy, you don't feel safe. The ax also may indicate hard work to get settled or the need for security measures.

Your aspirations are not yet fulfilled; you know that your current lodgings are not the proper place for you.

The general sense is that you will find temporary solutions that are acceptable but not very good.

Fifth Six

> He shoots a pheasant.
> Although the first arrow fails finally he is praised and given employment.

To shoot a pheasant means to seek employment by way of showing your abilities.

You may have some troubles demonstrating your value, but in the end you will get what you look for, after you prove what you are capable of.

In another interpretation level you will have to offer something of value before getting accepted.

"The shooting at a target was used in antiquity, for the election of feudatories and officials. The precision in shooting was supposed to represent the uprightness of the heart, and vice-versa." (*Wieger*).

Top Nine

> The bird burns its nest.
> The Sojourner laughs at first but afterward cries out and weeps.
> He loses his cow in *Yi*.
> Misfortune.

The nest indicates an elevated position, at the top of the hexagram. To laugh first and weep afterwards means that if you are being arrogant and careless you will lose your position, a thing that happens many times in the top line, when people cross the line of proper behavior. The reference to the lost cow in *Yi* is related to an historical-mythical Chinese figure, associated to birdlike characters, which took his herds to pasture in *Yi* and was murdered there.

To lose the cow means to lose the livelihood and to be unable to adapt to the exigencies of the time.

The character for bird, *niao*, who appears in this line, only is used four times in the *Yijing* and always indicates that extreme attitudes will cause misfortune.

57

xùn
Gentle Influence / Penetration / The Wind

This is one of the eight hexagrams that are comprised by the same trigram repeated twice, in this case *xùn*, The Gentle.

Associated meanings

Humble, yield, compliant, obedient, mild, bland, insinuating, bowing down, food offering, bending to enter.

Judgment

> Gentle Influence.
> Success in small things.
> It is favorable to have a place to go.
> It is favorable to see the great man.

Success in small things indicates certain attitude, compliant and humble, but persistent and determined. This means that you will achieve your ends little by little, but in a sure way.
To have a place where to go means that you should have perseverance and clear objectives; otherwise your gentle influence would dissipate soon without having any lasting effects.
To see the great man not only indicates to seek advice and help from a qualified source, but also to rise mentally and spiritually to be up to the situation.

The Image

> Winds that follow each other: The image of Gentle Influence.
> Thus the noble proclaims his commands and acts to carry out his tasks.

Confucius said: "The relation between superiors and inferiors is like that between the wind and the grass: the grass is bound to bend when the wind blows across it". This quotation indicates clearly the meaning of the image.
Wind influences the grass without being visible. In the same way, you should influence unceasingly the people that you are leading, inspiring and supporting them to perform their tasks.

The words "proclaims his commands" mean that you should be always behind your projects supporting them but also indicates the need to concentrate your mind in your objectives, avoiding unnecessary distractions.

First Six

> Advancing and retreating.
> The determination is favorable for a warrior.

To advance and then retreat indicates a state of indecision and hesitation and hence lack of stability.
What is required is the determination of a warrior: assume your duty firmly, be single-minded and valiant.

Second Nine

> Penetration under the bed.
> Using invokers and sorcerers in large number brings good fortune.
> No defect.

The invokers and sorcerers indicate the way to catch hidden factors or influences. Invokers can be also translated as "chronicles", which suggests unseen influences from the past.
The message is that you will need special methods and specialists to clarify the situation and uncover hidden forces. Also, this kind of work should be done with subtleness and finesse; a frontal assault would be useless.
You will make no mistake uncovering what is hidden beneath the surface, because such disclosure will benefit you.

Third Nine

> Repeated penetration.
> Humiliation.

If you can't accomplish your will and try to force you way blindly, you will be shamed.
In another interpretation level it also may indicate that you cannot reach a decision, and will ruminate without end about some matter. Such indecision will not allow you to do anything good and in the end will humiliate you.

Fourth Six

> Repentance fades.
> Captures three types of prey in hunting.

Traditionally, animals caught in real hunts were divided in three categories: a) for sacrifices; b) for guests and c) provisions for the sovereign's kitchen. A hunt that yielded enough for all purposes was considered very successful.
Applied to current situations it means to achieve very good results at all levels and to get all that you need.
Troubles will disappear.

Fifth Nine

> The determination is fortunate.
> Repentance fades.

> Nothing that is not favorable.
> There is no beginning, but an end.
> Before the seventh day, three days; after the seventh day, three days.
> Good fortune.

You should change your approach after you realize that your first intents were wrong. If you act with determination and flexibility you will avoid trouble.

The mention to the seventh day and the three days is related to the ancient ten-day week. It means that if you make adjustments by the middle of the week, by the end of it you will see good results –do not take the number of days literally–. It also means that any changes in your methods should be done gradually and that your new approach will take some time to produce visible results.

In ancient China, the ten days weeks in use was based only on numerical considerations, without any astronomic relation. The ten days were associated with the Ten Heavenly Stems *(tian gan)*, that are a Chinese system of cyclic numbers from the *Shang* dynasty.

Top Nine

> Penetration under the bed.
> He loses his belongings and an ax.
> The determination is ominous.

Penetration under the bed means to be obsessed with elucidating every detail of some issue before taking action.

If you waste all your energy and time in vain speculation you will have nothing left to face the real problems in your life.

In another interpretation level it means that if you follow some issue too far, you will generate more trouble than good results.

If you persist in your obsession you will lose your means of defense and attack, and will squander your resources.

58

duì
Joyousness / The Lake

This is one of the eight hexagrams that are comprised by the same trigram repeated twice, in this case *duì*, The Joyous.

Associated meanings

Joyousness, happiness, satisfaction; cheerful talk, openness, interaction, exchange, communication, mouth; barter.
"Good words that dispel grief and rejoice the hearer; hence the two meanings, to speak, to rejoice." (*Wieger*).

Judgment

> Joyousness.
> Success.
> Determination is favorable.

A joyous attitude is easily communicable to others and will help to foster good communications and friendly relations between people.
Joy should flow from within and not depend on external circumstances. If you run after joy you will not find true joy. The essence of joy is an open and cheerful nature, not a mindless search of external pleasures.
Determination is required to avoid joy from becoming immoderate and weakening.

The Image

> Two lakes together: The image of Joyousness.
> Thus the noble joins his friends for discussion and training.

As two lakes linked together mingle their waters and avoid stagnation, free communication with other people will enrich your ideas and give proper perspective to your thoughts, keeping your notions up-to-date and vital.
Open communication with friends will not only give you knowledge, will keep you happy as well.

First Nine

> Harmonious joy.
> Good fortune.

The word translated as "harmonious" also means "balance, rhythm, respond to, agreement", indicating that you are in tune with the current situation and with the people around you. You are free to do your will because you have inner calm and good balance.

Second Nine

> Sincere joy.
> Good fortune.
> Regrets go away.

Do not let others complicate your life with dubious pleasures. Follow what you think is best, disregarding what others say.
In that way you will avoid trouble and will enjoy good fortune.

Third Six

> Coming joy.
> Misfortune.

Excessive indulgence of your own appetites and desires will cost you dearly and will destroy your hopes.

Fourth Nine

> Haggling joy.
> Still not at peace.

After limiting your anxiety there will be happiness.
You are restless and undecided, trying to balance external pressures with your own desires. Choose wisely; select what will give you true and lasting value and not only temporary pleasure. Once you find the correct path you will be happy.

Fifth Nine

> Trusting degrading influences is dangerous.

To trust degrading influences means to trust unworthy people or to be involved in a dubious situation.
It also indicates overconfidence in your capacity and strength disregarding possible dangers.

Top Six

> Alluring joyousness.

Vain and fun loving people will only care about their pleasures and follies, dragging others with them in their wake.

59

huàn
Dispersion / Dissolution / The Flood

Associated meanings

Dispersion, dissolution, scattering; dispel misunderstandings, fantasies and fears; overcoming dissension; gush, splash; slack, relaxed.

Judgment

> Dispersion.
> Success.
> The king approaches his temple.
> It is favorable to cross the great river.
> The determination is favorable.

This hexagram has a double meaning:
To disperse the obstacles or misunderstandings that prevent an union.
Avoiding to be dispersed or separated by obstacles, illusions and prejudices.
People are keep apart by prejudices and petty intolerance, but the time of Dispersion is like a flood that will carry away such obstructions and melt the ice in the hearts of the people.
The king is a leader that gathers people around him. To join a mass of people, a sense of shared purpose and identify is required. The temple symbolizes such central point, which focuses the attention of the people in a single goal and brings people together.
In ancient China, crossing rivers, either at a ford or when the river was frozen, was not an easy task. It implicated dangers and hardships; hence crossing the great river means to carry out a difficult undertaking.

The Image

> Wind moving over the water: The image of Dispersion.
> Thus the ancient kings made offerings to the Supreme Lord
> and erected temples.

The wind blowing over the water melts the solid ice and pushes the water around. In the same way barriers between people should be overcame.

The ancient kings symbolize a pattern or model of good governance, which we should strive to follow.
To make offerings means to get over egoism, grudges and prejudices, to make a contribution for the sake of the community. The temple symbolizes a shared project or idea that summons peoples around.

First Six

> Uses the strength of a horse for rescue.
> Good fortune.

You are located at the beginning of Dispersion and you should try to prevent dissension. To help with the strength of a horse means to go quickly and energetically to fix the problems. Good fortune means that you can avoid further troubles by taking early care.

Second Nine

> Dispersion.
> Run to your support.
> Repentance fades.

You are in danger of becoming isolated and alienated from others, swept by the flood of the circumstances.
You should adjust your attitude to prevent trouble, get in touch with other people and help them instead ruminating and bearing ill will towards them.
Running to your support also means to use your energy in constructive ways, doing what is your real vocation.

Third Six

> Disperses himself.
> No repentance.

You will need all your energy concentrated in the undertaking that you are carrying out, do not waste time or energy regarding your own personal trivial interests.
Putting all your efforts towards the common good will benefit not only other people but yourself, in the long run.

Fourth Six

> Disperses his group.
> Outstanding good fortune.
> Dispersion is accumulation.
> Common people do not consider that point.

To disperse his group means to leave behind self-centered partisanship, and narrow factions, to be open-minded and ready to benefit others beyond your close friends. Also it indicates to overcome prejudices, outdated rules and customs.
By dispersing the benefits outside your own group of associates you will work for the common good and achieve far greater results in the end, which is the meaning of the phrase: dispersion is accumulation.
This can be only done by an enlightened person, who can see beyond what common people realize.

Fifth Nine

> Dispersing sweat, proclaiming aloud.
> Disperses the king dwellings.
> No defect.

"Dispersing sweat" can also be translated as "imperial edict". In the same way that sweating can break a fever, the king's edicts will break –disperse or dissolve– conflicts and grudges between his subjects.

Notice that the fifth line is the place of the ruler and symbolizes somebody with authority. To disperse the king dwellings means to share what you have with others, to give first and ask later, to take the first step in helping others.

Top Nine

> Disperses his blood.
> Going away, keeping at a distance, departing.
> No defect.

Blood symbolizes danger and hatred. To disperse the blood means that the risk of spilling blood (bitter conflicts) should be avoided by whatever means necessary.

Anything that can cause serious trouble should be put away. Risks should not be taken and caution should prevail.

You should be ready to give up, depart or discard some of your projects if that is necessary to avoid danger.

60

jié
Limitation

Associated meanings

Regulate, moderate, constraint, contain, restrict, articulate; moral integrity, self-control.
"The primary application of *jié* was to denote the joints of the bamboo; it is used also for the joints of the human frame; and for the solar and other terms of the year. Whatever makes regular division may be denominated a *jié*; there enter into it the ideas of regulating and restraining; and the subject of this hexagram is the regulation of government". (*Legge*)

Judgment

> Limitation.
> Success.
> A severe limitation cannot be applied with persistence.

Limitation means to put each thing in its right place at the proper time and to restrain all things to their proper spheres.
Restrictions should be applied to put order in your live, like when limiting how much you eat or controlling your temper. In other cases, temporary limitations are required to adapt to some circumstance, like when limiting expenditures in times of hardship.
Severe limitation refers to excessive control that can cause counterproductive results instead of being beneficial.

The Image

> Above the lake is water: The image of Limitation.
> Thus the noble establishes the number and measure
> and deliberates about morality and conduct.

The lake puts boundaries to the water inside it, defining its shape and depth.
In the same way, through self-imposed limitations, we shape our life and channel our energy in the chosen path.
To establish number and measure means to regulate properly our work along time. It also indicates to discard some things and to keep others, establishing proper priorities.

To deliberate about morality and conduct means to adjust our behavior to the present situation, to actualize the norms to the current necessities.

First Nine

> Not going out of the door to the courtyard.
> No defect.

Here, not stepping into the courtyard means to remain in a safe and familiar place.
Stay well inside your limits, wait for an opportunity, and do not make a false start.

Second Nine

> Not going out of the gate of the courtyard
> Misfortune.

If you do not act quickly you will lose a good opportunity.
The gate separates the courtyard from the outside world, crossing it means to venture in the world.
Open yourself to new possibilities, travel, be ready to meet new people and to take some risks. Do not let doubts and fears stop you from acting.

Third Six

> Disregarding the limits leads to sorrow.
> No defect.

Lack of self-control and moderation may put you in some embarrassing situations when relating to other people.
Each sphere of society has its own rules and if you ignore them you will create unnecessary conflicts.
In another interpretation level, self-indulgence may make you to violate your own rules and you will harm yourself.

Fourth Six

> Contented limitation.
> Success.

A realist attitude, accepting willingly the restraints imposed on your life will be successful.
Once you have learned to control your behavior in order to get the most of your life, self-control will come to you naturally and easily.
This also means being capable of following the leading of your bosses.

Fifth Nine

> Pleasant limitation.
> Good fortune.
> Going forward has praise.

A well-balanced person applies restrictions to himself before requesting them to other people. By setting the correct example he incites others to follow his good example. Going smoothly he will be able to achieve his goal and will gain the public esteem.

Top Six

>Bitter limitation.
>The determination is ominous.
>Repentance fades.

Exaggerated limitations will cause undesirable consequences, for that reason to continue this way will bring misfortune.

Treating others in a hard way will generate resentment and resistance; being too harsh on yourself may make you bitter.

Such bitter limitation can be useful only for a while and just in extreme cases.

61

zhōng fú
Inner Truth

Associated meanings

Inner sincerity; reliability, to inspire confidence in others, inner confidence.

Judgment

>Inner truth.
>Pigs and fishes.
>Good fortune.
>It is favorable to cross the great river.
>The determination is favorable.

This hexagram shows how inner reliability and confidence will be advantageous and will allow you to earn the trust of other people.

Pigs and fishes were presented to the Lord of Heaven by the common people, but these humble contributions, presented with inner sincerity were worthy of blessings. No matter how small is your contribution, if it is presented with sincerity it will be appreciated. Also, if you inner truth can even influence pigs and fishes, it is great indeed.

In ancient China, crossing rivers, either at a ford or when the river was frozen, was not an easy task. It implicated dangers and hardships; hence crossing the great river means to carry out a difficult undertaking.

If you are true to yourself and proceed with confidence you will be successful.

The Image

>Above the lake is the wind: The image of Inner Truth.
>Thus the noble discusses criminal cases and delays executions.

The two empty lines in the middle of this hexagram symbolize the heart and mind free from all preoccupations, without any consciousness of self, indicating inner truth.

A truthful person in a position of authority tries to understand deeply the conduct of people and is not hasty to condemn them, taking all necessary care to understand all the facts before taking action.

I Ching: Oracular Interpretation

First Nine

> It is auspicious to be prepared.
> If there is something else, it is unsettling.

Take preventive steps, don't leave anything to chance.
Rely in your own resources; do not depend on the support of others.
If you are focused and do not vacillate all will go well.

Second Nine

> A crane calling from the shadows.
> His young replies.
> I have a good cup.
> I will share it with you.

If you cultivate sincerity, all those who share the same temperament will answer your call.
You will prosper and receive help from others.
The crane is an emblem of longevity, wisdom and nobility. Also notice that the meaning of *fú*, the second character in the hexagram tag (*zhōng fú*) means "to brood over eggs", "to hatch".

Third Six

> Gets a mate.
> Sometimes beats the drum, sometimes stops.
> Sometimes weeps, sometimes sings.

Other translations for "mate" would be "comrade, antagonist or enemy".
If you depend on relations with other people for your happiness or self-confidence, your emotional stability will be erratic, according to the changes in the mood and esteem of the others toward you.
Try to be more independent.

Fourth Six

> The moon is almost full.
> One of the team's horses goes away.
> No defect.

The moon almost full indicates that a cycle is ending and changes are coming.
The horse going away means that somebody is going his own way. It may also indicate the end of a relation, society or project.
A lost horse also is an image of distress and loss of strength.
This is the proper time to choose a new path, leaving something behind and following higher goals.
Do not vacillate in accepting advice from wiser people, but in the end, trust your own opinion.

Fifth Nine

> He has truth that links them together.
> No defect.

This line is the place of the ruler. The truth that links them together is the confidence and sincerity of the leader that binds all his followers together under his leadership
This is the proper time to establish relationships and to attach associates.

Top Nine

> The cry of the pheasant rises up into heaven.
> The determination is ominous.

When reputation is higher than capability, promises can't be carried out. Sooner or later reality will take charge of the situation and misfortune will arrive.

Do not promise more than you can achieve, you will not accomplish anything good with only words.

The cry of the pheasant can be taken as a bad omen. Compare with the second nine where the crane and his young answering it are a sign of sincerity and comradeship.

xiǎo guò
Excess of the Small

Associated meanings

Preponderance of the small, keeping a low profile, small gains, scrupulous and humble work, small gets by.

Judgment

> The Excess of the Small.
> Success.
> The determination is favorable.
> Proper for small matters, not suitable for great matters.
> The flying bird leaves the message:
> It is not right to ascend, it is fit to go below.
> Great good fortune.

The Excess of the Small indicates lack of strength and resources for doing big things. Because the only two yang lines in this hexagram are placed in the center –the inner part of the hexagram– there is not enough strength to cope with the outer world.

The flying bird symbolizes the risk of carrying something too far, as a bird that flies too high and is shot down. The symbol of the bird (niao) only appears –besides this hexagram, where it is repeated three times– at the top line of the **hexagram 56**, where it indicates misfortune following hubris. In all cases it is a warning against the danger of ambition and reckless behavior. This is not the proper time to be bold.

Good fortune is the result of being focused on your daily routines with care and modesty, giving proper attention to detail.

The Image

> On top of the mountain is the thunder: The image of the Excess of the Small.
> Thus the noble in his behavior is exceedingly reverent,
> in mourning is exceedingly sorrow,
> and in his expenditures is exceedingly frugal.

This is a time to accept and respect the social norms to the utmost grade, a time for humbleness, prudence and conscientious work.

Be willing to accept your present limitations; do not try to force the situation or to stand out, instead flow with the current.

First Six

> The flying bird will have misfortune.

Being the first line, it describes what will happen to a beginner when he tries to carry out something that is beyond his capacity or knowledge.

Do not take any chances or you will suffer trouble. Stay where you are, if you try to move to a higher position, you will fail.

Second Six

> Passing by his ancestor, meeting his ancestress.
> Not reaching his ruler, meeting his minister.
> No defect.

To go towards the ancestress means to follow the hierarchies. To meet the ancestress instead of the ancestor or to meet the minister instead of the prince means that you should take exceptional care when approaching authority, not demanding too much. This also indicates to follow the line of minor resistance and to make the most with limited resources.

Third Nine

> If he is not exceedingly careful, somebody may follow and strike him.
> Misfortune.

If you do not take good precautions you will be harmed by an unexpected aggression. The Chinese character translated as "strike" also means "kill, injure, violent assault, maltreat".

The attack will come without warning, like a stab on the back, and it may come from somebody that you trust.

An alternative translation would be "Not passing, somebody...", meaning that if you go too far you will put yourself in danger.

Fourth Nine

> No defect.
> Not passing, meeting.
> Moving on is dangerous.
> One must be alert.
> Do not be unyielding.

This is a warning to be quiet and restrained. Do what you need to do and no more. Be humble, do not make others to lose face.

To be alert means to wait and see. This is not a good time for making any changes or to introduce new plans.

Fifth Six

> Heavy clouds but no rain from our western frontier.
> The prince catches the one in the cave.

Clouds without rain indicate that you have reached some results, but still you cannot achieve your final objective.

Search for something new that can help you; it may be hard to find, as if hidden in a cave. Perhaps some person can help you or you need some thing or knowledge to succeed.

Notice that the text neither prognosticates success nor error.

Top Six

> Passes without finding him.
> The flying bird is netted.
> Misfortune.
> This means disaster.

If you don't know where to stop and try to fly too high you will become entangled in trouble. Some translations say "the flying bird leaves" instead of "the flying bird is netted". The modern meaning for the character lí is "to leave, part from", but originally the phonetic element of this character showed a bird being caught in a net and some of its original meanings were "fall into, fasten, attach".

63

jì jì
Already Across

Associated meanings

After completion, after the climax, after crossing the river, already fording, already completed, mission accomplished.

Judgment

> Already Across.
> Success.
> The determination is favorable for small things.
> At first good fortune, at the end chaos.

In ancient China, crossing rivers, either at a ford or when the river was frozen, was not an easy task. It implicated dangers and hardships; hence having crossing the river means to have accomplished a difficult undertaking.

Success is achieved. Now you should handle the transition to a new stage. If you neglect to take precautions things may go downhill easily.

Do not take things or people for granted. Small things that are often overlooked can cause serious problems later on, take scrupulous attention to detail to stabilize the situation.

The Image

> Water over fire: The image of Already Across.
> Thus the noble meditates on misfortune in advance to prevent it.

Fire and water interacting usefully are used to cook or to produce vapor, but if the fire is too strong, the water will boil outside the cauldron, and if it is too weak the water will stop boiling. As a boiling cauldron must be tended with care to obtain proper results, all factors in the current situation should be kept working seamlessly and in their proper places to prevent trouble.

Do not wait until trouble gets out of hand; prevent small problems from getting worse by stopping them as soon they start.

First Nine

> Drag his wheels and wets his tail.
> No defect.

To drag the wheels means to contain the advance, to avoid rushing blindly forward. Take your time and advance with care.

The next hexagram –which is the specular image of this one–, depicts a fox crossing a stream in its Judgment. The tail mentioned in this line is a reference to the tail of that same fox, which is implied here in the text. The wet tail symbolizes minor inconveniences, but the main idea here is that by applying restraint you can avoid falling into danger and minimize your loses.

Second Six

> The woman loses the curtain of her carriage.
> Do not chase it; you will get it in seven days.

You will suffer a temporary setback that will stop you for a while. To lose the curtain means to get your plans exposed at the wrong moment, to be in danger, to lose strength.
Control your anxiety and be discreet, do not attract attention over yourself.
Instead of trying to press forward, bide you time and wait until the situation improves and you can advance without endangering yourself.
Besides this hexagram, the Chinese character for seven only appears in the **hexagram 24**, in the Judgment and in the second line of the **hexagram 51**. Here it indicates the return of the curtain of a carriage, in the hexagram 24 is related with a return and in the hexagram 63 with the return of money.

Third Nine

> The eminent ancestor attacks the Land of the Devil,
> after three years conquests it.
> Petty men must not be used.

The three years conquest campaign indicates a hard and dangerous enterprise. Three years symbolizes one long period of bitter conflicts. The triumph can be achieved, but not without paying a high cost.
The Land of the Devil indicates what is outside the laws, a factor of danger and corruption that must be subjugated by force.
To consolidate your gains you should use only reliable methods and people, otherwise you will endanger your achievements.

Fourth Six

> He has frayed silk and caulking rags.
> Be cautious until the end of the day.

The frayed silk and the rags are for stopping leaks in a boat that is crossing the river; they mean taking preventive measures when doing something dangerous.
You may find unexpected trouble along the way, be alert and take precautions beforehand.

Fifth Nine

> The eastern neighbor sacrifices an ox, but this falls short of the neighbor in
> the west with his small offering, whose sincerity receives blessings.

Sincerity will be rewarded, humble contributions presented with real feeling will fare better than pretentious exhibitions.

You don't need to do big things to cause a good impression, be sincere and modest.

Top Six

> He immerses his head.
> Danger.

You have gone too far and too deep and now you will pay the price for your carelessness.

If you wait too long to turn back or to take corrective action, you will fall into danger. You may have a serious setback at the end of the crossing.

wèi jì
Before Crossing

Associated meanings
Before completion, before the climax, before crossing the river.

Judgment
> Before Crossing.
> Success.
> If the little fox tail gets wet when finishes fording the river
> nothing is favorable.

In ancient China, crossing rivers, either at a ford or when the river was frozen, was not an easy task. It implicated dangers and hardships. Before crossing the river, careful preparations must be made and proper precautions should be taken.

In this case the crossing of the river symbolizes a difficult transition between chaos and order. The warning about getting the tail in the water points to the difficulties of the endeavor. You should have a surplus of strength and prudence to face such a task. If you can't carry the endeavor out to the end, everything done before will be in vain.

The Image
> Fire over water: The image of Before Crossing.
> The noble is careful discriminating things, so that each one is left in place.

Fire over water can't be used to cook food or anything useful because both forces are misplaced. To discriminate things placing them in its correct positions means to recognize the potential of each thing and to order and structure them in function of your objective.
In that way order can be obtained from chaos.

First Six
> He wets his tail.
> Humiliation.

The character that wets his tail is the little fox mentioned in the Judgment. The wet tail is the result of rash action, without planning and with ignorance.
Humiliation will serve you to know your own limits, and to turn back, avoiding further danger.

Second Nine

> Dragging his wheels.
> The determination is fortunate.

To drag the wheels means to contain the advance, to avoid rushing blindly forward and to advance with care.

Determination means to keep dedicated to your goals, to not skip any step and to keep full control.

Third Six

> Before Crossing.
> Attack brings misfortune.
> It is favorable to ford the great river.

Aggressive or unyielding advance will conduce to failure.

Be sure of getting support from good people and avoid being intransigent.

In this way you will be able to handle difficult endeavors, as symbolized by fording the river.

Fourth Nine

> The determination is fortunate.
> Repentance fades.
> Shock to conquer the Land of the Devil.
> Three years of rewards from the great kingdom.

The carefully planned advance will be successful, thus repentance will fade.

Shock means fast and strong advancement (lit.: "as a thunderbolt") that inspires fear in the foes that are going to be conquered. It also means that you will face a hard and difficult struggle to achieve your objectives.

The Land of the Devil indicates what is outside the laws, a factor of danger and corruption that must be subjugated by force.

The three years of rewards indicate that you will get plenty of gains for a long time. Notice the difference with the third line in the previous hexagram, where it takes three years to conquer the Land of the Devil but there is no mention about any rewards.

Fifth Six

> The determination is fortunate.
> There is no repentance.
> The glory of the noble is true.
> Good fortune.

The struggle was won by using harsh methods, but to administer your new domains it is better to use more diplomatic ways.

The light of the noble indicates sincerity, civility and enlightenment. The fifth line is the ruler of the hexagram, who empowers capable people on the basis of objective merit.

Abiding in the middle of the trigram of the light (the upper trigram), nothing is concealed from the perception of the ruler.

Top Nine

>They drink wine in confidence.
>No defect.
>But confidence will be lost if your head gets wet.

The new time is on the threshold, but the situation is still unfulfilled. To celebrate the end of the old stage and to get ready to receive a new time is not a bad idea. However, to wet the head indicates an unbalanced attitude and to lose control on the final step.

This line is a warning against getting dizzy when success is at hand.

The Principles of Astrological Geomancy

The Art of Divining by Punctuation

Franz Hartmann, M.D.

According to Cornelius Agrippa and others,
with an appendix containing 2,048 answers to questions.

This text and the accompanying illustrations are in the public domain in the
United States of America because they were published prior to 1923.

Foreword

The Principles of Astrological Geomancy was published in London, on 1889. It is still a very valuable text, but its language is a bit old-fashioned. We replaced many words by its modern equivalents when it could be done without changing the intended meaning, but as we want to be as faithful to the original text as possible, we did not rewrite the text. Some words, mainly used in the Appendix, cannot be replaced without changing the book substantially.

It is up to the reader to find the modern equivalence of some old-fashioned words that we could not change. Fads and mores change, but human society remains the same. We still care about the same things that our ancestors, although we may use different words.

Preface

The following book is not intended to be a "fortune teller", but an aid for the student of the higher science, who desires to develop his intuition. A book teaching the art of mixing colors would not make an artist out of a person who has no talent for painting; but to one who is an artist by nature such a book may be very useful. Likewise a work on Geomancy, teaching the rules by which certain truths which are spiritually perceived by the soul, may be brought within the understanding of the external mind, will be of little service to those whose souls have no power of perceiving the truth.

Nevertheless, there is at least a germ of truth in every human being, and every power is developed by exercise. The practice of Geomancy requires above all concentration of thought, and the use of that faculty of the mind by which several ideas may be grasped at once, and be brought to a focus within the field of consciousness, and those who follow the rules prescribed in these pages, may thereby expand their mental faculties and strengthen their intuition,so as to be able to correctly prophecy future ev ents and divine unknown things.

The superficial reasoner, whose mind is captivated by the external and illusive appearance of the world of phenomena, will naturally treat with contempt all knowledge claiming to have been derived from a source superior to reasoning from the base of external observation; but a deeper penetration into the realm of causes will disclose to the lover of truth, the Unity of the divine Law that governs all things, and according to which all external things, phenomena and events are nothing else but the ultimate outcome of pre-existing causes in the realm of ideas. The divine order of things in nature has left nothing to blind chance; the spirit may know the causes and the mind calculate the effects. God, the divine self-consciousness in the universe, knows All, and those who approach in spirit to the divine source of All will obtain more spiritual knowledge than those whose minds, wandering away from the center of Divine Wisdom, become forgetful of their own spiritual nature,and lost in the labyrinth of little external details. Those who desire to practice the art of Geomancy, should remember that spiritual truth is not found by external calculation and argumentation, but only by the knowledge of self.

> *"Why idly seek in outward things?*
> *The answer inner silence brings,*
> *So to the calmly gathered thought,*
> *The uttermost of truth is taught."*

Introduction

The term "divining," or "divination," comes from *"divine"*, and the art of divination is based upon the recognition of a universal divine principle acting within the soul. Man is said to be the crown of creation; in him are combined the quintessences of all the four kingdoms. He is at once a mineral, a plant, an animal, and a god, and each of these constituent parts has its own peculiar states of consciousness, its own sensations, desires, feelings, and perceptions. The divine Light which shines within the darkness of his material constitution is the eternal Spirit of God, in which there exists neither past nor the future time, but in whose consciousness all things are forever present. Its presence is felt within the soul as the divine power of Intuition, and if the Mind of man were to rise entirely above the realm of selfishness, to become illuminated by the Light of the Spirit, there would be no need for Geomancy or for any other artificial aids to bring the knowledge of the Spirit to the understanding of the material Intellect. We could then not only intuitively feel the truth, but see it and know it without any argumentation or mathematical reasoning.

There are, however, only a few saints or adepts in the world who are in possession of such a state of perfection, and the majority of men and women upon this globe have to go the roundabout way of speculation and calculation to obtain information in regard to things unknown. The psychological process by which the knowledge of the spiritual soul comes to the understanding of the human intellect appears to be very complicated; it seems that the divine ray of Light has to pass through many *strata* of matter, and is broken many times, before it is ultimately reflected within the field of external consciousness, and the more we are able to spiritually rise above these clouds of matter that darken the mental sky, the more will we become able to see the sunlight of truth in its purity.

By practicing the art of Geomancy in that state of mind and feeling which brings Man nearer to the perception of the Truth, the Intuition may teach the reasoning Intellect. The first four symbols of which the geomantic figure is constructed, are the products of Intuition, and from them the final result is obtained by intellectual labor. The condition for obtaining success is the full and entire concentration of thought and will upon the question which is to be answered.

In the art of Geomancy it is not the mind, but the soul which answers the question and the answer is received by means of the power of the living divine Spirit of God, whose temple is man. It is, therefore, clear that this magical art ought not to be practiced in any other frame of mind than that of worship, adoration, and faith in the eternal Law of order and harmony. If undertaken merely for the purposes of gratifying idle curiosity, or for selfish purposes, or from motives of greed or revenge, its results will be unreliable; because in such cases the intuitional ray becomes distorted by the perverted images existing within the mind. Like-wise the answers will only be reliable, if the whole strength of will and thought is concentrated upon the question asked; a vacillating mind has but little power, for the truth suffers no other loves, only those who rise up to it and embrace it with all their soul, with all their mind, and with their whole being, will receive true knowledge.

Finally, it may be well to state that the foreseeing of future events will not enable us to change their course; for if these events did not already exist in the future, they could not be foreseen, while if they were to be altered, the alteration would also be seen. Nevertheless, the art of Geomancy may be very useful to act as our guide in meeting future events, in enabling us to take courage in what we know to become a success, and to give up insisting in fruitless attempts to attain that which would end in a failure if carried out. It should, however, always be kept in mind that the reliability of all such arts depends on our own reliability of perception, and the decisions of Geomancy can be infallible only when all the conditions required to make them infallible have been complied with. Geomancy is not a substitute but an aid for divine Reason.

PLANETARY SIGNS

☉	The Sun	♀	Venus	♄	Saturn
☽	The Moon	♂	Mars	♅	Uranus
☿	Mercury	♃	Jupiter	♆	Neptune

SIGNS OF THE ZODIAC

Northern		Southern	
♈	Aries	♎	Libra
♉	Taurus	♏	Scorpio
♊	Gemini	♐	Sagittarius
♋	Cancer	♑	Capricornus
♌	Leo	♒	Aquarius
♍	Virgo	♓	Pisces

Astrology

The science of Astrology is based upon a correct under-standing of the true nature of Man and his position in the Universe. Natural man is not, as many vainly imagine, a self-existent being, creating his own ideas, thoughts and feelings; but as his physical body is the product of the confluence and assimilation of physical atoms, likewise the constitution of his mind is the product of the action of the intellectual and emotional elements entering his psychic organism. His visible and tangible form receives from the great storehouse of physical nature the four originally invisible elements, called: Earth, Water, Fire and Air (solid, fluid and gaseous essences, heat, electricity, life, etc.), and by means of the physiological processes going on in his visible form he transforms them into such substances and activities as are required by the nature of his corporeal body. These processes are taking place without the intellectual supervision of man; they are going on instinctively, involuntarily and even without his being conscious of it.

All this nobody will deny; because we see the food which we eat and the water we drink; we know of the existence of the air which we inhale, and we feel the heat that warms our bodies. These things are not our own creations, nature prepares them for us, lends them to us, and after we have made use of what we have borrowed, we restore them back to nature.

With the invisible principles that enter the invisible soul of Man, the same process takes place. We do not create our own thoughts, but the ideas which in pure, permanent and indivisible incorporeal ideal forms exist in the *Astral Light,* reflect their images in the individual minds of men and women, in the same way as a landscape may be reflected in a looking-glass, or the whole of the starry sky be mirrored forth in a drop of pure water. These images may enter the consciousness of man without any voluntary effort on his part, in the same sense as the air enters his lungs without man's conscious effort to breathe. They may even enter against his will and desire; for there are unwelcome thoughts that come when they are not wanted, and there are welcome ones difficult to retain. Animals only think the thoughts which enter into their minds without any efforts on their part; but man has the power to voluntarily rise in thought to the realm of ideas and grasp the images which he desires, and therefore it is said that man does not need to be governed by the stars, but that he can become superior to them.

The ideas which enter the field of consciousness act upon his Imagination, and his Imagination re-acts upon his Will; thereby producing certain states of feelings or emotions according to the nature of the idea, from the most gross and vulgar passion up to the highest state of exalted thought. As the food which he eats determines the state of purity or impurity of his physical organism, so likewise the thoughts which he harbors, and the feelings in which he indulges, determine the purity or impurity of his soul.

Man does not create his thoughts; but he elaborates them from the ideas which he absorbs, in the same sense as his physical body elaborates the food which he eats, and transforms vegetables and grains into blood and flesh and bones. Likewise the mind of man mixes and combines ideas, and infuses then with life by the power of his Will; and as an impure body may poison the surrounding atmosphere by the unhealthy effluvia coming from his impurities, so also the emanations of an impure mind will poison the mental atmosphere with the products of an impure Imagination rendered alive by an evil Will; for the products of thought are real and substantial things, even if they are invisible for gross material eyes, and the Will is a real power which may act as far as thoughts travel.

As the moon without the light of the sun is dark, so likewise the images produces by thought have no power unless they are strengthened by the will; while the Will is useless unless it is guided and brought into a form by thought. If thought and will are divided, they are both ineffective; but is thought and will are in unison, they become effective; they then constitute a Unity, and this unity is called *"Spirit"*.

According to the statements of the wise, all things in the universe are the products of Will and Imagination (Ideation) acting in unison, and therefore, all things are produced by Spirit. Spirit is the Reality; that which we call the material form is merely the shadow of the light of the divine Ideal. That which we call "Matter" is the same thing as "Spirit", only it is in a state of inertness or condensation, while the vibrations of Spirit are far higher than those of Matter, so as to transcend our physical power to perceive them, in the same sense as there are vibrations of sound too high to be heard by the external ear, and vibrations of color too high to be seen by the external eye. We are spirits ourselves, even if we are clothed in a gross material form; we live in a spiritual world; we are surrounded and permeated by Spirit. We are continually influenced by spiritual powers that come to us with or without our desire, and we have no other means to protect ourselves except Reason and Will. Man is a little world in which all the celestial and terrestrial powers and principles existing in the great universe may be reflected, and upon the perception of this truth rests the science of Astrology.

Everywhere in the universe rules the same fundamental law; everything is governed by order and harmony. The planets revolve in their orbits with mathematical precision, and each human being must follow the orbit in which it has to revolve. A man may oscilate to the right or the left as it traverses its orbit, but he cannot leave the line of his destiny, which is the result of causes produced in previous states of existence. There are ebbs and tides of the sea, and there are ebbs and tides in the ocean of thought. There are conjunctions and oppositions of spiritual influences in the world of ideas, as there are among the corporeal planets. There are times in which mankind as a whole rises up to a higher state of spiritual enlightenment, coming nearer to God ; and there are other times in which they sink deeper into ignorance and superstition

If the mathematical rules that govern in the realm of ideas were as well known as those that rule the revolutions of the visible planets, there would be as little difficulty in predicting future thoughts and the external events resulting therefrom, as there is in predicting an eclipse of the moon; but as long as the mind is too much captivated by the external sensual impressions to be attracted by the things that belong to the Spirit of Truth, its deductions and conclusions will be unreliable. As long as its imagination is captivated and its desire inflamed by the fire of the Astral plane, the thoughts and aspirations will not penetrate into the pure region of Truth.

Fortunately, however, there is a knowledge higher than that of the speculating brain; it is the knowledge of the soul, and if there were nothing to prevent the free communication of the Intellect with the Soul, man might intuitively know many things which now seem beyond the reach of his knowledge.

But it is written, that "those who desire to live from the altar must serve the altar," that means to say, that those who wish to know and be rendered alive by the truth must serve the truth by loving it with their whole heart, and manifest that love in thoughts, words, and actions. Those who desire spiritual knowledge, and to obtain the power to predict future events, must above all seek for the truth within their own souls. They should put away their passions and evil desires, their scientific, social, and religious prejudices, and the errors which have been engrafted into their minds by a false education, received in an age of so-called rationalism, during which there was but little comprehension of spiritual things; when the Sun of Divine Wisdom was obscured by the delusive shadow of the speculative semi-animal intellect, and when the voice of the Intuition was drowned in the noise made by the clamors of conceited ignorance assuming the place of science.

Fortunately the days of *Kakosophia* are approaching their end, and humanity as a whole is again coming nearer to the zenith of ☉. May all the lovers of truth make use of this opportunity to enjoy all the light which they are capable to receive, before the planet, following the law of order, will again descend into the shadow of ♄.

The principle upon which astrology is based, cannot be fully understood, unless the nature of the "planets" with which it deals is realized; but this realization wall not be the product of book reading, nor can a person give to himself knowledge or power which he does not possess; it will remain unattainable to the doubter, and can only be acquired by faith; that is to say, by the interior awakening of the *Spirit of Truth*.

The Seven Planets

The ancients recognized the presence of seven different states of the One Universal Spirit which constitutes the Soul of all things as well as all physical bodies, and they gave to these seven principles the following names and symbols, which are also those of the "seven planets" and of the seven days of the week:

♄	Saturn	Saturday
☉	Sun	Sunday
☽	Moon	Monday
♂	Mars	Tuesday
☿	Mercury	Wednesday
♃	Jupiter	Thursday
♀	Venus	Friday

It is almost unnecessary to say that these "seven planets" have little or nothing to do with the seven cosmic bodies in our solar system bearing the same names; for although the latter may to a certain extent be regarded as their external and visible representatives, the principles themselves are invisible, and rule not only within our solar system, and throughout the extent of the Macrocosms of the Universe; but also within the internal constitution of the Microcosm of Man. Their significations differ according to the aspects which we take of them. Generally speaking, they may be stated as follows:

The Sun is the emblem of Wisdom. In him are the powers of all the planets united; in him are love, will, and intelligence combined into one; in the same sense as the four sides of a pyramid all culminate in one point. The Sun is the center and source of all light and heat, and of all power; not only of the visible terrestrial light, but of the light of intelligence; not only of terrestrial heat, but of the heat of love. He attracts by his power all the planets in space and keeps them within their orbits. Those in whom the sun principle is strong are capable of becoming wise, strong, and powerful. It is therefore said that the Sun is a planet governing the souls of kings and noblemen, and conferring honors, powers, and titles. Its influence is decisive in all important questions in human life. In the mineral kingdom it is represented by gold; in the animal kingdom by the Lion, in the spiritual kingdom as *Sol-om-on*, the divine Sun of Wisdom.

The Moon is the symbol of imagination, illusion, and dreams. She has no light of her own, but borrows her light from the Sun. Without the light of the sun the moon would be cold and dark; without the power of the Will the products of the Imagination are without life. Thoughts become powerful only when the are infused by the will; they become luminous only when they are illuminated love; they can be wise only if permeated by wisdom. Under the influence of the moon are said to be especially dreamers and mediums, persons who live a great deal in the realm of imagination and fancy, ladies of rank, pleasure seekers and travelers; it is said to govern things in which there is little firmness and stability, especially water and ships. In the mineral kingdom the Moon is represented by silver, in the spiritual kingdom by *Luna* the queen of the night.

Mars represents strength. If unguided by wisdom it is a dangerous planet, inclined to deeds of violence, acting rashly and without consideration. It is a principle which causes anger and wrath. It has been regarded as the god of warriors, soldiers, lawyers, causing also the effects of violent medicines. Its action may become moderated by its union with ♀. Among the metals Mars is represented by iron, in the kingdom of spiritual powers by the god of war. It is of a fiery nature, and as fire does not combine with water, likewise an irate temper and the assertion of self-will is incompatible with that calm and peaceful thought necessary for the perception of the truth.

Mercury represents the Intellect, and it may be a good or evil planet according to the conditions under which it acts. If ☿ is under the influence of ♄, that is to say, if the intellect is subservient to selfish and material things, it becomes a source of evil; if combined with ♃ it will produce pride; if united with love ♀ it will become wise, and in this manner "crude mercury" may be transformed into the gold of wisdom.

Mercury without love is said to rule especially those who live by their wits; scientific speculators, sophists, merchants, thieves, intellectual but not necessarily moral persons, men of letters, students, etc. In the mineral kingdom i t is represented by quicksilver, in the spiritual realm by the god of trade.

♃

Jupiter represents power. Its qualities differ according tots aspects. Its symbol is an eagle; because it enables man to rise up by its power into the highest regions of thought, even to the throne of the Eternal. It is, or ought to be, therefore, the ruling planet for ecclesiastics and clergymen, and those who have to deal with the administration of justice. Its influence gives eloquence. It is friendly with all the rest of the planets except ♂; the latter being loved by none except ♀. In the mineral kingdom it is represented by tin; in the spiritual realm by Jupiter, the king of the gods, who obtain their power through him.

♀

Venus represents love. In its lowest state it is blind attraction, producing gravitation among the corporeal planets and instincts among animals. The more it becomes amalgamated with intelligence, the more does it become capable to manifest its divine qualities. Pure love is a divine and self-existent power which only gives and does not seek to receive. It has no desires; but it creates desires in the objects in which its power awakens. In its higher aspects it rules artists and true physicians, in its lower state it is active in all affairs of love and marriage and in pleasures of various kinds. Among the metals it is represented by silver, in the spiritual realm by the goddess of Love. As Power is the father of all the gods, like wise Venus is their mother. No being can exist without love. When their ♀ is departed they will all be swallowed up by ♄.

♄

Saturn represents the element of Matter. Not the visible tangible earth, but the primordial Substance out of which all things are made. It is also the principle of Life. It produces and destroys all forms, and is therefore represented as the god who eats his own children. Unless associated with ☉, Saturn is a cold, cruel and dark planet. It therefore rules old persons, misers, and usurers, gross material and vulgar people, and governs agricultural and mining pursuits. In the mineral kingdom ♄ is represented by lead; in the spiritual realm as the god of Time.

Saturn represents darkness and fear, melancholy, gloom,and death; but it is also the god of Life, for all so-called death is merely a change of state, and in the end of an old form, is the beginning of a new state of being.

Conjunctions

From the approximations and conjunctions of planets, or, in other words, from the combination of different emotions and mental states, result a great many varieties of powers,which again differ from each other in regard to their quality of gradation.

In every kingdom of nature we find sympathies and antipathies. Among the planetary influences they are as follows:

☉	sympathetic to	♃, ☿	antipathetic to	♂, ☿, ☽
☽	"	♃, ☿, ♄	"	♂, ☿
♂	"	♀	"	☉, ☽, ☿, ♃, ♄
☿	"	♃, ♂, ♄	"	☉, ☽, ♂
♃	"	☉, ☽, ☿, ♀, ♄	"	♂
♀	"	☉, ☽, ☿, ♀, ♃	"	♄
♄	"	☉, ☽, ☿, ♃	"	♂, ♀

The Colours of the Planets:

☉	yellow	☽	white	♂	red	☿	brown
♃	blue	♀	green	♄	grey		

One color may be changed into another by mixing it with one of a different kind; for instance, blue mixed with yellow will produce green, and likewise a planetary influence may be changed in its nature by coming in conjunction with one of another kind. Love and Imagination mixed together may in their exultation result in insanity, ♂ and ☽ produce hallucinations, ♃ and ☽ will make a man very vain, ♂ and ☿ may make a robber out of a thief, ♃ and ♀ maybe the source of the inspiration of an orator, and if ☿ is added, carry him up into the highest regions of thought. In this manner an almost endless number of combinations maybe formed in the alchemical laboratory of the soul. There is no action without reaction. Each planet has therefore a two-fold aspect, and may manifest a two-fold activity. There is no relative good without relative evil, and no evil without good. The same ☉ that is the source of all life may burn up living forms, ♀ coming in opposition to ☿ may turn into hate; the same ♃ that lifts the aspiring mind up to heaven may, by becoming perverted, turn into an angel of evil and drag him down into the abyss of self-conceit.

Thus the lover of astrology will find abundant material in his own mind to study the various states resulting from the approximation, conjunction, or opposition of planets, without the aid of books, and such a study will be found to be even more interesting and useful in the end than that of the stars in the sky, for however sublime the study of the latter may be, all the learning of external things in the world is far inferior to the knowledge of self.

The Twelve signs of the Zodiac

The twelve signs of the zodiac, or the circle through which the Earth travels in its annual revolution around the sun, are described in every almanac; but in their deeper signification they represent principles which form the basis of the evolution and involution of the Universe. Their names and signs are as follows:

♈	Aries	
♉	Taurus	
♊	Gemini	Ascending signs
♋	Cancer	
♌	Leo	
♍	Virgo	
♎	Libra	The point of equilibrium
♏	Scorpio	
♐	Sagittarius	
♑	Capricornus	Descending signs
♒	Aquarius	
♓	Pisces	

The twelve signs of the zodiac represent the powers of Man; but as these powers are of a spiritual nature, their qualities can he known only to those who in the course of evolution and unfoldment have become conscious of their existence. The more we enter the realm of spiritual knowledge, the more do we begin to realize that all terrestrial knowledge is but child's play in comparison with the true knowledge of the spirit; but the door to the temple in which the truth can be seen without a veil is guarded by the dragon of selfishness, and only those who are able to conquer the "beast" can enter the sanctuary.

No greater truth has ever been pronounced than that we must die before we can begin to live. The mysteries of the inner temple can never be divulged to the uninitiated, because they would not be understood even if an explanation were attempted. Sensual things may he perceived by the senses; intellectual verities may be intellectually understood; but only the Spirit of God in Man searches the depths of Divinity. Sciences may be taught, arts may be acquired by practice ; but divine Wisdom can only be attained by the grace of the divine spirit, and all that man can possibly do is to render himself capable for its reception,by seeking to eliminate from his constitution those elements which hinder the entrance of Light. Therefore the religious books advise us that man should seek above all the Kingdom of God (the divine consciousness), promising that then all other kinds of knowledge will be given to him ; but of the scoffer and skeptic who desires to prey with curious eyes behind the veil it is said that his safety is in his ignorance, for the knowledge which he might attain would prove to be the cause of his perdition.

To give a correct and complete description of the twelve signs of the zodiac would require the writing of a book greater than all the books in the world, nor could any amount of words be adequate to describe the sublimity and grandeur of thought and conception necessary to rise up to a comprehension of one of the greatest of all divine mysteries, the construction of the spiritual and material universe, or in other words, of Nature in her aspect as the living temple of God.

If we therefore attempt to describe our ideas in regard to the character of these divine principles, we are well aware of the difficulty of our task, and it must be left to the reader to ask for more light, by seeking within himself for the hidden truth.

♈

Aries, or Ram, represents the universal principle of Life or ☉, which is the source of all things. It may also be represented as ♄, or the universal element of living Matter or Substance, in which all things are, and by whose power they all exist. It is "Matter" and "Force" in one; for those terms do not represent two things essentially different from each other; they are merely two words representing two states of the eternal One, for which there is no name. "Matter" means relative inactivity; "Force" means a higher state of activity of the same principle. The spirit of man descends into "Matter", that is to say,it becomes relatively inactive and unconscious, and reascends again to its highest state as a self-conscious spiritual power. The process taking place in each individual monad corresponds to the grand process taking place in the evolution and involution of the universe as a whole.

♉

Taurus, or the Steer, represents Power. It symbolizes the divine power of that universal principle, which is at once the creator, preserver, and destroyer of forms. By the inherent strength of the divine principle in Man, humanity is enabled to aspire for something higher than merely material existence, and to rise up to its former divine as a spiritual self-conscious being. In one of its aspects, ♉ may, therefore, be compared to ☽; because the light of the Spirit begins to be reflected by the material mind. In another aspect it resembles ♀, for all power originally arises from Love, and in still another it may be compared to ♃, for in this sign Man begins to realize the glory of God.In fact, each of the zodiacal signs may be compared to all the planets; for Spirit is a Unity, and in each sign are,therefore, contained the powers of the other six. The distinction is not made on account of any difference in their essential nature; but in regard to the form of their manifestation.

♊

Gemini, or the Twins, represent the spiritual Man of whom the mortal body is merely an imperfect image or a reflection. It is the personal God of each man, the divine *Adonai* who is neither male nor female but in whom both sexes are united by the divine marriage of Intelligence and Love. It may be said to correspond to ☿ united with ♀, or to a union of Will and Thought. Its germs are within every man or woman, for in each human being are male and female elements; a being wholly male would have no Will, a being wholly female would have no Imagination. In its aspect as a universal power n represents the "Great Spirit", the universal bisexual *Man.*

♋

Cancer, the Crab, represents retrogression; that is to say,the final descent of the Spirit from its divine into a material state by the act of creation. It also represents the power of the *Word*", through whose action creation takes place. It is the α and Ω, the beginning and the end ; if the word had never been spoken, there would never have been any objective creation and God (resp. *Man*) would not have left his divine state of rest. Perhaps it may be compared to ♂, as it also represents Power acting regardless of personal danger, and without any consideration of the consequences that must result to itself from its entering the realm of darkness, the material plane; impelled as it is by the power of ♀; for thus has ♀ loved the world, that it sent its own essence and the power to enter the hearts of mankind, and to redeem them from the realm of illusions.

♌

Leo, Lion, represents that divine power of Christ, the Man anointed with spiritual knowledge, which enables him to rise again up to a conception of his own divine state. It may be compared to ♃, or the *Eagle*, who wings itself up to the throne of the Most High. It represents the true savior of mankind; for no one can enter the kingdom of heaven unless he has the power to do so, and no one can come to the unmanifested God except through the power of the Christ in whom God has become manifest. Let those who desire to enter the kingdom by force, meditate about the signification of ♌, and enter into this sign; for the kingdom of heaven can be gained only by violence.

♍

Virgo, the Virgin, represents the Spiritual Soul in Man and in the Universe, the celestial virgin, the eternal mother of man-made God. It may be compared to ☽, in which the power of ☉ is reflected, and becomes substantial light; it is divine Intuition, which saves from perdition the semi-animal Intellect; it is for ever immaculate, because it has nothing to do with external reasoning and argumentation; it knows the Truth, because it is one with it. It represents Isis, the eternal goddess of Nature, from whose womb will arise *Horus*, the time-born god. It is the eternal patroness of those who seek for salvation, as its exalting influence raises man up into a higher region of thought. It is one of the greatest mysteries of religion, and can form no object for external scientific research.

♎

Libra, the Balance, represents the point of equilibrium, the unimaginable state of Nirvana, which cannot be described, and for which we have no words in the language of mortals to explain its condition. If a planetary sign is to be compared with it, it must be ♀, for Love is the root out of which all powers spring.

When the Day of Creation (We purposely use the term "creator" for constructor of forms, because forms are nothing, they are merely appearances and in creating a form an illusion is *created*) is over, the celestial powers again retire to the bosom of their eternal Father, to rest in divine blissfulness until the equilibrium becomes again disturbed by the awakening of an internal desire for creation and a new evolution begins. The descent of Spirit into matter then recommences, producing once more the "fall of man", and this work of involution is represented in the following descending signs of the Zodiac.

♏

Scorpio, or Scorpion, represents that *Desire* for knowledge which again induces the celestial spirit to descend and to overshadow material forms. It is the *Snake* which eternally tempts *Eve* to break the fruit from the forbidden tree and to offer it to the Intellect for its comprehension. By its influence the attention of the Spirit of Man is again attracted to the realm of phenomena, and he again enters the wheel of evolution, but on a higher scale than before. In its universal aspect it represents that state of the Universal Mind in which the idea of a new creation begins to exist. If we had to compare it with any planetary sign we would choose for it , or Love acted upon by the Will.

♐

Sagittarius, the Archer, represents the divine Will to create a new world, for the thought alone would not be sufficient to produce a world existing in the imagination, unless the divine will were present to project it into objectivity. In a lower aspect it may represent that power by which the individual spirit, unable to create a world of its own, is impelled to form again a connection with Matter. In its aspect as a universal principle it may be compared to .

♑

Capricornus, or the Goat, represents the exercise of the constructive power of the universe: the universal Law of Evolution, which at the time of the beginning of a new creation again enters into activity. It also is the symbol of perversion, and in its lower aspect it may signify the power by which the disembodied spirit again builds up a mortal house of clay, and enters again into the world of formation.

Aquarius, the Waterman. The product of the imagination acting within the Will is Thought. Water is the symbol for Thought, and a "Waterman" therefore symbolizes a man formed of thought. All things are made of thought; the visible as well as the invisible world is the product of Thought and made up of the substance of Mind; material forms are merely the external expressions of internal principles which must necessarily be substantial, for forces are states of matter, and a state of a thing which does not exist is an impossibility. The whole universe is substantial thought, produced by the will and the imagination. ♒ may therefore be regarded as the creative power of divine Will and Thought, that is to say, as the *Word*, in its aspect as a universal divine Power. In its more limited aspect, it represents the power by which the Spirit again assumes a material form.

Pisces, Fishes. The fish lives in water; man is living in the ocean of thought, rendered more or less material by the influence of ♄. In one of its aspects, ♓ represents man as a being immersed in an ocean of spiritual ideas, and therefore those who are supposed to live in that higher region of spiritual and exalted thought have been called episcopes or bishops. In another aspect this sign may represent the world of ideas existing in the Astral Light. Gradually the wheel of evolution approaches again the sign of ♈, representing the realm of Matter; the descent of the spirit is then accomplished, and the ascension begins, unless man should allow himself to descend still deeper into the realm of darkness where those who willfully reject the light of the Spirit are doomed to perish. When the descending Spirit in whose idea the world of formation exists, expresses his thought in the act of creating, he finds himself like a fish in the water, in the world of forms which he has created himself, and then the reign of ♄ begins again, and with it the work of redemption by the ascending signs.

The Symbols of Geomancy

There are sixteen geomantic symbols, corresponding to certain planetary signs, as follows:

Symbol 1	Planet	Symbol 2
Fortuna Major	☉	Fortuna Minor
Via	☽	Populus
Acquisitio	♃	Laetitia
Puella	♀	Amissio
Conjunctio	☿	Albus
Puer	♂	Rubeus
Carcer	♄	Tristitia
Caput Draconis	☊ ☋	Cauda Draconis

Significations

◆ ◆ ◆◆ ◆◆	**Via,** Street or Way, is neither good nor bad; its quality, like those of all the rest, is determined by its position in the house of the astrological figure. Its nature corresponds to ☽, its element is watery, its zodiacal sign ♌, and its number 7.
◆◆ ◆◆ ◆◆ ◆◆	**Populus,** People, is likewise indifferent. Its nature correspond to ☌, its element is watery, its zodiacal sign ♑, its element is earthy, its zodiacal sign ♓, its number 12.
◆◆ ◆ ◆ ◆◆	**Conjunctio,** union or coming together, is rather good than bad. Its nature corresponds to ☿, its element is earthy, its zodiacal sign ♍, and its number 11.
◆ ◆◆ ◆◆ ◆	**Carcer,** prison, or to be bond, is good or bad, according to the nature of the question. Its nature corresponds to ♄, its element is earthy, its zodiacal sign ♓, and its number 10.
◆ ◆◆ ◆ ◆	**Fortuna Major,** Great Fortune, success, interior aid and protection, is a very good sign. Its nature corresponds to ☉, its element is earthy, its zodiacal sign ♒, its number 12.
◆ ◆ ◆◆ ◆	**Fortuna Minor,** Little Fortune, external aid and protection, is not a very good figure. Its nature corresponds to ☉, its element is fiery, its zodiacal sign ♉, and its number 10.
◆◆ ◆◆ ◆ ◆	**Acquisitio,** success, obtaining, absorbing, receiving, is a good figure. Its nature corresponds to ♃, its element is airy, its zodiacal sign ♈, and its number 7.
◆ ◆◆ ◆ ◆◆	**Amissio,** Loss, that which is taken away. It is a bad figure. Its nature corresponds to ♀, its element is fiery, its zodiacal sign ♎, and its number 8.
◆ ◆ ◆◆ ◆◆	**Laetitia,** Joy, health, laughing, is good. Its nature corresponds to ♃, its element is airy, its zodiacal sign ♉, and its number 15.
◆◆ ◆◆ ◆◆ ◆	**Tristitia,** Sorrow, grief, perversion, condemnation, is bad. Its nature corresponds to ♄, its element is earthy, its zodiacal sign ♒, and its number 14.
◆ ◆◆ ◆ ◆	**Puella,** girl, pretty face, is pleasant but not very fortunate. Its nature corresponds to ♀, its element is watery, its zodiacal sign ♎, and its number 2.
◆ ◆ ◆◆ ◆	**Puer,** Boy, rash and inconsiderate, is rather good than bad. Its nature corresponds to ♂, its element is fiery, its zodiacal sign ♈, and its number 3.

· · · · · ·	**Albus**, White Head, wisdom, sagacity, clear thought, is a good figure. Its nature corresponds to ☿, its element is watery, its zodiacal sign ♋, and is number 12.
· · · · · ·	**Rubeus**, Redhead, passion, vice, fiery temper, is a bad figure. Its nature corresponds to ♂, its element is fiery, its zodiacal sign ♊, and its number 13.
· · · ·	Caput Draconis, Dragon's head, entrance, threshold, upper kingdom, is good. Its symbol is ☊, its zodiacal sign ♍, its element earthy, and its number 4.
· · · · ·	**Cauda Draconis**, Dragon's tail, exit, lower kingdom, is bad. Its symbol is ☋, its zodiacal sign ♐, its element fiery, and its number 5.

The significations of these symbols differ to a certain extent according to the nature of their origin.

A good figure made of two good ones is good.

A bad figure made of two bad ones is bad.

A good figure made of one good and one bad figure mean success, but delay and vexation.

If the two witnesses are good and the judge bad, the result will be obtained; but it will be unfortunate in the end.

If the first witness is good and the second bad, the success will be very doubtful.

If the first witness is bad and the second one good, the unfortunate beginning will take a good turn.

Instructions for the Practice of Geomancy

Preparation

The art of Geomancy ought not to he practiced unless the mind is tranquil and calm. If the field of mental vision is clouded by fear or doubt, by grief or selfish desires, if the temple of the spirit is occupied by money changers or resounding from the quarrels of the pharisees and scribes, it will be difficult to hear the voice of the truth. Cornelius Agrippa says that Geomancy should not be practiced "on a cloudy or rainy day, or when the weather is stormy, nor while the mind is disturbed by anger or oppressed with cares". Neither should it be practiced for the purpose of gratifying idle curiosity, for mere amusement, or for giving tests to the skeptics. Finally, the same question ought not to be asked repeatedly in the same form.

It is, furthermore, desirable that for each question an appropriate day and hour should be selected; for instance, all questions in regard to agriculture or mines should be asked on the day, and in the hour of Saturn, all questions in regard to love and marriage on the day, and in the hour of Venus, etc.

The reason for this is that the soul of man stands in intimate relationship to the soul of the world, and that the influences of the higher world act correspondingly upon the lower. If man were in a perfectly natural state, and his soul in exact harmony with nature, he would be more sensitive to planetary influences, and the state of his thoughts and feelings would correspond to the states of the Universal Mind.

The clays of thee week are named by their ruling planets, and each planet rules the first hour of his day. To find the planetary hour, it is, therefore, merely necessary to divide the time from sunrise to sunset into twelve equal parts, adding, however, one hour for the twilight. The first planetary hour is then dedicated to the planet of the day, and then follow the other planets in their regular order: ♄, ☉, ☽, ♂, ☿, ♃, ♀, ♄.

Thus, if we imagine some Wednesday in summer, when the sun rises at five and sets at seven, we will have a day of fourteen hours, to which one hour is added. These fifteen hours are divided into twelve equal parts. The hour of ☿ then begins at 4.30 a.m. and ends at 5.45. Then follows ♃ ending at 6.60; next ♀, etc.

However useful it may be to observe the planetary hours, it is undoubtedly of still greater importance to pay attention to the constellation within, and to take care that no evil spirit enters the sphere of mind of the operator to interfere with his work.

The Practice of Geomancy

If it is desired to obtain by the art of Geomancy an answer to a certain question, it is, above all, necessary to be in tranquil state of mind, and to fix one's thought firmly, and without wavering, upon that question. While the mind is thus fixed, the right hand is used to make an indefinite number of points without counting them from right to left in the following manner:

. . . .

They may be made with a pencil upon a piece of paper, or following the old custom, with a stick on the ground, and it is from this old method that the term "Geomancy" (Divining by means of the earth) is derived; for it is believed by some that the Elemental spirits of Earth are guiding the hand of the operator. Four such lines are constructed, and each line will have either an even or an uneven number of dots.

If the number is even, two marks are made at the end of the line; if it is uneven, only one. The four lines produce one geomantic figure, as may be seen in the following example (in the example, the dots are separated by slashes to make it easier to see if its number is even or uneven):

../../../..	♦ ♦
./../../../../..	♦
../../../..	♦ ♦
./../../..	♦
This process is repeated three times.	
./../../../../..	♦
../../../..	♦ ♦
../../../../..	♦ ♦
../../../..	♦ ♦
../../../..	♦ ♦
../../../../..	♦ ♦
../../../..	♦ ♦
../../../../..	♦ ♦
../../../..	♦ ♦
./../../../../../..	♦
../../../..	♦ ♦
../../../../..	♦ ♦

The Principles of Astrological Geomancy

In this way four figures have been obtained; they are called the **Mothers**.

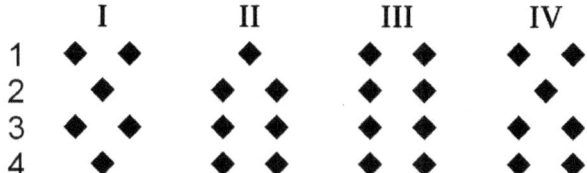

Each of these figures consists of four parts: 1, 2, 3, and 4. 1 is called the heads; 2, the necks; 3, the bodies; and 4, the feet. By taking the heads of the four mothers, and putting them below each other, the first daughter is produced; the necks produce the second, the bodies the thirds, and the feet the fourth daughter, as follows:

Daughters

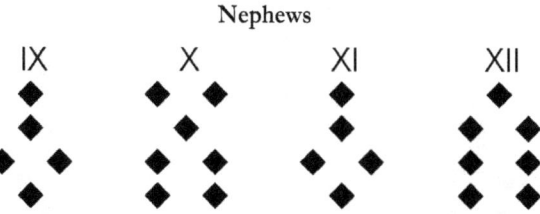

The Nephews are produced in a different manner. To produce the first nephew the heads of I and II are counted together and marked down as even or uneven, then the necks, next the bodies and the feet.

The second nephew is produced in the same manner from III and IV, the third from V and VI, the fourth from VII and VIII.

Nephews

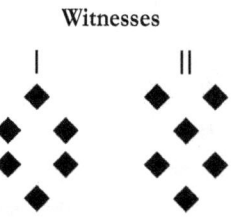

From the four Nephews are constructed the two witnesses in the same manner, namely the first witness from IX and X, and the second from XI and XII.

Witnesses

and from the two witnesses,

The Judge

To recapitulate we will seek the answer to the following questions:

Shall I succeed in my undertaking?

../../../..	♦ ♦
../../..	♦ ♦
../../../../.	♦
../../../../..	♦ ♦
../../../.	♦
../../../..	♦ ♦
../../../../.	♦
../../../..	♦ ♦
../../../../../.	♦
../../../.	♦
../../../../..	♦ ♦
../../../..	♦ ♦
../../../../..	♦ ♦
../../../../.	♦
../../..	♦ ♦
../../../../.	♦

We have, therefore, the

Mothers

I II III IV

Daughters

V VI VII VIII

The Principles of Astrological Geomancy

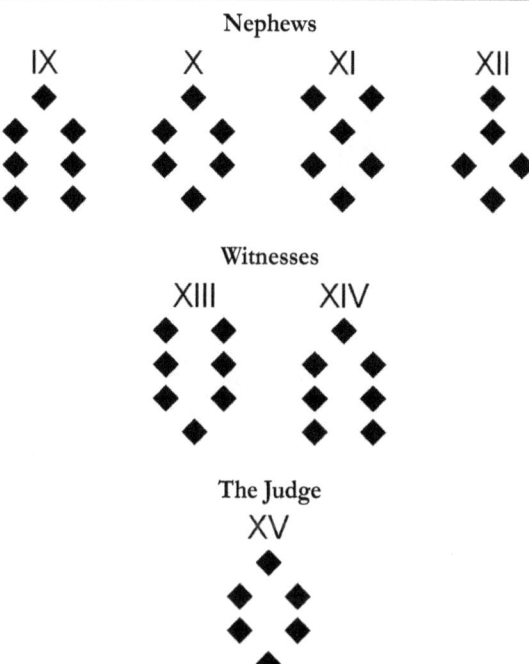

In this case the Judge is *Carcer*, meaning prison, capture, or attainment of the object desired. It has been made of *Tristitia* and *Laetitia*, meaning sorrow followed by Joy, and the answer is therefore:

The beginning is painful, but you will succeed in the end.

If analyzed still more we find:

I.   is *Albus*, signifying that the undertaking must be begun with wisdom.
II. is *Amissio* meaning that a sacrifice must be made.
III. is *Fortuna Major*, showing that the undertaking, if successful, is well worth the trouble involved.
IV. is an important figure; it always refers to the termination. Being in this case *Acquisitio*, it means that the object will be obtained, and thus it confirms the decisions of the judge.

Sometimes, if the answer is not satisfactory, a *Supreme Judge* may be constructed out of I and XV.

The above is a short and easy method, and sufficient to answer simple questions. If, however, any more detailed information is desired, a house is to be constructed according to astrological rules.

Astrological Geomancy

An astrological figure consist of twelve houses, and is constructed in the following manner:

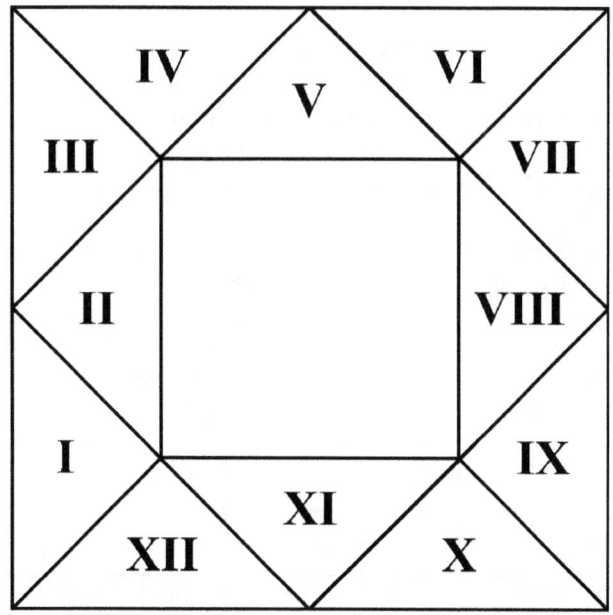

Each of these houses is under the predominating influence of some certain planet or planets, whose action is modified by their position in regard to the rest.

I. House 1. is the house of Life, and therefore represented by ☉.

II. Is dedicated to ☿.

III. The influence of ☽ is mixed with that of ☿ and ♄.

IV.   Is especially under the rule of ♄.
V.   Here the influence of ♀ is predominant, mixed with that of ♄ and ♃.
VI.   In this house ♂ is the principle ruler.
VII. Is dedicated to ♀.
VIII. Is dedicated to ♄.
IX.   Is dedicated to ☽.
X.   Is dedicated to the ☉.
XI.   Here the influence of ♃ is predominant.
XII. Is under the pernicious influence of ♄ in its evil aspect.

House I. Deals especially with the person of the questioner, also with matters regarding life, health, appearance, beauty, color, riches, fortune, success.

House II. With profit and loss, mercantile matters.

House III. Relatives, letters, little voyages.

House IV. Parents, property, treasures, agriculture, mines.

House V. Women, children, luxury, eating, drinking, pleasures, servants, legacies.

House VI. Diseases, servants, misfortunes, domestic animals.

House VI. Women, marriage, whores, thieves, robbers, dishonors.

House VIII. Death, legacies, trouble, suffering, poverty.

House IX. Religious matters, long voyages, dreams.

House X. Fortune, honors, kings, glory, fame, victory.

House XI. Protection, riches, presents, friends, joy, hope, confidence.

House XII. Loss, imprisonment, secret enemies, vagabonds, prostitutes, beggars, misfortune.

The usual way of proceeding is to insert the above-described 15 symbols in the order in which they have been received into the houses which their numbers indicate; namely, the 1st mother in the 1st house, the 2nd in the 2nd, etc., as may be seen in the figure below: The two witnesses and the judge are to be put into the middle field (see figure on the next page).

Cornelius Agrippa, however, recommends another method as being superior to this; namely, to insert the symbols into the houses in the following order:

Mother	I	into	house	I
"	II	"	"	X
"	III	"	"	VII
"	IV	"	"	IV
Daughter	I	"	"	II
"	II	"	"	XI
"	III	"	"	VIII
"	IV	"	"	V
Nephew	I	"	"	IX
"	II	"	"	VI
"	III	"	"	III
"	IV	"	"	XII

The Principles of Astrological Geomancy

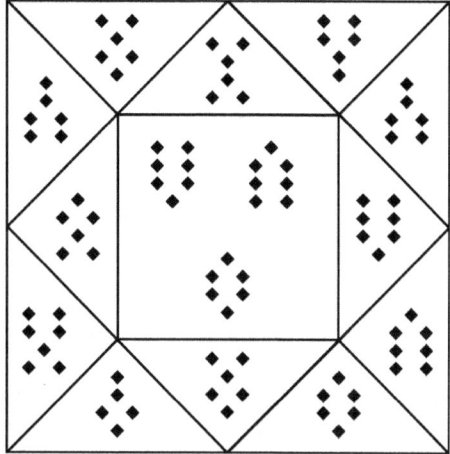

The above figure will then present the following aspect:

Mothers:

Daughters:

Nephews:

These symbols are inserted into the houses as described above:

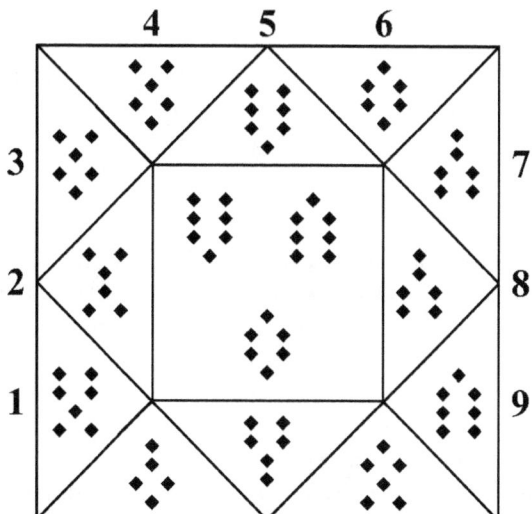

The figure is then amplified by adding the signs of the zodiac. The zodiacal sign of the first Mother is put next to House I. The others then follow in their regular order.

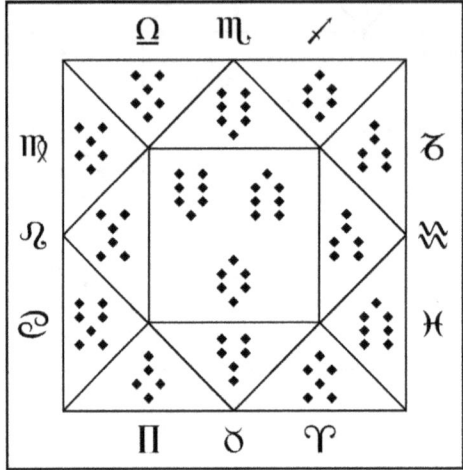

The figure may then be completed by inserting the planetary signs corresponding to each symbol.

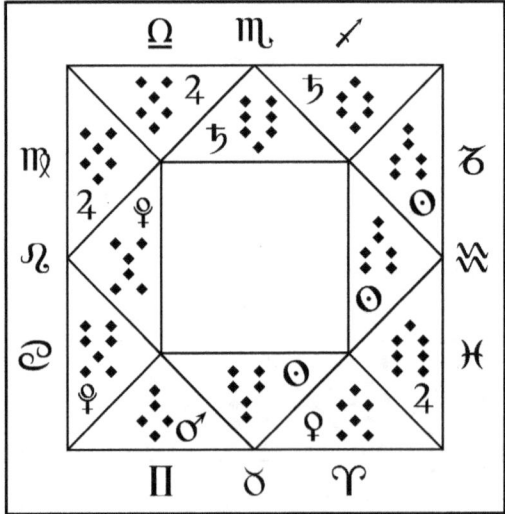

To find the Judge or Indicator according to this method, all the points of the whole scheme received by punctuation are counted together and divided by 12. The remaining points are divided off one by one into the houses, beginning by I, and the house which receives the last point, is the one whose symbol is to be the Judge.

In our scheme Shall I succeed in my undertaking?, the number of points amounts to 169. Divided by twelve there remains only one point. The symbol of the first house is therefore in this case the Judge, and his decision becomes intelligible by taking his position to the other houses and planets into consideration. If the aspects of the other planets are doubtful, the opinion of the judge alone is decisive.

Significations of the Geomantic Symbols according to their Positions

To practice successfully the art of Geomancy, it is necessary to keep in mind the significations of the planetary signs, the position which they occupy in regard to the signs of the zodiac, the houses in which they reside, and their constellations among each other. To become an experienced geomantist is a difficult undertaking, unless one possesses the necessary talents for it. Geomancy is an art, and, like all other arts, requires to be attained by practice. To facilitate this practice the meaning of the geomantic symbols, according to their position, is now given below:

Fortuna Major

In House I, signifies a noble character, long and happy life, a person of middle size, moral and benevolent.
In II. Riches and gain, being fortunate in recovering a thing that was lost, capture of a thief, etc.
In III. Noble and agreeable relatives, fortunate voyages, friends.
In IV. A noble and respected father, inheritance, success, recovery, success in mines.
In V. Joy from children, honors, fame, birth of a son.
In VI. Health, recovery; a good physician; faithful servants.
In VII. A rich, honest and amiable life; happy marriage, agreeable love affairs, gaining of lawsuits, and also powerful opponents.
In VIII. The person about whose death one inquires, still lives. It also signifies a painless and natural death, honors after death, legacies and a great dowry belonging to one's wife.
In IX. Extensive but fortunate voyages; safe return; a man faithful in religion; important dreams, visions, intuition; spiritual knowledge.
In X. Great honors; public and honorable positions; upright judges; the lawsuit will be quickly decided; fortunate kings; victory; long life of a noble mother.
In XI. True and useful friends; a rich and benevolent noble man; success at the king's court; happiness.
In XII. If the question is about enemies, it means that they are powerful and influential. If the question is, whether one will be victorious over one's enemies, it means a lucky escape. It also signifies faithful servants, escape from prison, and that an impending danger will be avoided or not become very serious.

Fortuna Minor

In I. Long life, but some troubles or ailments. A man or woman of small stature.
II. Money, but squandering; lavish expenses; the thief remains hidden; stolen articles are not recovered at all, or with great trouble.

III. Trouble and annoyances from relatives; threatening danger on a voyage, but escape therefrom. Reliable but reserved and uncommunicative persons.

IV. Loss to that which has been inherited from the father and other legacies; difficulty in obtaining lost or hidden things. No success in mines.

V. Only few children; a girl is to be born; honorable positions with but little remuneration. Small honors, little fame.

VI. Sanguinic or choleric diseases; the patient is in danger, but will escape; honest but lazy and useless servants.

VII. Marriage with a woman of good family, but some trouble connected with it. Inconstant loves. Procrastination. Tedious law-suits but final success.

VIII. Death in a foreign country ; legacies obtained with trouble and vexations; the dowry of the wife will soon be used up, or obtained with difficulty.

IX. Trouble on a voyage ; theological occupations; imperfect knowledge.

X. Powerful kings and nobles; gaining possession by force; great honors and positions but instability of fortune.' Tedious law-suits. Illness not serious.

XI. Many friends, but poor and useless ones. Favors from high personages. Inconstancy of fortune.

XII. Sly and smart enemies ; to a prisoner a long captivity but final freedom. Useless servants. Frequent changes.

Via

In I. Long and happy life. A stranger of tall figure, thin, liberal, agreeable, but not much inclined to labor.

IT. Increase of fortune; recovery of lost or stolen property, but escape of the thief.

III. Many brothers and relatives. Many fortunate voyages, sociability.

IV. An honest father; increase of fortune inherited from the father; good harvest; gain. Mines.

V. Numerous male children, a son will be born; honorable positions in foreign countries.

VI. Protection against diseases; the patient will quickly recover; useful servants and animals.

VII. A beautiful and agreeable wife, lasting happiness in marriage; favorable progress of law-suits, profitable settlements.

VIII. Death in consequence of phlegmatic diseases; great legacies; the person believed to be dead is still living.

IX. Long voyages on the water; profit; clerical positions; profit from church affairs; simple but firm faith: significant dreams; philosophical and grammatical knowledge.

X. Fortunate, kings and noblemen in peace with their neighbors; friendships; public honors; official positions, profitable money affairs; lawsuits will be quickly decided; a respected mother.

XI. Many useful friends ; confidence of superiors; business connected with traveling.

XI. Many enemies, doing, however, little harm; useful servants; escape of prisoner, protection in misfortune.

Populus

In I. Life of average duration; diseases and changes of fortune. A person of medium stature; thick.

II. Moderate fortune, obtained with much trouble. The stolen property will not be recovered, nor will that which has been lost be completely restored, the thief has not escaped, but is hidden.

III. An average number of relatives; little profit, a vacillating mind; loss by being cheated.

IV. A sickly father; no inheritance of real estate, but profit in things connected with water, Trouble about inheritance. No success in mining.

V. Ordinary, neither very profitable nor very respected positions; calumny, slander, gossip; wife bears no children; miscarriages.

VI. Cold diseases, especially of the lower extremities; a careless physician; danger of death; difficult recovery; dishonest servants.

VI. A beautiful and pleasant wife; but one who is not very faithful. Hypocrisy; pretended loves; impotent enemies.

VII. Quick death, perhaps by water. No inheritance. Legacies lost by lawsuits. Wife has very little dowry.

IX. Deceptive dreams; a vulgar and coarse person; in clerical matters low positions; indifference towards religion; not very conscientious.

X. Kings and noblemen who lose their positions; loss offices connected with water; tedious lawsuits; a sickly mother.

XI. Few friends, but many flatterers. No favors to be expected from superiors; weak and ignoble enemies; the prisoner will not escape; danger from water.

Acquisitio

I. Long life; happy old age. A man of medium size with a big head; marked features; spends much for himself, but gives little away.

II. Great riches. Lost or stolen goods will be restored.

III. Many relatives with ample means. Many fortunate and profitable voyages. Fidelity and sincerity.

IV. A considerable inheritance from the parents; great possessions, large harvests; a hidden treasure; mines can be found; a rich, but avaricious father.

V. Numerous children of either sex; but more boys than girls; a son will be born; profitable offices.

VI. Many long and serious diseases; danger of death; but an experienced physician. Many servants. Profit.

VII. A rich wife, a widow or advanced in years. Long and tedious lawsuits, a love affair or a concubine.

VIII. The person inquired after is dead. Quick death after a disease of only a few days duration. Profitable legacies. Rich dowry.

IX. Long and profitable voyages. The absent person will soon return. Profit from theologians and teachers. The person inquired after has considerable knowledge.

X. To kings augmentation of possession. In law a judge who is favorably inclined, but who expects presents. Profitable positions and business. A rich and happy mother.

XI. Many useful and profitable friendships. Favors from high personages.

XII. Many and powerful enemies. Recovery of lost animals. The prisoner will not escape.

Laetitia

I. Long, fortunate and joyful life. A person of tall stature, fine figure and features.

II. Riches, but also great expenses. Stolen things will be restored; but the thief escapes.

III. Agreeable but short-lived relatives; good voyages; fidelity and sincerity.

IV. Considerable parental fortune; possessions; a noble father. A rich mine may be found.

V. Obedient and good-natured children. A daughter will be born. A good reputation.

VI. The patient recovers. Useful servants.

VII. A young and beautiful wife; gaining of lawsuit; fortunate in love affairs.

VIII. Legacies. The person inquired after is still living.

IX. Few voyages. A man of a religious character, not very learned, but intuitive.

X. Kings and nobles of peaceful character. Honorable positions in the church or in law. If the mother is a widow, she will marry again.

XI. Many friends among the high. Protection.

XII. Victory over enemies; useful servants; freedom for the prisoner, protection against evils.

Puella

I. Rather short life. A man of middle size and feeble constitution, of a feminine character, full of sensual desires, and who often gets into trouble on account of his love for the other sex.

II. No increase of riches nor greater poverty. Lost or stolen things will not be restored. The thief has left the city.

III. More sisters than brothers. Agreeable voyages. Pleasant social surroundings.

IV. The inherited fortune is small. The harvest will be good.

V. The expected child is a girl. Favors received through the influence of ladies.

VI. The patient is very feeble, but will speedily recover. The physician is ignorant and inexperienced, but the vulgar people have great respect for him. Useful servants.

VII. A beautiful and agreeable wife, living in peace with her husband, but being of an amorous nature and having many admirers. No serious lawsuits of any kind.

VIII. The person believed to be dead still lives. The dowry is small, but the man is satisfied with it.

IX. Short voyages. A religious-minded man without great talents, except for music and singing.
X. Powerful and peaceful kings and noblemen loving sport. Honest judges. Positions with ladies of rank.
XI. Many friends among men and women.
XII. Only few enemies; but trouble with women. The prisoner will obtain his freedom through the influence of his friends.

Amissio

I. The patient will not recover. A short life. A man of irregular form, spiteful and disagreeable, having some blemish, such as a squint or limping, etc.
II. Loss or squandering of money. Poverty. That which is lost or stolen will not be restored; the thief will escape. No luck in mining.
III. Few relatives, or death of tee latter. No important voyages. A great deal of cheating.
IV. The inheritance from the father is rapidly lost. The father is poor, and dies suddenly.
V. Death of children. Miscarriages. Neither honors nor fame, but a great deal of slander.
VI. The patient will recover. Useless servants. Misfortune with domestic animals.
VII. An adulterous and quarrelsome wife, who, however, will die soon. Loss of lawsuits.
VIII. Death of an acquaintance. No legacies, or loss of the latter.
IX. No voyages, or if there are any they will be unfortunate. A person of vacillating mind, changing his belief frequently. A person ignorant in every respect.
X. Unfortunate kings or nobles, ending in exile or losing their positions. Ignorant judges, or such as can be bribed. Positions that will cause loss and harm the reputation. Death of the mother.
XI. Only few friends. Friendship easily lost. Favors, if any, will bring no profit.
XII. The enemies will be annihilated. The prisoner will be long in captivity, but is otherwise safe.

Conjunctio

I. Long life. A man of medium size; face long, agreeable and having many friends.
II. Neither riches nor poverty. The thief will be caught. Lost or stolen property will be returned. Success in mining.
III. Few relatives. Various voyages with changeful success. Reliability of character.
IV. Average fortune from parents; a good and intelligent father.
V. Intelligent children. The expected child is a son. Self-acquired honors, great fame, good reputation.
VI. Long and tedious diseases. An experienced physician; faithful servants.
VII. A well-educated and intelligent wife. Difficult law-suits with sly opponents.
VIII. The person inquired after is dead. An advantage to be derived from the death of a relative or friend.

IX. Few but long voyages. Knowledge of secrets in religion. An active mind.

X. Good and liberal-minded kings; upright judges; positions connected with instruction in natural sciences. A good and intelligent mother.

XI. Many friends and especially great favors from high personages.

XII. The enemies are prudent and sly. The prisoner remains in his prison. Escape from various dangers.

Albus

I. A person troubled with continual ailments or serious diseases. A person of small stature, a great talker, gay and amusing.

II. Gain from things that serve for amusement. Discovery of lost or stolen things. No success in mining.

III. Only few relatives; few but difficult voyages. A great deal of cheating.

IV. Little or no inheritance from the parents.

V. No children, or if there are any, they die. Miscarriage or birth of monstrosity. Slander and gossip. No honors to be expected.

VI. Tedious diseases. Useless and dishonest servants. The patient mistrusts his physician,

VII. A beautiful and beloved wife, but who will bear no children. Few but long-lasting lawsuits.

VIII. The person inquired after will die. The dowry of the wife is small, and will be the cause of a lawsuit.

IX. Voyages bringing but little profit. Obstacles. The absent person will not return. A superstitious man, adhering to false sciences.

X. No favors to be expected from kings or judges. Unprofitable positions or business. The mother is unchaste, or suspected of adultery.

XI. False friends. Hypocrisy, inconstant fortune.

XII. The enemies are impotent. Perversities of various kinds. The prisoner will not escape.

Puer

I. Life not very long, but full of trouble. A man of strong constitution. An excellent soldier.

II. Money not inherited but acquired. Escape of the thief. No success in mining.

III. Superiority. Dangerous voyages. Good reputation.

IV. Doubtful legacies and possessions. Irregularly acquired riches.

V. Good children, who will become prosperous. The expected child is a son. Military honors. Considerable fame.

VI. Serious diseases. Wounds; injuries; but easy recovery. A physician well versed in surgery. Useful servants.

VII. An honest and courageous wife, an order-loving housewife. Difficult lawsuits.

VIII. The person inquired after is alive. Death rapid. No legacies are to be expected.

IX. Dangerous but successful voyages. A person neither very religious or conscientious. Considerable learning in natural sciences, medicine and arts.
X. Powerful and victorious kings. Changes of fortune. Unmerciful judges. Positions in the army or in professions having to do with iron or fire. Danger to the mother.
XI. Friendship with nobles, especially in the military. Doubtful profit.
XII. Cruel and dangerous enemies. The prisoner escapes. Evasion of dangers.

Rubeus

I. Short life, and a bad end. A vicious, cruel and useless person; a villain ; being especially marked on some part of his body.
II. Poverty; thieves; robbers; counterfeiters; cheats. The thief escapes, and there is no fortune in mining.
III. Hated relatives; dangerous voyages; treachery.
IV. Loss of inheritance; bad harvest; sudden death of the father.
V. Numerous but bad and disobedient children.
VI. Mortal diseases or wounds. The patient dies. The physician makes a mistake. Treacherous servants.
VII. A wife of ill repute, adulterous and quarrelsome. The enemies are treacherous, and will by some trick get the best of tile querant.
VIII. Death forcible, in consequence of judicial decision, execution, hanging, etc. The person inquired after is dead. The wife has no dowry.
IX. Dangerous and difficult voyages. Robbery or imprisonment. A person of very little religion; one who does keep his promises; unfaithful. False and deceptive sciences.
X. Cruel tyrants, who will die a miserable death. Judges who must be bribed. Cheats, swindlers, thieves and usurers. The mother dies suddenly, and leaves a bad reputation behind.
XI. Intercourse with bad and disreputable people. Expulsion from good society.
XII. Cruel enemies and traitors. The prisoner will perish. Many obstacles and perversities.

Carcer

I. A short life. A vicious, ugly, and unclean person, who is an object of hate and contempt.
II. Extreme poverty. The thief will be captured.
III. Dislike among relatives. Evil company, Unfortunate voyages.
IV. No legacies to be expected. The father is a bad man, and will take an evil end.
V. Bad children. The woman is not pregnant. Miscarriage or infanticide. No honors; but much gossip.
VI. The patient has a long-lasting disease. The physician is ignorant. Bad and useless servants.
VII. The wife is hated by her husband. The lawsuit will be lost.
VIII. Death by a fall or by execution. Suicide. Neither dowry or legacy to be expected.

IX. The absent person will not return, having met with an accident on the way. A person devoid of religious sentiment. A very bad conscience. No culture.
X. Vicious kings and nobles, using their power for the gratification of evil desires; and who will take a bad ending. Falsifying judges and lawyers. A dishonest, adulterous mother. The person obtains neither honor nor position, but lives by begging, theft or robbery.
XI. No friends nor protectors.
II. Enemies. The prisoner will not escape. A great deal of misfortune.

Tristitia

I. The life is not necessarily short, but full of trouble. A good-natured person, but slow in everything; of an eccentric character; melancholy and avaricious.
II. Fortune and riches; but little benefit resulting from its possession, as it is not used, but hidden away. The thief escapes, and the stolen goods are not restored.
III. Few relatives, who will all die before the questioner. Unfortunate voyages.
IV. The expected legacy or possession will not be obtained. A very long-lived and avaricious father.
V. There are no children, or, if any, they will die young. The expected child is a girl. Honors and fame are small.
VI. The patient must die. Faithful but lazy servants.
VII. The wife will die soon. No advantage from lawsuits.
VIII. Death after a long and painful sickness. Legacies. The wife has a dowry.
IX. The absent person is dead, or has met with an accident. Unfortunate voyages. A man of good religion, and possessing considerable knowledge.
X. Severe but just kings and judges. Slow decisions in law. Many obstacles. The mother will have a long life, but various troubles. The positions obtained are important, but not of long duration. Occupation with water or agriculture, or with theological or philosophical matters.
XI. Few friends, and the death of the same.
XII. No enemies. The prisoner will be condemned. Battle with many difficulties.

Caput Draconis

I. Long life and fortune.
II. Riches. The thief escapes. Rich mines.
III. Several brothers. Voyages. Relations by marriage.
IV. Rich legacies. The father has a long life.
V. Many children. The expected child is a son, or there may be twins. Honor and fame.
VI. Diseases. An experienced physician. Many servants.
VII. Several marriages. Numerous lawsuits.

VIII. Certain death, legacies. A good dowry.
IX. Many voyages. Safe return. Religiosity. Knowledge.
X. Celebrated kings. Respected judges. A noble mother. Important affairs and remunerative occupations.
XI. Many friends and the favor of all.
XII. Many enemies. Many female acquaintances. The prisoner will not escape, but receive a severe punishment.

Cauda Draconis

This figure signifies in all its houses the exact opposite to that of the preceding one.

Note

In practicing geomancy it is necessary to seek the answer to the proposed question not merely by studying the figure in the house to which that question belongs; but also to take all the figures connected with it into consideration. The principal point in this art is the comparison of the various symbols and of their true signification, an art which is only possible to those who can call to aid the power of their own intuition.

EXAMPLE

Question: Will the proposed marriage be a success?

./../../../../..	♦
./../../../...../..	♦
../../../../../..	♦ ♦
../../../..	♦ ♦
../../../../..	♦ ♦
../../../../..	♦ ♦
./../../../..	♦
./../../../..	♦
../../../../..	♦ ♦
./../../../..	♦
../../../../..	♦ ♦
./../../../..	♦
../../../..	♦ ♦
./../../../..	♦
./../../..	♦
./../../..	♦

— 152 points (Typo: in fact there are only 151 points)

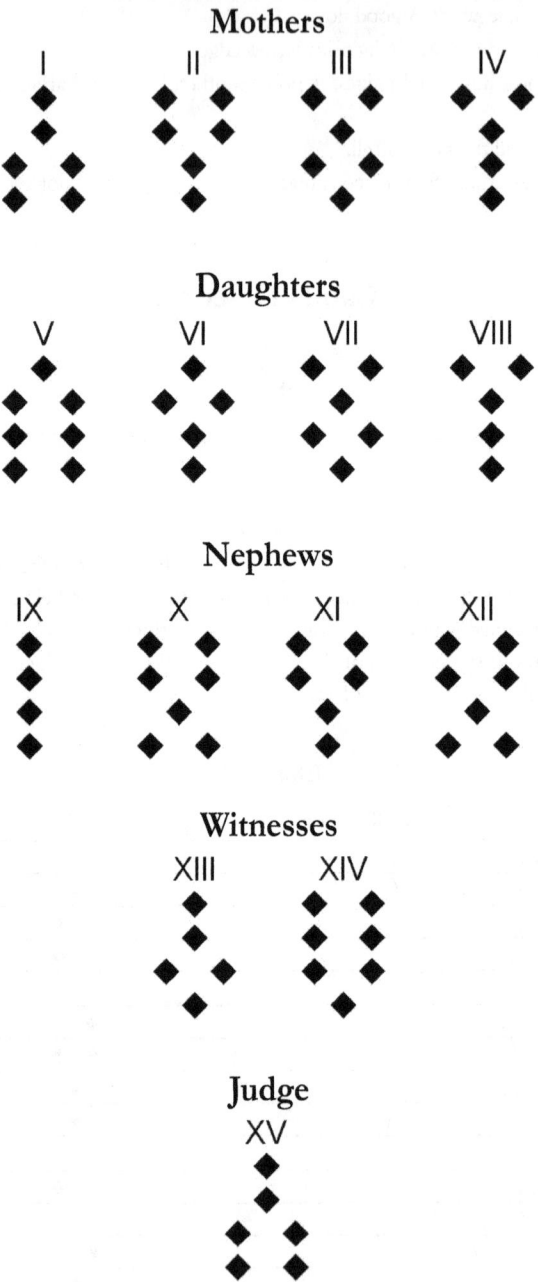

The answer is: *He will obtain her.*

If we desire to see this statement corroborated, and to know more particulars about the proposed marriage, we may construct an astrological house, and insert the symbols according to the directions given above:

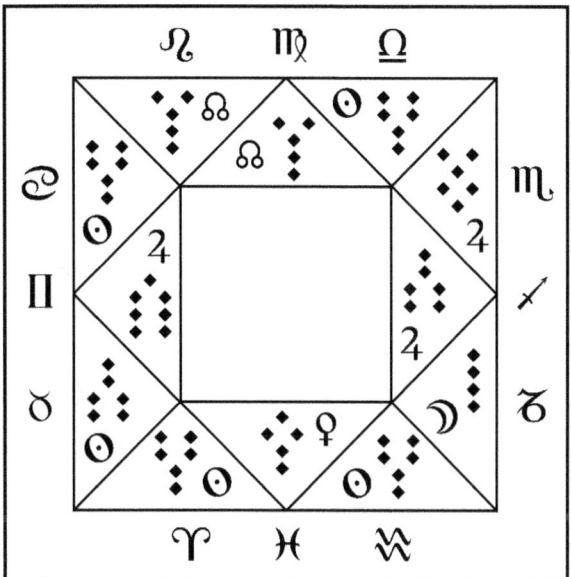

There have been 152 points obtained by punctuation. If we divide this number by 12, there will still remain 8 (working with whole numbers); 8 is, therefore, in this case the Judge or indicator. The symbol in house VIII, is *Acquisitio*. The answer is, therefore: *He will obtain her.*

Moreover, *Acquisitio* in the eight house means that the woman is rich, and a widow; the sign is if ♃, which means that there is a strong power active to produce the desired result. The termination is the fourth house, as indicated by ♌ is very favorable, and predicts that she will inherit a fortune from her father. The ☉ in the house of life (I) predicts a long and happy life, but not without some trouble; ♌ in house I indicates that children will be the result of the marriage. If the whole figure is carefully studied, according to the directions given above, numerous other details may be learned therefrom.

If we stand before a picture representing a landscape, we do not look at merely one house or one tree, to the neglect of the rest; but we see the whole picture at once, and then we may afterwards examine it in its details. Thus, to the experienced geomantist, such a table of figures represents a picture in which he can at once see the future life of the questioner represented in allegorical figures. As a whole, it has been grasped by his own internal spiritual perception during the process of punctuation. It has been resolved in its details by the science of Geomancy, and it now comes to his external consciousness, as a whole, by the power of his trained intellectual perception.

The soul may know a great deal, while man may know very little; the former sometimes communicates some of its knowledge to the latter by dreams and visions, when the mind is in that tranquil state between waking and sleeping. The mind is like a mirror, in which not only the images of external things, but also those projected by the soul may be reflected. If the Spirit retires within itself, the mind resembles an unclouded mirror; but as soon as the brain begins to think, the mirror becomes like a pool of water, whose surface is disturbed by falling rain. Man sees then only his own thoughts and not the thoughts of the soul. Those who desire to practice successfully the art of Geomancy should, during the process of punctuation, keep their own thoughts in abeyance, and let the divine soul do its thinking in them.

Astronomical Geomancy

There is still another method of practicing Geomancy described by Cornelius Agrippa. It is called the Astronomical Geomancy of Gerhard of Cremona. It is a very simple method, but to be successfully applied it requires a considerable knowledge of the character of the various planets and their constellation. The figure used is similar to those described above.

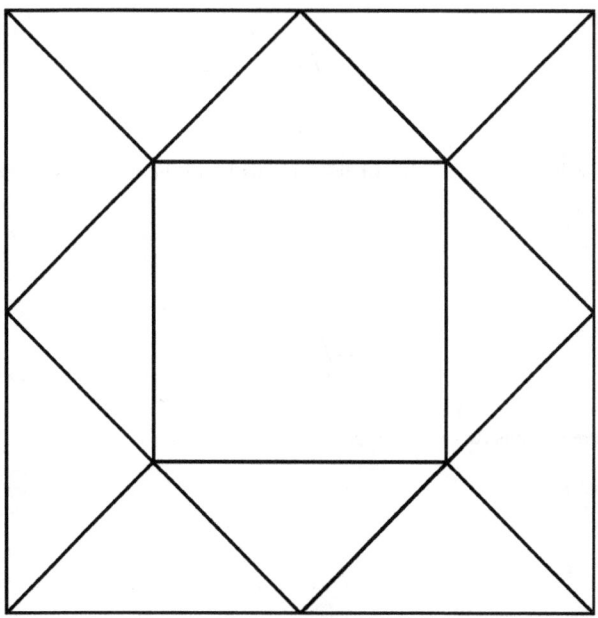

Four lines of points are made in the usual manner, and a geomantic symbol obtained. The zodiacal sign corresponding to it is then put into the first house, and the remaining signs into the other houses, from I to XII, in their regular order. For instance, if the symbol obtained is *Populus*, its corresponding sign, ♋, is put into the first house, ♒, in the second, ♓ in the third, and so forth to the end. The sign in the first house is called the *Ascendant*.

After this there are again four lines punctuated. The number of points is counted together and divided by twelve. The rest signifies the number of the house into which the first planet, ☉, is to be inserted.

In the same manner the house for the next planet ☽ is to be found, and the same process is repeated for all the planets in the following order:

☉, ☽, ♀, ☿, ♄, ♃, ♂, ☊, ☋

The houses and the planets and signs contained therein are then studied and compared together, as has been indicated above.

The manner of proceeding may be illustrated by the following example.

Question. Will the patient recover?

. / . . / . . / . . / . .	◆
. / . . / . . / . . / . .	◆
. . / . . / . . / . . / . .	◆ ◆
. / . . / . . / . . / . .	◆

The corresponding zodiacal sign is ♈. It is to be inserted into the first house and the other signs follow in regular order.

We now punctuate again to find the house of the Sun:

I.

            . . . / . . . .
            . . . . / . . . .
            . . / . . . .
            . . . / . . . .

After dividing the number of these points by 12 there remains 9, and ☉ is therefore inserted into the ninth house. Then follows:

II.

            . . . / . . . .
            . . . . / . . . .
            . . . / . . . .
            . . / . . . .

There remains two, and the ☽ belongs to the second house.

III.

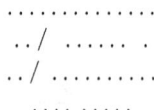

There remain 12, and ♀ is to be put into XII.

In this way the process is continued until the houses for all the planets are found. If two or more planets receive the same number, they are to be put into the same house.

The figure may then represent the following aspect:

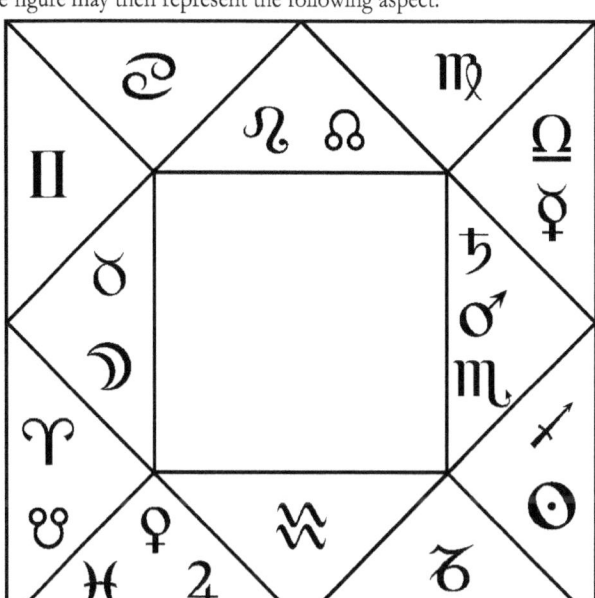

In this case the answer would be, that there is not the least possibility for the recovery of the patient. The presence of ☊ in I is a very bad sign, indicating an ignorant physician/ but the presence of ♄ and ♂ under the influence of ♏ in the house of death is extremely bad, indicating death by iron or fire, and the probability is, therefore, that he will be killed by a surgical operation.

In this way numerous complications may arise from the positions of the various planets in the twelve houses, and those who desire to enter deeper in the twelve houses, and those who desire to enter deeper into this subject will find information in regard to the meaning of the different constellations in books on Astrology. Those, however, whose intuition is sufficiently developed to grasp the true meaning of the symbols and signs, will require no further instruction.

Conclusion

If Geomancy was a truth once, it must still be true, and the answer to the question why it is so little practiced at present can only be either that man's intuition has been unfolded so much as no longer to require such artificial aids; or that he has become so much less intuitive as not to be aide to grasp truths spiritually, even with such artificial aid.

That the first answer cannot be the true solution of the riddle is self-evident, for there are few persons existing today who can correctly predict any future event, unless they base their prophecies upon calculations made from external observation. If the attention of the reader has been called to the existence of a higher power than the perishing intellect, and he has been encouraged to put more faith in the knowledge of God, the object for which these pages were written will have been accomplished.

Appendix

CONTAINING 2048 ANSWERS TO QUESTIONS

NOTICE

The following answers are obtained by constructing the I and II Witness, and subsequently the Judge according to the directions given on page 38 of the preceding part of this book. The middle figure is the Judge; the left-hand figure is the first, and the right-hand one the second Witness.

QUESTIONS

1. Will the person inquired about have a long life?
2. Will he become rich?
3. Will the proposed undertaking succeed?
4. How will the undertaking end?
5. Is the expected child a boy or a girl?
6. Are the servants (dependents, employees) honest?
7. Will the patient recover?
8. Will the lover succeed?
9. Will the inheritance be obtained?
10. Will the lawsuit be gained?
11. Will the desired position be had?
12. What will be the kind of death?
13. Will the expected letters (messages, emails) arrive?
14. Will the voyage be fortunate?
15. Will good news arrive?
16. Will the adversary be conquered?

Appendix - The Principles of Astrological Geomancy

♃
Acquisitio

♌
Populus

1. A long and happy life.
2. Will be rich in old age.
3. It will be successful.
4. The object will be slowly attained.
5. A boy.
6. Do not trust them too much.
7. He dies after a long sickness.
8. Success.
9. Yes, but it will take a long time.
10. Money will gain the day.
11. No success.
12. Dropsy.
13. Yes.
14. Fortunate, but slow.
15. Good news will arrive.
16. Yes.

☽
Populus

♃
Acquisitio

1. Feeble in youth, afterwards strong.
2. Wealthy in youth, afterwards poor.
3. Do not doubt.
4. The end is good.
5. Son.
6. Reliable, but greedy.
7. He will die soon.
8. After waiting a long time.
9. At last something will be had.
10. The judge is favorably inclined.
11. The aspect is favorable if it refers to lawyers.
12. Death by water or watery diseases.
13. Slowly.
14. Fortunate.
15. Tolerable.
16. Yes.

♀
Amissio

☽
Via

1. He will die early.
2. Inconstant fortune.
3. Many disappointments.
4. Difficult beginning but a good end.
5. Daughter.
6. Worthless.
7. Dies.
8. He may obtain her by strategy.
9. The legacy is bad.
10. Loses.
11. Inconstant fortune.
12. Fever.
13. Yes.
14. In no way favorable.
15. Trifles.
16. The adversary is stronger than you.

☽ Via

Acquisitio ♃

♀ Amissio

1. Average.
2. A little in the beginning, but nothing in the end.
3. Doubtful.
4. Tolerable.
5. Daughter.
6. They are thieves.
7. Dies.
8. She is inconstant.
9. The inheritance is not good.
10. Success through women.
11. Fortunate with ladies of high position.
12. The fever will kill him.
13. No.
14. A good voyage on land in female company.
15. Only tolerable news.
16. Victory.

♃ Laetitia

Acquisitio ♃

♂ Puer

1. Feeble in youth, stronger in old age.
2. Final success.
3. Success.
4. The beginning bad, the end good.
5. Son.
6. They are faithful.
7. Recovers.
8. Embrace.
9. Good inheritance gained by law.
10. Loses.
11. Fortunate with clergymen.
12. Febrile diseases.
13. No.
14. Beware of robbers.
15. Bad news.
16. The adversary gains.

♂ Puer

Acquisitio ♃

♃ Laetitia

1. Strong in youth, feeble in old age.
2. That which is inherited will nearly all be lost.
3. Fails.
4. A good beginning and a bad end.
5. Son.
6. Reliable.
7. Recovers.
8. He will obtain his wish.
9. A good inheritance.
10. Gains.
11. Success with clergymen.
12. Congestion or apoplexy.
13. They will arrive.
14. No obstacles.
15. News about advancement in office.
16. The adversary loses.

Appendix - The Principles of Astrological Geomancy

♄ Tristitia

1. Short and painful life.
2. Be not deluded.
3. Cease to think of it.
4. Bad end.
5. Son.
6. They steal secretly and openly.
7. He will have to go.
8. Vain hope.

♂ Rubeus

9. Obtains.
10. Loses.
11. Unlucky.
12. Cold steel.
13. Waits in vain.
14. Wounded during the voyage.
15. Bad news.
16. The adversary gains by cheating.

♂ Rubeus

1. Painful and feeble.
2. What you gain will be taken away.
3. The undertaking will be abandoned.
4. Bad ending.
5. Son.
6. Thieving and unreliable.
7. Dies.
8. Loss on account of neglectfulness.

♄ Tristitia

9. The legacy is worthless.
10. Gains, but receives no advantage from it.
11. No luck except in war.
12. Beware of fire and lead.
13. The messenger does not arrive.
14. The voyage will cost his life.
15. Worthless.
16. Victory by strategy.

☊ Caput Draconis

1. Long life.
2. Fortune acquired by writing.
3. Fortunate.
4. Good end.
5. Daughter.
6. Honest and industrous.
7. Recovers after a long illness.
8. Will ultimately succeed.

☿ Albus

9. A fat legacy.
10. Settlement.
11. Fortunate with mercurial people.
12. Dies quietly in bed.
13. Soon.
14. Good but slow.
15. Agreeable.
16. Adversary is feeble and desires to settle.

Acquisitio with Albus and Caput Draconis

1. Happy old age.
2. A fortune by marriage and employees.
3. Keep your undertaking secret.
4. The end is as it is desired.
5. Daughter.
6. Faithful and discreet.
7. Danger.
8. He will obtain her.
9. Slow success.
10. The adversary has the advantage.
11. Fortunate with clergymen and ladies.
12. Natural death.
13. Soon.
14. Fortunate.
15. Good.
16. You will wish to settle.

Acquisitio with Cauda Draconis and Puella

1. Not very long. Feeble old age.
2. Means by marriage.
3. Fortunate in love affairs.
4. The end very doubtful.
5. Son.
6. Unchaste and thieving.
7. Dies.
8. Obtains her.
9. Obtains the inheritance.
10. Gains through the influence of women.
11. Fortunate with ladies.
12. Dies of venereal diseases.
13. The letters will arrive.
14. Happy voyage, but great expenses.
15. News about love affairs.
16. You will be victorious over your malicious enemy.

Acquisitio with Puella and Cauda Draconis

1. Feeble youth, happy old age.
2. Your wife will cause your ruin.
3. If the object is robbery, it will succeed.
4. The end is better than the beginning.
5. Son.
6. Thievish and unchaste.
7. Dies.
8. There are enemies in the way.
9. The legacy will go into the hands of strangers.
10. You will lose because ♀ is against you.
11. No luck.
12. Beware of being wounded.
13. No letters.
14. The voyage is very dangerous.
15. News about war.
16. Your enemy is stronger than you.

Appendix - The Principles of Astrological Geomancy

☉
Fortuna Major

♄
Conjunctio

Acquisitio
♃

1. Long life.
2. Rich by trade.
3. Doubtful.
4. Tolerable.
5. Daughter.
6. Faithful.
7. Dies.
8. Certain success.
9. Obtains the legacy.
10. Settlement.
11. Fortunate by means of the pen.
12. Dies in his bed.
13. Soon.
14. Quick and fortunate.
15. Advantageous.
16. You will conquer.

♄
Conjunctio

☉
Fortuna Major

Acquisitio
♃

1. Happy and very old age.
2. Great riches.
3. Good success.
4. Good.
5. Daughter.
6. Useful.
7. Regains his health.
8. Success by negotiation.
9. Obtains an excellent inheritance.
10. Gains.
11. Fortunate in high places.
12. Natural death.
13. Not as soon as expected.
14. Fortunate but slow.
15. Happy news.
16. Meet him without fear.

☉
Fortuna Minor

♄
Carcer

Acquisitio
♃

1. Average.
2. Little gained by a great deal of trouble.
3. You will cease to think of it.
4. Success slow.
5. Daughter.
6. Lazy and vain.
7. Dies.
8. Yes, if she is a widow.
9. The legacy is poor.
10. The adversary gains.
11. Fortunate in the country.
12. Dies of a cold.
13. No letters.
14. Slow and a great deal of annoyance.
15. The news are worthless.
16. The enemy will be victorious.

♄ Carcer

Acquisitio ♃

☉ Fortuna Minor

1. Average.
2. Fortune through ladies.
3. Final success.
4. Tolerable.
5. Son.
6. Vain and idle.
7. Recovery.
8. Success.
9. The adversary obtains the legacy.
10. Gain.
11. Some success.
12. Dies of a fever.
13. No letters.
14. Tolerable.
15. Letters from high personages.
16. You will not gain.

Appendix - The Principles of Astrological Geomancy

♀
Amissio

Amissio
♀

☽
Populus

1. Short and feeble life.
2. Small fortune.
3. Disappointment.
4. Unsuccessful.
5. Boy.
6. Quick, but unchaste.
7. Dies.
8. Loses her on account of a long voyage.
9. Another person obtains the legacy.
10. Neither one of the opposing parties will have an advantage.
11. Unfortunate.
12. Danger of drowning.
13. Soon.
14. He will go to see his sweetheart.
15. News about voyages.
16. The enemy will do no harm.

☽
Populus

Amissio
♀

♀
Amissio

1. Feeble and short life.
2. Fortune easily lost.
3. Untimely love is injurious.
4. A bad end.
5. Son.
6. Careless and unfaithful.
7. Recovery.
8. He will obtain his wish.
9. The legacy will be very meagre.
10. The opponent has the advantage.
11. Success by being genteel.
12. Danger of death by venereal disease.
13. Delay.
14. Interference from water.
15. Contents are love affairs.
16. You will conquer all enemies.

♃
Acquisitio

Amissio
♀

☽
Via

1. Average.
2. Poor in youth and old age. Rich in middle years.
3. The chances are against it.
4. Tolerable.
5. Daughter.
6. Good but inconstant.
7. He regains his health.
8. Your inconstancy will cause you to lose her.
9. Not by you.
10. You will lose.
11. Fortunate on a voyage.
12. Dies in a foreign country.
13. Receives letters.
14. Rapid voyage on land and water.
15. Unimportant.
16. Powerful enemies.

☽
Via

♃
Acquisitio

Amissio
♀

1. Healthy youth, feeble old age.
2. The older he becomes, the poorer will he be.
3. The prospect is good.
4. Good.
5. Boy.
6. Yes.
7. A long disease.
8. You will get her.
9. Legacy obtained through females.
10. Victory.
11. You will be welcome.
12. Peaceful and natural.
13. Long delay.
14. Delayed.
15. Joyful contents.
16. You are superior to him.

♃
Laetitia

☿
Albus

Amissio
♀

1. Long, joyful life.
2. The older he becomes the richer he will be.
3. Very good prospect.
4. The end will show your ability.
5. Girl.
6. Honest and useful.
7. Dies.
8. Will get her through writing.
9. Another one will get the best part.
10. Amicable settlement.
11. Your pen will be your recommendation.
12. Natural death.
13. They have already arrived.
14. Fortunate.
15. Good.
16. You should try to obtain a settlement.

☿
Albus

♃
Laetitia

Amissio
♀

1. Long life and health.
2. Rich by services.
3. The wish will be fulfilled.
4. The beginning is better than the end.
5. Son.
6. Reliable and good.
7. Health.
8. Will get her.
9. You will get the best part.
10. Gains.
11. Honorable positions in the church.
12. Peaceful and easy death.
13. Certainly.
14. Very good.
15. Agreeable.
16. The enemy will do no harm.

Appendix - The Principles of Astrological Geomancy

♄
Tristitia

Puella ♀

Amissio ♀

1. Average duration. Troublesome.
2. Means by way of marriage.
3. Yes, if it is a love affair.
4. Tolerable.
5. Son.
6. Not very faithful.
7. Will gain strength.
8. Most certainly.
9. You may hope for a little.
10. Gains through ladies of rank.
11. All favors by female influence.
12. Melancholy.
13. Letters from ladies.
14. Tolerable.
15. The contents are love matters.
16. Look out for treachery.

♀
Puella

Tristitia ♄

Amissio ♀

1. Long but troubled life.
2. A little by agriculture and hard labor.
3. Useless.
4. Worthless.
5. Girl.
6. Idle and dishonest.
7. Recovery.
8. Lost on account of carelessness.
9. A little, but not much.
10. The adversary gains.
11. Unlucky in the country.
12. Gloom and discouragement.
13. No letters.
14. Slow.
15. Bad news.
16. The enemy gains the day.

☊
Caput Draconis

Puer ♂

Amissio ♀

1. Sickly in youth; afterwards stronger.
2. Nothing to be expected except by force.
3. Unsuccessful.
4. Bloody.
5. Son.
6. Average.
7. Will gain strength.
8. The marriage will take place.
9. There is nothing to be inherited.
10. The adversary gains.
11. Fortune in war.
12. Beware of fire.
13. Soon.
14. Dangerous.
15. News about war.
16. Your enemy is too sly for you.

♂ Puer

☊ Caput Draconis

1. Strong in youth, feeble afterwards.
2. A little by marriage.
3. This time you will have success.
4. Fortunate end.
5. Girl.
6. Good.
7. Recovers his strength slowly.
8. The marriage will not take place.
9. A small legacy.
10. Fortunate ending.
11. Fortunate at the court.
12. Natural death.
13. Slowly.
14. Fortunate.
15. Very agreeable.
16. You have the advantage.

☋ Cauda Draconis

♂ Rubeus

1. Long life. Feeble old age.
2. Considerable means.
3. Good success.
4. Fortunate end.
5. Daughter.
6. Average.
7. Dies.
8. It will come to nothing.
9. A small amount.
10. It will not be to your advantage.
11. A good position at the Court.
12. Taking cold.
13. Soon.
14. Fortunate.
15. Good.
16. You are superior to the other.

♂ Rubeus

☋ Cauda Draconis

1. Feeble youth, healthy old age.
2. Obtains some means in old age.
3. It will be abandoned.
4. Unfortunate.
5. Son.
6. Worthless.
7. Dies.
8. The marriage will take place.
9. Another person will get it.
10. The adversary has the advantage.
11. Go to the country or to the war.
12. A fever will make and end to his life.
13. Very slowly.
14. There is dangers from robbers and lewd women.
15. Disagreeable news.
16. Your enemy is too powerful for you.

Appendix - The Principles of Astrological Geomancy

1. A long life.
2. Means by agriculture and mines.
3. That which seems difficult now will become clearer.
4. Average and slow success.
5. Girl.
6. Good and useful.
7. Dies.
8. You ought to dismiss all thoughts of marrying.
9. The legacy is destined for your.
10. The adversary will receive the judgment.
11. Your fortune is to be found in the country.
12. A natural death.
13. No letters.
14. Fortunate but slow.
15. Letters on agricultural matters.
16. You had better remain away.

1. Long life.
2. Abundance.
3. There will be some success.
4. The end will be as desired.
5. Girl.
6. Good and useful.
7. This time he will escape.
8. He will not get his darling.
9. Persons of high positions will divide it with you.
10. The judgment will be in your favor.
11. Success in view.
12. Quietly.
13. No.
14. Fortunate but slow.
15. News speaking of persons of high rank.
16. Take courage.

1. Short life, full of disappointments.
2. Very little fortune.
3. Disappointment.
4. Only tolerable.
5. Girl.
6. Faithful.
7. Recovers.
8. It is very doubtful.
9. No.
10. The adversary succeeds.
11. Disfavor.
12. Dropsy.
13. Soon.
14. Tolerable.
15. Tolerable good news.
16. The enemy is stronger than you.

1. Average life.
2. Poverty.
3. Partly.
4. The end is better than the beginning.
5. Daughter.
6. Very vain.
7. Recovers.
8. She will be his.
9. Inheritance.
10. Favorable.
11. Some danger is connected with it.
12. Fever.
13. They are coming.
14. Fortunate.
15. Good news.
16. You will be victorious.

1. Long life.
2. Average fortune.
3. Yes.
4. Average success.
5. Son.
6. Honest and useful.
7. Dies.
8. He will get what he wants.
9. The profit will not be very great.
10. Settlement with loss.
11. Some success in mercantile positions.
12. Natural.
13. Soon.
14. Tolerable.
15. Tolerably good.
16. Seek a settlement.

Appendix - The Principles of Astrological Geomancy

☿
Conjunctio

Fortuna Major

♃
Acquisitio

1. Long life.
2. Sufficient money.
3. Success.
4. The end is good.
5. Son.
6. You may hire the servant.
7. He will die at last in spite of all hope.
8. The marriage will take place.
9. Unexpected inheritance.
10. You will gain by settling the matter.
11. Fortunate with lawyers.
12. Painless and peaceful.
13. The messenger is on the way.
14. Very good ending.
15. As desired.
16. Your enemy offers a settlement.

♃
Laetitia

Fortuna Major

♀
Puella

1. Fortunate and healthy.
2. Riches acquired by marriage.
3. If it is a love affair, it will succeed.
4. Pleasant.
5. Son.
6. Gay, but honest.
7. Will regain his health.
8. He will get his wish.
9. Fortunate.
10. The adversary gains.
11. Fortune through ladies.
12. Peacefully.
13. The messenger will arrive soon.
14. A gay and pleasant voyage.
15. They concern love matters.
16. The enemy is wise, just, and powerful.

♀
Puella

Fortuna Major

♃
Laetitia

1. Long and healthy.
2. Abundance.
3. Success.
4. As desired.
5. Son.
6. Good.
7. He will leave his couch.
8. She loves him very affectionately.
9. Inheritance and fortune.
10. A good end.
11. Fortunate with the clergy.
12. Dies in his bed.
13. The letters are detained.
14. Quick and successful.
15. Only good news.
16. The enemy is timorous and unjust.

♂ Rubeus — **Caput Draconis ☊**

Fortuna Major ☉

1. Short and sickly life.
2. What has been gained in youth will be lost in old age.
3. Some success.
4. Good.
5. Daughter.
6. Intelligent but dishonest.
7. Recovery.
8. Enjoyment.
9. Several legacies.
10. Favorable judgment.
11. Fortunate among ladies.
12. Natural death.
13. Slowly.
14. Fortunate.
15. Good.
16. You will get the best of your enemy.

☊ Caput Draconis — **♂ Rubeus**

Fortuna Major ☉

1. Short life, full of trouble.
2. Poverty in his youth, rich in old age.
3. The calculation was made without consulting the host.
4. The end will be the ruin of the whole thing.
5. Daughter.
6. Thievish.
7. Death will release him.
8. You are in danger of death on account of your sweetheart.
9. You may inherit a lawsuit.
10. The judge favors your adversary.
11. ♂ is against you.
12. Danger of forcible death.
13. Soon.
14. Dangerous.
15. The news are useless.
16. Your enemy seeks to destroy you.

♂ Puer — **☋ Cauda Draconis**

Fortuna Major ☉

1. Short and painful life.
2. Poverty and misery.
3. It will be a miscarriage.
4. Useless.
5. Son.
6. Lazy, idle, dishonest, thievish.
7. Let him make his preparations for death.
8. It will be useless to think of marriage.
9. The lawyers will divide it among themselves.
10. The lawsuit will be lost.
11. Unfortunate everywhere except in the war.
12. Death by water, drowning or dropsy, etc.
13. No letters will come.
14. A great deal of misfortune.
15. Nothing agreeable.
16. The enemy is too powerful for you.

Appendix - The Principles of Astrological Geomancy

☋
Cauda Draconis

Fortuna Major
☉

♂
Puer

1. Nothing but misfortune. A short life.
2. What he has will be taken from him by force.
3. Castles in the air.
4. The beginning bad; the end somewhat better.
5. Son.
6. Dishonest, useless.
7. He is on his dying bed.
8. There is many a slip between the cup and the lip.
9. It will not be worth the while to possess it.
10. The adversary loses.
11. There is nothing to be found.
12. Force, executioner, murder, or suicide.
13. You are waiting in vain.
14. You will do well to remain at home.
15. Severe disappointment.
16. You are superior to your enemy.

♄
Carcer

Fortuna Major
☉

♄
Amissio

1. Long but sickly life.
2. Inconstant fortune.
3. Useless thoughts about love.
4. Good ending.
5. Daughter.
6. Idle and dishonest.
7. Recovery.
8. The engagement will be broken up.
9. Vain hopes.
10. Neither one of the opponents will gain.
11. Cease to think of it.
12. In bed.
13. They will arrive at last.
14. It will be slow.
15. Trifles.
16. Doubtful ending.

♄
Amissio

Fortuna Major
☉

♄
Carcer

1. Short life, but a strong constitution.
2. Riches by agriculture or mining.
3. It will slowly succeed.
4. Tolerable.
5. Girl.
6. Average.
7. Dies.
8. There will be a wedding.
9. It amounts to very little.
10. The prospect is bad.
11. Go to the country.
12. Natural death.
13. The mail will not arrive.
14. Tolerable.
15. They are neither good nor bad.
16. The advantage is on your side.

♄ Tristitia

Fortuna Major ☉

☿ Albus

1. Long and healthy life.
2. Riches through writing.
3. Success.
4. The desired end.
5. Daughter.
6. Honest.
7. Will get well.
8. The marriage bells will ring.
9. Good luck.
10. Gains.
11. Fortunate in the legislation.
12. Natural death.
13. Good letters that will come quickly.
14. Fortunate and rapid.
15. Contents are good.
16. Victory.

☿ Albus

Fortuna Major ☉

♄ Tristitia

1. Long, melancholy life.
2. Great fortune by agriculture or mining.
3. Success, but slow.
4. Tolerably well.
5. Daughter.
6. Idle, but honest.
7. Dies.
8. Successful in the end.
9. Tolerably lucky.
10. He loses on account of his own neglect.
11. The country is more suitable for you than the city.
12. A natural death.
13. Slowly.
14. Good on the average.
15. Not worth much.
16. The enemy keeps the upper hand.

Appendix - The Principles of Astrological Geomancy

☉
Fortuna Minor

Fortuna Minor
☉

☽
Populus

1. Long life, considerably fortunate.
2. Some means by trading on the ocean.
3. It has no power to live.
4. Average.
5. Daughter.
6. They will do well enough.
7. Dies.
8. He will be disappointed.
9. Doubtful.
10. Loses.
11. Your fortune is on the water.
12. Painless.
13. The letters will come.
14. Quick and fortunate.
15. Tolerable.
16. The enemy will do no damage.

☽
Populus

Fortuna Minor
☉

☉
Fortuna Minor

1. Average duration. Changeable.
2. Considerable riches.
3. It will succeed.
4. The end is good.
5. Son.
6. Not the very best.
7. Dies.
8. The wedding will take place.
9. A good legacy will be obtained.
10. Gains.
11. Changeable.
12. Natural death.
13. No.
14. Fortunate and rapid.
15. Good news.
16. Beware of too many enemies.

♃
Acquisitio

Fortuna Minor
☉

♄
Carcer

1. Long and healthy life.
2. Rich by works belonging to ♄.
3. No.
4. Average.
5. Son.
6. Honest and industrious.
7. Dies.
8. It is useless to attempt it.
9. Vain hopes.
10. Loses by not coming in time.
11. Ill luck.
12. In bed.
13. No letters.
14. It will be slow.
15. Good on the average.
16. Stay away.

♄ Carcer

Fortuna Minor ☉

1. Long life and health.
2. Rich by practicing law.
3. It will take place.
4. A good ending.
5. Daughter.
6. They are good.
7. The tomb is waiting for him.
8. Marriage.

♃ Acquisitio

9. There is cause for hope.
10. Gains.
11. Fortunate with lawyers.
12. A natural death.
13. They will not arrive.
14. Fortunate.
15. Doubtful.
16. The enemy is harmless.

♃ Laetitia

Fortuna Minor ☉

1. Short, unhealthy life.
2. Loss of property.
3. It will go the wrong way.
4. Unfortunate.
5. Son.
6. Thievish.
7. Dies.
8. Marriage.

♂ Rubeus

9. Worthless.
10. Loss.
11. Fortunate in the army.
12. Forcible death.
13. The letters will be stolen.
14. Unfortunate.
15. Disagreeable.
16. The enemy will come out first best.

♂ Rubeus

Fortuna Minor ☉

1. Long and healthy.
2. Rich from rents.
3. It will take place.
4. The end is good.
5. Son.
6. Good.
7. Recovery.
8. You will be left in the cold.

♃ Laetitia

9. A good legacy.
10. Gains.
11. Fortunate among the clergy.
12. Dies a natural death.
13. Soon.
14. Fortunate.
15. Good news.
16. Your enemy will give way.

Appendix - The Principles of Astrological Geomancy

♄ Tristitia   *Fortuna Minor* ☉   **♂ Puer**

1. Short and painful.
2. He will have nothing whatever.
3. His attempts are useless.
4. The end is of no use.
5. Son.
6. Dishonest.
7. Dies.
8. He will marry the woman.
9. Not worth the while to take it.
10. Loses.
11. The starts are against it.
12. He will be killed in battle.
13. Soon.
14. Dangerous voyage.
15. Bad news.
16. The enemy has the advantage.

♂ Puer   *Fortuna Minor* ☉   **♄ Tristitia**

1. Long and very unfortunate life.
2. A little, obtained with great labor.
3. Extremely doubtful.
4. Doubtful.
5. Daughter.
6. They are lazy.
7. He must die.
8. There will be no marriage because he will be too careless.
9. A good legacy.
10. Will win at last.
11. Expect nothing.
12. Natural death.
13. No.
14. Delay.
15. Mournful news.
16. The enemy must succumb.

☊ Caput Draconis   *Fortuna Minor* ☉   **♀ Puella**

1. Average duration of life. Good circumstances.
2. A fortune through marriage.
3. Fulfillment of wish.
4. A good end.
5. Son.
6. Faithful.
7. Will recover his health.
8. The beloved one will be obtained.
9. Inheritance from ladies.
10. Gains.
11. There is some hope.
12. A natural death.
13. The letters will arrive.
14. Gay and happy voyage.
15. Agreeable news.
16. A settlement is advisable.

Puella	Fortuna Minor	Caput Draconis

1. Pleasant life but not very long.
2. Good circumstances.
3. Some is true and some of it false.
4. Slow.
5. Daughter.
6. They are good.
7. He will die.
8. He will have no success.
9. Obtains the legacy.
10. It will be settled.
11. Fortune smiles upon you.
12. Natural death.
13. Slowly.
14. Slow but fortunate voyage.
15. Good news.
16. The whole animosity is merely pastime.

Cauda Draconis	Fortuna Minor	Albus

1. Long but unhealthy life.
2. Rich by trade.
3. Success.
4. Good ending.
5. Daughter.
6. Dies.
7. Good.
8. Never in this case.
9. A good legacy.
10. Gains.
11. Some advantage is waiting for you.
12. A natural death.
13. Very soon.
14. Fortunate.
15. Good news.
16. You will be the master.

Albus	Fortuna Minor	Cauda Draconis

1. Short but healthy life.
2. Poverty and misery.
3. Wrongly calculated.
4. Worthless.
5. Boy.
6. They are useless.
7. Dies.
8. All his efforts are in vain.
9. He will get nothing.
10. Is already lost.
11. Ill luck.
12. Will be killed.
13. Nothing comes.
14. Unfortunate voyage.
15. Without any value whatever.
16. The enemy is too smart for you.

Appendix - The Principles of Astrological Geomancy

1. Average life. Unhealthy.
2. Average means.
3. Some success.
4. Average.
5. Twins.
6. They are of the average blood.
7. Dies.
8. The wedding will take place.
9. It is not very considerable.
10. It will be settled.
11. Fortunate in trading.
12. A natural death.
13. Soon.
14. Good on the average.
15. Neither good nor bad.
16. No harm will be done.

1. Short and feeble life.
2. Poverty.
3. All in vain.
4. Worthless.
5. Son.
6. They are worthless.
7. Recovery.
8. The marriage will be celebrated.
9. It is of no value.
10. Loss.
11. Bad luck.
12. A natural death.
13. The messenger does not arrive.
14. Unfortunate.
15. Worthless news.
16. A strong enemy.

1. Short life, but very fortunate.
2. Some fortune.
3. Will be abandoned.
4. Doubtful.
5. Daughter.
6. Average.
7. Must die.
8. He will not get her.
9. It is worthless.
10. Lost.
11. Unfortunate.
12. A natural death.
13. Soon.
14. Quick and happy.
15. Of the average kind.
16. Avoid him.

Via — ☽

Fortuna Minor — ☉

Fortuna Major — ☉

1. Long and healthy life.
2. Riches.
3. Fulfillment.
4. A good end.
5. Daughter.
6. Faithful.
7. Recovery.
8. Success.
9. Fortunate.
10. Gains.
11. Very fortunate this time.
12. Natural.
13. Slow.
14. Fortunate.
15. Good news.
16. You will conquer.

Appendix - The Principles of Astrological Geomancy

1. Long life.
2. Abundant means.
3. Your dreams will come to nought.
4. The end is doubtful.
5. Daughter.
6. Honest.
7. Dies.
8. A wedding.
9. You will be disappointed.
10. Things look very bad for you.
11. You will be fooled.
12. Natural.
13. Soon.
14. Fortunate and healthy.
15. They are of the average kind.
16. Both adversaries have equal chances.

1. Long and happy.
2. Abundance.
3. You will give up the idea.
4. Average success.
5. Girl.
6. Faithful.
7. Dies.
8. His wish will be granted.
9. A good inheritance.
10. Doubtful.
11. Fortunate.
12. Natural.
13. Delay.
14. Slow but fortunate.
15. Good.
16. You will do him no harm.

1. Very feeble health.
2. Poverty and misery.
3. The plans will be destroyed.
4. Worthless.
5. Girl.
6. They are useless.
7. Dies.
8. No prospect whatever.
9. Vain hope.
10. Lost.
11. He will obtain nothing.
12. Will be killed.
13. Soon.
14. Unfortunate.
15. Bad news.
16. Loss on both sides.

Tristitia / Populus / Tristitia

1. Long and troubled.
2. A little by hard work.
3. Missed.
4. Painful.
5. Girl.
6. Useless.
7. Dies.
8. He will not get her.
9. Worthless.
10. Lost.
11. Nothing to be expected.
12. Natural.
13. No.
14. Slow voyage.
15. Useless.
16. A tricky enemy.

Caput Draconis / Populus / Caput Draconis

1. Average healthy life.
2. Rich by services.
3. It will work, but slowly.
4. Good.
5. Girl.
6. Good.
7. Recovers.
8. He will get her in spite of everything.
9. A good inheritance.
10. Settlement.
11. Lucky.
12. Natural.
13. They are coming.
14. Unfortunate.
15. Good news.
16. Neither one harms the other.

Cauda Draconis / Populus / Cauda Draconis

1. Weak and feeble.
2. Poverty, misfortune.
3. Useless.
4. Unfortunate.
5. Son.
6. Dishonest.
7. Dies.
8. Great disappointment.
9. He will get nothing.
10. Lost.
11. Ill-luck.
12. Will be killed.
13. No.
14. Unfortunate.
15. Worthless.
16. The enemies are a worthless set.

Appendix - The Principles of Astrological Geomancy

♀ **Puella**   *Populus* ☽   ♀ **Puella**

1. Long and happy.
2. Rich.
3. Fulfillment
4. Good.
5. A son.
6. Good.
7. Recovery.
8. He will get her.
9. Yes.
10. Settlement.
11. Unlucky.
12. Natural.
13. They will arrive.
14. Gay voyage.
15. Joyful news.
16. He will do you no harm.

♂ **Puer**   *Populus* ☽   ♂ **Puer**

1. Wealth and feeble.
2. Poverty in consequence of theft.
3. Non-success.
4. Useless.
5. Son.
6. Worthless.
7. Dies.
8. He will be refused.
9. Gets nothing.
10. The judge is partial.
11. Fortune in war.
12. Forcible.
13. No letters.
14. Quick.
15. Useless.
16. The enemy is dangerous.

☿ **Albus**   *Populus* ☽   ☿ **Albus**

1. Long and happy.
2. Riches by service.
3. It will take place.
4. Good.
5. Daughter.
6. Good.
7. Dies.
8. He will succeed.
9. A good inheritance.
10. Settlement.
11. His pen will recommend him.
12. Natural.
13. Soon.
14. Happy.
15. Good.
16. Harmless.

♂ Rubeus  ♂ Rubeus

1. Short and unhealthy.
2. Loss by theft.
3. A wrong beginning.
4. A bad end.
5. Son.
6. Dishonest.
7. Dies.
8. He will be dismissed.
9. Nothing but law-suits.
10. The judge is against you.
11. No.
12. Dies in the war.
13. No letters.
14. Unfortunate.
15. Worthless.
16. A bloodthirsty enemy.

☉ Fortuna Major 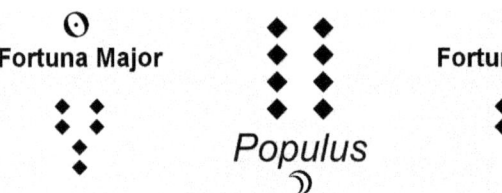 ☉ Fortuna Major

1. Fortunate and long.
2. Abundance.
3. It will go on.
4. Fortunate.
5. Girl.
6. Good.
7. Recovery.
8. He will surely get her.
9. A rich legacy.
10. it is already gained.
11. Fortunate among potentates.
12. Natural.
13. Slowly.
14. Unfortunate.
15. Good.
16. The enemy will give way.

☉ Fortuna Minor  ☉ Fortuna Minor

1. Average. Changeable.
2. Satisfactorily.
3. Incorrect.
4. Good.
5. Son.
6. Good.
7. He will gain strength.
8. He will be very fortunate.
9. Gained by a great deal of dispute.
10. A bad prospect.
11. Instability.
12. Natural.
13. Soon.
14. Quick and fortunate.
15. Not very good.
16. You will do him no harm.

Appendix - The Principles of Astrological Geomancy

☽
Via

Populus
☽

☽
Via

1. Long and happy.
2. Fortunate in the silver trade.
3. Worthless plans.
4. Tolerable.
5. Daughter.
6. Tolerable.
7. Dies.
8. He is going to marry her.

9. An average legacy.
10. Tolerable success.
11. No.
12. Dies in the water.
13. Soon.
14. Quick and happy.
15. Average.
16. You will get the best of him.

☿
Conjunctio

Populus
☽

☿
Conjunctio

1. Average length.
2. Tolerable.
3. Will turn out truly.
4. Good.
5. Son.
6. Good.
7. Dies.
8. He will obtain her.

9. Settlement with the opponent.
10. Settlement.
11. Fortunate in the mercantile business.
12. Natural.
13. The letters will arrive.
14. Tolerable.
15. Tolerably good.
16. Settlement.

♄
Carcer

Populus
☽

♄
Carcer

1. Long and full of trouble.
2. Riches by agriculture.
3. You will give up the idea.
4. Tolerable.
5. Daughter.
6. They work hard but stupidly.
7. Dies.
8. No prospects.

9. An average inheritance.
10. Unfortunate look-out.
11. No luck.
12. Natural.
13. Slowly.
14. Fortunate.
15. Tolerably good.
16. The enemy will not harm you.

☽
Via

♦
♦
♦
♦
Via
☽

☽
Via

1. Long life.
2. Sufficient means.
3. In vain.
4. Tolerable.
5. Daughter.
6. Average.
7. Dies.
8. He is going to obtain her.

9. Without any value.
10. Gained.
11. Changeable luck.
12. In bed.
13. Soon.
14. Quick and fortunate.
15. Tolerably good.
16. You are master.

☽
Populus

♦
♦
♦
♦
Via
☽

☽
Via

1. Short life.
2. Mediocrity.
3. Vain hope.
4. Unfortunate.
5. Girl.
6. Useless.
7. Dies.
8. Yes.

9. Amounts to nothing.
10. Missed the time.
11. Everything is against you.
12. Natural.
13. Soon.
14. Fortunate on land.
15. Trifles.
16. The enemy appears to be master.

♃
Acquisitio

♦
♦
♦
♦
Via
☽

♀
Amissio

1. Short but healthy.
2. Inconstant.
3. Useless to try it.
4. Deplorable end.
5. Son.
6. Faithful.
7. Recovery.
8. All attempts are in vain.

9. Will do more harm than good.
10. Lost.
11. It is worthless.
12. Natural death.
13. Soon.
14. Quick and fortunate.
15. Disagreeable.
16. The enemy remains on the top.

Appendix - The Principles of Astrological Geomancy

♀
Amissio

1. Long but not strong.
2. Tolerably good.
3. Good. success.
4. Average.
5. Son.
6. Good.
7. He will regain his health.
8. Of course.

Via

♃
Acquisitio

9. A good legacy.
10. Gained.
11. Success among lawyers.
12. Peaceful.
13. Slowly.
14. Delay, but fortunate.
15. As desired.
16. The enemy will run away.

♃
Laetitia

1. Average and healthy.
2. Sufficient.
3. A mistake.
4. Good.
5. Daughter.
6. Faithful.
7. Recovery.
8. He will.

Via

☊
Caput Draconis

9. It will come to him.
10. Settlement.
11. It is not a very god one.
12. In bed.
13. Slowly.
14. He will not regret it.
15. Pleasant.
16. The enemy becomes a friend.

☊
Caput Draconis

1. Long and joyful.
2. Abundance.
3. Success.
4. Excellent.
5. Son.
6. Good.
7. Recovery.
8. He will obtain his heart's desire.

Via

♃
Laetitia

9. A good legacy.
10. He will be fortunate.
11. Fortunate with the clergy.
12. Natural.
13. They are coming.
14. Fortunate.
15. Pleasant.
16. You will gain the upper hand.

♄ Tristitia

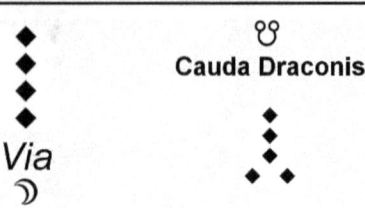

1. Short and painful.
2. Very little.
3. Non-success.
4. Misfortune.
5. Girl.
6. Treacherous and lazy.
7. Dies.
8. His sweetheart cheats him.

9. The inheritance is dangerous.
10. Loses the lawsuit.
11. No luck.
12. Forcible.
13. Soon.
14. Not very good.
15. Bad news.
16. A strong enemy.

☋ Cauda Draconis

1. Miserable, but long.
2. A little by hard work.
3. Carrying water in a sieve.
4. A bad end.
5. Girl.
6. Idle.
7. Dies.
8. She will refuse his offer.

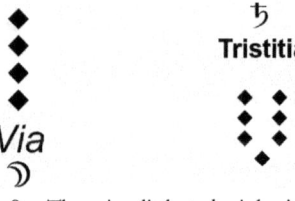

9. There is a little to be inherited.
10. Gains.
11. More luck on the land than on water.
12. Natural.
13. No.
14. Delay.
15. Mournful news.
16. The enemy loses.

♀ Puella

1. Short.
2. Bad.
3. Disappointment.
4. Entirely worthless.
5. Son.
6. Dishonest.
7. He will give up the ghost.
8. You may go ahead.

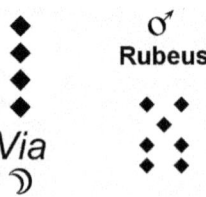

9. The inheritance escapes.
10. Loses.
11. High places are unhealthy for you.
12. Fever.
13. No letters.
14. Dangerous.
15. Bad.
16. The enemy has the advantage.

Appendix - The Principles of Astrological Geomancy

♂ **Rubeus**   ♀ **Puella**   *Via* ☽

1. Average.
2. Tolerable.
3. Good.
4. Very well.
5. Son.
6. Good.
7. Recovers.
8. You will soon rejoice.

9. Yes.
10. Gains.
11. Luck.
12. Natural.
13. Soon.
14. Happy.
15. Good.
16. You are superior to him.

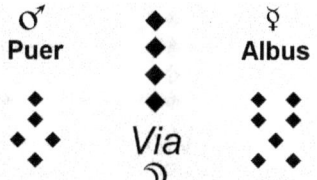

♂ **Puer**   ♀ **Albus**   *Via* ☽

1. Long but feeble.
2. Tolerable.
3. Failure.
4. Pleasant.
5. Girl.
6. Good.
7. Dies.
8. The marriage will take place.

9. Yes.
10. Gains.
11. A good prospect.
12. Natural.
13. Certainly.
14. Fortunate.
15. Good.
16. You will make him squirm.

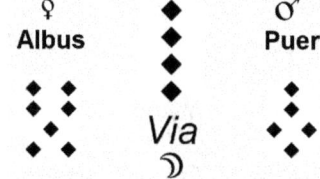

☿ **Albus**   ♂ **Puer**   *Via* ☽

1. Short.
2. Bad.
3. Failure.
4. Indifferent.
5. Boy.
6. Dishonest.
7. Dies.
8. Marriage.

9. Bad.
10. Lost.
11. Difficult.
12. Forcible.
13. None.
14. Worthless.
15. Bad.
16. He will conquer you.

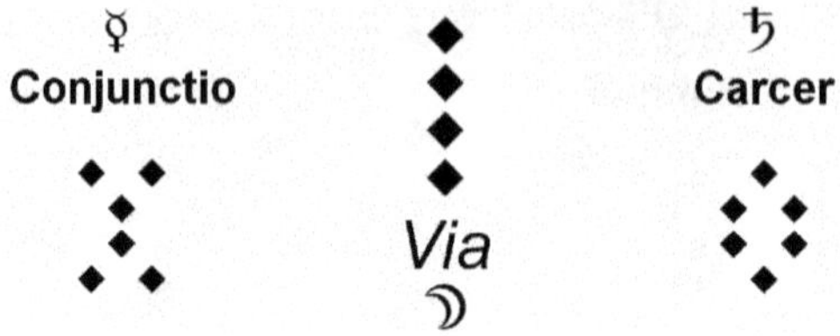
Conjunctio
Via
Carcer

1. Long.
2. Bad.
3. Failure.
4. Useless.
5. Girl.
6. Idle.
7. Dies.
8. A wedding.
9. Yes.
10. Settlement.
11. No.
12. Natural.
13. Yes.
14. Tolerable.
15. Bad.
16. The enemy succeeds.

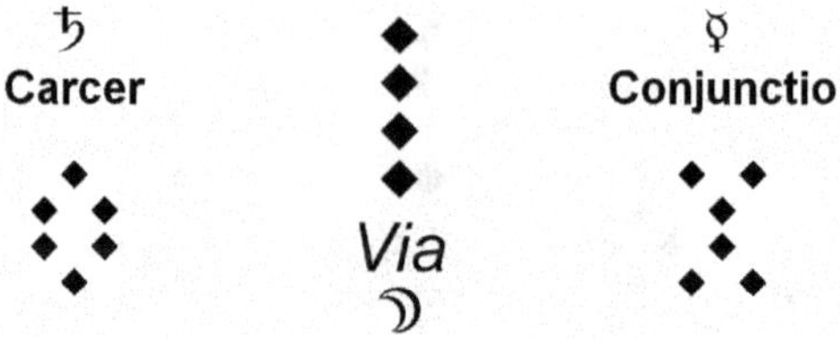
Carcer
Via
Conjunctio

1. Average.
2. Tolerable.
3. It will be accomplished.
4. Indifferent.
5. Girl.
6. Average.
7. He is going to travel.
8. He will be very lucky.
9. It comes in good time.
10. It will be decided in your favor.
11. A tolerably good prospect.
12. Natural.
13. Yes.
14. Tolerably good.
15. Indifferent.
16. The enemy is a loser.

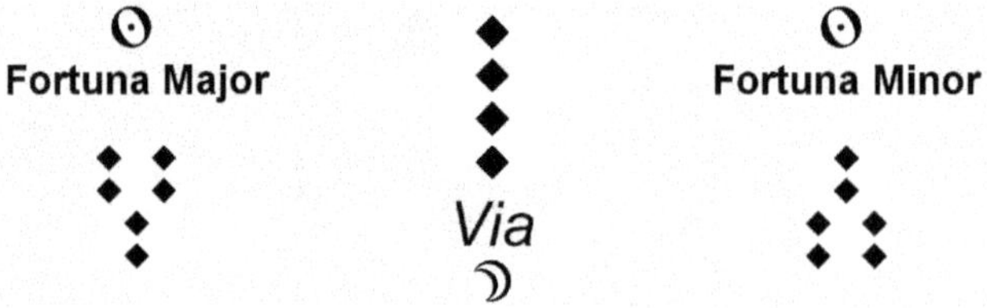
Fortuna Major
Via
Fortuna Minor

1. Good and long.
2. More than enough.
3. Will disappear.
4. Good.
5. Son.
6. Tolerable.
7. Recovery.
8. She cannot escape him.
9. Good.
10. Lost.
11. Inconstant luck.
12. Natural.
13. They will come.
14. Fortunate.
15. Tolerably good.
16. Victory for the enemy.

Appendix - The Principles of Astrological Geomancy

☉
Fortuna Minor

♦
♦ ♦
♦ ♦

♦
♦
♦
♦
Via
☽

☉
Fortuna Major

♦ ♦
♦ ♦
♦
♦

1. Long but unfortunate.
2. Sufficient.
3. Good.
4. Good.
5. Daughter.
6. Honest.
7. Recovers.
8. Success.

9. A good legacy.
10. Gains.
11. Luck.
12. Natural.
13. Slowly.
14. Delay.
15. Gladness.
16. Victory.

1. Long life, indifferent health.
2. Tolerable.
3. False.
4. Indifferent.
5. Daughter.
6. Average.
7. Dies.
8. He will get her.
9. Not much to be had.
10. Loses.
11. No luck.
12. Natural.
13. Soon.
14. Quick.
15. False reports.
16. The adversary desires the peace.

1. Average health, short life.
2. A little by trade.
3. A mixed-up affair.
4. Indifferent.
5. Twins.
6. Average.
7. Dies.
8. Marriage.
9. A good legacy.
10. Settlement.
11. A bad position.
12. Natural.
13. Soon.
14. Good.
15. Indifferent.
16. You will want a settlement.

1. Long and healthy.
2. Abundance.
3. Success.
4. Glad.
5. Girl.
6. Good.
7. Dies.
8. There is no one to take her from him.
9. Rich.
10. Gains.
11. Luck.
12. Natural.
13. Soon.
14. Fortunate but long.
15. As desired.
16. The adversary will be conquered.

Appendix - The Principles of Astrological Geomancy

☉
Fortuna Major

Conjunctio
☿

♃
Acquisitio

1. Healthy and fortunate.
2. Tolerable.
3. Some success.
4. Indifferent.
5. Son.
6. Good enough.
7. Dies.
8. Marriage.

9. Certainly.
10. Gains.
11. Luck among lawyers.
12. Natural.
13. Slowly.
14. Slow.
15. Good news.
16. Enemy remains victorious.

♀
Amissio

Conjunctio
☿

☉
Fortuna Minor

1. Feeble and short.
2. Little.
3. Deluded hope.
4. Tolerably good.
5. Son.
6. Not the best.
7. Recovers.
8. Obtains his wish.

9. A bad legacy.
10. Inconstant luck.
11. Success.
12. Natural.
13. Soon.
14. In vain.
15. Useless.
16. You will succeed.

☉
Fortuna Minor

Conjunctio
☿

♀
Amissio

1. Feeble and weak.
2. Little constancy.
3. Disappointment.
4. Doubtful.
5. Son.
6. Useless.
7. Dies.
8. Marriage.

9. Cease to think of it.
10. Loses.
11. Nothing.
12. Fever.
13. Soon.
14. Bad.
15. Worthless.
16. No.

Laetitia	Conjunctio	Cauda Draconis

1. Short but healthy.
2. Bad.
3. All in vain.
4. Useless.
5. Girl.
6. Treacherous.
7. Dies.
8. The engagement will be broken up.
9. The adversary gets it.
10. Lost.
11. Misfortune.
12. Forcible.
13. Soon.
14. Quick.
15. Good.
16. The enemy will be victorious.

Cauda Draconis	Conjunctio	Laetitia

1. Long and happy.
2. Enough.
3. Success.
4. Good.
5. Son.
6. Honest.
7. Recovery.
8. Success.
9. Success.
10. Gains.
11. A good prospect.
12. Natural.
13. They will come.
14. Fortunate.
15. Glad.
16. Enemy will have to leave the field.

Caput Draconis	Conjunctio	Tristitia

1. Long life.
2. Tolerable.
3. Failure.
4. Indifferent.
5. Daughter.
6. Unfaithful.
7. Dies.
8. Vain hope.
9. Bad prospect.
10. Loses.
11. The stars are against you.
12. Natural.
13. They are coming.
14. Disagreeable.
15. Worthless.
16. Your enemy will be your judge.

Appendix - The Principles of Astrological Geomancy

♄
Tristitia

☊
Caput Draconis

Conjunctio
☿

1. Long life.
2. Good circumstances.
3. Fulfillment.
4. Good.
5. Daughter.
6. Faithful.
7. Dies.
8. Success.
9. Success.
10. Success.
11. The fate is in his favor.
12. Natural.
13. They will come.
14. Fortunate.
15. Good.
16. The enemy loses.

☉
Fortuna Major

♃
Acquisitio

Conjunctio
☿

1. Long and happy.
2. Abundance.
3. It will be done.
4. Good.
5. Son.
6. Good.
7. Recovery.
8. Success.
9. Another will get the best.
10. The adversary gains.
11. The lawyers are in your favor.
12. Natural.
13. Slowly.
14. Delay.
15. Good news.
16. Your enemy will be master of the situation.

♃
Acquisitio

☉
Fortuna Major

Conjunctio
☿

1. Fortunate and long.
2. Sufficient.
3. Success.
4. Fortunate.
5. Daughter.
6. Honest.
7. Dies.
8. They will become a pair.
9. A good legacy.
10. A good prospect.
11. Favorable.
12. In bed.
13. They will come at last.
14. Postponement.
15. Glad.
16. The adversary gets the worst.

Rubeus ♂ — **Conjunctio** ☿ — **Albus** ☿

1. Long life.
2. Average riches.
3. Success.
4. Good.
5. Daughter.
6. Faithful.
7. Dies.
8. Marriage.
9. A good legacy.
10. Gains.
11. Favorable.
12. Natural.
13. Soon.
14. Dangerous.
15. Good.
16. The adversary loses.

Albus ☿ — **Conjunctio** ☿ — **Rubeus** ♂

1. Short.
2. Bad.
3. Wrongly calculated.
4. Bad.
5. Son.
6. Useless.
7. Dies.
8. Disappointment.
9. The inheritance will injure you.
10. Loss.
11. It will be a hell for him.
12. Forcible.
13. None.
14. Slowly.
15. Vexatious.
16. The adversary loses.

Via ☽ — **Conjunctio** ☿ — **Carcer** ♄

1. Short life.
2. A little by hard work.
3. From bad to worse.
4. Indifferent.
5. Daughter.
6. Idle.
7. Dies.
8. A wedding.
9. Tolerably good.
10. Gained at last.
11. Secret enemies.
12. Natural.
13. None whatever.
14. Delay.
15. Good.
16. Yes.

Appendix - The Principles of Astrological Geomancy

♄
Carcer

Conjunctio
☿

☽
Via

1. Short.
2. Bad.
3. Disappointment.
4. Indifferent.
5. Daughter.
6. Average.
7. Dies.
8. Marriage.

9. Nothing.
10. Lost.
11. Nothing to be expected.
12. Natural.
13. Certainly.
14. Quick.
15. Indifferent.
16. The enemy will gain nothing.

Carcer

1. Long life.
2. Good.
3. It will be interfered with.
4. Average.
5. Daughter.
6. Average.
7. Dies.
8. Undoubtedly.
9. The adversary inherits.
10. Lost.
11. Indifferent luck.
12. Natural.
13. A message.
14. Quick.
15. Indifferent.
16. The enemy must leave the field.

1. Long.
2. Tolerably good fortune in the country.
3. Backward.
4. Tolerable.
5. Daughter.
6. Average.
7. Must go.
8. Cease to think of her.
9. Things look bad.
10. Too late.
11. Nothing to be obtained.
12. Natural.
13. Letters.
14. Delay.
15. Bad.
16. The enemy conquers.

1. Short and happy.
2. Tolerable.
3. In vain.
4. Good.
5. Son.
6. Good.
7. Recovery.
8. Marriage.
9. The legacy is against you.
10. Lost.
11. Lucky, but inconstant fortune.
12. Natural.
13. Yes.
14. Soon.
15. Tolerable.
16. You lose.

Appendix - The Principles of Astrological Geomancy

☉
Fortuna Minor

Carcer
♄

♀
Acquisitio

1. Long life.
2. Tolerable.
3. It will go ahead.
4. Good.
5. Son.
6. Faithful.
7. Dies.
8. Wedding.

9. A good legacy.
10. Gains.
11. Nothing.
12. Natural.
13. Soon.
14. Fortunate.
15. Good.
16. The enemy returns.

♀
Amissio

Carcer
♄

☉
Fortuna Major

1. Long life.
2. Great fortune and durable.
3. It will slowly go on.
4. Happy.
5. Daughter.
6. As good as can be desired.
7. Recovery.
8. He will take the bride.

9. A fat legacy.
10. Gains.
11. A good star.
12. Natural.
13. Letters.
14. Fortunate.
15. Good.
16. Enemy succumbs.

☉
Fortuna Major

Carcer
♄

♀
Amissio

1. Short life.
2. Poverty and misery.
3. The idea is incorrect.
4. Bad.
5. Son.
6. Useless.
7. Must go.
8. ♀ is against you.

9. Another one will rejoice over it.
10. Gains.
11. An unlucky star.
12. In bed.
13. They have been captured.
14. It will cause you a loss.
15. Contents are vile.
16. Your enemy will step upon you.

♃ Laetitia

Carcer
♄

1. Long life.
2. Bad.
3. Disappointment.
4. Bad.
5. Daughter.
6. Lazy.
7. Good-bye.
8. At a very late hour.
9. Some success.
10. Decision against you.
11. Everything works against you.
12. Natural.
13. No.
14. Delay.
15. Bad.
16. Enemy comes out first best.

♄ Tristitia ... ♃ Laetitia

Carcer
♄

1. Long and painful life.
2. Abundant means.
3. Success.
4. Good.
5. Son.
6. Faithful.
7. Recovery.
8. No prospect.
9. Prospect very favorable.
10. Gains.
11. Good luck.
12. Natural.
13. Soon.
14. Fortunate.
15. Glad.
16. Enemy must give way.

♀ Puella ... ☿ Albus

Carcer
♄

1. Long life.
2. Good.
3. It is well thought out.
4. Good.
5. Daughter.
6. Good.
7. Dies.
8. The stars are against him.
9. It is not very big.
10. Gains.
11. We congratulate.
12. Natural.
13. Soon.
14. Fortunate.
15. Good.
16. The enemy will come out second best.

Appendix - The Principles of Astrological Geomancy

☿
Albus

Carcer
♄

♀
Puella

1. Short but happy.
2. Tolerable.
3. Good.
4. Indifferent.
5. Son.
6. Faithful.
7. Health.
8. He will get what he loves.
9. There is a little of it.
10. Gains.
11. Good luck.
12. Natural.
13. Soon.
14. Fortunate.
15. Good.
16. The victory is doubtful.

♂
Rubeus

Carcer
♄

♀
Puer

1. Short but unfortunate.
2. Poor and miserable.
3. Incorrect.
4. An arrest and imprisonment.
5. Son.
6. Dishonest.
7. Dies.
8. No success.
9. It is harmful.
10. Loses.
11. Obstacles.
12. Forcible.
13. No letters.
14. Unfortunate.
15. Useless.
16. The enemy will be victorious.

♀
Puer

Carcer
♄

♂
Rubeus

1. Long life.
2. Loss of property.
3. Let it alone.
4. Misery.
5. Son.
6. Thievish.
7. Dies.
8. The marriage will be postponed for ever.
9. Nothing but quarrels.
10. Gains, but will receive no advantage from it.
11. Avoid it.
12. Forcible.
13. None.
14. Dangerous.
15. Throw them into the fire.
16. Victory.

478 — The Principles of Astrological Geomancy - Appendix

Caput Draconis — *Carcer* — **Cauda Draconis**

1. Short.
2. Poverty.
3. A false calculation.
4. Bad.
5. Son.
6. Greedy.
7. Dies.
8. No success.
9. Nothing to inherit for you.
10. Loses.
11. The position is dangerous.
12. In prison.
13. None.
14. Unfortunate.
15. Useless.
16. The enemy is too cunning.

Cauda Draconis — *Carcer* — **Caput Draconis**

1. Short and unhappy.
2. Average means.
3. Succeeds.
4. Good.
5. Daughter.
6. Good.
7. Dies.
8. No marriage.
9. He will get it.
10. Gains.
11. Luck.
12. Natural.
13. Slowly.
14. Slow.
15. Agreeable.
16. The adversary loses the game.

Conjunctio — *Carcer* — **Via**

1. Short and painful.
2. Poor.
3. Disappointment.
4. Indifferent.
5. Daughter.
6. Average.
7. Dies.
8. The engagement will be discontinued.
9. Bad prospects.
10. Loses.
11. No luck.
12. Natural.
13. A message.
14. Quick.
15. Tolerable.
16. The enemy desires peace.

Appendix - The Principles of Astrological Geomancy

1. Average.
2. Tolerable.
3. Bad prospects.
4. Bad.
5. Twins.
6. Average.
7. Dies.
8. He will get her.
9. Pays for the mourning.
10. Decided to your advantage.
11. Everything looks bad.
12. Natural.
13. The messenger is near.
14. Profitable.
15. Good.
16. Victory.

Fortune Telling by Cards

Methods of Ancient and Modern Nations

P.R.S. Foli

This text and the accompanying illustrations are in the public domain in the United States of America because they were published prior to 1923.

Introduction

"This goddess Fortune frustrates, single-handed, the plans of a hundred learned men." In this saying the Latin author has given us the key to all the restless striving to search out the Unknown and the Unknowable which marks our own age, just as it has marked previous periods in history which we are apt to look back upon as being but little removed from the dark ages.

Of all the methods by which men and women seek to penetrate into the mysteries of Fate and Futurity, Cartomancy is one that can claim the distinction of having swayed the human mind from prehistoric times right down to this twentieth century of ours.

It may be that this book will fall into the hands of those who agree with the words of L'Estrange: "There needs no more than impudence on the one side and a superstitious credulity on the other to the setting up of a Fortune-teller." This attitude of cynical superiority is sometimes genuine, but in many cases if we could read what lies beneath the surface we should find that it is but a cloak worn to conceal a lurking fear, an almost irritated condition of mind, born of a half-confessed faith in the power at which it is so easy to scoff.

There is a vein of superstition in every human heart, and many men who have played a great part in the world's history have not been ashamed to seek help from occultists, when the tangle of life seemed too involved for them to unravel with the ordinary means at their disposal.

The pages of history are full of the penalties meted out by kings and rulers to those who were accused of working evil spells upon them. It needs but to mention the names of Wallenstein, Murat, King of Naples; Bernadotte, afterwards King of Sweden; and the merciless Robespierre, as types of a vast number over whom the fascinations of Astrology and Cartomancy, which are so closely allied, have cast their witching spell.

Pope treats the cards as sentient entities:

"*The king, unseen.*
Lurked in her hand and mourned his captive queen."

While in another passage he says:

"*Soon as she spreads her cards th' aerial guard*
Descend and sit on each important card."

In the following pages we have given information that will, we hope, afford interest and amusement to many. We have not dwelt on the gift of prophecy, or on the power of second sight claimed by apostles of the occult. We would in no case obtrude the subject of Cartomancy upon the notice of those whose susceptibilities would be wounded, or whose sense of right and wrong would be outraged by the practice, and we have ventured to speak a word of warning to the morbidly minded.

We give this method of Fortune-telling for what it is worth. It may be either a pastime seasoned with a flavor of mystery, a study in the weird ways of coincidence, or a test of skill quickened by intuition. We would have all our readers amused and interested, but none saddened or enslaved by it.

Chapter I
How we got our Pack of Cards

Where do they come from? – The Romany Folk – Were they made in Europe? – Suits and signs – The power of cards – Their charm and interest – Necessity for sympathy – Value of Cartomancy.

Where do they come from?

When we take up an ordinary pack of cards to deal them out for a rubber, or to lay them down in the careful deliberation of Patience, or when we watch them being used as the inexplicable instruments of a something that, with a feeling akin to superstitious dread, we prefer to call coincidence, we do not often stop to think of the varied and eventful history represented by those smooth, highly-glazed playthings.

The actual and authentic history of playing cards only goes back about five hundred years, and various theories have been mooted as to the source from which Europe obtained them. It is an established fact that in past ages many eastern peoples, notably those of India, China, and Chaldea, possessed cards which differed materially both in use and design from those known in the West at a later date. It is impossible to trace these prehistoric beginnings of card-lore, but there seems little doubt that the Wise Men of eastern lands regarded their cards with none of the contempt usually bestowed upon them in the West. They held them in high esteem as mediums for the partial revelation of the Unknowable, and included them as a part of their mystic lore.

The Romany Folk

It Is thought by many that we owe our cards to the gypsies, who are supposed to have been the offspring of a low caste of Hindus, and who, driven from their own land, found their way, as fugitives, through Western Asia into Egypt, and from Northern Africa into Europe. It is certain that all kinds of fortune-telling, whether by Cartomancy or whatever method, are inseparably connected with that curious, fascinating, highly gifted and elusive people. They excelled in music and all mechanical pursuits; they could learn a language, or distinguish themselves in metal work, with equal ease; but they had to live more or less on the defensive, as very children of Ishmael, and years of persecution only deepened their craftiness, sharpened their intuition, and rendered them more keen to assert their mysterious power over those who oppressed and yet inwardly feared them.

These Romany folk have preserved intact the ancient lore of the East, while incredulous Europe has turned the sacred pages of divination from the book of fate into mere instruments of amusement, and a vehicle for winning or losing money. The gypsy remains a past master in the art of Cartomancy, and though we may scoff, there are very few amongst us who do not feel a sense of disquietude when brought face to face with an instance of her uncanny power. We can afford to laugh when the sun of our lives is shining brightly and all is well in mind and body, but there come dark days in the lives of all, and then some are impelled to seek the aid of these weird sons and daughters of an unknown land.

By many, perhaps by the majority, this inexplicable gift has been vulgarized and debased to a mere means of extorting money from the ignorant and the credulous; but by some it is still held as a sacred faith-possibly no more superstitious than some forms of unenlightened or perverted Christianity.

Were They Made in Europe?

Another theory separates the cards of the West entirely from those of the East, and holds that the western were originally made in Europe. This is as it may be. A writer of the latter part of the fifteenth century says that cards were first known at Viterbo in 1379, and that they had been introduced by the Saracens, who, with the Arabs and Moors, have the credit of planting the seeds of Cartomancy in Spain. It is certain that at first cards were called by the name *naibi*; and the Hebrew and Arabic words, *Nabi, nabai nabaa*, signify "to foretell". It is also widely believed that the idea of playing games with cards was an afterthought, and that their original purpose was for the practice of divination.

The earliest cards were the Tarots, of which we speak in another chapter, and it is supposed that some one had the bright idea of adding the numeral to the symbolical cards, so as to play games with them. This addition was made about the middle of the fourteenth century, and at the beginning of the fifteenth century there was a pack in Venice composed of seventy-eight cards, twenty-two symbols and fifty-six numerals; with four *coat* (court) cards, king, queen, chevalier, and valet, and ten *point* or pip cards to each suit The fifty-six numerals were subsequently reduced to the present number, fifty-two, by the rejection of one of the picture cards.

The Spaniards discourteously abolished the queens, but the French, true to their reputation, kept the dame and rejected the chevalier. The early German packs were the same as the French, but the queens again were cast out in favour of a superior knave called the *Obermann*. England accepted the Spanish or French pack as she found it.

Suits and Signs

There have always been four suits, but there have been many changes in the signs used to mark them. The original quartette were: Cups, supposed to be emblematical of Faith; Money, representing Charity; Swords, figuring Justice; and Clubs, typical of Fortitude. These signs are still retained in the Tarots, and in Italian and Spanish cards. Old German packs have bells, hearts, leaves, and acorns; and during the fifteenth century the French adopted spades (*pique*), hearts, clubs (*trèfle*), and diamonds.

There is some difficulty in tracing how we come by the word spade in this connection. It has been thought to be a corruption of the Italian word *spade*, meaning swords. It is not known why the French should have called this suit *pique*. Our suit of clubs is known by the French is *trèfle*, from their drawing the sign like the trefoil; and the Germans call it *Eichel* from its resemblance to an acorn. Our name is supposed to show Italian influence, though where the connection between the word *bastoni* and our sign is to be found, I am at a loss to say. The heart sign needs no explanation, and is found in French, German, and English packs. It corresponds to the Spanish and Italian sign of cups. By some curious evolution the signs of money and bells were squared into the French *carreaux*, our diamonds.

Many of the packs used in the fourteenth century were of the most artistic and costly nature, and in some cases the court cards were drawn so as to represent historic characters.

The Power of Cards

Fierce controversies have ranged round these apparently simple pieces of glazed pasteboard. They have exercised such an irresistible fascination upon the minds of men and women of all grades and ages that others have risen in wild revolt against this power, which had no attraction for them, and which they longed to crush out of existence. There are still those amongst us who will not have a card in the house, and who, even if they do not use it, acquiesce in the term "the Devil's books," which has been applied to the pack.

With their use for gambling purposes we have nothing to do here. As the instruments of Cartomancy we give them our respectful consideration. We would urge those of a morbid and unhealthy turn of mind to beware of letting this practice take too strong a hold upon them. No reasonable being need be ashamed of confessing a certain fear of the Unseen and the Unknowable; but, on the other hand, no sane person would take a pack of cards as the rule and guide of life, the final court of appeal in any matters of moment

Their Charm and Interest

There is much amusement to be derived from the study of Cartomancy, and it is not to be denied that there are certain persons who appear to have the power of making the meaning of the cards vivid and convincing, while in the hand of others there seems neither rhyme nor reason in their manipulation of the most carefully shuffled pack. We may call things by what name we will, but strange coincidences meet us at every turn, and now and then there seems but the thinnest veil between us and the Future, which is so sedulously hidden from us.

There has been a great revival of interest in all matters relating to occultism in the immediate past, and if we are to believe what we read and hear, educated men and women of today are going to have their fortunes told as eagerly as did the great men and famous women of France during the stormy period of the Revolution, and under the sway of the great Napoleon himself. Many curious and convincing instances of accurate foreshadowing of future events are told with regard to the famous Mademoiselle Lenormand, and other cartomancers who held undisputed sway over the minds of society at a time when credulity was supposed to have been cast off with the trammels of a worn-out creed.

So when the fortune-tellers of the twentieth century take a pack of cards and proceed to read the mysteries revealed therein, they are following the example of the wise men of Chaldea, Egypt, and China, the Flowery Land of the East, to say nothing of their European predecessors.

Divination by cards, therefore, is of great antiquity and of worldwide popularity. Formerly it was combined with a knowledge of astrology; but now it is considered sufficient to follow the general rules laid down by one of two famous cartomancers, and to rely on intuition and experience for details.

Necessity for Sympathy

Any one with the slightest knowledge of occultism is aware that sympathy with the inquirer or subject is essential.

It is true that cold reason tells us that the cards are pieces of pasteboard and nothing more, and that it is the height of absurdity to expect any revelation; yet, in dealing with them, human sympathy may discern something of our perplexities, and all unconsciously set our feet on the right path.

Value of Cartomancy

In the following pages there are several methods of divination by cards. Any one observing the rules can learn the signification of the cards, and while a study of the combinations they resolve into in the hands of different people will always provide a fund of amusement, it may also –in all seriousness I say it– inspire hope in the place of despair, assuage sorrow, and send the inquirer away comforted; surely no insignificant result

Chapter II
What the Individual Cards Signify

Two systems – The English method – The foreign – Significations of the cards – Hearts – Diamonds – Clubs – Spades – A short table – Mystic meanings

Two Systems

There are two separate systems of explaining the cards individually: one which makes use of the whole pack of fifty-two cards, and another which only employs thirty-two, throwing out the plain cards under seven of each suit.

The English Method

The former plan is sometimes spoken of as the English method, and in it we do not find mention of reversed cards bearing a different meaning from those which come out in the ordinary way. This is probably to be explained by the fact that the larger number in use affords sufficient shades of meaning, and the task of remembering one hundred and four significations would be too heavy for many minds.

The Foreign

In the latter system, which is more distinctly traceable to foreign sources, we get the signification of each card modified, or even contradicted, by its position being upright or the reverse.

The following definitions apply to the use of the whole pack, and have been worked up from both ancient and modern sources of information. It must always be borne in mind that the reading of the cards has come down to us through many ages, has been passed on to us through countless hands and in varied tongues. Cartomancy has traveled from the East to the West, from the South to the North, and its secrets have been, for the most part, jealously preserved by oral tradition among its weird and fascinating votaries.

Significations of the Cards.

The following definitions are based upon one of the oldest authorities dealing with the subject, and have been amplified by some of the more modern meanings now in vogue.

Hearts

Ace.– An important card, whose meaning is affected by its environment. Among hearts it implies love, friendship, and affection; with diamonds, money and news of distant friends; with clubs, festivities, and social or domestic rejoicing; with spades, disagreements, misunderstandings, contention, or misfortune; individually, it stands for the house.

King.– A good-hearted man, with strong affections, emotional, and given to rash judgments, possessing more zeal than discretion.

Queen.– A fair woman, loving and lovable, domesticated, prudent, and faithful

Knave.– Not endowed with any sex. Sometimes taken as Cupid; also as the best friend of the inquirer, or as a fair person's thoughts. The cards on either side of the knave are indicative of the good or bad nature of its intentions.

Ten.– A sign of good fortune. It implies a good heart, happiness, and the prospect of a large family. It counteracts bad cards and confirms good ones in its vicinity.

Nine.– The wish card. It is the sign of riches, and of high social position accompanied by influence and esteem. It maybe affected by the neighborhood of bad cards.

Eight.– The pleasures of the table, convivial society. Another meaning implies love and marriage.

Seven.– A faithless, inconstant friend who may prove an enemy.

Six.– A confiding nature, liberal, open-handed, and an easy prey for swindlers; courtship, and a possible proposal

Five.– Causeless jealousy in a person of weak, unsettled character.

Four.– One who has remained single till middle life from being too hard to please.

Three.– A warning card as to the possible results of the inquirer's own want of prudence and tact

Deuce.– Prosperity and success in a measure dependent on the surrounding cards; endearments and wedding bells.

Diamonds

Ace.– A ring or paper money.

King.– A fair man, with violent temper, and a vindictive obstinate turn of mind.

Queen.– A fair woman, given to flirtation, fond of society and admiration.

Knave.– A near relative who puts his own interests first, is self-opinionated, easily offended, and not always quite straight. It may mean a fair person's thoughts.

Ten.– Plenty of money, a husband or wife from the country, and several children.

Nine.– This card is influenced by the one accompanying it; if the latter be a court card, the person referred to will have his capacities discounted by a restless, wandering disposition. It may imply a surprise connected with money, or if in conjunction with the eight of spades it signifies cross swords.

Eight.– A marriage late in life, which will probably be somewhat checkered.

Seven.– This card has various meanings. It enjoins the need for careful action. It may imply a decrease of prosperity. Another reading connects it with uncharitable tongues.

Six.– An early marriage and speedy widowhood. A warning with regard to second marriage is also included.

Five.– To young married people this portends good children. In a general way it means unexpected news, or success in business enterprises.

Four.– Breach of confidence. Troubles caused by inconstant friends, vexations and disagreeables.

Three.– Legal and domestic quarrels, and probable unhappiness caused by wife's or husband's temper.

Deuce.– An unsatisfactory love affair, awakening opposition from relatives or friends.

Clubs

Ace.– Wealth, a peaceful home, industry, and general prosperity.

King.– A dark man of upright, high-minded nature, calculated to make an excellent husband, faithful and true in his affections.

Queen.– A dark woman, with a trustful, affectionate disposition, with great charm for the opposite sex, and susceptible to male attractions.

Knave.– A generous, trusty friend, who will take trouble on behalf of the inquirer. It may also mean a dark man's thoughts.

Ten.– Riches suddenly acquired, probably through the death of a relation or friend.

Nine.– Friction through opposition to the wishes of friends.

Eight.– Love of money, and a passion for speculating.

Seven.– Great happiness and good fortune. If troubles come they will be caused by one of the opposite sex to the inquirer.

Six.– Success in business both for self and children.

Five.– An advantageous marriage.

Four.– A warning against falsehood and double-dealing.

Three.– Two or possibly three marriages, with money.

Deuce.– Care is needed to avert disappointment, and to avoid opposition.

Spades

Ace.– It may concern love affairs, or convey a warning that troubles await the inquirer through bad speculations or ill-chosen friends.

King.– A dark man. Ambitious and successful in the higher walks of life.

Queen.– A widow, of malicious and unscrupulous nature, fond of scandal and open to bribes.

Knave.– A well-meaning, inert person, unready in action though kindly in thought.

Ten.– An evil omen; grief or imprisonment. Has power to detract from the good signified by cards near it

Nine.– An ill-fated card, meaning sickness, losses, troubles, and family dissensions.

Eight.– A warning with regard to any enterprise in hand. This card close to the inquirer means evil; also opposition from friends.

Seven.– Sorrow caused by the loss of a dear friend.

Six.– Hard work brings wealth and rest after toil.

Five.– Bad temper and a tendency to interfere in the inquirer, but happiness to be found in the chosen wife or husband.

Four.– Illness and the need for great attention to business.

Three.– A marriage that will be marred by the inconstancy of the inquirer's wife or husband; or a journey.

Deuce.– A removal, or possibly death.

In connection with the foregoing detailed explanation of the meanings of each card in an ordinary pack, we append a short table, which may be studied either separately or with the preceding definitions. It gives at a glance certain broad outlines, which may be of use to one who wishes to acquire the art of reading a card directly it is placed before the eye:

A Short Table

Prudence	Wealth	Rejoicing	Early Marriage
Ace of clubs 6 of spades	9 of hearts 2 of hearts 7 of clubs 10 of diamonds 10 of clubs.	8 of hearts	2 of clubs 6 of diamonds 3 of clubs 5 of clubs
Credulity	Jealousy	Unfaithfulness	Late Marriage
10 of hearts 2 of hearts 7 or clubs 6 of clubs	5 of hearts	King of diamonds 4 of diamonds 4 of clubs 7 or hearts	8 of diamonds 3 of clubs

Prosperity	Discretion Needed	Presage Misfortune
10 of hearts 2 of hearts 7 of clubs 6 of clubs	3 of hearts 7 of diamonds 2 of diamonds 2 of clubs 4 of spades	10 of spades 9 of spades 8 of spades 7 of spades 3 of spades 2 of spades 3 of diamonds 9 of clubs

Mystic Meanings

There is fascination in certain calculations, and the following figures are not without a deep interest to those attracted by the study of Cartomancy.

The fifty-two cards in the pack correspond with the fifty-two weeks in the year.

The thirteen cards in each suit symbolize the thirteen lunar months, and the thirteen weeks in each quarter.

There are four suits, as there are four seasons in the year.

There are twelve court cards in the pack, just as there are twelve calendar months and twelve signs of the Zodiac

A Curious Calculation

Number of pips on the plain cards of the four suits	220
Number of pips on the court cards of the four suits	12
Twelve court cards, counted as 10 each	120
Number of cards on each suit	13
Equal to the number of days in the year	365

Chapter III
The Selected Pack of Thirty-two Cards

Reduced pack generally used – How to indicate reversed cards – Meaning of Hearts – Diamonds – Clubs – Spades

Reduced Pack Generally Used

The practice of using only thirty-two cards in telling fortunes is very general, especially in those systems which have been adopted from or based upon a foreign source. We here give the definitions used in these methods, as they differ in certain respects from those given with the entire pack of fifty-two cards. Special care must be taken when using the selected pack to notice which way the cards come out upon the table, whether upright or reversed, as the meanings of the two positions may be diametrically opposed.

How to Indicate Reversed Cards

In former days it was easier to distinguish between the top and the bottom of a card, but now that they are practically made reversible, with a few exceptions, it is necessary to mark the cards that are to be used for fortune-telling in such a way as to enable the dealer to say at a glance whether the card is reversed or not These marks should be made before the pack has been used, and need not be altered if the cards are kept solely for this purpose.

In the following pages this selected pack is required for several methods, and in the case of the Master Method it is augmented by the four twos taken from the excluded cards.

Meaning of the Hearts

Ace.– A love letter, good news; reversed, a removal or a visit from a friend.

King.– Fair man of generous disposition; reversed, a disappointing person.

Queen.– Fair, good–natured woman; reversed, she has had an unhappy love affair.

Knave.– A young bachelor devoted to enjoyment; reversed, a military lover with a grievance.

Ten.– Antidote to bad cards; happiness and success; reversed, passing worries.

Nine.– The wish card, good luck; reversed, short sorrow.

Eight.– Thoughts of marriage, affections of a fair person; reversed, unresponsiveness.

Seven.– Calm content; reversed, boredom, satiety.

Meaning of the Diamonds

Ace.– A letter, an offer of marriage; reversed, evil tidings.

King.– A very fair or white-haired man, a soldier by profession, and of a deceitful turn of mind; reversed, a treacherous schemer.

Queen.– A fair woman, given to gossip and wanting in refinement; reversed, rather a spiteful flirt

Knave.– Subordinate official, who is untrustworthy; reversed, a mischief-maker.

Ten.– Traveling or a removal; reversed, ill-luck will attend the step.

Nine.– Vexation, hindrances; reversed, domestic wrangling, or disagreement between lovers.

Eight.– Love passages; reversed, blighted affections.

Seven.– Unkindly chaff, cynicism; reversed, stupid and unfounded slander.

Meaning of the Clubs

Ace.– Good luck, letters or papers relating to money, pleasant tidings; reversed, short-lived happiness, a tiresome correspondence.

King.– A dark man, warm-hearted and true as a friend, straight in his dealings; reversed, good intentions frustrated.

Queen.– A dark woman, loving but hasty, and bearing no malice; reversed, harassed by jealousy.

Knave.– A ready-witted young man, clever at his work and ardent in his love; reversed, irresponsible and fickle.

Ten.– Prosperity and luxury; reversed, a sea voyage.

Nine.– An unlooked for inheritance, money acquired under a will; reversed, a small, friendly gift.

Eight.– Love of a dark man or woman which, if accepted and reciprocated, will bring joy and well-being; reversed, an unworthy affection calculated to cause trouble.

Seven.– Trifling financial matters; reversed, money troubles.

Meaning of the Spades

Ace.– Emotional enjoyment; reversed, news of a death, sorrow.

King.– A widower, an unscrupulous lawyer, impossible as a friend and dangerous as an enemy; reversed, the desire to work evil without the power.

Queen.– Widow, a very dark woman; reversed, an intriguing, spiteful woman.

Knave.– Legal or medical student, wanting in refinement of mind and manners; reversed, a treacherous character, fond of underhand measures.

Ten.– Grief, loss of freedom; reversed, passing trouble or illness.

Nine.– A bad omen, news of failure or death; reversed, loss of one near and dear by death.

Eight.– Coming illness; reversed, an engagement canceled or a rejected proposal, dissipation.

Seven.– Everyday worries, or a resolve taken; reversed, silly stratagems in love-making.

Chapter IV
The Signification of Quartettes, Triplets, and Pairs

Combinations of court cards – Combinations of plain cards – Various cards read together – General meaning of the several suits – Some lesser points to notice

Combinations of Court Cards

Four Aces.– When these fall together they imply danger, financial loss, separation from friends, love troubles, and, under some conditions, imprisonment. The evil is mitigated in proportion to the number of them that are reversed.

Three Aces. – Passing troubles, relieved by good news, faithlessness of a lover and consequent sorrow. If reversed, they mean foolish excess.

Two Aces.– These portend union; if hearts and clubs it will be for good, if diamonds and spades, for evil, probably the outcome of jealousy. If one or both be reversed, the object of the union will fail.

Four Kings.– Honors, preferment, good appointments. Reversed, the good things will be of less value, but will arrive earlier.

Three Kings.– Serious matters will be taken in hand with the best result, unless any of the three cards be reversed, when it will be doubtful.

Two Kings.– Cooperation in business, upright conduct and prudent enterprises to be crowned with success. Each one reversed represents an obstacle. All three reversed spell utter failure.

Combinations of Plain Cards

Four Queens.– A social gathering which may be spoilt by one or more being reversed.

Three Queens.– Friendly visits. Reversed, scandal, gossip, and possibly bodily danger to the inquirer.

Two Queens.– Petty confidences interchanged, secrets betrayed, a meeting between friends. When both are reversed there will be suffering for the inquirer resulting from his own acts. Only one reversed means rivalry.

Four Knaves.– Roistering and noisy conviviality. Any of them reversed lessens the evil.

Three Knaves.– Worries and vexations from acquaintances, slander calling the inquirer's honor in question. Reversed, it foretells a passage at arms with a social inferior.

Two Knaves. – Loss of goods, malicious schemes. If both are reversed the trouble is imminent; if one only, it is near.

Four Tens.– Good fortune, wealth, success in whatever enterprise is in hand. The more there are reversed, the greater number of obstacles in the way.

Three Tens.– Ruin brought about by litigation. When reversed the evil is decreased.

Two Tens.– Unexpected luck, which may be connected with a change of occupation. If one be reversed it will come soon, within a few weeks possibly; if both are reversed, it far long way off.

Four Nines.– Accomplishment of unexpected events. The number that are reversed stand for the time to elapse before the fulfillment of the surprise.

Three Nines.– Health, wealth, and happiness. Reversed, discussions and temporary financial difficulties caused by imprudence.

Two Nines.– Prosperity and contentment, possibly accompanied by business matter, testamentary documents, and possibly a change of residence. Reversed, small worries.

Four Eights.– Mingled success and failure attending a journey or the taking up of a new position. Reversed, undisturbed stability.

Three Eights. – Thoughts of love and marriage, new family ties, honorable intentions. Reversed, flirtation, dissipation and foolishness.

Two Eights.– Frivolous pleasures, passing love fancies, an unlooked for development. Reversed, paying the price of folly.

Four Sevens.– Schemes and snares, intrigue prompted by evil passions, contention and opposition. Reversed, small scores off impotent enemies.

Three Sevens.– Sadness from loss of friends, ill-health, remorse. Reversed, slight ailments or unpleasant reaction after great pleasure.

Two Sevens. – Mutual love, an unexpected event. Reversed, faithlessness, deceit or regret.

Various Cards Read Together

The ten of diamonds next to the seven of spades means certain delay.

The ten of diamonds with the eight of clubs tells of a journey undertaken in the cause of love.

The nine of diamonds with the eight of hearts foretells for certain a journey.

The eight of diamonds with the eight of hearts means considerable undertakings; with the eight of spades there will be sickness; and with the eight of clubs there is deep and lasting love.

The seven of diamonds with the queen of diamonds tells of a very serious quarrel; with the queen of clubs we may look for uncertainty; with the queen of hearts there will be good news.

The ten of clubs followed by an ace means a large sum of money; should these two cards be followed by an eight and a king, an offer of marriage is to be expected.

When the nine, ace, and ten of diamonds fall together we may look for important news from a distance; and if a court card comes out after them a journey will become necessary.

The eight and seven of diamonds in conjunction imply the existence of gossip and chatter to be traced to the inquirer.

When the king, queen, knave, and ace of one color appear in sequence it is a sign of marriage; should the queen of spades and the knave of hearts be near, it shows there are obstacles in the way; the proximity of the eight of spades bodes ill to the couple in question, but their happiness will be assured by the presence of the eight of hearts and the eight of clubs.

The ace of diamonds and the ten of hearts also foretell wedding bells.

The seven of spades, with either a court card or the two of its own suit, betrays the existence of a false friend.

The eight and five of spades coming together tell of jealousy that will find vent in malicious conduct

A number of small spades in sequence are significant of financial loss, possibly amounting to ruin.

The king of hearts and the nine of hearts form a lucky combination for lovers.

The nine of clubs joined to the nine of hearts is indicative of affairs connected with a will likely to benefit the inquirer.

The queen of spades is the sign of widowhood, but if accompanied by the knave of her own suit she is symbolical of a woman who is hostile and dangerous to the inquirer.

General Meaning of the Several Salts

Hearts, as might well be supposed, are specially connected with the work of Cupid and Hymen. The suit has also close reference to affairs of the home and to both the domestic and social sides of life.

Diamonds are mainly representative of financial matters, small and great, with a generally favorable signification.

Clubs are the happiest omens of all. They stand for worldly prosperity, a happy home life with intelligent pleasures and successful undertakings.

Spades, on the other hand, forebode evil. They speak of sickness, death, monetary losses and anxieties, separation from friends and dear ones, to say nothing of the minor worries of life. They are also representative of love, unaccompanied by reverence or respect, and appealing exclusively to the senses.

Some Lesser Points to Notice

When a number of court cards fall together it is a sign of hospitality, festive social intercourse, and gaiety of all kinds.

Married people who seek to read the cards must represent their own life partner by the king or queen of the suit they have chosen for themselves, regardless of anything else. For example, a very dark man, the king of spades, must consider his wife represented by the queen of spades, even though she may be as fair as a lily and not yet a widow.

Bachelors and spinsters may choose cards to personate their lovers and friends according to their coloring.

Two red tens coming together foretell a wedding, and two red eights promise new garments to the inquirer.

A court card placed between two cards of the same grade –for instance, two nines, two sevens, & c., shows that the one represented by that card is threatened by the clutches of the law, and may be lodged at His Majesty's expense.

It is considered a good augury of success when, in dealing the cards out, those of lesser value than the knave are in the majority, especially if they are clubs.

Should a military man consult the cards he must always be represented by the king of diamonds.

It is always essential to cut cards with the left hand, there being a long-established idea that it is more intimately connected with the heart than the right. A round table is generally preferred by those who are in the habit of practicing cartomancy. It is a matter of opinion as to whether the cards speak with the same clearness and accuracy when consulted by the inquirer without an intermediary. The services of an adept are generally supposed to be of great advantage, even when people have mastered the rudiments of cartomancy themselves.

Patience, the power of putting two and two together, a quick intuitive perception, and a touch of mysticism in the character, are all useful factors in the pursuit of this pastime

Chapter V
What the Cards can Tell of the Past, the Present, and the Future

A simple method – What the cards say – The present – The future

A Simple Method

There is a very simple and generally-accepted method of studying the past, the present, and the future in the light of cartomancy. The selected pack of thirty-two cards is required, and they must be shuffled and cut in the ordinary way. After the cut the packs must not be placed one upon the other until the top card of the lower one and the bottom card of the upper one have been placed aside to form the surprise. The remaining thirty cards are then to be dealt into three equal packs which, beginning at the left, represent respectively the Past, the Present, and the Future.

We will suppose that the knave of hearts, a pleasure-seeking young bachelor, is the inquirer.

The ten cards representing the Past are as follows:

The queen of clubs, reversed.
The king of diamonds, reversed
The ten of clubs, reversed.
The nine of diamonds.
The eight of clubs.
The ace of diamonds, reversed.
The ace of hearts, reversed.
The knave of spades, reversed.
The queen of spades, reversed.
The eight of diamonds.

There are three pairs among the ten. Two queens, both reversed, which remind the inquirer that he has had to suffer from the consequences of his own actions. The two aces, also both reversed, refer to some partnership into which he entered with good intentions but which was doomed to failure. The two eights speak of his frivolous pleasures and countless evanescent love affairs.

What the Cards Say

We will now see what the cards have to say, taken in order. We begin with the queen of clubs, reversed, a dark woman tormented by jealousy, in which she was encouraged by the king of diamonds, reversed, who is a treacherous schemer, wishing no good to the inquirer. The ten of clubs tells of a sea voyage, and is followed by the nine of diamonds, showing that there were vexations and annoyances on that voyage. The eight of clubs speaks of the Inquirer's having possessed the affections of a dark woman, who would have contributed largely to his prosperity and happiness. The ace of diamonds, reversed, represents evil tidings that reached him in connection with the ace of hearts, reversed, which stands for a change of abode, and emanating from the knave of spades, reversed, a legal agent who was not to be trusted. There was also the queen of spades, a designing widow, with whom he had, the eight of diamonds, certain love passages.

The Present

The ten cards in the center pack are as follows:
Ace of spades, reversed.
Seven of diamonds.
Eight of hearts.
Queen of hearts.
Seven of hearts.
Queen of diamonds, reversed.
Nine of spades.
King of hearts, reversed.
Knave of hearts, reversed.
Ten of diamonds.

The Future

In this pack we have only two pairs, two sevens speaking of mutual love; and two queens, one being reversed, which suggest rivalry.

Taken in order the pack reads thus:

The ace of spades, reversed, speaks of sorrow in which he will be treated with a certain amount of heartless chaff and want of sympathy, as it is followed by the seven of diamonds. The eight of hearts tells us that he is entertaining thoughts of marriage, with the queen of hearts, a fair, lovable girl; but the seven of hearts shows that he is very contented with his present condition and in no hurry to change it. He is amusing himself with the queen of diamonds, reversed, who is a born flirt, but more spiteful than he suspects, and who is next to the worst card in the pack, the nine of spades, indicative of the harm she does to him, and the failure of his matrimonial plans. He is cut out by the king of hearts, who thus causes him a serious disappointment, and we see him, himself, reversed as the lover with a grievance; the last card is the ten of diamonds, so he has decided to ease his heartache by traveling.

This pack contains the following cards:
The knave of diamonds, reversed.
The seven of clubs.
The eight of spades, reversed.

The seven of spades, reversed.
The ten of spades.
The nine of hearts.
The king of clubs.
The ten of hearts.
The king of spades.
The ace of clubs, reversed.

The presence of four spades foretells that trouble awaits our bachelor. We again have a pair of sevens, but one is reversed, so he may expect deceit to be at work. The two tens promise him an unlooked for stroke of luck to be met with in a new walk in life, while the two kings speak of cooperation in business, and of the success which will crown his upright and practical conduct. The wish card, the nine of hearts, and the ten of hearts in a great measure counteract the mischief represented by the spades.

The inquirer must beware of the knave of diamonds, reversed, who is a mischief maker, who will make use of the seven of clubs, trifling financial matters, either to break off an engagement or to cause an offer of marriage to be refused, as shown by the eight of spades, reversed. The chagrined lover will have recourse to silly stratagems in his love-making, the seven of spades, reversed, and this error will cause him grief, even to the shedding of tears, the ten of spades. The wish card, the nine of hearts, however, brings him better luck in his love affairs through the instrumentality of his trusty, generous friend, the king of clubs. His ill-fortune is further discounted by the next card, the ten of hearts, which promises him prosperity and success. He will find an enemy in the king of spades, a dark widower, who is a lawyer by profession, and none too scrupulous in his ways. He may expect a good deal of troublesome correspondence with this man, as shown by the last card, the ace of clubs, reversed.

The subject of this correspondence is possibly to be found in the surprise, which consists of the nine of dubs, reversed, meaning an unexpected acquisition of money under a will. He will do well to take heed when in the companionship oft he knave of clubs, reversed, the second card of the surprise for he is a flatterer and a somewhat irresponsible character.

Chapter VI
Your Fortune in Twenty-one Cards

A reduced pack – An example – The three packs – The surprise

This method requires a pack of thirty-two cards, although only twenty-one of them are actually used in the process. The whole pack must be well shuffled and cut with the left hand. The dealer then takes off the first eleven cards and throws them aside. From the twenty-one left in his hand he takes the uppermost card and places it apart for "the surprise" before dealing out the other twenty and placing them in order on the table before him. If the card representing the inquirer is not among them the whole process must be repeated from the beginning.

The signification of the cards must be read, taking care to notice any set of two, three, or four of a kind, as their collective meaning should be added to the individual explanation. After this has been done the twenty cards should be taken in order, starting from the left, and their meanings linked up together as a continuous message.

The cards must now be taken up again, shuffled, and cut as before. The dealer then makes them into three packs, having been careful to place the first card apart for "the surprise". Two of the packs will consist of seven cards, the third of only six. The inquirer is then asked to choose one of the packs, which must be exposed face upwards, moving from left to right, and these six or seven cards, as the case may be, should be read according to their significations. This operation is repeated three times, so that at the finish "the surprise" consists of three cards, which are exposed and read last of all.

An Example

The accompanying example will make the foregoing explanation more lucid and interesting.

We will take the knave of clubs as the representative of the inquirer, a dark, clever, well-intentioned young man. The twenty-one cards come out in the following order, beginning from the left:

The king of spades.
Queen of hearts, reversed.
Ace of hearts.
Knave of clubs.
Ace of spades, reversed.
Ace of clubs.
Knave of hearts.
King of hearts.
Queen of spades, reversed.
Nine of hearts.
Knave of diamonds.
Ten of spades.
Ace of diamonds, reversed.
King of diamonds.
Seven of diamonds.
Eight of diamonds.
Eight of spades, reversed.
Seven of clubs, reversed.
Nine of clubs, reversed.
Nine of diamonds.
The surprise, placed apart

Before taking the individual significance of each card we will look at some of the combinations. There are the four aces, telling of bad news, relating to trouble through the affections, but two being reversed mitigate the evil, and give a ray of hope to the inquirer. The three kings tell of an important undertaking which will be discussed and carried through successfully by the young man, who has excellent abilities. The two queens, both reversed, warn the inquirer that he will suffer from the result of his own actions, more especially as the queen of spades in an inverted position represents a malicious and designing widow. It will be found as the process develops that she is very much to the fore with regard to the inquirer's affairs. The three knaves confirm the foregoing reading, for they betoken annoyances and worries from acquaintances, ending even in slander. The three nines, one of them reversed, speak of happiness and entire success in an undertaking, though the inversion shows that there will be as light, passing difficulty to overcome. The two eights refer to flirtations on the part of the inquirer, and one being reversed warns him that he will have to pay for some of his fun. The two sevens tell of mutual love between the young man and the lady of his choice, but as the one is reversed there will be deceit at work to try and separate them.

Now let us see what the twenty cards have to say taken consecutively. We start off with the king of spades, a clever, ambitious, but unscrupulous man who has been instrumental in thwarting the love affairs of the fair, lovable, and tender-hearted woman, the queen of hearts, upon whom the inquirer has set his affections. The ace of hearts following her is the love letter she will receive from the inquirer, the knave of clubs; but he is next to the ace of spades, reversed, foretelling grief to him, which may affect his health, and the ace of clubs coming immediately after points to the cause being connected with money. The next three cards are court cards, and that means gaiety, in which the inquirer will be mixed up with a lively young bachelor –the knave of hearts– a fair, generous, but hot-tempered man –the king of diamonds– and the malicious, spiteful widow represented by the queen of spades, reversed. The inquirer will meet with pleasure, caused by success, the nine of hearts; but this is closely followed by the knave of diamonds, an unfaithful friend, who will try to bring disgrace, the ten of spades, upon his betters, and will write a letter containing unpleasant news –the ace of diamonds, reversed– which will concern or be prompted by the king of diamonds, a military man who has a grievance with regard to his love affairs and who is not above having recourse to scandal, the seven of diamonds, to avenge his wounded vanity. The next card is the eight of diamonds, the sign of some love-making, but our young people are not at the end of their troubles yet, for the eight of spades, reversed, tells us that this offer of marriage will be rejected. The seven of clubs is a card of caution, and implies danger from the opposite sex, so we gather that the spiteful widow has been at work, and is possibly to blame for his rejection; this idea is further strengthened by the nine of clubs, also reversed, coming immediately, which suggests letters that may have done the mischief. The nine of diamonds tells of the annoyance caused by these events, and their effect upon the affections of a dark person, the inquirer, who is a man well worth having.

The Three Packs

In the first deal the inquirer chooses the middle pack, which contains the following cards: the knave of diamonds, the seven of diamonds, the ace of clubs, the queen of spades, reversed, the ace of spades, the ace of diamonds, the eight of diamonds.

We notice that three aces come out in this pack and show passing troubles in love affairs. The knave of diamonds, an unfaithful friend, is mixed up in scandal, the seven of diamonds, conveyed in a letter, the ace of clubs, written or instigated by the spiteful widow, the queen of spades. The ace of spades betokens sickness, but it is followed by the ace of diamonds, the wedding ring, and the pack closes with the eight of diamonds, telling of a happy marriage for the inquirer after all his worries.

In the second deal he again selects the middle pack, and we see the following: the queen of spades, reversed as usual, the nine of clubs, reversed, the seven of clubs, reversed, the nine of hearts, the seven of diamonds, the eight of clubs.

There are two nines, one reversed, speaking of small worries, and two sevens, one reversed, which show there is deceit at work. The pack reads thus: the queen of spades, the spiteful widow, who seems to be ubiquitous, is followed by the nine of clubs, representing the letter referred to above, and the seven of clubs standing next to it sounds a word of caution to the inquirer as to his lady friend, so-called; he will probably succeed in outwitting the widow, for the next card is the nine of hearts, implying joy and success in spite of scandal, the seven of diamonds with reference to his affections represented by the eight of clubs.

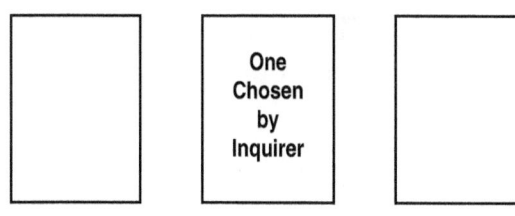

What the first selected pack contains:

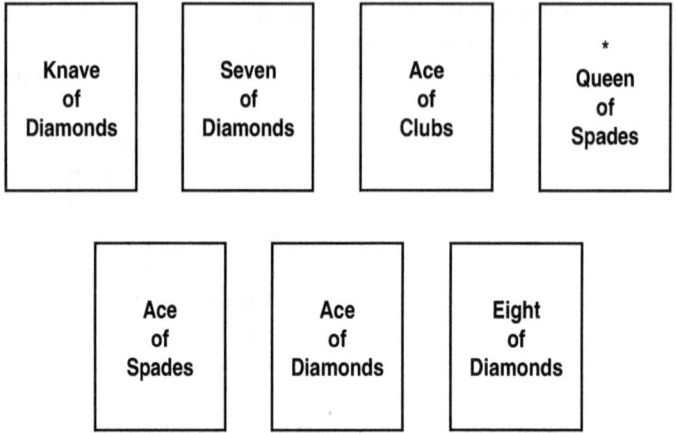

The three cards forming the Surprise:

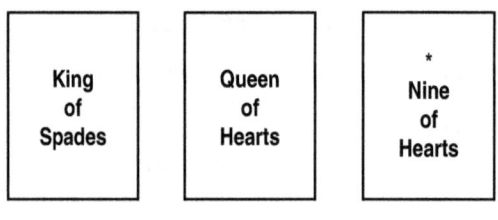

* Means "reversed"

In the third deal the inquirer still is faithful to the middle pack, and we find the following cards: the ace of diamonds, ten of spades, reversed, queen of spades, reversed, nine of diamonds, reversed, seven of clubs, reversed, ace of clubs, reversed.

The two aces, one of them reversed, tell of a union between two parties, but as the colors cross and one is reversed the result will not be known at present. Here we get the wedding-ring, the ace of diamonds, followed by the ten of spades, reversed, which speaks of brief sorrow, occasioned doubtless by the spiteful widow, who again appears reversed, and intent upon mischief; next to her comes the nine of diamonds, reversed, signifying a love quarrel; the seven of dubs, reversed, gives a word of caution to the inquirer with regard to the opposite sex; the last card is the ace of clubs, reversed, which means joy soon followed by sorrow.

It is remarkable that the queen of spades comes out in each of the packs and is reversed every time.

The Surprise

The surprise is now turned up and contains the king of spades, a dark, ambitious unscrupulous man who has interfered with the love affairs of the fair woman, the queen of hearts, to whom the inquirer has made an offer, so far without success; the third card is the nine of hearts, reversed, which tells that it will be but a passing cloud that will separate the lovers.

Chapter VII
Combination of Sevens

A method with selected cards – General rules – How to proceed – Heading of the cards – Signification of cards – Some combinations – A typical example – Further inquiries – The seven packs

A Method with Selected Cards

This method is very simple, and as it takes but a short time, is more suitable when there are many fortunes to read. A little practice will soon enable a would-be cartomancer to construe the various combinations, as there are so few cards to remember.

It may be objected that meanings are now given different from those taught in the first method. This is certainly a fact, but it also an advantage; one method may suit one person's abilities and intuitiveness better than another, and so enable a more comprehensive reading to be given from the diminished pack than from the full pack.

General Rules

Thirty-two cards only are selected from an ordinary pack of playing cards. In each suit the ace, king, queen, knave, ten, nine, eight, and seven are retained; all the others, those from two to six inclusively, are discarded.

The cards must be shuffled and cut into three sections by the inquirer, each cut being turned face upwards. The manipulator must carefully note the result of these cuts, as they give an indication of what is coming. Then the center pack is to be taken first, the last next, and the first last of all.

Holding this newly arranged pack in the left hand, draw off three cards, and facing them upwards, select the highest card of any suit that may appear. Retain this one and put the others aside for the next deal. Proceed in this way until you have finished the pack, then shuffle all the discard together, and repeat until you have any number over twenty-one on the table. If three cards of any suit should appear, or three cards of the same value, they are all to be taken.

It must not be forgotten that the cards are also selected from the "cuts," and should the lifting of one card reveal another of greater value of the same suit exposed, then that also is retained.

How to Proceed

The first question to decide is which card will represent the inquirer. This is generally settled according to the complexion: diamonds for the very fair; hearts, those of medium coloring; clubs for brunettes with brown hair; and spades for those of dark complexion. This suit also represents elderly people. A king represents a man, and a queen a woman. This representative card is not to be drawn out; it is shuffled with the others, and taken when it is the highest of its suit. The only exception to this rule is, when there have been already twenty-one or more cards selected, then it must be taken from the remainder and placed last of all

Reading of the Cards

The reading in this method is from left to right, and the cards are to be placed in a semi-circle or horse-shoe, in the order they are drawn.

Court cards represent people, and the numbers relate to events. Generally diamonds relate to money and interest; hearts, to the affections; clubs, to business; spades, to the more serious affairs of life.

The signification of each card is given separately, as well as of some of the combinations, and an example of a fortune is worked out, the study of which will more easily enable a student to understand this method.

Signification of Cards

Hearths

King	A man with brown hair and blue eyes.
Queen	A woman of similar complexion.
Knave	A friend with good intentions.
Ten	Marriage.
Nine	Wish.
Eight	Affection.
Seven	Friendship.
Ace	House.

Diamonds

King	A fair man.
Queen	A fair woman.
Knave	A friend.
Ten	Wealthy marriage.
Nine	Rise in social position.
Eight	Success with speculation.
Seven	A good income.
Ace	A wedding or present of jewelry.

Clubs

King	A man who is neither fair nor dark.
Queen	A woman in middle life.
Knave	A business friend.
Ten	Journey by water.
Nine	Successful business.
Eight	Preasure in Society.
Seven	A business affair.
Ace	A letter, cheque, or legal document.

Spades

King	A dark man.
Queen	A dark woman (or widow).
Knave	Personal thoughts.
Ten	A journey by land.
Nine	Illness or sorrow.
Eight	A loss.
Seven	A disagreement.
Ace (right way)	Responsible position in the service of the Crown.
Ace (upside down)	Sorrow or death.

Some of the Combinations

Three kings: a new friend; two kings and a knave: meeting with an old friend; three knaves: legal business; three queens: a disagreement with women; three tens: very fortunate combination. If the ten of clubs and the ten of hearts appear with the ten of diamonds, it will easily be seen that a wealthy marriage will take place after a journey across the water.

Three nines: very speedy good news; three eights: a removal; three sevens: speedy news, but not altogether satisfactory; three aces: very good fortune; the ace of clubs and the ace of diamonds would signify an offer of marriage by letter.

The ace and nine of hearts mean that you will have the realization of your heart's desire in your own house; the ace and nine of spades: that sorrow and death will come to your family; the king and queen of any suit, with the ten of hearts, is a sign that you will hear of a marriage shortly.

A Typical Example

Now we will proceed to read a fortune, and for the subject we will take the queen of hearts. The first shuffle and division of the pack into three reveals three hearts –king, knave, and seven– which indicates that the lady whom the queen represents has a firm man friend, who is neither fair nor dark. These three cards are taken and laid in order, beginning on the left hand.

Then the packs having been taken in order as described, and held in the left hand, the fortune-teller proceeds to draw off three cards, and make his selection according to the rule. The pack being finished, the process is repeated twice more.

In three deals the fortune of the queen of hearts revealed the following cards, and if a student will take a pack of cards and select the same, he can judge how the various combinations may be read.

King, knave, seven of hearts, ace of clubs, king of spades, queen of clubs, queen of diamonds, queen of spades, king of clubs, knave of diamonds, ace of hearts, knave of spades, king of diamonds, knave of clubs, queen of hearts, ace of diamonds, ten of hearts, eight of clubs, seven of spades, ace of spades, ten of clubs, ten of spades, ten of diamonds.

Now, from the queen of hearts we will proceed to count seven, taking into consideration the way the lady's face is turned It is to the left, consequently the seventh card from her is the queen of spades, the seventh from which is the king of hearts, and the seventh again is the ten of hearts. I read this that the lady has some good friends; but that the woman whom the queen of spades represents will resent her marriage, but without effect. The next card is the knave of diamonds, followed by the seven of hearts and the seven of spades –a combination which represents some speedy news, not exactly to the advantage of the inquirer. The knave of spades, followed by the king and the ten of clubs, denotes that a dark man, who is separated from the queen of hearts, is constantly thinking of her and hoping for a speedy reunion.

The knave of clubs and the queen of diamonds come next. Knaves and women form a conjunction that never brings good luck; but in this case they are followed by the ten of diamonds, one of the most fortunate cards in the pack. The ace of diamonds and the king of clubs follow, which means an offer of marriage shortly. The queen of hearts is indeed a sad coquette, for there is no indication that she accepts this, as the knave of hearts, with the eight of clubs and the ace of hearts, are quickly on the scene. It appears that there is another wooer who comes to her home and is received with pleasure.

More serious affairs appear now; the ace of clubs, with the ace of spades and the king of diamonds, signify that the lady is likely to have some business with which a woman darker than herself is connected. This will lead to a considerable journey, which she will immediately take, as the card denoting this counts seven directly to her.

Now we will look at the cards as they lie on the table. For a reading taken at random they foretell a very good future. All the court cards and the aces and tens are out, with the seven of hearts and the eight of clubs, and all are cards of favorable import

Three queens together generally betoken some mischief or scandal, but as they are guarded by kings it will probably not amount to much. The ace of diamonds and the ten of hearts placed so near the representative card would surely tell us of a forthcoming marriage, except that the queen has her face turned away from it. The three tens placed as they are tell of prosperity after journeys by land and water.

Now we will pair the cards and see if any more meaning can be extracted from them. On land and on the water this lady will meet a rich man who will entertain a strong affection for her. I must not omit to mention that the cards are paired from the extreme ends of the horse-shoe. Thus the king of hearts and the ten of diamonds, knave of hearts and ten of spades, &c. The business appears again, and a dark man seems to be in some perplexity. The three queens are not yet separated and are in closer connection with the inquirer than ever. Oh! there will be chatting over the tea-cups about a marriage. The fair damsel herself appears to be a little more inclined to matrimony, but the three knaves imply that she will have some difficulty in settling her affairs.

The two kings imply that she has some staunch friends, and that the result will be quite satisfactory. A general reading gives the impression that the queen of hearts is of a lovable disposition and fond of society, as so many court cards came out, and if the three queens meant a little gossip it was in a kindly spirit

Further Inquiries

There is another little ceremony to be gone through which will tell us if she is likely to have her "heart's desire" realized. The nine of hearts, which is the symbol of a wish, did not appear, so that she is apparently very cool, and neutral. However, the other cards may tell us something.

The used cards are to be shuffled and cut once by the inquirer, and she may wish for anything she likes during the process. Then the cards are laid out one at a time in seven packs –six packs in a semicircle, and one in the centre– the cards of the last are to be turned face upwards, but none of the other cards are to be exposed until the end.

The Seven Packs

The seven packs represent respectively: "yourself", "your house," "what you expect," "what you don't expect," "a great surprise," "what is sure to come true," and "the wish".

The cards, having been shuffled and cut once, are dealt out in the manner described, and these are the combinations we get:

First Pack.– Queen of, spades, queen of hearts, ten of clubs, seven of hearts.
Second.– Ace of spades, knave of clubs, ace of diamonds and ten of spades.
Third.– Knave of spades, king of diamonds, knave of hearts.
Fourth.– Queen of clubs, seven of spades, king of spades.

Fifth.– Ten of diamonds, eight of clubs, and queen of diamonds.
Sixth.– King of hearts, ten of hearts, king of clubs.
Fifth.– Ace of hearts, knave of diamonds, ace of clubs.

The first pack represents to me the meeting of the inquirer with a dark or elderly woman, for whom she has a strong affection. Water is crossed before that meeting takes place.

The second pack reads as if a dark man would offer a ring or a present of jewelry, and also that he is meditating a journey by land. He is probably a professional man, or in the service of the Crown.

The third pack, with its combination of knaves and king, has reference to business transactions which will most probably be favourable to the interests of the queen.

The fourth pack presages some slight disappointment, illness, or unhappiness in connection with some friends.

The fifth pack tells us that some brilliant fortune is awaiting a fair friend that will lead to a higher social position.

The sixth pack tells us that, perhaps, our seemingly indifferent queen of hearts has a slight tenderness for some one. He is older than she is, and is only waiting for an opportunity to declare his affection. If the wish related to such a man as I have described, she may be certain of its fulfillment, even should there be a slight delay.

The seventh or wish pack is extremely good, and tells us that many affairs will be transacted by writing.

The future of the queen of hearts is fair and bright, her disposition is lovable, and she will bring happiness to other people.

This example is not made up of selected cards. They were shuffled, cut, and drawn in the ordinary way. I say this because so few cards of bad import have appeared, and it might be thought these were chosen in order to avoid prophesying disappointments.

In the foregoing example twenty-three cards were dealt out, but the number may vary. It must, however, be an uneven number. Sometimes only fifteen or seventeen cards are taken, and with the smaller quantity of selected cards there is an optional way of concluding operations. After having read the pairs, the cards are gathered up, shuffled, and cut into *three packs* instead of seven. These three are placed in a row, and a fourth card is put apart for *the surprise*. The inquirer is requested to choose one of the three packs, which represent respectively: For *the house*, For *those who did not expect it*, and For *the inquirer* –the last being decided by the choice of the person in question.

When these three packs have been duly read, all the cards are again taken up except The Surprise (which is left face downwards on the table), and dealt out again, the same process being repeated three times until there are three cards set aside for the surprise. These are read last of all, and form the concluding message to the inquirer. Let's hope it may be a cheerful one.

Chapter VIII
Another Method

General outline – Signification of cards – How to consult the cards – An illustration – Its reading

Here again the pack of thirty-two cards is used, the cards from two to six inclusively being discarded, as in "The Combination of Sevens".

General Outline

The general meaning pertaining to each suit is as follows: The court cards bear the signification of people, and the king, queen, and knave in each suit suggest relationship. The kings indicate the profession followed.

Thus, the king of spades denotes a literary man, or one whose desires would lead him to the pulpit or the platform.

The king of hearts is the symbol of a wealthy man –one who deals with large sums of money– for instance, a banker, capitalist, or stockbroker.

The king of clubs indicates the mental side of business, and here we look for the lawyer or barrister.

The king of diamonds is a business man –one who will depend on both his brain and hands for work. Diamonds are eminently the practical suit, and must always be consulted with reference to the subject's condition in life. They signify the material side of life, and according to the needs, so this suit indicates success, or the absence of it –failure.

There is a very slight variation in the signification of the cards as given in the preceding method, but it is well too observe it carefully, as the mode of procedure is entirely different

Signification of Cards

	Hearts
Ace	Quietness and domestic happiness.
Seven	Love.
Eight	A surprise.
Nine	A wish.
Ten	A wedding.
	Diamonds
Ace	A letter or ring.
Seven	A journey.
Eight	Society.
Nine	Illness, or news of a birth.
Ten	Money, joy success.
	Spades
Ace	Service under the Crown.
Reverse ace	A death.
Seven	Unpleasant news.
Eight	Sorrow or vexation.
Nine	Quarrels.
Ten	A disappointment.
	Clubs
Ace	A present.
Seven	Gain; good business.
Eight	Pleasure.
Nine	A proposal.
Ten	A journey by water.

How to Consult the Cards

The inquirer is to shuffle the pack of cards and cut it into three. Take up the cards and let your subject draw any chance card that he pleases. Place this card on the table, and the suit from which it is drawn will determine the representative card, as it is an indication of the character of your subject.

Fortune Telling by Cards

A lady is represented by a queen, a man by a king, and the knave stands for the male relations or thoughts.

After the card is drawn, place the remainder on the table in four rows, beginning each row from left to right.

The cards that immediately surround the king or queen aid us in our judgment of the inquirer; and remember that the right hand card is the more important one.

An Illustration

A practical illustration will exemplify my meaning, and again we will suppose a lady has cut the cards to have her fortune read.

The cards being shuffled and cut into three, the card was drawn, and as this proved to be a seven of clubs, so the queen represented the subject in this instance. When the cards were placed in order this is how they appeared.

First line.– Seven of clubs, eight of clubs, king of clubs, seven of hearts, king of diamonds, nine of diamonds, ten of diamonds, king of hearts.

Second line.– Seven of spades, nine of spades, knave of hearts, king of spades, eight of spades, queen of spades, ten of spades, ace of diamonds.

Third line.– Ace of spades, knave of clubs, queen of clubs, ten of hearts, ace of hearts, queen of diamonds, ace of clubs, nine of hearts.

Fourth line.– Knave of spades, seven of diamonds, eight of hearts, nine of clubs, eight of diamonds, knave of diamonds, queen of hearts, ten of clubs.

Its Reading

Now we can proceed with the reading:

As the suit of clubs is a pleasant one, we may conclude the lady is of a cheerful temperament. The seven itself signifies gain and prosperity, and the eight pleasure, which come to the inquirer through the king of clubs –typical of a solicitor. The seven of hearts indicates that a fair man is in love with the inquirer. The nine of diamonds, with the joyful ten beside it, seems to foretell a birth, and the king of hearts stands for a good friend. But the seven and nine of spades, in conjunction, inform us that some annoyance is coming which is possibly connected with the king of hearts.

The king of spades, accompanied by the eight of that suit, tells that this man is suffering considerable grief and vexation on account of the queen of clubs, suffering which will cause another woman to be jealous.

The queen and ten of spades, with the ace of spades, imply disagreeable tidings; but as the knave of clubs appears side by side with the queen of that suit (the inquirer), and they are followed by the ten of hearts, it will in no wise disturb the affection of either. The knave here may be taken to indicate the thoughts or intentions of the king. The ace of hearts seems to promise great tranquility and happiness in the domestic life. A near relation, one deeply interested in the queen of clubs, is represented by the queen of diamonds. The ace of clubs shows that a letter is on its way.

The nine of hearts, the wish or betrothal card, follows, and from this I should infer that a proposal of marriage will come by letter, and one which will most probably be accepted. The knave of spades is followed by the seven of diamonds and the eight of hearts, which shows that the queen of clubs has been much loved by some one, and that an offer of marriage will have to be considered either directly before or immediately after a journey. The inquirer will have a great deal of pleasure on a journey. The queen of hearts and knave of diamonds indicate good friends who show her much kindness, and there will be welcome tidings for her across the water.

Now, count the rows, and should the betrothal card (the nine of hearts) appear in the third or fourth row, that number of years must elapse before becoming affianced.

Count the rows again until the one in which the ten of hearts (the marriage card) appears. In this example the betrothal and marriage card both appear in the third row, which indicates that the inquirer will be engaged in about three years and marriage will take place soon after.

Chapter IX
A French Method

French system – The reading – An example

French System

Take the pack of thirty-two cards, shuffle them thoroughly, then cut them in the usual way and deal them out in two packs of sixteen cards each. The inquirer must choose one of the packs and the first card is placed apart to supply the surprise. The remaining fifteen cards must then be turned face upwards, and placed in order, from left to right, before the dealer. It is essential that the card representing the inquirer should be found in the pack selected by him or her, otherwise it is useless to proceed; so the cards must be shuffled, cut, and dealt out over and over again, until the representative card is found in the right quarter.

The Reading

The reading is conducted as follows. First, take any two, three, or four of a kind, kings, knaves, eights, or whatever may appear, and give their explanation as pairs, triplets, or quartettes; then start from the representative card, and count in sevens, moving from right to left; thirdly, pair the end cards together and consider their meaning. The next move is to shuffle the fifteen cards again, cut, and deal them out into three packs, each of which will naturally have five cards. The uppermost card of the three packs is removed, and placed with that which has been set apart for "The Surprise", and by this arrangement there will be four packs containing an equal number of cards.

The inquirer must then be asked to choose one of these packs for himself or herself, after which the four cards are exposed on the table from left to right, and their individual and collective meanings are read. The left hand pack will be for "The House," the third pack is "For Those Who do not Expect It," and the fourth supplies "The Surprise."

An Example

Here is an example of the way in which the packs may turn out. We will suppose that the inquirer is represented by the queen of clubs. Her choice falls on the middle pack, which contains the following cards: the knave of clubs, the eight of diamonds, reversed, the eight of hearts, and the queen of spades.

I. For the Inquirer

| Knave of Clubs | Eight of Diamonds (reversed) | Eight of Hearts | Queen of Spades (reversed) |

The reading will be thus, taking the cards in the above order: The thoughts of the inquirer are running upon an unsuccessful love-affair, and, though moving in good society, she is exposed to the interference of a dark, malicious widow.

The next pack, standing for "The House", is made up of the knave of spades, the ace of spades, the king of spades, and the knave of hearts. We will take their significations as they stand. The three spades mean disappointment. The presence of two knaves together speaks of evil intentions.

The legal agent, knave of spades, is employed In some underhand business by his master, king of spades, the dishonest lawyer, who is an enemy to the inquirer just as he is that of her friend, the festive, thoughtless young bachelor, knave hearts, who follows him.

II. The House

| Knave of Spades | Ace of Spades | King of Spades | Knave of Hearts (reversed) |

The third pack is composed of the nine of clubs, reversed, the ace of clubs, the ten of spades, and the queen of hearts. We find short-lived joy and good news, followed by tears, for the fair, soft-hearted lady, who is susceptible to the attractions of the other sex.

III. For Those who do not Expect

| Nine of Clubs (reversed) | Ace of Clubs | Ten of Spades | Queen of Hearts |

Fortune Telling by Cards 519

"The Surprise" is very closely connected with the inquirer herself, for we find her included in the four cards. There are the ace of hearts, the queen of cubs, the nine of diamond and the seven of diamonds. From this we gather that there is a love letter for the inquirer, which, however, may be delayed by some accident, and she will thus be exposed to the foolish ridicule of tactless, unkindly persons. Bat she will get the letter all the same.

IV. The Surprise

| Ace of Hearts | Queen of Clubs | Nine of Diamonds | Seven of Diamonds |

Chapter X
The Grand Star

The number of cards may vary – The method – The reading in pairs – Diagram of the Grand Star – An example

The Number of Cards may Vary

There are various ways of telling fortunes with cards arranged in the form of a star, and whichever of these may be preferred, it will always be found necessary to use an uneven number of cards in addition to the one representing the inquirer. Some stars are done with thirteen cards, some with fifteen, and so on, but the real Grand Star must have twenty-one cards placed round the representative one.

The Method

Suppose the inquirer be a fair man, the king of hearts would be the card selected to form the centre of the star. This representative card is placed face upwards on the table, and the remaining thirty-one cards of the pack (the twos, threes, fours, fives, and sixes having been previously removed) must then be shuffled, and cut with the left hand.

In the accompanying diagram the cards are numbered in the order that they are placed in upon the table, taking the representative as No. 1. The mode of withdrawing the cards from the pack is as follows: The first ten cards are thrown aside after the first cut, and the eleventh card is placed *below* No. 1; then cut out a second time, and place the *top* card of the pack on the table above No. 1; cut a third time, take the bottom card of the pack in the hand and place it to the left of No. 1. The cards must be cut every time a card is to be withdrawn, and they are taken alternately from the top and bottom of the pack as above directed. Great care should be observed in the placing of the cards in due order, as any deviation will affect the reading at a subsequent stage of the process. The last card, No. 22, is placed across the foot of the representative.

The Reading in Pairs

When the Grand Star has been thus formed, the cards must read in pairs, taking the outside circle in this order: 14 and 16, 21 and 19, 15 and 17, 20 and 18. Then take the inner circle, moving from left to right thus: 6 and 10, 9 and 12, 8 and 13, 7 and 11; the four centre points are paired thus: 4 and 2, 5 and 3; and the last card, No. 22, is taken separately. The significations are, of course, taken with regard to the relative positions of the cards, and their special reference to the central figure of the inquirer. This is a picturesque and simple way of consulting the cards, and will probably be a favourite with most people.

Diagram of the Grand Star

The central card, No. 1, represents the inquirer, and each card is numbered in the order in which it is taken from the pack.

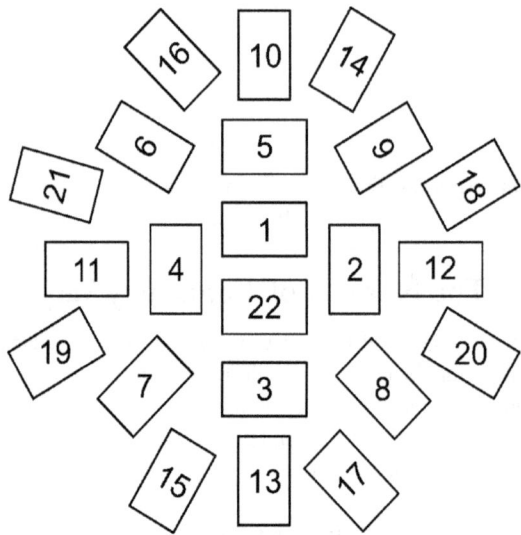

An Example

We will take the king of hearts as representative of the inquirer, and the twenty-one cards come out in the following order:
1. King of hearts.
2. Ten of spades.
3. Ten of hearts.
4. Ace of hearts.
5. Nine of spades.
6. Ace of spades.
7. Nine of diamonds, reversed.
8. Queen of hearts.
9. Knave of diamonds.
10. Queen of spades.

11. Knave of clubs.
12. King of clubs.
13. Eight of clubs.
14. Queen of diamonds.
15. Nine of clubs, reversed.
16. King of spades.
17. Queen of clubs.
18. Eight of diamonds, reversed.
19. Ace of diamonds.
20. Knave of spades.
21. Knave of hearts
22. Ace of clubs.

Before taking the above in pairs as directed, it will be well to glance at the groups contained in the star as it lies before us. We find:

Four aces.– Love troubles and hasty news for the inquirer.

Three kings.– Success in an important undertaking.

Four queens.– A good deal of social intercourse.

Four knaves.– Somewhat noisy conviviality.

Two tens.– Unexpected good luck.

Three nines.– Health, wealth, and happiness discounted by imprudence as one is reversed.

Two eights.– Passing love fancies, one being reversed.

The king of hearts, a fair, open-handed, good-natured man is the starting-point in reading the pairs which surround him. He is connected with (14) the queen of diamonds, a fair woman with a tendency to flirtation. She is amusing herself with (16) a very dark man, probably a lawyer, of an ambitious and not too scrupulous character, who does not wish well to the inquirer. The next pair (21) shows the knave of hearts, representing Cupid, or the thoughts of the one concerned, linked with (19) the ace of diamonds, a wedding ring. While this important item is occupying his thoughts he gives a small present (15), the nine of clubs, reversed, to (17) the queen of clubs, a charming dark lady, who is the real object of his affections. (20) The knave of spades, figuring a legal agent, or the wily lawyer's thoughts, makes mischief, and (18) the eight of diamonds, reversed, causes the inquirer's love-making to be unsuccessful. (6) The ace of spades warns the inquirer against false friends who will frustrate his matrimonial projects, and in (10) we find one of them, the queen of spades, a widow with possible designs upon him herself; (9) the knave of diamonds, reversed, shows the mischief-maker trying to breed strife with the inquirer's trusty friend (12), the king of clubs, and (8) the queen of hearts, a fair lovable woman possessing (13) eight of clubs, a dark person's affections; (7) the nine of diamonds, reversed, tells of a love quarrel, owing to (11) the knave of clubs, reversed, a harmless flirt. The inquirer will get (4) the ace of hearts, a love letter, but his happiness will be succeeded by (2) the ten of spades, a card of bad import; (5) the nine of spades, tells of grief or sickness, possibly news of a death; but (3) the ten of hearts, counteracts the evil, and promises happiness to the inquirer, who shall triumph over the obstacles in his path, and find (22) joy in love and life.

Chapter XI
Important Questions

How to answer them – Specimen questions – Cupid and Venus at work

How to Answer Them

When an answer to an important question is required, and the inquirer wishes to consult the cards on the subject, the following simple method may be adopted.

Let the question be asked by the inquirer, then let the dealer take the pack of thirty-two cards, which must be shuffled and cut in the usual manner. The dealer throws out the first eleven cards, which are useless, and proceeds to turn up the others upon the table. The answer is determined by the absence or presence of the special cards applying to each question among the exposed twenty-one.

Specimen Questions

We will give some examples. Suppose the question to be:

"How far off is the wedding?"

The needful cards in this case are the queen of spades, who should come out with or near the queen of hearts, and the ace of spades, which should accompany the eight of diamonds. These must be taken in conjunction with the other eights –each of which signifies a year; the four nines –each of which stands for a month; and the four sevens –each of which represents a week. Supposing the above-named cards –the two queens, the ace of spades, and the eight of diamonds– should not come out in due order, or be absent altogether, it may be feared that the date is postponed to vanishing point.

"Have I real cause for jealousy?"

If the seven of diamonds comes out in the first fifteen cards, the answer is "Yes." If the five of hearts and the seven clubs appear instead among the first fifteen, it means "No."

"Shall we be parted?" or *"Shall I sustain the loss of my goods?"*

If the four nines are included in the twenty-one cards, the answer is "Yes." Should the four kings and the four queens come out, the meaning is "No, never!".

"Shall I succeed in my present or projected undertaking?"

To ensure a favourable answer the four aces and the nine of hearts must come out. Should the nine of spades appear just before the card representing the inquirer, it prognosticates failure, sure and certain.

"Will the change of residence or condition that I am considering be satisfactory?"

Should this question be asked by the master or mistress of a house, or an employer of labour, a favourable answer is secured by the presence of the four knaves, the eight and ten of diamonds, and the ten of clubs. In the event of the inquirer being an *employé*, or a paid worker of any grade, the twenty-one cards must include the ten and seven of diamonds, the eight of spades, and the four queens, to ensure a satisfactory reply. In both cases the nine of diamonds means hindrances and delay in attaining success.

"What fortune does the future hold for this child?"

The four aces foretell good luck and a suitable marriage. If the child in question be a girl, the four eights and the king of hearts should come out to secure peace and concord for her in the home of her husband.

Cupid and Venus at Work

Among the many ways in which cards can be used to provide entertainment, seasoned with a spice of the unexplainable, the following round game may be given a prominent place:

The ace of diamonds is the most valuable asset in winning tricks, as it takes all the other cards. The pack of fifty-two cards is used.

The queen of hearts represents Venus.
The knave of hearts stands for Cupid.
The knave of diamonds represents sweethearts.
The knave of clubs represents sweethearts.
The knave of spades represents sweethearts.
The ace of hearts –a new house.
The ace of clubs –conquest.
The two of diamonds –the ring and marriage.
The twos of clubs, spades, and hearts –good luck.
The threes –show surprise.
The fours –that present conditions will remain unchanged.
The fives –lovers' meetings.
The sixes –pleasure.
The sevens –disappointment.
The eights –mirth.
The nines –changes.
The tens –marriage settlements.
The queens represent women.
The kings represent men.

Any number may take part in the game. The dealer is chosen by lot, and when this has been settled, he or she proceeds to deal out the cards, leaving ten face downwards on the table. The stakes are agreed upon, and each player puts into the pool, the dealer being expected to pay double for the honour done to him by the fates.

The cards are then taken up, and each player looks at his own hand. The dealer calls for the queen of hearts, Venus, who ranks next to the ace of diamonds in value. Should any one have the ace of diamonds in his hand, he plays it straight out. Should the ace not be among those that have been dealt round, the queen of hearts is supreme, and the happy holder of Venus may look confidently forward to standing before the altar of Hymen during the current year. The ace of diamonds only counts as one card, but should any lucky player hold both Cupid and Venus in his hand he is entitled to clear the pool, and so end the game right off. In the event of the holder of these cards being married, their presence promises him some special stroke of good fortune.

When the matrimonial cards are out, or proved absent, the game is played on similar lines to whist, the same order of precedence being observed in taking tricks, and the larger the number secured the better the luck of the winner during the current year.

The nine of spades is the worst card in the pack, and the unfortunate holder has to pay for its presence in his hand by a treble stake to the pool. Should any player fail to win any tricks, he must pay in advance the stakes agreed upon for the next game.

Marriage by Lot

For this appeal to the fates we require a pack of cards, a bag, and stakes either in money or counters. When the players have fixed upon their stakes and placed them in the pool, one of those playing must thoroughly shuffle the pack of cards and place them in the bag. The players then stand in a circle and draw three cards in turn from the bag as it is handed to each of them. Pairs of any kind win back the stakes paid by the holder, and promise good luck in the immediate future. The knave of hearts is proclaimed to represent Hymen. He wins double stakes, and is a happy augury that the holder will soon be united to the partner of his or her choice. Should Venus, the queen of hearts, be found in the same hand, the owner takes the pool and wins the game. Fours and eights are losses and crosses, compelling a pre-arranged payment to the pool in addition to the usual stakes. A lady who draws three nines may resign herself to a life of single-blessedness, and the one who has three fives must prepare to cope with a bad husband.

Your Fate in Twenty Cards

Only three or four girls are required to pursue this search for hidden knowledge. All the kings, queens, knaves, aces, and threes must be taken from the pack and dealt round to the players. Each one examines her hand for an answer to her inward questionings. The one who holds the most kings possesses the largest number of friends. The one with most queens has a proportionate number of enemies. Where kings and queens are united, there is the promise of speedy and happy marriage. Should a queen come out with knaves, we may be sure that intrigues are being woven round some unlucky person. Knaves by themselves represent lovers. Threes are evil omens betokening great sorrow. A knave with four threes means that the fair holder will not enter the holy estate. A king with four threes encourages her to hope, for she has a good chance of matrimony. A queen with four threes is the worst combination a girl can draw, for it speaks of sorrow deepened by disgrace. Mixed hands have no special significance, nor is there any great meaning attached to the four aces. Where only two or three of one kind of card fall together, the meaning ascribed to the four collectively is lessened in proportion to the number held.

Hearts are Trumps

This game might by some be called an apology for whist Four players, or three and a dummy, are necessary, and the whole pack is dealt out in the usual way. Hearts are trumps in every deal, and carry everything before them. The highest card is the queen, who is the goddess of love, and takes precedence of the ace, which only counts as one. The person on the left hand of the dealer leads trumps, and the stronger the hand the better the chances for love and marriage. The one who wins the largest number of tricks has, or will have, the most lovers. The presence of the king and queen of trumps in one hand is the sign of a speedy union of hearts, and of the approaching sound of wedding bells. A sorry fate awaits the luckless maid or youth who is without a heart –in the hand– for Cupid and Hymen have turned their faces away, and no luck will come of a love affair in that quarter. Where only one or two small trumps can be produced, the holder will have to wait long for wedded bliss. Each one plays quite independently of the others, and the one who undertakes dummy must not connect its cards in any way with those he holds himself.

Another Lottery

Put a well-shuffled pack of cards into a bag deep enough to prevent the contents from being seen. An uneven number of girls must then form a ring round the one holding the bag, and each must draw a card. The cards thus drawn must then all be exposed, as they have to be compared. The lucky lady who draws the highest card will be the first to be led to the altar. She who draws the lowest will have to emulate Mariana of the Moated Grange, and resign herself to the fact that "he cometh not" for many weary days to follow. Anyone drawing the ace of spades may cheerfully prepare for the pleasures of a bachelor life. The nine of hearts is the presage of serious trouble, coming to the holder through loving "not wisely but too well".

Chapter XII
How They Tell Fortunes in Italy

Italian method – An example – Notice the groups – How the pairs work out – The five pack

Italian Method

Only thirty-two cards are used for the Italian method of fortune-telling, all the numbers under seven, except the ace, being taken out of each suit. This reduced pack –containing the ace, king, queen, knave, ten, nine, eight, and seven of the four suits– must be carefully shuffled and cut, with the left hand of course, by the inquirer. The one who is going to act as interpreter then takes the pack, and turns them up three at a time. Should three cards of one suit be turned up at once, they are all laid upon the table, face upwards; if only two of a suit come out together, the higher card is selected; if all three belong to different suits, they are all rejected.

When the pack has been dealt out in this manner the cards that have not been chosen are taken up, shuffled, and cut a second time. The deal by threes is then repeated until there are fifteen cards upon the table. They must be placed inline, from left to right, as they appear.

It is absolutely necessary that the card representing the inquirer should be among those on the table. Some authorities maintain, however, that in the event of its not coming out during the deals, the whole process must be repeated until it makes its appearance. Others again take the card out, and place it on the table when fourteen others have been selected.

The next step is to count five cards from the representative one, and to continue counting in fifths from each fifth card until all have been included, or the counting has come back to the representative. The signification of every card is read as it is reached, due notice being taken as to whether it is reversed or not, and the surrounding circumstances must also be balanced by the interpreter.

When this reading is complete the fifteen cards must be paired, one from each end of the line being taken and read together, while the remaining odd one must be dealt with separately.

The third process is to shuffle and cut the fifteen cards, and deal them out into five small packs: one for *the lady herself;* one *for the house;* one *for those who do not expect it;* one *for those who do expect it;* one *for the surprise;* and one, which is not to be covered, for *consolation.* When the fifteen cards have been dealt out, it will be seen that four of the packs contain three cards, and the fifth only two. These must all be turned face upwards and read in separate packs, but with the connecting idea that they all refer to the fortune of the inquirer.

An Example

Let us imagine that a very fair lady, represented by the queen of diamonds, is seeking to read her fortune.

The fifteen cards come out in the following order:

The queen of diamonds; nine of diamonds, reversed; queen of hearts; king of spades; ten of diamonds; seven of diamonds, reversed; knave of hearts, reversed; ten of hearts; knave of diamonds; ace of diamonds, reversed; knave of spades; nine of spades; king of clubs; ten of spades, reversed; ace of hearts.

We begin to count from the queen of diamonds, the representative card, and find the nine of diamonds to be the fifth from it. By this first count we see from the nine being reversed that there is a love quarrel troubling the inquirer. Starting again from the nine we come to the queen of hearts, a mild, good-natured, but not very wise woman, who is probably the tool of the next fifth card, the king of spades, a crafty, ambitious man, and an enemy to the queen of diamonds.

Our next count is to the ten of diamonds, which speaks of a journey for the inquirer. Passing on to the seven of diamonds, reversed, we get hold of a foolish scandal connected with, if not entirely caused by, the next count, which is the knave of hearts, reversed, and stands for a military man who is very discontented with the treatment he has received at the hands of the fair inquirer. She will, however, triumph over this foolish annoyance, for the ten of hearts comes next in order, and counteracts the harm involved by the other cards.

Our gentle lady has, unfortunately, an unfaithful friend in the knave of diamonds; and he is followed by the ace of diamonds, reversed, which portends a letter on the way containing bad news. The writer of this is a dark young man of no social position, and he probably is the servant of one who is dear to the queen of diamonds. The bad news is found in the next count, the nine of spades, which tells of sickness affecting the king of clubs, the warm-hearted, chivalrous man who occupies the first place in the inquirer's affections. The last count but one brings us to the ten of spades, reversed, by which we know that the lady's sorrow will be but brief; and it is followed by the ace of hearts, a love letter containing the good news of her lover's recovery.

Notice the Groups

Before proceeding to pair the cards, we may as well note the groups as they have come out in the fifteen. The six diamonds point to there being plenty of money; the two tens tell of a change of residence, either brought about by marriage, or by the journey read in the ten of diamonds; the presence of three knaves betokens false friends, though as one is reversed, their power of doing harm is lessened; two queens indicate gossip and the revealing of secrets; the two aces imply an attempted plot, but it is frustrated by the one being reversed; the two nines also point to riches.

How the Pairs Work Out

The two end cards of the fifteen are taken up together, so that the pairs shall work out thus: The queen of diamonds and the nine of spades, implying that sickness and trouble will affect the inquirer; the ten of diamonds pairs with the ten of hearts, and they signify a wedding; the knaves of diamonds and spades coming together show evil intentions towards the inquirer; the king of clubs and the ace of hearts tell of the lover and the love letter; the inverted nine of diamonds pairing with the knave of spades, tells of a love quarrel, in which a dark young man, wanting in refinement, is concerned; the reversed seven of diamonds pairs with the knave of hearts, also inverted, and tells of a foolish scandal instigated by the ungallant soldier who is suffering from wounded vanity; the inverted ace of diamonds comes out with the queen of hearts, telling of a letter containing unpleasant news from a fair, good-natured woman; while the remaining card, the ten of spades, being inverted, speaks of brief sorrow for the inquirer.

The Five Packs

Our next step is to deal out the five packs as already directed. The first one *–for the lady herself–* contains three cards, two of which are bad, but their harm is largely discounted by the ten of hearts. In the nine of spades we read of the trouble caused by her lover's illness; the ten of spades betokens the tears she will shed while the beloved life is in danger; the ten of hearts speaks of happiness triumphing over sorrow.

The second pack *–for the house–* contains a flush of diamonds, the ten, the ace, and the knave. There is plenty of money in the house: the ten speaks of a journey, possibly resulting in a change of residence; the ace, being reversed, tells of a letter on the way containing unpleasant news (probably connected with the removal), from the knave, who is a faithless friend, and is to blame for the annoyance.

The third pack *–for those who do not expect–* consists of three court cards, which taken together foretell gaiety of some sort. We find the inquirer, personated by the queen of diamonds, in the society of the knaves of spades and hearts, the latter reversed, and consequently we know that she will be troubled by some unfriendly schemes, in which the dark, undesirable young man and the disappointed officer will be concerned. The inversion of the one knave counteracts the intended harm.

The fourth pack *–for those who do expect–* contains the queen of hearts, the king of spades, and the seven of diamonds, inverted. These indicate that the fair woman of gentle and affectionate nature will be exposed to scandal, seven of diamonds reversed; through the agency of the king of spades, an ambitious untrustworthy lawyer who is her enemy.

The fifth pack, consisting of only two cards (the ace of hearts and the nine of diamonds), is for *the surprise*, and we learn that a love letter, the ace, will be delayed, the nine but the consolation card is the king of clubs, the dark, warm-hearted man, who will come in person to his lady-love.

The above example has been taken in the plainest, most straightforward manner with just the most apparent reading of the cards given as an illustration of the method. Those who spend time and thought on the subject will soon get to see more of the "true inwardness" of the cards with respect to their relative positions, and their influence one upon another. Various experiments with this plan of fortune-telling will give rise to curious combinations, and perhaps startling developments, as the one acting for the inquirer gains in knowledge and confidence.

Chapter XIII
The Master Method

Knowledge is power – Four twos added to the usual pack – The thirty-six squares and their significance – Tendencies of the suits

Knowledge is Power

We have here a detailed and exhaustive method by which the cards can be read. The beginner may feel somewhat alarmed at the mass of explanatory matter there is for him to study, but when once the information has been acquired, the would-be cartomancer will find he possesses a sense of power and comprehension, that will give both confidence and dexterity to his attempts to unravel the thread of destiny.

Four Twos Added to the Usual Pack

The selected pack of thirty-two cards, which have been mentioned in connection with several of the preceding methods, are in this case augmented by the addition of the four twos, one of which is sometimes taken as the representative of the inquirer. There is no hard and fast rule about this, however, and another card may be taken if preferred. The accompanying table shows that not only has each card its own signification, but that every position upon the table within the cube in which the cards are arranged has its own meaning. These must be carefully studied, first separately and then together. It would be a help to the beginner to make a separate chart for his own use, and to have it at hand when laying the cards according this system.

Table of the Positions and their Several Meanings

No. 1 Project in hand	No. 2 Satisfaction	No. 3 Success	No. 4 Hope	No. 5 Chance Luck	No. 6 Wishes Desire
No. 7 Injustice	No. 8 Ingratitude	No. 9 Association	No. 10 Loss	No. 11 Trouble	No. 12 State or Condition
No. 13 Joy	No. 14 Love	No. 15 Prosperity	No. 16 Marriage	No. 17 Sorrow Affliction	No. 18 Pleasure Enjoyment
No. 19 Inheritance Property	No. 20 Fraud Deceit	No. 21 Rivals	No. 22 A Present Gift	No. 23 Lover	No. 24 Advancement A rise in the world
No. 25 Kindness A good turn	No. 26 Undertaking Enterprise	No. 27 Changes	No. 28 The End (of Life)	No. 29 Rewards	No. 30 Misfortune Disgrace
No. 31 Happiness	No. 32 Money Fortune	No. 33 Indifference	No. 34 Favour	No. 35 Ambition	No. 36 Ill-health Sickness

The thirty-six cards must be shuffled and cut in the usual way, and then placed upon the table in six rows of six cards each, starting from the left-hand corner where square No. 1 is marked on the chart. The position of the inquirer must be carefully noted, and then all the cards in his immediate neighborhood must be read in all their bearing, individually, and with regard to their position, and their influence upon the representative card.

The Thirty-Six Squares and their Significance

We will take the meanings of the thirty-six squares in connection with the several cards that may cover them.

No. 1. The Project in Hand

When covered by a heart, the inquirer may hope that the project will be successfully carried out.

When covered by a club, kind and trusty friends will help forward the project.

When covered by a diamond, there are serious business complications in the way of the project's accomplishment.

When covered by a spade, the inquirer will have his trust abused and those in whom he has confided will play him false, to the detriment of the project in hand.

No. 2. Satisfaction

When covered by a heart, the inquirer may look for the realisation of his brightest hopes and his dearest wishes.

When covered by a club, satisfaction will be derived by the help of true friends, who will do all in their power to promote the inquirer's happiness.

When covered by a diamond, there will be jealousy at work to mar the inquirer's satisfaction.

When covered by a spade, the hope of success will be well-nigh shattered by deceit and double-dealing.

No. 3. Success

When covered by a heart, the inquirer may hope for complete success.

When covered by a club, any success will be due to the help of friends.

When covered by a diamond, the success will be but incomplete.

When covered by a spade, all chance of success will be eventually destroyed by underhand means.

No. 4. Hope

When covered by a heart, the inquirer may look for the fulfillment of his dearest hopes.

Covered by a club, hopes will be realised through the agency of helpful friends, or be due to the obstinate determination of the inquirer.

Covered by a diamond, it shows that the hopes are groundless and impossible of realisation.

Covered by a spade, wild hopes are indicated, tending to mania, and provocative of grave trouble, or even tragedy.

No. 5. Chance – Luck

Covered by a heart, good luck will attend the hopes and plans of the inquirer.

Covered by a club, means moderately good luck, especially due to the kindly offices of friends.

Covered by a diamond, does not promise much luck to the inquirer; rather an evil than a good influence.

Covered by a spade, bad luck, robbery, financial ruin, disaster, and possibly death.

No. 6. Wishes – Desire

Covered by a heart and surrounded by good cards, it promises the immediate fulfillment of the inquirer's highest desires.

Covered by a club, a partial gratification of the inquirer's wishes may be expected.

Covered by a diamond, the earnest efforts of both the inquirer and his friends will only be crowned with imperfect success.

Covered by a spade, disappointment and non-fulfillment of desires.

No. 7. Injustice

Covered by a heart, any injustice done to the inquirer will be rectified and withdrawn, so that the passing cloud will turn to his ultimate advantage.

Covered by a club, the wrong already done will require long and courageous efforts to efface its effects, and the inquirer will need the support of his best friends.

Covered by a diamond, the harm done will not be entirely remedied, but the inquirer's good name will be re-established.

Covered by a spade, injustice will bring about sore trouble and serious misfortunes.

No. 8. Ingratitude

The four suits have exactly the same influence upon the situation in this number as in the preceding one.

No. 9. Association

Covered by a heart, the partnership will be successful and have the best results.

Covered by a club, good results of cooperation or partnership will be effected through the agency of true friends.

Covered by a diamond, the inquirer will need to use all possible caution and diplomacy, and even then the results will be but unsatisfying.

Covered by a spade, the connection will not benefit the inquirer, in fact he may suffer terribly from it, but his friends will profit thereby.

No. 10. Loss

Covered by a heart, shows loss of a benefactor, which will be a great grief to the inquirer.

Covered by a club, the loss of dear friends and the failure of cherished hopes.

Covered by a diamond, loss of money, goods, property, and personal effects.

Covered by a spade, the best interests of the inquirer will be seriously compromised, and he will have to renounce them.

No. 11. Trouble

Covered by a heart, very great trouble caused by near relations, or born of love for another.

Covered by a club, trouble with friends.

Covered by a diamond, money troubles.

Covered by a spade, trouble arising from jealousy.

No. 12. State or Condition

Covered by a heart, the conditions of life are steadily improving.

Covered by a club, the improvement will be slower and more uncertain; hard work and good friends are essential to ensure advancement.

Covered by a diamond, the inquirer will only attain to a satisfactory position in life after he has overcome numerous and powerful enemies. He will never get very far however.

Covered by a spade, the inquirer's circumstances are bound to go from bad to worse, in spite of all he may do.

No. 13. Joy – Delight

Covered by a heart, deep, unruffled delight, joy of a pure and disinterested nature.

Covered by a club, joy from material causes, better luck or greater prosperity.

Covered by a diamond, joy springing from success in profession or business, gained in spite of jealous opposition.

Covered by a spade, joy from having been able to render a service to a superior, who will not forget it.

No. 14. Love

Covered by a heart, the inquirer will be blessed and happy in his love.

Covered by a club, he may rely absolutely upon the fidelity of his beloved.

Covered by a diamond, love will be troubled by jealousy.

Covered by a spade, love will be slighted and betrayed.

No. 15. Prosperity

Covered by a heart, the inquirer will enjoy complete and well-merited prosperity.

Covered by a club, betokens moderate prosperity, due to hard work and the kindly offices of friends.

Covered by a diamond, prosperity will be damaged by the jealousy of others.

Covered by a spade, serious misfortunes will arise in business, brought about by the malice and fraud of other people.

No. 16. Marriage

Covered by a heart, the inquirer may look forward to a happy and well-assorted marriage.

Covered by a club, foretells a marriage prompted by practical or financial considerations alone.

Covered by a diamond, the married life will be troubled by the jealousy of one or both partners.

Covered by a spade, inquirer will lose the chance of a wealthy marriage, through the deceit and jealousy of his enemies.

No. 17. Sorrow – Affliction.

Covered by a heart, the inquirer will pass through a love trouble, but it will only be of short duration.

Covered by a club, trouble will arise from a quarrel with a dear friend, but it will end in complete reconciliation.

Covered by a diamond, there will be sorrow caused by jealousy.

Covered by a spade, bad faith and underhand dealings will bring affliction upon the inquirer.

No. 18. Pleasure – Enjoyment

Covered by a heart, the inquirer will enjoy the bliss of mutual love, undimmed by even passing clouds.

Covered by a club, there will be love of a more imperfect and superficial character.

Covered by a diamond, love will be tormented and distracted by jealousy.

Covered by a spade, love will be unreal and evanescent, unable to bear the test of time, or to survive the first disagreement

No. 19. Inherited Money or Property

Covered by a heart, the inquirer will come into a large inheritance, to which he has a legitimate and undisputed right.

Covered by a club, a friend will bequeath a portion of his property or money to the inquirer.

Covered by a diamond, the inquirer will lose part of his rights, owing to the jealousy of another person.

Covered by a spade, an entire estate will be stolen from the inquirer by intriguing rivals.

No. 20. Fraud – Deceit

Covered by a heart, the deceiver will be caught in the trap he has laid for the inquirer.

Covered by a club, by the aid of true friends the inquirer will escape from the effects of an act of treachery.

Covered by a diamond, the inquirer will have to suffer great pain from the consequences of deceit, but it will only be a passing trouble.

Covered by a spade, deceit and underhand dealings will culminate in calumny which will cost the inquirer many friends, and have serious consequences for him.

No. 21. Rivals

Covered by a heart, the inquirer will obtain his desire in spite of powerful or puny rivals.

Covered by a club, rivals will be overcome with difficulty, and with the help of generous friends.

Covered by a diamond, a rival will so far outwit the inquirer as to obtain some of the advantage, wealth, or favour for which he is striving.

Covered by a spade, the rival will triumph over the inquirer, robbing him, and plunging him into disgrace both with his benefactors and with members of his own immediate circle.

No. 22. A Present or Gift

Covered by a heart, the inquirer will have a very handsome and unexpected present.

Covered by a club, the inquirer will receive a gift that is bestowed upon him from motives of self-interest, or in a spirit of vulgar display.

Covered by a diamond, points to a gift intended to act as a bribe.

Covered by a spade, indicates a present which is given to further the deceitful ends of the donor.

Covered by a heart, the lover or the lady, as the case may be, will be both fond and faithful in life and death.

Covered by a club, the beloved will be faithful, but somewhat faulty in other respects.

Covered by a diamond, the inquirer may be prepared to find the beloved both jealous and disposed to sulk.

Covered by a spade, the beloved will prove faithless, selfish, and vindictive.

No. 24. Advancement

Covered by a heart, the inquirer will soon see a rapid improvement in his worldly position, and it will exceed his wildest hopes.

Covered by a club, there will be a moderate and satisfying advance in the inquirer's circumstances, which will be the result of his own hard work, aided by the sympathy and help of his friends. He will be contented and happy.

Covered by a diamond, advancement will only be obtained after a hard struggle against difficulties, caused by the jealous ill-will of others.

Covered by a spade, the underhand dealings of his enemies will destroy all hope of a rise in the world.

No. 25. Kindness – A Good Turn

Covered by a heart, the inquirer will receive a kindness which far exceeds both his expectations and his deserts.

Covered by a club, this good turn will be well deserved, but only obtained by the help of disinterested friends.

Covered by a diamond, the inquirer will only obtain a modicum of kindness, and that after he has surmounted serious obstacles built up by the jealousy of his enemies.

Covered by a spade, the inquirer will not benefit by the good turn which he well deserves, but he will have to see it diverted from him by double-dealing.

No. 26. Undertaking – Enterprise

Covered by a heart, whatever undertaking the inquirer has in hand will meet with signal success.

Covered by a club, the enterprise will be a financial success, owing to the help of friends.

Covered by a diamond, the success of the undertaking will be hindered and decreased by the jealousy and self-seeking of some people concerned in it.

Covered by a spade, the inquirer must prepare for failure in his enterprise, owing to the malicious intrigues of his rivals.

No. 27. Changes

Covered by a heart, the change contemplated by the inquirer is a good one.

Covered by a club, a change for the better will take place in the inquirer's circumstances, owing to the good offices of friends.

Covered by a diamond, the inquirer will make an earnest attempt to change his position in life, but his efforts will be fruitless.

Covered by a spade, a change, very much for the worse, is to be apprehended. It will be brought about by the malice and double-dealing of those who seek to harm him.

No. 28. The End (of Life)

Covered by a heart, by the death of a relation or friend the inquirer will come into a considerable fortune.

Covered by a club, a handsome legacy from a friend may be expected by the inquirer.

Covered by a diamond, one who wishes ill to the inquires will depart this life.

Covered by a spade, this portends the untimely death of the inquirer's greatest enemy.

No. 29. Reward

Covered by a heart, the inquirer will be rewarded out of all proportion to his efforts.

Covered by a club, a due and fitting reward will be meted out to industry and perseverance.

Covered by a diamond, a well-merited reward will be hindered and reduced, by the unscrupulous action of others.

Covered by a spade, the inquirer will be done out of his just reward, by the double-dealing and dishonesty of certain people.

No. 50. Disgrace – Misfortune

Covered by a heart, misfortune will come to the inquirer, but it will not do him any permanent harm.

Covered by a club, the inquirer will suffer through the disgrace of a friend.

Covered by a diamond, misfortune will be brought about by jealousy, and will indirectly affect the inquirer.

Covered by a spade, dishonesty and double-dealing will cause disgrace, from which the inquirer will suffer long and acutely.

No. 31. Happiness

Covered by a heart, the inquirer will experience unexpected happiness which will be both deep and lasting.

Covered by a club, a stroke of luck will come to the inquirer, through the good offices of friends.

Covered by a diamond, the jealousy and ambition of false friends will result in good fortune to the inquirer.

Covered by a spade, the life of the inquirer will be in danger from the malice of his enemies. Their murderous schemes will be happily defeated by the vigilance of his friends.

No. 32. Money – Fortune

Covered by a heart, the inquirer will rapidly acquire a large fortune, by making a hit in his profession, or by a lucky speculation.

Covered by a club, by hard work and sustained effort the inquirer will secure a competence, and will receive both help and encouragement from his friends.

Covered by a diamond, through misplaced confidence in unworthy friends the inquirer will see his fortune pass into dishonest hands.

Covered by a spade, not only will the inquirer be tricked out of his money by dishonest acquaintances, but he will have to suffer for their misdeeds in his business or profession.

No. 33. Indifference

Covered by a heart, thanks to his indifference and want of heart the inquirer will lead an unruffled, if somewhat joyless, life.

Covered by a club, lack of interest and energy will allow the inquirer to let slip things that would give him pleasure.

Covered by a diamond, the inquirer will forfeit the love and regard of valuable friends owing to indifference and utter unresponsiveness.

Covered by a spade, as a result of culpable indifference the inquirer will be robbed and impoverished.

No. 34. Favour

Covered by a heart, the inquirer will enjoy all that love can bestow upon the beloved.

Covered by a club, the inquirer will honestly seek and acquire the favour of influential persons.

Covered by a diamond, the favour of the great will be long and earnestly sought by the inquirer, who will not succeed single-handed.

Covered by a spade, no effort of any kind will admit the inquirer to the favour to which he aspires.

No. 35. Ambition

Covered by a heart, the inquirer will shortly arrive at the highest point of his ambition.

Covered by a club, the moderate ambition of the inquires will be realised.

Covered by a diamond, the lawful ambitions of the inquirer will be partially frustrated, by the ill-will and jealousy at certain acquaintances.

Covered by a spade, the principal ambition of the inquirer will be defeated by underhand transactions, and he will even suffer from the consequences of perfectly justifiable steps which he may take to accomplish his desire.

No. 36. Sickness – Ill-health

Covered by a heart, the inquirer will suffer from passing ailments, that will leave no bad results.

Covered by a club, a rather serious illness may be expected.

Covered by a diamond, an acute attack of a definite disease.

Covered by a spade, a very severe illness, that may materially interfere with the inquirer's career or happiness.

Tendencies of the Suits

It will be seen in the foregoing definitions that hearts are almost invariably the sign of good luck, love, and happiness. Even where the position is indicative of misfortune, the presence of a heart has a mitigating effect upon the evil. Clubs rank next in order of good fortune, and seem specially connected with the precious gift of true friendship. Diamonds seem accompanied by the disquieting elements of jealousy and rivalry, which strew obstacles in the path to success and happiness, while for sheer bad luck and dire disaster the ill-omened suit of spades stands unrivaled.

Chapter XIV
Signification of Suits in the Master Method

Court cards – Plain cards – An example of the Master Method

Hearts

The King of Hearts.– In this method he represents a married man or a widower. Should the inquirer be a woman, and this card fall upon either of the squares, 14, 22, 23, 24, or 32, he then denotes a lover. Should the inquirer be a man, the king falling in the above-named squares signifies a rival.

When this card falls on either of the following numbers; 2, 3. 4, 13, 14, 15, 16, 18, 19, 23, 24, 29, 31, 32, 34, the situation is favourable, and the inquirer will have his wishes granted with respect to the special meaning of the square.

When the king falls on No. 1, 5, 6, 9, 12, 22, 26, 27 or 28, it foretells a satisfactory solution of any matter connected with the subject represented by the squares.

Should he fall upon an unlucky square, namely, No. 7, 8, 10, 11, 17, 20, 21, 30, 33, 35, or 36, he mitigates the evil fortune of the positions.

The Queen of Hearts.– She signifies a married woman or a widow who desires the happiness of the inquirer, and does her best to promote it

If the inquirer is a man, this card falling on the squares 14, 22, 23, 24, or 32, represents his lady-love. In the event of his being already engaged, his fiancée will possess all the most lovable and desirable qualities.

When the inquirer is a woman, and the queen of hearts falls on either of the above-named squares, it shows that she has a rival to reckon with. Should she be engaged, it indicates that her future husband is both young and well equipped for social and professional success.

When a very elderly person consults the cards, the above combination foretells a peaceful, contented old age.

To any one interested in agriculture, the same combination promises abundant crops.

The Knave of Hearts.– This card represents a good-natured, amiable, but rather insipid young man, devoid alike of violent passions and exalted aspirations.

When a young girl consults the cards, this knave falling on the squares 14, 22, 23, 24, or 32, may be taken to personate her fiancé.

When the inquirer is a young, unmarried man, the same combination indicates that he will marry the object of his choice, after he has surmounted considerable obstacles by hist act and quiet determination.

The Ten of Hearts.– The signification of this card does not differ from that given in the general definitions save in the following cases:

When it falls on square No. 10, it signifies success.

When it falls on square No. 14, it signifies success in love.

When it falls on square No. 16, it signifies a happy marriage. If, in the last-named case, a knave or a seven falls on No. 7, 15, 17, or 25, there will be several children born of the union.

If the ten of hearts falls on squares 18, 19, 31, or 30, it foretells wealth, intense enjoyment, and real happiness.

The Nine of Hearts.– The only addition to the general signification is, that when this card falls near the seven of clubs, it denotes that a promise already made to the inquirer will shortly be fulfilled.

The Eight of Hearts.– This card is the special messenger of good things when it falls on one of the following squares: 5, 9, 15, 18, 19, 22, or 31.

The Seven of Hearts.– If this card falls on No. 14, 22, 23, 24, or 32, when the inquirer is a bachelor, it signifies that he will very soon take unto himself a wife.

The Two of Hearts.– This is frequently taken as the representative card, and in that case is entirely influenced by its position on the chart, taken in connection with the cards that touch or surround it.

The Ace of Hearts.– This card represents the house of the inquirer as it does in other methods. It is very important to note its position on the chart and its surroundings.

Clubs

The King of Clubs.– Taken generally, this card represents a married man or a widower, whose worth as a friend is not to be excelled.

When the inquirer is a young girl, and this king falls on No. 14, 3 2, 23, 24, or 33, she may rejoice, for she will shortly be united in marriage to the man she loves.

Should a young man be consulting the cards, this king falling on any of the above-named squares denotes a generous, high-minded rival who will meet him in fair fight, and who is far above anything like taking a mean advantage.

When this card falls on No. 18, 19, 30, 27, or 28, it represents the guardian of a minor, whose line of conduct will be determined by the cards which surround or touch it

The Queen of Clubs.– When a bachelor consults the cards, and this queen falls on No. 14, 22, 23, 24, or 32, it promises him a lady-love whose beauty shall be her strongest attraction.

Should a woman be seeking to know her fate, this queen falling on either of the above-named squares warns her that she has a rival. In the case of the inquirer being a married man or woman, this card represents a woman of high position and great influence who is attractive to the inquirer, and who will be the means of bringing him or her valuable and pleasing intelligence.

In the case of a business man the above combination denotes that he will be entirely successful in the enterprise which is engrossing all his thoughts at the moment.

The Knave of Clubs.– This card may be taken to represent a sincere and lasting friendship founded upon a basis that will endure.

When the inquirer is a young girl, and this card falls upon either of the matrimonial squares, namely, 14, 22, 24, 24, or 32, it signifies some man who wants to marry her.

In the case of a bachelor, this card on the same squares tells him that he has a rival, either in love or in his business career.

The Ten of Clubs.– This card is the harbinger of good luck if it falls on No. 3, 5, 13, 18, 19, 22, 25, 28, 31, or 32.

Should this card fall on squares 10, 17, or 36, it implies the inquirer will be asked for a loan in money, which he will be unable to lend.

The Nine of Clubs.– This card means a present, and if it follows a club, the gift will be in money; if it follows a heart, the inquirer may look for a present of jewelry; if it follows a diamond, the gift will be but trifling in value; and if it follows a spade, the recipient of the present will derive no pleasure from it

The Eight of Clubs has no special significance outside the general definition.

The Seven of Clubs.– This represents a young girl capable of the highest self-devotion, even to risking her life in the interests of the inquirer. The exact nature of her relations and services to the object of her affection will be decided by the surrounding cards.

In the case of a bachelor, this card falling on any of the squares 14, 22, 23, 24, or 32, represents the lady of his choice.

In the case of an unmarried girl or a widow, the same combination points to a generous rival.

Whenever this seven comes out near the nine of hearts, the wish card, it is a token of some signal success for the inquirer.

The Two of Clubs.– This represents the trusted friend of the inquirer, and the square on which it falls will give the requisite information, if its meaning be taken in conjunction with those of the surrounding cards.

The Ace of Clubs.– This card is the sign of a well-ordered life and legitimate hopes, and foretells success in an ordinary career, or the attainment of celebrity in special cases.

Should the inquirer be a soldier by profession, it signifies a fortunate turn of events, that will secure him a rapid rise in the army.

To one interested in agriculture, it promises plentiful crops.

To a traveler, it foretells a most satisfactory result from his journey.

To an actress, it promises phenomenal success in a leading role. Should the inquirer or one of his parents be a dramatic or lyrical author, this card is the augury of theatrical success.

Diamonds

The King of Diamonds.– Should the inquirer be a young girl, she will do well to note whether this card falls on any of the matrimonial squares, 14, 22, 23, 24, or 32, for in that case her present admirer is not to be trusted, unless he has cards of good import touching him, or is preceded by either a heart or a club.

The Queen of Diamonds.– If this card falls on any of the matrimonial squares, 14, 22, 23, 24, or 32, it signifies to a bachelor that he will be engaged to one whose character is to be read in the surrounding cards. If this queen be preceded by a heart or a club, it promises good luck on the whole; but if by a diamond or a spade, the augury is bad.

Should the inquirer be a young unmarried woman or a widow, this card falling on the above-named squares indicates that she has a rival whose character is revealed by the cards touching it.

The Knave of Diamonds.– For an unmarried woman or a widow, this card represents a lover from a foreign country. If it is accompanied by a heart, he has many good points to recommend him; if by a club, he is kind and generous; if by a diamond, he is bad-tempered, exacting, and jealous; if by a spade, he is an undesirable, and she had better have nothing to do with him.

The Ten of Diamonds.– The general meaning of this card is a journey.

If it falls between two spades, the journey will be long.

If it falls between two hearts, the journey will be short.

If it falls between two clubs, the journey will be successful.

If it falls between two diamonds, the journey will have bad results.

The Nine of Diamonds.– This card signifies news. If preceded by a heart or a club, the news will be good. If preceded by a diamond or a spade, the news will be bad.

The Eight of Diamonds.– This card signifies a short journey.

If it falls between two hearts, the expedition will be an enjoyable pleasure trip.

If between two clubs, it denotes a satisfactory business journey.

If between two diamonds, it signifies a trip begun for pleasure and ending in misadventure.

If between two spades, it signifies an unsuccessful business journey.

The Seven of Diamonds.– This card stands for a young girl of foreign birth and breeding. Taken by itself it means love-sorrows and heart-searchings.

Should the inquirer be a bachelor, and this card fall on one of the matrimonial squares, 14, 22, 23, 24, or 32, it signifies a lady-love as above described.

This seven is an excellent augury when it falls on No. 2, 3,15, 16, 18, or 27.

The Two of Diamonds has practically the same signification as the deuce of clubs, unless it be selected as the representative card.

The Ace of Diamonds.– The signification of this card is a letter.

If preceded by a heart, it is a letter from a lover or friend.

If preceded by a club, it is a letter on business or one containing money.

If preceded by a diamond, the letter is dictated by jealousy.

If preceded by a spade, the letter contains bad news.

Spades

The King of Spades.– When the inquirer is an unmarried woman or a widow, this card falling on one of the squares, 14,22, 23, 24, or 32, is indicative of a false lover whose character is mean and base.

When the inquirer is an unmarried man, the above combination signifies that he has a rival.

This card falling on the squares numbered 10, 18, 19, 20, 27, 28, or 29, represents a guardian or the executor of a will.

To a married man, this king is a warning that there are domestic ructions in store for him.

To a married woman, the card cautions her to be very much on her guard when in the society of an attractive but unprincipled man whom she has to meet frequently, and who will bring scandal upon her if she is not most careful.

The Queen of Spades.– When the inquirer is a bachelor, this card falling on No. 14, 22, 23, 24, or 32, represents the lady to whom he will be engaged.

In the case of an unmarried woman or a widow, the combination signifies a rival in love.

The Knave of Spades, the Ten of Spades, the Nine of Spades, and the *Eight of Spades* have no special signification other than that given in the general definitions.

The Seven of Spades.– This card signifies all troubles and worries connected with the tender passion.

Should the inquirer be a man, this seven falling on squares 14, 22, 23, 24, or 32 foretells faithlessness on the part of his *fiancée*, a betrayal of trust by some other woman, or a robbery.

When the inquirer is a woman, this card on any of the same squares points to a rival who will be preferred before her.

The Two of Spades may be taken as a representative card, but otherwise has no special signification.

The Ace of Spades is a card of good omen, meaning perseverance followed by possession, a happy marriage, success, and rapid advancement in business or profession.

An Example of the Master Method

We have taken the deuce of hearts as the representative card of the inquirer, who is a fair young girl seeking to know her fate. We will give the order in which the thirty-six cards come out, but intend to leave the bulk of them for the reader to solve according to the instructions given.

We have taken the inquirer and her immediate surroundings as an example of the working of the method, and feel sure that any intelligent reader will be able to complete the reading for himself.

No. 1. Ace of clubs.
No. 2. Eight of spades.
No. 3. Two of clubs.
No. 4. Knave of hearts.
No. 5. King of diamonds.
No. 6. King of hearts.
No. 7. Eight of diamonds.
No. 8. Ten of clubs.
No. 9. Ten of hearts.
No. 10. Seven of spades.
No. 11. Nine of spades.
No. 12. Two of spades.
No. 13. Nine of hearts.
No. 14. Eight of clubs.
No. 15. Queen of diamonds.
No. 16. Two of hearts.
No. 17. King of spades.
No. 18. Queen of hearts.
No. 19. Ace of spades.
No. 20. Ten of spades.
No. 21. Knave of spades.
No. 22. King of clubs.
No. 23. Nine of clubs.
No. 24. Eight of hearts.
No. 25. Queen of clubs.
No. 26. Knave of diamonds.
No. 27. Queen of spades.
No. 28. Seven of diamonds.
No. 29. Seven of hearts.
No. 30. Ten of diamonds.
No. 31. Knave of clubs.
No. 32. Ace of diamonds.
No. 33. Ace of hearts.
No. 34. Seven of clubs.
No. 35. Two of diamonds.
No. 36. Nine of diamonds.

We find the inquirer in No. 16, which square when covered by a heart indicates a happy and well-suited marriage. On her left in No. 15 (prosperity) she has the queen of diamonds, a very fair woman who is fond of gossip, and somewhat wanting in refinement of feeling. She will interfere with the inquirer's prosperity through jealousy, but on the whole she will bring good luck because she is preceded by a club. To the right in No. 17 (sorrow) we have the king of spades, a dark, ambitious, but unscrupulous man, who is the inquirer's legal adviser, and will bring grave sorrow upon her by his underhand dealings. Immediately above her we have in No. 10 (loss) the seven of spades, a card representing troubles connected with a love affair. This square being covered by a spade indicates that she will be unjustly compelled to relinquish her rights, and her chance of marriage may be lessened or postponed by the loss of her fortune.

On the left above her we get in No. 9 (association) the ten of hearts, a most cheering and excellent card, promising her success and happiness in a partnership which she is contemplating. On the right, above, in No. 11 (trouble) we have the nine of spades, a bad omen, signifying the failure of her hopes through the jealousy of some other person.

Immediately below her we find in No. 22 (a gift) the king of clubs, who is her true and valued friend, either a married man or a widower. He will make her a present, and will be actuated by certain motives of self-interest in so doing; but she may keep a good heart, for his presence in that position on the chart indicates that she will soon be united to the man of her choice. On the left, below, in No. 21 (rival) we find the knave of spades, a legal agent whose influence will be instrumental in enabling a rival to triumph over and bring discredit upon the inquirer. On the right, below, we have in No. 23 (a lover) the nine of clubs, which in this case means a gift in money. We may take it that her faithful lover, uninfluenced by her pecuniary losses, has decided to make her a present, probably in the form of marriage settlements.

The remainder of the chart will provide the student with many more interesting particulars regarding the fate of this fair inquirer, and at the same time prove an excellent exercise in the art of cartomancy.

No. 1	No. 2	No. 3	No. 4	No. 5	No. 6
No. 7	No. 8	No. 9 Ten of Hearts	No. 10 Seven of Spades	No. 11 Nine of Spades	No. 12
No. 13	No. 14	No. 15 Queen of Diamonds	No. 16 Inquirer Deuce of Hearts	No. 17 King of Spades	No. 18

Fortune Telling by Cards

No. 19	No. 20	No. 21 Knave of Spades	No. 22 King of Clubs	No. 23 Nine of Clubs	No. 24
No. 25	No. 26	No. 27	No. 28	No. 29	No. 30
No. 31	No. 32	No. 33	No. 34	No. 35	No. 36

Chapter XV
Combination of Nines

How to Work it

The fifty-two cards must be shuffled and cut into three packs by the person who wishes to have his or her fortune told, and the fortune-teller must be careful to note what cards appear as the various packs are turned face upwards, as this will be found to assist the reading.

The card representing the inquirer must first be selected according to the rules given in Chapter VII; it is not to be withdrawn, but shuffled and cut with the pack.

Then lay the cards nine in a row, beginning from right to left with each row; only seven will be in the last row.

The cards being in order on the table, you must begin by counting nine from your representative card and nine again from the ninth, until you come to a card that has already been counted.

The court cards represent the various people with whom the inquirer is brought into contact, and their relation and attitude are easily determined by the import of the cards between. Three deals are necessary for a good reading.

An Example

I give an example of fortune-telling by the combination of nines, because an illustration is of practical help.

The pack having been dealt with in the manner described, we find the cards have resolved themselves thus, reading from left to right in each row:

First line.– Seven of clubs, seven of spades, king of spades, ace of diamonds, ace of hearts, knave of clubs, four of hearts, eight of hearts, knave of spades.

Second line.– Two of diamonds, three of diamonds, two of hearts, six of hearts, king of diamonds, five of clubs, two of clubs, five of spades, three of hearts.

Third line.– Five of hearts, six of diamonds, four of clubs, queen of clubs, five of diamonds, three of spades, king of hearts, four of diamonds, ten of spades.

Fourth line.– Nine of spades, queen of spades, eight of diamonds, six of clubs, ace of spades, queen of diamonds, king of clubs, knave of hearts, six of spades, nine of hearts.

Fifth line.– Ten of diamonds, eight of clubs, seven of diamonds, ace of clubs, nine of clubs, nine of diamonds, knave of diamonds, ten of hearts, ten of clubs.

Sixth line.– Eight of spades, queen of hearts, seven of hearts, four of spades, three of clubs, two of spades.

We will take the queen of hearts to represent the inquirer, and, as she is in the lowest line of all, will count upwards. The ninth card is the knave of clubs, and the next ninth the six of hearts, then the three of spades, the ace of spades, and nine of clubs, which last brings us back to our queen.

According to the signification given by this method the reading would be as follows:

Knave of clubs:	A generous friend.
Six of hearts:	Implies credulity.
Three of spades:	An unfortunate marriage.
Ace of spades:	Difficulties. Be careful in making friends.
Nine of clubs:	Displeasure of friends.

The First Reading

My general reading of this would be that if the queen of hearts were an unmarried woman she was in danger of making an unhappy marriage, which would bring the displeasure of her friends upon her. If she will avoid forming hasty friendships, and take the advice of a man who is older and darker than herself, she will avoid much misfortune.

If married, the queen is the victim of an ill-assorted union, but she must be careful not to give too much credence to the reports of friends, and must guard her own conduct carefully.

We will now proceed with the next deal, to see if we can find a more favourable augury in the Book of Fate.

The Second Reading

First line.– Eight of clubs, queen of hearts, six of spades, eight of spades, eight of hearts, six of diamonds, ten of hearts, nine of clubs, six of hearts.

Second line.– Three of spades, ace of spades, three of diamonds, king of spades, ace of diamonds, ace of hearts, king of diamonds, king of clubs, ace of clubs.

Third line.– Ten of spades, five of clubs, two of hearts, five of hearts, ten of diamonds, four of hearts, two of clubs, knave of spades, three of hearts.

Fourth line.– Five of spades, four of clubs, six of clubs, queen of hearts, four of diamonds, king of hearts, nine of spades, five of diamonds, seven of clubs.

Fifth line.– Knave of clubs, ten of clubs, three of clubs, nine of diamonds, queen of spades, seven of spades, knave of hearts, eight of diamonds, seven of diamonds.

Sixth line.– Seven of hearts, four of spades, queen of clubs, two of spades, knave of diamonds, two of diamonds, nine of hearts.

Here our inquirer does not prove to be a very wise person. In spite of the warning and displeasure of friends, regardless of the affection of a good man, and elated through unexpected riches, she listens with credulous mind to one who will cause her much unhap-

Fortune Telling by Cards

piness. Let us hope she will stop short of one fatal step, and take the good honourable love that is awaiting her.

The ninth card is the king of clubs, and the five of the same suit following in our arranged plan, then the five of diamonds, the ten of clubs, the two of diamonds, the six of hearts, and the three of spades complete this reading. A reference to the signification will show the importance of these cards.

Perhaps in the third reading we may have more success.

The Third Reading

First line.– Ace of clubs, eight of clubs, queen of hearts, ten of spades, king of clubs, five of diamonds, ten of clubs, nine of spades, knave of spades.

Second line.– Three of spades, two of spades, six of hearts, eight of spades, five of spades, knave of clubs, seven of hearts, four of spades, queen of clubs.

Third line.– Five of hearts, two of diamonds, three of diamonds, queen of diamonds, eight of hearts, three of clubs, five of clubs, ace of diamonds, six of diamonds.

Fourth line.– Four of diamonds, six of clubs, seven of clubs, seven of diamonds, six of spades, nine of diamonds, knave of diamonds, nine of hearts, eight of diamonds.

Fifth line.– Ten of hearts, king of spades, two of hearts, ten of diamonds, ace of hearts, four of hearts, king of hearts, king of diamonds, queen of spades.

Sixth line.– Two of clubs, seven of spades, knave of hearts, nine of clubs, three of hearts, four of clubs, ace of spades.

The cards here are of better promise, though still full of warning. The ninth card is the seven of hearts, which means unfaithfulness, followed by another card indicating domestic dissension. The next is the knave of diamonds, and treachery is to be apprehended. But there is considerable success if care is exercised, and later on there appears to be a happy marriage with comfort and even luxury.

Throughout her life the inquirer would have to be on her guard against forming hasty friendships, and refrain from listening to scandal about those near and dear to her. In this case I should think there would be two marriages, the first not happy (which would probably be dissolved by the law), then a happier time later on in life, with one who had been content to wait.

Chapter XVI
Your Heart's Desire

The wish with fifteen cards – Another way – The wish with thirty-two cards – What the four aces tell – The wish in seven packs – The wish card again

The Wish with Fifteen Cards

Having shuffled the cards well, select according to the second method the card which will represent the inquirer –a king for a man, a queen for a woman– and place this card on the table; then request your subject to wish for some one thing whilst he or she is shuffling the pack (which must only include the selected thirty-two cards). The pack must be cut once.

Take the cards, and holding them easily in your own hands, let the inquirer draw fifteen cards, placing them face downwards on the table, one on top of the other in the order drawn. The fifteen cards having been drawn, discard the others, and place the selected ones in position according to the following plan: The representative card is to be in the centre, and the other cards are to be placed to the left – to the right – above – below – and on the centre, one by one. Thus on the left you will have the first, sixth, and eleventh; on the right, the second, seventh, and twelfth; above, the third, eighth, and thirteenth; below, the fourth, ninth, and fourteenth; and on the representative card you will have placed the fifth, tenth, and fifteenth.

Then take the left packet and turn and read according to the meaning in the combination of sevens. The next packet to be taken is the one on the right, then the one above, and following that the packet below. The left and top packets represent events that may influence your wish in the future; the packets on the right and below show those events which have influenced it in the past; whilst those cards covering the representative card indicate affairs that may be expected immediately, and are to be read in strict reference to the wish.

The Fifteen Cards diagrams is shown in the next page.

555

			13th			
			8th			
			3rd			
11th	8th	1st	Inquirer's Card, covered by 5th, 10th and 15th	2nd	7th	12th
			4th			
			9th			
			14th			

Another Way with Fifty-two Cards

Let the inquirer shuffle the cards well, and cut them into three packs, having first selected your representative card, as in the former method, and placed it in the centre of a circle.

Take up the packs and lay the cards in a circle, using forty-two, and with the remaining nine form a triangle inside the circle. The cards must be laid face down.

Now let the inquirer choose any fifteen cards, which must be faced upwards as he makes his selection. When fifteen cards are chosen, read the signification according to the meaning given in the combination of nines.

Generally speaking, if diamonds predominate the fortune will be fair; if hearts appear in the ascendant, love affairs are prosperous; clubs will show how material interests are progressing; and spades will prepare us for sorrow.

The Wish with Thirty-two Cards

Take out all the twos, threes, fours, fives, and sixes from an ordinary pack. The inquirer must then shuffle the remaining thirty-two, cut with the left hand, and wish from the depths of the heart. The dealer places eight cards, face downwards, upon the table in a row before him. He next turns them up one by one, beginning from the left, and as soon as a pair of any kind, it does not matter what, be exposed, they must both be covered by cards taken from the pack in his hand. If they all pair off exactly, it may be taken as a sign that the inquirer's wish will be gratified, but if at any moment there are no pairs exposed, the fates are unpropitious, and the search for a favourable answer must be abandoned. Should most of the cards pair off, leaving only one, two, or three unmated, it portends delay and disappointment before the realization of the desire.

What the Four Aces Tell

Take the thirty-two cards up again, shuffle them, and mentally register your wish. The first thirteen cards must be turned up, and a careful search made for any aces that maybe there. If found, place them on one side. The rest of the cards must be shuffled again and thirteen more dealt out, with a second search for aces. This is done a third time if all the four have not appeared; and if they still refuse to come, there is no hope of the wish being granted. It is the best possible omen if the four aces come out in the first deal, and very good luck if they arrive with only two attempts; but the third is the last chance, so the turning up of those thirteen cards is fraught with much excitement.

The Wish in Seven Packs

This is a very simple method, but it is by no means always propitious to the inquirer; if however, he *does* get the desired answer, we take it that the capricious goddess is in a very smiling mood.

Thirty-two cards are required, and they must be arranged in suits in the following order: Ace, king, queen, knave, ten, nine, eight, seven. The cards must not be shuffled, but the arranged pack is cut, with the left hand, into seven smaller packs, and all are placed face downwards upon the table.

The dealer must then proceed to turn up the top cards of each pack, and as a pair of queens, nines, knaves, or whatever they may happen to be becomes visible, he must remove them from the packs. Should all the cards pair off in this manner, the wish may be taken as one that will speedily be granted. Should the cards come out awkwardly, literally in sixes and sevens instead of pairs, the inquirer must adapt his desires to the inevitable with the best grace he can.

The Wish Card Again

Yet a sixth way, which will give some idea if the heart's desire will be gratified, is as follows:

Shuffle the whole pack of cards and give them to the inquirer, who must then divide the pack into three, wishing intently all the time. Take up the packs separately and glance through them; the nine of hearts is the most important card, as that is the symbol of the wish. Should this be in juxtaposition to the card –the king or queen– representing the inquirer, and with favourable surroundings, then you may conclude that the things hoped for will come to pass. Also, if the wish card is in combination with cards that are an indication of the inquirer's desires, it is a favourable augury.

For instance, if the wish referred to business, and the suit of clubs surrounded the nine of hearts, then it might be concluded that the matter would terminate in a prosperous manner. Diamonds, as they foretell wealth, would also promise prosperity; hearts imply good wishes and good will, whilst spades carry a sinister import.

Chapter XVII
A Rhyming Divination

Diamonds – Hearts – Spades – Clubs

There are those to whom the more elaborate form of fortune-telling by cards may seem a trifle wearisome, or possibly too intricate to be followed without a somewhat exhausting effort of attention. The method which we give in this chapter has the advantage of being at once simple, diverting, and varied.

As the rhyming significations concern both sexes, a great deal of fun can be provided where there is a party of young people, and who can tell whether the long arm of coincidence may not use this old-time practice to bring some loving pair together?

Take a new pack of cards, or at any rate one in which there are no tell-tale marks on the reverse sides, and spread them face downwards upon the table. Before any one draws a card, he or she is requested to close the eyes, place the right hand on the heart, and say, "Honi soit qui mal y pense." The card must then be drawn with the left hand, and its meaning will be read by the one who holds the key contained in the verses which we now give.

Diamonds

Ace	Since that this ace is now your lot, / You will wed one that's fierce and hot, / But if a woman does draw it, / She will wed one with wealth and wit.
Two	Hast thou not drawn the number two? / Thy spouse shall be both just and true. / But if a woman this now have, / Beware a sly and crafty knave.
Three	You that have drawn the number three / Great honour will your fortune be; / But if a female draw the same, / She must beware of fickle shame.
Four	The man that draws the number four / Shall quite forsake his native shore; / But if the same a woman finds, / Both hand and heart in love she joint.
Five	He that draweth the number five, / Where he was born he best will thrive; / But if it's drawn by womankind, / Good luck abroad they sure will find.
Six	He that can catch the number six / Will have cunning and crafty tricks; / But if a woman draw the same, / It will show that she is free from blame.
Seven	Since that the seven does appear, / Crosses thou hast great cause to fear; / Women, whene'er the same they draw, / Shall not fear crosses more than straw.
Eight	Hast thou then drawn the number eight? / Thou sure wilt be a rascal great; / Females that chance the same to take, / They never will the truth forsake.
Nine	Hast thou turn'd up the merry nine? / Then guineas will thy pocket line; / She that doth draw it to her hand, / Will die for love or leave the land.
Ten	O brave! the ten, 'tis very well! / There's none in love shall thee excel. / Only the maid who draws the ten / May wed, but nobody knows when.
King	This noble king of diamonds shows / Thou long shalt live where pleasure flows / But when a woman draws the king, / Sad, melancholy songs she'll sing.

Queen	Now is the queen of diamonds fair, She shows thou shalt some office share Oh, woman, if it fall to you, Friends you will have not a few.
Knave	Is now the knave of diamonds come? Be sure beware the martial drum; Yet if a woman draw the knave, She shall much better fortune have.

Hearts

Ace	He that draws the ace of hearts Shall surely be a man of parts; And she that draws it, I profess, Will have the gift of idleness.
Two	He who can draw the deuce shall be Endowed with generosity; But when a woman draws the card, It doth betide her cruel hard.
Three	The man who gets hold of this trey Always bound, always obey; A woman that shall draw this sort Will sure drink brandy by the quart.
Four	He that draws this four shall make A faithful love for conscience' sake; But if it's drawn by womenkind, They will prove false, and that you'll find.
Five	Note that this five of hearts declares Thou shalt well manage great affairs; But if it's drawn by fair women, They sure will love all sorts of men.
Six	The six of hearts surely foretells Thou shalt be where great honour dwells; If it falls on the other side It then betokens scorn and pride.
Seven	Now this old seven, I'll maintain, Shows that thou hast not loved in vain Thou shalt obtain the golden prize, But, with the maids, 'tis otherwise.
Eight	Having drawn the number eight, Shows thou'rt servile, born to wait; But if a woman draw the same, She'll mount upon the wings of fame.
Nine	By this long nine be well assured The lovesick pains must be endured; But the maid that draws this nine Soon in wedlock hands shall join.

Ten	This ten it is a lucky cast, For it doth show the worst is past; But if the maids the same shall have, Love will their tender hearts enslave.
King	King. By this card surely 'twill appear Thou shalt live long in happy cheer; And if a woman draw this card, She shall likewise be high preferred.
Queen	Now by this card it is well known Thou shalt enjoy still all thine own; But women, if they draw the same. Shall sure enjoy a happy name.
Knave	He that doth draw the knave of hearts Betokens he hath knavish parts; But if a woman draw the knave, Of no man shall she be the slave.

Spades

Ace	Thou that dost draw the ace of spades Shall be sore flouted by the maids; And when it is a damsel's lot, Both love and honour go to pot.
Two	Always this deuce betokens strife, And with a scolding, wicked wife; But if a woman's lot it be, Honour, great love, and dignity.
Three	Thou that art happy in this trey Shalt surely wed a lady gay; Whilst maids who now the same shall take, Join marriage with a poor town rake.
Four	Now this same four betokens you Shall lead a dissipated crew; Maids that do draw the same shall meet With certain joys always complete.
Five	The five of spades gives you to know That you must through some troubles go But, if a woman, it foretells Her virtue others' far excels.
Six	The six foretells whene'er you wed You'll find your expectations fled; But if a maid the number own She'll wed a man of high renown.

Seven	Now as the seven comes to hand, It does entitle you to land; But maids with this shall wed with those That have no money, friends, or clothes.
Eight	This eight of spades foretells you shall Wed a young maid fair, straight, and tall; If to a maid the same shall come, She weds the brother of Tom Thumb.
Nine	Now by this nine thou art foretold, Thou shalt wed one deaf, lame, and old. Females, when they draw this odd chance, Shall of themselves to wealth advance.
Ten	'Tis seen by this long ten of spades That thou shalt follow many trades, And thrive by none. But women, they By this chance shall not work but play.
King	By this brave king observe and note, On golden streams you e'er shall float; But women, by the self-same lot, Shall long enjoy what they have got
Queen	Here is the queen of spades, likewise Thou soon shalt unto riches rise; A woman by the same shall have What her own heart doth sorely crave.
Knave	This is a knave, pray have a care That you fall not into despair; Women, who the same shall choose, Shall prove great flats, but that's no news.

Clubs

Ace	He that doth draw the ace of clubs, From his wife gets a thousand snubs; But if maids do it obtain, It means that they shall rule and reign.
Two	Two. Note that this deuce doth signify That thou a loyalist shalt die; The damsels that the same shall take Never will their good friends forsake.
Three	You that by chance this trey have drawn Shall on a worthless woman fawn. A maiden that shall draw this trey Shall be the lass that ne'er says nay.
Four	Now by this four we plainly see Four children shall be born to thee; And she that draws the same shall wed Two wealthy husbands, both well-bred.

Five	Now by this five 'tis clear to see Thy wife will but a slattern be. This same five drawn by virgins, they Shall all wed husbands kind and gay.
Six	By this six thou'rt wed, we know, To one that over thee will crow; Maids that can draw the same shall be Blest with good husbands, kind and free.
Seven	Thou that hast now the seven drawn Shall put thy Sunday clothes in pawn; Maids that draw the same shall wear Jewels rich without compare.
Eight	By this club eight, tho' Whig or Tory, Thy life will prove a tragic story; Ye maids that draw the same, are born To hold both fools and fops in scorn.
Nine	By this brave nine, upon my life, You soon shall wed a wealthy wife; She that shall draw the same shall have One that is both fool and knave.
Ten	Now for this number, half a score, Shows that thou wilt be wretched poor; Maids that can draw this number still Shall have great joy and wealth at will.
King	Here comes the king of clubs, and shows Thou hast some friends as well as foes; Maids that do draw this court card shall Have very few, or none at all.
Queen	If the queen of clubs thou hast, Thou shalt be with great honour graced. And women, if the same they find, Will have things after their own mind.
Knave	See how the surly knave appear! Pray take care of both your ears! Women, whene'er the same they see, Will be what oft they used to be.

Chapter XVIII
The Tarots

Derivation of name – Remote origin – The great Etteilla

Derivation of Name

These immediate predecessors of our own playing cards were primarily used for divination, and are supposed to have been the invention of one Jacques Gringonneur, an astrologer and cabalist, who was probably of Jewish extraction, as the Tarot packs extant in Europe are of an Israelitish character. Various derivations are given of the name. A simple one is that they were called Tarots because of the crossed diagonal lines upon the back of the cards, a design known by the word *tarotée*. There were Roman numerals in the margin above the symbolic devices. The game played with them after the numeral cards had been added was called *tarrochi*.

Remote Origin

Cartomancers and occultists trace the Tarots back into the dim and distant past. The science of hieroglyphics was based upon an alphabet in which the gods were letters, the letters were ideas, the ideas numbers, and the numbers perfect signs. This alphabet is supposed to date from the days of Abraham, and is called the famous "Book of Thoth." Moses, who was learned in all the lore of the Egyptians, took it back to his own people and guarded the secret jealously. It is supposed to have come down to us in the Tarots, which have been changed and modified by the time and place of their adoption.

Another theory is given by the famous cartomancer Etteilla, who says: "On a table or altar in the temple of Ptah at Memphis, at the height of the breast of the Egyptian Magus, were, on one side, a book or collection of cards, or plates of gold (the tarots), and on the other a vase, &c." According to this authority the name tarot is derived from the pure Egyptian word *Tar*, a path; and *Ro, Ros, Rog*, royal, the combined meaning reading "The Royal Path of Life."

A writer of the eighteenth century, Count de Gibelen, says: " If it were known that there exists in our day a work of the ancient Egyptians, which had escaped the flames that devoured their superb libraries, and which contains their purest doctrines on the most interesting subjects, every one would doubtless be anxious to acquire the secrets of so valuable a work... . This work is composed of seventy-eight illustrations..."

Count de Gibelen here refers to the "Book of Thoth," or the Tarot pack of cards. A writer on occult subjects (Macgregor Mathers) believes that the title of this book is derived from *taru*, an Egyptian word which means "to require an answer" or "to consult"; and that the second "t" is added to denote the feminine gender.

"Papus," in his "Key to Occult Science", tells a quaint story as to the reason why the ancient Egyptians came to confide their secrets to the "Book of Thoth." When the overthrow of the kingdom was at hand, the priests met in solemn conclave to decide what means might be used to preserve their secrets inviolate for the initiates of all future ages.

After much deliberation it was held to be best to confide these secrets to something which appealed to vice in man and not to his nobler qualities, so thus the "Book of Thoth" was compiled.

And, indeed, to those interested in occult science it is evident that many solemn mysteries are here symbolized, the explanation of which would be out of place in book principally designed for amusement, as this is.

The Great Etteilla

Le Célèbre Etteilla was the great exponent of the mysteries of the Tarots in the time of the French Revolution. He was well known in Paris as a hairdresser, but he had a mind above his trade, and proceeded to steep himself in the study of the occult. Having mastered much of the mystic lore then available, he started to evolve a system of his own, invented mystic signs, made cabalistic calculations, drew diagrams, and produced weighty volumes to further the cause to which he had devoted himself. His principal work appeared in 1783, and from being somewhat of a celebrity as Alliette the fashionable hairdresser, he mounted to the top of the ladder of popular favour, and reigned supreme for thirty years as *Le Célèbre Etteilla*. So much for spelling your name backwards! Disciples and rivals grew up and thronged around him. In the perilous days of 1789, men came to him with blanched lips and drawn features, asking if they might hope to live through the morrow. There were but few "smooth things to prophesy in those dark days. One cannot help wondering whether he helped any to evade the doom that threatened them.

Etteilla used the Tarots, and adapted them to his own system. Some students of the occult think that he mishandled the sacred emblems of ancient wisdom, but most cartomancers look upon him as one of the chief authorities on fortune-telling by cards, and his method has been made the basis of several subsequent and modern experiments.

It is to be observed that the Tarots are not universally known in the present day, and at the few places where they are sold a fairly high price is asked for them, in comparison with the cost of an ordinary pack of playing cards. For this reason those systems which can only be worked with the Tarots have not been dealt with at length in these pages. The following chapter gives an outline of the way in which these symbolical and mysterious cards can be used, together with some of the significations attached to those composing the major and minor arcana.

Chapter XIX
Etteilla's Method

The Major Arcana – The Minor Arcana – General rules – The second deal – The third deal or great figure – The fourth deal

The Tarot pack is divided into two parts, called the major and minor arcana, the first consisting of twenty-two cards and the latter of fifty-six, which are again divided into four suits.

We will take first the major arcana, and here we are confronted by some curious figures, each bearing a distinct meaning, typical of man himself and his moral and material life. The first seven cards refer to the intellectual side or mental power of man, the second seven to the moral side, or his attitude towards his fellow-man, whilst the third seven are relative to the various events of his material life. The remaining card is the symbol of the greatest heights it is given to man to reach.

The first step is to learn the actual meaning of each separate card, and remember to which group it belongs.

The Major Arcana

First	
The Juggler	Male inquirer.
High Priestess	Woman.
Empress	Action; initiative.
Emperor	Will.
Pope or Priest	Inspiration.
Lovers	Love.
Chariot	Triumph; Providential protection.

Second	
Justice	Justice.
The Hermit	Prudence
The Wheel of the Fortune	Destiny.
Strength	Fortitude; courage.
The Hanged Man	Trial or sacrifice.
Death	Death.
Temperance	Temperance.
Third	
The Devil	Immense force or illness.
The struck Tower	Ruin and deception.
The Stars	Hope.
Moon	Hidden enemies; danger.
Sun	Material happiness; marriage.
Judgment	Change of position.
The Universe	Success.

The Minor Arcana.

This consists of four suits, known as scepters, cups, swords, and pentacles, which correspond to the four suits of the pack of playing cards in general use. Each suit also bears a symbolical meaning, which I give:

Sceptres	corresponds to	diamonds	and mean	enterprise.
Cups	"	hearts	"	love.
Swords	"	spades	"	misfortune.
Pentacles	"	clubs	"	interest.

The court cards consist of king, queen, knight, and knave, and represent respectively man, woman, youth, and childhood. These also have another meaning, which is interesting:

King	Divine world (spirituality).
Queen	Human world (vitality)
Knight	Material world (materiality)
Knave	Transition stage, i.e. life passed on.

The remaining cards in each suit count from one to ten inclusively, and these must be considered in relation to the suit and their face value. "Papus," in his "Key to Occult Science", has given a few suggestions which considerably simplify fortune-telling with the Tarot pack.

By dividing the ten cards of each suit into four sets, we get the relation which they bear to the court cards. The first three, 1, 2, 3, relate to man, which signifies creation and enterprise. The second division, 4, 5, 6, pertain to woman, in opposition to man, that is, reflection and negation. The third division, 7, 8, 9, represent youth and materialism, whilst the ten in each suit makes the fourth set, and relates to the knave or childhood, a transitory or neuter period.

Having thoroughly studied the meaning of each section and each card, it is now necessary to consider some of the methods of divination.

General Rules

As stated in the preceding chapter, Etteilla, the famous cartomancer, used the Tarot pack, and we can scarcely do better than follow his general rules and method.

The whole pack of seventy-eight cards is to be shuffled and cut into three packs, each consisting of twenty-six cards. Take the centre pack and place it to the right. Then the inquirer must again shuffle the remaining cards and divide into three packs of seventeen cards. Take again the centre pack and place on the right hand, keeping it separate, however, from the first. Another shuffle, and again cut into three packs of eleven cards each, and take the centre pack.

Before proceeding further, it is necessary to explain what to do with the cards that are over. 78 will divide into three times 26 evenly; but three times 17 = 51, therefore there is one card over. This card is to be shuffled with the pack for the third time, and when cut there will be found two over, which two cards must remain as a discard until the centre pack of eleven has been selected. There will now be three packs of cards on the right hand –one of twenty-six, one of seventeen, and one of eleven; the discard will consist of twenty-four cards.

Take the first pack of 26 and draw off each card separately, laying it on the table from right to left The second and third packs must be dealt with in similar fashion, only placing them under the first, thus:

26
17
11

The cards being placed, and the signification of each card being kept in mind, the reading can be given. In this figure the lowest line refers to the body or material needs of the inquirer; the second or middle line to the minds or to the affairs on which the thoughts are more specially directed; and the upper line to the unseen or spiritual sense.

The Second Deal

Shuffle the whole pack and let the inquirer cut once. Then draw off the first seventeen cards, and look at the eighteenth and also at the last card in the pack. These two cards will show you if you have established any sympathy between yourself and the inquirer –a fact which must be judged from the signification the cards bear to the inquirer.

Lay out the seventeen cards selected, and place them in order from right to left, then give the interpretation. Pair, by taking the 1st and the 17th, and and 16th, and so on to the end. The pairing should either enhance or modify the deductions already drawn.

The Third Deal or Great Figure

This method is more elaborate than any of the others. Let all the cards be well shuffled and cut by the inquirer, then arrange in the following order:

On your right hand, working upwards, place eleven cards.

Opposite to the first card, but leaving a space between (see next diagram), place the 12th card, and work upwards from that until you have arranged another column of eleven cards.

From the 11th card on the right, begin and place eleven cards across, which arrangement will give you the three sides of a square formed by thirty-three cards. Then form the circle by commencing with the 34th card, and placing it in a line with the centre card of the top row. Sixty-six cards will now have been used. One card must represent the inquirer, and should be placed in the centre, and the more satisfactory plan is to take the juggler to represent a man, and the high priestess a woman, instead of simply drawing any card by chance. Eleven cards now remain, and with these the triangle inside the circle can be formed. The apex of the triangle will be towards the manipulator, as shown in the diagram.

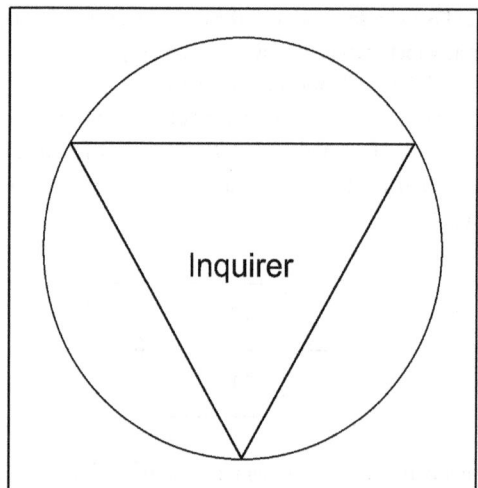

This figure will give a reading of the past, present, and future –the right referring to the events that have passed, the left to things as they are at present known, and the third to what is to come.

The first card placed on the square and the first card placed on the circle are paired, then the 2nd and the 35th, the 3rd and 36th, and so on until you have taken all the cards on the right, which will give you a reading of the past. Pair the 13rd card with the 45th, and proceed until you have finished with the section referring to the present

For the future, take the 1st card and the 66th, and read the indication of events to come.

The triangle formed of the eleven cards is an innovation on Etteilla's method, but, read in reference to the deductions made, it will probably confirm the cartomancer's opinions.

This figure requires much attention and patience, especially if the more symbolical meaning of the cards is studied.

The Fourth Deal

This refers only to the wish. Let the inquirer shuffle the cards, then draw off the first seven and lay them from right to left, and read according to the meaning.

www.ingramcontent.com/pod-product-compliance
Lightning Source LLC
Chambersburg PA
CBHW060827190426
43197CB00039B/2525